Geopolitics

Geopolitics

The Geography of International Relations

Third Edition

Saul Bernard Cohen

Dev Publishers & Distributors
New Delhi

Published by
Dev Publishers & Distributors
Second Floor, Prakashdeep,
22, Delhi Medical Association Road,
Darya Ganj, New Delhi – 110 002

www.devbooks.co.in

ISBN 978-93-5944-944-9

This edition, 2024

Printed in India.

Contents

List of Figures viii

List of Tables ix

List of Abbreviations and Acronyms x

1 Overview **1**
Geopolitical Analysis 1
Four Pillars of Power 2
Hierarchical Order of Power 3
Impact of Geography 4
Geopolitical Map of the Future 6
Geopolitics and Geographical Change 7
Developmental Stages 9
Globalization 11
Notes 13

2 Survey of Geopolitics **15**
Definitions 15
Stages of Modern Geopolitics 16
Conclusion 33
Notes 33

3 Geopolitical Structure and Theory **37**
Structure 38
Proliferation of National States 55
Geopolitics and General Systems 59
Equilibrium, Turbulence, and World Order 60
Notes 63

4 The Cold War and Its Aftermath **65**
Geopolitical Restructuring 65
Phase I: 1945–56 65
Phase II: 1957–79 72
Phase III: 1980–89 83

The Collapse of the Soviet Superpower 87
Transition into the Twenty-First Century 88
Notes 93

5 North and Middle America 95
The United States 95
Canada 124
Economic Exchange 132
Mexico 136
Middle America 148
Notes 159

6 South America 161
United States–South American Relations 161
The Geographical Setting 163
Geopolitical Features 165
Geopolitical Forces of Separation and Attraction 168
Prospects for South America's Geopolitical Independence 172
Conclusion 177
Notes 178

7 Maritime Europe and the Maghreb 179
Geopolitical Features 183
European Integration 191
Immigration Patterns 200
Merging of Eastern and Western Europe within the European Union 203
State Proliferation 204
The Maghreb: Maritime Europe's Strategic Annex 209
Conclusion 214
Notes 216

8 Russia and the Eurasian Convergence Zone 217
The Changing National Territory 220
Geopolitical Features 234
The Eurasian Convergence Zone 245
Eastern Europe 249
The Trans-Caucasus and Central Asia 257
Mongolia 264
Conclusion 265
Notes 269

9 The East Asia Geostrategic Realm 271
China 271
The East Asia Rim Periphery 298
Conclusion 309
Notes 312

10 The Asia-Pacific Rim 315
Evolution of the Region 317
Linking Australia to Asia Pacifica 319

A Region of Trading States 320
Political Stability and Instability 323
Geopolitical Features 333
Conclusion 342
Notes 347

11 South Asia 349
Historical Background 350
Regional Geopolitical Overview 352
Geopolitical Features 359
Challenges to National and Regional Unity 369
Conclusion 372
Notes 374

12 The Middle East Shatterbelt 375
Modern Colonial Penetration 376
Great Power Rivalry: Cold War Period 378
The Geographical Setting 382
Geopolitical Features 390
Major Conflicts 398
Selected Countries 402
Oil, Pipeline Routes, and Politics 410
Conclusion 411
Notes 416

13 The Sub-Saharan African Shatterbelt 417
Colonial/Imperial Background 418
Postcolonial Political Frameworks 419
Geographical Background 423
Geopolitical Features 426
Regional Subdivisions 433
Southern Africa 434
West Africa 437
Central Africa 440
East Africa and the Horn of Africa 441
Conclusion 443
Notes 445

14 Epilogue 447
Mapping the Future 450
Notes 457

Bibliography 459

Index 467

About the Author 491

Figures

2.1	Mackinder's World: 1904	18
2.2	Mackinder's World: 1919	20
2.3	Mackinder's World: 1943	21
2.4	Changing Heartland Boundaries	22
3.1	The Geopolitical World: Beginning of the Twenty-First Century	45
3.2	The World's Major and Regional Powers	52
4.1	Realm and Regional Changes from the End of World War II to the Present	67
5.1	North and Middle America: Major Geopolitical Features	97
5.2	Keystone XL Pipeline/Bakken Formation	102
6.1	South America: Major Geopolitical Features	166
7.1	Maritime Europe and the Maghreb: Major Geopolitical Features	184
8.1	Heartlandic Russia and Periphery: Major Geopolitical Features	235
8.2	Eurasian Convergence Zone	246
8.3	Ukraine Ethnic Divide	252
9.1	China Air Defense Identification Zone	281
9.2	East Asia: Major Geopolitical Features	286
10.1	Asia-Pacific Rim: Major Geopolitical Features	334
11.1	South Asia: Major Geopolitical Features	361
12.1	Middle East Shatterbelt: Major Geopolitical Features	391
12.2	Sudan/South Sudan Boundary Dispute	414
13.1	Sub-Saharan African Shatterbelt: Major Geopolitical Features	427
14.1	World Geopolitical Map by the First Quarter of the Twenty-First Century	451

Tables

3.1	Second-Order Power Rankings	53
3.2	Gateways and Separatist Areas	57
3.3	Potential Confederations	59
4.1	State Targets of Major Terrorist Actions since World War II	92
5.1	Four Stages of US Geopolitical Development	106
7.1	Maritime Europe Population and Trade in European Union Key States	196
7.2	Potential European States and Quasi States	205
8.1	Post–World War II Soviet Land Annexations	227
10.1	The Asia-Pacific Rim: A Region of Trading States	321
10.2	Asia-Pacific Rim Population and GDP	322
11.1	South Asia Population and Trade	351
12.1	Current Middle East Boundary Disputes	396
12.2	Recent Middle East Dispute Territorial Resolutions	396
12.3	Middle East Irredentism	397
13.1	Sub-Saharan Africa: Current Boundary and Territorial Disputes	429
13.2	Sub-Saharan Africa: Latent Boundary and Territorial Disputes	430

Abbreviations and Acronyms

ABM	Antiballistic Missile (Treaty)
AFRICOM	United States Africa Command
AKP	Adalet ve Kalkınma Partisi (Justice and Development Party)
ANZUS	Australia, New Zealand, United States
APEC	Asia-Pacific Economic Cooperation Forum
ARAMCO	Arab-American Oil Company
ASEAN	Association of Southeast Asian Nations
ASSR	Autonomous Soviet Socialist Republic
AU	African Union
BRICS	Brazil, Russia, India, China, South Africa
CAFTA-DR	Dominican Republic-Central America Free Trade Agreement
CAP	Common Agricultural Policy
CARICOM	Caribbean Community
CASAREM	Central Asia-South Asia Regional Electricity Market
CENTO	Central Treaty Organization
CIA	Central Intelligence Agency
CIS	Commonwealth of Independent States
COMECON	Council for Mutual Economic Assistance
COMESA	Common Market for Eastern and Southern Africa
CTBT	Comprehensive Test Ban Treaty
DEW	Distant Early Warning Line
DMZ	Demilitarized Zone (especially Korea)
EAC	East African Community
ECOWAS	Economic Community of West African States
ECSC	European Coal and Steel Community
EEC	European Economic Community
EEZ	Exclusive Economic Zone
ELN	Ejército de Liberación Nacional (People's Liberation Army)
ENT	Effective National Territory
ERT	Effective Regional Territory
ETA	Euskadi Ta Askatasuna
EU	European Union

FARC	Fuerzas Armadas Revolucionarias de Colombia (Revolutionary Armed Forces of Colombia)
FATA	Federally Administered Tribal Areas of Pakistan
Frelimo	Mozambique Liberation Front
FSU	Former Soviet Union
GAP	Guneydogu Anadolu Project
GATT	General Agreement on Tariffs and Trade
GDP	gross domestic product
GNP	gross national product
GUAM	Georgia, Ukraine, Azerbaijan, Moldova
GUUAM	Georgia, Ukraine, Uzbekistan, Azerbaijan, Moldova
ICBM	intercontinental ballistic missile
ICJ	International Court of Justice
ISI	Interservice Intelligence
ISIL	Islamic State in Iraq and the Levant
ISIS	Islamic State in Iraq and Syria
KIZ	Kaesong Free Trade Industrial Zone
LNG	liquefied natural gas
MAD	mutually assured destruction
MED	mutual economic dependence
Mercosur	Mercado Común del Sur
MPLA	Movimento Popular de Libertação de Angola (People's Movement for the Liberation of Angola)
MSD	mutual strategic dependence
NAFTA	North American Free Trade Agreement
*NATO	North Atlantic Treaty Organization
NMD	National Missile Defense (system)
NMS	new member states of the European Union
NORAD	North American Aerospace Defense Command
OAS	Organization of American States
OAU	Organization of African Unity
OMS	old member states of the European Union
OPEC	Organization of Petroleum Exporting Countries
PAN	National Action Party (Mexico)
PEMEX	Petróleos Mexicanos
PJAK	Partiya Jiyana Azad a Kurdistanê (Party for Freedom and Life in Kurdistan)
PKK	Partiya Karkerên Kurdistan (Turkish Workers Party)
R&D	research and development
RSFSR	Russian Soviet Federative Socialist Republic
SAARC	South Asian Association for Regional Cooperation
SACU	Southern African Customs Union
SADC	South African Development Community
SALT	Strategic Arms Limitations Talks
SDF	(Japanese) Self-Defense Force
SEATO	Southeast Asia Treaty Organization
SLORC	State Law and Order Restoration Council
SNAP	Supplemental Nutrition Assistance Program
SSR	Soviet Socialist Republic

START II	Strategic Arms Reduction Treaty II
SWAPO	South West Africa People's Organization
TANU	Tanganyika African National Union
UAV	unmanned aerial vehicle
UGV	unmanned ground vehicle
UN	United Nations
UNASUR	Unión de Naciones Suramericanas (Union of South American Nations)
UNITA	União Nacional para a Independência Total de Angola (National Union for Total Independence of Angola)
UNTAC	United Nations Transitional Authority in Cambodia
USSR	Union of Soviet Socialist Republics
VAT	value-added tax
WTO	World Trade Organization

CHAPTER 1

Overview

On September 11, 2001, nineteen al-Qaeda terrorists hijacked two airliners, crashing them into the New York City World Trade Center and claiming 2,977 victims. A third hijacked plane crashed into the Pentagon building a few minutes later, killing 125 people. Washington's immediate reaction to the bombings was to declare war against the Afghan-based terrorists who were sheltered by the Taliban regime. This war began on October 7, 2001, with air bombing and special strike-force actions.

These attacks exposed the vulnerability of the country that had become the world's sole superpower following the breakup of the Soviet empire in 1989. The bombings triggered a series of developments that have led to geopolitical shifts that have affected the relationships among states and the balance of power in the world.

Geopolitical Analysis

Geopolitical analysis does not predict the timing of events, crises, and flash points that force radical changes in the geopolitical map. Such events have been the sudden invasion of South Korea by North Korea and the popular uprisings that overthrew the Ben Ali regime in Tunisia, initiating the Arab Spring. What such analysis can do is focus the attention of policy makers on conditions that are likely to bring about geopolitical change. For example, the attempted rebellion in Bahrain, quashed by Saudi Arabia, was energized by the Arab Spring. The underlying condition was repression of the Shia majority by the Sunni monarchy, aggravated by the large immigrant worker underclass. This set of circumstances is common to the Gulf states. Saudi Arabia's reaction was predictable because its easternmost province is largely Shiite, and Shiite Iran has historic claims to Bahrain. This kind of geopolitical analysis should alert the United States to the fragility of its naval base in Manama, Bahrain, and the advisability of relocating it to the eastern Mediterranean.

Changes in the balance within the international system can also be anticipated by geopolitical analysis. The United States, along with its NATO allies, had early military successes in ousting the Taliban from Afghanistan and two years later launched a war against Iraq, toppling the Saddam Hussein regime. However, the United States soon became bogged down in costly guerrilla warfare that extended into the next decade. Meanwhile, China experienced a meteoric rise as an economic giant.

Four Pillars of Power

A nation's claim to power rests on four pillars: (1) overwhelming military strength and the willingness to use it; (2) surplus economic energy to enable it to provide aid and invest in other states; (3) ideological leadership that serves as a model for other nations; and (4) a cohesive system of governance.

The first pillar is the military. This period of transition from a world dominated by superpowers to a polycentric power system is marked by significant changes in the nature of warfare. The United States, by far the world's strongest traditional military power, has overwhelming strength in tanks, aircraft, naval fleets, and superbly equipped armed forces. Nevertheless, it failed to attain its political goals in Iraq and Afghanistan as guerrilla warfare and terrorism has torn those two countries apart. In Iraq, the American occupation has been unable to impose a peace upon this regionally and ethnically fragmented land. In Afghanistan, US and NATO troops and weaponry, which so easily dislodged the Taliban, were unable to overcome the guerrilla forces in this tribally and ethnically torn country. The Afghan Taliban are poised to regain a powerful foothold within Afghanistan with the withdrawal of US and NATO combat troops from the country in 2014.

US success in killing key al-Qaeda leadership, including Osama bin Laden, who was killed in 2011 by US special strike forces in Abbottabad, western Pakistan, neutralized the centralized al-Qaeda organization in Afghanistan and western Pakistan. Nevertheless, the movement lives on. It has morphed into a decentralized network extending throughout the Middle East, the Maghreb, East Africa, and the African Sahel and has now been superseded by ISIS (Islamic State of Iraq and Syria).

The lessons learned from America's military experience in Afghanistan and Iraq are twofold. First, soft power may yield greater success than warfare, and second, weapons of warfare are radically changing. In wars against guerrillas and terrorists, drones—unmanned aerial vehicles (UAVs) with surveillance and missile capacities and robots—and unmanned ground vehicle (UGVs), combined with special strike forces and cyberwarfare, have proven more effective than traditional weapons and massed armed forces.

The second pillar, economic capacity, is even more important than the military. The United States, Europe, and Japan have yet to recover fully from the deep recession of 2008. This is reflected in the caution which Washington has recently displayed in responding to political and military crises throughout the world. Its foreign policy has been strongly influenced by high domestic unemployment and huge indebtedness that have preoccupied the country while turmoil rages in the Middle East. The fear that countries like China and Japan will withdraw their bond holdings also tempers Washington's geopolitical actions.

The third pillar is ideological leadership. Americans have taken pride in their ideals, which are a blend of the principles of freedom of expression and religion, concern for human rights, the rewards of free enterprise, and the practice of democracy in governance. Since the founding of the republic, these principles have been widely embraced throughout the world. However, much of US foreign policy has often not been true to them. While preaching democracy, Washington has long supported dictatorships and overthrown governments not to its liking. It has tolerated widespread corruption in supporting allies. The Arab Spring was only the last of the upheavals that laid bare the contradiction between the myth of American exceptionalism and its practice of *realpolitik*.

The fourth pillar is political cohesiveness. In the United States the recent stalemate between the two major parties has been a factor in undermining America's ability to provide international leadership. A government that can suddenly be shut down, budgets that cannot be agreed upon, and a proposed health system that has divided the nation are poor models for international friends and foes alike.

With respect to these pillars, China, for its part, lacks the capacity to apply military power beyond its contiguous Asian borders. Instead, it relies on economic trade and investment to extend its influence. In doing so, the Chinese have used their sovereign funds to purchase or invest in natural resources throughout the world. While such economic initiatives have been welcomed, the political fallout from these actions has often been rising suspicion and opposition on nationalistic and environmental grounds. Moreover, the need for China to focus on building its own national infrastructure and realign its populace from rural agricultural to urban industrial and service pursuits sets a limit on China's foreign aid capacities. Although the mixture of state and private capitalism as practiced in China has been adopted in many other countries, the repressive nature of the Chinese Communist regime has been widely rejected as an ideological model by people who yearn for individual freedom as well as economic advancement.

Hierarchical Order of Power

Pundits have debated whether the new century is destined to become the Chinese era or whether the United States will retain its global dominance. Recently, this debate faded from the public agenda as it became plain that both countries have exhibited substantial weaknesses along with their inherent strength. The United States is beset by war weariness, economic problems, and political dysfunction. China has failed to match its economic power with commensurate military strength, and its economic growth, overly dependent upon exports, has slowed down. Its repressive Communist regime also has failed to be embraced as a model by other nations of the world.

Instead of a world ordered by superpowers, an international geopolitical system that is emerging is polycentric and polyarchic. It is built on a hierarchical combination of great and regional powers. The major powers are first-order states with the capacities and ambitions to expand their influence beyond the regions within which they are located. Competing with major powers are the regional powers, or second-order states. Their geopolitical reach is regionally confined. The United States, China, the European Union, Russia, and Japan are major powers. Iran, Turkey, Australia, and South Africa are representative examples of regional powers. India and Brazil are at an intermediate stage. While their reach currently is regional, they have the potential to become major powers. In time, they gain enough strength and ambition to try to influence affairs throughout their regions by the application of military and/or economic muscle. Examples are Iran's actions within Iraq and Ethiopia's in Somalia.

A third order of states has also arisen—those with unique ideological or cultural capacities to influence their neighbors. Examples include Cuba and North Korea, whose military power is maintained by ideological rigor. Ukraine derives its third-order status from playing off its two adjoining major powers, Russia and the EU. Fourth-order states are generally incapable of applying pressure upon their neighbors, and those of the fifth order depend upon outside sustenance for survival.

This hierarchical system is dynamic, not static. States such as Nigeria and Venezuela, once regional powers, have lost these positions. Nigeria is torn apart by the conflict between its Christian south and Muslim north so that it possesses little geopolitical energy to influence its neighbors. The government of Venezuela, having lost much of its popular appeal with the death of its charismatic leader, Hugo Chávez, is mired in debt and plagued by shortages of basic commodities and by inflation.

Without the dominant American superpower to play the role of global peacemaker, prepared to intervene militarily in conflict situations and to invest financial and diplomatic energies aimed at stabilizing the international system, the world is now like a ship without a rudder. Such disequilibrium is inevitable in this period of geopolitical transition. Great and regional powers are focused on redefining their own national security interests, economic strategies, and ideological goals.

Impact of Geography

Geography is the study of the features and patterns formed by the interaction of the natural and human-made environments. An example of a simple feature/pattern relationship is a gorge straddled by a bridge which forms of a transit way. At a more complex level, the features of a coastal embayment located at the edge of a broad basin which is rimmed by the escarpment of a plateau provides the setting for an urban metropolis. Its features, consisting of a port, a dense central city, and suburbs within the basin, extend onto the plateau as exurbia. Collectively these features form a pattern.

The importance of geographic proximity in waging war and conducting trade is reflected in many ways. US launching pads for drones are placed in Djibouti to strike al-Qaeda in Yemen, and France has developed a similar cite in Niger for its operations against terrorists in northern Mali. Empty desert landscapes serve as the locale for space exploration bases, as is the case for Russia's Baikonur Cosmodrome in northern Kazakhstan. The US southwest desert is a prime site for military pilot exercises.

Population density is another important geographic consideration in international relations. High densities inhibit drone strikes for fear of causing many civilian casualties. Consequently, such densities provide safe havens for Afghan Taliban leadership in Pakistan's Karachi, with a population of twenty million. Narrow seas, such as the Gulf of Aden, offer targets for pirates based in Somalian fishing ports. The vast deposits of North Sea oil and gas that adjoin the east coast of Scotland encourage Scottish separatists to seek independence from Britain.

Seoul's location so close to the North Korean border influences the cautious diplomatic policies of South Korea toward its erratic northern neighbor. There are countless examples of how geography affects international relations, but none more striking than the geographical fact that the United States is the only great power in the world with access to the two world oceans.

Changes in the natural environment have profound geopolitical implications. Global warming has made possible navigation of Russia's Arctic Northern Sea Route during the summer. With continued global warming, this is likely to evolve into a full-year transit way, strengthening the economic ties between Europe and China. The physiographic features and patterns of ethnic and religious distribution in both Afghanistan and Iraq have demonstrated the impact of geography upon war and politics. The Afghan war continued to rage because the Taliban and al-Qaeda were able to regroup in the sheltering and welcoming mountainous areas of Pakistan's Federally Administered Tribal Areas (FATA) of fellow Pashtuns when the focus of US attention shifted to Iraq.

Driven by dreams spun by neoconservative theorists of a US twenty-first century and propelled by the shock of September 11, 2001, the Bush administration embraced with evangelical fervor policies of unilateralism and preemptive war. The action in Afghanistan, undertaken under the umbrella of NATO and with the support of China, Russia, and neighboring Muslim states, conformed to geopolitical reality. This was not the case with Iraq, where the hastily planned and poorly executed war launched in 2003 did not have widespread external support or internal logic. Saudi Arabian opposition forced the United States to abandon all of its strategically important bases early in the action. Turkey refused to join the coalition. It did allow overflights and transshipments of supplies but did not permit land forces to traverse its territory. With the exception of Britain, the input of other coalition forces was trivial. The speedy defeat of Saddam Hussein's army, rather than ending the conflict, unleashed fierce sectarian warfare and widespread hostility toward US occupation. Rationalized as a war against terrorism, the invasion provided a breeding ground for terrorism in a geographic area more accessible than Afghanistan. The Sunni western desert of Iraq hosts "al-Qaeda of Iraq" and other militant Islamic groups which, along with the Shia-Sunni sectarian violence, dragged the United States into a military and political quagmire. By removing the Iraqi Sunni from power, the United States eliminated the region's major bulwark against the spread of Iranian influence in the Arab Middle East.

Whereas the United States may see little strategic value in some parts of the world, it must be sensitive to the concerns of other powers. Australia is an important strategic ally. Yet Washington paid little attention to its vital interest in the conflict in East Timor. The United States sought to appease Indonesia rather than help stop the massacres that took place after the East Timorese voted for independence. This ignored Australia's strategic stake in East Timor because of its proximity to the Australian north and prospective joint development of oil and gas resources within the Timor Sea. While the United States stood back, it was Canberra that pressed for UN intervention and has since assumed the military burden of peacekeeping. Even though Washington may not be moved to act out of humanitarian considerations it considers to be strategically unimportant, it may have to involve itself in deference to the interests of allied regional states that are important to global geopolitical equilibrium.

The geopolitical perspective is dynamic. It evolves as the international system and its operational environment changes. The dynamic nature of geographical settings accounts, to a considerable extent, for changes in geopolitical patterns and features. These settings change in response to such phenomena as the discovery or depletion of natural resources, the movement of people and capital flows, and long-term alterations in climate. Thus, the shift from rural to urban landscapes or from manufacturing to service economies represents geographical change that becomes reflected in changing national ideals and objectives. So does the impact of large-scale immigration. The decline of manufacturing in the United States, its greater reliance on imported goods, its enormous national debt—all have increased the dependency on international trade to the point where "going it alone" as a superpower is not a practical, or even possible, foreign policy. This is a reality that the US administration has confronted in Iraq, Afghanistan, and counterterrorist actions throughout the world as well as in its efforts to contain the spread of nuclear weapons. With respect to the negotiations over Iran's nuclear threats, the participation of the European Union in the imposition of sanctions has been critical.

Geographical dynamism has also influenced changing national and regional outlooks in Maritime Europe as well as in South Korea and Taiwan. In the latter case, the massive outsourcing of manufacturing to mainland China's southern and central coasts has pressed Taipei and Seoul, as well as Tokyo and Washington, to be cautious in their diplomatic relationship with China. China, in turn, has been forced by changes in the geographical setting of its high-tech "Golden Coast" to open itself to the outside world. It has also been forced to focus on the development of its rural interior and to grant greater rights to temporary workers who have been drawn to job opportunities in the cities. At the same time, the United States has had to play a delicate diplomatic role in seeking to curb China's aggressive actions over control of the East and South China Seas.

Geopolitical Map of the Future

The geopolitical structure of the twenty-first century will not be under the aegis of an American empire, in which order is maintained by the benign, omnipotent superpower. What world geopolitical patterns and features may then be anticipated? What mechanisms for maintaining global equilibrium can be established as alternatives to the top-down world order that is implicit in the structure of empires? While no single discipline can claim to have the answers to these questions, they can surely be informed by the political-geographical perspective.

Washington's announcement of its "Asian pivot" is an example of a premature declaration of strategic geopolitical shift. It foreshadowed the downgrading of America's role in the Middle East and the reduction of its military forces in Europe. The struggle between Russia and the EU for influence over Ukraine, and the emergence of ISIS, has stymied this downgrading. The US commitment to maintain freedom of shipping in the waters between China and the island countries of the Asia-Pacific Rim requires a delicate balancing act, maintaining peaceful relations with Beijing while fulfilling America's security guarantees to such Asia-Pacific Rim countries as Japan, South Korea, the Philippines, and Australia.

Washington's greater focus on diplomatic soft power rather than military power reflects recognition of its new international strategy. The promotion by the Obama administration of transatlantic and transpacific free-trade pacts reflects a strategic focus on those regions which are parts of the maritime realm.

The path to a new global equilibrium is tortuous. Progress is being made as the most important equilibrial force is no longer military, but economic and cultural. These forces operate at both the global and regional levels. Socioculturally, such communications networks as Facebook and Twitter leap national boundaries. They influence the behavior of people on a global scale, stimulating challenges to repressive national systems and influencing consumer tastes and demands. Publication of Edward Snowden's revelations on the US National Security Agency's sweeping cyberspying activities spread resentment among America's most important friends and allies.

Large-scale transborder immigration flows also affect the equilibrium equation. These movements are spurred by those escaping war, famine, and floods or searching for greater economic opportunities. Although some of this movement is on a global scale, most of it is regionally confined. Refugees from Syria threaten the shaky political balance within Lebanon and Jordan and are a heavy financial burden on Turkey. Refugees from Eritrea and Somalia into Italy have become a disruptive political issue there. A handful of young Somalian refugees who found their way to Minneapolis only to become disaffected returned to southern Somalia and joined al-Shabab there.

On a positive note, Mexican migrants, legal and illegal, play an important role as farm and day laborers within the United States. Similarly, workers from Central Asia, although they face discrimination, are important to the Russian economy. So are migrants from Eastern Europe who have filled job needs in Western European states and those from the Maghreb to France. Of equal importance, cash remittances from immigrants to the developed world help to keep the economies of underdeveloped countries afloat and enable families in home countries to improve their living standards. Besides benefiting from unskilled labor, the United States has attracted highly skilled professionals from many parts of the world who contribute to advancing American technological innovation in Silicon Valley and other parts of the United States.

As their power cores wax and wane, states may be added to the region or shifted to other regions. This chain may be likened to tides that flow in and out, but unlike the tidal phenomenon, their timing is unpredictable. With the passing of Fidel Castro and Hugo Chávez, the regional compression zone that extended from Cuba through Venezuela to Ecuador is likely to disappear, leaving South America as an integrated geographical region under the leadership of Brazil.

Despite the global reach of trade and investment, media, and advanced weaponry, the present hierarchical system is based upon a dynamic geopolitical structure of geopolitical realms and regions, not globalism. The boundaries of this system expand and contract in response to changes within their core states, and its patterns and features are geographically framed. It is in this context that geography plays such a key role in international affairs.

Geopolitics and Geographical Change

The changes in the world geopolitical map have been more rapid and sweeping during the past century than during the previous two and one-half centuries, when the modern, sovereign national state emerged and the European colonial system was imposed on much of the world. In the twentieth century, the seeds of destruction of the colonial system were planted in the savage conflict of World War I, from which the European powers emerged drained economically and in manpower. The Bolshevik Revolution, world economic depression, and the rise of Nazi Germany led to World War II and the complete collapse of the European-imposed world order. The end of that war saw the emergence of the two great superpowers—the United States and the Union of Soviet Socialist Republics (USSR). Unlike their European colonial-imperial predecessors, these Cold War powers dominated their spheres of influence through regional clusters of formally independent allies and vassal states. After half a century, the Soviet Union imploded, laying the groundwork for a new world order, the outlines of which are still being drawn.

The clues to the geopolitical map of the future lie in the patterns of restructuring that have taken shape during the past half century. The bipolarity that characterized the world system in the years that immediately followed World War II gave way to multipolarity as new or revived power centers arose within the geopolitical networks established by the two superpowers. China broke off from its Soviet masters, and Maritime Europe and Japan became economic powers linked to, but also in competition with, the United States. Small satellites also struck independent courses from their former overlords, Yugoslavia and Albania from the USSR and Cuba, and then Venezuela from the United States. Yugoslavia, in turn, imploded into six independent units. In recent years, South Africa and Nigeria have taken more assertive roles in Sub-Saharan African affairs, Brazil has become the "powerhouse" of South America, and Iran is asserting its power in the Middle East. It has extended its influence in a chain that extends from Iraq through Syria to Hezbollah in southern Lebanon and Hamas in Gaza. India is slowly moving toward becoming a world power.

Especially within the developing world, regional powers have achieved dominance over neighboring states, carving out independent spheres of influence in political and economic affairs. While they possess the capacity to wage wars, most have been loath to do so and tend to assume the roles of conflict mediators rather than imposing peace upon their neighbors.

Regional geopolitical unity is far more advanced in Maritime Europe than in any other part of the world. Such unity was advocated by Europe's leadership as a prerequisite to the economic recovery that was attained through massive American aid. While loss of colonial empires stimulated the process, what propelled the movement toward unity was the devastation of World War II, followed by the US Marshall Plan aid. The Europeans recognized the complementary nature of the region's national economies and the benefits to be derived from economies of scale and larger markets. An additional motivation was the recognition that regional political and military institutions would bind West Germany tightly to its neighbors, especially France. This would minimize the threat that a revived Germany might someday plunge Western Europe once again into conflict with the USSR over the issue of German reunification or that German national resurgence might resurrect dreams of dominance over Western Europe. The policy has succeeded.

Far from being a military threat, the unified Germany that has emerged as the unchallenged political and economic leader of the European Union. With only 7 percent of the world's population, it accounts for one quarter of the world's manufacturing output and maintains a surplus trade balance that was even greater than that of China in 2013. Berlin has used its fiscal strength to prop up eurozone countries, such as Greece, Cyprus, Spain, and Portugal, that have plunged into recession. While many Germans resent this burden, the fact that the Merkel government received overwhelming endorsement in the 2013 election reflects Germany's commitment to the evolving united Europe.

The world map was also changed significantly by the proliferation of national states that occurred in the wake of the collapse of colonial empires. These states vary from sovereign entities as large as India and as small as Nauru or Singapore and include highly successful as well as "failed" states. This multiplicity of national nodes and their external links has led to greater system complexity.

The ancient weapon of terrorism was used by many colonial peoples in their drives for independence. It continues to be an important force in the struggles of separatist movements to wrest sovereignty from the national states within which they are located and is often transferred to the international arena. Terrorism is also used to quell rebellious groups as well as to overthrow existing regimes in order to impose political-ideological or religious systems. What is new is that terrorism is no longer confined to local or regional arenas. Ease of global communication and movement leaves no place in the world immune from international terrorist attack. It has also become an expression of internal discontent within countries.

Also contributing to system complexity have been developments at the subnational level, where metropolitan entities emerged with the revolution in highway and air transportation. Such urban agglomerations often compete with state and federal governments, sometimes conducting independent economic activities that have historically been within the province of higher government levels. Prominent among these activities are the promotion of capital investment, overseas markets, and tourism. Examples in the United States are the northeastern coastal megalopolis from southern New Hampshire and southern Maine to northern Virginia and its central and southern California urban complexes.

A related phenomenon is the transnational megalopolis, large conurbations whose interests often compete with those of their national governments. Examples in Maritime Europe include the London, Paris, and Ruhr basins, the urban-industrial triangle from Benelux through the Rhine to Luxembourg and Strasbourg, and the Rhine-North Italy axis.

Another feature of the contemporary world geopolitical map is the "shatterbelt"—a region torn by internal conflicts whose fragmentation is increased by the intervention of external major powers. The interveners seek to extend their influence over the region by offering military, political, and economic support to their clients. At a lesser geographical scale are "compression zones"—smaller atomized areas that lie within or between geopolitical regions. Such zones are torn apart by the combination of civil wars and the interventionist actions of neighboring countries.

In historic terms, the age of balanced superpower competition was relatively brief—only four and one-half decades. But it was an age of sweeping scientific, technological, economic, and ideological change. Nuclear weapons and space-age capacities, dominated by the United States and the Soviet Union, created a strategic standoff between the two. For a brief period, the equilibrium that was struck was static. This remained so until the Soviet Union leapfrogged the areas surrounding the continental Eurasian center to penetrate southward into the Middle East and, together with Communist China, eastward into Korea and southward into Southeast Asia. This was later followed by the spread of Soviet influence into Sub-Saharan Africa and Latin America.

The global system became more complex and its structure more flexible, as the new balance struck between the superpowers depended upon a nested system of geopolitical levels whose units were tied to the superpowers as well as to emerging regional powers. This bipolar system was precariously balanced by "mutually assured destruction" (MAD), or nuclear deterrence, whereby they avoided direct conflict while engaging in a weapons race and arming their allies. The system ended with the dismantling of the Warsaw Pact in 1989 and collapse of the Soviet Union in 1991. This end of the Cold War briefly left the United States as the world's sole military and economic superpower.

Developmental Stages

With the emergence of new geopolitical structures and equilibrial forces, the developmental principles that guided the evolution of the global system during the Cold War retain their validity and provide the basis for anticipating the contours of the geopolitical map of the twenty-first century. Essentially, the principles hold that systems—both human and biological—evolve in stages, from atomization and undifferentiation to differentiation, specialization, and specialization-integration.

Applying these principles to the geopolitical map is complex, for various parts of the world are at different developmental stages. The differences in developmental pace are compounded by different spatial orders, along which geopolitical relations are forged. Broadly speaking, such orders occur at the macro, meso, and micro, or local, levels. The macro order embraces geostrategic realms, the meso order covers geotactical regions, and the micro order includes states and subnational unit areas. As a result of such complexity, change occurs in fits and starts, not in a smooth, orderly fashion.

The capacity of different parts of the system to evolve relates, in great measure, to their distinctive operational environments. Today, three geostrategic realms embrace much, but not all, of the world. The United States is a great power whose geopolitical arena is the maritime world of the Atlantic and Pacific basins. It both derives strength from its allies within its realm and provides them with strength. Maritime Europe, organized around the European Union (EU), has achieved economic parity with the United States, although it has yet to match it in military might, so Washington continues to treat Brussels as its geopolitical satellite.

For much of the Cold War, and even at times of ideological and military rivalry, the USSR and China were joined together in a continental Asian geostrategic realm. While they still have common strategic interests in the Northwest Pacific, their paths have diverged. Russia is the core of the continentally rooted realm of the Eurasian heartland that embraces Central Asia. China, the core of East Asia, has developed a powerful, maritime-oriented economic base that is combined with its continental qualities. This has enabled it to carve out a separate continental-maritime geostrategic realm, extending its influence into Southeast Asia. Japan, another great power owing to its economic strength, does not hold sway over a geopolitical region because of the historic mistrust that underlies its relations with neighbors that it previously occupied, especially South Korea and Indonesia, and because it is constitutionally blocked from building a strong military. The boundaries of these three geostrategic realms include the areas that the major powers consider to be vital to their national interests. Such interests represent a mix of security, economic, cultural-ethnic-religious, and ideological imperatives. Regional, national, and subnational entities have their own identified self-interests within the framework of the realm. If these are highly incompatible with those of the realm's major power(s), structural geopolitical changes may result. For example, new shatterbelts could emerge where competing realms converge, or former ones may reemerge. At the same time, where converging realms find mutual self-interest in fostering cooperative relationships, such intermediate regions could become bridges or "gateways."

Within the geostrategic realms, economic gaps may be closed by surplus energies from core powers that can be directed toward areas of need. Less energy is generally directed to parts of the world that lie outside the realm, especially if they do not adjoin it. The losers in this situation have been the southern continents of South America and Sub-Saharan Africa. Their teeming populations are mired in poverty and illiteracy, ravaged by disease, and torn by rebellion. In countries torn apart by warring armies and terrorist bands, such as Somalia, the Democratic Republic of Congo, Sierra Leone, Mali, and Colombia, governments have lost effective control of large parts of their national territories, and their states scarcely function as organized geopolitical entities.

Following World War II, the southern continents emerged from colonial and pseudocolonial status to become Cold War battlegrounds. With the collapse of the Soviet Union and the Communist movements in most countries on the southern continents, the days in which American, European, and Soviet powers waged surrogate wars, propping up satellite regimes or rebellious groups and extending vast amounts of military and economic assistance, are now history.

Because the countries were perceived to have little military importance, the major nations of the world have had less incentive to become deeply involved in directly addressing the poverty, illiteracy, and disease that ravage most of these lands, delegating the amelioration of such problems to international agencies. These agencies, however, lack the massive funding commitments that are needed and that only the major industrialized states can provide.

The strategic significance of Africa and South America has been rediscovered with the rising world demand for their natural resources, such as oil, gas, minerals, and timber. Africa has once again become a shatterbelt—an economic battleground between China and the West. South America is a focus of US attention for both the dangers of its drug traffic and the challenge posed by Venezuela, joined by Cuba, in the use of its energy wealth to promote its socialist revolution within the region. In addition, China's growing trade and investment in the region and Brazil's rise as a regional power poised to become a great power challenge the historic claim of the United States to Pan-American dominance.

The independent geopolitical region of South Asia has risen to geopolitical prominence because of the emergence of India as a major power and US dependence on a fragmented Pakistan while the war in Afghanistan raged. The United States has made an effort to create a strategic alliance with India, including the sharing of civilian nuclear technology. Nevertheless, it is likely that New Delhi will maintain its traditional posture of neutrality and seek to extend its own influence among the Indian Ocean lands.

In time, a fourth geostrategic realm dominated by India is anticipated. South Asia's importance as a region is ensured by the size of its population and the historical-cultural uniqueness of its civilizations and peoples. While beset by major economic and social problems, the region, led by India, already a high-tech global power, has the capacity for modernization and economic growth.

Globalization

The rapidly evolving globalization of the world's economy and the transformation of communications networks into globe-spanning information systems will not erase national or regional boundaries and identities. Globalization does not spell the end of geography and geopolitics, as some have argued.[1] Rather, it makes for a much more complex geopolitical system. Within it, national states have to deal with extensive external and internal pressures and forces, including domestic and international terrorism.

Globalization does not override geography. Rather, it adjusts to geographical settings and changes them. Its effects are selectively felt within national states and regions rather than having across-the-board impacts. Capital flows and outsourcing of manufacturing do not touch all parts of the world equally. The movement is largely toward coastal sections of states and regions that possess mass markets, ease of access, and large pools of cheap but trainable labor. Some of these areas have been the homelands of immigrants who have become successful entrepreneurs in the United States, Maritime Europe, and the Asia-Pacific Rim.

The diffusion of modern industry also takes place in response to political as well as economic considerations. South Korea, Taiwan, and Japan were the objects of US outsourcing when it suited Washington to build up these key portions of the Asia-Pacific Rim to stave off Soviet-Chinese pressures. This, too, was the case for the American initiatives in aiding the reconstruction of Western Europe immediately after World War II. Later, US economic attention shifted to other parts of Asia-Pacifica, such as Indonesia, Thailand, Malaysia, and the Philippines. It then turned toward its southern borderland—to Mexico and Central America. Washington is once again beginning to shift its attention—this time to transatlantic and transpacific free-trade partnerships.

Maritime Europe first focused its interests on its Maghreb borderland and on Southeast Asia, the former because of geographical proximity and colonial ties, the latter as a continuation of economic links forged during the age of imperialism. With the eastward expansion of the EU, Western Europe turned its attention to strengthening the economies of most of Central and Eastern European countries as well as serving as outlets for their surplus labor. Nevertheless, Europe's security and economic interests in the Maghreb remain important.

The rapid military response of France in expelling Islamic extremist rebels from Mali is an example of these strategic concerns. They are linked to the large presence within France of Muslim migrants who are vulnerable to jihadist influences. In recent years, the United States, the European Union, and Japan/Taiwan/South Korea have extended the global economy to China's "Golden Coast" and India's centers of information technology. However, vast parts of the world remain untouched by economic globalization and are unlikely to be drawn into the world economy for the foreseeable future.

Even in those parts of the developing world that have been strongly affected by globalization, there have been some adverse consequences. Progress is manifested in the creation of large middle and working classes and pockets of new wealth, despite charges by critics that globalization is another form of capitalist exploitation. However, the gap between the benefiting classes and the low-paid urban and farm workers in these countries has widened, creating new social strains—an inequality gap being felt in wealthier countries. In addition, the dependence of developing economies on the consumer markets of the world's wealthy countries as well as on foreign capital and loans has become dangerously high. When foreign markets shrink due to recession and decreased demand or to debt overload, there is little to cushion the impact. The economies and finances of Thailand, Indonesia, and Malaysia suffered severe declines in the late 1990s as a result of this vulnerability. They recovered, only to be affected once again by the 2008 recession in Europe and the United States. Entry into the world market economy has had an adverse effect on agriculture in many of the countries that have benefited from globalization, which is linked to freer trade and involves the opening of domestic markets to low-cost farm products from overseas. The output from highly efficient, modernized agricultural sectors, such as those of the United States, Canada, and Australia, has undermined more backward domestic farm economies. The result is growing opposition to free-trade agreements by such modernizing countries as Brazil that are reluctant to abandon protective farm tariffs.

While farm protection and preservation of the rural landscape are major concerns in some advanced industrial countries, such as Spain, Italy, France, Japan, and the United States, their economies can absorb displaced farm workers. This is not the case within the developing world. There, industrial job creation cannot keep pace with the demand for jobs. Displaced farmers flock to cities that cannot absorb them or seek relief through emigration, much of which is illegal.

The use of information technology, another aspect of globalization, is also not as far reaching as some assume. Thanks to the Internet, individuals in the most repressive of states can learn about developments in other parts of the world. However, the wider access to the hardware and software is lacking for much of the world's populace and tightly controlled if not absent. In settings such as China, many along the coastal region are tuned into the global information network and so act as pressure points against the restrictive aspects of the regime. This applies to a lesser degree to the poorer populations of the north and the interior, who remain rooted to their Communist traditions. Ultimately, the geographically framed gap between the economic and information "haves" and "have-nots" could lead to deep political fissures within China.

Another side of the information revolution is that, while it exposes parts of the developing world to the fruits of economic freedom and consumerism, it also reinforces the realization of the vast gaps in living standards and opportunities between the two worlds. In a country such as Russia, where the introduction of the free market economy led to such great abuse, including the looting of former state companies by corrupt entrepreneurs, the regime of Vladimir Putin used information technology to highlight these excesses and tighten its grip on the government. At the same time, the technology makes it harder for the government to hide its own abuses.

Still another example of the differential impact of the forces of globalization has to do with global warming. The "greenhouse effect," which causes rising surface and water temperatures, is an accepted scientific fact, but its impact will vary geographically. Bangladesh could be inundated by rising oceans as ice caps melt. At the same time, the warming might enable agriculture to be extended over more northerly areas and for longer periods in the Great Plains of the United States, Canada's Prairie Provinces, and Russia's west and central Siberia. While the United States is now reducing its overseas military bases for strategic and economic reasons, it may have to make common cause with Canada in expanding its Arctic military presence as the latter becomes a major ocean highway. Thus, while globalization is a most important force and will become increasingly so, its impact will vary with specific national states and regions. In subsequent chapters on the world's geopolitical regions, these variations will be amplified in the discussions on geopolitical patterns and features.

While the United States surely holds considerable responsibility for stabilizing the world system, it cannot be its sole manager. Proponents of the thesis that there is no credible alternative to the American role as linchpin and guarantor of the global system grossly overestimate the current US capacity. The United States was overstretched militarily in Iraq and Afghanistan, with limited capacity to use military force in trouble zones such as Darfur, Libya, and Syria, let alone be drawn into war with Iran. It is deeply in debt, has an unfavorable trade imbalance, and is overly dependent on its service economy. In efforts to maintain global equilibrium, the United States must join with other geopolitical actors, each with their own goals and immediate spheres of interest. United States partnerships with Maritime Europe and the Asia-Pacific Rim will be strengthened by the proposed free-trade pacts. This will enable it to give leadership to this multipolar world, but it cannot unilaterally impose order on the system. Indeed, in cases in which a single stronger power may not be able or willing to apply military force to gain particular objectives or to use it as a means of halting conflict, international and regional bodies may often be more effective in stabilizing the system. Alan Henrikson has made a cogent case for the increasingly vital role of diplomacy, as distinct from military deterrence, in achieving international equilibrium through the framework of the United Nations and other bodies.[2] It was China and South Korea which took the lead in the negotiations with North Korea. Negotiations with Iran involve six states. If international and regional diplomacy cannot stave off military intervention, it surely has proven a necessary adjunct in separating warring parties and leading them toward peace.

This volume seeks to identify the nature of the world's complex geopolitical structure and the roles and capacities of its various components. It is the hope of its author that a better understanding of the geopolitical forces that shape the international system can lead to shared national strategies that promote the maintenance of global equilibrium.

Notes

1. R. O'Brien, *Global Financial Integration: The End of Geography* (New York: Council on Foreign Relations Press, 1992), 1–35, 101–15.
2. Alan K. Henrikson, "Diplomacy for the 21st Century: 'Re-crafting the Old Guild'" (paper presented at the 503rd Wilton Park Conference, "Diplomacy: Profession in Peril?"); published in *Current Issues in International Diplomacy and Foreign Policy*, Wilton Park Papers, Vol. 1 (London: H.M. Stationery Office, 1998).

CHAPTER 2

Survey of Geopolitics

The true value of modern geopolitics is as a scholarly analysis of the geographical factors underlying international relations and guiding political interactions. Such analysis does not determine the directions that statecraft must take. It does, however, present desirable directions and alerts policy makers to the likely impact of their decisions on these relations and interactions.

Geography as a discipline has had to overcome some controversial roots. Introduced a century ago as a deterministic field of study and a recipe for statecraft, it was first offered as a set of geographically determined laws governing a state's strategic destinies and evolved as the geographical underpinnings of *realpolitik*. Presented as a science, its scholarly legitimacy was challenged on the grounds that it lacked empirically based principles in its development of doctrines that served the singular needs of particular states. In addition, the focus on *realpolitik* was criticized for the absence of a moral and ethical basis.

Later, in Nazi German hands, *geopolitik* became a distorted pseudoscience, with no scientific bounds. During and since the Cold War, the field has diverged into two competing schools of thought—one nation centered, the other offering universalistic perspectives.

Definitions

Geopolitics is a product of its times, and its definitions have evolved accordingly. Rudolf Kjellén, who coined the term in 1899, described geopolitics as "the theory of the state as a geographical organism or phenomenon in space."[1] For Karl Haushofer, the father of German *geopolitik*, "Geopolitics is the new national science of the state, . . . a doctrine on the spatial determinism of all political processes, based on the broad foundations of geography, especially of political geography.[2] On the eve of World War II, Derwent Whittlesey, the American political geographer, dismissed geopolitics as "a dogma, . . . the faith that the state is inherently entitled to its place in the sun."[3] Richard Hartshorne defined it as "geography utilized for particular purposes that lie beyond the pursuit of knowledge."[4]

In contrast to geographers Whittlesey and Hartshorne, political scientist Edmund Walsh espoused an American geopolitics based upon international justice and that was "a combined study of human geography and applied political science . . . dating back to Aristotle, Montesquieu and Kant."[5]

For Geoffrey Parker, geopolitics is "the study of international relations from a spatial or geographical perspective,"[6] while John Agnew defined the field as "examination of the geographical assumptions, designations and understandings that enter into the making of world politics."[7] Gearóid Ó Tuathail, an exponent of critical geopolitics, argues that "geopolitics does not have a singular, all-encompassing meaning or identity. Its discourse is a culturally and politically varied way of describing, representing and writing about geography and international politics."[8] Robert Kaplan, a national security specialist, takes a deterministic approach in asserting that "geopolitics and the competition for space is eternal."[9] This ignores the reality that the content, and therefore the importance, of certain spaces may be radically reduced over time.

Statesmen and scholars who view geopolitics as a vehicle for integrating geography and international politics may find it useful to define geopolitics not as a school of thought, but as a mode of analysis, relating diversity in content and scale of geographical settings to exercise of political power and identifying spatial frameworks through which power flows.

"Geopolitics" is defined in this volume as the analysis of the interaction between, on the one hand, geographical settings and perspectives and, on the other, political processes. The settings are composed of geographical features and patterns and the multilayered regions that they form. The political processes include forces that operate at the international level and those on the domestic scene that influence international behavior. Both geographical settings and political processes are dynamic, and each influences and is influenced by the other. Geopolitics addresses the consequences of this interaction. In this analysis, geography is defined in spatial terms as "places" and the "connections" between and among them. "Places" are bounded settings in which the interactions between humans and natural environments occur. "Connections" refers to the circulation of people, goods, and ideas that tie places together and have an impact on them.

The approach that has been taken in this work is regional and developmental. It treats the world's geopolitical structure as an evolving system composed of a hierarchy of levels. National states and their subnational units are framed within geostrategic realms and geopolitical regions.

Because geopolitics straddles two disciplines—geography and politics—its approaches vary according to frameworks of analysis common to each discipline. Since most early theories and concepts of geopolitics grew out of geographical thought, later applications by historians and political scientists often failed because they did not adapt their theories to the dynamic, complex nature of geographical settings.

Stages of Modern Geopolitics

Modern geopolitics has developed through five stages—the race for imperial hegemony; German *geopolitik*; American geopolitics; the Cold War–state centered versus universalistic geographical; and the post–Cold War period.

STAGE 1: THE RACE FOR IMPERIAL HEGEMONY

Geopolitical thinking can be traced back to Aristotle, Strabo, Bodin, Montesquieu, Kant, and Hegel. Its nineteenth-century precursors include Humboldt, Guyot, Buckle, and Ritter.

However, the founders of modern geopolitics were Ratzel, Mackinder, Kjellén, Bowman, and Mahan, whose writings reflected their era of intense nationalism, state expansionism, and overseas empire building. The principles and laws of these leading theoreticians reflected their national perspectives and experiences, including command of modes of transportation and communication for world outreach as well as the influence of social Darwinism.

Ratzel

Friedrich Ratzel (1844–1904), the German "father" of political geography and a natural scientist, was the first to treat space and location systematically, in his comparative studies of states.[10] He provided successor geopoliticians with a scientific basis for state expansionist doctrines that reflected Germany's nineteenth-century experiences and its ambitions for the future. During the last half of the nineteenth century Germany had emerged as the chief economic and military power on the European continent. Unified under Bismarck's leadership and victorious in its wars with Austria and France, it had enlarged its territory, expanded its heavy industries, and enacted social reform. With the aid of a new, powerful naval fleet, Germany posed a serious threat to Britain and France as it acquired an overseas empire in East and West Africa and the West Pacific, and sought commercial footholds in East Asia.

Ratzel based his system upon principles of evolution and science.[11] He viewed the state as an organism fixed in the soil whose spirit derived from mankind's ties to the land. His geographical "laws" focused on space (*raum*) and location (*lage*), the former dependent upon and contributing to the political character of groups living in the space, the latter providing space with its uniqueness. Frontiers were the "skins" or peripheral organs of states, reflecting growth and decline. When correlated with continental areas organized under a single government, states would generate vast political power. These "organic" theories of state growth fitted Germany's view of its future as a youthful, aggressive, capitalist "giant state."

Mackinder

Halford Mackinder (1861–1947), who established geography as a university discipline in Britain, foresaw the ending of the Victorian era. His concern was safeguarding the British Empire's political, commercial, and industrial primacy at a time when command of the seas no longer appeared to guarantee world supremacy. With the advent of the transcontinental railroad age (the Union Pacific, 1869; Berlin-Baghdad via Anatolia, 1896; and the Trans-Siberian, 1905), Mackinder viewed the rise of Eurasian continental states as the greatest threat to British world hegemony.

For Mackinder, geographical realities lay in the advantages of centrality of place and efficient movement of ideas, goods, and people. In 1904, he theorized that the inner area of Eurasia (the great Eurasian lowland), characterized by interior or polar drainage and impenetrable by sea power, was the "pivot area" of world politics (figure 2.1). This area included basically the forests of Siberia in the north and its steppes of the south, bounded by the deserts and subarid steppes of Turkestan. He warned that rule of the heart of the world's greatest landmass could become the basis for world domination owing to the superiority of rail over ships in terms of time and reach. A Eurasian land power (be it Russia, Germany, or even China, and especially an alliance of the first two) that gained control of the pivot area would outflank the maritime world.[12] Eleven years later, the English geographer James Fairgrieve, who introduced the term "heartland," opined that China was in an excellent position to dominate Eurasia.[13]

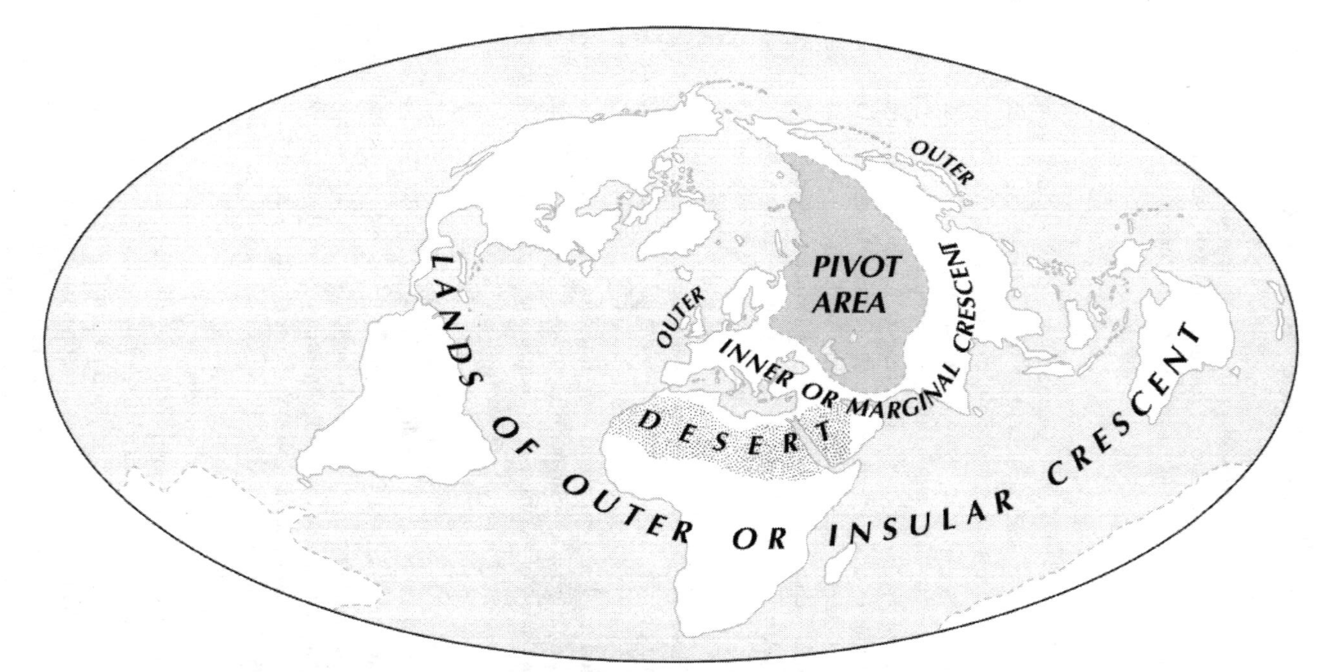

Figure 2.1. Mackinder's World: 1904

In *Democratic Ideals and Realities* (1919), Mackinder, now using the term "heartland" and taking into account advances in land transportation, population increases, and industrialization, enlarged his map to include Eastern Europe from the Baltic through the Black Sea as Inner Eurasia's strategic annex (figure 2.2). This became the basis for his dictum, "Who rules Eastern Europe commands the Heartland: Who rules the Heartland commands World-Island: Who rules World-Island commands the world."[14] The warning to Western statesmen was clear—the key to world domination lay in the middle tier of German and Slavic states, or Mitteleuropa—a region as accessible to Germans as it was to Russia.

Mackinder described the world as a closed system. Nothing could be altered without changing the balance of all, and rule of the world still rested upon force, notwithstanding the juridical assumptions of equality among sovereign states. Mackinder called himself a democratic idealist in advocating equality of opportunity for nations to achieve balanced economic development. He also described himself as a realist who feared that the League of Nations would degenerate into an unbalanced empire as one or two of the great powers bid for predominance. As a safeguard, he urged smaller powers to federate to increase the number of significant players on the world scene and make it more difficult for hegemony to be attained by potential tyrants. Foreseeing the decline of Britain as the world's leading power, he called for Western Europe and North America to become a single community of nations—a forerunner of the North Atlantic community.

Mackinder remained steadfast in his commitment to the concept of balance. In looking at the shape of the post–World War II order, he foresaw a world geopolitically balanced between a combination of the North Atlantic ("Midland Ocean") and Asian heartland powers. By working together, they could keep future German ambitions in check. The monsoonal lands of India and China represented an evolving third balancing unit within the world system. He also speculated that the continental masses bordering the South Atlantic might eventually become a unit within the balancing process. The "Mantle of Vacancies," a barrier region extending from the Sahara through the Central Asian deserts that divides the major communities of humankind, might emerge as a fifth component of the system. Mackinder forecast that this barrier region might someday provide solar energy as a substitute for exhaustible resources.

These thoughts were sketched out in a 1943 article titled "The Round World and the Winning of the Peace."[15] In it, Mackinder discarded his famous 1919 dictum that rule of Heartland meant command of World-Island. He drew no map to accompany his article. Therefore, a map that cartographically expresses what he wrote is presented here (figure 2.3). First, he detached Lenaland (the central Siberian tableland) from Heartland. Thus, Heartland now consisted largely of the cleared forest and steppe portions of Eurasia. More important, Mackinder's concept of the map of the world had changed, as he introduced the concept of a world balanced by a multiplicity of regions, each with a distinct natural and human resource base.

The yardsticks that Mackinder used in drawing the boundaries of his Heartland indicate that the original concept of the pivot area of the world had changed from that of an arena of movement (i.e., as a region of mobility for land forces) to one of a "power citadel" based upon people, resources, and interior lines. The three boundaries (figure 2.4) that reflect Mackinder's changing views of the earth indicate that he was well aware of technological developments, including air power. To place Mackinder's views in historical and contemporary perspectives, Cold War US containment policy was based on his Heartland worlds of 1904 and 1919. Post–Cold War American balance-of-power goals are more in consonance with his 1943 global view.

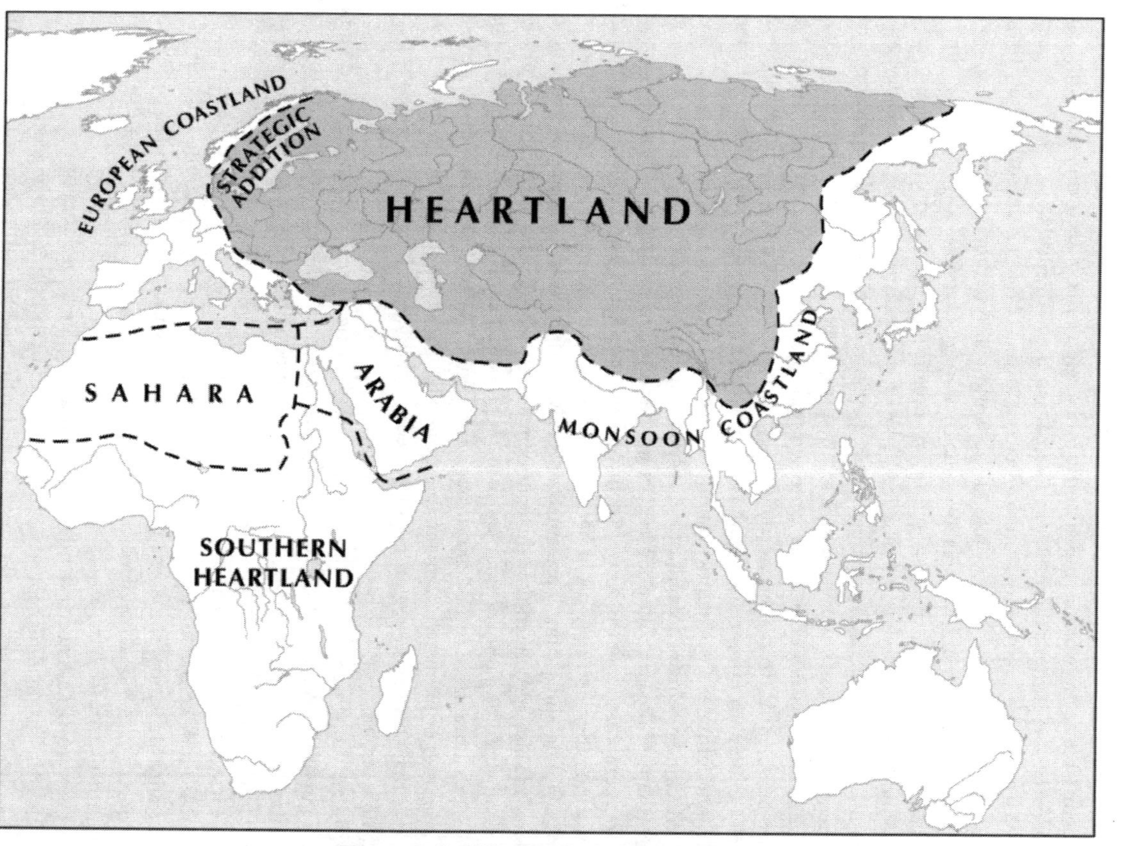

Figure 2.2. Mackinder's World: 1919

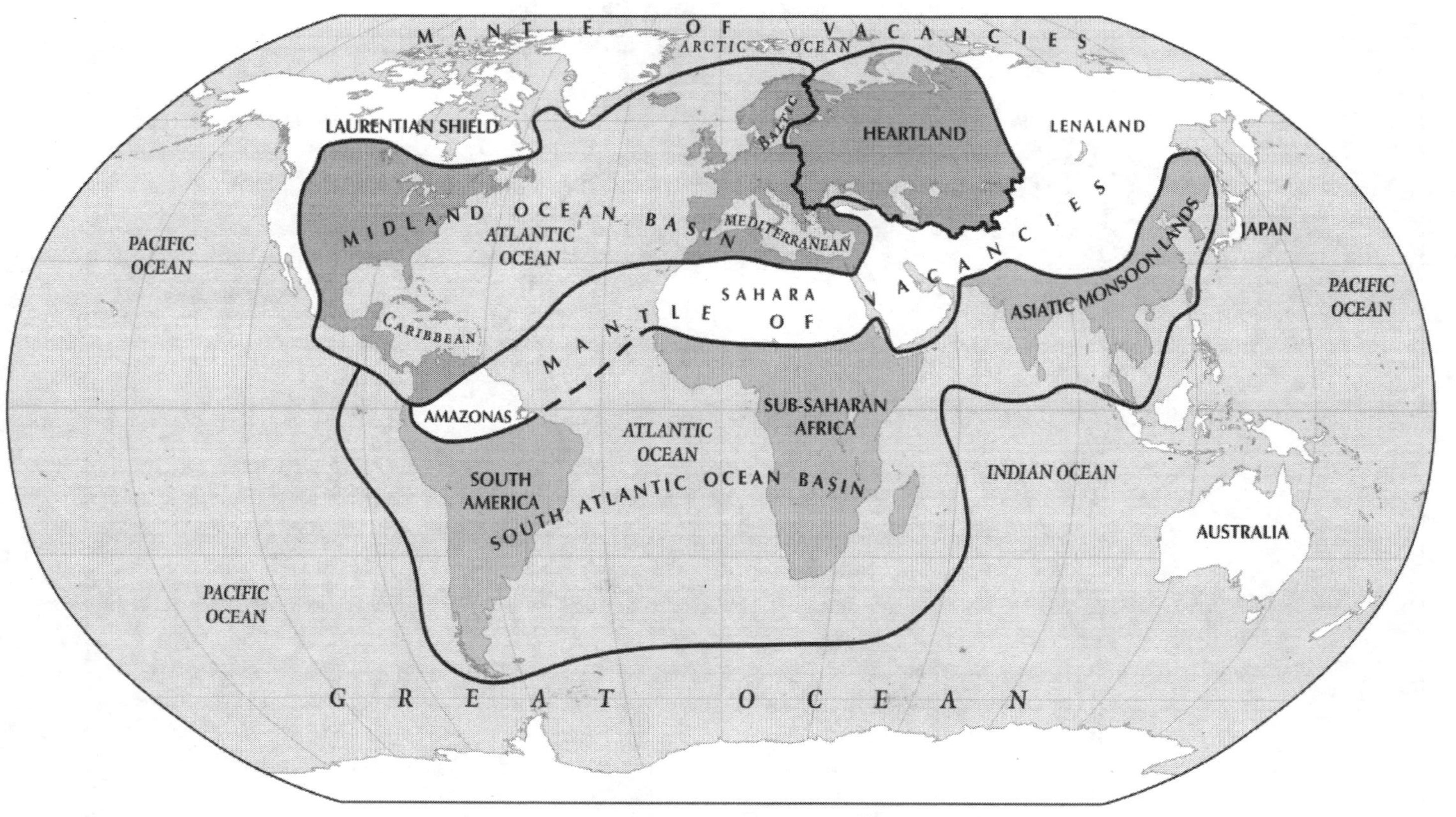

Figure 2.3. Mackinder's World: 1943

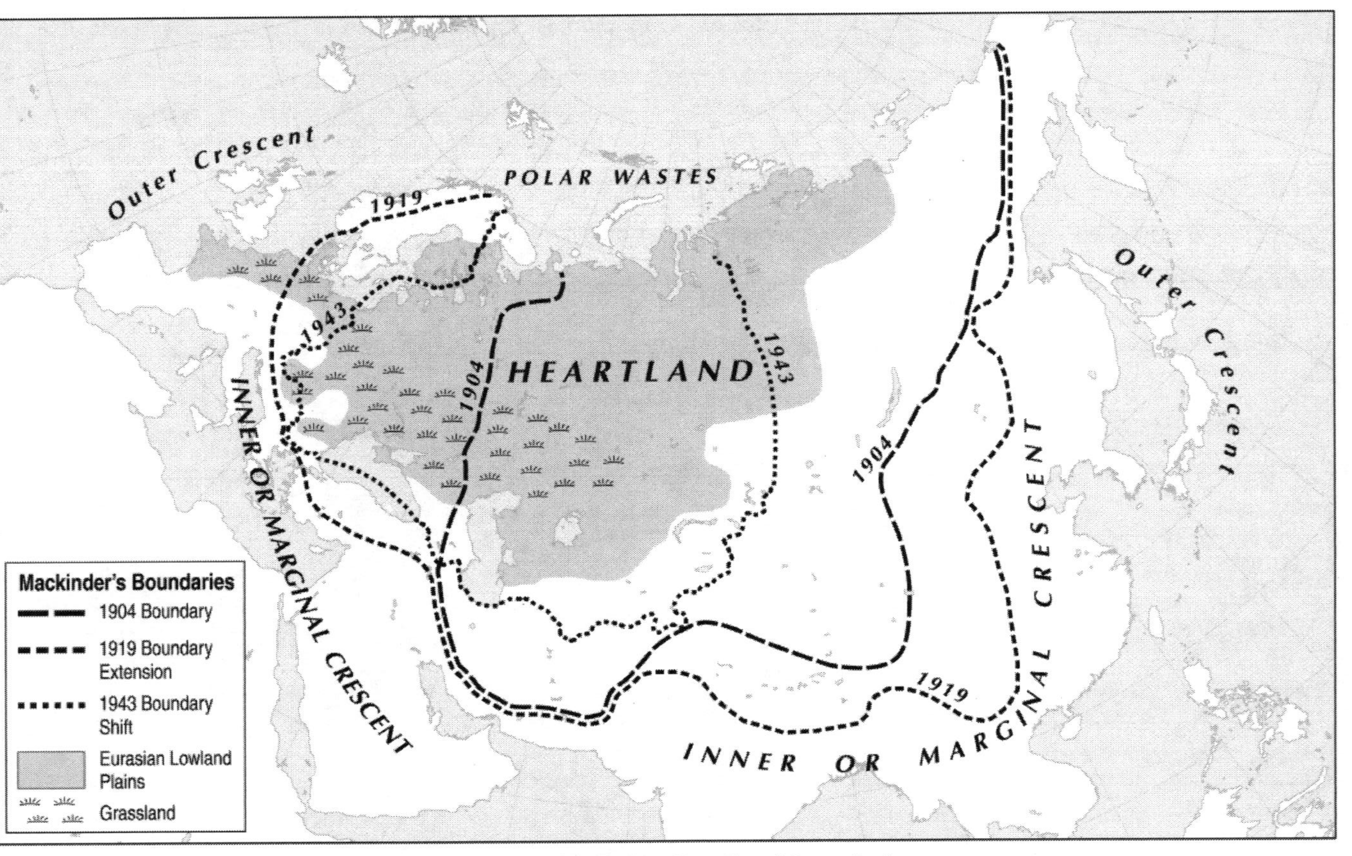

Figure 2.4. Changing Heartland Boundaries

Whereas Ratzel's theories of the large state were based on concepts of self-sufficiency, closed space, and totalitarian controls, Mackinder was strongly committed to cooperation among states, democratization of the empire into a commonwealth of nations, and preservation of small states. He bridged the academy and politics, serving as a Conservative and Unionist member of Parliament (1910–22) and as British high commissioner for South Russia (1919–20). While he was an advocate of open systems, he exhibited ambivalence over trade issues. Initially a Liberal imperialist and proponent of free trade, he eventually became committed to a preferential tariff system to protect British imperial unity.[16]

The impact of Mackinder's thinking spanned half a century, and his ideas were the cornerstone for generations of strategic policy makers. His view of the world became the basis for Lord Curzon's imperial strategies in South Asia and South Russia, for German *geopolitik* between World Wars I and II, and for Western containment strategies of the post–World War II era.

Mahan

Admiral Alfred T. Mahan (1849–1914) was a naval historian and second president of the United States Naval War College. His global perspective was also Eurasian centered.[17] For Mahan, the northern land hemisphere, the far-flung parts of which were linked through the passageways offered by the Panama and Suez Canals, was the key to world power; within that hemisphere, Eurasia was the most important component. Mahan recognized Russia as the dominant Asian land power, whose location made it unassailable. However, he felt that Russia's landlocked position put it at a disadvantage because, in his view, sea movement was superior to land movement.

For Mahan, the critical zone of conflict lay between the thirtieth and fortieth parallels in Asia, where Russian land power and British sea power met. He argued that world dominance could be held by an Anglo-American alliance from key bases surrounding Eurasia. Indeed, he predicted that an alliance of the United States, Britain, Germany, and Japan would one day hold common cause against Russia and China.

Mahan developed his geopolitical views as America's frontier history was drawing to a close and the country had begun to look beyond its continental limits to a new role as a world power. He considered the United States to be an outpost of European power and civilization, regarding its Pacific shore and islands to be extensions of the Atlantic-European realm. The United States thus lay within the Western half of a twofold global framework, the Oriental (Asian) being the other half. In many ways, Mahan's view of the world's setting anticipated Mackinder's. Their diametrically opposed strategic conclusions stemmed from different assessments of the comparative effectiveness of land versus sea movement.

Espousing a "blue water strategy," Mahan strongly supported US annexation of the Philippines, Hawaii, Guam, and Puerto Rico; control of the Panama Canal Zone; and tutelage over Cuba. His writings helped bring an end to American isolationism and were highly influential in shaping US foreign policy during the McKinley and Theodore Roosevelt administrations. Roosevelt, in particular, endorsed the Mahan call for a larger navy as well as his broader geopolitical concepts.[18]

Bowman

Isaiah Bowman (1878–1949), the leading American geographer of his period, was also engaged at policy levels in an attempt to fashion the new world order envisaged by Woodrow

Wilson: "The effects of the Great War are so far-reaching that we shall have hence-forth a new world. . . . [T]he new era would date from the years of the First World War, just as Medieval Europe dates from the fall of Rome, or the modern democratic era dates from the Declaration of Independence." Describing the war as the combination of assassination, invasion, and Germanic ambitions "colored by the desire to control the seats of production and the channels of transportation of all those products," he viewed the relations among states as an evolutionary struggle.[19]

Bowman did not believe that the League of Nations was, in and of itself, the framework for a new world. Rather, he saw different leagues emerging for functional purposes, each designed to advance cooperative plans that would reduce the causes of international trouble. "The world's people are still fundamentally unlike," he wrote, "and the road to success passes through a wilderness of experiment."[20]

No grand theory here, as was Mackinder's, but rather the prescription of an empiricist, of a practitioner grounded on boundaries, resources, national minorities—a world of shifting international parts that was disorganized, unstable, and dangerous and requiring mediating international groups to minimize the dangers. Bowman's idea of a new world was essentially a map of the world as it was, with greater attention to the sovereign interests of certain nationalities and to a need for coordinated international action. His work was, in effect, an explication of what problems would be encountered by Woodrow Wilson's fourteenth point—the call for a general association of nations to guarantee the peace of the world.

Kjellén

Rudolf Kjellén (1864–1922), the political scientist who coined the term "geopolitics" in 1899, was influenced both by his Swedish background and by Germany's growth into a giant state. He viewed the impending breakdown of the Concert of Europe and the drift toward war and chaos as the death knell for a small state like Sweden. Adopting Ratzel's organic state concept, he considered Germany's emergence as a great power inevitable and desirable. The needs of Sweden would be fulfilled within the framework of a new Mitteleuropean bloc from Scandinavia and the Baltic through Eastern Europe and the Balkans, dominated by an ascendant Germany.

A Conservative member of the Swedish parliament, Kjellén viewed geopolitics as the "science of the state," whereby the state's natural environment provided the framework for a power unit's pursuit of "inexorable laws of progress." Geopolitics was initially conceived by Kjellén as one of five major disciplines for understanding the state, the others being termed econo-, demo-, socio-, and crato- (power) politics. As the mainstay of the five, geopolitics came to subsume the others.

The dynamic organic approach led Kjellén to espouse the doctrine that political processes were spatially determined. Moreover, since giant states in Europe could only be created by war, he viewed geopolitics as primarily a science of war.[21]

STAGE 2: GERMAN *GEOPOLITIK*

German *geopolitik* emerged in reaction to Germany's devastating defeat in World War I. Humbled by the Treaty of Versailles, Germany was stripped of its overseas empire and important parts of its national territory. Alsace-Lorraine was returned to France, small border areas were annexed by Belgium, and North Schleswig was returned to Denmark in a plebiscite. Historic Prussia was divided. In West Prussia, Poznan (Posen) went to Poland, as did the land that constituted the Polish Corridor. Danzig became a "free city" and, in the easternmost part of East Prussia, the Memel Territory first came under the League of Nations, administered by France, and was then annexed by Lithuania. Parts of Upper Silesia went to Poland and Czechoslovakia. The Saar was put under French administration, pending a plebiscite to be held in 1935 to determine its final status, and the Rhineland was occupied by Allied forces. Germany was now but a shadow of the expanding giant state of Ratzel's and Kjellén's imperial era.

In addition, the social cohesion forged by Bismarck's policies was shattered. The socialist Weimar Republic was beleaguered by class warfare and attempts to overthrow it by Communists on the left and racist militant nationalists and aristocratic conservatives on the right. Unemployment was rampant and inflation raged. This was the setting within which Karl Haushofer and his colleagues established the *Zeitschrift für Geopolitik* (1924–39) and the Institute for Geopolitics at the University of Munich. Undoing Versailles by restoring the lost territories and rebuilding Germany as a world power undergirded the pseudoscientific "laws" and principles of *geopolitik* that served Nazi Germany.

Haushofer

Karl Haushofer (1869–1946), the former military commander who became a political geographer, was not an original thinker. The *geopolitik* of the group of German geopoliticians whom he led (Otto Maull, Erich Obst, Ewald Banse, Richard Hennig, Colin Ross, Albrecht Haushofer) was based essentially upon the writings of Kjellén, Ratzel, and Mackinder. Others whose teachings he invoked included Mahan, Fairgrieve, and such geographical determinists as Ellen Churchill Semple, who was Ratzel's leading American disciple.

Much of the organismic Hegelian philosophy of *geopolitik* came from Ratzel directly or via Kjellén. *Lebensraum* (living space) and autarchy became slogans for doctrines whose consequences were conflict and total war. Three geographical settings permeated the literature of *geopolitik*: Ratzel's large states, Mackinder's World-Island, and panregions. The organic growth of Germany to its west and east was regarded as inevitable. To gain mastery over World-Island, it was necessary for Germany to dominate the USSR and destroy British sea power. The geopoliticians posited that German control over Pan-Europe (including Eastern Europe) would force the Soviet Union, regarded as an Asian power, to come to terms.

During most of the 1920s and 1930s, Haushofer espoused continental panregionalism based upon complementarity of resources and peoples: Pan-America, Pan-Eur-Africa, and Pan-Asia, with the United States, Germany, and Japan as respective cores. His position on the USSR was ambiguous. He proposed variously a German-Russian alliance, a Pan-Russia-South Asia grouping, and a Japan-China-Russia bloc. His call for Germany, the USSR, and Japan to form a Eurasian panregion that would dominate World-Island influenced the German-Soviet pact of 1939 but was made moot by Hitler's subsequent invasion of the Soviet Union.

The German school could overlook these contradictions because *geopolitik* made no pretense of objectivity. Its principles were designed to fulfill German national and imperial aims. Doctrines such as *blut und boden* (blood and soil) and *rasse und raum* (race and space) became ideological foundations for the murderous Nazi regime, which plunged the world into history's most devastating war and perpetrated the Jewish Holocaust and the murder of millions of Slavic peoples.

While Karl Haushofer was the key figure in *geopolitik*, there were other important contributors. Otto Maull was a cofounder and coeditor of the *Zeitschrift* and subscribed to the theory of the organic state as a collection of spatial cells (regions, cities, etc.) with a life of its own. Erich Obst, the third cofounder of the *Zeitschrift*, sought to establish "objective" standards for *lebensraum*. Richard Hennig developed a doctrine in which land, space, and economics were deemed more important than racial considerations, for which he was bitterly attacked by some of his colleagues. Ewald Banse outlined the strategy and tactics for the coming *blitzkrieg*. Albrecht Haushofer focused on the Atlantic world and on translating geographic data into expansive power politics. An American contributor to the *Zeitschrift* was Colin Ross, an early advocate of Japan's freedom to develop its own "laws of life," independent of German direction. Nevertheless, it was Karl Haushofer who was the architect and mastermind of the *Zeitschrift* and the Institute for Geopolitics—he held the main responsibility for the content and direction taken by German *geopolitik*.

Haushofer's extraordinary influence derived from his close ties to Rudolf Hess, his aide-de-camp in World War I and, subsequently, his student at the University of Munich. Through Hess, he had contact with Hitler from 1923 to 1938. Many of Haushofer's doctrines, especially *lebensraum*, were incorporated into *Mein Kampf*, and Haushofer advised Hitler at Munich in 1938.[22] With Hess's flight to England in 1941, the influence of the geopoliticians upon Hitler ended. Indeed, Haushofer was imprisoned briefly at Dachau (ironically, he had a Jewish wife). His son Albrecht, also a geographer with links to aristocrat military circles, was involved in the generals' plot to assassinate Hitler in 1944 and was killed by the SS. Haushofer and his wife committed suicide in 1946.

STAGE 3: GEOPOLITICS IN THE UNITED STATES

Spykman

Most American academic geographers vigorously repudiated German *geopolitik*, resulting in a general reluctance to pursue the study of geopolitics. Nicholas Spykman, a US scholar of international relations who had been born in Amsterdam, was one of the few who did work in the field during this period (1942–44). His "rimland" theory reflected Mahan's view of the world and was presented as an antidote to the concept of heartland primacy.[23]

However, Spykman's terminology, his detailed global geographical setting, and the political conclusions that he derived from his views of the world show that his basic inspiration came from Mackinder, whose strategic conclusions he attempted to refute. Essentially, Spykman sought to arouse the United States against the danger of world domination by Germany.[24] He felt that only a dedicated alliance of Anglo-American sea power and Soviet land power could prevent Germany from seizing control of all the Eurasian shorelines and thereby gaining domination over World-Island.

Spykman considered that the Eurasian coastal lands (including maritime Europe, the Middle East, India, Southeast Asia, and China) were the keys to world control because of their populations, their rich resources, and their use of interior sea-lanes.

In essence, Spykman had the same global view as Mackinder, but he rejected the land-power doctrine to say, "Who controls the rimland rules Eurasia; who rules Eurasia controls the destinies of the world." To Spykman, the rimland (Mackinder's "Marginal Crescent") was the key to the struggle for the world. In the past, the fragmentation of the Western European portion of rimland and the power of the United Kingdom and the United States (parts of what Spykman considered the offshore continents and islands) had made unitary control of the rimland impossible. (This offshore region, which included the New World,

Sub-Saharan Africa, and Australasia, was equivalent to Mackinder's "Outer Crescent.") Now, however, Spykman feared that a single power, such as Germany, might seize control of the European rimland and then sweep onto the other portions through various combinations of conquests and alliances, using ship superiority and command of a network of naval and air bases around Eurasia.

Certainly there is still much to be said in favor of sea communication as far as the movement of goods is concerned. Also, aircraft carriers and submarines have given a mobility in the use of aircraft and missiles to ocean basin powers that fixed land bases cannot. The inadequacy of Spykman's doctrine was and remains the fact that no Eurasian rimland power is capable of organizing all of the rimland because of the vulnerability of the rimland to both the heartland and the offshore powers. A united maritime Europe would have to have complete control of the Mediterranean, North Africa, the Middle East, Sub-Saharan Africa, and Australia before it could attempt to exert its strategic dominance upon the remainder of the South and East Asian portions of the rimland. It could succeed only if the heartland or the offshore New World's American power did not intervene. He also held that a rimland China that swept into control of offshore or South Asia would be at a disadvantage in seeking to control the Middle East against heartland-, Western European–, or African-based pressures.

The importance of interior lines of land communication, even between parts of the rimland, looms greater today than it did in Spykman's considerations. Thus, the Chinese land base was able to sustain North Korea and North Vietnam in spite of the control of the seas and the air by offshore powers. Communist networks of rails and modern highways (as well as jungle and mountain trails) in South China and North Vietnam were the sinews of politico-economic penetration that ultimately defeated the United States in Vietnam and that have drawn Vietnam, Laos, and Cambodia into China's strategic oversight.

Other Theoreticians

The impact of the air age upon geopolitical thought produced a variety of views. In 1942, George Renner suggested that the air lanes had united the heartland of Eurasia with a second, somewhat smaller heartland in Anglo-America, across Arctic ice fields, to form a new, expanded heartland within the northern hemisphere.[25] A major attribute of this new heartland was the mutual vulnerability of its Eurasian and its Anglo-American portions across the Arctic. According to Renner, not only would the expanded heartland be the dominant power center of the world, but it also possessed the advantages of interior air, sea, and land routes across the polar world. Thus the Arctic, as the pivotal world arena of movement, was the key to heartland and therefore to world control.

Another opinion, that of Alexander de Seversky, has been described by Stephen Jones as "the airman's global view."[26] De Seversky's map of the world, which he presented in 1950, is an azimuthal equidistant projection centered on the North Pole. The western hemisphere lies to the south of the pole, Eurasia and Africa to the north. Here again was an Old World-New World division. North America's area of "air dominance" (its area of reserve for resources and manufacturing) is Latin America; the Soviet Union's area of air dominance is South and Southeast Asia and most of Africa south of the Sahara. De Seversky considered the areas where North American and Soviet air dominance overlapped (this includes Anglo-America, the Eurasian heartland, maritime Europe, North Africa, and the Middle East) to be the "Area of Decision." According to this view, air mastery and, therefore, global control could be gained.[27]

In one sense, this is an extension of Renner's air-age view. In another, however, it led to two different and highly questionable conclusions. The first stems from the distortion of the map projection, which suggests that Africa and South America are so widely separated that they are mutually defensible by their respective senior partners, the Soviet Union and the United States.

Second, de Seversky's view was that air supremacy, and with it control of the northern hemispheric Area of Decision, could be achieved by one power through all-out aerial warfare. While he spoke of only the United States, the USSR, and perhaps the United Kingdom as having the potentialities of being great powers, in theory any country with the necessary military hardware, recuperative strength, and will could achieve dominance. Thus de Seversky's theories lead to two conclusions: (1) "air isolationism," which suggested a viable division of the world into two, and (2) "a unitary global view," suggesting that, in the event of all-out war, the power that led in military hardware, regardless of its location, could dominate the world. De Seversky's major work, written in 1950, did not anticipate that several powers might achieve the capabilities of mutual destruction.

There are those who held that air power did not add a third dimension to land and sea movement but simply a complementary dimension to each of these channels. Particularly if all-out nuclear warfare is eliminated, this view of what Jones called the "air-first moderates" held that air power could be decisive only as it lends a comparative advantage to land or sea powers. An influential spokesman for this point of view within the North Atlantic Alliance was the British strategist, air force marshal Sir John Slessor. He was a strong advocate of airborne nuclear weapons as the "great deterrent" against total war.[28] Thus ruling out total war, he concluded that the role of air power is to supplement sea- or land-based forces. He held that even an invasion of Western Europe could be countered by a limited type of air attack and land defense to arrest invasion without nuclear war. To Slessor, whose strategic doctrine followed a rimland-heartland equilibrium theory, the likely arenas for limited war were the Middle East and Southeast Asia, with air power being the key supplement to sea-supported land actions.

STAGE 4: THE COLD WAR–STATE-CENTERED VERSUS UNIVERSALISTIC APPROACHES

Onset of the Cold War reawakened Western interest in geopolitics. This came from historians, political scientists, and statesmen, not from geographers, who had distanced themselves from geopolitics because of the taint of German *geopolitik.*

State-Centered Geopolitics

American Cold Warriors embraced geopolitics as a basis for a national policy aimed at confronting the Soviet Union and international Communism. Building on early, geographically derived geopolitical theories and holding static interpretations of global and regional spatial patterns, they introduced such political-strategic concepts as containment, domino theory, balance-of-power linkages, and linchpin states into the lexicon of Cold War geopolitics. In this context, Halford Mackinder's heartland theory played an instrumental role. In 1943, William C. Bullitt, the first US ambassador to the Soviet Union, cited Mackinder in his efforts to persuade Roosevelt that Stalin was not to be trusted owning to Soviet long-range plans for the global conquest by Communism. Roosevelt rejected Bullitt's recommendations that the United States should take measures to block the expansion of Soviet influence into Eastern Europe that Bullitt anticipated.

George Kennan's 1946 warning of the historical imperative of Soviet expansionism from its Russian Asiatic center was embraced by American anti-Communists as the intellectual basis for containment of the USSR around every point of the heartland.[29] This was formalized in the Truman Doctrine of 1947. Winston Churchill, in his 1946 speech in Fulton, Missouri, also issued a call for containing the expansionist tendencies of the Soviet Union, coining the expression "Iron Curtain."[30]

As a member of the policy planning staff of the US Department of State during the Truman administration, Kennan had promoted the idea of containment. He was the first in a long line of US policy makers to embrace the concept. Other early proponents were Dean Acheson, Paul Nitze, John Foster Dulles, Dwight Eisenhower, Walt Rostow, and Maxwell Taylor. They were later joined by Henry Kissinger, Richard Nixon, Zbigniew Brzezinski, and Alexander Haig, and containment became the keystone of American foreign policy.[31] These versions of the heartland-rimland theory remained a tool for containment strategy long after that strategy had proved wanting, as the Soviet Union and China leaped across the rimland to penetrate parts of the Middle East, Sub-Saharan Africa, the Caribbean and Central America, and Southeast Asia.

Western foreign policy therefore could not confine itself to containment of the Eurasian continental power along its heartland borders. Instead, it adopted a strategy of checking the spread of Communism throughout the Third World. The idealistic vision that had prompted the United States to support the freedom and democratization of colonial peoples quickly gave way to expedient *realpolitik*—propping up right-wing dictatorships in order to stop the threat of Communism wherever that threat was perceived to exist.

Another popular geopolitical doctrine, "domino theory," was first proposed by William Bullitt in 1947. He feared that Soviet Communist power would spread via China into Southeast Asia. The concept was adopted by both the Kennedy and Nixon administrations, which rationalized American intervention in Vietnam as a measure to "save" the rest of Southeast Asia.[32]

The domino theory was an important argument for extending Western containment policy well beyond the Southeast Asian and Middle Eastern shatterbelts into the Horn of Africa and Sub-Saharan Africa, Central America and Cuba, South America, and South Asia. These areas became battlegrounds for the two superpowers, as each supported local surrogates militarily, politically, and economically. The goal was to protect or gain sources of raw materials and markets while denying military bases to the enemy overseas. The imagery of dominos survives. The threat of the spread of Kosovar Albanian irredentism to Macedonia, Bulgaria, and Greece was one of the factors, along with humanitarian considerations, which precipitated NATO's air war against Yugoslavia in 1998. Without using the term, the George W. Bush administration applied this theory as one of its rationales for toppling Saddam Hussein. It argued that a free, democratic Iraq would foster democracy and peace throughout the Middle East as well as help to resolve the Arab-Israeli conflict. Toward the end of his administration, President Bush shifted course, arguing that American troops had to remain in Iraq to prevent Islamic terrorism from spreading. This argument is also the basis for the efforts of President Obama to retain American military trainers in Afghanistan after withdrawal of nearly all of the US and NATO troops in 2014.

A third principle, "linkage," was introduced into geopolitics by Henry Kissinger in 1979.[33] Indeed, Leslie Hepple suggested that Kissinger almost single-handedly reintroduced the term "geopolitics" as synonymous with global balance-of-power politics.[34] Linkage is based upon the theory of a network that connected all parts of the world's trouble spots to the Soviet Union and on the premise that American involvement in any single conflict needed to be viewed for its impact upon overall superpower balance. For Kissinger, display of Western impotence in one part of the world, such as Asia or Africa, would inevitably erode its credibility in other parts of the world, such as the Middle East. Linkage was used to rationalize the Nixon administration's clinging to the war in Vietnam long after the conflict had clearly been lost. The threat of credibility loss continued to resonate with the West, serving as a driving force in NATO's war against Yugoslavia.

Linkage theory was also applied to détente with the Soviet Union and accommodation with China. To maintain the balance of power, the Nixon administration sought Moscow's agreement on strategic arms limitations and mutual nuclear deterrence and tried to play China off against the USSR. The logical consequence of this policy was acquiescing to the Brezhnev Doctrine, which held that military force was justified to keep the socialist countries of Eastern and Central Europe within the Soviet camp.

Zbigniew Brzezinski's geopolitical worldview was based on the struggle between Eurasian land power and sea power. For him, the key to containment and preventing Soviet world dominance lay in US control of "linchpin" states. He defined these by their geographical position, which enabled them to exert economic/military influence, or by their militarily significant geostrategic locations. The designated linchpins were Germany, Poland, Iran or Pakistan-Afghanistan, South Korea, and the Philippines. Their dominance by the United States would effectively contain the Russian "imperial" power, protecting Europe and Japan and, in the case of South Korea and the Philippines, preventing encirclement of China.[35]

For Brzezinski, the US-Soviet conflict was an endless game, and linchpin control was a necessary part of the US geostrategic game plan. In this approach to geopolitics, there is little consideration of the geopolitical complexity of the global system and of the multiplicity of forces beyond superpower reach that had become active agents in the system. It particularly ignored the innate geopolitical positions and strengths of China and India and surely underestimated the costs of superpower alliances with weak and unstable regimes.

Universalistic Geopolitics

When geographers reengaged in geopolitics in the 1960s and 1970s, they introduced theories based upon universalistic/holistic views of the world and the dynamic nature of geographical space. Three approaches predominated: (1) a polycentric international power system; (2) a unitary economically based world system; and (3) an environmentally and socially ordered geopolitics.

Because these fresh geographical theories challenged bipolar Cold War geopolitics, they had little appeal to the Cold Warriors and failed to make their way into popular "political" geopolitics as practiced by statesmen and popularly disseminated through the press. The polycentric or multinodal/multilevel power approach rejected the heartland theory of world domination, as (ironically) had Halford Mackinder in his last published work in 1943.

In 1963, this writer proposed a flexible hierarchy (refined in 1973) of geostrategic realms, geopolitical regions, shatterbelts, national states, and subnational units within a system that evolved through forces of dynamic equilibrium.[36] A decade later, a comparative developmental approach was added that drew on the developmental psychology theories of Heinz Werner and the general systems principles of Ludwig von Bertalanffy.[37] The expanded geopolitical theory posited that the structural components of the global system evolve from stages of atomization and undifferentiation with relatively few parts to specialized integration with many parts at different geoterritorial scales. Equilibrium is maintained by moving from one stage to another through responses to short-term disturbances. Regionalism, not globalism, is the primary shaper of geopolitical relations—a view reinforced by the current focus of great powers, especially the United States, on regional trade pacts.

In England, G. R. Chrone presented a geopolitical system of ten regional groupings that were also hierarchically ordered and had a historical and cultural basis.[38] In Chrone's view, the world power balance was shifting from Europe and the West toward Asia and the Pacific. He predicted that the Pacific Ocean would become the future arena of confrontation for the USSR, the United States, and China.

Two decades later, Peter Taylor, the English geographer, broke away from the "realistic" approach to power-centered geopolitics when he applied a world-systems approach based upon global economics. He drew upon the 1983 work of Immanuel Wallerstein, who argued that the world economy means a single global society, not competing national economies. Integrating the Wallerstein model with George Modelski's cycles of world power, Taylor presented power and politics within the context of a cyclical world economy in which nation-states and localities are fitted.[39]

Both Taylor and Wallerstein viewed global conflict in North-South terms (rich nations versus poor nations) rather than in Mackinder's earlier East-West model. Accepting the thesis that capitalist core areas aggrandize themselves at the expense of the peripheral parts of the world, Taylor's radical perspective was offered as a basis for "informing" the political issues of the day.[40]

An environmentally and socially oriented geopolitics was promoted by Yves Lacoste in France with the establishment of the journal *Hérodite* in 1976. In moving toward a "new" *géopolitique*, Lacoste sought to overcome the national chauvinism of the "old" geopolitics by focusing on the land, not on the state. *Hérodite* linked geopolitics to ecology and broader environmental issues, as well as to such matters as world poverty and resource exhaustion.[41] Much of Lacoste's work was inspired by the French human geographer and political anarchist Élisée Reclus, who believed it essential to reshape the world's political structure by abolishing states and establishing a cooperative global system.[42] While this French geopolitics did not produce systematic geopolitical theory, it did put the spotlight on applying geopolitics to significant global problems.

STAGE 5: POST–COLD WAR ERA: COMPETITION OR ACCOMMODATION?

The end of the Cold War era has generated a number of new approaches to geopolitics. For Francis Fukuyama, the passing of Marxism-Leninism and the triumph of Western liberal democracy and "free marketism" portended a universal, homogeneous state. In this idealized worldview, geographical differences, and therefore geopolitics, have little role to play. Fukuyama has more recently theorized that for the next couple of decades, authoritarianism will become stronger in much of the world, especially Russia and China, and that the United States cannot do much to arrest it.[43]

For others, the end of the Cold War has heralded a "new world order" and the geopolitics of US global hegemony. President George H. W. Bush, addressing Congress in 1990, defined the policy behind the war against Iraq as envisaging a new world order led by the United States and "freer from the threat of terror, stronger in the pursuit of justice, and more secure in the quest for peace, . . . a world in which nations recognize the shared responsibility for freedom and justice."[44]

Still another approach is Robert Kaplan's geopolitics of anarchy. From the perspective of a world divided into the rich North and the poor South, Kaplan concludes that the South, especially Africa, is doomed to anarchy and chaos. His map of the future, dubbed the "last map," is an "ever mutating representation of chaos." He argues that only the United States has the power to stabilize the world system, pushing back the spreading autocratic tide and standing up to Islamic antimodernism.[45]

None of these three scenarios has come to pass. In most cases, the overthrow of Communist regimes has not led to stable, free-market economies. The restraints upon the unilateral application of US military, economic, and political power are evident from the failures to gain US objectives in Iraq, Afghanistan, Somalia, and Haiti, while a geopolitics of chaos gives inadequate attention to the systemic regional and global forces that keep turbulence in check and absorb its positive aspects into the system.

The main thrust of post–Cold War geopolitics, however, continues to follow the two streams of the previous era—the nation-centered/political and the universalistic/geographical. Political geopoliticians advocate projection of Western power into Central and Eastern Europe to weaken Russia's heartland position at its western edge. They also advance strategies for penetrating the Caucasus and Central Asia and for playing China off against Russia.

Brzezinski's prescription for maintaining US global hegemony is to achieve primacy in three parts of the "Eurasian chessboard": the West, or Europe; the South, or the Middle East and Central Asia; and the East, or China and Japan.[46] To this end, he advocates pulling Ukraine and the Black Sea into the Western orbit, strong US engagement in Central Asia and the Caucasus (described as "the Eurasian Balkans"), and support of China's aspirations for regional dominance in peninsular Southeast Asia and Pakistan. Despite its expanded influences, China would still be limited to regional power status by the globally framed US-Japan strategic alliance. The objective is to prevent Russia from reasserting strategic control over "near abroad" states or from joining with China and Iran in a Eurasian anti-US coalition. Kissinger's recent oversimplistic foreign policy prescription is for the United States to ensure that no power emerges regionally or globally to unite with others against it.[47]

Advancing a geopolitics of "the West against the rest," Samuel Huntington argues that world primacy can be maintained by dividing and playing off the other civilizations.[48] His thesis is that the fundamental sources of conflict in the world will not be ideological. Instead, the great divisions will be cultural, and the fault lines between civilizations will be the battle lines. In dividing the world into Western, Confucian, Japanese, Islamic, Hindu, Slavic-Orthodox, Latin American, and possibly African civilizations, he makes little allowance for internal religious, ethnic, economic, or strategic divisions. He also assumes the permanence of these cultural fault lines, despite the massive demographic changes brought about by migrations and modernization.

Geographical geopolitical theory also continues to reflect the universalistic approaches advanced during the Cold War. Building on the work of Taylor and Lacoste, the "critical" geopolitics represented in the writings of John Agnew and Gearóid Ó Tuathail applies social scientific critical thinking to ask how power works and might be challenged.[49] Analyses of discourse—of rhetoric, metaphors, symbolism; of feminist approaches to the subject of national security; and of the geographies of social movements, particularly in relation to newly radicalized and participative democracy—are viewed by Joe Painter as central to geopolitical studies.[50]

Neil Smith offers a vigorous critique of "neocritical" geographers, such as Ash Amin and Nigel Thrift,[51] for abandoning "critical geographic theory for the concept of a flatter earth." Dubbing the neocritical proponents as the "heterarchical left" that has bought into Thomas Friedman's neoliberal flat-earth globalization theory, he argues that this "'de-spatializes' the globe." For Smith, the power of class, race, gender, and other hierarchical characteristics of capitalism remain the reality of society, which must be restructured. He holds that this should continue to be the focus of critical geographical analysis.[52]

Conclusion

The reality-based geographical geopolitics that is espoused in this volume is based on multipolarity and regionalism. It builds upon the continuous proliferation of the various parts and levels of the world and their geopolitical development. The current number of 200 national states could increase to 250 within the next quarter of a century. As the pace of devolution quickens, some of these new geoterritorial entities will be highly autonomous "quasi states." In addition, the network of global cities—centers of capital flows and financial services linked ever more closely by cyberspace, tourism, and immigrant communities—will emerge as a major new geopolitical level, promoting policies sometimes contradictory to national interests. International social movements, such as environmentalism, will also become more influential in shaping national and regional policies, including military ones.

Within this framework, radical geopolitical restructuring is a continuing process. Thus, China has emerged as a separate geostrategic realm, while Southeast Asia is no longer a shatterbelt. The Middle East has become even more fractured as a shatterbelt. One prong extends from Iran through Iraq to Bahrain and the Eastern Province of Saudi Arabia. The other extends through Alawite-controlled Syria to Hezbollah-dominated southern Lebanon. Sunni-ruled Gaza was also part of this Iranian bloc but broke with Tehran in 2011 when Hamas supported the Sunni rebels in Syria.

The presently atomized Sub-Saharan Africa could ultimately subdivide into four regional units—east, west, central, and south. The convergence zone that extends from the Baltic through Eastern Europe, the Trans-Caucasus, and Central Asia could either become a new shatterbelt or evolve into a gateway between the West and Russia. Maritime Europe could extend into the Levantine eastern Mediterranean to include Lebanon, Israel, coastal Syria, and Egypt as part of a Euro-Mediterranean geopolitical region.

Whatever the course of geopolitical restructuring, we are entering an era of power sharing among a wide variety of regions, states, and other political territorial entities of different sizes and functions. Reality-based geopolitical theory will continue to be a valuable tool for understanding, predicting, and formulating the structure and direction of the world system.

Notes

1. Rudolf Kjellén, *Staten som Lifsform*, 1916. Published in German as *Der Staat also Lebenform* (Leipzig: Hirzel, 1917), 34–35, 203; also cited in Hans Weigert, *Generals and Geographers* (New York: Oxford University Press, 1942), 106–9.
2. Richard Hennig, *Geopolitik: Die Lehre vom Staat als Lebewesen* (Leipzig: Hirzel, 1931), 9; also cited in Andrew Gyorgy, *Geopolitics* (Berkeley: University of California Press, 1944), 183.
3. Derwent Whittlesey, *The Earth and the State* (New York: Henry Holt, 1939), 8.
4. Richard Hartshorne, *The Nature of Geography* (Lancaster, PA: Association of American Geographers, 1939), 404.
5. Edmund Walsh, "Geopolitics and International Morals," in *Compass of the World*, ed. H. W. Weigert and V. Stefansson, 12–39 (New York: Macmillan, 1944).
6. Geoffrey Parker, *Geopolitics: Past, Present and Future* (London: Pinter, 1998), 5.
7. John Agnew, *Western Geopolitical Thought in the Twentieth Century* (New York: St. Martin's, 1985), 2.

8. Gearóid Ó Tuathail, Simon Dalby, and Paul Routledge, *The Geopolitics Reader* (London: Routledge, 1998), 3.
9. Robert D. Kaplan, *The Revenge of Geography* (New York: Random House, 2012), 88.
10. Friedrich Ratzel, *Politische Geographie*, 3rd ed. (Munich: Oldenbourg, 1923), 4–12.
11. Friedrich Ratzel, "Die Gesetze des Raumlichen Wachstums der Staaten," *Petermanns Mitteilungen* 42 (1896): 97–107. Translated by Ronald Bolin under the title "The Laws of the Spatial Growth of States," in *The Structure of Political Geography*, ed. Roger Kasperson and Julian Minghi (Chicago: Aldine, 1969), 17–28.
12. Halford Mackinder, "The Geographical Pivot of History," *Geographical Journal* 23, no. 4 (1904): 421–44. Reprinted in Mackinder, *Democratic Ideals and Reality* (London: Constable, 1919; New York: Norton, 1962), 265–78.
13. James Fairgrieve, *Geography and World Power* (London: University of London Press, 1915), 329–46.
14. Halford Mackinder, *Democratic Ideals and Reality* (London: Constable, 1919; repr., New York: Norton, 1962), 104–14, 148–66.
15. Halford Mackinder, "The Round World and the Winning of the Peace," *Foreign Affairs* 21, no. 4 (1943): 595–605. Reprinted in Mackinder, *Democratic Ideals and Reality*, 265–78.
16. Brian Blouet, *Halford Mackinder: A Biography* (College Station: Texas A&M University Press, 1987), 140–45.
17. Alfred T. Mahan, *The Influence of Sea Power upon History: 1660–1783* (Boston: Little, Brown, 1890), 25–89; Mahan, *The Problem of Asia and Its Effect upon International Policy* (Boston: Little, Brown, 1900), 21–26, 63–125.
18. Neil Smith and Jan Nijman, "Alfred Thayer Mahan," in *Dictionary of Geopolitics*, ed. John O'Loughlin (Westport, CT: Greenwood, 1994), 156–58.
19. Isaiah Bowman, *The New World* (Yonkers-on-Hudson, NY: World Book, 1922), 1–2, 8.
20. Bowman, *New World*, 11.
21. Parker, *Geopolitics*, 10–19.
22. Andrew Gyorgy, *Geopolitics* (Berkeley: University of California Press, 1944), 180–86; Gearóid Ó Tuathail, "Introduction," in The *Geopolitics Reader*, ed. Gearóid Ó Tuathail, Simon Dalby, and Paul Routledge (London: Routledge, 1998), 19–24.
23. Nicholas Spykman, *America's Strategy in World Politics: The United States and the Balance of Power* (New York: Harcourt, Brace, 1942), 457–72.
24. Nicholas Spykman, *The Geography of Peace* (New York: Harcourt, Brace, 1944), 38–43, 51–61.
25. George T. Renner, *Human Geography in the Air Age* (New York: Macmillan, 1942), 152–54.
26. Stephen B. Jones, "The Power Inventory and National Strategy," *World Politics* 1, no. 4 (July 1954): 421–52.
27. Alexander de Seversky, *Air Power: Key to Survival* (New York: Simon & Schuster, 1950), 11, map facing 312.
28. John Slessor, *The Great Deterrent* (New York: Praeger, 1957), 264–85.
29. George Kennan, "The Sources of Soviet Conduct," *Foreign Affairs* 25 (1947): 566–82.
30. Winston Churchill, "Iron Curtain" speech (graduation address given at Westminster College, Fulton, MO, March 5, 1946). Excerpts in *Internet Modern History Sourcebook* (August 1977), 2 pp.
31. Seyom Brown, "Inherited Geopolitics and Emergent Global Realities," in *America's Global Interests*, ed. Edward K. Hamilton (New York: Norton, 1989), 166–97.
32. Patrick O'Sullivan, "Antidomino," *Political Geography Quarterly* 1 (1982): 57–64.
33. Henry A. Kissinger, *The White House Years* (Boston: Little, Brown, 1979), 127–38.
34. Leslie Hepple, "Geopolitics, Generals and the State in Brazil," *Political Geography Quarterly* 5 (supplement 1986): S79–S90.
35. Zbigniew Brzezinski, *Game Plan* (New York: Atlantic Monthly Press, 1986), 52–65.
36. Saul B. Cohen, *Geography and Politics in a World Divided*, 2nd ed. (New York: Oxford University Press, 1973), 59–89.
37. Saul B. Cohen, "A New Map of Geopolitical Equilibrium: A Developmental Approach," *Political Geography Quarterly* 1, no. 3 (1982): 223–42; Heinz Werner, *Comparative Psychology of Mental Development*, rev. ed. (New York: International University Press, 1948), 40–55; Ludwig von Bertalanffy, *General System Theory* (New York: Braziller, 1968), 30–53, 205–21.
38. G. R. Chrone, *Background to Political Geography* (London: Pittman, 1969), 234.
39. Peter J. Taylor, *Political Geography*, 2nd ed. (Harlow, England: Longman Scientific and Technical; New York: Wiley, 1989), 2–41; Immanuel Wallerstein, "European Unity and Its Implications for the Interstate System," in *Europe: Dimensions of Peace*, ed. B. Hettne (London: Zed, 1988), 27–38; Wallerstein, "The World-System after the Cold War," *Journal of Peace Research* 30, no. 1 (1993): 1–6; George Modelski, "The Study of Long Cycles," in *Exploring Long Cycles*, ed. George Modelski (Boulder, CO: Lynne Rienner, 1987), 1–15.
40. Taylor, *Political Geography*, 157–69.
41. Yves Lacoste, "Editorial: Les Géographes, l'Action et la Politique," *Hérodite* 33 (1984): 3–32.
42. B. Giblin, "Élisée Reclus, 1830–1905," in *Geographers Bibliographical Studies*, ed. T. W. Freeman, vol. 3 (London: Mansell, 1979), 125–32; Gary Dunbar, *Élisée Reclus, Historian of Nature* (Hamden, CT: Archon, 1978), 47–53, 69–97, 112–22.

43. Francis Fukuyama, *The End of History and the Last Man* (New York: Free Press, 1992), 199–208, 287–99; Fukuyama, *The Great Disruption: Human Nature and the Reconstitution of Social Order* (New York: Free Press, 1999), 10–26, 187–93, 249–82. See also Fukuyama, "After Neoconservatism," *New York Times Magazine* (February 19, 2006), 5 pp.

44. George H. W. Bush, "Toward a New World Order," September 11, 1990, in *Public Papers of the Presidents of the United States, George H. W. Bush, 1990* (Washington, DC: Government Printing Office, 1991).

45. Robert D. Kaplan, "The Coming Anarchy," *Atlantic Monthly* 273, no. 2 (1994): 44–46; Kaplan, *The Coming Anarchy: Shattering the Dreams of the Cold War* (New York: Random House, 2000), 37–41, 51–57.

46. Zbigniew Brzezinski, *The Grand Chessboard* (New York: Basic, 1997), 30–56.

47. Henry Kissinger, *Does America Need a Foreign Policy? Towards a Diplomacy for the 21st Century* (New York: Simon & Schuster, 2001).

48. Samuel P. Huntington, "The Clash of Civilizations?," *Foreign Affairs* 72 (1993): 22–49.

49. John Agnew, *Geopolitics: Re-visioning World Politics* (London: Routledge, 1998), 23–30; Gearóid Ó Tuathail, "Thinking Critically about Geopolitics," in Ó Tuathail et al., *The Geopolitics Reader*, 1–11.

50. Joe Painter, *Politics, Geography and "Political Geography"* (London: Arnold, 1995), 151–79.

51. Ash Amin and Nigel Thrift, "What's Left? Just the Future," *Antipode* 37 (2005): 220–38.

52. Neil Smith, "Neo-critical Geography, or the Flat Pluralist World of Business Class," *Antipode* 37 (2005): 887–99.

CHAPTER 3

Geopolitical Structure and Theory

The subjects of this chapter are the geopolitical structures that are formed by the interaction of geographical and political forces and the developmental processes that guide the changes that take place within those structures. Geopolitical structures are composed of geopolitical patterns and features. "Pattern" refers to the shape, size, and physical/human geographical characteristics of the geopolitical units and the networks that tie them together, and these distinguish geopolitical units from other units. Features are the political-geographical nodes, areas, and boundaries that contribute to the unit's uniqueness and influence its cohesiveness and other measures of its structural effectiveness.

For the most part, geopolitical structures are organized along the following hierarchically ordered spatial levels:

1. the geostrategic realm—the most extensive level, or macro level;
2. the geopolitical region—a subdivision of the realm that represents the middle level, or meso level;
3. national states, highly autonomous regions, quasi states, and territorial subdivisions within and across states at the lowest level, or micro level.

Outside of this ordering of structures are regions or clusters of states that are not located within the realm or regional frameworks. These include regions such as shatterbelts, whose internal fragmentation is intensified by pressures of major powers from competing realms; compression zones, which are even more severely torn apart by internal divisions and the interference of neighboring states within the region; and gateways, which serve as bridges between realms, regions, or states. Convergence zones are regions caught between realms and whose ultimate status is yet to be determined.

The maturity of a geopolitical structure is reflected in the extent to which its patterns and features support the unit's political cohesiveness. The developmental approach posits that structures evolve through successive stages—from atomization/undifferentiation to differentiation, specialization, and, finally, specialized integration. Revolutionary or cataclysmic breaks in the process may result in de-development and the beginning of the cycle anew. Another result of such breaks could be rapid movement to a higher stage.

Structure

GEOGRAPHICAL SETTINGS

The earth's two major physical/human geographical settings are the maritime and the continental. These settings provide the arenas for the development of distinctive geopolitical structures. The civilizations, cultures, and political institutions that have evolved within these two settings are fundamentally different in their economies, human cultures and traditions, spirit, and geopolitical outlooks.

Maritime settings are exposed to the open sea, either from coastal reaches or from inland areas with access to the seas. The vast majority of peoples who live there have benefited from climates with moderate temperatures and adequate rainfall and ease of contact with other parts of the world, often behind the protective screen of inland physical barriers. Sea trade and immigration have flourished in such settings, contributing to the diversity of their peoples in terms of race, culture, and language. They have also sped up the process of economic specialization. The trading and other systems of exchange that have emerged from this specialization have had open, politically liberalizing effects. Of the world's major and regional powers, only the United States has direct access to the Atlantic and Pacific Oceans and the Caribbean Sea. Much of its interior is linked to these waters by the Great Lakes and the Mississippi and Missouri inland waterway systems.

Continental settings are characterized by extreme climates and vast distances from the open seas. Such settings often suffer from lack of intensive interaction with other parts of the world because of the barrier effects of mountains, deserts, and high plateaus or because of sheer distance. Historically, their economies have been more self-sufficient than maritime ones, while their political systems, more isolated from new influences and ideas, tend to develop as closed and autocratic.

Urbanization and industrialization have come much later to the continental arena than to the maritime one. The lag continues in the present postindustrial age. While maritime areas have forged ahead by generating and diffusing high-technology innovations, many continental areas remain heavily rural or are characterized by aging industrial bases that drag down the economies of their urban areas.

Geopolitical structures are shaped by two forces—the centrifugal and the centripetal. At the national level, both are linked to the psychobiological sense of territoriality.[1] The centrifugal force is the drive for political separation that motivates a people to seek territorial separation from those whom they consider outsiders, who might impose different political systems, languages, cultures, or religions upon them. In this context, space with clear boundaries serves as a defining and a defensive mechanism. The centripetal force promotes the drive for political unity that is reinforced by a people's sense of being inextricably linked to a particular territory. Such territoriality is expressed through symbolic as well as physical ties of a people to a particular land.

At one geographical scale, forces of separation may dominate, while forces for unity may prevail at another scale. Thus, centrifugal forces may drive a people to secede from another state in order to protect their unique identity. Immigration into countries by groups which either resist or are excluded from cultural and national absorption are also likely to have a centrifugal effect. At the same time, centripetal forces may propel nations toward a unity of regional action in such areas as commerce, military defense, or confederation with another state.

While drives for separation and unity are intertwined, they are not always in balance. The imperialist system that kept its form of world balance was destroyed by World War II. Global disequilibrium then followed. Balance was restored when a unifying Europe and a recovering Japan joined in strategic alliance with the United States to counter the Soviet-Chinese drive for Communist world hegemony.

The flow of ideas, migrations, trade, capital, communications, and arms takes place beyond, as well as within, the different structural levels of realm, region, and state. States may move from one level to another. Such change reflects the interplay of political power and ideological, economic, cultural, racial, religious, and national forces, as well as national security concerns and territorial ambitions. The geopolitical restructuring subsequent to the end of the Cold War is testimony to this dynamism. Demise of the former Soviet Union widened the opportunity for China to emerge as leader of an independent geostrategic realm, combining continental and maritime characteristics, thus enhancing Beijing's role in world affairs. The collapse of the Democratic Republic of Congo (DRC) has provided Nigeria with an opening to expand its role as a regional power, thereby extending its influence from West into Central Africa. However, Nigeria has not been able to exploit this opening because of the widening divisions and fighting between its Muslim north and Christian south. The rift has been exacerbated by the terrorist actions of Boko Haram, the Islamist jihadist movement of the north.

The Iraq War has strengthened Iran's position as a regional power, with the potential for becoming the leader of the Shiite eastern half of the Middle East. At the same time, the war in Afghanistan has played a major role in weakening the already vulnerable central government of Pakistan because it has led to the emergence of a Pashtun-based Pakistani Taliban.

GEOPOLITICAL FEATURES

Despite variations in function and scale, all structures have certain geopolitical features in common:

Historic or Nuclear Cores. These are the areas in which states originate and out of which the state idea has developed. The relationship between the physical environment of the core and the political-cultural system that evolves may become embedded and persist as an important element of national or regional identity and ideology.

Capitals or Political Centers. Capitals serve as the political and symbolic focus of activities that govern the behavior of people in politically defined territories. While its functions may be essentially administrative, the built landscape of a national capital—its architectural forms, buildings, monuments, and layout—has considerable symbolic value in mobilizing support for the state. Capitals may be selected for a variety of reasons—for their geographic centrality to the rest of the national space, for the defensive qualities of their sites, or for their frontier locations, either as defensive points or springboards for territorial acquisition.

Ecumenes. These are the areas of greatest density of population and economic activity. Ecumenes have traditionally been created and expanded by dense transportation networks to reflect economic concentration. In today's postindustrial information age, the boundaries of ecumenes can be expanded to include areas that are linked by modern telecommunications, and therefore ecumenes are less tied to transportation clustering. Because the ecumene is the most advanced portion of the state economically as well as its most populous sector, it is usually the state's most important political area.

Effective National Territory (ENT) and Effective Regional Territory (ERT). These are moderately populated areas with favorable resource bases. As areas of high development potential, they provide outlets for population growth and dispersion and for economic expansion. Their extent is an indication of future strength, especially when they are contiguous to the ecumene.

Empty Areas. These are essentially devoid of population, with little prospect for mass human settlement. Depending on their location and extent, they may provide defensive depth and sites for weapons testing. Some are important as sources of minerals and for tourism.

Boundaries. These mark off political areas. While they are linear, they often occur within broader border zones. Their demarcation may become a source of conflict.

Nonconforming Sectors. These may include minority separatist areas within states and isolated or "rogue" states within regions. In many cases, these minority areas are concentrated at the periphery of the country, far removed from the economic advantages provided within the ecumene and parts of the ENT. Even where such areas possess riches of natural resources, their fruits tend to flow to the national center.

The degree to which geopolitical features are developed and the patterns formed by their interconnections are the bases for determining the stage of maturity of a geopolitical realm or region.

Structural changes produced by these features and patterns may be likened to geological changes that are brought about by the movement of underlying plates and subplates, which eventually regain a new state of balance or equilibrium known as "isostasy." These geopolitical structures are formed by historic civilization-building processes and reconfigured by both short- and long-term geopolitical forces. Geostrategic realms are, in effect, the major structural plates that cover most of the earth's surface. Their movement may result in the addition of some areas to one realm at the expense of another; new realms will be formed when the movements are revolutionary. Shatterbelts, which form zones of contact between realms, may be divided into separate subplates, such as compression zones, by such movement or totally subsumed within one realm. Regions, or medium-sized plates, may also change their shapes and boundaries as they shift within realms or from one realm to another, becoming convergence zones. Compression zones, or regional subplates, may be formed or disappear with shifting within regional plates.

The most radical shifting of geopolitical plates in recent decades has taken place at the geostrategic level. Following World War II, the world divided into a bipolar and rigidly hierarchical structure. The end of the Cold War signaled a revolution of equal magnitude. With the collapse of the Soviet Union and the crumbling of its empire, the maritime realm overrode the Eurasian continental realm, detaching most of Eastern Europe from the sway of Russia. The boundary between the two realms continues to be fluid, as Russia seeks to pull Azerbaijan, Armenia, Georgia, Ukraine, and Moldova into its Eurasian Economic Community/Eurasian Customs Union, while the EU attempts to attract them to its fold through trade partnerships. The Eurasian Customs Union was founded with Kazakhstan and Belarus in 2010. In addition, the continental "plate," which had already been weakened by the Sino-Soviet schism, has now broken in two, with East Asia emerging as a separate realm. With the weakening of the Russian core, China has been able to pull away from the heartland and move partly toward the maritime realm through the force of international trade and technology. As a further result of this shifting, the strategic and economic interests of the West, Russia, India, and China now compete within the South Caucasus and Central Asian Eurasian convergence zone. This represents a challenge to Russia, which commands this zone militarily and continues to consider it as belonging to the continental plate.

Another way of looking at how structures divide and redivide at different levels is to consider the world not as a pane of glass but as a diamond. The force of blows shatters glass into fragments of unpredictable sizes and shapes. Diamonds, by contrast, break along existing lines of cleavage, forming new shapes. Geopolitical boundaries follow combinations of physical, cultural, religious, and political cleavages. These boundaries change with shifts in the power balance between political cores, and new boundaries then follow latent cleavages that now come to the surface.

STRUCTURAL LEVELS

The Geostrategic Realm

In the spatial hierarchy of the global structure, the highest level is the geostrategic realm. These realms are parts of the world large enough to possess characteristics and functions that are globally influencing and that serve the strategic needs of the major powers, states, and regions they comprise. Their frameworks are shaped by circulation patterns that link people, goods, and ideas and are held together by control of strategically located land and sea passageways.

The overriding factor that distinguishes a realm is the degree to which it is shaped by conditions of "maritimity" or "continentality." In today's world, three geostrategic realms have evolved: the Atlantic and Pacific economically advanced maritime realm; the Eurasian continental Russian heartland; and the mixed continental-maritime East Asia. India, an international high-technology powerhouse, has a huge impoverished farm populace and remains essentially continental in terms of trade and outlook. Its progress has been stymied by cultural, linguistic, and religious divisions as well as its long-standing conflict with Pakistan. This has limited the ability of India to extend its reach throughout the Indian Ocean and the fringes of Africa and Southeast Asia that border it.

Realms have been a factor of international life from the time that empires first emerged. In modern times, geostrategic realms have been carved out by British maritime and czarist Russian land-power realms. The United States created a mixed realm consisting of both transcontinental power and maritime sway over part of the Atlantic, the Caribbean, and much of the Pacific. Today's trade-dependent maritime realm, which embraces the Atlantic and Pacific Ocean basins and their interior seas, has been shaped by international exchange. Mercantilism, capitalism, and industrialization gave rise to the maritime-oriented national state and to economic and political colonialism. Access to the sea facilitated circulation, and moderate coastal climates with habitable interiors offered living conditions that aided economic development. The open systems that ultimately developed within the leading states of this realm have facilitated the struggle for democracy, and movements across the seas have spawned the creation of pluralistic societies.

Expanding international trade and investment, reinforced by mass-migration movements, has defined the maritime realm for the past century and a half. From the mid-1890s to World War I, European (and then US) imperialism created a global trading system that was imposed by military force and enhanced by revolutionary advances in transportation and communications. This system was shattered by World War I and the Great Depression of the 1930s.

The global economy was rebuilt under US leadership following World War II. By the 1970s, the share of world goods that entered the arena of international trade had climbed back to its pre-1914 levels. This proportion surged in the 1990s, due in large part to the General Agreement on Tariffs and Trade (GATT) and its successor organization, the World Trade Organization (WTO). It has continued to climb.

The world's leading exporters and importers, the members of the Group of Seven (G-7), are all maritime realm nations—the United States, Japan, Germany, France, the United Kingdom, Italy, and Canada. China has joined these ranks, owing to the unprecedented economic strength of its maritime south and central coastal regions.

Since the lifting of Mao's restrictive policies in the late 1970s by his Communist successors, maritime China has once again become the main engine for China's economic growth and entrance into the world of labor-intensive manufacturing of consumer items, high technology, and financial services. The coastal regions, collectively known as the "Golden Coast," have reinforced the maritime component of the Chinese setting, allowing Beijing to break the economic grip of Eurasian continentality and assume separate geostrategic status. Guangdong/Hong Kong, Fujiang, and Shanghai have been the historic foci of China for trade and cultural exchange with the outside world. The coastal regions have drawn millions of migrants from the interior of the country. They have been the source of large-scale emigration, many of whose participants have maintained strong familial and village links with the home country.

In recent years, industrialization has been extended northward into the Beijing-Tianjin area and to Xian, deep in the interior. Trade is the most important measure of China's economic rise. While China's share of world trade is 11 percent, its share of the maritime realm totals 18 percent. The United States and China are equal in percentage of total trade only because US service exports are three times those of China. Such data do not measure China's much lower productivity per person in terms of output and its far lower per capita incomes than enjoyed in the large maritime powers as well as in South Korea and Taiwan. Nevertheless, through its favorable balance of trade, China has been able to accumulate huge capital reserves, which provides great economic and political leverage in world affairs. The frenzy for development has resulted in a high level of pollution, especially in the large coastal cities—a consequence that will be difficult and expensive to cope with.

Of significant geopolitical importance is the fact that China has both maritime and continental orientation. China lay within the continental Eurasian orbit for much of the Cold War, even after the Sino-Soviet schism in the 1960s. With the introduction of capitalism by Deng Xiaoping after Mao's death in 1976, foreign contacts and international trade were grafted onto China's closed, continental character. Continentality has been associated historically with political authoritarianism. Despite economic liberalization, which has fostered a private capital sector, state capitalism and authoritarian government persists in China as it does in Russia and its former republics.

The people of China's continental, inland-oriented north and interior, which are essentially rural with urban pockets of now-antiquated heavy industry, have until recently been more supportive of autocratic Communist governmental state policies than are the peoples of the south, the east, and the central coastal regions, which have long been opened to the influences of the outside world.

China has not become part of the maritime world (as predicted by Mackinder and Spykman in their times and Richard Nixon in his) despite its dramatic rise as a trading nation during the past quarter of a century. Nearly half of China's populace remains mainly engaged in small-scale agriculture, and most reside in the continental regions. The remarkable economic growth and prosperity enjoyed by coastal China has widened the economic gap with the rural interior, bringing on unrest and strikes. Beijing has adopted new policies aimed at closing this gap through developing the interior, with the help of high-speed rail and air systems. Urbanization and industrialization of this region, which is now taking place, remains a formidable challenge.

For the continentally oriented Chinese, the mountains and grasslands, not the sea, hold spiritual, mystical attractions. And it is the common border with Russia that serves as both lure and threat. The Sino-Soviet clash over the present-day boundary had historic roots that go back to Chinese claims on lands annexed by czarist Russia between 1858 and 1881—1.5 million square kilometers in the regions east of Lake Baikal and the far eastern provinces. When the rift took place between the two continental Eurasian realm powers, beginning with Stalin's death in 1953 and culminating in the breaking of diplomatic relations in 1960, the issue was more than ideology and strategy. It was also China's resentment at being treated as a subordinate power. Reinstitution of diplomatic ties between Moscow and Beijing in 1989 reflected the reality that they had become equals. Most recently, the two powers have grown closer to one another as Russian pipelines have begun to deliver oil and gas to China, and the two countries have forged common policies toward Syria.

Withdrawal of American and Soviet power from Indochina has enabled China to extend the new continental-maritime East Asian geostrategic realm southward to include the Indochinese states of Vietnam, Cambodia, and Laos and eastern Myanmar. These constitute a separate geopolitical region within the East Asian realm. The boundaries of the East Asian realm are forged by China's reach to other parts of Asia. Tibet and Xinjiang afford contact with South and Central Asia. In the northeast Pacific, where the maritime, Eurasian, and East Asian realms meet, North Korea is part of East Asia. A reunified Korean Peninsula, however, could become either a gateway among the three realms or a compression zone.

The Eurasian continental realm, which is anchored today by heartlandic Russia, is inner oriented and less influenced by outside economic forces or cultural contacts. Until the mid-twentieth century, the major modes of transportation there were land and inland river. The self-sufficient nature of the economy, belated entrance into the industrial age, and lack of sea access to world resources all contributed to politically closed systems and societies. Highly centralized and generally despotic forms of government through the ages became the breeding grounds for the emergence of Communism and other forms of authoritarianism in the cores of the realm.

The continentality that pervades the Eurasian heartlandic realm is both a physical and a psychological condition. Russia/the former Soviet Union has historically been hemmed in. Even when technology alters the previous reality (e.g., Soviet conquests in outer space, nuclear and conventional weapons achievements, and energy wealth), the earlier mentality persists. The breakup of the Soviet Union and the threat of North Atlantic Treaty Organization (NATO) expansion reinforce the Russian perception of being boxed in by the outside world. Russia's international trade is only 3 percent of the world total. Its GDP is based heavily on the export of oil and gas, which reflects inflated energy prices that are likely to fluctuate.

The boundaries of the heartlandic Russian realm have changed substantially. To its west, with the exception of Belarus and Transnistria, the Eastern European states are no longer within the political grip of Moscow, while the boundary between the heartland and the maritime realm has become a zone rather than a line. The accession to NATO of the Baltic states, Slovakia, Slovenia, Bulgaria, and Romania, intensified Moscow's suspicions of Western actions that penetrate its traditional sphere of interest. US plans to place an antiballistic missile shield in the Czech Republic and Poland have increased tensions, as has the prospect of admission of Ukraine and Georgia to NATO. While a new Cold War is not in the offing, Moscow has already used and will continue to use its vast energy resources as political leverage to block expansion of NATO further into Russia's Black Sea borderlands, particularly Ukraine and Georgia.

Elsewhere along the boundaries of the realm, the former Soviet republics of the Trans-Caucasus and Central Asia are not free of Russia's strategic oversight, although they have gained their independence. The efforts of the West to penetrate these regions in pursuit of oil and gas wealth, as well as the need for military bases for the war in Afghanistan, required Russian cooperation in order to succeed. In the Middle East, such cooperation is also needed, as has been demonstrated by Moscow's initiative in persuading Syria to dismantle its chemical weapons. Moscow also has considerable influence in Iran and is a major arms supplier to several Middle Eastern countries. The West cannot discount Russia's strategic assets in the convergence zone and the Middle East should competition between Washington and Moscow be rekindled.

The Geopolitical Region

The second level of geopolitical structure is the geopolitical region. Most regions are subdivisions of realms, although some may be caught between or independent of them. Regions are connected by geographical contiguity and political, cultural, and military interactions and in many cases by the historical migration and intermixture of peoples and shared histories of national emergence.

The regions of the maritime realm are North and Middle America, South America, maritime Europe and the Maghreb, and the Asia-Pacific Rim. Geographically they are framed by the world's two great oceans, the Atlantic and Pacific. The Eurasian continental realm now consists of the heartlandic Russian region, which extends into Belarus and eastern Ukraine, and the breakaway Transnistrian province of Moldova, which has declared independence with Russia's support. Two more regions lie within the realm—Central Asia and the Trans-Caucasus. The East Asian realm is divided into two regions—mainland China and Indochina (the latter consisting of Vietnam, Cambodia, and Laos and extending into eastern Myanmar).

South Asia stands apart from the three geostrategic realms as an independent geopolitical region. It includes India, Pakistan, Sri Lanka, and western Myanmar. The long-term prospect for this region is to evolve into a realm led by India that embraces the African and Southeast Asian coastlands of the Indian Ocean basin. As previously noted, India must first address its internal fragmentation.

The Middle East and Sub-Saharan Africa are shatterbelts. The future of the Eurasian convergence zone is yet to be determined—it may become a shatterbelt or a gateway geopolitical region (figure 3.1).

Regions range in their stages of development from those that are cohesive to those that are atomized. The prime example of a tightly knit region is maritime Europe and the Maghreb. Its core, the twenty-eight-member European Union (EU), has begun to create a "European" culture and identity through regional laws, currency, and regulations. It is unlikely that the union will evolve into a highly centralized body with a constitution that would override some of the cherished national and political values held by its member states. On the other hand, the EU has already demonstrated that it is far more than a loose federation by the establishment of the eighteen-member eurozone and the euro currency. Euro skeptics have been strengthened by the crisis over the deep recessions in Greece, Cyprus, Spain, and Portugal. This has been reinforced by the clamor of many in Britain to opt out. These challenges to the future of the EU are likely to slow the pace of centralization, but Europeans are highly unlikely to abandon the goal of a loosely unified Europe with a strong central bank to help stabilize the region's economy.

In contrast, a part of the world such as Sub-Saharan Africa has no geopolitical cohesion. The end of European colonialism, followed by Cold War–stimulated conflicts and the wars

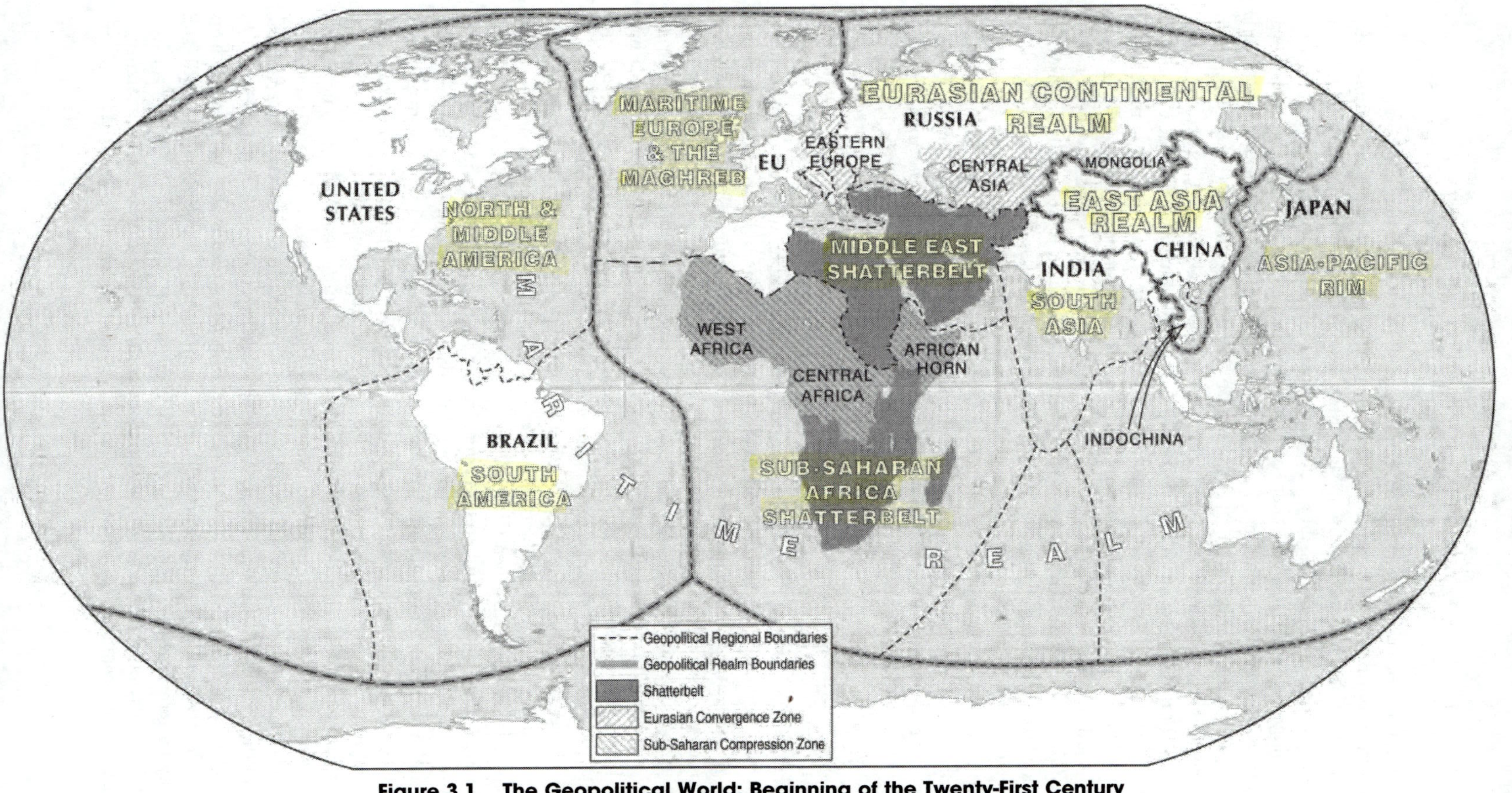

Figure 3.1. The Geopolitical World: Beginning of the Twenty-First Century

and revolutions that have since raged, have produced a process of de-development and atomization. Efforts during the early years of independence to create subregional federations failed, and current ones, such as the Common Market for Eastern and Southern Africa (COMESA), have little prospect of developing into meaningful economic units, let alone geopolitical ones.

Certainly, regional trade and other economic agreements can help foster regional unity. Just as the Common Market ultimately led to the creation of the European Union and the eurozone, so has the North and Middle American Free Trade Agreement (NAFTA) strengthened the geopolitical sinews of the North American geopolitical region. Canada and Mexico account for nearly 30 percent of all US trade in goods. Washington's proposed Free Trade Area of the Americas, which would embrace South America, has failed because of the wide differences in cultural, political, and social traditions as well as the distances between the northern and southern continents. Instead, some bilateral free-trade agreements have been forged.

Within South America, the strongest prospects for regional unity rest with Mercosur, the trade bloc formed by Brazil, Uruguay, Paraguay, and Argentina. Under the lead of Brazil, this group could develop sufficient political as well as economic cohesion to emerge as a separate geopolitical region. Venezuela and Cuba have attempted to create a socialist bloc that straddles the Caribbean and Andean regions of South America, but the prospects are problematic. This is especially the case since the death of Hugo Chávez has weakened the Bolivarian revolution and Communist Cuba without Fidel Castro is slowly opening itself to privatization.

Distinctions between realm and region are distinctions between the strategic and the tactical. States operate at both regional and realm levels, and sometimes they can maintain ties with two regions and/or two realms. For example, Australia is part of the Asia-Pacific Rim. However, because it belongs also to the maritime realm, it is able to benefit from its ties to the two other regions of that realm. Strategically, it serves as a crucial link within the maritime world's global network. Culturally, politically, and ethnically it retains its historic British roots as well as its bonds with the United States forged in World War II.

With their continuing development, geopolitical regions have become more important forces within the international system. The larger European states, Japan, and China have gathered sufficient strength and independence of action to focus their attentions on their regional surrounds and to organize them more effectively as well as to become more assertive on global issues. The emergence of geopolitical regions as power frameworks enhances global stability by strengthening the balance-of-power system. Soviet hegemonic control over the Eurasian realm was broken when China asserted its strategic independence. The result was that the two former allies began to restrain one another's actions in South and Southeast Asia, East Africa, and Taiwan. They have, however, acted in concert, joining the United States, Japan, and South Korea in negotiations which led to an agreement over the dismantling of North Korea's nuclear facility that North Korea subsequently renounced. They have also sought to protect the Syrian and Iranian regimes from Western pressures.

The European Union has been of similar importance in limiting US hegemonic control over the maritime realm. In reaction to its loss of global power and its economic and military dependence on the United States, postwar Europe began to build a series of economic and political institutions with an eye to regaining its strength through regional unity.[2] As a renewed center of geopolitical power, Western Europe has been able to reestablish its influence in strategically important areas, such as the Middle East, Sub-Saharan Africa, and especially Eastern Europe.

The Asia-Pacific Rim has developed its geopolitical unity out of a complementarity of needs among the countries of the region and its common dependence on the US military shield. The role of Japan in the economic development of the region has been pivotal in this process, overriding the long-standing political antagonism between Tokyo and Seoul. This antagonism is based on the annexation of Korea by Japan in 1910 and its exploitation of Korean slave labor and "comfort women" during World War II. Japan, Taiwan, South Korea, and Australia have become heavily engaged economically with China through capital investments, outsourcing production and technology, and exporting raw materials, despite political and strategic tensions with China. The ten-member ASEAN bloc includes member states from both the rim and the Indochinese states, and ASEAN and China are negotiating to create a broader free-trade area.

Of all the world's geopolitical regions, South Asia is the only one that is independent of the three major realms. It is the unit that consciously sought to become a world balancer, with mixed results. India's attempt to project itself as an independent force dedicated to achieving a peaceful, balanced world fell far short of its goal. Rejecting pressures by both the United States and the USSR to join their respective blocs, India adopted a policy of neutrality and became a leader of the Afro-Asian bloc of nations that sought a "third way" in world affairs.

What undermined India's hopes of becoming a balancer was not only that the superpowers rejected the proffered role. India also found itself in a struggle to exercise its control over the entire continent that had once been British India but had become politically fragmented when the British Raj left. India has been embroiled in wars with Pakistan over Kashmir and East Bengal, and the two nuclear powers continue to share an uneasy relationship. It has had unsuccessful interventions in Sri Lanka, engaged in two border conflicts with China, and is torn internally by ethnic and religious violence. Despite these setbacks in its efforts to play a balancing role on the world scene, India did partly succeed in the sense that it never fully joined either superpower's camp during the Cold War. While its dependence upon the Soviet Union for military, economic, and diplomatic support often tilted it toward the latter, it more recently forged a strategic partnership with the United States, enabling it to secure nuclear materials and know-how for its civilian nuclear power industry. Washington policy makers should be cognizant of the fact that such an agreement is unlikely to wean India away from its culture of political neutrality.

A legitimate question is whether the enhanced role of geopolitical regions may become a factor that will divide, not help to unite, the world system. For example, fears have been expressed that a united Europe, especially with its common currency, growing opposition to immigration from outside the region, farm bloc pressures, and commitment to an independent military force, might raise its barriers toward the rest of the world. While there is some basis for such concern, there are powerful offsetting forces. Forces mitigating against a "Fortress Europa" include the special relationships that individual Western European powers have historically enjoyed with such areas as the Maghreb, Sub-Saharan Africa, Latin America, and the Middle East. So do the historical, cultural, and political-military bonds that link Europe to the North Atlantic world. Indeed, the direction of EU policies is to expand world trade in order to cope with the unemployment that accompanies the downsizing of inefficient industries as well as to expand its membership into Central and Eastern Europe with the aim of improving the economies and opening the political systems of those countries and attracting new pools of labor.

While Europe is hardly typical of the world's geopolitical regions, it should be noted that most of the other regions would be far less capable of attaining higher standards of living and security were they to become more isolated. As regions evolve and become more specialized, their external outreach becomes more, rather than less, of a necessity.

Shatterbelts

While most geopolitical regions have varying degrees of cohesiveness depending on their stages of maturity, this is not the case for shatterbelts. Such deeply fragmented regions are global destabilizers.

The concept of the shatterbelt has long held the attention of geographers, who have also used the terms "crush zone" or "shatter zone." Alfred Mahan, James Fairgrieve, and Richard Hartshorne contributed pioneering studies of such regions. As early as 1900, Mahan referred to the instability of the zone between the thirty- and forty-degree parallels in Asia as being caught between Britain and Russia.[3] Fifteen years later, Fairgrieve used "crush zone" to describe small buffer states between the sea powers and the Eurasian heartland, from Northern and Eastern Europe to the Balkans, Turkey, Iran, Afghanistan, Siam, and Korea.[4] During World War II, Hartshorne analyzed the "shatter zone" of Eastern Europe from the Baltic to the Adriatic, advocating a post–World War II federation for this region.[5]

The operational definition for shatterbelts used here is *strategically oriented regions that are both deeply divided internally and caught up in the competition between great powers of the geostrategic realms*. This competition increases the intensity of the fragmentation by supplying weapons, economic rewards, and political backing to their respective clients. In shatterbelts, conflicts between countries are more likely to spread to neighboring ones because of the heterogeneous nature of most of these states.

By the end of the 1940s, two such highly fragmented regions had emerged—the Middle East and Southeast Asia. They were not geographically coincident with previous shatterbelts because the global locus of strategic competition had shifted. The East and Central European shatterbelt had fallen within the Soviet orbit, as the maritime and continental worlds became divided by a sharp boundary in the part of Europe that lay along the Elbe River. Soviet influence in Indochina was exercised through its ally, Communist China.

In discussions of the typology of the shatterbelt, it has been pointed out by Philip Kelly that other parts of the world are also characterized by high degrees of conflict and atomization.[6] It is true that wars, revolts, and coups are chronic in the Caribbean, South America, and South Asia. The distinguishing feature of the shatterbelt, however, is that it presents an equal playing field to two or more competing global powers operating from different geostrategic realms.

Not all areas in turmoil are shatterbelts. Despite the conflicts in South Asia, it is not a shatterbelt because India's dominance within the region is not seriously threatened by the United States, Russia, or China, let alone by Pakistan. Similarly, the Caribbean did not become a shatterbelt despite Communist regimes in Cuba, Nicaragua, and Grenada, socialist rule in Venezuela, and leftist uprisings elsewhere because the Soviet Union could not threaten US dominance there.

Shatterbelts and their boundaries are fluid. During the 1970s and 1980s, Sub-Saharan Africa became a shatterbelt as the Soviet Union, Cuba, and China penetrated deeply into the region to compete with European and US influences. Following the collapse of the Soviet Union, war-torn Sub-Saharan Africa briefly lost its role as a shatterbelt because it had become strategically marginal to the major Western powers. While China has strongly penetrated the region economically and Western interests in oil and nonferrous minerals have increased, the outside powers have little strategic stake in the region. They no longer compete for influence through supporting military allies. Indeed, it has become strategically marginal to the major Western powers. Southeast Asia, too, has lost its Cold War shatterbelt status and is now divided between the East Asian and maritime realms. Indochina has emerged as a separate geopolitical region within East Asia, while western and southern peninsular Southeast Asia and Indonesia are aligned with the Asia-Pacific Rim.

Sub-Saharan Africa has reemerged as an atomized shatterbelt region. Its energy and mineral resources are the objects of keen competition between the West and China. This competition is economic, not ideological or military, as it was during the Cold War. Much of the region consists of highly fragmented compression zones that form an uninterrupted belt from the African Horn through Central Africa to West Africa. Many of the countries within this zone are failed states, whose unstable, corrupt, and dictatorial regimes magnify the poverty, disease, and famines which plague them. The Middle East remains a shatterbelt, its fragmentation reinforced by the Arab-Israeli conflict, the wars in Iraq, Afghanistan, Lebanon, Syria, and the Horn of Africa, and the rise of Iran as a major intrusive force. In recent years, the "Arab Spring" swept away dictatorships, but those have been replaced by chaotic political conditions wherein the military continues to jockey for power, as well as by the emergence of ISIS as a serious threat to regional stability.

The future may bring additional shatterbelts onto the world scene. A possible candidate is the new/old zone from the Baltic through Eastern Europe and the Balkans. A second possibility is the region from the Trans-Caucasus through Central Asia that borders the Russian-dominated heartlandic realm but is so tempting to Western, Chinese, and Russian energy interests. The emergence of such shatterbelts within the Eurasian convergence zone depends upon whether the West tries to overreach by penetrating these regions geostrategically. Such regions are pivotal in world politics and warrant advance-planning strategies rather than ad hoc reactions to crises. Should Afghanistan and Pakistan implode, the Pashtun homeland of western Pakistan is likely to be drawn into the Middle East shatterbelt. Other imploding areas might be Indonesia and Caribbean-northern Andean South America.

NATIONAL STATES

In modern times, the linchpin of the world geopolitical system has been the national state. However, some see the state's demise as a consequence of the rising strength of world and regional governmental bodies, the increased influence of nongovernmental organizations, and the globalization of information and economic forces. Predictions of this demise are hardly novel. Karl Marx held that with the victory of the workers over the bourgeoisie and the emergence of a classless society, the state would wither away as an instrument of centralized control. More contemporaneously, Peter Drucker says that the new "knowledge society," which transcends national borders, will relegate the state to a mere administrative instrument.[7]

Michael Hardt and Antonio Negri advance the thesis that supranational, not national, powers rule today's global system. They hold that a new political structure and power ranking is emerging that constitutes a fluid, infinitely expanding, and highly organized system, embracing the entire population of the world. They reason that because power is so widely dispersed, it is possible for anyone to affect the system's course and that the potential for both revolution and democracy is therefore far greater than it was during the era of nation-states and imperialism.[8]

In reality, globalization is not an independent force. It is the handmaiden of the nation-state system, which influences state policies but not to the point that it undermines nationalism. On the contrary, backlash to globalization has reinforced nationalism in countries such as France, Mexico, and the United States and led to the strengthening of regional structures. The global corporations that outsource capital and manufacturing are subject to antitrust laws in their home countries and in many of the countries in which they operate. While the WTO does place restrictions on the application of national quotas, tariffs, and subsidy systems, national restraints continue to affect world trade patterns. Where the national state has agreed to limit its independence of action, this has taken place at the regional, not the global, scale. A prime example is the European Union, whose regional structure is federated, not centralized.

The other major regional framework, the North American Free Trade Agreement (NAFTA), is even more subject to national directions and controls and even calls for its termination by particular interest groups. To dismiss the power of the national state is to ignore the political and economic weight as well as the decision-making capacities of the major states and regional bodies in the economic, political, military, and cultural arenas.

Theories of globalization present the picture of an emerging world system based upon a seemingly unlimited number of nodes and lines of economic interaction and communication that have the capacity for reshaping global culture and politics. This construct is based, in essence, upon a notion of a structureless world network, devoid of hierarchy, directedness, and spatial differentiation. Globalization may better be described as anomie, or the collapse of structures that govern the world system, rather than as the portent of a new, evolving system.

The geopolitical viewpoint of this volume differs markedly from the notion of an emerging world system of globalization. It views the world as organized around core areas that are hierarchically arranged in space and whose functions vary in accordance with the power and reach of these cores. The patterns of interconnection among the nodes are strongly affected by regional settings as well as by historic and contemporary flows that extend beyond these regions to realms. The major cores of the globalized trading system are the United States, the European Union, Japan, and China, while secondary cores include such countries as South Korea, Taiwan, Singapore, Turkey, Iran, and South Africa.

Awash with petrodollars, Qatar and the United Arab Emirates, especially Dubai, are seeking to become specialized secondary cores as centers for tourism, air traffic, and finance. The economies of the Pacific Rim secondary cores first developed as foci for outsourcing but then expanded to the point where they became independent sources of capital accumulation and have themselves become outsourcers. While neither realms nor regions are self-contained, they nevertheless set the overall geopolitical spatial configurations within which the great majority of political, military, economic, and cultural connections take place.

The role of the national state continues to command vigorous defenders. Peter Taylor argues that the territorial state is vital to the capitalist system and, therefore, to the operation of the world economy.[9] Historian Paul Kennedy also holds the view that a nationalist-based, mercantile world order will persist.[10]

However, economics is not the only, or even the major, reason for the national state—the sense of belonging to something socially and territorially is even more important. The state fulfills the cultural and psychological yearnings of particular people, strengthened by their historic memory. While economic and political interdependence does pose a threat to national cultures, it also provides people with the resources to hold on more tightly to what they most value. For countries that have recently emerged from colonialism or whose economies were dominated by the West, this issue is especially acute. Edward Said cogently observed that, for such countries, there is need for a reconquest of space through a new, decolonized identity.[11] Today, political control of their own territories permits the nations of the former colonial world to be selective in what they accept or reject of Western culture.

There is no question that what transpires within a national state is increasingly influenced by global and regional forces—by international ideological movements, such as environmental and human rights; by global economic institutions and multinational corporations; by the internationalization of politics through foreign monies and other forms of pressure by the world financial markets; and by the media. These forces can also be turned to advantage by the state in advancing its own goals. In the last analysis, the national state remains the glue of the international system, the major mechanism that enables a people to achieve a self-realization inextricably bound with its sense of territoriality. Even the breakup of existing national states, while upsetting the status quo temporarily, is testimony to the power of nationalism, not its decline.

ORDERS OF NATIONAL POWER

The state system consists of five orders or levels. The first consists of major powers—the United States, the collectivity of states embraced by the European Union, Japan, Russia, and China. These all have global reach, serving as the cores of the three geostrategic realms. India, the core of an independent geopolitical region, is en route to forging a South Asian realm. Brazil has the potential of becoming the core of a South American realm, although currently its control is limited to the eastern part of the continent.

The second order of states consists of regional powers whose reach extends over much of their respective geopolitical regions and, in specialized ways, to other parts of the world (see figure 3.2). The third, fourth, and fifth levels are those states whose reach is generally limited to parts of their regions only. In assessing the strategic importance of states, policy makers need to recognize their appropriate levels of power, still keeping in mind that lower-order states are capable of upsetting the system by serving as terrorist bases.

The rank of a nation in this hierarchy can be assessed through a number of socioeconomic, political, and military measures, including possession of nuclear weapons While power rankings suffer from being somewhat mechanistic, they are commonly used in international assessment. The ranking system used here includes value and political behavior characteristics that reach beyond the traditional emphasis on population, area, economic resources, and military expenditures and technology. Such a ranking method cannot account for idiosyncratic factors, like the length to which the dictator of an impoverished country such as North Korea, or fanatics like the Taliban, will go to influence regional and even global events through threats of war, support of rebellions, and offerings of a base for terrorism. For the most part, however, "rogue" state leaders must have either access to resources, such as oil, or patrons who will provide them with the needed backing to intervene in affairs outside their borders, for example, Cuba and North Korea's dependence upon the USSR during the Cold War.

The increased importance of second-order, or regional, states has come at the moment in world history when major powers have begun to distance themselves from regions they no longer consider vital to their own national interests (see figure 3.1). Second-order powerdom is a reflection of the inherent military and economic strength of a state relative to that of its neighbors. It is also a function of its centrality or nodal role in regional transportation, communication, and trade. As important as any of these factors, however, is the ambition and perseverance of the state not only to impose its influence on others but also to persuade them of their stakes in regional goals and values. Egypt's leadership in the Middle East has derived in great measure from its espousal of the pan-Arabism to which the other Arab states also subscribed. This leadership has been eroded by the chaotic conditions that have beset the country since the overthrow of the Mubarak and Morsi regimes. Saudi Arabia's influence comes from its use of petrodollars to support rigid Islamic law, while Venezuela's has been based on its willingness to spread its oil wealth within the Caribbean and the Andes.

Another criterion for measuring the strength of a regional power is its ability to gain sustenance from one or more major powers without becoming a satellite or through extrare-

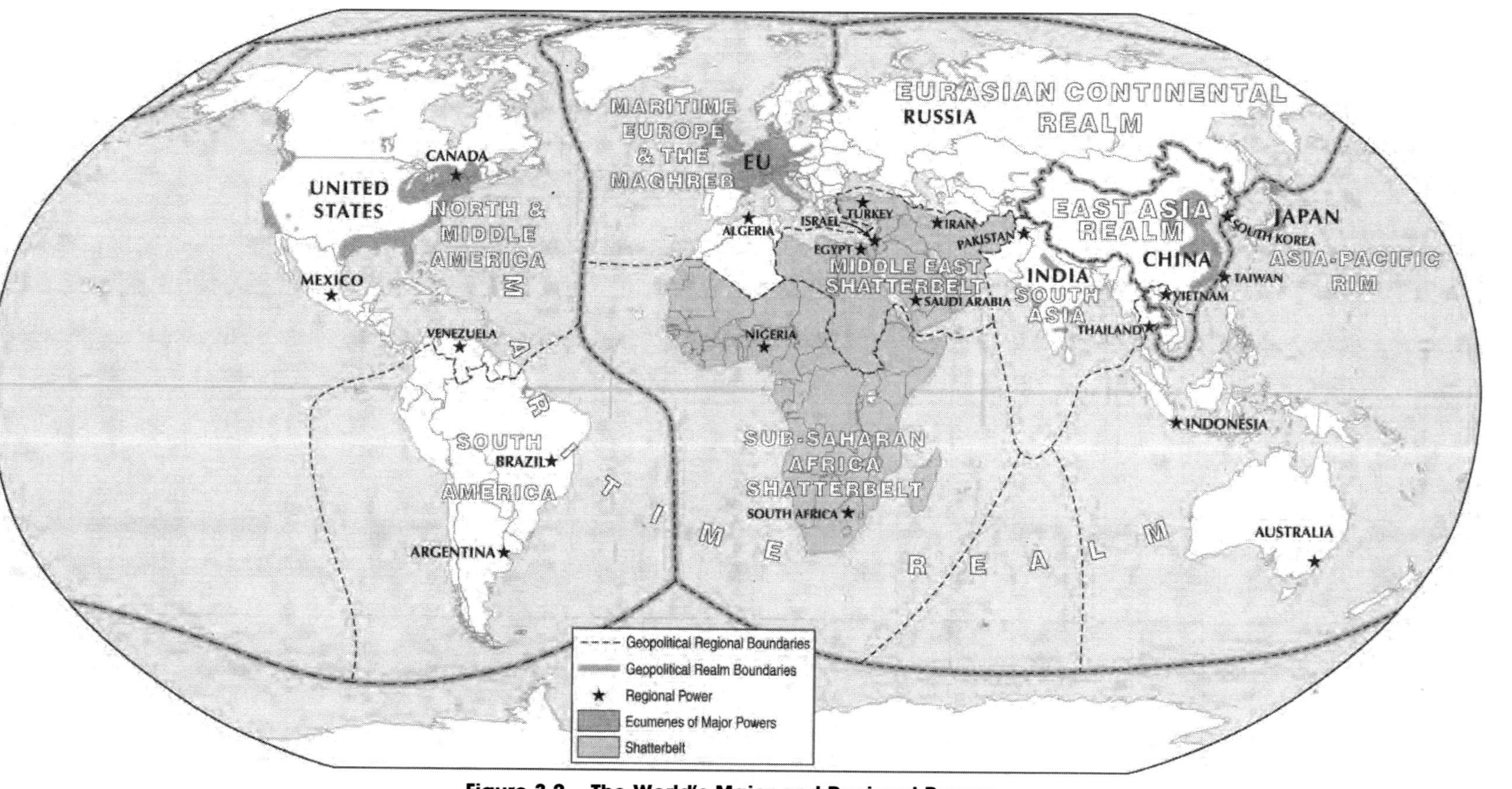

Figure 3.2. The World's Major and Regional Powers

Table 3.1. Second-Order Power Rankings

High	*Medium*	*Low*
Brazil	Indonesia	Algeria
Canada	South Korea	Thailand
Turkey	Vietnam	Argentina
Australia	Israel	Taiwan
Iran	Mexico	
South Africa	Pakistan	
Nigeria	Egypt	
	Venezuela	
	Saudi Arabia	

Note: States are also ranked within categories.

gional political-military alliances, trade links, or ideological links. When India took the lead in fostering the concept of Third World neutrality, its inherent power was increased, just as South Africa's attempts to be a leader of peace movements is part of its inherent strength.

Not all regional powers are equal. Table 3.1 is an attempt to rank them in three categories. Members of the European Union are omitted, as the EU is treated collectively as a major power. Were they to be included, Germany would rank as a great power, while France, Britain, and Poland would be regional ones.

Certain regions contain more than one regional power, and some states in such regions have developed highly complementary relations with the first-order powers located within the region. This is the case for the US relationship with Canada and Mexico; both of the latter states have gained in strength as a result of their close ties to the North American superpower. Others vie with major powers located within the same realm, for example, Vietnam with China. Still others are heavily influenced by support received from distant first-order states—for example, Israel and Egypt by the United States, Nigeria by the EU. Proximity is important in the capacity of first-order states to influence second-order states militarily and politically psychologically, but it is less of a factor in extending economic influence because trade more easily spans distance.

Although second-order states may have regional hegemonical aspirations, their goals are constrained by geopolitical realities. With the exception of Brazil and India, which have the capacity to become first-order powers, second-order powers are unlikely to achieve dominance over an entire geopolitical region. Rather, they can hope to exercise broad regional influence, with hegemony having practical significance only in relation to proximate states.

Third-order states influence regional events in special ways. They may compete with neighboring regional powers on ideological and political grounds or by having a specialized resource base, but they lack the population, military, and general economic capacities of second-order rivals and depend on more powerful patrons for support. Examples of third-order states are Ethiopia, Cuba, Ukraine, Angola, Chile, Argentina, Colombia, North Korea, and Malaysia. Oil-rich Qatar also belongs in this category because it derives influence from supplying military weapons to Sunni groups throughout the Middle East, especially Syria.

Fourth-order states such as Sudan, Ecuador, Zambia, Morocco, and Tunisia have impact only on their nearest neighbors. Fifth-order states, such as Nepal, have only marginal external involvement.

Membership in the various orders is fluid. China is now a first-order power. It has gained economic strength through the opening of its system to world market forces, and its military strength has grown through expansion of its air power and its drive to create a "blue ocean" navy. India is moving from second-order status to that of a major power, especially since Pakistan is rapidly losing its stability and cohesiveness due to the clash between its Islamic fundamentalists and its military regimes. Some Western foreign policy makers downgraded Russia as a great power because of the economic chaos that prevailed after the fall of Communism. However, its rapid economic recovery, political stability, nuclear arsenal, armaments industry, energy resources, and strategic centrality within Eurasia have enabled it to maintain its first-order status.

Morocco, the Democratic Republic of Congo (then Zaire), and Cuba have fallen from the ranking or never attained it. The German Democratic Republic and a greater Yugoslavia have disappeared altogether from the map. At the same time, South Korea, Taiwan, Vietnam, and Thailand have now achieved regional power status. Among the most prominent regional states that are extending their influence to neighboring areas are South Africa, Turkey, and Nigeria. However, Turkey has failed in its efforts to become peacemaker in the Arab world, and Nigeria has not been able to sustain its regional influence because of its domestic instability.

Third-order status is also ephemeral. Tunisia, Tanzania, Zimbabwe, Ghana, and Costa Rica have enjoyed and then lost such ranking with the waning of their ideological influence.

The impacts of major powers and second- and third-order states give regionalism increasingly important geopolitical substance. States that are ideologically at odds with the other states in the region play a special role. They promote turbulence by challenging the norms and injecting unwelcome energy into the system. Examples are pre-1990 revolutionary Cuba, Titoist Yugoslavia, and the market-oriented Côte d'Ivoire of the 1970s.

GATEWAY STATES AND REGIONS

Gateway states play a novel role in linking different parts of the world by facilitating the exchange of peoples, goods, and ideas (see table 3.2). Should Russia and the EU come to a compromise over Ukraine, the latter would become a gateway. This applies also to an independent Palestinian state, which could be a bridge between Israel and the Arab world.

The characteristics of gateway states vary in detail but not in the overall context of their strategic economic locations or in the adaptability of their inhabitants to economic opportunities. They are distinct politically and culturally and may often have separate languages or religions as well as relatively high degrees of education and favorable access to external areas by land or sea.

Small in area and population and frequently lying athwart key access routes, gateways usually possess highly specialized natural or human resources upon which export economies can be built. Lacking self-sufficiency, they depend upon trade with other countries for many of their raw materials, finished goods, and markets, as well as on specialized manufacturing, tourism, and financial services. Especially when they are sources of out-migration because of their overpopulation, they acquire links to groups overseas that can provide capital flows and technological know-how. The models for such states have existed in such ancient centers as Sheba, Tyre, Nabataea, and Palmyra; in the medieval Hanseatic League and Lombard city-states; in Venice (twelfth to fifteenth centuries); in Manila (seventeenth, eighteenth, and nineteenth centuries); and in Zanzibar (nineteenth century). In the twentieth century, Lebanon was an important gateway until torn apart by civil strife and war.

Among today's most prominent gateways are Singapore, Hong Kong, Monaco, Finland, Bahrain, Dubai, Qatar, Djibouti, Trinidad, and the Bahamas. The latter two, because of their focal location within the Caribbean, proximity to the United States, ease of access to Western Europe and South America, and favorable climates, have become centers for tourism, offshore financial services and banking, and international corporate headquarters as well as, unfortunately, the drug trade. The Cayman Islands also serves as an offshore financial address.

Hong Kong, although now part of China, continues to play its powerful gateway role, owing to its special political status. As economic relations between Taiwan and China have greatly expanded and Taipei has become the major source for capital investment on the mainland, Taiwan's role as a gateway linking the maritime and East Asian realms has taken on added significance.

The emergence of gateways helps to convert former barrier boundaries to borders of accommodation. Estonia is beginning to serve such a role as a link along the geostrategic boundary between the European portion of the maritime realm and heartlandic Russia, and Slovenia plays such a role between Central and Southeast Europe.

The concept of gateway regions is a logical extension of the gateway state concept. Such regions do not yet exist. But Eastern Europe, for example, could develop into a gateway region between heartlandic Russia and maritime Europe rather than into the shatterbelt that it once was if it is treated by the major powers as an area of cooperation and not of competition. The countries of such a gateway, especially the Baltic states and Poland, have successfully made their transitions to market economies. Ukraine is already a gateway for Gazprom pipelines to the EU. A forward-looking Russia would build on Ukraine, the Baltic states, and Poland as a trade bridge to the West, including the development of joint enterprises with Western companies.

Gateways, for the most part, play positive economic or social roles. Some, however, may be more problematic. For example, Spain's Canary Islands are jumping-off places for West African illegal immigrants seeking to enter maritime Europe through Spain. The perilous journey taken by these "boat people" all too often ends in drowning at sea or being sent back upon reaching the islands. Similarly, Turkmenistan and Uzbekistan serve as the gateways through which much of Afghanistan's heroin is exported through various routes to Europe. Jamaica and the Cape Verde Islands are gateways for the transfer of Andean cocaine for the European market. Honduras, Mexico, and Puerto Rico are gateways for South American cocaine destined for the US market as well as sources of immigration to the United States.

Proliferation of National States

The number of national states in the world has trebled in the past half-century. In 1945, there were sixty-eight states and the United Nations had fifty-one members, including three memberships allotted to the USSR. In 1991, there were 165 states, and currently there are close to 200, including a few claimants which have not been internationally recognized. As of 2013, the United Nations' formal membership numbered 192. The increase in the number of national states is likely to continue to slow down as central governments offer separatist areas high degrees of autonomy rather than risk the loss of important territories. Paradoxically, the continuing devolution of existing states will also provide long-range opportunities for new kinds of loose confederations as smaller units feel driven to come together in cooperative frameworks.

State proliferation is the consequence of two forces—the drive of dependent territories for independence and the division of existing sovereign states. Often, although not always, this devolution comes about only after conflict. More than one hundred former colonies and territories have achieved self-determination either as sovereign states or through association with other states. There are approximately sixty remaining dependencies, many of which have very small populations or provide their administering powers with strategic military bases so that the latter are reluctant to give up control. Others are so highly dependent economically that they cannot afford the luxury of national independence. Those non-self-governing territories most likely to opt for independence are ones that are sufficiently resource rich, have favorable tourist bases, or are financial havens. As the world becomes a more open system, the advantages that such territories currently enjoy from retaining colonial ties decreases.

POTENTIAL NEW STATES AND QUASI STATES

Table 3.2 identifies states that are possibilities for independence or quasi statehood. For many separatist movements, the high degree of autonomy that may be offered to them through quasi statehood is likely to be accepted.

Those territories whose prospects for independence are greatest contain peoples who have operated from historic core areas in which they have maintained their cultural, linguistic, religious, or tribal distinctiveness. Many of the prospective states and quasi states listed in table 3.2 are economically viable because of the strength of their resource bases—for example, in Indonesia, Aceh's oil and natural gas; in West New Guinea, Irian Jaya's copper and gold; Democratic Republic of Congo's eastern province of Shaba's copper, tin, uranium, diamonds, and fertile grasslands; South Nigeria's oil and gas; Scotland's offshore North Sea oil; and the grain of Punjab, known as the "granary of India," where the Sikh majority aspires to create a separate country known as Khalistan. The trade, tourism, and revenue from smuggling enjoyed by some Caribbean islands are also bases for national status.

Those states that achieve only qualified forms of sovereignty thus become quasi states both because they lack the military capacities to gain their full objectives and because they are too important to the home country to be allowed full independence. Spain's approval of greater autonomy for Catalonia in 2005 offered promise as a useful model for resolving other separatist conflicts. The revised autonomy law recognizes the Catalan nation, increases to 50 percent its share of income and VAT that are collected within the province, and guarantees that national investments in Catalonia will be equal in proportion to the region's contribution to the national GDP. In addition, the region is given jurisdiction over culture, education, health, local government, and police. However, this law has not been fully implemented. As a consequence, increased Catalan pressures for an independence referendum poses a major challenge to the unity of Spain.

Political latitude might offer special diplomatic status, including UN membership to quasi states, as was the case for Belarus and Ukraine when they were within the Soviet Union. Such status might be especially appropriate for Taiwan, although it would surely be opposed by Beijing.

Another form of organization for some quasi states could be the "condominium," whereby two larger powers share oversight for such functions as defense and foreign relations. The Kashmir dispute between India and Pakistan might be resolved by such an arrangement.

In maritime Europe, the proliferation of quasi states in such countries as Spain, Italy, France, and the United Kingdom could reinforce the developmental process of regional specialization and integration. These semi-independent entities would be free of some of the restraints that currently limit their specialized potentional, thus strengthening the EU rather than being impediments to integration.

Table 3.2. Gateways and Separatist Areas

Present Region	*Present Gateway*	*Potential Gateway*	*Independent/ Quasi States*
North and Middle America	Bahamas Trinidad Jamaica Guyana Cayman Islands Honduras	Bermuda	Puerto Rico* Quebec*
South America			S. Brazil*
Maritime Europe and the Maghreb	Malta Lampedusa Monaco Finland Canary Islands Azores	Gibraltar**	Crete* Catalonia* Greenland N. Ireland‡ Euskadi* Scotland* Galicia* Brittany* Corsica* Faero Islands* Madeira Islands* Flemishland* Trentino-Alto Adige Adige* Wales* Wallonia* Kabylla (Algeria)*
Asia-Pacific Rim	Taiwan Singapore	Guam S.W. Australia* Unified Korea	S. and W. Mindanao* Aceh* Irian Jaya S. Moluccas
Heartland		Russian Far East*	Chechnya* Tuva* Sakhlin*
Caucasus/ Central Asia	Turkmenistan Uzbekistan		
China	Hong Kong	China "Golden Coast"*	Tibet* Xinjiang*
Indochina			
South Asia		Pakhtoonistan	Kashmir‡ Nagaland* Kalistan* N. Afghanistan* E. and S. Afghanistan*
Middle East	Bahrain Cyprus Dubai Qatar		Arab Palestine Kurdistan (Iraq)* W. Iraq*
Central and Eastern Europe	Austria Estonia Finland Slovenia	Ukraine	Transnistria* Abkhazia**
Sub-Saharan Africa	Djibouti Cape Verde	Zanzibar	Puntland* Somaliland† Shaba N.E. Nigeria*

*Quasi state (statelet)
**Condominium
†Two stages: quasi state to independence
‡Two stages: condominium to independence

One unfortunate consequence of the proliferation process has been the creation of "failed" nation-states. These are deeply divided, war-torn states, lacking in national cohesiveness, whose governance institutions have collapsed to the point of anarchy or near anarchy. Some divisions are so entrenched and long-standing that they defy international and regional efforts at amelioration. Somalia, which was patched together from three colonial territories and then unified as an independent state, has once again fallen apart.

One index for measuring such states is the Failed State Index of 2013.[12] It includes such indicators as demographic pressures, refugees, uneven economic development, deterioration of services, violation of human rights, and political factionalism. In this index, ten of the top fifteen states are located within Africa, all but one (Zimbabwe) within the region's compression zones. Four are located within the Middle East and one (Haiti) in the Americas. Somalia leads the list, followed by the Democratic Republic of Congo.

Models for addressing the "failed state" syndrome include full-scale nation building, as attempted by the United States in Afghanistan and Iraq, and the NATO peacekeeping effort in Bosnia. It remains to be seen how successful these remedies can be. For the most part, the international community lacks the capacity and geopolitical motivation to mount such operations in most of the world's failed states. It is more likely that massive intervention will continue to be pinpointed for lands that are global geopolitical flash points and that elsewhere the burden will be left to regional powers to try to mediate conflicts and restore domestic stability.

A strategy of early identification of emerging states would permit advance action by international and regional bodies to mount comprehensive infrastructure development programs within prospective states. This could help ward off potential political instability and prepare them to become viable members of the world community when they gain independence. Timely and effective international action could include commitment to technological and capital support for building and maintaining water, sanitation, health, transportation, communications, and education infrastructures. Such comprehensive development efforts would require that when new states emerge, their fledgling governments demonstrate a "best effort" to share responsibility for these programs, with agreed-upon international monitoring and auditing. This is especially critical for countries with valuable resources that might be siphoned off by ruling cliques.

This continuing struggle for independence has profound implications for US foreign policy making. Concomitant with the objective of eradicating global terrorism, it will be necessary for Washington to promote new approaches that will encourage separatist movements to negotiate their goals peacefully. In many cases, American pressures, sanctions, and rewards by themselves will not be able to dictate peaceful resolutions of irredentist conflicts. Neither is the United Nations equipped to shoulder such a burden. However, a hands-off policy by Washington that simply awaits the implosion of many countries is a recipe for global instability.

The challenge is to find new mechanisms for mediating these separatist disputes, based upon a partnership of effort among the United States in alliance with the EU and Japan, other major and regional powers, and regional organizations. Afghanistan and Iraq are evidence that outside military force alone cannot resolve disputes. A confederation of highly autonomous Shiite, Sunni, and Kurdish areas appears to be the only alternative to a Shiite-dominated Iraq. A similarly loose confederation may be the optimal solution to the struggle in tribalized Afghanistan, with its Pashtun population in the east and south and Tajiks and Uzbeks in the north. Alternatively, an independent Pakhtoonistan, linking the Pashtuns of Afghanistan and western Pakistan, could emerge, leaving the rest of Iraq to a new Tajik-Uzbek state.

State proliferation is a stage in the evolution of the global system toward specialized integration. States now trying to break away might one day seek confederal ties with their for-

Table 3.3. Potential Confederations

Region	*Potential Confederations*
North and Middle America	"Westindia"
Maritime Europe and the Maghreb	N. and S. Cyprus
Heartland	• Russia, Belarus, Kazakhstan • "Greater Turkestan" (Uzbekistan, Tajikistan, Kyrgyzstan, Turkmenistan) • GUAM (Georgia, Ukraine, Azerbaijan, Moldova)
China	• China, Taiwan *or* • Continental China, the "Golden Coast," Taiwan
Middle East	• Afghanistan, Pashtun E. and S., Tajikistan and Uzbekistan N. and W. • Saudi Arabia, Gulf States, Syria, Lebanon, W. Iraq • W., Central, and N. Iraq • Israel and Independent Palestine
Central and Eastern Europe	• Baltic states (Estonia, Latvia, Lithuania) • Former Yugoslav states (Serbia, Croatia, Montenegro, Bosnia, Kosovo)

mer hosts, especially to fulfill mutual economic self-interest. Table 3.3 suggests possible future confederations.

The creation of up to fifty additional fully independent or quasi states over the coming few decades will change the territorial outlines and functions of many major and regional powers. With the exceptions of Nigeria, Indonesia, Iraq, Syria, and Pakistan, these changes are likely to have only limited impact on the power rankings of these states or on world equilibrium.

Geopolitics and General Systems

Treating the geopolitical world as a general system provides a model for analyzing the relationships between political structures and their geographical environments. These interactions produce the geopolitical forces that shape the geopolitical system, upset it, and then lead it toward new levels of equilibrium. To understand the system's evolution, it is useful to apply a developmental approach derived from theories advanced in sociology, biology, and psychology.

The developmental principle holds that systems evolve in predictably structured ways, that they are open to outside forces, that hierarchy, regulation, and entropy are important characteristics, and that they are self-correcting.

In 1860, Herbert Spencer was among the first to set forth a development hypothesis that drew an analogy between the physical organism and social organization. His evolutionary ideas came from physiology and the proposition that organisms change from homogeneity to heterogeneity. Using the organic growth analogy, Spencer argued that social organizations evolve from indefinite, incoherent homogeneity to relatively definite, coherent heterogeneity. In this hypothesis, state and land meant the combination of social organization and physical organisms.[13]

Combining organismic concepts from Herbert Spencer, sociologist, with those of Heinz Werner, psychologist, and Ludwig von Bertalanffy, psychobiologist, provides the foundations for a spatially structured geopolitical theory.[14] It is a theory that is holistic, is concerned with the order and process of interconnecting parts, and applies at all levels of the political territorial hierarchy, from the subnational, to the national, to the supranational. Adapting this developmental principle to geopolitical structures, the system progresses through the following.

The earliest is *undifferentiated* or atomized. Here, as in feudalism, none of the territorial parts are interconnected, and their functions are identical. The next stage is *differentiation*, when parts have distinguishable characteristics but are still isolated. The post-Westphalian states in Europe or the postcolonial states of the 1950s through the 1970s all sought to be self-sufficient and to mirror one another. The next stage is *specialization*, which is followed by *specialized integration*. In this last stage, exchange of the complementary outputs of the different territorial parts leads to an integration of the system. The parts of the system are hierarchically ordered, increasing its efficiency, as one level fulfills certain functions but leaves other functions to units belonging to different levels. What helps to bring balance to the system is the drive of less mature parts to rise to higher levels.

Currently, the world geopolitical regions operate at the following stages:

1. specialized integration—maritime Europe and the Maghreb;
2. specialization—North and Middle America, Asia-Pacific Rim;
3. differentiation—heartlandic Russia, East Asia, the Middle East, South America, South Asia;
4. undifferentiation—Trans-Caucasus-Central Asia, Indochina; and
5. atomization—Sub-Saharan Africa

Geopolitical systems behave like physical systems in that they may exhaust the material and human resources that are the bases of their power unless they are able to recharge their systems with outside energies. In the past, empires did so by exploiting colonies and conquests. In today's world, such energies are best secured through exchange. The Soviet Union collapsed because, in trying to penetrate the far reaches of the globe, it expended its resources and manpower far beyond the benefits it could reap from such penetration. In contrast, a state like Singapore recharges itself through the import of goods and ideas in exchange for the products and services that it exports. The advantage of most states within the maritime world is that they can maintain their energy through international exchange. Continental countries, however, especially those that develop closed political systems, have found themselves with less and less energy not only to influence the world outside but also to maintain their domestic systems.

Equilibrium, Turbulence, and World Order

The collapse of Soviet Communism, the end of the Cold War, and the successful entry of China into the global economy have inspired the hopes that a new order is dawning and fired the debate about the form that such an order will take. The rhetoric is not novel—peace and security, reduction of military weapons, sharing the wealth, justice for national groups. It is the mechanism that is at question. Can there be a truly global system in which the world acts in concert through the United Nations? Is it now feasible to save the world through a Pax Americana, or can we count on the world's major power centers—the United States, the

European Union, Japan, a reconstituted heartlandic Russia, China, and emergent India and Brazil—to take collective action to stabilize and enhance the international system?

The greater promise for a stable world system lies in the collaborative efforts of these power centers, with Washington and the EU taking the initiative. In this effort to gain consensus, the UN Security Council, while it may not have a clear collective interest, nevertheless has proved its importance by serving as a forum that requires agreement among its permanent members and thus has an important role to play in stabilizing the global system.

How we treat the new era's prospects for global stability is very much a matter of conceptualization and perspective. Instead of discussing "world order," we should be speaking of "global equilibrium" because global stability is a function of equilibrium processes, not order. Order is static. It speaks to a fixed arrangement, a formal disposition or array by ranks and clusters that requires strong regulation and implies a sharply defined set of niches separated by clear-cut boundaries. The niches fit together in an elaborate structure that follows a blueprint designed by some body that operates either hegemonically or consensually. Essentially, order implies outside regulation.

Equilibrium, by contrast, is dynamic. The term, as applied here, is not being used in the physical or psychophysical sense that the natural state of an organism is rest or homeostasis. Such equilibrium characterizes closed systems but does not fit human organizations or most natural systems. In these, equilibrium is the quality of dynamic balance between opposing influences and forces in an open system. Balance is regained after disturbance by the introduction of new weights and stimuli. Under ideal conditions, such balance is regained through self-correction—through what Adam Smith referred to as the "invisible hand," or the rational self-interest of peoples.

Because of inertia of the self-interest of governing elites, self-correction may not always take place. War, terrorism, economic greed, energy crisis, illegal immigration, and environmental devastation may bring people to the breaking point in the absence of reason. So may human interference with the regenerative powers of the natural environment. When things have gone too far, there is reaction, correction, and new regulation. Whether equilibrium is maintained through self-correction or a new level is produced by cataclysmic forces, the balance is accompanied by change, and change by turmoil.

A great deal of turmoil and conflict has taken place in the world since the end of the Cold War. The collapse of the Soviet Union was not so cataclysmic as to bring on global conflagration, as hypothesized by such economic determinists as Immanuel Wallerstein and George Modelski.[15] Communist rule disappeared from the Soviet sphere with a whimper, not a "big bang." Even where Communist regimes still prevail, their economies are being liberalized and their systems opened. When these regimes come to an end, the attendant disturbances are likely to be minor tremors.

The difference in the turmoil that plagues the post–Cold War world from that during the Cold War is not that wars, civil disturbances, and terrorist activities are less numerous or less lethal, but that their geographical locations have shifted.[16] During the Cold War, the major conflicts raged in the Korean Peninsula and in the Southeast Asian and Middle Eastern shatterbelts. With the end of the Cold War, the locus of conflict moved to the Balkans and the periphery of the former Soviet Union (FSU) and intensified in the Middle East and Sub-Saharan Africa.

At the same time, as global terrorism has become more sophisticated and more lethal, it has reached into the farthest corners of the earth, affecting major powers and small, weak states alike. It was naive to assume that the end of the Cold War would usher in an era of global peace and harmony. Change and turmoil are intertwined, an unfortunate characteristic of the process of dynamic equilibrium. Because of overlapping spheres of influence and global trade and communications, hierarchy becomes more flexible and national and regional systems become more open. At the same time, the diffusion and decentralization of power make the system increasingly complex.

In addition to war, terrorism, and cyberwarfare, massive illegal migration flows have become world system destabilizers. The number of international migrants is estimated at two hundred million, or 3 percent of the world population. More than half these immigrants have settled in developed countries, mainly Europe and the United States. Cultural absorption has become a serious problem within many of these countries. On the other hand, nearly three quarters of the cash remittances generated by these immigrants goes to the poorer countries of the world, helping to stabilize their political and economic systems. Concern that immigration flows, legal or illegal, facilitate the spread of terrorism is legitimate. However, on the whole, international migrations to the developed world perform a positive role in providing needed labor.

War refugees, however, have a destabilizing effect. Refugees from the Iraq War had an impact on the economic and political stability of Jordan and Syria, as do the Afghan refugees upon Pakistan now. This applies also to those who have gone from Darfur to Chad, from Somalia to Kenya, or from Rwanda and Burundi to Congo, and most recently from Syria to Lebanon, Jordan, and Turkey. These human tragedies have their impact on local and regional stability but not on global equilibrium.

Another threat to the stability of the world is climate change due to global warming. It is estimated that flooding of coastal areas and inundation of low-level islands could displace as many as one billion people from their homes and farmlands. Record low ice cover in the Arctic is partially caused by global warming. If by 2100 the sea level rises by two meters—the high end of prediction—Manhattan could be inundated, and much of the island state of Kiribati submerged. Some of its villages have already been swept away by rising tides, and the government has purchased land in Fiji where its citizens can grow food and eventually settle. In other parts of the world, climatic shift due to natural variability increases drought, water shortages, and famine. Where this has occurred in the United States, this can also be explained by greenhouse gas emissions. Unless serious steps are taken to slow or arrest this greenhouse effect, the geopolitical system would be greatly destabilized.

The immediate challenge is to develop a global consensus on how to deal with global warming, but the will to do so is very uneven. Europe has already imposed emission quotas; US attention seems finally to be engaged, but effective government action has yet to be taken; China, India, and Russia continue to place their highest priority on economic growth, despite the impact of pollution on the health, safety, and living conditions of their people. Real progress depends on a commitment by all of the world's highly developed nations to take strict measures within their own countries but also to assist the developing world technologically and, where needed, financially to enable them to balance their needs for economic growth with rigorous antipollution standards.

With all of the looming threats, what is the possibility of maintaining global equilibrium? There is no threat of war among the major powers of the world. Despite economic and political competition, the interdependence of their economies has become the bulwark against large-scale conflict. In addition, they face similar and sometimes mutual threats of terrorism, a need to stabilize the energy resources of the world, and the danger of instability in neighboring countries. Thus, even with the continued turbulence of world events and problems, including governmental upheavals and rebellions, it is possible for the great powers to cooperate in maintaining global dynamic equilibrium.

Notes

1. Robert Ardrey, *The Territorial Imperative* (New York: Atheneum, 1966), 3–41, 108–17.
2. Geoffrey Parker, *A Political Geography of Community Europe* (London: Butterworth, 1983), 1–17, 41–61.
3. Alfred T. Mahan, *The Problem of Asia and Its Effect upon International Policy* (Boston: Little, Brown, 1900), 21–26.
4. James Fairgrieve, *Geography and World Power* (London: University of London Press, 1915), 329–30.
5. Richard Hartshorne, "The United States and the 'Shatter Zone' in Europe," in *Compass of the World*, ed. H. Weigert and V. Stefannson (New York: Macmillan, 1944), 203–14.
6. Philip Kelly, "Escalation of Regional Conflict: Testing the Shatterbelt Concept," *Political Geography Quarterly* 5, no. 2 (1986): 161–86.
7. Peter F. Drucker, *The New Realities* (New York: Harper & Row, 1989), 173–86, 255–64.
8. Michael Hardt and Antonio Negri, *Empire* (Cambridge, MA: Harvard University Press, 2000).
9. Peter J. Taylor, *Political Geography*, 2nd ed. (Harlow, England: Longman Scientific and Technical; New York, Wiley, 1989), 7, 16–41.
10. Paul Kennedy, *Preparing for the Twenty-First Century* (New York: Random House, 1993), 122–34.
11. Edward Said, *Culture and Imperialism* (New York: Vintage, 1994), introduction, 3–61.
12. Fund for Peace, "Failed States Index, 2013," *Foreign Policy Magazine* (2014).
13. Herbert Spencer, "The Social Organism," reprinted in *The Man versus the State*, ed. Donald Macrae (Baltimore: Penguin, 1969), 195–233.
14. Heinz Werner and Bernard Kaplan, "The Developmental Approach to Cognition," *American Anthropologist* (1956): 866–80; Heinz Elau, "H. D. Lasswell's Developmental Hypothesis," *Western Political Quarterly* 21 (June 1958): 229–42; Saul B. Cohen, "Assymetrical States and Geopolitical Equilibrium," *SAIS Review* 4, no. 2 (Summer/Fall 1984): 193–212; Ludwig von Bertalanffy, *General System Theory* (New York: Braziller, 1968), 194–213.
15. Immanuel Wallerstein, *The Capitalist World-Economy* (Cambridge: Cambridge University Press, 1979), 6–15, 61–71; George Modelski, *Long Cycles of World Politics* (Seattle: University of Washington Press, 1987), 18–50, 215–48.
16. Dan Smith, *The State of War and Peace Atlas* (London: Penguin, 1997), 16–29, 32–61.

CHAPTER 4

The Cold War and Its Aftermath

Geopolitical Restructuring

The memory of the Cold War has faded rapidly with the conflicts in the former Yugoslavia, Iraq, Afghanistan, Syria, and Somalia and the concerns with global terrorism. Nevertheless, it is the geopolitical restructuring that took place as a result of World War II and the Cold War that has shaped the outlines of the current world geopolitical map. The forces behind this restructuring remain important guides to future changes in this map. The Cold War is divisible into three phases: (1) the maritime realm's ring of containment along the near periphery of the continental Eurasian realm; (2) Communist penetration of the maritime realm; and (3) Communist retreat from the maritime realm and the waning of Soviet power. The geopolitical patterns and features that developed during these phases reflected the changing ideological postures, military capacities, and economic/technological advances among the major Cold War protagonists and other states that had been drawn into the competition.

Phase I: 1945–56

NUCLEAR STALEMATE AND DETERRENCE: DRAWING THE RING OF CONTAINMENT

It was widely assumed that the end of World War II would herald the onset of a peaceful era, free of the virulent nationalism that led up to the war, and would permit national energies to be dedicated to rebuilding lands and societies. However, the territorial exchanges and boundaries that were agreed to by the Western Alliance and the Soviet Union sowed the seeds of dissension. The USSR received eastern Poland in exchange for the award of East Prussia and Silesia to Poland. Very soon the United States' fear of the spread of Communism and the Soviet fear of containment led to the onset of what would be known as the Cold War (a term coined by Walter Lippmann in 1945).

The first decade of the Cold War confirmed the mutual fears and distrust that prevailed between the American and Soviet superpowers. For Washington, clear evidence of the Soviet threat to world peace was the Berlin blockade (1948), Soviet detonation of an atom bomb

(1949), North Korea's invasion of South Korea (1950), the Soviet hydrogen bomb (1953), and the Warsaw Pact (1955). Moscow perceived as major threats to its security the Truman Doctrine and Marshall Plan (1947), NATO (1949), American involvement in the Korean War, and the US hydrogen bomb (1952). The various events and perceptions that were formed by the two superpowers during this period resulted in a balance of nuclear terror and nuclear deterrence.

The global geopolitical map of phase I and most of phase II reflected the rigid, hierarchical, bipolar structure imposed on the rest of the world by the United States and Soviet superpowers (figure 4.1). Most of the world was included within two geostrategic realms—the Eurasian continental, dominated by the USSR, and the trade-dependent maritime, dominated by the United States. The status of South Asia was that of a geopolitical region independent of the two realms but subject to continuous pressure from them.

The Eurasian Continental Realm consisted of two geopolitical regions—the Soviet inner Eurasian heartland, with its Eastern European strategic attachment, and East Asia. The economic core of the Soviet heartland had been expanded from its Ukrainian-western Russian base to the Urals when Soviet industry had to be relocated there during World War II. The spread of Communism into Central and Eastern Europe immediately after the war provided the USSR with a new, advanced position from which to threaten Western Europe and to seek to undermine the North Atlantic Alliance.

Through its Communist Chinese and North Korean allies, Moscow also posed a major threat to Japan and to the strategic positions of the United States in the Western Pacific. Vulnerability to Soviet power of North and interior China emphasized China's dependent status. Moreover, Beijing also needed the alliance with Moscow because of its vulnerability to Western naval and air power and the exposure of its coastal reaches to the nationalists based on Taiwan and US forces based in South Korea.

The trade-dependent maritime realm included the Atlantic and Pacific basins and their Caribbean and Mediterranean extensions. From its intermediate location between the two oceans, the United States could reinforce its North Atlantic European partners, cast its strategic net over South America, and provide military and economic cover for Japan and other allies along the Pacific Rim.

The regional geopolitical divisions of the maritime realm included Anglo-America and the Caribbean, maritime Europe and the Maghreb, offshore Asia and Oceania, and South America. Sub-Saharan Africa also lay within the realm but lacked a distinct geopolitical framework since it remained divided among the various European colonial powers. The cores of the realm were the manufacturing belt of the northeastern and midwestern United States and the recovering industrial triangle of northern Europe. They were connected via the sea-lanes of the North Atlantic.

The Caribbean was tied to the eastern United States by proximity, capital investment, trade, and US naval bases in Puerto Rico and Guantánamo Bay. South America was under the political and economic shadow of the United States, and the cultural and economic ties between Europe and such countries as Brazil and Argentina reinforced the influence of the maritime realm.

The Maghreb was still ruled by France, although independence movements had gathered momentum in Tunisia and Morocco (soon to gain their independence) and rebellion had broken out in Algeria. The presence of large numbers of French settlers, especially in Algeria, plus economic ties helped to keep the Maghreb within France's geopolitical orbit and thus within maritime Europe's sphere of influence.

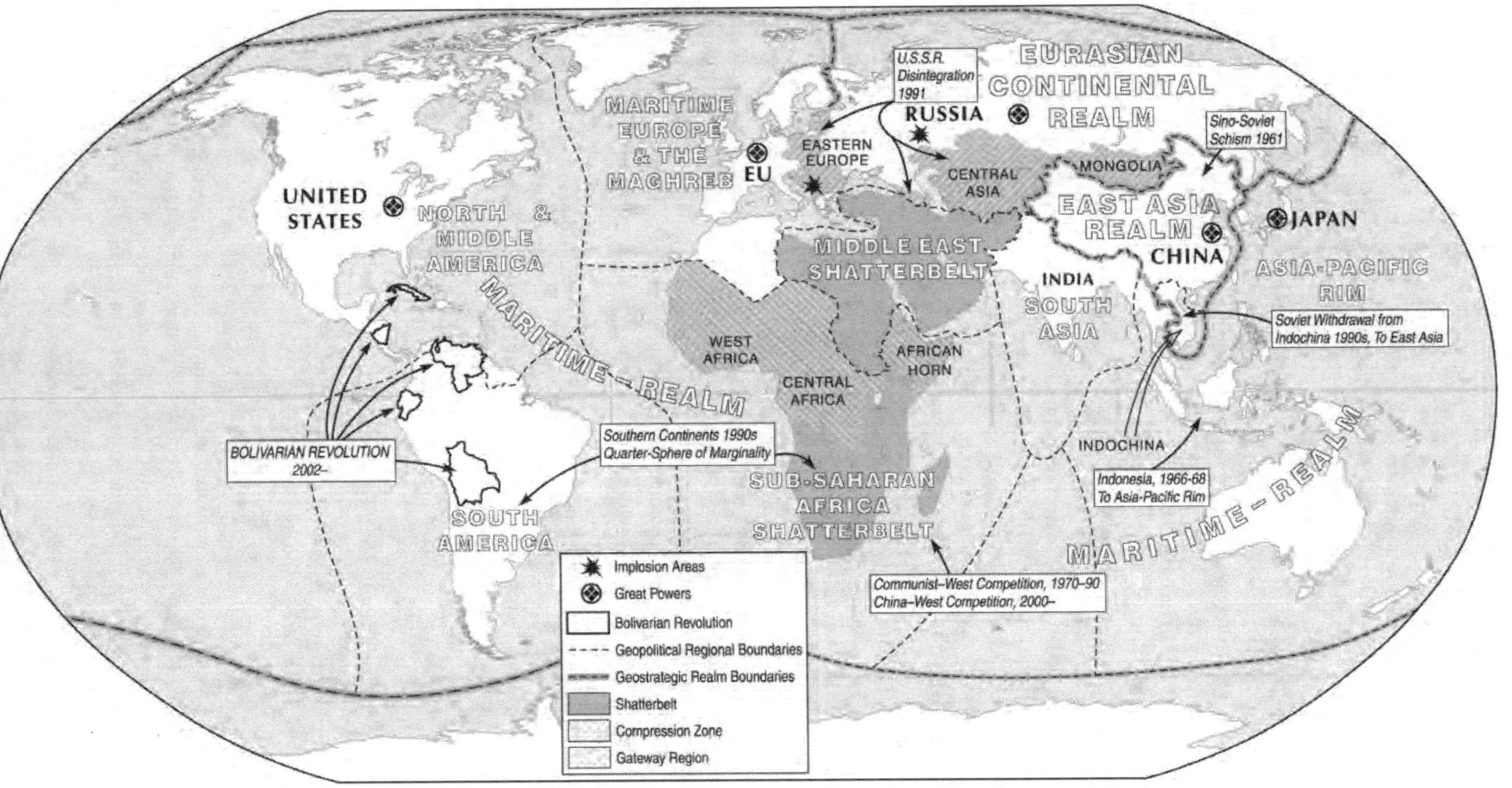

Figure 4.1. Realm and Regional Changes from the End of World War II to the Present

In the Pacific, American military power was firmly anchored in South Korea, Japan, Taiwan, the Philippines, Australia, and New Zealand. It was backed by European colonial positions in Malaya, North Borneo, New Guinea, and East Timor. Another important base was Thailand, which had emerged from its World War II occupation (an occupation that it had invited) by Japan. Thailand shook off its historic isolationism and forged a military alliance with the United States. In 1954, Bangkok became the headquarters for the Southeast Asia Treaty Organization (SEATO), which had been established under the leadership of the United States, Britain, and France immediately after the withdrawal of the latter from Indochina. SEATO also included Australia, New Zealand, Pakistan, Thailand, and the Philippines. The stated purpose of the new alliance was to contain the further spread of Communism into Southeast Asia. It ultimately proved helpful to the United States in sanctioning its military presence in Vietnam.

The fundamental weakness of the treaty organization was the fact that only two Southeast Asian states had joined it. Instead, the regional defense role was assumed by Asia-Pacific Rim, consisting of South Korea, Taiwan, Japan, the Philippines, peninsular Thailand and Malaya, Australia, and New Zealand. These countries were linked bilaterally to the United States and Britain through economic and military alliances. (In 1977, toward the end of phase II and in the aftermath of the US withdrawal from Vietnam, SEATO was disbanded.)

The countries of Southeast Asia—Indonesia plus the three Indochinese states of Vietnam, Cambodia, and Laos—that were not part of the new offshore Asian region were soon to become the contested arena between the Eurasian continental and maritime realms and would take the form of a shatterbelt.

Most of the Middle East had gained independence by the early 1950s, but the region still lay within the orbit of the maritime realm. In 1955, under the sponsorship of Great Britain and the United States, Turkey, Iraq, Iran, and Pakistan forged the Baghdad Pact in an effort to create a northern regional screen against the expansion of Soviet influence. This pact was short-lived, collapsing in 1959 when its only Arab member, Iraq, withdrew to pursue a policy of nonalignment. The remaining members were organized within the Central Treaty Organization (CENTO).

Elsewhere within the Middle East, Britain still maintained its rule over the Persian Gulf states, Aden, and the Sudan; its military alliance with Jordan; and its troops in the Suez Canal (although they were in the process of being withdrawn). Saudi Arabia was a firm client state of the United States, and both Israel and Lebanon looked to America as their main supporter. Sub-Saharan Africa, still subject to European colonial rule, was also very much part of the maritime realm and especially important for the realm's strategic minerals and other natural resources.

South Asia, the only independent geopolitical region in the world, stood apart from the two geostrategic realms. Under the leadership of Jawaharlal Nehru, the force of India's commitment to neutrality in the global struggle gave the region unique status. Burma (Myanmar) also took a neutralist course, refusing to join SEATO. Ceylon (Sri Lanka) sought to carve out a role as a leader in the economic development of South and Southeast Asia when it served as host for the Colombo Plan program. However, beset by rebellions, economic crises, and governmental instability, the country had little energy to take on regional initiatives. Nepal, which had for the previous century deliberately isolated itself from foreign influence, continued to pursue nonalignment upon gaining independence. Bhutan, fearing China's claims upon its territory, became even more dependent on India in matters of defense and foreign relations but remained fairly closed and inaccessible.

Among the states of South Asia, only Pakistan became embroiled in Cold War alliances. This was due, in part, to its geographic split personality as both a Middle Eastern and South Asian state. The seminomadic Pashtuns (Pathans) of Pakistan's North-West Frontier Province, the Tribal Areas, and the northern borderlands of Balochistan, as well as the Balochi tribesmen in the southwest were culturally and linguistically oriented to the Middle East lands. In contrast, the farmers of Pakistan's Punjab, while Muslims, were culturally and geographically linked to the Indian portion of the Punjab. Similarly, the Muslim Bengali were culturally and linguistically linked to the Hindu Bengali of India. This internal tension eventually erupted in the civil war that brought independence to East Pakistan, which then became firmly tied to India.

During phase I, the USSR and its Communist China ally sought to forge a *cordon sanitaire* around the Sino-Soviet realm by pushing outward from the heart of continental Eurasia to its surrounding inner seas and passageways to the oceans. With the USSR still reeling from the devastation wrought by the invading armies of Nazi Germany during World War II, Joseph Stalin's goal was to erect a strong defensive screen between the Soviet Union and Western Europe. This was to guard against a recurrence of the *blitzkrieg*, with which the Germans had so recently swept across the Baltic, lain siege to Leningrad (St. Petersburg), penetrated Moscow's suburbs to within twenty miles of the city, reached the Volga at Stalingrad (Volgograd), and seized most of the northern Black Sea coast.[1]

Poland was the key to the Soviet defensive screen. The Allied attempts at Yalta to secure a postwar representative government came to naught, as the controlled elections for the provisional government in 1947 assured a Communist victory.

There were a number of catalysts for the decision of the West to try to block further Soviet expansion by creating a "ring of containment" around the near-periphery of the heartland. They included the establishment of the Soviet Zone in Germany in 1945, the outbreak of the civil war in Greece the following year, and the blockade of West Berlin in 1948–49.

The major territorial objective of the Soviet Union during phase I was Eastern and Central Europe—the region that Mackinder had described as the "middle tier of states" between Germany and Russia, populated by Slavs and South Slavs, Bohemians, and Magyars and constituting a strategic addition to the heartland (figure 4.1).

At the end of World War II, East Prussia was taken from Germany, its northern half, including Memelland, being annexed by the USSR and its southern half being annexed by Poland. The defeat of Germany also enabled the Soviets to retain the Finnish territories that they had seized during the Finnish-Russian War of 1940 and the Baltic republics that they had added during that same year. These annexations provided the USSR with a firm grip on the Baltic and gave greater defensive depth to Leningrad. Not only were the Karelian Isthmus and Finnish Karelia acquired, but Finland was forced to lease the Porkkala Peninsula for a Soviet naval base. In the far north, the Finns lost Pechenga and the Ribachy Peninsula, adding to the security of Murmansk, which had been so important as the lifeline terminus for supplies from the United States during World War II.

Elsewhere in Europe, the Soviets annexed a wide strip of land from eastern Poland, adding it to Belarus and Ukraine. Prior to Poland's regaining its independence in 1919, these territories had belonged to czarist Russia and the Austro-Hungarian Empire. In addition, eastern Transcarpathia was seized from Poland and parts of Bessarabia and Bucovina from Romania to complete the zone of annexation. With the acquisition of these lands, the USSR gained considerable defensive depth along the invasion routes to Moscow, Stalingrad (Volgograd), and Odessa, as well as the Crimea, which had been taken by the invading Nazi armies during the war.

To compensate Poland for its losses in the east, the Soviets added to western Poland thirty-nine thousand square kilometers (twenty-five thousand square miles) of the Third Reich's 1939 territory. The new lands lay east of the Oder and Neisse Rivers and, at their northern end, included Gdansk (Danzig) and southern East Prussia. All of these border changes were approved by the West at the 1945 Potsdam Conference.

Soviet security objectives were further satisfied between 1945 and 1948 by Moscow's imposition of Communist regimes upon the belt of Eastern and Central European countries extending from the Gulf of Lübeck and the Elbe River to Thuringia, the Ore Mountains and the Bohemian Forest, the Middle Danube, the Julian Alps, and the Adriatic. Most of the Black Sea now lay within the Soviet orbit save its southern Turkish shores. Included were the single-party, vassal Communist states of East Germany, Czechoslovakia, Hungary, Poland, Albania, Yugoslavia, Bulgaria, and Romania. This represented fulfillment of the Soviet strategy of establishing a *cordon sanitaire* along its highly vulnerable western border. Toward the end of phase I, in 1955, the Warsaw Pact formally linked the Eastern European Communist bloc countries militarily with the USSR as a direct response to remilitarization of West Germany.

Along the southwestern reaches of Soviet power, however, the attempts to draw Greece into the Communist orbit through a civil war launched by Communist rebels and to pressure Turkey failed. Instead, the North Atlantic Treaty Organization (NATO), which had been created in 1949 in response to the Soviet blockade of Berlin and to defend Western Europe from Soviet expansionism, was enlarged in 1952 to include Greece and Turkey. In addition, Yugoslavia, which had been expelled from the Comintern in 1948, signed a separate military pact with Greece and Turkey in 1954, strengthening the Western containment effort.

During phase I, the Western ring of containment was extended eastward to include Iran. In 1946, the Soviet Union withdrew its troops from the northern part of the country, where they had been stationed during World War II, at the time when British and American troops secured the southern part of the country. The Soviet withdrawal came only after intense pressure from the United States and Britain, acting through the United Nations, and with the promise by Iran (which was never fulfilled) to grant Moscow oil concessions. This then enabled the Iranian military to depose Soviet puppet Communist regimes in the Kurdish and Azerbaijani sectors of Iran that had been set up in 1945. In 1952, the anti-US government of Mohammad Mosaddegh took power, nationalizing the oil industry and seeking to overthrow the Shah. Two years later, Mosaddegh was overthrown, largely by covert activities of the US Central Intelligence Agency (CIA) with British help, and the Shah was returned to power. The next year (1955), Iran joined with Turkey, Britain, Iraq, and Pakistan in the Baghdad Pact, with the United States as an associate member, strengthening the ring of containment along the northern borders of the Middle East.

In South Asia and peninsular Southeast Asia, Indian and Burmese neutrality and Communist revolutionaries in North Vietnam prevented the West from extending containment to the borders of China. The pervasive influence of Mohandas K. Gandhi's philosophy of nonviolence was not the only source of the Indian policy of neutrality. It related also to New Delhi's ideological differences with the Soviet Union, fears of the Chinese threat to India's territorial integrity, and suspicions that the United States was intent on achieving strategic dominance and imposing American-style capitalism upon the world.

Indian fears of world Communism were also fanned by China's annexation of Tibet in 1950 on the basis that the 1914 McMahon Line had deprived China of lands that were rightfully its own. Not only was China now perched on India's Himalayan border, but also it laid claim to Indian, Nepalese, and Burmese territories, as well as Bhutan in its entirety. In phase II, this dispute would erupt into conflict between India and China. At the same time, New Delhi's distrust of the United States and its former British colonial ruler was fanned by the inclusion of Pakistan within SEATO and the Baghdad Pact. The military support provided by the United States to Pakistan in connection with these pacts was, from the Indian perspective, a direct threat.

Burma maintained its neutrality, refusing to join SEATO and identifying with the other nonaligned Third World states. While recognizing the People's Republic of China diplomatically, it kept its distance, being itself plagued by internal Communist and tribal rebellions. A particular problem for the Burmese was the presence of Nationalist Chinese troops who had fled across the border after their defeat in 1950. The troops remained there for three years until forced to leave by the United Nations.

In Southeast Asia, the boundary between the Communist and Western worlds remained in flux as the French-Indochina War raged from 1946 to 1954. With the fall of Dien Bien Phu in 1954, France agreed to an armistice, the terms of which divided Vietnam along the seventeenth north-latitude parallel. The north, with its core in the Red River Delta and Hanoi, went to the Communists under the leadership of Ho Chi Minh, while the south, whose core was Cochin China, centering on the Mekong Delta and Saigon, became a French puppet regime led by Bao Dai.

The armistice boundary did not long hold as a line of containment. The very next year the Saigon regime, now led by Ngo Dinh Diem, was recognized by the West as the legal government of all of Vietnam, while North Vietnam began to receive considerable economic as well as military support from the USSR and China. What followed during much of phase II was conversion of all of southern peninsular Southeast Asia into a shatterbelt region as the Vietnam War engulfed the great powers as well as the Vietnamese rivals.

In insular Southeast Asia, the former Dutch East Indies were also part of this shatterbelt. Indonesia had achieved its independence from the Dutch in 1949, but during the first part of the Cold War it was preoccupied with uniting its diverse peoples in the face of sporadic uprisings and the threat of a highly influential local Communist Party. Moreover, President Sukarno, who had led the fight for Indonesian independence, adopted a socialist and neutralist platform, which fanned Western suspicions.

The northeastern boundary between the Sino-Soviet realm and the United States and its allies was forged by war. Japan's northern limits were drawn after World War II. Then, at Yalta, the Allies agreed to the Soviet annexation of the southern half of the island of Sakhalin and the Kuril Islands as part of the price for the Soviets having entered the war against Japan. In 1951, the US-Japan Security Treaty committed Washington to the defense of Japan from external attack.

The victory of the Chinese Communists over the Nationalists in 1949 extended the Eurasian continental Communist power to the limits of the East Asian mainland and was quickly followed by Beijing's occupation of Tibet in 1950. Offshore, however, the ring of containment was sharply drawn during the same year, when the Chinese Communist plans to invade Nationalist-held Taiwan were frustrated by the patrols of the US Seventh Fleet. Thus was the boundary established in the Western Pacific between the two geostrategic realms—down the centers of the Sea of Japan and the East China Sea through the Taiwan Strait. The line was hardened in 1955–56, when the US response to Communist shelling of the Nationalist-held islands of Quemoy (Jinmen) and Matsu (Mazu) was to enter into a mutual security pact with the Nationalists and a promise to defend Taiwan against outside attack.

In the Korean Peninsula, the boundary was stabilized only after a bitter conflict that directly involved American and Chinese forces in the fighting on the ground and in air combat, in which Soviet pilots also joined. While most of the northern boundary divided China from

Korea, Soviet concerns over the entry of American troops into the fighting were heightened by the fact that a ten-mile stretch at the eastern end of the boundary that followed the mouth of the Hunchun River served as North Korea's boundary with the USSR, only ninety miles from Vladivostok. After the seesaw battle that raged up and down the peninsula ended, the 1953 armistice line along the thirty-eighth parallel became the basis for the boundary between the two Koreas that persists to this day.

There were unanticipated consequences for the USSR as a result of helping build up the Chinese air force and army. That air force became the third largest in the world, and the large Chinese army became battle hardened. This new strength was instrumental in changing China's view of itself from that of a Soviet satellite to that of a partner. It was an important factor in Mao Zedong's break with Moscow after the death of Joseph Stalin.

The southern end of the ring of containment in offshore Asia included the Philippines, which had received independence in 1947 but continued to house US military, naval, and air bases. These positions overlooked the South China Sea and the shorelands of southern China and Indonesia. The threatened spread of Communism to the Philippines was halted in 1954, when indigenous Communist guerrillas (the Hukbalahap, who operated in Central Luzon) were defeated by the government's forces. However, they regrouped and conducted a campaign of terrorism for the next decade and a half until crushed by the Philippine military in 1969. They ceased to function the following year.

Rounding off the heartland's near-periphery was the Arctic. There, the Cold War balance was maintained through mutual deterrence, as nuclear weapons capable of being delivered by long-range bombers and submarines prowling under the Arctic ice cap became available to both sides. The US-Canadian Distant Early Warning (DEW) line air defense system, begun in 1955, was an important element of the American transpolar security system. Similarly, Soviet meteorological, radio, and scientific posts based on ice floes backed up the country's air, nuclear icebreaker, and submarine defenses.

Expansion of the Communist realm into its near-periphery during phase I was greatly facilitated by Moscow's buildup of its nuclear capacity as well as by the rapid rebuilding of its war-shattered heavy industrial economy. Reconstruction of the economy, including reindustrialization of much of the western Soviet Union, was marked by rapid advances in military technology.

Phase I came to an end in 1956, when Soviet nuclear weapons development led to the establishment of a balance of terror between the two superpowers. Also marking the period's conclusion was the beginning of the Sino-Soviet schism.

Phase II: 1957–79

COMMUNIST DEEP PENETRATION OF THE MARITIME REALM

During this phase, substantial change in the geopolitical map of the world took place, as the Cold War leapfrogged continental Eurasia's near-periphery and spread to the inner and outer reaches of the maritime world. The bitter rivalry between the superpowers was fanned by a number of events. The 1957 launching of Sputnik, the first artificial satellite, a year before the US launching of Explorer I, was considered a wake-up call to American science and education. In the same year, Moscow announced the development of the first intercontinental ballistic missile (ICBM). In addition, it broke a voluntary moratorium on nuclear testing, which it had signed in 1958, when it resumed testing in 1961. US fears of the Soviet threat were also heightened by the building of the Berlin Wall (1961), the Cuban missile crisis (1962), and the invasion of Czechoslovakia (1968). Soviet fears in turn were intensified by the Bay of Pigs (1961), by US entry into the Vietnam War (1965), and by the American role in the overthrow of Indonesia's President Sukarno (1965).

The penetration of the maritime world by the Eurasian continental powers was facilitated by a number of developments. The European colonial era was ending in the Middle East, Southeast Asia, and Sub-Saharan Africa. At the same time, Marxist influence was gathering strength within Third World national liberation movements. The ability of the United States to become directly engaged in additional Cold War conflicts was limited by negative American public opinion stemming from the involvement in the Vietnam War. Development of a massive Soviet arms export industry cemented the dependence upon Moscow of many Third World countries.

The schism between Moscow and Beijing set up a competition between the two for Third World influence. This break began with Mao's ideological opposition to the de-Stalinization policy introduced by Nikita Khrushchev in 1956 and widened with Mao's promotion of the Great Leap Forward. For Mao and his successors, Khrushchev's disavowal of Stalinism represented abandonment of Marxism. These events led to the withdrawal of Soviet economic aid and technicians from China in 1960. Hostility intensified as China became allied with Albania in 1961 in the wake of the rift between Moscow and Tirana. It increased still further in the late 1960s, when Chinese hard-liners took objection to Leonid Brezhnev's call for peaceful coexistence with the West. Finally, the decade-long border dispute between the two Communist powers erupted into fighting.

A marked ideological shift gave impetus to Moscow's strategic ambitions. The move away from the ideological commitment to support only revolutionary Marxist parties was signaled by the 1956 dissolution of the Cominform. Instead, by joining hands with all who were enemies of imperialism, the USSR could support nationalist movements that were hostile to Communism as well as those that were led by Marxists. The banner was no longer the "World Communist Revolution"; it was the "War against Capitalism-Imperialism."

The Soviet Union developed its arms industry to the point of becoming the world's second-largest supplier of arms. Whereas in phase I Soviet arms shipments had been limited primarily to the Warsaw Pact countries and China, in phase II, the direction of the flow of weapons shifted to the Third World and to India. While Moscow could not compete with the United States and its allies in trade or in economic assistance to its Third World clients, Soviet military transfers to its clients in the form of sales and grants were generous. Moreover, its improved logistics capabilities enabled it to move large numbers of Cuban troops to Angola and Ethiopia and to ship large quantities of arms and military supplies by sea and air.[2]

Much of what happened in phase II can be traced to the rising influence of Nikita Khrushchev after the deaths of Stalin and Lavrentiy Beria. Khrushchev's 1956 speech to the Twentieth All-Union Congress denounced Stalin's dictatorial rule and personality cult and called for decentralized management of the Soviet economy. The address followed up on efforts initiated in the previous year to introduce greater flexibility to Soviet foreign policy. This had included a peace treaty with Austria, diplomatic relations with West Germany, and return to Finland of the site of the Porkkala naval base.

Khrushchev also made efforts to place relations with Eastern Europe on more of a partnership basis. The result was establishment of the Council for Mutual Economic Assistance (COMECON) as a broadening of the Warsaw Pact, which had been initiated in response to the remilitarization of West Germany. However, Eastern European hopes that this presaged a loosening of the Soviet grip were quickly dashed when uprisings in Poland by disaffected students and workers were repressed by the Soviets. In Hungary, an anti-Communist revolution that had declared Hungary neutral and withdrew Budapest from the Warsaw Pact was also crushed by Soviet troops.

With Eastern Europe still securely in its hands, the Soviet Union could now challenge the United States and its allies diplomatically and politically, within their own backyard—the maritime realm. Soviet aggressiveness was strengthened by advances in military technology, including ICBMs, so that by the 1970s the USSR had achieved nuclear parity with the West.

REGIONS OF SOVIET PENETRATION

The Soviet strategy of penetrating the maritime world gathered momentum in the years that followed, as the United States became increasingly bogged down in Vietnam. In addition, starting in 1969–71, the Nixon and Brezhnev administrations pursued a policy of détente in Europe through strategic arms limitation talks (SALT), while the American-supported *ostpolitik* of Germany's Willy Brandt aimed at reducing US-Soviet tensions and achieving mutual force reductions in Europe.

As a general strategy, the Soviet Union sought to establish political and military positions along key maritime world waterways. Such areas included:

1. the Middle East and the African Horn—the eastern Mediterranean and the Suez Canal, the Red Sea, Bab el-Mandeb, and the Gulf of Aden
2. Southeast and offshore Asia—the Strait of Malacca and the South China Sea
3. the Caribbean—the Florida Straits and the Yucatán Channel

To carry out such a strategy, a major naval buildup was undertaken.[3] Forming the core of the new Soviet "blue water" navy were missile-carrying nuclear-powered submarines and guided missile cruisers, as well as intelligence and survey ships. The fleet was backed by long-range naval and giant cargo aircraft. In addition, Soviet shipyards produced one of the largest merchant fleets in the world, including many ships with military mission capabilities. In addition to the Northern, Pacific, Baltic, and Black Sea fleets, the Soviet navy kept permanent forces in the Mediterranean and the Indian Ocean.

The rise of Soviet naval power took place at a time of decline for the US naval program, the fleet having been reduced in number and threatened with obsolescence. Cold War proponents in the United States saw the Soviet buildup as an effort to gain control of the oceans and as a major threat to the security of the seas. However, their call for a strong response to the challenge through the expansion of the US Navy was not answered until the Reagan administration.

Fears of the USSR's threat to Western dominance of the oceans may have been overblown. A more likely explanation for the Soviet naval buildup is that it was done to help defend the footholds that had been secured within the maritime world, rather than to use naval power as the basis for broader expansion within the realm. A major problem for the Soviet fleets was the undependability of their overseas bases, which were vital to their operations, for they had no independent deep-water capacities. Alexandria, Berbera, Aden, Aseb (Assab), and Massawa were gained and later lost. Cienfuegos was more than offset by the US bases in Guantánamo and Key West; Cam Ranh Bay was neutralized by American air and naval operations in Guam, Okinawa, and the Philippines; and the Conakry base was offset by the

US facilities in the Azores and Ascension Island. Soviet anchorages in the Indian Ocean and the Mediterranean were at the mercy of Western air and sea power.

In the late 1960s and early 1970s, China shifted from a revolutionary policy to a vigorous diplomatic foreign policy, extending aid to selected parts of the underdeveloped world in South America, Africa, and Asia. This new Chinese political assertiveness was facilitated by the self-confidence derived from its development of nuclear bombs and satellites in the 1960s and by the Sino-US détente initiated by President Richard Nixon's dramatic visit to Beijing in 1972.

SHATTERBELTS

During phase II, Soviet penetration of the maritime realm resulted in the creation of three shatterbelts—the Middle East and the African Horn, Sub-Saharan Africa, and Southeast Asia.

The Middle East and the African Horn

The Middle East was the first place in the maritime realm where the Soviets penetrated the Western ring of containment. There, Syria, Egypt, and South Yemen were Moscow's main targets for extending its influence. Egypt, the largest and most powerful of the Arab states, was the prime objective. As early as 1955, the USSR began to provide aid to Egypt and also to Syria.

Withdrawal of US and British financial support for the proposed Aswan Dam, the centerpiece of Gamal Abdel Nasser's development plans in Egypt, opened the door for the Soviets to provide the funding. Moscow went on to give military support to Cairo after the Egyptian army had been defeated in the 1956 Sinai War with Israel. During the next decade and a half, Soviet influence upon Egypt was all-embracing, with vast military, technical, and economic aid. In return, the Soviets acquired access to Egyptian naval bases on the Mediterranean coast, which supported its Mediterranean squadron, a self-contained detachment of the Black Sea fleet.

This penetration of the Arab world's leading nation ended in 1972, when President Anwar Sadat made preparations for another war with Israel against the wishes of the USSR. Sadat ousted Soviet forces and took over their bases. After the defeat of Egypt in this war, the United States moved into the vacuum and, at Camp David, brokered a peace between Egypt and Israel. Egypt then returned to the maritime orbit through a new alliance with the United States.

Soviet relations with Syria were longer lasting. The Baath Party, which combined socialism and nationalism, had gained power in the mid-1950s. In 1960, its radical wing seized control with Moscow's help. Subsequent economic and military accords provided the Soviets with a strong foothold in Syria, although President Hafez al-Assad, who had seized power and become president in 1971, feared an internal Communist coup and therefore remained wary of Soviet long-range intentions. These fears played a role in Syria's decision to join with Egypt and Libya in the short-lived Federation of Arab Republics (1969–70).

Unlike Egypt, which had swept out Soviet influence in favor of peace with Israel and strong support from the United States, Syria remained at war with the Israelis over possession of the Golan Heights. As a consequence, the USSR continued to maintain considerable influence with Damascus, which still remains heavily dependent on Russian arms.

When Lebanon became embroiled in civil war among Christians, Muslims, and Palestinians in the mid-1970s, Syria seized the opportunity to extend its influence over the country.

The Syrian military intervened in 1976 at the invitation of the Christian community to prevent its being overrun by the Lebanese Muslims and Palestinians. Damascus then switched its support to the Muslims and the Palestinians when the Christian-dominated Lebanese army leadership sought to oust the Syrian forces from the country.

Soviet penetration into South Yemen began with the independence of the colony of Aden from Britain in 1967. The new state included the Arab Emirates of South Arabia in the Hadhramaut, which lay to the east of Aden. The historic trading center for the southern part of the Arabian Peninsula, Aden had an excellent natural harbor that would well serve Soviet strategic aims in the Red Sea and Indian Ocean.

In 1979, a twenty-year accord between the Soviets and the South Yemen regime provided for Soviet naval bases to be installed. These gave support to the eastern Mediterranean Soviet fleet as it entered or exited the Red Sea at Bab el-Mandeb en route to the Suez Canal. With complementary Soviet bases that had developed earlier, first in Somalia and then on Ethiopia's Eritrean coast, oversight of the southern end of the Red Sea was strengthened.

In Libya in 1969, Muammar al-Gaddafi's overthrow of King Idris and seizure of power led to the closing of the remaining British military bases there, as well as of the US Wheelus Air Base. (Most British troops had been withdrawn three years previously.) This paved the way for the short-lived alliance with Egypt and Syria and for Libya to become a base for international terrorism against Israel and the West.

Gaddafi espoused socialist principles but was strongly anti-Communist. While he forged military ties with the USSR, which supplied him with vast amounts of advanced military equipment, including missiles, his major interests lay in extending Libya's influence into the Arab world and providing support to Palestinian guerrilla movements. A formal Soviet-Libyan alliance was forged much later, in 1980, when the Libyans came into conflict with Tunisia, and it continued in subsequent years of Libya's conflict with Chad. However, by 1980 the alliance was of little strategic value to the Soviets, inasmuch as Egypt had already made peace with Israel and had become a major client state of the United States.

Relations between the USSR and Iraq took various turns. Initially, in 1955, Iraq severed ties with the Soviet Union over the latter's support of the Kurdish revolt in northern Iraq. Later, in 1972, when Iraq broke its diplomatic links with Britain and Iran, it signed a friendship pact with the Soviets, although its various Baathist regimes continued to be wary of possible Communist coups. Given the strength of the alliance between Washington and the Shah of Iran, Iraq saw its links to the USSR as a valuable countermeasure and purchased substantial amounts of arms from Moscow. The situation changed drastically in 1979, when the virulently anti-American Khomeini regime overthrew the Shah. As Saddam Hussein prepared for war against Iran, the United States considered support of Iraq both desirable and feasible.

During this period of major Soviet inroads into the Arab world, the West maintained its position through strategic alliances with Turkey, the Shah's Iran (until his ouster), Israel, Saudi Arabia, and the Gulf states. The importance of Iranian oil to the West had been underscored at the beginning of this era when Prime Minister Mohammad Mosaddegh nationalized the British-owned Anglo-Iranian oil company. Elected by the deputies of the Majlis in 1951, with strong support for his nationalization program, Mosaddegh was overthrown by a combined CIA-British action two years later. He was convicted of treason by the new government. Far from being the Soviet tool that he was accused of being, he had rejected Moscow's bid to win an oil concession.

It was in early 1979, at the very end of phase II, that the US-Iran alliance was shattered by the overthrow of the Shah and the establishment of the fundamentalist Islamic Republic, led by the Ayatollah Khomeini. Seizure of the American embassy by Iranian militants and the keeping of 52 American hostages for 444 days embittered the relations between the two nations for years to come.

From the 1950s onward, oil from the eastern Arabian Peninsula and the Gulf waters, as well as from Iraq and Iran, had become of such global importance that the West had to maintain a strong Middle Eastern presence. In addition, Turkey, the region's largest military power, served as NATO's eastern cornerstone and defensive bastion against the Soviet Black Sea positions.

US support for Israel had begun out of domestic political and humanitarian concerns. However, with American help, Israel had developed a formidable military machine, supported by a strong intelligence capacity which was superior to those of its combined Arab enemies It therefore constituted a valuable Cold War military asset to counter Soviet influence among most of the Arab states. Saudi Arabia and the Gulf states were completely dependent upon Washington for military support and arms to guard against continuing threats from Iraq (and, after 1979, from Iran), providing the West with a firm strategic presence in the Persian/Arab Gulf.

Soviet penetration also extended into the Horn of Africa, where its strategic objective was full command of the southern end of the Red Sea. This involved Moscow in countries bordering the sea along both the Arabian Peninsula and the Horn of Africa. Even though the Suez Canal was now closed, the Horn, a transitional region between the Middle East and Sub-Saharan Africa, was a tempting prize. By linking positions on the coast of the Horn to those held in South Yemen, the Soviet navy would acquire control of both sides of the Gulf of Aden through surveillance installations monitoring the movements of US and allied air and naval power in the Arabian Sea and Indian Ocean.

In the Horn of Africa, the opening for the USSR came in Somalia in 1969, when a military coup brought General Mohamed Siad Barre to power and established a Marxist-Leninist state that developed strong ties with the Soviet Union. Soviet assistance included considerable arms to build up the Somali forces. In exchange, Moscow was given the right to build naval and missile bases in the north in the port of Berbera (in former British Somaliland), opposite Aden, and in Mogadishu in the south.

Events in Ethiopia soon placed the Soviets in a quandary, forcing them to choose between two allies, Ethiopia and Somalia. In 1974, a Soviet-backed military junta had overthrown Emperor Haile Selassie and installed a Marxist regime headed by Mengistu Haile Mariam. Two years later, the Ethiopians formally ended their alliance with the United States and formed one with the USSR. In the long-standing dispute between the Somalis and Ethiopians over the latter's control of the Ogaden Desert, which lay between them, the USSR and Cuba opted for Ethiopia. The Soviets flew in twenty thousand Cuban troops and provided advisers, enabling the Ethiopians to retake the Ogaden in 1978.[4] As the conflict continued, the Somalis turned to Egypt, Saudi Arabia, Iran, and the United States for help.

In 1978, Soviet-Cuban assistance also enabled the Ethiopians to defeat the Eritrean rebels, who had seized most of Eritrea, and clear the way for the Soviets to gain naval and military bases on the Red Sea at Massawa and Aseb.

Sub-Saharan Africa

Sub-Saharan Africa became a second shatterbelt during this period. With the reopening of the Suez Canal in 1975, the USSR gained direct access to the Red Sea by way of the eastern Mediterranean and the Black Sea. Together with land proximity, this provided the Soviets with a strategic advantage in the Middle East over the more distant Western powers. In most of Sub-Saharan Africa, however, Moscow was at a strategic disadvantage relative to Western Europe. France, Belgium, and Britain were much closer geographically to West and Central Africa and could apply military power there more quickly. In addition, the Europeans had strong economic and cultural ties to those regions. The Soviets, however, had to use lengthy sea routes or overfly the continent to provide military support to Communist movements there.

Only in relatively distant southern Africa did Moscow and its Cuban allies have equal strategic access. There, however, the Soviets had to contend not only with the European powers backed by their transatlantic US partner but also with white-ruled South Africa, which could directly support the anti-Communist forces in nearby Mozambique and Angola.

An early opportunity for a Soviet foray into Sub-Saharan Africa presented itself within Central Africa, in Congo. Congo attained independence from Belgium in 1960, and its first government was headed by Patrice Lumumba, a Marxist. His Soviet-backed regime was immediately beset by the secession of the mineral-rich Katanga (Shaba), but the USSR's capacity to provide military help was limited. Lumumba was soon overthrown and subsequently murdered, and a new national government was established through a combination of covert US help, Belgian troops, and white mercenaries. Two years later, Mobutu Sese Seko seized power and the United States became the main supporter of the country (renamed Zaire). This ended Soviet hopes of gaining a foothold in Congo—an important source of such strategic minerals as copper, uranium, cobalt, and tin as well as industrial diamonds, petroleum, and rubber.

The adjoining Republic of the Congo-Brazzaville had received its independence from France at the same time as had Congo. Although a Marxist-Leninist government took power, it steered a neutral course between Moscow and the capitalist world, especially because of its economic dependence upon France. Only at the beginning of phase III of the Cold War did Congo sign a friendship pact with the Soviet Union, a relationship devoid of strategic significance.

In West Africa, Guinea, which had been led to independence from France in 1958 by Ahmed Sékou Touré's radical union movement, cultivated relations with the Soviet Union. In 1961, Touré expelled the Soviet ambassador for seeking undue influence in the country, but relations were restored, and Conakry became a base for Soviet military surveillance aircraft and a permanent Soviet naval patrol off the Guinea coast.

Ghana provided no opening for the Soviet Union, although under Kwame Nkrumah (1957–66) it took a strong anticolonial, Pan-African stance, unfriendly to the West. Elsewhere within West Africa, Mali had a flirtation with the USSR in the 1960s and 1970s, when Soviet military advisers provided a small number of tanks and aircraft. While there was a Soviet market for some of its exports, such as hides, groundnuts, and canned fish, the impoverished country still depended mainly upon France for imports and credits as well as for trade with neighboring African states.

In the latter part of phase II, Benin, which had adopted a Marxist ideology in 1975, sought support from the Communist world. Little was forthcoming except for a handful of Soviet small naval craft, so the country remained economically tied to Europe. Neither Benin nor Mali offered any strategic advantages for the USSR.

In East Africa, which received its independence from Britain in 1963, only Tanganyika and Zanzibar were realistic targets of opportunity for Communist penetration, as major ethnic divisions rather than ideology were the basis for turmoil in Kenya and Uganda. Immediately following independence, Zanzibar was the scene of a leftist revolt, some of whose participants were Cuban trained. However, the island was quickly merged with Tanganyika into Tanzania (1964), and the mainland gradually took control of the island's affairs.

Chinese influence grew in Tanzania, as China provided the aid for building the Tazara (Tan-Zam) Railway from the coast at Dar es Salaam to Zambia in the late 1960s. Nevertheless, the Communist influence was kept within limits, as Julius Nyerere preferred to follow his own brand of socialism, free of great-power entanglements. Nyerere and his successors continued to steer a course of nonalignment in the great-power clash. The country did become embroiled in border clashes with Uganda that erupted into full-scale war in 1978–79. It also served as a support base for liberation movements in other parts of Africa.

In the mid-1970s, southern Africa provided the USSR with a new window of opportunity. In Angola, the Communist guerrillas who had led the war of independence from Portugal gained control of the government. In its struggle to keep power against opposition rebel movements, the Marxist regime received large amounts of aid from the Soviet Union and Cuba. In 1976, the opposition National Union for Total Independence of Angola (UNITA) nearly succeeded in capturing Luanda with the help of South African troops and US support. However, Cuban soldiers were flown in by Soviet planes, backed by seaborne supplies, to save the capital and to enable the regime to gain control of the north and much of the rest of the country. With the assistance of Cuba and the USSR, Angola also provided a base for Southwest African guerrillas (the South West Africa People's Organization, SWAPO) in their battle for independence from South Africa.

A Marxist government was also installed in Mozambique when the Mozambique Liberation Front (Frelimo) came to power in 1975. The new regime received aid, equipment, and training support from the USSR and help from Cuban air force personnel. Beira became a base for the Soviet Indian Ocean squadron. The country soon became a haven for the rebels of the Marxist Zimbabwe African National Union, precipitating a brief but devastating invasion from white-dominated Rhodesia.

The Soviet bases on the two coasts of the two southern African allies, Angola and Mozambique, were strategically valuable. From Beira overlooking the Mozambique Channel, the Soviets presented a challenge to the US Fifth Fleet and to its air arm based on the Indian Ocean Island of Diego Garcia, which had been leased from Britain. In addition, Beira provided oversight of the shipping lanes from the eastern Mediterranean and Indian Ocean through the channel to the Cape of Good Hope and of traffic destined for the Atlantic. Angola enabled the Soviet Union to monitor the trans-Cape route from the Atlantic side.

By the end of phase II, the Soviet position in Sub-Saharan Africa had become shaky, despite these widespread efforts to penetrate the region. Its Communist satellites in Ethiopia and Angola remained locked in combat with powerful rebel forces within their countries. Moscow incurred high costs in keeping large numbers of Cuban troops to sustain these regimes while pumping arms and economic assistance into them. Moreover, in white-dominated South Africa, the Soviets had encountered a regional power with the military capacity and the logistical advantages to help the rebels in both Angola and Mozambique fight the Marxist governments and their Communist allies to a standstill.

The geopolitical actions of the Soviet Union in Sub-Saharan Africa during phase II had converted the region into a shatterbelt. Moscow's goals had been twofold—to support Marxist and anticolonial movements of national liberation wherever they took place and to fulfill Soviet geostrategic objectives by securing footholds along the Horn of Africa and other lands and offshore islands bordering the Indian Ocean, thus threatening sea-lanes vital to the maritime world. The success of these efforts proved to be mixed, however, as so much of Africa continued to depend upon the West for its economic survival and was unwilling to forgo ties with European investors and markets.

Southeast and Offshore Asia

During phase II, the Southeast Asian peninsula and the western portions of offshore Asia emerged as the third shatterbelt. Communist control of North Vietnam had been affirmed in the 1954 partition of Vietnam. This partition served as the initial stage of the war that would then engulf all of Indochina and divide the region between the Communist world and the West. The United States failed to contain the spread of Communist power, although it spent over $150 billion in more than a decade of combat.[5]

Despite the rift between the Soviet Union and China, both provided massive military and economic aid to North Vietnam. In 1978, three years after the war's end, China broke with Vietnam over the latter's invasion of Cambodia in support of a Communist faction, led by Hun Sen, that had ousted China-backed Pol Pot and his Khmer Rouge regime. In China's stead, the Soviet Union became Vietnam's chief ally and source of aid, receiving in return a long-term lease for the Cam Ranh Bay naval base overlooking the South China Sea.

Not only had much of the northern half of the Indochinese portion of the Southeast Asian peninsula fallen to the Communists during phase II, but the southern half of the peninsula and Indonesia were also drawn into the East-West conflict.

In Malaysia, a Communist insurrection that lasted through the 1950s ended with the forced resettlement of nearly five hundred thousand Chinese and the emergence of a strongly Western-supported state that had gained its independence as a member of the Commonwealth of Nations in 1957. Thailand, threatened by its proximity to China and Communist gains in Vietnam, had used SEATO early on for protection. During and following the Vietnam War, it received considerable military and economic aid from the United States. While Communist insurgencies in several parts of the country, especially in the northeast, plagued the Thai regime in the early 1970s, they were eventually put down. The Philippines, though wracked by intermittent uprisings, remained resolutely anti-Communist. The Communist-led Hukbalahaps rose up again in the late 1960s and fought intermittently before being finally quashed in 1979. Since that time, the major rebel groups have been the Muslim Moros of Mindanao and the Sulu Archipelago.

During this phase, Indonesia veered from neutralist to pro-Communist to pro-Western stances. The shift toward the West took place in 1966 as a result of an attempted Communist coup, which was repressed by the army, led by General Suharto. Up to three-quarters of a million, many of them ethnic Chinese, were killed in Java and Bali. General Suharto took advantage of the turmoil to strip President Sukarno of his powers and put him under house arrest. He assumed the presidency himself the following year. Suharto then developed close ties with the United States and helped to found ASEAN. This regional bloc of anti-Communist countries included Malaysia, the Philippines, Singapore, and Thailand. (Today, ASEAN also includes Vietnam, Cambodia, Laos, Myanmar, and Brunei.)

OTHER GEOPOLITICAL REGIONS

South Asia

While not of the same strategic imperative to the USSR as the Middle East, Sub-Saharan Africa, and Southeast Asia, South Asia nevertheless became more deeply drawn into the Cold War during this phase. It was China, rather than the Soviet Union, that represented a threat to India. While New Delhi continued its policy of nonalignment, its fears of China were increased as Tibet became more tightly controlled by Beijing, with the settlement there of hundreds of thousands of Chinese.

The ongoing border disputes between India and China erupted into border clashes in Ladakh and Assam in 1959 and a limited war in 1962, whereby China gained some territory in Ladakh. As India's relations with Beijing worsened, its ties with Moscow improved. In 1966, for example, the USSR brokered a troop withdrawal between India and Pakistan that took their forces back to the lines that had been held prior to their war of 1965.

Five years later, Soviet political support and an airlift of military equipment was of assistance to India in its third war with Pakistan, this one over Bangladesh. A new economic assistance plan was subsequently concluded between Moscow and New Delhi. At the same time, India's relations with the United States became increasingly strained over the latter's continuing military and economic support of Pakistan. In spite of all of this, India maintained its posture of neutrality, and ties with the United States gradually improved.

Burma (Myanmar) was not only physically and historically identified with the Indian subcontinent, but it also shared India's commitment to neutrality. In addition to Burma's distrust of Britain, its neutrality had been influenced by its fears of China. Communist rebels and tribal groups, such as the Karens, rose up against the Burmese government shortly after independence and continued their insurgencies over the next two decades with support from Beijing. The military junta that seized power in 1962 increasingly shifted the orientation of the country from its earlier contacts with the nonaligned world to complete isolation.

Latin America

Latin America was another focus for Soviet penetration efforts during phase II. Extending the Cold War to the Caribbean, which lay within the immediate tactical and strategic reach of the United States, represented a daring and costly challenge. Cuba, which overlooks the Straits of Florida and the Gulf of Mexico, provided the USSR with the opportunity to challenge the United States on its own doorstep. When Fidel Castro overthrew Fulgencio Batista in 1959, he nationalized American landholdings and financial and industrial companies, breaking relations with Washington and declaring allegiance with the Eastern bloc. The subsequent failure of the US-sponsored Bay of Pigs invasion in 1961 emboldened Nikita Khrushchev to strengthen the Cuban armed forces significantly and to build Soviet missile bases on the island.

The immediate response of President John Kennedy was to demand that the Soviets dismantle their missiles and to impose a naval blockade, forcing the USSR to back down. In addition, the naval base at Guantánamo remained in US hands, thus allowing the United States control of the Windward Passage and the lanes between the Atlantic and the Caribbean as well as securing the Panama Canal from the north. While Cuba continued to be a base for Soviet naval and surveillance activities until the disintegration of the Soviet Union, the 1962 missile crisis was a lesson to both superpowers. To avoid similar nuclear confrontations, both adopted strategies of relying upon surrogates in their competition wherever possible. It was Cuba that then took on the mantle of spreading the revolution to other parts of Latin America. However, while Castro became completely dependent upon Soviet arms, economic aid, and fuel and on the sugar market of the Communist bloc, he was by no means a puppet in the sense that the Eastern European regimes were. Indeed, geographical distance, which was such a considerable liability to the USSR in its efforts to sustain Cuba and spread the revolution within the Western hemisphere, proved to be a political asset to Castro in pursuing some of his domestic and foreign initiatives. This freedom of action was unavailable to Eastern European satellites because of the presence of Soviet forces on their doorsteps or within their territories.

The Bay of Pigs incident stimulated the United States to take an aggressive stance against the Marxist rebellions that began to sweep Latin America. While Cuban influence in Jamaica and Guyana was not negligible, Castro failed to convert the socialist governments there to overt allies. In Venezuela, where two Communist-inspired naval revolts in 1962 and subsequent hit-and-run terrorist actions threatened the Social Democratic government, Washington provided support to suppress the threats.

Elsewhere, the United States had intervened in Guatemala as early as 1954 to topple a Communist-influenced government. Guatemalan bases were then established with US assistance to train anti-Castro guerrillas in the early 1960s. When left-wing terrorism broke out within the country in the mid-1960s and continued in the following years, American support of its military strongly shaped Guatemalan politics.

Only at the very end of phase II, in 1979, did two radical left-wing governments emerge in the Caribbean that were to become closely allied to Cuba and the Soviet Union during phase III. The Sandinistas gained control of Nicaragua after the lengthy Somoza rule, while a leftist coup supported by Cuban troops seized power in Grenada, to be ousted by US and Caribbean troops four year later.

In South America, Soviet penetration efforts were singularly unsuccessful. In Bolivia, the United States aided the rightist military junta in the struggle against Communist guerrillas led by Castro's chief lieutenant, Che Guevara, who in 1967 was killed in the fighting. Three years later, a leftist coup resulted in the attempt to develop ties with the Soviet Union, but that government was toppled by a rightist countercoup the following year.

In Chile in 1970, Salvador Allende became the first popularly elected Marxist president in Latin America. He sought close ties with the Communist bloc only to be overthrown and murdered after three years by the Chilean military with covert US support. The Marxist revolution spread to Uruguay in 1967 with the establishment of a terrorist group there. Ultimately, the campaign of the Tupamaros urban guerrilla movement was put down by a repressive regime installed by the military.

In Argentina, Communist as well as Peronista parties were banned in the 1963 elections by the right-wing regimes that took power. In Brazil, leftist guerrillas were ruthlessly suppressed during the 1960s and early 1970s.

The failure of the Soviet Union to expand its influence in Latin America outside of Cuba (and later Nicaragua) was due, to a considerable extent, to the vigorous countermeasures taken by Washington. Military and police leaders trained by the United States in the Panama Canal Zone's School of the Americas were significant forces in providing security support for the right-wing regimes that dominated most of the countries of the region. An example of the impact of this training was "Operation Condor," a system developed to share in intelligence and antileftist security actions among Brazil, Argentina, Chile, Paraguay, Uruguay, and Bolivia. The security establishments of these countries and their Washington backers often made little distinction between real and imagined security threats in the effort to stop the spread of Soviet and Cuban-supported Communist movements.

THE ARMS RACE

It was in phase II that the Soviet Union achieved parity with the United States in its military and nuclear buildup. While US arms expenditures had escalated rapidly during the Korean

War, they were then scaled back, as President Dwight Eisenhower sought to rein in the "military-industrial complex." By 1961, Soviet military expenditures had nearly caught up with those of the United States. During the 1960s, the two powers kept pace with one another. From 1956 through 1970, for example, Washington's defense outlay totaled $861.7 billion and Moscow's $812.8 billion.[6] The United States forged substantially ahead only during the administration of President Ronald Reagan. US foreign arms sales, mainly to the Middle East, increased exponentially during the 1970s, exceeding those of the USSR.

While the largest portion of Soviet increases in military expenditures was in missiles and air power, and while nuclear parity had been achieved, the buildup of the Soviet fleet also required substantial outlays. The price of this buildup placed a heavy strain on the Soviet economy and society. With a reported gross domestic product that was half that of the United States and a per capita income that in real terms was probably only one-third that of its rival, the USSR succeeded in matching the United States in military expenditures during phase II. Increasingly plagued by food and consumer goods shortages and lagging in high technology, the Soviet Union was ill prepared to compete under the further strains that would result from the arms buildup of the Reagan administration.

Phase III: 1980–89

COMMUNIST POWER RETREAT FROM THE MARITIME REALM

In the 1980s the world geopolitical map again underwent major restructuring. Most significantly, China broke away from the Eurasian continental world to establish a separate East Asian geostrategic realm. Other hallmarks of phase III were the hard-line stance taken against the Soviet Union and other Communist states by the Reagan administration and the rapid decline of Soviet influence in the Middle East, Sub-Saharan Africa, and Latin America.

This phase followed upon the period of détente between the United States and the USSR during the 1970s, which resulted in SALT I and SALT II—accords that banned new ICBMs and launchers. The détente ended in early 1980 with the Soviet invasion of Afghanistan and the US boycott of the Moscow Summer Olympics.

If phase II marked the apogee of Soviet penetration of the maritime world, phase III was its nadir. The USSR's bloody and ultimately unsuccessful war in Afghanistan left it with little surplus energy to devote to its other Cold War pursuits. Considerable pressure was put on Moscow by the decision of the Reagan administration to scrap détente and greatly increase US military expenditures, for it triggered an arms race that the Soviet Union could neither afford nor win.[7] By 1989, the end of phase III, the annual defense expenditures of the United States were $275 billion. The Soviet figure was $190 billion—significantly higher than its average annual expenditures during the previous phase but inadequate to prevent the arms gap from widening. The United States had extended its lead, particularly in the application of high technology and telecommunications to modern warfare, as it would demonstrate in the Gulf War.

Economically, the situation was worsening in the Soviet Union, as living standards dropped, consumer goods were in short supply, and Soviet agriculture failed to meet the needs of the nation. While the defense budget of the USSR was two-thirds that of the United States, its gross national product had dropped to one-sixth that of the United States. By the end of the decade, it had become evident to Soviet leadership that the costly and uneven arms race could not be sustained, that the country would not have both "guns and butter."

EMERGING MAJOR POWERS

The multilateral nature of the international system began to emerge clearly during phase III, as the European Union, Japan, and China became recognized as global power centers. The extraordinary economic growth and prosperity of maritime Europe and Japan were important factors affecting the Cold War balance during this period. The economic success of Western Europe and the buildup of its military forces within NATO put new pressures on the Soviet position in Eastern Europe. There the unrest over lack of consumer goods, the rise of the Solidarity movement in Poland, and "creeping capitalism," especially in Hungary, were beginning to undermine the foundations of the "command economies" and the stability of the Soviet Union's satellite Communist regimes.

Japan's startling economic and technological success in the 1980s, during which its gross domestic product expanded to become the second largest in the world, enabled it to increase its influence in Southeast Asia as well as in its own offshore Asian region. By the end of the decade, Tokyo had forged important economic links with Communist Vietnam, providing investment capital and aid. These links came about as Vietnam redirected its state economy toward privatization and reached out for foreign investment when Moscow was forced to reduce its substantial subsidies. Rebuffed by China, from which it had requested help, Hanoi shifted toward the development of a market economy and turned to Japan. The latter had the financial capacity and the political and economic interest to respond positively, and it did so.

Relations between Moscow and Beijing continued to worsen in the 1980s, not only over Vietnam and Cambodia but also over the need for the USSR to maintain a large military force along the border with China. The Soviet buildup there had started in 1969, with clashes between the former allies in Manchuria and Xinjiang. Hostility between the two was also fanned by China's opposition to the Soviet invasion of Afghanistan.

During the previous two Cold War phases, China had shared the Eurasian continental realm with the Soviet Union, first as its satellite and then as a hostile competitor. While tensions between China and the Soviet Union were high over ideological differences and boundary disputes, their mutual vulnerability along what was then their 4,500-mile land border had served to keep them geostrategically linked. Moreover, each operated behind closed political and economic systems, reinforcing their common distrust of the maritime realm powers.

China's strategic position vis-à-vis the USSR began to change after the mid-1970s, when the United States withdrew from Southeast Asia and Vietnam was reunified under a Communist regime. For China, this was a major geostrategic victory. The perceived Western military threat to its southern provinces was removed, and Beijing was free to pursue expansionist aims within the South China Sea region. Deng Xiaoping, Mao's successor, could also now enter into a new political relationship with the United States and other maritime states that would enable him to introduce badly needed economic reforms into the stagnant socialist state economy. In 1979, diplomatic ties between the United States and China were established and four coastal economic zones were created to attract foreign investment and to spur international trade.

These developments were the necessary preludes to China's vigorous economic growth during the 1980s—a growth that coincided with a period of unprecedented economic expansion throughout the Asia-Pacific Rim. Expansion in that region enabled Japan, Taiwan, Hong Kong, and Singapore to join the United States in providing China with the capital and technology that expanded its manufacturing base and stimulated its export economy.

The foreign policy impact of China's sweeping economic reforms was that it began to seek political accommodation with nations of the maritime realm, balancing off its traditional continental orientation. The strategic consequence was the emergence of East Asia as the world's third geostrategic realm and a new balancer in the global power equation.

THE WANING OF SOVIET INFLUENCE

Southeast Asia

The northern half of peninsular Southeast Asia—Indochina—remained a shatterbelt, but now the major external interveners were not the Communist powers and the West but the two opposing Communist states. The Soviet Union was able to maintain some of its past influence in Vietnam, serving as its main political ally and military supplier. Relations between China and Vietnam, on the other hand, worsened because of the dispute between the two over Cambodia. After the Vietnamese invaded the country in 1978 to oust Pol Pot and the Khmer Rouge, their troops remained in Cambodia for the next decade. The Vietnamese also established a military presence in Laos. In addition, Vietnam and China skirmished over territorial claims in the Paracel and Spratly archipelagoes of the South China Sea.

The southern parts of peninsular Southeast Asia, by contrast, became more firmly tied to the maritime realm's Asia-Pacific Rim. Singapore, Malaysia, and Thailand benefited from their close economic relations with Japan, as they participated in the region's remarkable economic resurgence. Indonesia, too, made rapid progress as a modernizing industrial power and trading state within offshore Asia and the broader maritime world system.

Middle East

Within the Middle East, Soviet influence became substantially diminished during phase III. Moscow's greatest setback came from the entry of Egypt into the Western bloc. Another major Soviet setback in the Middle East was the weakening of its Iraqi ally as a result of the Iran-Iraq war, which lasted from 1981 to 1988. Taking advantage of the turmoil in Iran, the Iraqis launched an invasion to seize the disputed Shatt-al-Arab waterway. Rather than gaining the expected speedy victory, they became mired in a bloody conflict. Ironically, as matters later turned out, Iraq received considerable backing from the United States in this war.

Syria was left as Moscow's main Middle East ally during this period. Damascus was fully dependent upon arms purchases from the Soviet Union to support its military presence in Lebanon and its continuing conflict with Israel. The Syrians were helped by Soviet-maintained economic surveillance stations within the country. However, Syria's economic ties became more balanced. Even though it had formed economic alliances with the USSR and Libya in 1980, and even though the Soviet Union still constituted its largest export market, because of the faltering Soviet economy Damascus forged stronger trade ties with the West, especially the countries of the European Union. During this period, Syria tightened its grip on Lebanon both militarily and economically, bringing an end to the civil conflict that had continued to rage between the Christians and the Lebanese Muslim and Palestinian communities.

South Yemen was the other remaining Soviet ally within the region during the 1980s. The Marxist regime continued to provide Moscow with the naval base at Aden and sites for communications and electronic intelligence facilities. This enabled the Soviets to retain a strategic presence in the Red and Arabian Seas. A peace treaty was subsequently signed with North Yemen, initiating talks that ultimately led to the unification of the two countries in

1990. When the Marxist state disappeared, the Soviet strategic foothold on the Arabian Red Sea and Gulf of Aden coasts disappeared with it.

Sub-Saharan Africa

In the Horn of Africa, the Marxist regime in Ethiopia, led by Mengistu Haile Mariam, remained in power. However, it was beset by famine and bitter rebellions in Tigre and Eritrea, placing in peril the Soviet African Red Sea bases. Moreover, as economic aid from Moscow and Havana declined during this period, the Ethiopian regime had to look to other sources for economic help.

Elsewhere on the continent, and especially in West Africa, Soviet influence declined rapidly as Marxist regimes were overthrown in many countries and severely weakened in others. The diminished military and economic support of the Soviet Union and its Cuban ally forced African Marxist regimes to turn to the West economically, thus rebuilding the region's geostrategic ties to the maritime realm. Moscow continued to strongly support the Communist regimes in Angola and Mozambique as well as the Cuban troops who continued to fight side by side with governmental forces against the rebels, who received considerable aid from South Africa.

Toward the end of the decade, however, the Marxist fervor of the Angolan regime weakened as it began to implement land and industrial privatization programs. In addition, the United States entered the scene directly by providing arms to the UNITA rebels. In Mozambique, as Soviet and Cuban influence faded, the Communist government turned to Zimbabwe for help. The radical leftist regime there responded by sending troops to guard the railway and oil line that extended into Zimbabwe from the port of Beira.

Latin America

During much of the 1980s, Communist attempts to penetrate Latin America had some successes. However, by the end of the decade, these also had largely dissipated. While Cuba remained the Soviet's major power base, in Nicaragua right-wing guerrilla actions and a US trade embargo undermined the economy of the Sandinista government. Economic distress and dissatisfaction with the repressive regime led to the ouster of the regime in the general election held in 1990. In Grenada, the Marxist regime of Maurice Bishop was toppled in a coup following the invasion and occupation of the island by the United States.

The 1980s were a period of rising strength for leftist rebel movements in Colombia and Maoist guerrilla forces in Peru. However, these terrorist groups were internally generated and directed, offering little scope for the Soviet Union and Cuba to extend their influence within the western Andes. Without outside aid, the guerrillas became increasingly dependent on the drug trade to finance their endeavors.

THE WAR IN AFGHANISTAN

Afghanistan was the major focus of Soviet military energies abroad during phase III. While only one of several factors that eventually contributed to collapse of the Soviet empire, the Afghan war had a traumatic effect upon the Soviet military. The conflict began in 1979, when thirty thousand Soviet troops entered Afghanistan to save the Marxist regime that had seized power the previous year and aligned itself with the USSR. Moscow installed Babrak Karmal as prime minister and gradually increased the number of its troops so that at the height of the conflict as many as one hundred thousand members of the Soviet armed forces were engaged in the fighting. Immense technological power was brought to bear against the outnumbered mujahideen, who depended upon arms originating from the United States, Saudi Arabia, and China and funneled through Pakistan, which also provided the rebels with their main training bases. In the course of the war, over one million Afghans were killed, and over five million (one-third of the prewar population) fled the country as refugees. Soviet losses were fifteen thousand killed and thirty-seven thousand wounded.

By the time that Mikhail Gorbachev rose to power in 1985 and instituted his policies of *glasnost* (openness) and *perestroika* (restructuring), it was too late to save the situation. The Soviet Union had exhausted both its capacity and rationale for pursuing the war. Recognizing its futility and burdened by the enormous cost of trying to maintain in power an unpopular Afghan regime, Gorbachev withdrew the Soviet troops in 1988–89, leaving the way clear for the mujahideen to sweep into power.

For Moscow, the price of the Afghan war was political as well as economic and military. The unpopularity of the war at home fueled the popular dissatisfaction with the Soviet government's repressiveness and economic failures. The latter had become patently evident with Gorbachev's liberalization policies. Abroad, much of the developing world viewed the Soviet invasion of Afghanistan as an imperialist venture, undermining Moscow's credibility as the patron of anticolonialism.

The Collapse of the Soviet Superpower

While these events were taking place in the Soviet Union, its grip on its Eastern European satellites was weakening. In 1989, democratic movements had gathered stunning momentum. By the end of the year, the Communist governments had been toppled in every one of those countries and the Berlin Wall had fallen, wrenching the European near-periphery of the Soviet heartland from its grasp.

The following year, the Baltic republics demanded independence from the USSR, and Moscow signed a pact accepting the reunification of Germany. Thus the heartland's Eastern European strategic adjunct was lost without a shot being fired, the mighty nuclear arsenal that the USSR had built up having proved valueless. Now the continental Eurasian realm has shrunk inland toward the continent's center, and geographically it resembles the "pivot area" that Halford Mackinder described a century ago.

The dogged determination of the Soviet Union to pursue its strategy of deep penetration of the maritime realm proved to be a geostrategic blunder of the greatest magnitude. In extending the Cold War to arenas where the West had an overwhelming military, logistical, and economic advantage, the USSR played to its enemy's strength.

Could the Soviet Union have maintained its superpower status? One alternative strategy for doing so would have been to concentrate on its near-periphery and develop the Eurasian continental realm into a cohesive unit on a partnership basis. Such a strategy might still have failed, given the sociopolitical rot and the economic weaknesses of the Marxist-Leninist revolutionary state. Indeed, the Brezhnev regime widened the schism through confrontational policies that assumed that Mao could be brought into line by pressure.

The Soviets failed to recognize that Chinese and Soviet Communism had emerged from fundamentally different cultures, refusing to respect the ideological legitimacy of Maoism, which focused on its agricultural peasant base and the principle of continuing revolution. Mao's policies of dispersing industry into the interior in the Great Leap Forward of 1958 and the Cultural Revolution of 1966 were clearly resounding failures. The famine of 1958–62 was brought on by a combination of inefficient farm methods, waste, and bad weather. It resulted in the deaths of millions by starvation. But from the point of view of Moscow, recognition of the principle of separate revolutionary pathways might have cemented a Sino-Soviet partnership and not led the two powers into seeking to play one another off against the United States.

A strategy that sought to craft alliances of equals between the USSR and Eastern Europe and the USSR and China would have altered the course of the Cold War. From this perspective, one may conclude that Soviet policies had more to do with losing the Cold War than United States policies had to do with winning it.

Thus geographical factors shape events but are not deterministic. Within those parameters, it is the policies and decisions of political leaders that determine the geopolitical structures of the globe.

Transition into the Twenty-First Century

THE DECADES OF THE 1990S AND EARLY 2000S

The end of the Cold War brought a reordering of the world's geopolitical structures and concomitant changes in expectations and attitudes toward international relations. Three transformations characterized the period. This reordering is in contrast to the instability imposed upon the system by the competition between the two superpowers. There had been important changes in the geopolitical spheres of influence during the Cold War, but the two superpowers knew the limits that mutual nuclear deterrence placed upon them. They avoided direct military conflict, which would have thrown the world into chaos. Today's dynamic system is more complex, but its multilateral great and regional powers provide the base for regional cooperation that contributes to greater global equilibrium.

The dissolution of the Warsaw Pact, followed by the disintegration of the Soviet Union, left only one world superpower—the United States. Many expected the United States to impose a Pax Americana on the world. It has tried to do so but has stumbled in its effort. Although turmoil and conflict have continued, it is not among great and regional powers that this takes place and is therefore more limited in scope and geostrategic implications. More open borders allow globalization and regionalization to flourish, with both positive and negative consequences. The negative is the absence of great-power control combined with ease of communications, movement, and capital flows, all of which give more scope to international terrorism.

These transformations effected change in the world geopolitical structures. With the shrinking of the Eurasian realm through the implosion of the former Soviet Union and former Yugoslavia, the status of Eastern Europe and Central Asia was significantly altered. In the East Asian realm, the weakening of Russian pressures enabled China to become more assertive in its relations with the Asia-Pacific Rim and to draw Indochina into its orbit geostrategically. Vietnam has become a strong economic competitor with China and is in dispute with Beijing over the sovereignty of offshore islands. Nevertheless, it remains strategically subordinate. Within the maritime world, expansion of NATO as well as the enlargement of the European

Union has affected the existing balance between maritime Europe and the United States as well as between Europe and the Russian heartlandic realm.

During this decade, Sub-Saharan Africa and South America became geostrategically marginal to the maritime powers, even though they were still within the maritime realm. The Western powers have stood by passively as Central Africa has broken into a compression zone, its internal divisions being reinforced by the intervention of neighboring eastern and southern states.

At the onset of the post–Cold War era, the world's sole remaining superpower—the United States—assumed the mantle of global leadership. It quickly met the first international challenge—Iraq's invasion of Kuwait in August 1990. Washington organized and led the coalition of forces that pushed the Iraqis out of Kuwait in January 1991 and, through an unprecedented demonstration of electronic air power, devastated Iraq's major military installations, ports, and cities.

However, in Iraq, Saddam Hussein continued in power behind his Republican Guard, which escaped virtually intact from the massive Allied air bombardment of the Gulf War. In 1992, Saddam ruthlessly crushed the US-encouraged Kurdish rebellion in the north and the Shia uprising in the south.

When the Somali military warlord Mohamed Siad Barre was overthrown in 1991, the country fell into chaos, and the American response was rapid. Somalia was swept by intertribal warfare and then devastated by the worst drought that Africa had experienced during the century. To protect relief supplies and restore order, Washington dispatched US troops to the stricken country.

These early American initiatives were widely heralded as harbingers of a stable "new world order" guaranteed by a Pax Americana imposed by US global economic, military, and informational hegemony. What followed instead was the turbulence that is characteristic of systems undergoing fundamental structural change. The American superpower could neither prevent nor easily put an end to the conflicts that broke out during the 1990s and escalated in the first decade of the twenty-first century.

In 1994, the US expeditionary force was shocked by an ambush during street fighting in Mogadishu in which eighteen rangers were killed and seventy-five wounded. The troops were quickly withdrawn, as the American public made it clear that it had little stomach for interventions of a humanitarian nature that would cost American lives. The following year, the UN forces also pulled out. Elsewhere, wars in several of the former Soviet republics, especially Georgia, Armenia, and Azerbaijan, were followed by the dismemberment of Yugoslavia, with bloody conflicts in Croatia, Bosnia, and Kosovo.

Where conflict has broken out as the aftermath of the Cold War, its geographic scope has been generally limited. Even in Bosnia, Kosovo, and Rwanda, and in the bloody civil wars in Liberia and Sierra Leone, all of which caused extensive casualties, the conflicts did not spread beyond their own regions. In Rwanda, the genocide of hundreds of thousands of Tutsis by the ruling Hutus was followed by the expulsion of equal numbers of Hutu, who fled to eastern Congo and Burundi.

In Afghanistan, the fighting between the Taliban and its tribal opponents did not result in the deaths of hundreds of thousands or the displacement of millions of refugees, as occurred in that country during the Soviet invasion. Nonetheless, the optimism that had given birth to the idea of a new world order quickly gave way to pessimistic scenarios. Zbigniew Brzezinski promoted the view of a world in perpetual turmoil; I. Lukacs predicted that the international system would be ruled by intransigent nationalism; Samuel Huntington saw a future marked by bloody global struggles between great world civilizations and culture; and Robert Kaplan predicted global chaos.[8]

Events since the 1990s suggest that neither the optimists nor the pessimists are correct in their reading of the world geopolitical map. There has indeed been considerable turmoil as the result of the profound changes that the international system has undergone. That turmoil, especially the wars in Iraq and Afghanistan as well as global terrorism, do threaten global stability but are not likely to lead to global chaos because all of the great and most of the regional powers have stakes in containing it.

A balanced perspective of the Cold War's aftermath must also take into account the many peaceful transitions of rule and territorial reconfigurations that have taken place. These include secessions from the FSU by Ukraine, Belarus, the Baltic states, and the former Soviet Central Asian republics; from Yugoslavia by Slovenia, Croatia, Bosnia, and Macedonia; and from Czechoslovakia by Slovakia. The reunification of Germany was accomplished with minor economic or political disruption, and the changeover from Communist regimes was relatively smooth in Poland, Romania, Bulgaria, and Mongolia.

Elsewhere, South Africa's transformation to a black government was peaceful, as democracy has taken root in that land. As the twenty-first century unfolds, seemingly intractable conflicts have wound down in Angola, Sierra Leone, Aceh, Northern Ireland, Peru, Sri Lanka, and Nepal. An agreement was also reached to end the conflict between North and South Sudan in 2005, but it was not immediately honored. It took six years for the division of the two countries to be formalized following a referendum that the southerners overwhelmingly approved. South Sudan then became an independent state and a member of the United Nations. However, the 1,250-mile border between the two countries has not yet been ratified owing to a dispute over control of Abyei. This is a 4,000-square-mile region, the majority of whose population is Ngok Dinka southern black farmers. The northern part of the province is populated by nomadic Arab Misseriya tribes, who come with their herds only during the dry season. Abyei also has oil reserves, but their production has declined significantly in the past few years, so the intractable nature of this border dispute is now principally demographic rather than over energy resources.

While major wars continued to rage in Afghanistan and Iraq, conflict continued to plague the African Horn, Sudan's Darfur, Georgia, Israel and Arab Palestine, and Lebanon. The war in Iraq wound down with the withdrawal of US troops in 2011, and most US/NATO troops are scheduled to withdraw from Afghanistan at the end of 2014. Nevertheless, the future of these two countries is bleak. Iraq continues to be torn by sectarian conflict. An independent, tribally dominated Afghanistan is likely to be wracked by instability. The turmoil in Egypt and Libya as well as the rebellion in Syria takes place in the absence of strong great-power involvement.

Other significant elements of post–Cold War transformation, globalization and regionalization, were present in the 1980s but could not develop fully until systems became more open and borders could be more easily crossed in those parts of the world that bore the brunt of Cold War competition. Networks of economic and cultural interaction have expanded exponentially since then, bringing prosperity to parts of the developing world. In such areas, international capital flows have facilitated investment and stimulated the outsourcing of manufacturing. The information revolution has broadened the horizons of individuals and made it easier to challenge entrenched authority.

Some of these same factors have their negative aspects. The open system makes it more difficult to contain arms and drug smuggling and to prevent the spread of international terrorism across more open borders. The transfer of technology has speeded the emergence of

India and Pakistan as nuclear powers and enhanced the abilities of North Korea and Iran to develop their own nuclear and biological weapons and advanced missile systems. Corruption and the ease with which capital can be illegally expatriated initially undermined the Russian economy, but its recovery has been unexpectedly rapid thanks to its energy wealth and restoration of political stability. Opposition to incursion of foreign cultures has deepened the fissures within traditional societies, leading to the spread of Islamic fundamentalism in such countries as Turkey, Afghanistan, Iraq, Pakistan, the states of Central Asia, Nigeria, Mali, the Philippines, and Indonesia. Egypt, in contrast, has ousted the Muslim Brotherhood government.

Absent the Cold War competition that stirred up so many wars, conflict mediation has become more widespread. Russia has become involved in helping to mediate regional crises. The first Gulf War was contained with Russian collaboration, and Moscow's influence also helped to moderate Serbia's behavior in its fighting with Croatia and, in the latter stages of the war, in Bosnia. It played an important part in bringing Slobodan Milošević to the negotiation table and eliminating in 2013 Syria's stock of chemical weapons. NATO, Russia, and China have been supportive of the United States in its conduct of the war in Afghanistan. They have also participated in negotiations with North Korea to halt production of nuclear weapons, which the North later repudiated.

The United States has played a key mediating role in Northern Ireland. In the Middle East, it has organized "the Quartet"—the United States, EU, UN, and Russia—in the commitment to achieve a two-state solution in the Arab-Israeli conflict. The EU has cooperated with Washington in the imposition of heavy sanctions which brought Tehran to the nuclear weapons negotiation table in 2013. South Africa has taken the lead in mediating the conflict in Congo. Governments at all levels, as well as the United Nations and regional bodies, are all more fully engaged in the process.

GLOBAL TERRORISM

Terrorism, both domestic and international, is an age-old phenomenon. Its purposes have ranged from grasping for political power and struggles for national freedom, to the exercise of ideological and religious beliefs, to sheer brigandage. It has been practiced by individuals and small groups, national and transnational movements, empires and states. Practitioners employ surprise and increasingly lethal weapons and techniques to produce widespread panic and fear within the target publics. Kidnappings and ambushes are traditional stratagems, but aircraft and other vehicular hijackings, suicide missions, and the use of planes as weapons of direct assault are of recent origin. Even more potentially lethal are biological, chemical, and nuclear weapons of mass destruction.

Approximately one hundred states have been targeted by terrorist attacks since the end of World War II. Terrorism, war crimes, and violations of human rights, ignored during the Cold War, have become important items on the international agenda, although the international community is often notably slow to act. Table 4.1 lists countries that have been exposed to major terrorist actions during this period, nearly two-thirds of which have taken place within the past two decades, or remain highly vulnerable to them. Thirty-four of the countries enduring terrorism are Muslim dominated, a reflection of the vulnerability of Muslims themselves to Islamic terrorism.

Despite historic episodes of assassination and other terrorist activities, it was not until the 1980s and 1990s that American citizens and facilities became exposed to large-scale terrorist activities. For the most part, they occurred overseas—in Beirut; in West Germany; over

Table 4.1. State Targets of Major Terrorist Actions since World War II

Region	*Countries*
North and Middle America	El Salvador, Guatemala, Mexico, Nicaragua, United States
South America	Argentina, Bolivia, Chile, Colombia, Ecuador, Peru, Uruguay
Maritime Europe and the Maghreb	Algeria, Austria, France, Germany, Greece, Italy, Morocco, Netherlands, Spain, United Kingdom
Eastern Europe	Albania, Croatia, Cyprus, Kosovo, Macedonia
Heartlandic Russia and Periphery	Armenia, Azerbaijan, Georgia, Kazakhstan, Kyrgyzstan, Russia, Tajikistan, Uzbekistan
Middle East and African Horn	Afghanistan, Bahrain, Djibouti, Egypt, Eritrea, Ethiopia, Iran, Iraq, Israel, Jordan, Kuwait, Lebanon, Palestine (West Bank and Gaza), Saudi Arabia, Somalia, Sudan, S. Sudan, Syria, Tunisia, Turkey, Yemen
South Asia	Bangladesh, Burma, India, Pakistan, Sri Lanka, Nepal
East Asia	Cambodia, China, Laos, Vietnam
Asia-Pacific Rim	Indonesia, Japan, Korea, Malaysia, Philippines, Thailand, Timor-Leste
Sub-Saharan Africa	Angola, Burundi, Chad, Congo, Guinea, Kenya, Liberia, Mali, Mozambique, Namibia, Niger, Nigeria, Rwanda, Sierra Leone, South Africa, Tanzania, Uganda, Zimbabwe

Lockerbie, Scotland; in Dar es Salaam, Tanzania; in the Khobar barracks, Saudi Arabia; in the harbor of Aden, Yemen; in the Westgate Mall of Nairobi, Kenya; and in Moscow. Bombings and other terrorist attacks took more than one thousand lives in fourteen major incidents, with embassies, aircraft, airports, and vessels as major targets. While there was much public surprise and concern within the United States over the attacks, the response from Washington was relatively muted as it failed to recognize the danger of international terrorism to the stability of the global system.

Nor did scattered incidents at home serve as wake-up calls. The terrorist bombings of Fraunces Tavern and the federal courthouse and the 1993 attack on the World Trade Center, all in New York, as well as a fray outside CIA headquarters in Virginia cost a limited number of lives and minimal physical dislocation.

It took the events of September 11, 2001, for Americans to feel the agony of terrorism and to recognize that it was also their problem. September 11 severely shook the American public and government. The loss of an approximately three thousand lives and the devastation wrought upon the country's financial and military nerve centers, as well as the boldness of an attack using terrorist-seized aircraft, had a stunning psychological effect. The Atlantic and Pacific moats, which had lulled the nation into a feeling of security, had been breached. The terrorism that the English, Italian, French, Irish, Israeli, Spanish, Somalian, Pakistani, and Indian people had so long endured, not to speak of the atrocities perpetrated upon innocent civilians throughout the developing world, had suddenly become part of the American experience.

The 2012 bombing of the US consulate in Benghazi, Libya, which resulted in the killing of the American ambassador and three others, brought renewed attention to this threat. This was followed by the 2013 Boston Marathon bombing that killed three and injured many others, further heightening public concern.

Under the US Anti-terrorism and Death Penalty Act of 1996, the secretary of state is required to designate foreign terrorist organizations that threaten the country's interests and security. In 2000, twenty-nine such organizations were identified. The largest number of these are Muslim groups, mostly with Arab roots.[9] With the killing of Osama bin Laden and most of his leading confederates, al-Qaeda, the most lethal of terrorist organizations, has become an increasingly loose network whose cells operate in thirty-seven countries (some estimates go as high as sixty countries). This decentralized system of jihadist movements has increased the difficulty of coping with international terrorism.

Organized terrorist groups do not operate in a geographical vacuum but are based in certain countries from which they reach out to others. They derive much of their strength from support obtained from states that sponsor them or offer safe havens. The US State Department's most recent list of such sponsors cites Cuba, North Korea, Iran, Sudan, and Syria. US law requires that sanctions be imposed on these states. On the list to be sanctioned, although they control areas that are not states, are Hezbollah in southern Lebanon and Hamas in Gaza. Pakistan, Lebanon, Qater, Saudi Arabia, and Somalia sponsor, finance, or knowingly shelter terrorist groups. Ironically, the United States sought to engage such backers of terrorism as Syria and Iran in developing a regional approach to stabilizing Iraq. Beyond the military expedience of seeking support from these states, the position of Washington is that coalition building provides an opportunity to wean some of them away from the support of terrorism. Examples are Libya and Yemen. With the overthrow of Gaddafi, Libya has reverted to being a source of terrorism, and American withdrawal has given room for al-Qaeda in Iraq to operate.

For the global war on terrorism to succeed, states that support or turn a blind eye to it will have to be pressured to change their behavior or be isolated by the world community. Collective world action is required to address the easy availability of communications, financial instruments, and weaponry to the perpetrators as well as the economic and political conditions that breed terrorism.

The multilateral approach taken by the United States in its war against the Taliban and the various al-Qaeda and other jihadist movements has enlisted not only most nations of the maritime world but also Russia, China, and Muslim nations, especially Saudi Arabia. The rejection by Saudi Arabia of a Security Council seat, for which it had lobbied, reflects its deep disappointment at the inability of the council to mediate the Syrian rebellion. They all have much to fear from home-grown and neighboring terrorist groups. Self-preservation is an imperative for every sovereign state. A state's own vulnerability to terrorism as well as its desire for economic support and trade with the economically advanced countries of the world are incentives to act against terrorism.

Since September 11, 2001, some states that sponsor or harbor terrorists have announced a change of direction. Despite the devastation and hardship that they incur, the number of wars and armed conflicts throughout the world has declined by nearly half since its peak in the early 1990s.[10] This is a hopeful sign in the long-term campaign against global terrorism, provided that the United States stays the course in leading the effort.

Notes

1. B. Liddell Hart, "The Russo-German Campaign," in *The Red Army*, ed. B. Liddell Hart (New York: Harcourt, Brace, 1956), 100–126.

2. Andrew J. Pierre, *The Global Politics of Arms Sales* (Princeton: Princeton University Press, 1982), 256–62.

3. Paul H. Nitze, Leonard Sullivan Jr., and the Atlantic Council Working Group on Securing the Seas, *Securing the Seas* (Boulder, CO: Westview, 1979), 31–118.

4. Daniel A. Korn, *Ethiopia, the United States and the Soviet Union, 1974–1985* (London: Croom Helm, 1986), 23–47.

5. All dollar figures in this work refer to US dollars.

6. Paul Kennedy, *The Rise and Fall of the Great Powers* (New York: Random House, 1987), 384.

7. Peter Trubowitz, *Defining the National Interest* (Chicago: University of Chicago Press, 1998), 225–34.

8. Zbigniew Brzezinski, *Out of Control: Global Turmoil on the Eve of the Twenty-First Century* (New York: Scribner's, Macmillan, 1993), 181–231; Robert Kaplan, *The Coming Anarchy: Shattering the Dreams of the Cold War* (New York: Random House, 2000), 3–57, 169–85; Samuel P. Huntington, "The Clash of Civilizations," in *The Clash of Civilizations? The Debate* (New York: Council on Foreign Relations, Simon and Schuster, 1996), 12–25; Huntington, *Clash of Civilizations?*, 56–67; John Lukacs, *The End of the Twentieth Century and the End of the Modern Age* (New York: Ticknor and Fields, 1993), 242–91.

9. US Department of State, *Patterns of Global Terrorism—2000* (Washington, DC: Office of the Coordinator for Counterterrorism, 2001).

10. World Watch Institute, *Vital Signs 2006–2007* (New York: Norton, 2006), 82–83.

CHAPTER 5

North and Middle America

The United States

The United States and the North and Middle American geopolitical region within which it is located will be discussed first. As the world's leading military and economic great power, the United States is uniquely suited to leading the maritime realm because of its central location within that realm. The United States is the only major power that fronts on the world's two great oceans—the Atlantic and the Pacific. In addition, much of its interior is drained by the Mississippi-Missouri-Ohio River system, leading to the Gulf of Mexico, the Caribbean, and the Panama Canal. This provides the geographical framework within which the United States serves as the core of the maritime realm. This Atlantic and Pacific position enables it to link the maritime European and Asia-Pacific Rim geopolitical regions. Moreover, the United States is the only major power possessing both a highly advanced maritime sector and a fully developed continental interior. However, it is not the superpower that dominates the world scene; it must share its global influence with strategic allies and competitors. It can retain its position as "first among equals" only as long as it enters into equal partnerships with the other power centers of the maritime realm.

The United States has entered its postindustrial age at a time of considerable geopolitical upheaval. Washington must therefore adjust its domestic socioeconomic policies while at the same time rebalancing its foreign policy strategy. Waning US influence in the Middle East, the military assertiveness of China in the East and South China Seas, and the competition between Russia and the European Union over Ukraine are some of the challenges to be addressed. This is taking place at a time of domestic economic strain, political dysfunction, and demographic change.

The economy is entering the era of deindustrialization as manufacturing shifts to services. Manufacturing now accounts for only 12 percent of the US economy, in contrast to its 1953 peak of 28 percent. Services represent 70 percent of the economy and government another 18 percent. Millions of well-paid union factory jobs have been lost, as cheaper imported goods have flooded the country, to be replaced largely by lower-paid health service, retail, restaurant, and entertainment work. To be sure, the service economy has created new jobs for well-paid media and information technology workers as well as creating unparalleled wealth for innovative entrepreneurs. On the whole, however, deindustrialization has not only increased unemployment and led to international trade imbalance but also widened the gap between rich and poor. The shrinking manufacturing base is increasingly dependent upon automated and sophisticated knowledge to be competitive with imports from countries with far lower labor costs. To do so requires employees with technological skills that many young people entering the labor force lack because the American public educational system is not geared to provide such training.

The geopolitical significance of the state of the US economy cannot be overemphasized. In many ways, economics has outstripped the military as the most important of America's four power pillars (military, economic, political, and ideological). This has in turn led to the need for greater emphasis on "soft power" in Washington's conduct of international relations. In exercising such power, the size and breadth of a nation's international trade, together with its foreign aid and investment, play the key roles. While the United States had a global trade of nearly $5 trillion in goods and services in 2012, its share of world exchange dropped from a peak of 20 percent to 10 percent. The European Union has become the world's leading trading center while China ranks second, the United States third, and Japan fourth. Moreover, the United States suffers from a chronic trade imbalance while the EU and China both have positive balances.

The thirsty American consumer economy absorbs three-quarters of the country's manufactured goods, while the figure for China is 50 percent. Neither a reduction in American demand for goods nor pursuit of a "buy American goods" campaign is a viable option. A realistic policy is one that seeks to increase domestic production through expanded global trade in high-end goods and services. It is in this context that the success of Washington's efforts to forge transpacific and transatlantic free-trade partnership agreements are so crucial to maintaining America's role as the world's premier great power.

To better understand the role that geography plays in assessing the four pillars that constitute America's power base, one first has to turn to an assessment of its geopolitical features and their spatial patterns, especially those of its core area. As a nation's core changes demographically, economically, and politically, so do its geostrategic outlooks and policies.

GEOPOLITICAL FEATURES

The geopolitical features of the United States include its historic core, current political capital, ecumenes (areas of economic and population concentration), effective national territory (ENT), empty areas, and boundaries. The structural patterns laid down by these features provide the basis for analyzing the interrelationships between geography and politics in the United States. Unique among all of the world's great powers is that these features provide the country with a highly advanced maritime sector, accessible to both of the world's great oceans, and a fully developed continental interior. Moreover, most of this interior has water access to these oceans via the Great Lakes, the Mississippi-Missouri-Ohio River system, and the Gulf of Mexico.

Historic Core

Bostonians are wont to claim Massachusetts as the historic (nuclear) core of the United States on the basis of Faneuil Hall (the scene of revolutionary meetings), the Boston Massacre, and the Boston Tea Party. Most scholars, however, accord Philadelphia the status of the historic core around which the United States was organized. Independence Hall was the scene of the Declaration of Independence in 1776 and the meeting place of the Continental

Figure 5.1. North and Middle America: Major Geopolitical Features

Congress and the Constitutional Convention. Moreover, Philadelphia served as the new nation's first capital.

Whether the honor goes to Massachusetts or Pennsylvania, the birthplace of the revolutionary American state was in the northeastern and middle colonies, not the plantation South. It was among the small merchants and farmers of the colonies that lay along the northeastern coast that the unique American state ideas were formulated—freedom, individual liberty, religious tolerance, and egalitarianism.

Political Capital

With the establishment of the Union, the question of where to locate the new federal capital had to be addressed. There were other candidates to be the capital, but the debate was resolved in favor of what is now Washington, a site that would serve as "neutral ground" between the northern and southern states. The site lay on the fall line of the Potomac River, nearly equally accessible to North and South and only about fifty-five miles south of the Mason-Dixon line. It was hoped that the new capital would help to bridge the differences between the urbanizing, manufacturing North and the rural, slaveholding South. In the end, however, it was not the geography of the capital that would assure the unity of the nation, but the Civil War.

The federal capital was laid out in 1790, first occupied by Congress a decade later, and became coincident with the District of Columbia in 1878. It is now far from the geographical population center of the country. Moreover, it does not house all of the federal government buildings, which sprawl into nearby Maryland and Virginia, where most federal employees live. Today, slightly more than half of DC's 630,000 inhabitants are black Americans, many of whom are poorly housed, jobless, and impoverished. This percentage of black Americans has dropped from 60 percent as middle-class whites, together with minorities of similar classes, have returned to rejuvenate some of the capital's decaying neighborhoods.

For years, the citizens of the district have clamored for political "independence." They have won the right to vote in presidential elections and elect their mayor and city council but have only a nonvoting delegate in the Congress, which also reviews the council's annual budget. The federal government maintains control over its own buildings, and the district's attempts to gain statehood and voting representation in Congress have failed.

It is ironic that the most prosperous nation in the world has a national capital whose population is now overshadowed by its wealthier white suburbs and in a city where the gap between rich and poor is so great. If the capital is to play a new "bridging" role, reflecting the egalitarian ideas of its founding fathers, it is not geographical location that can provide the answer, but socioeconomic and political action.

Ecumenes

At the close of World War II, the US ecumene extended along the Atlantic Seaboard from southern New England to Washington, DC, and westward across New York State and Pennsylvania in two prongs—along the Great Lakes to Detroit and then Chicago, and from Pittsburgh across the southern parts of Ohio, Indiana, and Illinois to St. Louis.

Over the past half century, this ecumene has filled in and expanded, and the California ecumene has emerged. The older ecumene now extends along the northeastern megalopolis from southern Maine and New Hampshire through Virginia and into the North Carolina piedmont. There, two major prongs have developed. One is the research triangle of Raleigh-Durham-Chapel Hill, a major high-tech, pharmaceutical, medical, and scientific center.

The other is Charlotte, a leading national financial headquarters city and air transport hub. The southward growth of this ecumene is beginning to extend across the South Carolina and Georgia piedmont to Greater Atlanta, while south Florida and Houston-Dallas have emerged as exclaves.

This economic and population core region has also spread westward from Chicago to the Milwaukee-Madison area of Wisconsin; northward from Buffalo and Detroit to merge with the Canadian ecumene that runs along the northern shores of Lakes Ontario and Erie; and southward from Cincinnati along the lower Ohio valley to Louisville and then west to St. Louis. Nashville and Memphis are exclaves that may soon be included within the core region. Much of the industrial vitality of the older part of the ecumene has been sapped by the demise of textile and shoe manufacturing in the Northeast as well the emergence of the rust belt of western New York, Pennsylvania, and the Midwest. Michigan's automotive industry has suffered serious decline owing to foreign competition, high labor costs, and the opening of new motor vehicle plants in the South and California. So dire has the economic situation become in Detroit that in 2013 the city declared bankruptcy. Once a thriving center with a population of 1.8 million that made it the country's fourth-largest city, Detroit now ranks seventeenth in population size, over 80 percent of whom are African Americans. In contrast, across the river from Detroit, the Canadian province of Ontario, led by Toronto, thrives as Canada's leading economic center.

The second US ecumene is southern and central California. It extends from San Diego to Los Angeles and Santa Barbara. After a gap along the coast, much of which is taken up by National Forest Service lands and military reservations, the region connects to Silicon Valley (the high-tech hardware and software industry center extending from San Jose to Palo Alto to San Mateo) and then to San Francisco-Oakland. From there, it follows eastern and northeastern prongs into the Central Valley to Sacramento. Las Vegas, Nevada, and Phoenix, Arizona, are exclaves of the California region. In addition to being the hub of a rich irrigation and agricultural region and a leading center for tourism and recreation, Phoenix's high-tech and aerospace industries are spillovers from California centers. While the economies of Las Vegas and Reno dropped precipitously in the 2007–9 recession, their rapid recoveries since are testimony to the strength of the second ecumene's eastern desert prongs.

An information-age view of the dual ecumenes is that their growth and prosperity has in recent years been spurred by two poles—California's Silicon Valley and New York City's "Silicon Alley," the computer graphics and information center of the media age. With the increasing decentralization of high-tech and, in particular, software industries, the core areas continue to extend their boundaries substantially.

Some parts of the eastern core have been rejuvenated. These include the Greater Boston technology hub supported by a research-based university system; Pittsburgh, which has reinvented itself from a highly polluted former steel center to one based on mixed clean-air high-tech industries; and Milwaukee, which has become a global hub focusing on water control systems and research. Spartanberg-Greenville in South Carolina has attracted automobile and tire plants, and the Miami exclave has become the capital for Latin American finance and logistics. The growth of this eastern ecumene is nourished by New York City, the world's leading financial center and focus of networks of air hubs and the interstate highway system, as well as the emergence of Atlanta as the world's busiest airport.

While the eastern ecumene is not a major mineral producer, the Marcellus Shale has recently become a significant resource. This rock extends in an area one hundred thousand square miles from Illinois, Indiana, and Ohio, through Pennsylvania and into New York. The shale, which now produces nearly 40 percent of US natural gas supplies, is a marine sedimentary rock that lies close to the surface and is amenable to fracking technology. Over the past few years it has become the country's largest source of natural gas, providing cheap energy for generating electricity for home consumers and the steel, automotive, chemical, and shipbuilding industries. The rapid increase in natural gas has considerably lowered its price and begun to replace many highly polluting coal-fired electricity-generating plants as well as being the fuel of choice for new plants. As a result of this increase, the United States has joined Russia as the world's leading natural gas producer. Plants in the US Gulf Coast which recently imported liquid natural gas (LNG) are now being refitted to prepare American natural gas for export. California, the second ecumene, is underlain by the country's largest gas and oil reserve—the Monterey Shale. This resource awaits state regulatory legislation before the shale can be fracked.

Effective National Territory

The continental United States does not lack for effective national territory (ENT). Approximately two-thirds of the country that is not taken up with its ecumenes is ENT. Within the ENT, Texas and the lower Mississippi valley, much of the Pacific Northwest, and the western Midwest and eastern Great Plains are capable of absorbing substantial population growth, as their large cities and isolated industrial centers expand into the vast farmland acreage of rural America. The shrinkage of farmland within the ENT was arrested in 2007 as a result of the sudden demand for corn-kernel-based ethanol, and farm area has remained fairly constant since then. New corn storage bins and ethanol plants now dot the farm belt from Illinois to South Dakota and Nebraska. The duration of this boom will depend on how quickly more cost-effective substitutes such as cellulose-based switchgrass, straw, or wood ethanol or ethanol derived from imported sugarcane from such countries as Brazil are introduced to the market.

The ENT also includes the dry western high Great Plains, which extend from the one hundredth meridian to the Rockies. They are used for extensive farming and ranching and are underlain by vast petroleum and natural gas fields. Within the ENT, the Dallas/Austin/Houston triangle, an ecumene exclave, is a rapidly growing financial, high-tech oil and chemical center whose economic and political power rivals that of the declining industrial sections of the ecumene's western extension.

A major geographical feature within the ENT is the Ogallala Aquifer—a vast shallow water table beneath the high Great Plains that extends from South Dakota to Texas. It underlies a semiarid region with an annual rainfall of ten to twenty inches whose farmers suffered greatly from the droughts and dust storms of the 1920s and 1930s. The region's recovery came with the tapping of the aquifer for irrigation agriculture, industry, and the urban development that followed World War II. However, over-irrigation has depleted 30 percent of the aquifer, and Great Plains farmers are beginning to shift back to dry farming.

A revolutionary impact upon the Great Plains' economy has been the oil production boom experienced in the fifteen-thousand-square-mile Bakken rock formation. This is centered on North Dakota and extends westward into eastern Montana and northward into Saskatchewan and Alberta. Fracking technology has made it economically feasible to recover oil from the Bakken shale deposits. This shale lies under the subsurface of the Williston Basin and is easily tapped. In a matter of a few years, North Dakota has become the second largest oil-producing state within the United States, following Texas, while outstripping third-place California and fourth-place Alaska. The Bakken output, combined with reduced oil demand due to energy saving programs and the use of natural gas, led to a drop in the country's crude oil imports from 60 percent of the country's needs to slightly over one-third in 2013. This has played a major role in keeping crude oil prices down. Moreover, the United States has become a net exporter of finished petroleum products. Partnering with Canada and Mexico, the United States is likely to become self-sufficient in crude oil in a few years and may well leapfrog Saudi Arabia and Russia as the world's leading oil producer.

The carbon-rich Canadian tar sands oil basin represents a major source of petroleum for the United States. The Keystone XL pipeline has been proposed in order to transport the oil to the United States. A pipeline already exists in Canada, extending from Hardesty, Alberta, through Saskatchewan, across the border through North and South Dakota to a terminal at Steele City, Nebraska. The proposed Keystone XL line would shorten the distance between the border and Steele City and then run directly to refineries at the Gulf of Mexico (see figure 5.2). Current plans call for the 1,700-mile line to carry 830,000 barrels per day with the intention of eventually doubling its capacity.

The building of Keystone has triggered considerable controversy in the United States. Environmentalists argue that its development would sharply accelerate the emission of carbon dioxide from burning the tar sands as part of the production process. They fear that this would have negative global climate consequences. Proponents contend that the line will increase US and North American energy security and that the environmental impact would be minimal. They point out that if the line to the United States is not built, the Canadians are likely to develop the tar sands anyway and construct a connection to the Pacific coast to export the oil to East Asia. Because Keystone involves crossing an international border, US State Department approval is necessary. The department granted such approval on the grounds that the carbon increase would be insignificant. The political delicacy of the controversy is such that President Obama, whose approval is also necessary, has announced that no decision will be made until after the congressional election of November 2014. He would be inclined to grant approval.

Empty Areas

Another major feature for the United States is its empty areas. Within the "lower forty-eight" states, the empty area covers approximately one million square miles from the Rocky Mountains west to the Sierra Nevadas and the Cascades, embracing mountains and deserts to the west of the 105th meridian. It includes the Mojave Desert, the Great Basin of Nevada, which extends into the Salt Lake Desert, and the semiarid to arid Colorado Plateau of Arizona and New Mexico.

This empty area plays an important role in the defense strategy and economy of the nation. Militarily, the region provides vast spaces for bombing and missile ranges, weapons proving grounds, and nuclear test sites. Yucca Mountain, which is located within the Mojave Desert, ninety miles northwest of Las Vegas, was proposed as a national depository for the nuclear weapons wastes and spent fuels from the 104 US nuclear reactors by the US Department of Energy in February 2002. Permits for nearly 180 additional reactors have been awarded, but construction dates remain uncertain. It remains to be seen whether the plan, which proposed opening the site by 2010, will ever be implemented in the face of opposition from local and environmental groups, including the governor of Nevada. White Sands Missile Range in south-central New Mexico, which is also a landing site for space shuttles, was the scene of the first atomic explosion in 1945. The spectacular scenery of the region is a major asset for its recreation and tourist industry, and such minerals as copper, coal, lignite, zinc, and nickel, along with petroleum, natural gas, and timber, strengthen the national economy.

The other empty area, which extends over most of Alaska (the total land area of the state is over 650,000 square miles), was bought from Russia in 1867 and dubbed "Seward's

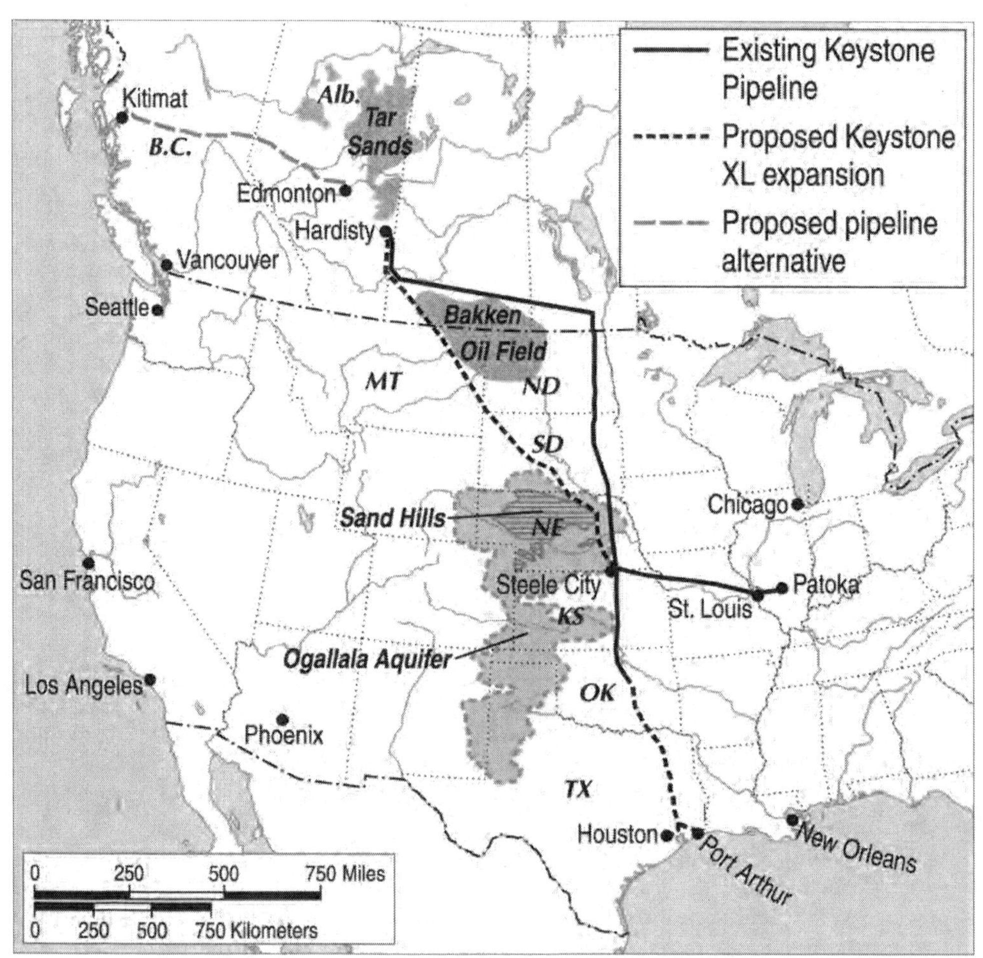

Figure 5.2. Keystone XL Pipeline/Bakken Formation

Folly" for many decades. It has proved to have considerable strategic and economic value. Alaska provides a military foothold, with a thousand-mile coastline that overlooks the Arctic Ocean. It hosts defense installations that provide surveillance over the North Pacific. With global warming, the opening of Arctic waters to shipping, oil and gas development, and fishing presents economic opportunities as well as geopolitical challenges over the division of the Arctic by the abutting countries.

Fort Greely in central Alaska, near Fairbanks, is the command center and testing ground for land-based interceptors designed to shoot down possible North Korean intercontinental ballistic missiles. Kodiak Island in south Alaska is another center for deploying antiballistic missile defenses. In addition, the Arctic North Slope near Prudhoe Bay, an inlet of the Arctic Ocean's Beaufort Sea, has become the most important petroleum-producing area in the United States. The eight-hundred-mile oil pipeline from Prudhoe Bay to the port of Valdez on the Gulf of Alaska was completed in 1977. From there, oil is shipped to the continental United States via the Inside Passage, the narrow shipping lane between the coastal and offshore islands that connects Anchorage and the Gulf of Alaska via Prince Rupert Sound to the waters of British Columbia and Seattle.

The environmental hazards involved in using this waterway for shipping oil were dramatized in 1989, when the *Exxon Valdez* tanker ran aground in Prince Rupert Sound, creating the worst oil spill in US history and causing severe damage to the Alaskan ecosystem. Efforts to exploit the natural gas and oil reserves of the Arctic National Wildlife Refuge farther inland have met with vigorous objections from environmentalists. As Prudhoe Bay production declines, the proponents of opening up the refuge to energy exploitation have gathered force.

Most of the state's population is located along the Gulf of Alaska, centering on Anchorage, with an outlying cluster in the south-central region around Fairbanks. Travel within the interior is mainly by air. However, an important strategic and economic land link is the Alaska Highway (or Alcan), the all-weather graveled road that extends for 1,523 miles from Dawson Creek in British Columbia near the Alberta border to Fairbanks. It was built in the early 1940s as a joint US-Canadian enterprise to supply American military forces in Alaska. Existing highways south of Dawson Creek linked the highway to the US Pacific Northwest and Midwest, while from Fairbanks the Alaskan road system connected it to Anchorage and the Gulf of Alaska. The Alcan route was critical in World War II in supplying US military bases on the gulf, the Bering Sea, and the Aleutians, from which the Japanese attacks on the Aleutian islands of Attu and Kiska were repelled. The US Coast Guard was able to operate its first Arctic operating base near Barrow on the North Slope owing to climate warming and the resulting ice melt.

The central and western Pacific represents another empty area for the United States, one that extends from islands in Polynesia to those in Micronesia. A most important American facility is the Kwajalein Atoll missile range—a Micronesian coral atoll in the Marshall Islands where launching pads for intercontinental missile testing and clusters of radars are located. The Marshalls became self-governing in 1979 under US military protection before being linked to the United States in "free association" seven years later. Bikini and Enewetak, Marshall Island atolls two hundred and four hundred miles to the west of Kwajalein, were used by Washington as test sites for atomic and hydrogen weapons from 1946 to 1979. The military-strategic significance of Kwajalein was demonstrated once again in July 2001. The atoll served as the base for the testing of the new US antiballistic missile defense system. One of its interceptor missiles succeeded in destroying a dummy nuclear warhead that had been launched from Vandenberg Air Force Base. Vandenberg, located on the Pacific coast, with Los Angeles to the south and the Mojave Desert to the east, may be regarded as the eastern anchor of a gigantic missile range, 4,600 miles wide, whose western anchor is Kwajalein.

International Boundaries and External Territories

The international boundaries of the United States with Canada and Mexico are mainly boundaries of attraction, not barriers. Between Canada and the continental United States, the four-thousand-mile border (excluding Alaska, whose border with Canada extends another fifteen hundred miles) has been a model of peaceful accommodation for over a century and a half, despite its length and complexity. The western half follows an artificial line, the forty-ninth parallel, across mountains and plains. The Red River settlement of 1821 fixed the eastern half of this western boundary. In the far West, the parallel was extended to Vancouver Island when Britain and the United States settled their dispute over the Oregon Territory.

The eastern part of the US-Canada border is, for the most part, a water boundary that at its western end extends from the Lake of the Woods and the Great Lakes to the upper St. Lawrence. From there, it briefly runs along the forty-fifth parallel to mark the New York-Vermont border, takes a jog along New Hampshire's northern and Maine's northwestern ends, and then follows the St. John and St. Croix Rivers to Passamaquoddy Bay and the Bay of Fundy.

In a unique case of international comity, the boundary that was a fighting front between Britain and the United States in 1812 has evolved into today's unfortified border between the United States and Canada, across which people, goods, and ideas flow to the benefit of both countries. Border demarcation has not been uncomplicated, especially in the water areas, and minor adjustments continued to be made by many treaties and conventions until final delimitation in 1925. The long-standing free flow of movement between the two countries has been complicated by concerns of security and immigration.

The Alaskan boundary between the two nations extends for over fifteen hundred miles. Its northern half follows the 141st meridian from the Arctic Ocean through the Yukon region to British Columbia. The southern half follows the Coast Mountains between southeastern Alaska and British Columbia to the Washington State border. While both nations agreed that the boundary would follow the range's main watershed, its demarcation was complicated since there is no single crest along which to draw that line.

What is remarkable about this international border of 5,500 miles (including Alaska) is that the remaining disputes are so minor. They center on the precise locations of four maritime borders: the northern end of the Alaska-Canada border in the Beaufort Sea; the Dixon Entrance, between Alaska's southernmost islands and Prince Rupert in British Columbia; the Strait of Juan de Fuca, between Vancouver Island and the northern tip of the state of Washington; and, on the Atlantic side, Machias Seal Island, at the southern end of the Bay of Fundy, on which Canada operates a lighthouse.

The US-Mexican border was established in 1848 by the Treaty of Guadalupe Hidalgo, which ended the US-Mexican War. This confirmed the US annexation of New Mexico, Utah, and Spanish Upper California. The southernmost strip of this US region was acquired later via the Gadsden Purchase of 1853. The eastern sector of the 2,075-mile boundary follows the Rio Grande for approximately 1,000 miles, from 20 miles north of El Paso to Brownsville at the Gulf of Mexico. The western portion of the border extends from the Rio Grande to the Pacific along artificial lines between New Mexico, Arizona, and California and the Mexican states of Chihuahua, Sonora, and Baja California. While for the most part the boundary traverses semiarid or desert lands, it also cuts across the heavily irrigated farm areas of the Imperial Valley and the lower Colorado River.

The boundary delimitation of the Rio Grande presented problems because the 1848 treaty defined the line as following the center of the normal channel. Since the river was subject to continuous shifting as a result of flooding, there was continuing dispute until 1933, when it was resolved that the deepest continuous channel, the thalweg, would become the agreed-upon boundary. Over the decades, the US-Mexico International Boundary Commission has taken responsibility for straightening and stabilizing the river. In addition, the two countries signed a water-sharing pact in 1945 and in 1968 settled their dispute over the location of the border at El Paso.

The US-Mexican border has become a major focus of tension between the two countries centering on the flow of illegal immigrants and drugs from Mexico and through Mexico from Central America into the United States. Efforts to control this penetration include border controls, cameras, and other security measures. A security fence is being built along a portion of the boundary, parts of which are walls that cut through border twin cities. The fence currently extends for 350 miles, and another 350 miles are contemplated. A major problem for US farmers is that this border barrier could not be built along the Rio Grande because of its constant shifting. Instead, the fence has been located at the outer edge of the floodplain, which contains lands used for agriculture. To provide access for the farmers to their lands, gaps in the fence have been provided, which weaken its security functions.

At the western end, in southern California, where the boundary ran through a heavily populated area, it was completely re-demarcated between 1891 and 1896. However, wrangling over the use of a canal that had passed through Mexican territory was only resolved when the eighty-mile All-American Canal was built entirely within US territory (1934–40) to tap the waters of the Colorado River.

Off the North American mainland, the United States has two territorial disputes in the Caribbean. Haiti claims US-owned Navassa Island, a tiny islet located between Haiti and Jamaica that once contained guano deposits that have long been mined out and is now used only for its lighthouse. A far more serious dispute is over the US base at Guantánamo Bay. The site covers forty-five square miles at the southeastern end of Cuba. Leased to the United States in 1903, it has become a source of considerable tension between the two countries since Cuba sought its return in 1960 and refused to accept the annual token lease rent.

Another growing source of tension has been the Puerto Rican island of Vieques, off the eastern coast of Puerto Rico. Its use by the US Navy as a bombing range as well as a training ground for land and air forces sparked considerable local opposition. Washington agreed to close down the range in 2008. Since then, it has expended large sums of money to clean up ordnance remains from the vast site, and Vieques residents are attempting to develop the island as a tourist center.

The status of the US Trust Territories in the Pacific Ocean has undergone significant change in recent years. In 1986, the Northern Mariana Islands became a commonwealth in political union with the United States. In the same year, the Federated States of Micronesia signed the Compact of Free Association with the United States, as did the Republic of the Marshall Islands. Palau entered into a similar compact in 1994.

Elsewhere in the Pacific, a number of islands remain dependencies (as do the US Virgin Islands in the Caribbean). These include Guam, Midway, and Wake. Guam is by far the most strategically important to Washington. Part of the Marianas chain, Guam is closest to the Philippines and the rest of the Asia-Pacific Rim and possesses major air and naval bases that provide the United States with long-range reach capacity. Wake has both a military and a commercial air base, Midway a military base.

American Samoa remained under US control when the New Zealand Trust Territory of Western Samoa gained its independence in 1990, even though the US eastern portions of the island chain had long ago lost their strategic value. Pago Pago had served the American navy as a fishing and repair base but was closed in 1951, when administration of the dependency was transferred to the US Department of the Interior. There is now little reason for Washington to retain control of this eastern half of the Samoan chain, whose islanders derive their livelihood from tourism and tuna canning.

THE FOUR STAGES OF US GEOPOLITICAL DEVELOPMENT

The pace of settlement and landscape use in the United States has shaped its geopolitical postures in world and hemispheric affairs. Four successive stages mark the development of the US geopolitical posture: (1) the maritime, (2) the continental, (3) the continental-maritime, and (4) the maritime-continental.

Table 5.1. Four Stages of US Geopolitical Development

	Inland		*Geopolitical*	
Stages	*Time Period*	*Transport*	*Power*	*Orientation*
Maritime	Colonial to 1803 (Louisiana Purchase)	River, road, hose	Manual, watermills	Securing Atlantic Seaboard
Continental	1803 to 1898 (Spanish-American War)	Rail, river, canal, horse	Coal, watermills	Continental unification and expansion
Continental-Maritime	1898 to World War II outbreak	Rail, highway	Oil, gas, coal, hydroelectric power (penstock turbines), internal combustion engine	Continental development, Caribbean and Pacific expansion
Maritime-Continental	1941 to present	Highway, rail, air, ocean shipping	All of above plus nuclear, wind, solar	US maritime ring and global reach

The Maritime Stage

This stage prevailed from colonial times through the Revolutionary War and the Louisiana Purchase of 1803. Expansion of the English colonies from their coastal and piedmont bases involved a series of campaigns against the French and the Indians in the mid-eighteenth century (1745–63). The western limits of colonial settlement were imposed by the Proclamation of 1763, in which the British established a boundary to separate the English settlers from the Indians, with whom the British sought to develop stable relations. Through this edict, Britain tried to put a halt to colonial expansion west of the headwaters of streams flowing into the Atlantic.

The boundary was a watershed line that followed the Appalachians from their southernmost point in northwest Georgia north to the Allegheny Mountains of central Pennsylvania, to northern New York, and then to the Green Mountains of Vermont. This line was substantially breached, both before and after 1763, as settlers pushed out to the Ohio, Tennessee, and Kentucky Rivers.

In the aftermath of the Revolutionary War, the inexorable drive of the settlers in the "western lands" pushed the frontier of settlement to the Mississippi, overrunning the Indian lands that had been set aside by the British. Settlement also penetrated the area north of the Ohio to the Upper Great Lakes, which had been claimed by Britain as an extension of Quebec but which was ceded to the United States at the end of the Revolutionary War.

Despite the ferment revolving around the westward expansion of the "Old Frontier," the weight of population and economic activities remained along the East Coast and piedmont. Whether acting in concert with Britain or apart from it during the years that led to separation and independence, most Americans had an Atlantic Seaboard outlook. Commerce, the main factor in the economy, was based on the export of such agricultural commodities as tobacco, rice, cotton, food grains, cattle, fish, and furs. The imports were manufactured articles from England and sugar, molasses, and rum from the West Indies. For most Americans of this era, therefore, the colonies and then the fledgling states of the new nation were part of an exploitable world whose main concern was to secure the Atlantic Seaboard.

The Continental Stage

Highlights of the continental stage were the Louisiana Purchase of 1803, the Lewis and Clark expedition of 1803–6, and the War of 1812. For nearly a century afterward—until the Spanish-American War—the focus was on conquest of the continental interior, to expand the nation's borders from "sea to shining sea." The era was touched off by the purchase from France of the vast area from the Mississippi to the Rocky Mountains and from the Gulf of Mexico to British-controlled North America. The 828,000 square miles thus acquired doubled the land area of the United States and whetted the appetite for more.

Results of the War of 1812 and annexation of Spanish-held West Florida in 1821 sealed US control over its Atlantic and Great Lakes frontiers, as well as over most of the Gulf of Mexico's northern coastlands. Britain's war strategy had included a plan to seize the Mississippi and block the expansion of its former colony into the continental interior. The strategy called for troops to seize New Orleans and move upstream to meet forces coming southward from Canada. It failed when Andrew Jackson's sharpshooters repelled the best of the Duke of Wellington's seasoned veterans at the Battle of New Orleans, which ironically took place two weeks after the signing of the Treaty of Ghent and the technical end of the war.

In 1818, the United States and Great Britain came to an agreement over the continental interior boundary west of the Great Lakes. The line ran westward from the Lake of the Woods along the forty-ninth parallel to the crest of the Rocky Mountains. As a result of the accord, most of the Red River valley of the North, south of Winnipeg, became US territory. From the Rockies, the boundary extended along the parallel to the Pacific coast but excluded Vancouver Island. This line assured US ownership of the middle and lower Columbia River basin.

In the South, the United States gained full control of the northern Gulf Coast when Texas joined the Union in 1845, after American settlers had driven Mexican troops from the territory and declared their independence in 1836. The treaty that followed the US-Mexican War (1846–48) confirmed the Rio Grande as the southern border of Texas. The new boundary ran westward from the Rio Grande at the New Mexico line to the Colorado River, turned to the Colorado's junction with the Gila River, and then followed west to the Pacific just south of San Diego. Thus, all of Upper California was ceded to the United States, while Baja (Lower) California remained within Mexico. Two years later, California entered the Union. Unification of the land from sea to sea had to await the Union victory in the Civil War and the building of the transcontinental railroad system. The earlier system, based on roads, the

Erie Canal, and the Ohio-Mississippi-Missouri Rivers, affected only the eastern half of the country and was a slower system of transportation. Construction of the continent-spanning rail line, which had been interrupted by the Civil War, was completed in 1869. On May 10 of that year, the Union Pacific, starting from its Omaha base, met the Central Pacific, which had originated in Sacramento.

Each line had to contend with daunting engineering challenges. Employing Irish laborers, the Union Pacific had to traverse the Laramie and Wasatch ranges after crossing the plains. The Central Pacific, which had brought in Chinese laborers from Canton (Guangzhou), had to climb across the Sierra Nevadas before traversing the deserts of Nevada and Utah. When the two lines met at Promontory Summit, Utah, on the eastern face of the Rockies, development of the interior of the country could progress full scale. Settlements, farming, ranching, mines, commerce, and then industry followed the east-west continental spine and then the north-south railroads that became linked to it.

In 1893, after nearly a century of efforts by pioneers to settle the continental interior, Frederick Jackson Turner called attention to the passing of the American frontier, based upon his evaluation of the 1890 census.[1] Only Utah, Oklahoma, New Mexico, and Arizona remained to be admitted to the Union, and all these states were admitted between 1896 and 1912. Elsewhere on the continent, Alaska, which had been purchased from Russia in 1867, also awaited statehood but did not receive it until 1959, when Hawaii was also added. The march across the continental interior was fueled by the belief of many Americans that it was their "Manifest Destiny" to expand—by force where necessary.

While the continental outlook dominated this period, there was also a strong belief, held over from the earlier maritime stage, that American vessels had the right to ply the high seas without interference. This maritime focus led to efforts to strengthen the navy as well as to develop the merchant marine to carry the increasing products of the American economy in US vessels. After trade wars with Britain had taken a heavy toll, the United States successfully promoted reciprocal trade policies with England, the West Indies, and Canada. But this drive for freedom of the seas and expansion of international trade was secondary to and derived from the overriding quest to unlock the riches of the continental interior and achieve self-sufficiency in agriculture, mining, and manufacturing.

In the development of the interior, the agricultural revolution came first, as settlers moved into the midwestern prairies and, in the latter part of the century, into the Great Plains beyond. Construction of the Erie Canal in 1825 was a major stimulus for the region's first stage of development. This was followed in 1848 by the construction of the ninety-six-mile Illinois and Michigan Barge Canal connecting Chicago to the Mississippi by linking the Chicago and Illinois Rivers. It helped to establish Chicago as the transport hub of the United States but soon became outmoded by the railroad boom that connected Chicago to the rest of the nation and provided manufacturing with efficient access to raw materials and markets. By the time of the Civil War, manufacturing in the Northeast and Midwest already equaled farm production in those areas in value. The war itself gave a tremendous boost to the intensification of industrialization in these regions, and by the 1880s the United States had emerged as the world's largest producer of steel and farm machinery.

The Continental-Maritime Stage

The next stage, the continental-maritime stage, was foretold by the German geographer Friedrich Ratzel. Speculating on the relationship between continentality and maritimity, he saw the two elements as complementary. To Ratzel and his American disciple, Ellen Churchill

Semple, the conquest of the interior was made possible by the unifying qualities of the Mississippi drainage system, which had oceanic outlets. The vast North American continental interior could be viewed not in land-oriented isolation but in a maritime-connected framework.[2]

This stage began with the Spanish-American War of 1898. Victory in that conflict enabled the United States to project its influence into the Caribbean and the Pacific in pursuit of an expanded version of Manifest Destiny. The era ended with the transitional decades between World Wars I and II.

The continental-maritime era was marked both by continuing development of the interior and outward reach for foreign markets, raw materials, and political influence. Railroad trackage increased from 52,922 miles in 1870 to a peak of 266,381 miles in 1916, to serve both grain exports and new manufacturing centers. (Since World War II, trackage has decreased so precipitously that only 148,000 miles of class I lines now exist.) The railroads enabled agriculture and industry to expand. As a result, farm acreage increased by over one hundred million acres between 1900 and 1920. In addition, Chicago strengthened its position as "Second City" (with New York City the acknowledged "first"), attracting large-scale heavy industry and pioneering American architectural forms that included the skyscraper. Detroit became a leading producer for the military in World War I, and St. Louis, already America's fourth-largest city by the turn of the century, expanded its position as a center for transportation, commerce, and diversified industry.

This urban growth depended to a considerable extent upon access to a large labor pool, much of which came from new immigrants from Central and Eastern Europe. From 1900 to 1920, 14.5 million immigrants were admitted to the United States, bringing the foreign-born population to 14 percent of the 106 million total. This was a peak percentage never again to be exceeded, as the proportion declined to 4.7 percent in 1970. The current legal immigration rate of approximately one million per annum consists mainly of professionals, entrepreneurs, and those admitted on the basis of family reunions. The recent waves of immigrants, legal and illegal, from Mexico, Central America, and the Caribbean account for half of this total, and Asians another 25 percent.

Washington's involvement in regional and global politics began with the Spanish-American War and came to full fruition with entry into World War I on the Allied side. However, this involvement did not come at the expense of the focus on the continental interior. Instead, it accelerated development of the interior. World War I stimulated production of corn in the Midwest and wheat in the eastern Great Plains. It also gave considerable impetus to the industrial growth of Chicago and other interior centers.

With the decisive role of the United States in the Allied victory and Woodrow Wilson's rallying cry for the United States to "make the world safe for democracy," it was widely assumed that the global/maritime orientation would displace the domestic focus. This was not to be. While Wilson took the lead in establishing the League of Nations, the US Senate in 1919 refused to approve the Treaty of Versailles, including US membership in the league. This turn inward continued with the strict limitations that were imposed on immigration in 1924 and the Smoot-Hawley Tariff bill in 1930, which raised barriers to world trade. The distancing of Washington from global affairs was reinforced by the Second and Third Neutrality Acts of 1936 and 1937.

This spirit of isolationism and continentality continued the focus on the interior. Flush with the farm prosperity of World War I and the economic boom that followed, the nation converted an additional hundred million acres in the southern Great Plains to cropland in the 1920s. Aided by the large-scale introduction of tractors and other mechanical equipment, this expansion took place in the area from the Texas Panhandle, western Oklahoma, and western Kansas to eastern New Mexico and eastern Colorado. This raised the total US farm acreage to 990 million in 1930. It has slowly declined since then, amounting to 920 million acres in 2010.

The postwar era of the 1920s also produced an industrial boom economy for the nation, based upon new techniques of mass factory production of consumer goods—home appliances, automobiles, trucks, and tractors. Most of this new production was centered in the Midwest. As a result, the region, which by 1870 had become the most populous in the United States owing to agricultural settlement, was now able to maintain its lead through the urbanization that accompanied industrialization. By 1920, Illinois, Ohio, Michigan, and Missouri ranked among the most populous states, and Chicago, Detroit, Cleveland, and St. Louis enhanced their positions as major metropolitan centers. Collapse of the US stock market in 1929 triggered the Great Depression, which became worldwide by 1931 and led to overproduction and falling prices in the farm belt. Conditions were further aggravated by the Dust Bowl of 1934 and succeeding years—a product of not only wind and drought but also of soil erosion due to the stripping away of the natural grasslands through cultivation.

During the Depression, the nation had little energy to devote to external affairs. US foreign trade dropped from $6.9 billion in 1930 to $4.3 billion in 1935. (The peak up to this time had been $13.5 billion in 1920, in the aftermath of World War I.) Rampant unemployment reached 25 percent, and the displacement of the rural population was especially severe in the interior. In the southern plains during the 1930s, the record heat, drought, and conversion of grasslands to wheat cultivation that had created the Dust Bowl produced a mass exodus. An estimated quarter of the plains populace, mainly tenant farmers known as "Okies" and cotton sharecroppers from the Mississippi valley (the "Arkies"), pulled up stakes and migrated to California.

Although the emphasis during this stage was continental, an important maritime component also developed. Alfred Mahan was a vigorous proponent of the notion that the future of the United States was as a maritime power. In his view, the world was divided into two geopolitical frameworks—the Western or maritime and the Oriental or continental.[3] In such a framework, the United States was an outpost of European power and civilization, while its Pacific coastland and the mid-Pacific islands were simply extensions of Atlantic Europe. In keeping with this view, the "Manifest Destiny" of the United States was to expand into the Caribbean and the Pacific, with a canal across Panama serving as the strategic link between the two borders.

During the early twentieth century, Cuba was freed from Spanish rule and, under the Platt Amendment (1901), became a virtual US protectorate. The Platt Amendment also provided for construction of a naval base at Guantánamo Bay. In addition, Spain ceded Puerto Rico to the United States, while in the Pacific it ceded the Philippines, Guam, and Wake Island. At the same time, the United States gained American Samoa through a treaty with Germany and Britain and established a naval base at Pago Pago. This Pacific presence was further expanded by the 1898 annexation of Hawaii, which became a territory two years later. Absorption of Hawaii came after three-quarters of a century of heavy US investment in the sugar industry and the securing of US naval rights to maintain a coaling and repair center at Pearl Harbor in 1887. The facility became a full-scale naval base after 1900.

In 1899 the United States took the initiative in promoting the Open Door trade policy in China. This move was designed to help the United States break into the European and Japanese spheres of influence that had been forced on China. For the most part, the success of the policy was limited because it was ignored by the major European powers, which continued to divide China into their own zones of trade to the exclusion of American commercial activity.

US influence in the Caribbean was extended in 1903, when the United States obtained the right to build the proposed Panama Canal and lease the Canal Zone from newly independent Panama, whose successful insurrection against Colombia had been aided by the protective presence of an American warship. The canal was completed in 1914 and was held by the United States until it was returned to Panamanian control on December 19, 1999. It is in the process of being expanded and deepened with a third lock that will enable giant container ships to pass through it.

While the Panama Canal is being enlarged, another canal in Nicaragua is in the offing. Nicaragua's Sandinista leader, Daniel Ortega, has offered a Chinese company a hundred-year concession for such a canal. Its construction would be handled by Chinese labor and would include two ports, a railway, an oil pipeline, roads, and free-trade zones.[4] The proposed canal would be three times as long as Panama's but would take advantage of several rivers as well as forty-mile-wide Lake Nicaragua. Rationale for its economic feasibility is that it would handle container and other cargo ships larger than those that will be handled by the new locks of the Panama Canal and that increases in global shipping make two canals economically viable.

For Nicaragua, the canal would be a major source of income. While ostensibly it would be built by a private Chinese company, there is no doubt that such a project, costing tens of billions of dollars, would need the financial backing of the Chinese government. A Chinese-controlled canal in the Americas would add considerable geopolitical weight to China's growing presence in Latin America. It would represent a major extension of China's "String of Pearls"—the series of ports, railways, and highways that China has built, expanded, or leased in Europe, Africa, and Asia. The US State Department has been circumspect in its reaction to the prospect of a Chinese-controlled canal in the Western Hemisphere. However, it is clear in the light of China's other activities in Latin America that the Monroe Doctrine is no longer enforceable.

The United States invaded Haiti in 1915 to protect US investments and properties in a military occupation that lasted until 1934. Another rationale for the invasion was fear that Germany would seize Haiti and threaten the security of the Panama Canal. The American Virgin Islands were purchased from Denmark in 1917.

Cuba, Haiti, and Panama were not the only Caribbean countries to feel the weight of US military intervention. Protection of American corporate interests in bananas, sugar, coffee, cotton, and tobacco in 1912 brought American marines into Honduras, Santo Domingo, and Nicaragua, where they remained for years. Troops were also sent into Mexico in 1914 and 1916.

Hegemony over the islands of the Caribbean and coastal Central America was justified by the Roosevelt Corollary to the Monroe Doctrine, whereby President Theodore Roosevelt asserted that instability in a Latin American country might tempt European intervention and therefore justified preemptive military action. The Taft and Wilson administrations used this corollary extensively in intervening militarily and politically within the region, as did subsequent administrations during the 1920s and 1930s. Even after the United States renounced the corollary (the Clark Amendment, 1928) and President Franklin D. Roosevelt introduced the "Good Neighbor" policy, Washington continued to regard the region as its special preserve.

The American presidency itself is a reflection of the pull during this period between the continental interior and the maritime interests of the United States. From the Spanish-American War to the outbreak of World War II, four of the eight presidents had their origins and power bases in the continental interior. Their terms for the most part were marked by inward-facing national concerns. The other four presidents were Northeast based and served during interventionist periods. Since World War II most US presidents have followed interventionist policies regardless of their political party. This reflects the emergence of the United States as a world superpower and the American public's expectation that its presidents will be the stewards of the country's global interests, especially during the Cold War.

The Maritime-Continental Stage

The maritime-continental stage began with the outbreak of World War II, as the United States geared up industrially and politically for the global war effort. During the war and into the 1950s and 1960s, the continental interior maintained its economic and political parity with the coastal regions of the country. The American manufacturing belt—from Buffalo, Cleveland, and Pittsburgh to Ohio, Indiana, Illinois, and Michigan—gained access to the Atlantic when the Saint Lawrence Seaway was opened in 1959. This belt served as the backbone of the US defense industry. By the end of World War II, its steel mills had produced eighty million tons, or 50 percent, of annual world steel production. With the opening of the seaway, this figure rose to over 130 million tons in 1965, as heavy industry produced motor vehicles, machine tools, rubber, glass, building materials, and a wide variety of appliances, such as washing machines and television sets. Most of these came from the factories of the Midwest.

The prosperity of the interior was augmented by the grains and beef of the prairies and eastern plains, which met the needs of both growing domestic consumption and the recovering economies of maritime Europe and Japan. Adding to the strength of the interior's economic base were the petroleum and natural gas of Texas and Oklahoma, the coal of Wyoming, Montana, and Utah, and the timber of the Upper Great Lakes.

This growth period seemed to confirm the doctrines that the "continentalists" of the midcentury had promoted. Historian James Malin, who drew much of his inspiration from the writings of Frederick Jackson Turner, held that the latter's "closed space" theory was based upon the continental agricultural realm of the nineteenth-century United States and held little relevance to the urban industrial scene of the twentieth century. Instead, he argued, the continental interior held the same wealth of raw materials for industry that it had held for agriculture previously. In Malin's analysis, the open space of the interior would therefore still be the dominant factor in American life.[5]

Malin drew the picture of a central power axis running north to south from Winnipeg to Dallas-Fort Worth, with "power potential distributed along the length of the axis" and the effective center shifting to fit changing requirements. He predicted that industry would migrate deeper into the interior and that population distribution would accompany the shift. According to this hypothesis, population would move toward the supply of food and toward lightweight metals, petroleum and gas, alloys, plastics, and hydropower, which all lay in the interior. Moreover, north-south mobility would be enhanced by the expansion of major commercial air centers along the central axis.

Giving support to the midwestern isolationist forces of the interwar period, Malin described the United States as a landmass state that should not extend its commitments across the Pacific or the Atlantic or south of the Amazon. He felt that the postwar world would hold room for seven or eight major powers—North America, Japan, China, Russia, Germany, Latin Europe, and the British Empire.

An expanded view of the geopolitical significance of the continental interior was offered by the geographer George Cressey in 1945.[6] He hypothesized that North America had become the real heartland of the world. Redefining Mackinder's "Heartland" as a "World Citadel," he argued that North America, not Eurasia, contained this citadel because the core of North

America was the one area in the world that possessed all the advantages of interior space, size, and resources, and access to the sea.

Alexander de Seversky, basing his theories on the supremacy of air power in world affairs, felt that the dominance of the United States over the rest of North and South America was balanced by Soviet air superiority over Africa and South Asia.[7] The area of mutual vulnerability for both powers was the North Pole. He argued that superiority in intercontinental bombers and missiles would prevail in an all-out war and that the basis for achieving such superiority lay in the continued development of the US interior. Indeed, he placed the future center of American power in Kansas.

Theories of the primacy of the continental interior were soon to be overtaken by new economic and demographic realities. Starting as early as the 1960s, industry, population, and markets began to grow outside the interior. Even though the St. Lawrence Seaway had provided the Great Lakes manufacturing area with oceangoing transportation access and attached it geographically to the country's ocean-oriented maritime coastal ring, it could not retain its industrial monopoly. By the beginning of the 1980s, plant closings or consolidations along with accompanying job losses foreshadowed the transformation of the Midwest into a rust belt. When new technologies were developed for the steel and motor vehicle industries, most served to spur industrial growth outside the traditional centers of the Great Lakes and the Ohio valley.

The impact of deindustrialization was particularly devastating for the steel and motor vehicle economy of Michigan, Ohio, Indiana, and Illinois. US raw-steel production dropped from its 1965 peak of 131 million tons to a low of 88 million tons two decades later, due to both the inefficiencies of the older American steel plants and the coastal locations of new industrial centers that used imported steel. With greater efficiencies and the introduction of new technologies, US output rose again to 109 million raw tons of steel in 1998, only to drop once more, to 90 million tons in 2012, when foreign producers in Japan, Russia, South Korea, India, China, Taiwan, Brazil, and Ukraine provided approximately thirty million tons to meet the needs of US industry. The Bush administration introduced tariffs of up to 30 percent in 2002 to try to arrest the erosion of the domestic steel industry, whose workforce had dropped from a peak of over one million to 440,000. This caused an angry outcry from foreign producers but did not provoke countermeasures against US exports. Tariff protection could not save the large, out-of-date, integrated American steel operations. Only smaller, modernized plants can survive in the highly competitive steel market. China now produces almost half of the world's raw steel, the European Union 12 percent, Japan 11 percent, and the United States only 6 percent. Moreover, half of the industry in the United States is owned by European, Japanese, and Indian corporations that remit much of their profits to home countries.

Similarly, the United States has lost its position as the world's largest producer of motor vehicles. The European Union and China are now the world leaders, while Japan and the United States are close behind. Vehicles in the United States reached their peak with sales of seventeen million in 2006. In 2007 Toyota became the world's largest automobile manufacturer, surpassing General Motors. Since then, the two companies (Toyota and General Motors) have alternated as the world's leading manufacturers.

While vehicle sales in the United States have climbed back to nearly sixteen million following the recession of 2008, only about three-quarters of these vehicles were produced in the United States. Considerable vehicle assembly and parts manufacturing capacity has been moved to Canada and Mexico. This began with the US-Canada Auto Pact of 1965 and accelerated with the establishment of NAFTA. Currently, imports from Canada and Mexico account for half of the vehicle imports to the United States. Japan and Europe provide most of the remainder.

In addition, much of the American vehicle manufacturing has shifted from its midwestern base to the South. This move was initiated by Japan, which built an assembly plant in Georgetown, Kentucky, nearly two decades ago, to be followed by the major Japanese, European, and South Korean automakers. Such cities as Chattanooga and Nashville, Tennessee, Spartanburg, South Carolina, Tuscaloosa, Alabama, and West Point, Georgia, attracted these foreign-owned companies because of their lower wage rates and non-union shops. Another example of the attraction of the South to foreign investment is the Airbus assembly plant built by the French aircraft corporation in Mobile, Alabama. Blocked by these foreign-owned companies from expanding their American market, the US auto manufacturers have invested heavily in Europe, China, and Brazil, either with local partners or through acquisitions.

In addition, the Midwest has experienced a drastic decline in defense spending, which had supported much of its industrial base during the Vietnam War, although military procurements have risen substantially as the result of the Afghanistan and Iraq wars. The nature of defense procurement shifted heavily from the tanks and armaments made in Michigan and neighboring states to products made in the Atlantic, Gulf, and Pacific sections of the maritime ring—for example, aircraft, electronic weapons systems, and ships. Continental-state awards represent less than 20 percent of the total defense budget.

The interior and the Great Lakes states have also lost economic and political influence due to the changing nature of the agricultural sector. Postwar farm production and productivity have increased owing to mechanization, application of fertilizers and pesticides, crop hybridization, and farm consolidation. During the same period, the farm population has declined drastically. In 1940, the farm populace represented 23 percent of the total US population. By 1970, the figure had dropped to 5 percent, and it is now under 2 percent.

Farm population losses in the grain-growing continental interior have been especially heavy since the agriculture there is so highly mechanized and the labor input relatively minimal. With the help of low transportation costs as a result of access to the St. Lawrence Seaway and the growth of world market demand for food products, US agriculture has become increasingly export oriented, making it the world leader in farm exports. In 2012, agricultural exports totaled over $136 billion, two-thirds of which were in food and feed grains, oilseeds, soybeans, and animal products from the interior and the Great Lakes/midwestern states. Still, farm products represent only 5 percent of all US exports. Moreover, the shift to corn-based ethanol at the expense of corn, wheat, and soybean food exports has raised prices and contributed to the 2008 world food crisis within the poorest nations, along with rising demand from China and India.

Despite its decline relative to the rest of the economy, the political leverage and influence of the interior's farm bloc remains strong. The era of the fiercely independent American farmer with roots in homesteading has passed. Today's two million farmers, especially the very largest corporations with their powerful lobbies, depend heavily on increasingly generous federal subsidies. One-quarter of all subsidies go to 1 percent of the farmers and three-quarters to 10 percent. Thus, a program that was introduced in 1933, when 40 percent of Americans lived in rural areas and was essentially a welfare program for needy farmers, has morphed into a support vehicle for a privileged few, including some owners who do not even farm their land. Farm aid payments are made for keeping land out of agriculture, for drought relief, and for subsidies to large farm corporations to compete in overseas markets. In 2012, subsidies amounted to $15 billion, representing 5 percent of the total value of US agricultural production and 12 percent of agricultural exports. Over one-third of these subsidies go to farm belt states. This policy also reduces market prices for small farmers in the United States and in developing countries. The Agricultural Act of 2014 calls for elimination of subsidies, whether crops are grown or not, in favor of crop insurance. At the same time, it reduces the Supplemental Nutrition Assistance Program (SNAP), on which up to forty-five million American poor depend. This playing off of agricultural support against SNAP reflects a mean-spirited effort to link two independent sets of need in a single farm bill.

While US farm support surely warrants considerable criticism, one should not ignore its international importance. These subsidies help to preserve the world's most efficient large-scale farming system. This system not only provides American consumers with low-cost food but also supports an agricultural industry which is the world's largest producer and exporter of soybeans, meat-poultry, and corn. Washington can support massive foreign food-aid programs, particularly in times of emergencies due to overseas droughts and floods. Because they help make the United States the world leader in food aid, these exports are important components of soft-power diplomacy.

THE MARITIME RING

What has shifted the balance away from continentality and toward maritimity in recent decades has been the dramatic growth of population, industry, services, and political power along the nation's coastal reaches. This geographical change has created, in effect, a maritime ring that surrounds and dominates the continental interior. Specialization has linked the parts of the ring so that their various economic and political interest groups act in concert across regional lines rather than dividing along such lines, as in the past. The ring also provides the United States with a central and interconnecting position in relation to the rest of the maritime realm—a geostrategic realm that includes two-thirds of the earth's water and land surface and one-third of its population.

Contrary to predictions of the continentalists of days gone by, the use and value of space has been most marked within the highly urbanized and metropolitan maritime ring, where most of the population lives, and not within the continental interior. This is not to minimize the negative impact of overcrowding within the ring. The pollution of urban environments is a serious problem, and the density of industrial operations directly contributes to smog and water contamination and has prompted many to relocate to the desert and mountain reaches of the western interior. But a concerted effort by industry and local and state governments can ameliorate the problems, and federal pressures through the Environmental Protection Agency are beginning to show some positive results.

The maritime ring might well be described as the "United States of the Four Seas"—the Atlantic, the Gulf of Mexico, the Pacific, and the Great Lakes (since the 1959 opening of the St. Lawrence Seaway). These coastlands vary in many ways—climate, elevation, landforms, natural vegetation, agriculture, and minerals. But they are similar in very important features—dense population; high degree of urbanization; large number of usable ports and well-integrated land, sea, and air connections; strong concentration of manufacturing and services; tourism; and international trade.

Among the common physical elements are humidity, natural harbors, and the barrier effects of mountains, such as the Appalachians and the western ranges. Average annual rainfall for the maritime ring is over thirty inches (save in southwestern Texas and along the southern California coast). In most instances, the rainfall is over forty inches. Such precipitation is adequate for the water needs of both urban centers and productive agricultural hinterlands. The best natural harbors occur along the highland-framed northeast and Pacific coasts and where the coastal plain has been joined to the ocean through submergence—from Buzzards

Bay to the James River. The South Atlantic, Gulf Coast, and Great Lakes have poorer natural harbors, which have required dredging and, in many cases, upstream locations. Nonetheless, as we consider the ring in its entirety, we find that no single maritime state, except perhaps Mississippi, lacks a good deepwater port, be it natural or artificial.

The completion of a third set of wider and deeper locks to the Panama Canal by 2014 is expected to double the canal's capacity. This will enable giant container ships to use the canal. The US East Coast ports of Miami, Jacksonville, Savannah, Charleston, Norfolk, and New York/New Jersey, as well as Houston, are all being expanded and deepened to compete for this trade, much of which is with China. Currently Los Angeles and Long Beach, which have expanded their ports to handle giant vessels, account for 40 percent of all container trade. Substantial shifting of this trade away from the West Coast will decrease the heavy overland truck and rail traffic that now brings goods from China and the Pacific Rim to the United States' interior and East Coast, reducing energy expenditures and attendant pollution.

While the mountains have not served as complete barriers between the seas and the interior, they have directed the alignment of land transportation lines along specific avenues. The Southeast's Atlantic coast has poor overland connections with the Midwest. This has, in turn, given stronger impetus to north-south movement along the Atlantic Seaboard. Where the Great Lakes and the Atlantic come closest together—the New York, New England, Pennsylvania, and Maryland corridors—excellent east-west land links complement the traffic of the St. Lawrence Seaway. Because of the north-south trend of the West's mountain-desert-plateau reaches, land links between the Gulf and the Pacific Northwest coasts have been weak.

Complementary resources and products also help to unify the maritime ring. The sorts of materials that are interchanged include petroleum, natural gas, coal, forest products, sulfur, cotton, copper, lead, zinc, phosphates, iron, steel, fruit, vegetables, dairy, beef, and poultry.

All of the states within the maritime ring have areas that are directly exposed to the open oceans, including those Great Lakes states that have gained access through the seaway. These thirty maritime states (including the District of Columbia) account for well over 80 percent of the nation's 2013 population of over 317 million and an even higher share of the country's urban populace. Nine of the ten states that achieved the largest absolute growth in population over the past two decades are maritime ring states, and nine of the ten largest metropolitan areas contain maritime ring ports. The ring states account for over 90 percent of both the population and the value added by manufacturing and an even higher proportion of financial services.

Some of the larger cities and population concentrations that are oriented to the maritime ring are as much as 150 to 250 miles from the sea. Examples are the inner lowland cities of Texas, such as San Antonio and Dallas; the piedmont centers of Charlotte and Atlanta; and the "central place" cities and towns of the farm belt of the Great Lakes states, such as Columbus and Indianapolis. However, most of the ring's population lives within a two-hour drive of open water in the coastal ocean and Great Lakes counties.

There are 673 counties defined by the US National Oceanographic and Atmospheric Administration as having at least 15 percent of their land in a coastal watershed or interwatershed (interior watershed that leads to the open sea). These counties alone contain over 160 million people, or approximately half of the country's total population.

Growth of the ring has been led in recent decades by the population explosions of California, Texas, and Florida. New York is almost even with Florida for third place among the most populous states, with nineteen million people, while there are over thirty-eight million Californians and twenty-six million Texans. Today the South and Texas, most of whose populations live in the maritime ring, is the most populous region, with one-third of the nation's total.

Population growth of the ring has been spearheaded by high-tech industry, as well as by immigration, retirement relocation, financial, educational, and medical services, and tourism. Not all of the region has experienced such growth. There have been only moderate to almost no increases in the populations of Great Lakes states such as Michigan, Illinois, and Ohio and in Pennsylvania and Connecticut. However, one must look to the county level to understand the impact of demographic decline. In their study of US counties from 1990 to 1995, Richard Lonsdale and Clark Archer noted that 635 counties, out of a total of 3,141, lost population.[8] With consolidations, the total has now been reduced to 3,034 counties. The great majority were within the continental interior—in the Great Plains, the Western corn belt, and Appalachia.

The demographic picture within the interior is not one of across-the-board population stagnation. Nevada, Arizona, Colorado, Utah, Wyoming, and Idaho have experienced population growth, and North Dakota's oil boom has brought many newcomers. Much of the surge in Nevada and Arizona is a consequence of the spillover of high-tech industry from California as well as the attractiveness of the environment to retirees, tourists, and gamblers. Colorado and Utah have also attracted high-tech industry in addition to those who relocate to experience life in the "great outdoors." However, by far the greatest population increase has been experienced in the newer parts of the ecumenes—in the southeastern United States, Florida, Texas, California, Arizona, and Nevada—the American Sunbelt.[9] The growth of the western interior, along with central city revival, has been cited by some as proof that the digital age has created a "new geography."[10] According to this view, the American landscape is undergoing profound change in scattered, small, uncrowded towns of this part of the interior because high-technology industry, tourism, and retirees are free of the older geographical constraints that have focused industry and population within the metropolitan portions of the ecumene. In fact, however, the digital age has done little to alter the geographical population patterns of the nation. The exception is Utah, which has attracted high-tech industries, and Idaho, which has enjoyed a boom from tourism and recreation. Information-age, back-office customer centers in such states as South Dakota and Iowa have not brought major population growth to the Great Plains. And home-based software developers attracted to the uncrowded milieus of the western interior are far less numerous than the retirees who have moved there.

Neither has the digital age been responsible for gentrifying the landscape of parts of older central cities. Instead, the time-honored banking, financial service, legal, and medical professions provide most of the jobs that draw the gentrifying class into these hubs.

For the most part, the high-tech growth takes place in the suburban metropolitan centers of the ecumenes, in their outliers such as Phoenix, Tucson, and Atlanta, and in independent metropolises such as Seattle-Portland, Salt Lake City-Provo, or Denver. These industries are attracted by the dense road, air, and rail networks; highly developed telecommunications infrastructures; skilled labor pools; educational and cultural amenities of metropolitan life; and advantages of industrial agglomeration. So powerful is the role played by the 319 largest US metropolitan regions that their goods and services now account for 85 percent of the national GDP.

There is little likelihood that the digital age will change the overall patterns of the nation's population distribution. Certainly it has energized the national economy and either filled in vacant lands within metropolitan areas or helped to expand metropolitan boundaries. However, this by no means represents a "new geography." It is simply part of the ongoing process of metropolitanization that is tied to those geographical features that initially attracted manufacturing and commerce to favored locations. These centers were linked by transportation and communication networks, allowing them to grow into the continually expanding ecumenes of the country. Now their metropolitan outliers shape and reshape the American landscape.

Diversity of people is a major feature of the two US ecumenes and the nation's ENT. The highly diverse religious, racial, and ethnic character of the ring was marked early on by the immigration from Ireland a century and a half ago and swelled by the immigration from southern and eastern Europe during the period that began in the 1880s and ended in the 1920s. The 1965 Immigration and Nationality Act lifted the immigration quotas that had restricted Asians and other non-Northern Europeans. The ecumene has been refreshed by the resultant infusion of immigrants from Latin America, Asia, Europe, and Africa. In 1990 the number of new legal immigrants was 1,586,000, and in 1991 it peaked at 1,827,000. Annual entries still total over one million legal immigrants. For example, New York City's population of over 8.3 million is 37 percent foreign-born. The Dominican Republic and China are its two leading sources of immigration, followed by Mexico, Guyana, and Jamaica. Chinese immigration is surging, having increased by one-third over the past decade, nearly half through the granting of asylum. Much of the city's revival in recent years is attributed to these new immigrants.[11] Nationwide, official immigration figures do not include approximately twelve million illegals, half of whom are estimated to come from Mexico. All of this has contributed to a new demographic profile in which the non-Hispanic white population of the United States has decreased to approximately two-thirds of the country's total and continues to decrease. It is anticipated that by 2043, the white population will no longer be a majority.

Throughout the ring, vast numbers of newcomers now cluster within large and medium-sized cities and are developing new political power bases that are changing local, state, and congressional political maps.[12] Hispanics are now vying for political power with black populations in Los Angeles, Chicago, Houston, Philadelphia, Newark, and New York. Arab Americans and South Asians are beginning to make an impact upon black-dominated Detroit. In New York City, the majority African Americans, Hispanics, and Asians are successfully challenging the old-line white-dominated machines, and Asians are also a growing force in such areas as Seattle, San Francisco, Los Angeles, and San Diego.

This diversity has also brought contrasts in standards of living, educational levels, sociopolitical outlooks, and traditions, changing American society from a melting pot to a society that is challenged and reshaped by cultural pluralism, giving new meaning to democracy. The burden of absorbing less-advantaged immigrants is heavy, requiring massive investments in education, health, and welfare. But the historic results of such processes have been the refreshing and reenergizing of the nation as a whole. These immigrants have also effected change in America's culinary tastes as restaurants and retail food stores reach out beyond the traditional immigrant neighborhoods. In addition, millions of recent immigrants to the United States have brought with them the scientific and technological skills that enable them to make immediate contributions to national development.

The rapid growth of racial and ethnic minorities, the vast majority of whom are concentrated within the maritime ring, has added a far richer meaning to the concept of maritimity than mere trade and climate. For America, maritimity connotes continuing outreach to peoples and ideas from all parts of the world and feedback by the immigrant communities to the lands of their origin. This gives a unique cast to the role of the ring as the nation's twenty-first-century frontier.

All along the maritime ring, the changes that have taken place have reshaped the nature of America's global economic power. The location base of the industries that drive the economy is not determined by proximity to the raw materials of the interior but by proximity to markets and a highly educated labor force. Within the northeastern megalopolis, financial services, electronics, pharmaceuticals, and chemicals have become the engines of economic growth, spearheading the economic boom that began in March 1991, which, with temporary downturns, continues the nation's longest period of expansion. The South, too, participated in the surge. North Carolina, while still a major textile center, has emerged as a center also for high technology, insurance, and banking and has become an integral part of the ecumene. South Carolina's main industries remain textiles and paper. However, the state has also attracted foreign-owned motor vehicle and tire industries, as well as a Boeing civilian aircraft assembly plant. In addition, while its Savannah River nuclear site at Aiken no longer produces new nuclear materials, the plant still reprocesses nuclear wastes. In Tennessee, Memphis has emerged as America's "aerotropolis." The home of FedEx, its international airport is the world's second-biggest cargo shipper (Hong Kong is the largest). Louisville, Kentucky's two airports, the hubs for UPS, follow on its heels. These two cities have attracted scores of distribution centers which handle scores of shoes, clothing, health products, and a wide variety of online purchases. This has rejuvenated Memphis, which long ago lost its cotton base, and Louisville, which had owed its earlier prosperity to rail and river transportation. In Georgia, telecommunications, aircraft assembly, motor vehicles, and finance are among the leading industries. Florida has added defense and space-oriented electronic plants to its tourist and agriculture base, and Cape Canaveral is the principal US launching site for space satellites. In Alabama, manufacturing now exceeds agriculture in importance, with products that range from paper and chemicals to motor vehicles. Louisiana's rich crude oil and natural gas deposits are the basis for its important oil refining and petrochemical industries, but high-tech and auto industries are also located there.

A major setback has been the devastation wrought by Hurricane Katrina. In New Orleans, the poor, African American sections were the hardest hit, and many of those residents who sought refuge in other cities, particularly in Texas, have not returned. This exodus and the slow recovery of the city have changed the makeup of the city. Even in Mississippi, long a rural and economically depressed state, manufacturing has overtaken agriculture as the leading economic sector, although the emphasis is upon traditional manufacturing activities such as apparel, furniture, and chemicals.

The most rapidly growing parts of the maritime ring have been Texas and the West Coast. In Texas, the aircraft industry that was established in World War II has been surpassed in importance by the high-tech computer and electronics industries in the Dallas-Fort Worth and Austin areas. Houston, the South's largest metropolitan area, is the center for the oil, petrochemical, and heavy industries of East Texas as well as for finance, electronics, computer technology, and motor vehicle parts. The National Aeronautics and Space Administration's Lyndon B. Johnson Space Center has stimulated a vital aerospace industry. The port of Houston, which extends along the Houston Ship Channel, a fifty-mile dredged waterway to Galveston Bay, is the third busiest in the United States and the focus for much of the country's Latin American trade.

Building upon its base as the nation's leading agricultural state, a center for the defense industry, and the world center for motion picture and television production, California has emerged as one of the world's industrial powerhouses. Were it an independent country, it would be ranked sixth among nations in GDP. Silicon Valley, stretching from San Jose to San Mateo, remains the world's leading producer of semiconductors and software. While the region was considerably depressed by high-tech industry cutbacks and closings during the recession of 2001, it has since recovered and spread northward to San Francisco. Other key manufacturing activities are motor vehicle and other transportation modes, electronic equipment, machinery, and food processing. That the port of Los Angeles-Long Beach, the country's largest, handles 40 percent of all US foreign trade reflects the role of transpacific trade in balancing the importance of the two American ecumenes. Washington, with Greater Seattle as its economic core, is the globe's leading aircraft producer and is a major focus for computer software, including the e-commerce industries, as evidenced by the presence of Microsoft, the world's most highly capitalized company. It has also been the beneficiary of the rapid expansion of the Pentagon budget.

California's growth in population and industry has not been an unmixed blessing, for it has created considerable pressures on the landscape. Land and housing costs in southern California and Silicon Valley have escalated, and urban sprawl has placed a heavy strain on the transportation systems and other elements of infrastructure. With this growth, demand for electricity and water has increased rapidly, leading to power shortages. While the state came to the aid of the utility companies in the spring of 2001, the long-range problem is far from resolved. California imports much of its power from out-of-state, gas-fired electric plants, which are an insufficient supply. The problem is compounded because drought in the Pacific Northwest has reduced the hydroelectric power surpluses that are usually transmitted to California.

Even in agriculture and mining, the maritime ring now substantially outstrips the continental interior in value of product. Maritime states contribute nearly two-thirds of the nation's farm output. California, by far the most important farm state in value of both crops and livestock, produces two and one-half times as much as Iowa, the leading continental farming state. Reflecting the intensive nature of California's highly irrigated agriculture, the total acreage used there is only one-third that of Iowa.

The bulk of the agricultural products grown in the maritime ring is consumed domestically, with only 25 percent being exported, the exports consisting mostly of fruit and vegetables, cotton, rice, and tobacco. The majority of US agricultural exports are still the corn, animal feeds, soybeans, wheat, beef, poultry, and hides of the continental interior and the Great Lakes states. However, this is balanced by national imports of agricultural commodities.

The intensive movement of goods by sea and air, along with the region's heavy dependence upon railroads and trucking, is a major feature of the maritime ring. Interstate 95, the fifteen-hundred-mile highway from Maine's Canadian border to Miami, Florida, is the primary artery that links the Eastern Seaboard and the most heavily trafficked route within the federal highway system. Traffic is especially heavy along the stretch from Portland, Maine, to North Carolina. Much of the sea traffic is local and intracoastal. Indeed, of the tonnage handled by the sixty busiest ports in 1997, half of the total traffic was domestic. On the whole, the goods that are moved by land or water within the maritime ring far exceed the movement of products between the ring and the continental interior, reflecting the complementary nature of the trade that takes place within the highly specialized sections of the US seaboards.

National political power, as measured by population concentration, is firmly within the maritime ring. In the US Electoral College, the ring states, including the District of Columbia, have 401 votes of the 538 total. The closeness of the 2000 and 2004 presidential election results can be attributed to the fact that while the Democrats received nearly 60 percent of those 401 ring state electoral votes, the Republicans secured over 90 percent of those from the continental interior, in great measure due to the strength there of the Evangelical Christian movement. The balance between the two parties, reflected by the fact that Gore won a slightly larger popular vote than Bush in 2000, was maintained by Republican victories in Texas, Florida, North Carolina, and Virginia. This trend was reversed in the 2012 presidential elections when Barack Obama won Florida and Virginia. All told, the Democrats gained 363 electoral votes in that election while the Republicans won 172 seats. With 53 percent of the popular vote, Obama was victorious in 22 of the 30 maritime ring states. This was offset by the Republicans having gained control of the House of Representatives (242 to 193 members) in 2010, leading to subsequent governance stalemates.

The politics of the four largest maritime ring states, California, Texas, New York, and Florida, are strongly influenced by the role played by international trade of goods, financial services, and tourist services. In addition, these states are the destinations of approximately two-thirds of all legal immigrants and a considerably higher proportion of illegals. Thus their politics is also increasingly influenced by the ties that their immigrants have to their home countries and communities.

Effect of Ethnicity on US Foreign Policy and Trade

US foreign policies toward Latin America, Israel, and, to a lesser extent, Asia have certainly been influenced in recent years by the pressure of ethnic and religious groups from the leading states of the maritime ring. The interests of such groups are manifested in pressures upon foreign policies dealing with national immigration and trade toward Mexico, political and military support of Taiwan in its dispute with China, and trade with China, as well as on such domestic issues as bilingual education and health and welfare policies. In New York, similar pressures are generated that contribute to shaping the US outlook toward Puerto Rico and Israel; in Florida such pressures influence policy on Cuba; and in Texas Hispanic Americans had an impact on Washington's embrace of NAFTA's *maquiladoras* system.

There is growing controversy within the United States over Washington's lax policies toward illegal immigrants, who are both an exploited labor class and, in some cases, involved in the drug trade. US law entitles children of illegals to free public schooling; the amnesty under the 1986 immigration law allowed some, especially farm workers, to gain green cards. The weight of the Hispanic vote has much to do with the reluctance of Congress and administrators to take a hard line on illegal immigration. This is reinforced by the interests of many US farm, construction, and factory employers in exploiting the cheaper labor source. On the other hand, the standoff between the Republican-controlled House and the Democratic-led Senate has blocked proposals of immigration reform that both parties acknowledge is so pressing. The key differences revolve around proposed citizenship for the nearly twelve million illegals, half of whom are from Mexico, and the measures adopted to interdict the ongoing flow of illegals across the country's southern border.

International Trade

International trade has become the mainstay of the American economy, foreign trade representing one-fourth of the nation's GDP. The trend line has been especially steep in recent years, with the import of low-cost goods from China and other emerging economies and of increasingly costly petroleum. This growth in foreign trade has brought benefits to the American consumer but also a serious loss of manufacturing jobs. The accumulated trade imbalance in merchandise goods has skyrocketed. While there has been a favorable balance of trade in the service sector, the future is uncertain because many jobs in the communications and medical sectors are being outsourced. This imbalance is responsible for the rapid increase in the US national debt to $17 trillion in 2014—approximately the same as the country's gross domestic product.

In accounting for 10 percent of the world's international merchandise trade as well as being the leader in exporting direct capital investments, the United States is inextricably tied to the world economy, and vice versa. The country's primary trade remains with the maritime realm allies, particularly Canada, Mexico, the EU, and Japan. However, trade with China and other parts of East Asia, South Asia, and the Middle East is growing rapidly. China alone accounts for 20 percent of US imports and purchases and 13 percent of its exports. Washington must therefore balance its geopolitical goals with economic realities in dealing with countries with whom it has political friction.

The maritime-continental setting of the United States supports the proposition that the United States' destiny is now heavily weighted toward the Atlantic and Pacific worlds as well as balanced between them. Events of the past half century have drawn the United States to the Pacific in definitive ways. The 1959 conferral of statehood on Alaska and Hawaii had significant geopolitical consequences, placing US security interests squarely in the North Pacific and the Arctic. Hawaii's nearest neighbors, the Micronesian Islands, are only one thousand miles away. Alaska's Seward Peninsula juts into the Bering Strait, only fifty-five miles from the northeasternmost tip of Siberia, and is also a short fourteen hundred miles from Hokkaido. These are short air distances. Alaska's 1,060-mile Arctic coastline not only extends US offshore claims in a fifty-mile exclusive fishing zone but also possible control of a two-hundred-mile seabed zone. This also gives Washington a claim to a sector that extends to the North Pole, should the Arctic region be divided into sectors by its abutters—Russia, Canada, Norway, Denmark, and the United States. As the oil, gas, and fisheries of the region become accessible with rapid ice melt stemming from global warming, competition for its resources will intensify.

Another important factor that draws the United States to Asia is the rapid growth of the US Pacific coast states in population, economy, and political power. The increased number of Asian American citizens, especially in California, increases the transpacific pull. Historic forces are also powerful Pacific magnets. The occupation and reconstruction of Japan, the Korean and Vietnam Wars, and the defense of the Taiwan Strait all were early Cold War involvements that left their psychological and political imprints on American public consciousness. Japan, South Korea, and the Philippines are now closely tied to the United States through security treaties. This calls for a delicate diplomatic balancing system with China in the face of the latter's territorial and water air claims in the East and South China Seas.

President Nixon's opening of China in 1972 signaled a first step in the evolving and sometimes tumultuous relations with that nation, from which neither nation can afford, economically, to step back. Washington's efforts to help China gain entry into the WTO in 2001 were not based on altruism. China now ranks first as the source of US imports and is first in accounting for the US trade deficit. On the Chinese side, the fact that the United States is its second-largest trading partner after the European Union reflects the importance of the United States to Beijing's continued modernization and development. Thus, the volume of Chinese imports makes imperative the opening of the Chinese market to American goods.

The shifting of the American frontier is a continuing process. The frontier of the colonists of the Northeast lost its innovative character as the focus of pioneering moved, first to the trans-Appalachian region and then to the continental interior. The decline of the frontier quality of the continental interior began with the collapse of small Midwestern farms during the Dust Bowl and the virtual abandonment of small prairie and plains farm and cattle towns. This trend was sealed when the adjoining heavy industrial centers of the Great Lakes fell into decline and technological innovation shifted to the coasts, first through the chemical-plastics revolution and then through the computer-technology, information-age, and financial-services revolutions.

This new frontier is augmented by its extension to offshore reaches developed by US initiative, as well as by innovations that are generated offshore that become adopted and adapted to the US scene.

To extend United States military reach around the world, a vast network of more than seven hundred overseas bases has been created, ranging from small mobile radar sites to gigantic land and air bases in Iraq, Britain, Germany, Okinawa, and Diego Garcia, naval bases in Djibouti and Bahrain, and air bases in Qatar. In addition, there are thirteen naval task forces organized around aircraft carriers that ply the world's oceans from the western Pacific to the Mediterranean and to the Persian/Arab Gulf.

Advocates of "hard power" in US foreign relations call for continued heavy defense expenditures. They cite such challenges as China's heavy investment in a "blue water navy," Russia's military positions in Central Asia, the Trans-Caucasus and Kaliningrad, and the existence of rogue regimes such as ISIS that sponsor terrorism. The Pentagon calls for being prepared for all conceivable exigencies—traditional conflict, asymmetrical warfare (guerrilla tactics and terrorism), space-based antiballistic systems, and "fourth-generation" or "net-centric" warfare. These budget requests have been supported not only by some military strategists but also by the lobbying power of the US private military-industrial complex about which Dwight Eisenhower warned half a century ago. However, it is increasingly clear to most US policy makers that America can no longer afford its military expenditures that amount to nearly half of the world's total. The slow recovery from the economic recession of 2007–9, coupled with the strategic geopolitical pivot of the United States away from the Middle East and Africa toward East Asia, and the shift in military hardware requirements for massive supplies of aircraft tanks and naval ships to drones, robots, and strike forces makes a drawdown in the Pentagon's expenditures inevitable.

In response to these challenges, Washington is increasingly turning to soft power in its outreach to the rest of the world. The Obama administration has been cautious in its approach to the Syrian rebellion, deferring to Moscow in the initiative to eliminate Syria's chemical weapons. It has also enlisted the EU in the negotiations with Iran aimed at persuading Tehran to abandon its nuclear weapons capacities. It "led from behind" in the war that contributed to the downfall of the Gaddafi regime in Libya in 2011 and has been ambivalent in its relations with the Egyptian military that overthrew the Morsi-led Muslim Brotherhood government. While decrying the military action, it continues to supply Egypt with over a billion and a half dollars in weaponry. The United States has also sought to reassure China that its security commitments to its Asia-Pacific allies are not aimed at undercutting China's strategic interests. Rather, the American position is aimed at freedom for all shipping in the waters between the East Asian and Pacific Rim coastlands.

The United States is no longer the world's sole superpower with the capacity and appetite to maintain a worldwide reach. However, in comparing its standing with other great powers, it is clearly the leading one. With respect to the four pillars that shape a nation's power, the United States ranks first militarily and is on a par with the European Union economically. Politically, its checks-and-balances system has been paralyzed in recent years by the deep division between the Democratic and Republican parties and the internal schism between the Republican moderate and Tea Party wings. Washington can no longer claim that its praxis of governance is the most effective. Ideologically, the American commitment to democracy has been corrupted by Washington's support of dictatorships in its practice of *realpolitik* and the National Security Agency's widespread spying practices, as well as by the widening domestic gap between rich and poor. However, despite the current problems, no other power has produced a more effective governmental system or more robust ideals. The United States is still the country of first resort for both political asylum seekers and those who wish to better themselves economically.

Washington's new focus on transatlantic and transpacific free-trade agreements is aimed at more than increasing trade with its two regional partners. It heralds a geopolitical strengthening of the maritime realm. The elimination of tariffs and trade barriers will inevitably draw the involved nations more closely together politically. While the agreement between the United States and the European Union is focused on agriculture and services, at the political level, increased economic interdependence is likely to bring about better balance in the relationships between the two partners which have been skewed in favor of the United States since the creation of the Atlantic Alliance following World War II.

As the United States moves toward oil self-sufficiency, its strategic need to be the dominant external Middle Eastern power decreases. Europe, China, India, Japan, and Russia are likely to replace the United States as the major forces within that region. American control of South America is also slipping away. Brazil is emerging as that continent's power core. The expansion of the Panama Canal will speed the emergence of the Caribbean as a gateway region bridging the United States, Europe, South America, and China. Europe and China have a greater stake in Sub-Saharan Africa than the United States. This is evidenced by the military initiatives taken by France in Mali and the Central African Republic and is likely to extend to the Republic of the Congo. China is second to Europe as the leading outside investor in Africa and very prominent in key construction projects. The redrawing of the world geopolitical map is likely to be a lengthy and tortuous process requiring considerable soft power guidance from the United States. Such a map can enhance world stability and therefore be of extraordinary benefit to generations of Americans to come.

Change is the most striking characteristic of a frontier. Since the maritime ring is the most significant generator of change, then surely the new frontier of the United States is the maritime ring, the urbanized area which must cope with mounting social, educational, employment, and environmental problems. Its overseas links also necessitate the reorienting and reordering of US regional and global priorities.

Canada

Few nations are as closely linked geopolitically as the United States and Canada. For over a century and a half, they have enjoyed peaceful and open borders, the conflicts between the two over continental land boundaries being now only historical memories.

This border is a border of attraction, not a barrier. Most US citizens are allowed to enter Canada without a visa for ninety days or less, and most citizens of Canada do not need visas for entry to their southern neighbor. Well over three-quarters of Canada's merchandise trade is with the United States, while Canada is Washington's single largest trade partner. But the links between the two countries extend well beyond economics. They are sociocultural. This is expressed in multiple ways, from the number of vacationers and day visitors to team membership in major-league sports. Citizens feel at home in one another's country. Despite these close relations, Canada is different. It is far from a satellite of its giant neighbor, with a history and system of governance that sets it apart from the United States.

With the signing of the British North America Act of 1867 (which was absorbed by the Constitution Act of 1982), Canada emerged as the Dominion of Canada, an independent, loosely joined federation, remaining geopolitically oriented to Britain up to the US entry into World War II. Its economic ties were reinforced by preferential tariffs accorded by London for raw materials and manufactured goods. As a member of the (British) Commonwealth of Nations, Canada followed Britain into World War I and joined the League of Nations at the war's end. Ottawa followed Britain's lead in declaring war against Germany on September 10, 1939, and immediately dispatched troops to the United Kingdom. A Canadian regiment was part of the 325,000-man British Expeditionary Force that invaded Dunkirk on May 26, 1940, only to be defeated in battle by the Germans.

The Canadian Confederation (simply known as Canada) that emerged after World War II was a substantially more centralized nation, following a process that had begun with Ottawa's initiatives in promoting stronger federal economic policies during the Depression years of the 1930s. Links with Britain loosened as a result of Britain's weakened postwar economic situation and its loss of empire, although Canada remained a constitutional monarchy with a parliamentary system consisting of a Senate and House of Commons. London's 1973 entry into the European Common Market (now the European Union) further diluted the significance of Commonwealth ties. By the Canada Act of 1982, the British Parliament made Canada fully sovereign, with the right to amend its own constitution. The act replaced the British North America Act of 1867 and made possible the 1982 Constitution Act, which absorbed the British North America Act, as well as subsequent amendments. This act gives the federal government authority in all matters not specifically reserved for provincial governments. Those governments have power over civil rights, education, property, and local government taxes. But the federal government may veto any provincial law. This only validated the reality of the independent status that Canada had enjoyed since World War I, evident in its membership in the United Nations and NATO. The fully sovereign country already had a strong social welfare commitment and was engaged in coping with Quebec separatism and the issue of native and minority rights, and it needed the new constitutional tools to deal with them, which the act provided.

STRATEGIC AND ECONOMIC TIES WITH THE UNITED STATES

Canada's geopolitical reorientation toward the United States began during World War II, when the two nations developed a close strategic partnership. Ice-free Halifax harbor, the largest in North America, was used as the marshaling and take-off point for American convoys in their crossings of the Atlantic, and Canadian escort vessels shared with the US Navy the task of guarding them. US and Canadian military bases were also established in Labrador and Newfoundland (which voted to join Canada in 1949) as aircraft were ferried across the North Atlantic from Newfoundland and Sydney, Nova Scotia. Canada also provided the vital land link to Alaska during the war, when the Alaska (Alcan) Highway was built through its territory. Canadian troops played an important role in the US-led Allied efforts in Europe. While their first foray, the Dieppe raid of August 1943, was mainly a Canadian operation which resulted in a resounding defeat, they went on to distinguish themselves in the following battles for Sicily, the spine of Italy, Normandy, and Germany.

The Cold War thrust the Canadian Arctic into new strategic prominence. The DEW Line was constructed as a defense against a transpolar attack and consisted of a series of roughly concentric circles of antiaircraft and antimissile bases in Canada and the northern United States. The North American Aerospace Defense Command (NORAD) became a cornerstone of US strategic policy as some of its most important bases, both defensive and offensive, were placed on Canadian soil. In addition to the air component, American missile-carrying nuclear submarines prowled the waters below the Arctic ice cap as they maintained their watch over the transpolar rival, often to the concern of environmentalists and Canadian nationalists.

A complication of this defense partnership is Washington's proposed defense system against ballistic missiles that, at the outset, would be based in Alaska. One Canadian view is that NORAD should be responsible for the new shield and that if Ottawa opposes the Alaska system development of the project, Canada should leave NORAD. Many Canadians object to the new defense scheme on the grounds that it would endanger the Anti-Ballistic Missile Treaty with Russia and also endanger nuclear arms control, triggering a new arms race. As a consequence, in 2005, Prime Minister Martin refused to join President Bush's proposed system.

Even more important than common strategic concerns, it is the economic interdependence between Canada and the United States that has sealed their common geopolitical destiny. The postwar demand of the booming US economy for raw materials could not be met by domestic resources. This provided the opportunity for large-scale Canadian exports to the United States of petroleum, natural gas, hydropower, timber, pulp, paper, and such minerals as copper, lead, zinc, and uranium. In turn, US manufacturers of consumer goods found a ready market in Canada. They also began to invest in Canadian mineral resources and in lower-cost manufacturing plants north of the border. This provoked some political resistance among Canadians in the years that followed. However, the resistance was overcome and the process was accelerated with the subsequent signing of various free-trade agreements. The most important of these are the US-Canada Free Trade Agreement of 1987 and, ultimately, NAFTA in 1994.

The interdependence of the two nations in trade is now inextricable. Canada ranks first for the United States as the source of imports and a destination for exports. Twenty percent of all imports to the United States come from Canada, and 22 percent of all US exports flow to its northern neighbor, even though the Canadian market offers a population of only thirty-six million. For Canada, the importance of US trade is even greater. Eighty-five percent of all Canadian exports go to the United States and three-quarters of its imports come from there. Because much of the economy in manufacturing, energy, and mining is now controlled by US interests, the economic fate of Canada is increasingly dependent on economic fortunes and market swings in the United States.

Geopolitical unity has presented Canada with the challenge of maintaining its national cultural distinctiveness and its independence from the United States in foreign policy making, while at the same time it has had to contend with the threat to its national unity by Quebec separatism and by rising demands of its northern indigenous peoples for self-government.

Ottawa has endeavored to assert a separate position in certain aspects of international affairs while at the same time maintaining its close political partnership with the United States. For example, when NORAD was first created, Canada resisted basing nuclear-tipped missiles on its soil, changing its policy only in 1963. Canadians were also widely opposed to the Vietnam War. This was expressed not only in public outcry and in welcoming US citizens who fled to Canada to avoid the draft but also through recognition of Communist China in 1970. Canada also maintains diplomatic and trade relations with Cuba and opposed the Reagan administration's intervention in Central America. It has split with the United States by supporting the International Court of Justice and the Kyoto Agreement.

It sent combat troops to Afghanistan but opposed the US invasion of Iraq. Although not joining the US-led coalition there, it reduced tensions with Washington by continuing to participate in naval patrol of the Persian/Arab Gulf which began during the first Gulf War and has helped to train Iraqi police.

As an expression of its commitment to world peace, Canada has been in the forefront of promoting international arms control, anti–nuclear weapons programs, and peacekeeping missions. It was Ottawa that first raised the idea of a UN Emergency Force to replace British and French troops in the wake of the 1956 Suez Canal invasion; Canadian peacekeepers have participated in most such UN actions since then. Moreover, Canada has led the anti–land mine campaign and been an outspoken proponent of international human rights and multilateralism. As a result of these policies, Ottawa has succeeded in shaping a unique and respected role in global affairs while continuing to enjoy the trust and confidence of its US ally.

Thus, the Canadian culture and sense of nationhood that was forged over two and one-half centuries of French and then British rule remains distinct from that of the "Colossus of the South." However, it has also had to make significant adaptations in the light of geopolitical realities.

GEOPOLITICAL FEATURES

Canada has made remarkable progress in little more than half a century as a maturing geopolitical state. Its 1940 population of ten million has more than tripled. Its east-west rail and highway networks, especially the latter, have been considerably extended and improved, while the Prairie Provinces, as well as Ontario and Quebec, have benefited substantially from the St. Lawrence Seaway. In addition to the development of these east-west lines of movement, north-south transportation and communication links have become fully developed—a step vital to the integration of the US and Canadian economies that has resulted from the various free-trade agreements between them.

Any discussion of Canada's geopolitical features must take into account not only Canada's relationship to the United States but also the historical development of its French- and English-speaking communities. Profound distinctions characterize the political outlooks of the two Canadian cultures.

Historic Cores

It is in the historic core that the Canadian state idea emerged. For French Canadians, Old Quebec, the lower part of Quebec City, is their historic core. Samuel de Champlain established a French colony there on what is now called the Lower Town, at the foot of a bluff that rises three hundred feet above the St. Lawrence River. By the mid-seventeenth century, Quebec City had emerged as the capital of New France and the center of the fur trade. The city remains the ideological heart of modern-day Quebec separatism.

The location of the historic core for English Canada is more ambiguous. For some, it is the Plains of Abraham, which now underlay the upper part (Upper Town) of Quebec City. It was on this high ground that the English general James Wolfe defeated the French, under the command of General Louis Montcalm, giving birth to English supremacy in Canada. However, a strong argument can be made, as did Derwent Whittlesey, that it was the flight to Canada of American loyalists during and at the end of the Revolutionary War that created the present Canadian state.[13] This would place the birthplace of the Canadian state idea in either the Eastern Townships of south-central Quebec or the upper St. Lawrence and lower Great Lakes.

The townships attracted large numbers of United Empire Loyalists, who settled south of the St. Lawrence between Montreal and Quebec. The area extends for about one hundred miles from Granby to Lake Megantic on a line that is approximately thirty miles north of Vermont, New Hampshire, and the border of Maine. These loyalists and their descendants were tenacious guardians of English culture and gave the area a marked British tinge for over a century.

Another candidate for historic core, the limestone lowland of the upper St. Lawrence and the lower Great Lakes, became the seat of Upper Canada. The site of today's Toronto was purchased by the British from Native Americans in 1787 and became the home of many loyalists who had settled in the area after 1783–84.

Still others look to Charlottetown, Prince Edward Island, as the historic core of the Canadian Confederation and therefore the country's nuclear core. In 1864 representatives of the Maritime Provinces (New Brunswick, Nova Scotia, and Prince Edward Island) met at the Charlottetown Conference to seal a union. The conference was also attended by delegates from other provinces and served as the forerunner of the Canadian Confederation that was formed three years later.

Political Capital

Ottawa, Canada's federal capital, owes its status to the Constitution Act of 1867, which split Quebec into Lower Canada (present Quebec Province) and Upper Canada (Ontario). The Ottawa River was selected as the boundary divide. The city of Ottawa was founded in 1827 on the south bank of the Ottawa River, fifty miles from its junction with the St. Lawrence, midway between Toronto and Quebec City. It became the capital, first of the United Provinces of Canada (1858) and then of the Dominion of Canada, which was established by the British North America Act of 1867, displacing Quebec City and Montreal, which had briefly served as the capitals of a United Canada after the creation of the union in 1841.

The selection of Ottawa as federal capital was dictated by the desire for a political center that would be located on "neutral ground" and be able to serve as a link between the two parts of the country. The choice followed an unsuccessful rebellion by the Québecois in 1837. From the onset, however, it did not become the hoped-for bridge, as rebellions in Quebec broke out again in 1870 and 1884. Despite its bilingual status today, Ottawa does not serve as the emotional capital for the Quebec separatists, who remain focused on Quebec City as their future capital.

Ecumenes

Canada's ecumenes are extensions of core portions of the major US ecumene. The main Canadian ecumene, which lies within the Province of Ontario with a population of over twelve million, runs from the northern shores of Lake Ontario westward along the shores of Lake Erie, via Hamilton and London, to Windsor. Its major nodes are Toronto-Hamilton, Kitchener-Waterloo, and Niagara, which are linked to New York's Buffalo area, and Windsor, which is linked to Detroit and Toledo, Ohio. Much of the ecumene's recent development has been stimulated by the growth of the motor vehicle industry in such southern Ontario centers as

Oshawa, Alliston, Cambridge, London, and Windsor, all of which are also hosts to a variety of machinery, chemicals, and electronics manufacturing. Toronto-Hamilton is both the ecumene's industrial powerhouse and its leading financial and services center. Kitchener-Waterloo is the center for the country's many small and medium information technology companies. Ottawa, an outlier of the ecumene, is also a major focus for Canada's high-tech industry, along with Greater Toronto. The prosperity and economic strength of the heart of the ecumene, from Oshawa through Toronto to Niagara, is such that Canadians refer to it as "the Golden Triangle."

In addition to the major southern Ontario ecumene, Canada has two secondary population and economic core areas—Greater Montreal and Vancouver-Victoria. As the cultural, commercial, financial, and industrial center of French Canada, Montreal's varied industries include steel, electronics, information technology, pharmaceuticals, textiles and apparel, refined petroleum, and transportation equipment. While it has been outstripped by Toronto, it remains Canada's second most important economic center and its leading port. Should the Province of Quebec, with its population of 7.9 million, eventually vote for independence, the connections of Greater Montreal's ecumene with the New York-New England portion of the US ecumene are likely to expand.

The Vancouver-Victoria area in southern British Columbia is Canada's third leading economic center. Vancouver, the chief Canadian Pacific port, has an excellent year-round harbor. A diverse city with a large Asian, especially Chinese, population, its industries include shipbuilding, fish processing, machinery, wood and paper milling, and oil refining. The city has developed as Canada's gateway to China and the Asia-Pacific Rim thanks to its location at the western terminus for the trans-Canada railroad system and the oil pipeline from Edmonton. Grains, petroleum, and minerals from the Prairie Provinces are thus able to tap the growing Asian market. Victoria, the capital of the province, is a major tourist center as well as the base for a deep-sea fishing fleet and the site of naval installations, grain elevators, and fish-processing plants.

Nearly all of the 4.3 million population of British Columbia is concentrated along its border with the United States, the remainder of the province being heavily forested, with the Rockies and the Coastal Range extending from the south to the province's northern end. This border location has enabled Vancouver-Victoria to benefit from its economic and commercial ties with Seattle and Portland. Separated from Ontario by twenty-two hundred miles of mountains, grasslands, and the Canadian Shield, and by the Rockies from Alberta four hundred miles to the east, Vancouver-Victoria has developed a distinct political-cultural outlook that reflects both its isolation from the rest of Canada and its proximity to the United States. Should the province respond to separatist stirrings—at this moment a highly unlikely event—it has the potential to become an important gateway state, bridging the North American and Asian-Pacific fringe lands.

Effective National Territory

While Canada is the world's third-largest country at 3,851,787 square miles, a large proportion is empty area. This leaves a relatively small proportion of the territory to be classified as effective national territory, most of which lies within the Prairie Provinces and southwestern Ontario west of Lake Superior. The readily developable parts of the Prairie Provinces are presently their wheat and general farming areas of southern Manitoba, southern and central Saskatchewan, and southeastern and east-central Alberta.

In addition to the fertile grasslands that have supported large-scale wheat and general farming, the region has a wealth of minerals—especially Alberta's vast oil, natural gas, and coal reserves; Saskatchewan's copper, lead, and zinc; and southwest Manitoba's large oil deposits. The region, which contains Canada's fastest-growing provinces, also has direct access to the sizable timber, precious metals, and minerals resources that lie to their north. These resources are a major share of Canada's raw materials that account for 40 percent of Canadian exports. Natural resources have supplanted manufacturing as the engine of economic growth. Alberta's oil patch, in particular, has become a focus for large-scale investment, including the construction of gas and oil pipelines and the extension of rail connections.

The five major metropolitan centers of the provinces—Winnipeg, Edmonton, Calgary, Regina, and Saskatoon—now contain well over half of the ENT's total population. The continued expansion of these cities and the growth of secondary urban centers can support the expansion of the ENT. Other stretches of ENT include the lands between Lake Ontario and Montreal, with Ottawa as focus, and the lower St. Lawrence between Montreal and Quebec City.

Empty Areas

Canada's empty area covers more than three million square miles, or more than 80 percent of the country's total land area. Within this region, the small, scattered populations of Yukon and the Northwest Territories, Nunavut, Labrador, most of British Columbia, the northern and central parts of the Prairie Provinces, northern Ontario, and much of Newfoundland are largely indigenous hunters and fishermen or those engaged in mining. Newfoundland and Labrador, which joined the Canadian Confederation in 1949 as its tenth province, has benefited from the proceeds of offshore oil production to the extent that it expected to be free from federal assistance by the end of 2009. This did not take place, and oil revenues were offset by the province's dependence on a collapsing cod fishing and packing industry that has suffered from overfishing and therefore requires continuing federal support.

This Canadian North, which extends across the Canadian Shield to the Arctic, consists largely of bare, windswept rock and treeless tundra. The retreat of the last ice sheet depressed much of the central part of the region's land surface, covering it with lakes and the great Hudson Bay embayment. The southernmost portion is in thick forests, while the northernmost reaches are covered with ice. For the most part, the North is dry—from under ten inches of rainfall in the Arctic to under twenty inches in the vast areas from the Rockies to Hudson Bay.

While this emptiness cannot sustain population to any extent, it is nevertheless valuable to Canada. The vast space of the North is a storehouse of minerals, proven and potential, from gold, oil, and natural gas to iron, copper, nickel, and uranium. It also serves as the country's defense shield. Its Arctic ice and waters contain the fabled Northwest Passage. With global warming, it could become an important Atlantic-Pacific route for surface oil tankers and general cargo vessels. This would shorten the Europe-Asia Panama Canal route by nearly 2,500 miles. In the summer of 2007, for the first time in its history, ice melt enabled the waters of the Northwest Passage to be open, and Canadian vessels, with international scientists aboard, traversed its length from both the east and west ends. Ottawa has long asserted its claims over large portions of the Arctic and particularly its sovereignty over the Northwest Passage. Both the United States and Russia have claimed the right of international transit through its waters, which lie between Canada's northern mainland and the Canadian Archipelago. While long a focus for exploration and attempted sea crossings, the passage was fully traversed only in 1969, when the USS *Manhattan* icebreaker tanker crossed from the eastern end to Prudhoe Bay and then returned, accompanied by Canadian and US icebreakers. The treaty signed between the two countries in 1988 did not address the issue of sovereignty, permitting the United States to use the passage on a case-by-case basis and with the proviso that such vessels carry Canadian scientists.

For Canadians, sovereignty over the Northwest Passage and parts of the Arctic beyond the Canadian Archipelago is a highly sensitive policy issue. In 2006, the Canadian military announced that it would no longer refer to the waters as the "Northwest Passage" but as "Canadian Internal Waters." In August 2007, on the heels of the placement of a Russian flag on the North Pole seabed by a Russian submarine, adding the doctrine of discovery to their Lomonosov Ridge claim, Canadian prime minister Harper announced the establishment of two military bases. One is at the port of Nanivisk in the territory of Nunavut at the eastern end of the passageway, and the other is at Resolute Bay, which is a training center for the army and the Canadian Rangers (an Inuit volunteer body) overlooking the center of the archipelago. Harper put the issue clearly: "Canada's Arctic is central to our national identity as a northern nation. . . . [T]he first principle of Arctic sovereignty [is] use it or lose it. . . . It is part of our history, and it represents the tremendous potential of our future."[14]

Thanks to the oil tar sand resources of the northern Alberta sector of the empty area, the importance of Canada as a major petroleum supplier to the United States is likely to increase over the next decade. The oil-impregnated sands of the Athabasca region of northeastern Alberta, which center on Fort McMurray, hold vast reserves, perhaps even greater than those of Saudi Arabia. Until now, the cost of recovering the oil has been prohibitively expensive. However, new technologies for separating the oil from the sand deposits have reduced production costs to one-fourth of what they were when the first pilot plant was constructed in 1970.

At the present high OPEC-driven price levels, Athabasca's energy resources have reached a competitive cost level and provide over one million barrels per day, surpassing the output of Alaska's North Slope. By the end of the decade, Athabasca's output is expected to reach two million barrels. To market this additional oil to the United States, the Keystone XL pipeline is planned to have the capacity of handling 830,000 oil barrels per day.

In addition, the North's extensive hydropower resources are just beginning to be tapped. The most important of these is the James Bay hydroelectric development in northern Quebec—a colossal project that has been planned in four stages. Phase one, completed in 1985, already supplies more generating power than all of Quebec's coal and nuclear power plants combined. Although the completion of the entire project was scheduled for 2004, objections from environmental groups brought phase two to a halt. Since then, Vermont and Massachusetts have contracted to purchase power from Hydro-Québec, but New York State continues to hold out, blocking full development of the James Bay project.

Migration

Canada's open border with the United States not only furthers economic exchange, including tourism, but it also facilitates the flow of migrants. In the eighteenth and nineteenth centuries, the movement was of American loyalists and blacks to Canada. For most of the twentieth century, with the exception of US youth seeking to avoid the draft during the Vietnam period, the flow has been from north to south. US immigration law has eased since the signing of the free-trade accords, applying to temporary workers as well as permanent migrants. While the years of heaviest out-migration of Canadians, from 1950 to 1970, reflected Canada's immature and still depressed economy, in more recent years, especially the 1990s, Canada has experienced a "brain drain" of professionals. This has been offset by the in-migration of foreign professionals to Canada, especially since US immigration laws have become more stringent.

Other migration factors, both domestic and global, affect the Canadian system. From the mid-1970s to the mid-1990s, the tensions resulting from the Quebec separatist movement prompted over four hundred thousand English speakers to leave the province for other parts of the country. Toronto in particular was the beneficiary of a substantial inflow of businesspeople and professionals as well as capital.

An even greater force for demographic change has been immigration from abroad. After World War II, Canada became the generous host to hundreds of thousands of Europeans. That welcome mat is still out for immigrants seeking work or refuge at a rate of over 250,000 persons per annum. However, the pattern of immigration has changed. Over the past decade, the vast majority of immigrants has come from the developing world, especially China, the Philippines, India, and Pakistan. In 2012, 36 percent of the country's population was either foreign born or had a foreign-born parent. This figure is expected to rise to nearly 50 percent by 2030. So great has been the impact of immigration that half the population of Toronto, which contains one-fourth of all immigrants in Canada, are foreign born, and over half the city population is nonwhite. Metropolitan Vancouver's population is now one-third Chinese and offshore Asian. These immigrants and the capital that many have brought with them have expanded trade and given Canada's Pacific coast a strong transpacific orientation.

GEOPOLITICAL FORCES OF ATTRACTION

The following discussion deals with the major elements that shape the intimate geopolitical ties between Canada and the United States. These ties are rooted in the nations' geographical relationships as well as the depth of the commitment of their people to democratic principles and institutions.

Population Distribution

Canada's population of thirty-six million is distributed in widely separated clusters, confined by the Laurentian Upland to a narrow zone along the country's lengthy, 3,926-mile southern border with the United States. Much of this population resides within fifty miles of the international boundary. Included in the clusters are the country's leading metropolitan regions—Toronto, 5.2 million people; Montreal, 3.4 million; Vancouver, 2.2 million; Calgary, 1.1; Edmonton, 966,000; and Ottawa, 935,000. More than 85 percent of the population lives within two hundred miles of the border, and very few live more than three hundred miles away.

These population clusters in the maritime provinces, the middle St. Lawrence, the Ontario Peninsula, and the Pacific coast, are linked not to one another but to US population concentrations to the south. The distance of these Canadian clusters from one another is reinforced by physical barriers—the bays and gulfs of the Atlantic and the Appalachians; the two prongs of the Laurentian Upland (the Algonquin Park-Adirondacks district and the upper Great Lakes-Superior highlands); and the Rocky Mountains. Calgary and Edmonton, each with populations of over one million, are the only two major metropolises located more than fifty miles from the border.

Economic Exchange

As the United States continues to draw down much of its natural resource base, Canada's abundant natural resources have become vital to the US economy. These include freshwater, hydropower, fish, timber and pulp, oil, natural gas, and such minerals as uranium, zinc, potash, asbestos, and nickel. Canada ranks first among petroleum exporters to the United States, accounting for 37 percent of all US imports. Gas from the Canadian Rockies is piped to Chicago and then eastward to the Pennsylvania border, via the big TransCanada pipeline. A major exception to this exchange of resources is the grain production of the Prairie Provinces, which competes with US commodities for world markets.

Much to the consternation of Canada's western prairie farmers, the Canadian government has responded to free-market agreements by cutting wheat subsidies drastically. Meanwhile, the US wheat subsidy remains high, at 38 percent. While Canada still produces about twenty-five million tons of wheat and serves 20 percent of the world market (two-thirds of the market for durum), the economic pressures on its prairie farmers are heavy, and farm population has dwindled. Indeed, what has long been called Canada's "breadbasket" is now more urban than rural. In Manitoba, for example, the value of grains and seed oils is exceeded by far by the value of such manufactured goods as buses, aircraft parts, furniture, and books. In fact, the single greatest obstacle to manufacturing is the shortage of labor. Ottawa has made the choice—because of its substantial trade balance with the United States, rescuing its western farmers through a reversal of its low-subsidy policy has taken second place to preserving a free market for Canadian goods exported to the United States.

With the implementation, first of the Canada-US Free Trade Agreement in 1989 and then NAFTA in 1994, Canada's manufacturing industries have become heavily geared to the US market and now account for 20 percent of the nation's GDP. Motor vehicles and parts, located mostly in southern Ontario, are the leading industry. The growth of this industry preceded NAFTA, having begun with the signing of the US-Canada Auto Pact in 1965. However, it was NAFTA that provided the major impetus for the increase in production. The Canadian-based industry's annual output of 2.5 million vehicles, most of which go to the United States, makes Canada a major motor vehicle producer. It ranks behind only Germany, Japan, South Korea, and Mexico as an exporter of autos. Bombardier, the world's third-largest civilian aircraft producer and a major manufacturer of transportation equipment, has a global reach. While its major plants are in Ontario and Quebec, it also has assembly facilities in New York State. Other manufactured products include paper, newsprint, aluminum, chemicals, electronics, machinery, and apparel. This growth of manufacturing is heavily dependent upon US investment. The reverse flow of investment dollars from Canada to the United States, though smaller, is also substantial, although much of it may originate with Canadian companies whose capital base is in the United States.

As a result of industrial expansion, the nature of the Canadian economy has changed dramatically over the past quarter century. This shift to manufacturing and services, as well as the export of energy, wheat, and forest products, has made Canada highly dependent on foreign trade. The value of imports and exports now represents 60 percent of GDP. Since over three-quarters of Canada's exports and over 60 percent of its imports are with the United States (the EU, Japan, China, and Mexico account for the rest), it is clear that Canada's economic destiny lies with its southern neighbor. Canada is negotiating with the EU for a free-trade agreement. Even if this is consummated, the impact on trade with the United States is likely to be minor. Washington inexplicably has chosen to exclude Canada (and Mexico) from its Transatlantic Trade and Investment Partnership negotiations with the EU, even though harmonizing all of NAFTA's trade relations with Europe seems to be a more sensible strategy.

The complementary and interdependent nature of the economies of the two countries is reinforced by north-south rail, highway, pipeline, airline, water, and telecommunications routes and networks. The exceptions to this directional orientation are the east-west

St. Lawrence Seaway and the TransCanada gas pipeline. However, even as the seaway has stimulated Canadian global bulk exports, it has also facilitated transborder trade within the Great Lakes region.

THE CHALLENGE OF GEOPOLITICAL PARTNERSHIP

US-Canadian relations appear to be proceeding inexorably in the direction of increasing interdependence. However, given the absence of power symmetry between the two countries, the fear that some Canadians have of sinking from partnership to satellite status is not unwarranted. Environmental issues have become especially contentious. The proposed James Bay Phase II power project to supply energy to New York State raised so much opposition from Canadian (and US) environmentalists and Cree Indians that in 1992 the New York State Power Authority backed away from signing a promised purchase contract. The following year, the government of Quebec decided to shelve the New York project.

Environmental issues yet to be resolved include the opposition in Canada to US proposals to import pure freshwater from Canada's Lake Winnipeg and to US Army Corps of Engineers flood-control plans to divert floodwaters in North Dakota into the Red River. The latter would direct polluted waters into Canada. Another issue is the Alaska-bound cruise ships and commercial vessels operating from the US Pacific coast, which pose environmental threats when they traverse Canada's portion of the Inside Passage—the waterway formed by a deep structural trough that extends along the Canadian coast from Vancouver Island to Prince Rupert and then follows the Alaskan shore to Juneau. The Canadian government cannot allow foreign vessels to continue dumping and spilling.

A recent area of controversy has been the proposed extension of the TransCanada natural gas pipeline from Chicago and under Lake Erie through New York State to the southern counties north of New York City. Suburban environmentalists there have argued that the pipeline's construction would have an adverse impact on the landscape.

None of these issues is unsolvable. The export of power and freshwater can be of benefit to Canada if environmental concerns are properly addressed. The use of the Northwest Passage might well lend itself to technological breakthroughs that would permit transit via giant submarine tankers of oil, liquefied gas, and even water, between the Atlantic and Pacific. For the US-Canadian geopolitical partnership to endure, there must be a mutuality of interest. This calls for understanding, sensitivity, and accommodation. Because northern British Columbia and the Yukon Territory do not have direct access to the Pacific, some Canadians have called for the granting of a corridor across Alaskan Panhandle territory. Although this may be passed off as being neither economically nor strategically important to Canada, it is still a sore point in some Canadian circles that the landward boundaries of Canada, which were confirmed in 1903, are denied access to the sea.

Canadian interest in a corridor centers on the Chilkoot and White Passes, which link Whitehorse in the Yukon to the Lynn Canal and the sea via Skagway, Alaska. The granting of a corridor to Canada would not affect the strategic or economic position of the United States, because the major land link, the Alaska Highway, already passes through Canada. A farsighted US policy that respected Canadian political-psychological yearnings in this instance would be a small but significant expression of mutual understanding.

The most significant issue currently dividing Ottawa and Washington is the proposed Keystone XL oil pipeline. This 1,179-mile, 36-inch line is to extend from Hardisty in Alberta to Steele City, Nebraska, connecting there via existing lines to Gulf Coast and Midwest refineries. Its projected output could increase US oil imports from Canada by over a third. The environmental controversy over Keystone is bitter. The oil is embedded in tar sand, which is a mixture of clay and sand, and sticky, heavy, high-sulfur oil. It sits beneath boreal forest that is inhabited by extensive wildlife. To extract, upgrade, and produce one ton of this bitumen tar sand requires removing four tons of soil as well as the forest cover and toxic sludge. In addition, the process would release considerable carbon dioxide and methane gases. Another point of environmental controversy is that the line would pass over the Ogallala Aquifer, exposing this major source of irrigation and drinking water to the danger of oil spills.

US regulatory authorities must weigh the benefits of adding such a substantial amount of oil from a secure source against the environmental risks. The rapid increase of oil production within the United States coupled with Canadian and Mexican oil would free the United States of dependence upon imports from Venezuela, Africa, and the Middle East. In addition, the Canadians have argued that they have an alternative should Keystone's extension into the United States be blocked. This would be swinging the line westward to the coast of British Columbia, from which the oil could be exported to China—a lucrative market. For Washington, this goes beyond the pipeline issue. It touches upon the more general relations with Canada. Rejecting the pipeline for environmental reasons could undermine the geopolitical partnership which has served both nations so well.

It behooves Washington to be especially sensitive and attuned to political developments in Canada. This includes respect for the federalism that characterizes the Canadian body politic and that helps to distinguish Canada from the United States. Much of Quebec's drive for separation has had to do with the economic imbalance between French Canada, which accounts for 22 percent of the population, and Ontario, with 34 percent. That imbalance has persisted, as US investment and industry has focused on southern Ontario. An example is the motor vehicle assembly and parts industry, three-quarters of which is located in southern Ontario. Washington's encouragement of capital flows and trade expansion with Quebec can yield political as well as economic dividends, for the closing of the economic gap between Ontario and Quebec will help reduce the political tensions between English- and French-speaking Canada. Greater political stability within Canada strengthens the foundations of geopolitical unity between the two countries.

Such capital and trade flows have already begun to help stimulate Montreal's economy. The city has become, in recent years, a major exporting center for the US Northeast, based on its lower labor costs, cheap energy, strong university and research and development (R&D) centers, and proximity to New York City and Boston, where Montreal's fashion and knit goods, as well as subway cars, find a ready market. Another important basis for exchange is Montreal's growth as a center for finance, the high-tech industry, and tourism. As a result of this recent spurt of activity, Quebec's exports to the United States have risen to one-fourth of the province's GDP; the continued growth of such exchange can play a vital role in closing the gap between French- and English-speaking Canada.

The population of Quebec is almost evenly divided with respect to the independence issue, so the issue is far from settled. At the end of 1999, the Canadian government tabled a bill seeking to clarify the conditions under which a province might secede. The draft of the proposed legislation revealed some of the complexities of secession—negotiating Quebec's borders and share of the federal debt and guaranteeing the rights of Indians and linguistic minorities. Quebec separatists would have to grapple with the possible loss of the province's border areas with Ontario and New York as well as northern parts of the province, where the Indians and Inuit oppose breaking ties with Ottawa. The Clarity Act, passed by the Canadian Parliament in 2000, essentially eliminates the possibility of Quebec's legal separation because the federal government must approve a referendum calling for Quebec's independence. Nevertheless, the political situation remains tense. The separatist Parti Québécois won the 2012 provincial elections and continues to promote independence. For Washington to be drawn into such political negotiations on any basis save as mediator would be a diplomatic disaster that could jeopardize the geopolitical unity that now prevails.

Nunavut was carved out from the eastern portion of what was the Northwest Territories in 1999. Its boundaries extend along a zigzag line running from the Saskatchewan-Manitoba border to the North Pole, encompassing lands from this boundary east to Hudson Bay. The nearly 30,000 Inuits who inhabit Nunavut have outright title to 20 percent of the territory's 772,260 square miles, including 13,896 square miles of mineral rights. They also receive royalties from the petroleum, natural gas, gold, diamonds, and uranium produced in all of the territory's federally owned land and compensation of over one billion Canadian dollars between 1993 and 2007. This agreement—creating Nunavut—called for its government to receive 50 percent of the first two million dollars earned in royalties and 5 percent of additional revenues. The Inuit are now seeking a fifty-fifty split of all royalties.

Progress has also been made with respect to the political status and land claims of Canada's other indigenous peoples, close to a million Indians and Métis, many of whom continue to live on reservations. Abandoning past policies of assimilation, Ottawa began to address their land claims in the 1990s, coming to agreements on land ownership and revenue sharing. Despite these agreements, tensions remain between the Canadian government and the indigenous people, the most recent being Ottawa's actions in delaying a UN declaration which would recognize indigenous national rights. Establishment of Nunavut has important geopolitical implications for the United States. In positioning new antiballistic radar systems as well as maintaining current monitoring systems, the United States needs to be mindful of the rights of the citizens of the new territory while it negotiates with Ottawa. Iqaluit, the new capital of Nunavut, is accessible only by air or sled for most of the year. Formerly, Iqaluit was only an outpost for a DEW station. Washington now must take into account the views of the Nunavut government on how the Inuit environment should be used with respect to future joint US-Canadian defense facilities.

The confederal nature of the Canadian system may complicate the political dealings between the United States and Canada, but if the common geopolitical destiny of the two countries is to be fulfilled, it is crucial that the decision-making process include all of the relevant constituent parts of the Canadian confederation. The strength of the geopolitical relations between Canada and the United States owes much to the geographical settings of the two countries—their complementary resource bases; the openness of their borders, which encourages exchange of ideas, goods, and people; and the merging of ecumenes. However, it is their common outlooks on such fundamental issues as the democratic process, protecting human rights, and international aid, and their mutual respect for those matters on which they differ, that has enabled the two countries to take advantage of the geographical factors that bind them. Above all, the political ties between the two must continue to be built on a genuine partnership rather than the dominant-subordinate relationship that so often has been the fate of smaller powers that have lived in the shadow of far larger and stronger neighbors.

Mexico

Geographically and culturally, Mexico belongs to Middle America. Geopolitically, however, its fate has been closely tied to the ambitions and policies of the United States, a condition that made for stormy relations between the two for much of the nineteenth and twentieth centuries. The US-Mexican War of 1846–48 resulted in the US annexation of 40 percent of Mexico's territory and initiated a century of US intervention in Mexican economic and political affairs.

What Mexico lost territorially to the United States is now being reclaimed in an unforeseen but geopolitically significant way. Mexican immigration to the United States is altering the American political voting map. The number of Mexican Americans is thirty-five million without accounting for several million undocumented Mexican residents. They constitute two-thirds of the entire Hispanic and Latin population of the United States. Most Mexican Americans are concentrated in California, Texas, New Mexico, Arizona, and Nevada, as well as parts of Colorado, Utah, and Wyoming—the very territories seized from Mexico in the nineteenth century. Both the Democratic and the Republican parties are vying for Hispanic American support in those states, especially their Mexican American voters, current and potential.

With the economic rise and increased political awareness of second- and third-generation Mexican Americans, we can anticipate greater pressure on Washington not only to reduce domestic economic and social discrimination but also to adjust its policies toward the Mexican motherland. Until now, the US government has focused its energies on fighting drug cartels, gun wars, and corruption within Mexico—and with little success. It has failed to address the roots of many of Mexico's problems, which relate to the uncontrolled export of guns from the United States as well as the demand of Americans for drugs. The emergence of a sizable Mexican American local, state, and national leadership concerned with ameliorating the upheavals within their homeland as well as supporting Mexican economic development is to be anticipated. Progress in this direction can only strengthen the geopolitical partnership between the two countries.

For nearly two centuries following its 1821 War of Independence that overthrew three centuries of Spanish rule, Mexico's development has been heavily influenced by its northern neighbor. This began with the influx of American settlers into Texas, which was then Spanish territory. The colonial government gave a land grant to Stephen F. Austin to settle three hundred families. The colony prospered. Following the war, the fledgling Mexican government welcomed the settlement by offering land grants to American entrepreneurs. The settler population in Texas grew so rapidly, however, that by 1830 it was three times as numerous as that of the Mexican settlers.

Conflict over land title between the American and Mexican settlers led the Mexican government to try to stop the American influx, leading to the Texas Revolution in 1835. The siege of the Alamo and the killing of its 180 defenders was followed by the defeat of the Mexicans at San Jacinto in 1836 and the declaration of independence. Because Texas was a slave state due to cheap land and the rapid expansion of the cotton-based plantation economy, antislavery forces opposed its admission to the United States until 1845, when it was annexed to the United States as a slave-holding state.

This, in turn, brought on the US-Mexican War (1846–48), which ended with Mexico's loss of 40 percent of its territory. In that war, the Battle of Chapultepec (1847) became a centerpiece in the narratives of both Mexican and US nationalism. The US Marine hymn that begins "From the halls of Montezuma" commemorated their victory over the Mexicans when they captured the ancient Aztec ruler's residence in the center of what is now Mexico City. For the Mexicans, this battle became a symbol of glory for its heroic young defenders of the castle, who preferred death to surrender—comparable to the "remember the Alamo" symbolism for Texans.

The war ended with the Treaty of Guadalupe-Hidalgo, which confirmed US claims to Texas and set a new boundary between the two countries. This line followed the Rio Grande from its mouth to what is now the US state of New Mexico. It then ran west to the Gila River, following it to the Colorado River, and then serving as the boundary between Upper and Lower California to the Pacific. The Gadsden Purchase of 1853 absorbed lands south of the Gila River toward what is the current border. The purchase was urged by American railroad interests because the most practical route from Texas to California was the Gila Valley that runs through New Mexico and Arizona to the mouth of the Colorado River. Most of the Mexicans living in these areas were descendants of early Spanish colonists who lived in Texas, the Upper Rio Grande Valley, and California. They remained in situ, retaining their property and, to some extent, their cultural rights. They are the first of the Mexican Americans.

While the Monroe Doctrine (1823) is generally identified with American interventionist policy in the Caribbean and Central and South America, it was also directed to concerns over European intrusion into Mexico. Washington feared that Britain and France would try to prevent annexation of Texas and were interested in penetrating the Yucatán. While the attention of the Union was fully focused on the Civil War, France, Britain, and Spain captured Veracruz to collect debts owed them by the Mexican government (1861). During the course of the war, the South's cotton was shipped through Mexico for export to Europe because of the Union blockade of the Atlantic and the US Gulf coasts. This was another irritant in US-Mexican relations.

Three years later, Napoleon III installed Maximilian, a Habsburg prince, as emperor of Mexico in response to an appeal by Mexican conservatives to overthrow the liberal, anticlerical government of Benito Juarez, who had led the War of Reform (1858–61). At that time Washington invoked the principles of the Monroe Doctrine. Its pressure caused the French government to withdraw support from Maximilian. His empire collapsed in 1867, and Juarez was reelected president.

From much of the rest of the nineteenth century and into the first quarter of the twentieth, the United States played a strong economic and political interventionist role in Mexico. The oligarch president, Porfirio Diaz (1876–1911), favored large landowners and invited large-scale foreign investment. This resulted in the acquisition of large ranches and valuable silver and iron mines by Americans, as well as the building of railroads from Mexico City through northern Mexico to the US border. Foreign investors also developed the country's eastern and western ports and light manufacturing in the center of the country, especially textiles and food.

In the late 1800s, Mormon settlements from the United States and Canada were encouraged. They engaged in cattle ranching in the arid north as well as in mining and forestry in the adjoining mountain slopes. The Mormon colonies prospered, but most of them had to be evacuated in 1912 due to the anti-US sentiment of that revolutionary period.

Another group of settlers in the region were the Mennonites, who also were concentrated in the north in Chihuahua and Sonora. They were Germans who had settled in Texas when it was under Spanish rule and left for Mexico in 1848. A much larger group of Mennonites, numbering 25,000, moved from Canada to Mexico, having been invited by President Álvaro Obregón. They were attracted by cheap land and freedom from taxation. They now number one hundred thousand and engage in farming, work in machine shops, and use motorized vehicles for transporting produce. These groups of settlers as well as Spanish descendants who developed large ranches are the forerunners of today's conservative PAN (National Action Party).

During the Mexican Revolution of 1910–20, the country was torn by factionalism within the revolutionary parties. In 1914, Pancho Villa gained control of northern Mexico but broke with his former ally Venustiano Carranza, who had been recognized as president of the country by Woodrow Wilson. In response, Villa led a raid across the border into the town of Columbus in southern New Mexico. This part of the US-northern Mexico borderland region had served as a haven for Mexican rebels and a jumping-off place for those opposing the regime during the Mexican Revolution. President Wilson ordered military retaliation, but the expedition, led by General John Pershing, failed to capture Villa. This invasion embittered the relations between the two countries.

Tension between the two countries was exacerbated by the strong pro-German sentiment that prevailed in Mexico during World War I, a tension inflamed by the Zimmerman telegram. This message, dated January 19, 1917, was purportedly sent by Germany's foreign minister, Arthur Zimmerman, to the German minister in Mexico City. The message was intercepted and passed on to Washington by a British encryption team; its contents proposed that Mexico be encouraged to form an alliance with Japan and the Central Powers against the United States should the latter enter the war to aid the Allies. In return, Germany would offer to help Mexico regain the territories that it had lost in 1846. Some have held that the Zimmerman telegram was a forgery designed to help justify Woodrow Wilson's decision to enter the war. Whatever the truth, the affair increased the hostility between Washington and Mexico City. This hostility was heightened further that year when Carranza proposed a constitutional change (never enacted) that would have nationalized the country's mineral resources.

Serious controversies over petroleum rights continued from the early 1920s into the 1930s, when the Mexican oil boom offered tempting financial rewards to US companies. Tensions reached new heights when Lázaro Cárdenas became president in 1934 and instituted sweeping reforms centering on land redistribution. He nationalized the railroads and foreign holdings and expropriated the petroleum fields, albeit with compensation. The oil industry came under control of a new state-owned company—Petróleos Mexicanos (PEMEX)—and private and foreign companies were prohibited from exploring or producing oil and natural gas.

This action put to the test Franklin D. Roosevelt's "Good Neighbor" policy. The policy had been articulated in 1933 when the United States repudiated Theodore Roosevelt's corollary to the Monroe Doctrine which justified US intervention in Latin America. The "Good Neighbor" policy held that no neighbor had a right to intervene in the internal or external affairs of another. FDR resisted pressures to intervene in Mexico's oil expropriation policies.

Relations between the two countries improved in the 1940s as Mexico entered World War II in 1942 on the Allied side. In return, Mexico received substantial economic aid from the United States, for which Mexican oil had become especially important in supplementing Texas and Oklahoma production. The Inter-American Highway, from Nuevo Laredo, Mexico, to Panama City, played an important logistical role during the war. While much of it had been completed before 1941, US funds were appropriated to assist its completion to meet the needs of the war effort. A later example of the growing convergence of the two countries was in the political arena, when Mexico firmly supported Washington's position in the Cuban missile crisis.

The Bracero program, which enabled large numbers of Mexican farm laborers to work temporarily in the fields of California and adjoining states, was initiated during the war and was extended until 1964. The program's peak years were in the 1950s, when close to 450,000 farm workers were recruited annually. Ultimately, over four million migrant laborers were involved in the program. With its ending, they lost their legal work status and were deported. Denied the possibility of legal entry, many Mexicans, especially from the northern part of the country, began to cross into the United States illegally. This initiated a wave of illegal immigration, which continues to this day and now totals several million Mexicans.

The most important factor in increasing the economic interdependence of the two nations is the North American Free Trade Agreement (NAFTA), which was signed in 1992 by the United States, Mexico, and Canada, and put into effect on January 1, 1994. That historic accord, coupled with a wave of privatization that had begun in the late 1980s, triggered a rapid growth in the Mexican economy. This trade expanded exponentially. The agreement called for erasing trade barriers and creating what was then a trading bloc of 370 million people. This bloc now has a population of 460 million. NAFTA called for the removal of all trade barriers within fifteen years. This was strengthened by an agreement in 2010 whereby all nontariff barriers to agricultural trade between Mexico and the United States were eliminated. The benefits of NAFTA to Mexico are clear. The United States is now, by far, Mexico's largest trading partner, as 80 percent of Mexico's exports go to the United States and half its imports come from there. China and Canada lag far behind as Mexico's second and third trading partners.

The 1980s and 1990s, especially after the signing of NAFTA, were marked by growth of the *maquiladora* system, initiated as a small industrial border program in 1965. The *maquiladoras* are free-trade zones located mainly along Mexico's border with the United States. At its height, the system had nearly four thousand assembly and manufacturing plants, employing nearly one million workers.

The number of border factories began to decline precipitously because of rising labor costs, moving electronics and textiles to such areas as China, Vietnam, Central America, and the Caribbean. This decline affected the border cities, whose prosperity had increased with the service jobs that were added and the large numbers of cross-border daily visitors. Drug war violence in the border cities has reduced this flow of visitors even further. In the past few years border *maquiladoras* have revived somewhat and now number approximately three thousand. Plant ownership, initially largely American, has in recent years attracted Chinese, Japanese, and European investors seeking to penetrate the US market.

Many Mexicans have expressed considerable resentment about the techniques used by the United States to curb illegal immigration. These techniques include strict border security measures which hamper trade flows as well as the movement of people. However, such tensions are overridden by mutual needs. The United States requires Mexican oil and laborers, and Mexicans depend heavily upon remittances from emigrants and US financial aid, markets, and tourists.

GEOPOLITICAL FEATURES

Capital and Historic Core

In the first stages of the postwar period, US attention was focused on the Mexico City national political core and the Bay of Campeche, which contains the country's major oil- and gas-producing areas and rich reserves. The capital, which is coterminous with the Federal District, is located in the high valley and former lake bed that is the site of Mexico's historic core. As the historic core, the site dates back to the fourteenth century, when the Aztecs built their capital on the ruins of a pre-Aztec site. When the Spaniards conquered the city in 1521, they expanded the site by filling in the lake with the rubble that covered most of the valley and by draining the lake, and made the city the political center of the viceroyalty of New Spain.

Mexico City's urban agglomeration now has a population of over twenty million. Its suburbs extend outward for as much as one hundred miles in all directions. The crowded metropolis, much of which is in the Valley of Mexico and surrounded by hills and mountains, is plagued by endless traffic jams and serious air pollution. Despite the pressures on land, air, and water, some demographers expect the metropolis to grow into a megalopolis of fifty million by the mid-twenty-first century and to reach out in a radius of up to 150 miles.

Ecumene

The nation's ecumene—the area containing the highest densities of population and economic activities—has formed around Mexico City. In addition to the Federal District, the ecumene contains the surrounding states of Mexico, Puebla, Morelos, and Tlaxcala and extends out to the Gulf Coast at Veracruz. It also contains parts of Michoacán, Hidalgo, and Querétaro.

The total population of the ecumene now exceeds 35 million, or one-third of the country's nearly 120 million inhabitants. The region contains much of Mexico's manufacturing, such as food products, textiles and apparel, motor vehicles, machinery, chemicals, pharmaceuticals, steel, paper, and consumer products. In addition, Mexico City serves as the financial-services and commercial center of the nation.

The center of the coastal extension of the ecumene, the city of Veracruz on the Bay of Campeche, is one of the country's two major ports (Tampico is the other) and is a focus for iron and steel, chemicals, and tourism. It is connected by rail and highway to Mexico City. In the northern coastal part of the state, a pipeline from the older oil fields of Tampico and Tuxpan provides refined oil to the capital. The basis for the country's petrochemical industry, however, is the newer oil and natural gas fields south of Veracruz City and extending into the adjoining state of Tabasco, where vast offshore reserves were discovered in 1972. These Bay of Campeche oil discoveries triggered the country's second oil boom, which lasted from 1973 to 1982. During that period, oil shipments accounted for three-quarters of the nation's export earnings. Growth then dropped sharply as international prices declined, and Mexico's ability to meet its foreign indebtedness became severely strained. The industry then recovered, and production stabilized at the earlier peaks. Since 2004, however, crude production has steadily declined to 2.25 million barrels per day in 2013, two-thirds of which is exported to the United States. This still represents one-third of all Mexican government revenues.

In response to the lessons learned from the sharp fluctuations in oil prices and its over-dependence on oil, the government put in place an industrial diversification policy aimed at increasing the export of manufactured goods, metals, and agricultural products, which has succeeded in reducing oil dependence. To a considerable measure, this success now depended upon Mexico's import of foreign capital as well as upon the access to markets provided by NAFTA. The capital flow has been substantial. Among low- and middle-income countries, Mexico is one of the world's leading importers of private capital, most of which comes from the United States. In addition, access to foreign markets has been broadened by a free-trade agreement that was signed with the European Union in 1999 and by agreements with many Latin American countries, such as Chile, Colombia, Venezuela, Uruguay, Bolivia, Costa Rica, and Nicaragua.

A major factor in the decline of Mexico's oil and gas production can be attributed to the monopoly position held by PEMEX, which is responsible for all of the country's oil and gas production, refining, and distribution. In keeping out foreign energy companies it has deprived itself of access to new production technologies. These are especially needed in order to tap the abundant oil and gas reserves contained in its deepwater shale. In 2013 the Mexican government introduced legislation that allows foreign companies to bid for licenses to explore and drill for energy. The below-ground hydrocarbon deposits remain state property, so partnership arrangements between PEMEX and foreign investors will probably have to be made. Estimates are that exploiting the shale deposits with the most up-to-date technologies will enable the country's production to rise to four million barrels per day.

Effective National Territory

The concept of a "free zone" dotted with *maquiladoras* (processing factories) originated with Mexico's Border Industrialization Act of 1965. However, it was NAFTA's establishment three decades later which stimulated the explosive growth of the *maquiladoras* that has been so instrumental in expanding Mexico's ENT to the US border. Most of northern Mexico remains a sparsely inhabited, semiarid to arid grazing region dotted with peasant farms that are heavily dependent upon irrigation. However, its urban clusters and centers of industry have converted what was a backward and largely empty area into part of the country's ENT.

From a geopolitical standpoint, the agreement has drawn the United States and Mexico more closely together, as Mexico's focus on industrial growth has shifted northward to the border zone between the two countries. Thanks to the rapid increase in *maquiladoras*—the assembly plants that import the bulk of their raw materials and parts from the United States and export the finished products on a duty-free basis—this northern border zone has attracted major manufacturing and urbanization.

Few cities and towns located along the boundary lack *maquiladoras*, and many, such as Tijuana, Otay Mesa, Mexicali, Nogales, Nuevo Laredo (the country's busiest inland port), and Matamoros, have enjoyed economic booms. This northern border zone also extends southward to cities that have easy access to the border. Monterrey, Mexico's second most important industrial city and its leading iron and steel center, is only 75 miles from the border; Chihuahua is 125 miles away; and Hermosillo is 175 miles distant. However, the greatest concentration of activity and employment is in the four border cities—Ciudad Juárez, Tijuana, Nuevo Laredo, and Matamoros.

The growth of the *maquiladoras* was so rapid that, by 2001, they accounted for over half of all Mexico's new manufacturing jobs, from textiles, apparel, household appliances, and television sets to high-tech products, chemicals, and metals. In particular, the *maquiladoras* stimulated the expansion of electronics and motor-vehicle assembly and parts plants. Mexico now produces 2.25 million motor vehicles per annum in plants located in such northern centers as Hermosillo, Chihuahua, Saltillo, Reynosa, and Monterrey, as well as in those in the center of the country, in Puebla and Guanajuato. Japanese automakers have transferred considerable production to Mexico, and the country is well on its way to becoming the world's third leading motor vehicle exporter, behind Japan and Europe.

The impact of all this activity has been relative prosperity and a higher standard of living for these northern urban centers. Monterrey, for example, where the *maquiladoras* program began, now employs over half a million workers in such industries as glass, cement, steel, chemicals, and furniture, as well as motor vehicles, and has become a center of wealth and capital formation.

This manufacturing growth has created, in effect, a new, industrialized border region between the United States and Mexico. On the Mexican side of the border, the population has increased by nearly 50 percent over the past decade. The growth is concentrated in the dozen Mexican border cities that extend from Tijuana and Mexicali on the Pacific side to Nogales and Ciudad Juárez in the center and to Nuevo Laredo, Reynosa, and

Matamoros on the Gulf of Mexico. The populations of their twin cities on the US side of the border, from San Diego and Calexico, to Nogales and El Paso, to Laredo, McAllen, and Brownsville, have grown by 20 percent during this period, largely through Hispanic migration—legal and illegal—drawn by US factories and farms in and around these centers. A striking feature of the US side of the border is that it also has shifted rapidly from being an agricultural area to being a mainly industrial area.

Some of the *maquiladoras* are located in the center of the country, in such cities as Aguascalientes, Guadalajara, and Mexico City. They employ only about 40 percent of the number of workers employed in the northern border zone, nearly half of them in clothing and textiles. In contrast, the better-paying, higher-technology industries, such as electronics and motor vehicles, are the dominant ones of the northern zone. A limited number of *maquiladoras* are located in the far south, in Yucatán, where they take advantage of their proximity to the US East Coast by air and sea.

While ownership of the *maquiladoras* is largely a mixture of US and Mexican interests, the ownership share varies with the distance from the border. US companies own over 60 percent of the equity in border centers, with 30 percent owned by Mexican firms and the remainder controlled by foreign interests, mainly Japanese. In the center of the country, Mexican interests own nearly 80 percent. The proportions in the north reflect not only geographic proximity but also the emphasis of US capital on electronics and motor vehicle industries.[15] The *maquiladoras* program in Central America, as well as in Mexico, is not without its critics. Low wages and substandard workplaces have aroused the opposition of liberal and labor forces within the United States. This has led to sporadic boycotts of firms that contract for or sell goods to US consumers. However, the general response in the producing countries is that the job opportunities afforded by the program to poverty-stricken, jobless native workers outweigh whatever abuses may be taking place.

The *maquiladoras* formally ceased to exist on January 1, 2001, when tariffs on manufactured goods between the United States and Mexico were completely phased out under NAFTA. However, the industrial structural and locational patterns that were set during the 1990s remain firm. In all likelihood, Mexico will continue to emphasize its export industry and the northern border zone will benefit from partnership with the United States. In the near future, the zone may well be converted from ENT to the country's second ecumene.

This is not to imply that the *maquiladoras* have been an unmixed blessing for Mexico's north. The higher-wage structure in the zone has contributed to the geographical shift of *maquiladoras* to lower-wage areas within the country's center and south and to Central America. When the peso strengthened against the dollar in 2003, a large transfer of factories to Malaysia, Thailand, Sri Lanka, and the Philippines took place. About 300,000 jobs were lost, as the *maquiladoras* workforce declined from a 2001 peak of 1.2 million to 900,000. Losses were especially heavy in the apparel and textile industry, which is footloose and dependent upon cheap labor. Since then there has been a recovery so that the labor force along the northern border has risen to 1.1 million, accounting for nearly half of Mexico's merchandise exports. The high-added-value industries, such as electronics, transportation vehicles, and chemicals have led to this rise. The program had been designed in part to slow legal and illegal immigration from Mexico to the United States but may have provoked the opposite effect. Some urbanized Mexican factory workers who have recently enjoyed higher living standards and now find themselves unemployed feel greater pressures than ever to seek work north of the border. Nevertheless, the export base of northern Mexico's industries is now solid. The greatest challenge lies in strengthening the urban fabric of the cities that have grown because of the *maquiladoras*. Tijuana, for example, has doubled in size and cannot handle the housing, educational, social, and environmental problems caused by its sudden growth. Many workers live in shacks, and there are severe shortages of power and clean water. Neither the Mexican government nor the United States, which have so enthusiastically sponsored the program that provides free land, power, and water to US factory owners, have taken significant steps to remedy the problems of the border cities.

While vast disparities of income characterize Mexico, the gap is greatest between the Spanish-Amerindian and white population and the indigenous Amerindian population, who constitute 30 percent of the total population. This disparity is most keenly felt in the ENT's southernmost part, especially in the states of Oaxaca and Chiapas. Poverty has been the driving force in sustaining the Zapatista rebels of Chiapas, drawn from indigenous Indian peasants who have long been exploited by wealthy landholders. Chiapas is a state steeped in ancient Maya traditions, and the Zapatista National Liberation Army, which raised the flag of independence in 1994, thrives on this Indian sense of separateness in dialect and social customs.

By 1996, the Mexican army had driven the Zapatistas into jungle hideouts. In the Accord of San Andrés, the Mexican government offered limited political autonomy, in response to which the leadership of the Zapatistas adopted a policy of nonviolence. The offer was never put into law by the administration of President Ernesto Zedillo, and discussions broke down. However, after the election of President Vicente Fox in 2000, peace talks were renewed. In a dramatic march to Mexico City in 2001, the Zapatistas declared an end to the war and the conversion of their movement into a political, rather than military, one. Renouncing their use of weapons, most of the Zapatistas have shifted their focus to political action, trying to organize a broad leftist coalition, with the goal of gaining power through the ballot. They have persisted in this policy despite police crackdowns in 2006 on some rebel remnants.

Empty Areas

Mexico has a number of empty areas that are either too mountainous or too dry to support populations. The most extensive ones are in the northwest and far south. One of the largest is the arid and desolate Baja California Peninsula, which is separated from the rest of the country by the Gulf of California (Mar de Cortés). Stretches of the coast in Sonora, along the eastern side of the gulf, are also desert.

Farther east, the Sierra Madre supports few people, as do its arid interior-facing slopes and the desert basins that lie beyond. In the far south, the empty areas include the tropical lowlands of Chiapas that border Guatemala and contain the sites of ruined Mayan cities as well as the interior tropical hardwood forests of southern Campeche State in the Yucatán Peninsula, which adjoin Belize and Guatemala.

Boundaries

Mexico's formal boundaries are not now in dispute. Conflicting claims over the boundary around El Paso were settled in 1964 and 1967, and in 1965 the treaty was signed, committing the United States to maintaining the freshwater content of the Colorado River, whose waters are used for irrigation and household needs in Mexico. These waters are vulnerable to salinity and chemical pollution from the runoff that upstream American farmers return to the river after drawing its waters for irrigation and applying fertilizers and pesticides to the fields.

Policing the 2,075-mile border between the United States and Mexico is not, however, without difficulty, as US immigration officials seek to stanch the flow of illegal Mexican and Central

American immigrants. For the most part, Mexican authorities cooperate with their northern neighbors, although without the resources or level of commitment of the northern country.

Another boundary of some concern is the border between Chiapas and Guatemala, which has been used as a transshipment zone for drug traffickers and immigrant smugglers. One of the points at issue in the negotiations between the Mexican government and the Zapatistas has been the latter's demand that Mexican troops be withdrawn completely from Chiapas. The government is reluctant to meet this demand fully because of the need to maintain security along the national border.

GEOPOLITICAL FORCES OF ATTRACTION

Trade ties with the United States have deepened with Mexico's industrial diversification. Most of the petroleum that is exported goes to the United States. This represents approximately one-fifth of total US imports, which is nearly on a par with US imports from Canada, Venezuela, and Saudi Arabia. Mexico's declining oil-field production and increasing domestic consumption do not pose an imminent supply problem for the United States because of the rapid increase in US oil production. On the other hand, Mexico has become a net importer of natural gas via pipeline from the United States. Over half of the motor vehicles produced go to the United States, one-third are reserved for the domestic market, and the remainder are exported to Latin America. In level of trade, Mexico is topped only by the EU, Canada, and Japan as a leading trading partner of the United States. The fact that two-thirds of the country's export and import trade is with the United States creates an overwhelming economic dependence of Mexico on its northern neighbor. While this dependence offers considerable benefits to Mexico in terms of economic growth and prosperity, it carries with it the risk of sharp economic declines when the United States suffers serious recessions, as was the case in 2001–2 and 2007–9. These trade ties are likely to continue to expand as European, Japanese, and South American companies, seeking access to a tariff-free US market, locate factories in Mexico.

Three other important geopolitical forces of attraction between the two countries are tourism, immigration, and drugs. Mexico is now the country of origin of the largest number of immigrants to the United States, generating approximately one-quarter of the annual immigration. If illegal immigrants were counted, the annual figure would be far higher.

So heavy is this flow of immigrants that Hispanics, the majority Mexican, account for one-third of registered voters in New Mexico, over 20 percent in Texas, and over 15 percent in California and Arizona. (Hispanics now account for 15 percent of the total US population, while African Americans represent 13 percent.) Many of the immigrants come from Mexico's northern tier of border states. Despite the growth of the economy in this area, the United States remains a magnet for unemployed urban *maquiladoras* workers and Mexicans from the northern rural areas, where limited arable land combined with overpopulation have produced a large, impoverished populace. Even greater numbers of immigrants to the United States originate from the arid, poverty-stricken farm areas of central Mexico, north of the capital. Population in many parts of such drought-parched agricultural states as Zacatecas, Jalisco, and Guanajuato has declined precipitously as illegal migrants from this region have found their way to the United States.

Proximity of the United States and contacts with friends and relatives already living there represent another "pull" factor, as do employment opportunities in agriculture, construction, and services. To complete the loop, the "migro-dollars" that are remitted from the United

States stimulate economic activity, especially in the northern section. These remittances are second only to oil as the country's source of foreign earnings. Representing 20 percent of all persons of Mexican origin, the American-Mexican citizens in the United States have a powerful political as well as economic impact on their homeland. Indeed, there is a movement within some Mexican political circles to allow migrants who reside in the United States to vote in state and national elections and to draw some of the successful émigrés back into the country to seek public office.

Another interactive force is the flow of drugs across the border from Mexico to the United States. This has increased as Colombian drug cartels have shifted some of their bases to Mexican border cities. To monitor and interdict the flow, US authorities need the cooperation of their Mexican counterparts. While such cooperation has been given only grudgingly in the past, it seems to have been strengthened recently. It is hard to measure the value of such cooperation in monetary terms, but Washington's help in refinancing Mexico's external debt when its economy collapsed in 1995 reflected an acknowledgment that Mexico's importance to the United States had risen with US dependence on Mexico's help in the war against drugs. The results, however, have been disappointing. In fact, some Mexicans argue that US support for the war against the cartels has served only to increase the bloodshed.

Recognition of mutual need is a powerful factor in bringing nations together, and the geopolitical ties between the United States and Mexico reflect such need. The political importance of Mexican-US relations was underscored in the summer of 2001, when the US administration began to consider legalizing up to three million Mexicans working illegally within the United States. Development of a rational immigration policy has been widely discussed ever since, but strong support and opposition to any proposal have stalled legislative action. In favor of a more open policy, which would include pathways to citizenship as well as a guest work program, are farm and factory employers and Hispanic lobbying groups. Strongly opposed are labor unions and residents of border states. General US citizen opinion is wide ranging, including those who take a humanitarian position, those who argue against current illegals coming "to the front" of the line in proposed amnesty programs, and those who fear infiltration by smugglers and terrorists. The last general amnesty, enacted in 1986, granted legal immigrant status to nearly three million persons who had entered the country illegally prior to 1982. This status was also extended to those who had worked as farm laborers for over ninety days. The rationale offered at that time was that such a program would reduce the tide of illegal immigrants, but this did not prove to be the case. Infiltration from Mexico and elsewhere will continue as long as conditions of extreme poverty persist. Mexico's small farmers continue to be battered by NAFTA free-trade policies and plummeting market prices for such crops as corn, rice, coffee, and sugarcane. Thus farm abandonment is not likely to slow down or to cease affecting the annual movement of illegals.

A genuine partnership between Mexico and the United States would benefit both countries. In the past the relationship has been one sided and summed up in the saying "When Uncle Sam catches a cold, Mexico sneezes." Today's reality is that when either catches a cold, both sneeze. Mexico's economic importance to the United States manifests itself in many ways—it is the third-largest trading partner of the United States, a secure provider of 10 to 12 percent of its oil imports, an indispensable source of farm labor, and a favored tourist destination. Mexicans who have migrated to the cities and suburbs of Chicago, New York, Los Angeles, Houston, and Dallas are a reliable pool of workers in construction, trucking, and landscaping.

The need to put an end to the flow of drugs across the border is a joint problem. Mexican drug cartels, which have taken control of much of northern Mexico's border states from Colombian cartels, have created chaos there. This has spilled over into the United States, the cartels' largest market for their wares. The violence in Ciudad Juárez extends into El Paso, and Tijuana drug gangs are active in San Diego neighborhoods. Matamoros, which is twinned with Brownsville, has become a battleground as cartel gangs kidnap, kill, or press-gang migrants from central Mexico and Central America who seek work in the fields and factories of northeastern Mexico or use it as a passageway into the United States. It is estimated that as many as three hundred thousand Mexicans are now employed in the drug business, many recruited from jobless youth in the North. Elsewhere, in the state of Michoacán, local self-defense militias have been organized to battle drug cartels such as the Knights Templars. Federal troops have entered the fray, disarming the militias and taking up the battle directly.

While much of the cocaine traffic that used to go from Colombia to the United States via the Caribbean has now declined, Bolivia and Peru have taken up some of the slack. Much of this traffic now goes through such Mexican Pacific ports as Mazanillo and Acapulco, and Merida and the Yucatán on the Atlantic side serve as transit points for the drugs destined for the US market.

While war rages in this borderland region, Washington is held hostage by the American gun lobby, which enables the selling of weapons to the cartels that are more sophisticated than those in the hands of the Mexican army and police.

That Mexico is rife with corruption is not debatable, and US assistance to the Mexican government to uproot this corruption is imperative. However, when 40 percent of the Mexican population earns less than $2.00 a day, of whom 18 percent live on $1.00 per diem, it is no mystery that illegal immigrants and drugs flow across the border. Real and virtual fences do not prevent the one million illegal border crossers who are apprehended each year from trying repeatedly, while countless others succeed. It is in the interests of the United States as well as Mexico to fight the dire poverty.

US priorities in foreign economic aid are askew. In 2009, Washington provided Afghanistan with $3 billion in economic assistance, $2.2 billion to Iraq, $1.5 billion to Egypt, and $1.3 billion to Pakistan. Mexico received $465 million, reduced to $205 million in 2013. This is not to speak of the cost of the wars in Iraq and Afghanistan, which have amounted to over $2 trillion since 9/11, while the drug war rages on our border. Much of these moneys should be diverted to a Marshall Plan for Mexico.

Without large-scale American economic aid and investments, China could become a major economic force in Mexico through investments and economic aid and thereby influence its foreign policy. Indications of this are the negotiations between Colombia, Peru, and Chile, which are being joined by Mexico to create an integrated Latin American financial system and ultimately a common market. A major and stated objective in these negotiations is to create instruments to attract foreign investment and trade, especially with China.

What will probably awaken US politicians to the need to shift resources and inject massive economic aid into Mexico is a change not in global strategic thinking but in American electoral politics. Addressing the anti-Hispanic immigration sentiment in key states is becoming ever more urgent. The US census of 2010 reveals that the country has 50 million persons of Hispanic origin, which is 16 percent of the total population of 320 million. Thirty-eight percent live in California and 25 percent in Texas. It is estimated that about two-thirds of the US Hispanic population is of Mexican origin. The US Mexican populace consists of two groups—the descendants of Mexicans whose roots as US citizens go back over two centuries to the time of the Mexican Cession, and the Chicanos—the first- and second-generation working-class immigrants. Led by the more affluent and politically sophisticated earlier Mexican Americans, both groups are pressing for immigration reform and increased economic aid, and the weight of this political bloc may succeed in shifting Washington's priorities.

The US Census Bureau has projected that given current birthrates, by 2019 the minority population of the United States under the age of eighteen will become the majority. The single largest increase in this age group is among Hispanics, whose birthrates are far above those of non-Hispanic whites. Given the preponderance of Mexicans in this group and their concentration in California, Texas, New Mexico, Arizona, and Illinois, as well as a strong presence in many other states, the meaning of "Montezuma's revenge" may well shift from a stomach disorder to their political dominance in key US states. Will Washington take the steps now to forge the necessary partnership with Mexico or wait until pressured to do so by demographic realities?

Middle America

Middle America, while geographically distinct, is a subregion that is geopolitically part of North America; both are within the maritime realm. The area includes the islands of the Caribbean, Central America, and the northern coastlands of South America, from the Gulf of Darién through Venezuela and the Guyanas. Colombia might also be pulled into the region because of the growing intensity of its relations with the United States.

Venezuela is a "bridge" country that geographically could be considered part of either Middle or South America. Its highlands and Orinoco savannas and jungles are extensions of South America; its coastlands are part of the Caribbean. The geopolitical consequences of this position as well as oil wealth enabled the late president Hugo Chávez of Venezuela to extend his socialist "Bolivarian revolution" from Cuba and Nicaragua into the southern continent.

Approximately a century ago, Ellen Churchill Semple noted the geographical similarities between the New World's Gulf of Mexico-Caribbean basin, which she termed "the American Mediterranean," and the interior sea of the Old World Mediterranean.[16] Nicholas Spykman described the American Mediterranean geopolitically as the area over which the United States held absolute hegemony.[17]

THE FOUR STAGES OF US-MIDDLE AMERICA ASSOCIATION

There is no doubt that the United States has acted as the hegemon of Middle America throughout the twentieth century. Its involvement in Caribbean affairs, however, antedates the era of hegemony, as reflected in the four stages of association that have marked their relationships.

Stage 1: The Era of Defensive Posture

With the emergence of the United States as an independent nation, Americans had a legitimate fear of European states using their Caribbean island bases and Mexico to dominate the Gulf of Mexico and Mississippi, thereby confining the United States to the Eastern Seaboard. In addition, Americans themselves were attracted by the wealth of the Indies—sugar, rum, and slaves—to which the subsistence colonial economy stood in marked contrast.

Stage 2: The Era of Aggressive Intervention

After the issue of slavery had been resolved in the United States by the Civil War, northern as well as southern voices were raised in favor of US expansion into the Caribbean and Central America. The interests were commercial, humanitarian, and strategic. By the turn of the century and following the Spanish-American War of 1898, military and economic considerations had become sufficiently pressing to inspire a series of US interventions in Cuba, Haiti, the Dominican Republic, Nicaragua, and Panama. The weight of the strategic considerations increased with the growth of population and industry in the US Gulf states and the opening of the Panama Canal in 1914. The canal permitted California to be more closely tied to the eastern United States and helped Washington to extend its influence across the Pacific. The Good Neighbor policy of the 1930s represented a less emotional and more sympathetic approach to US relations with Latin America but without any essential change in its aggressive actions toward the rest of the hemisphere.

Stage 3: The Cold War Fear of Counter-encirclement

Fidel Castro overthrew the regime of Fulgencio Batista in 1959 and soon declared himself a Marxist-Leninist and allied the country with the Soviet Union. Communist Cuba, in and of itself, represented no military challenge to US security. But the United States indeed would have been threatened had the USSR succeeded in basing nuclear missiles on the island in 1962, as the Soviets attempted to do, following Cuba's crushing of the US-sponsored Bay of Pigs invasion. However, Washington's instantaneous challenge to the Soviet incursion caused Moscow to back off. In so doing, the Soviet Union recognized American strategic primacy within its geopolitical region. US retention of its Guantánamo Bay naval base at the southeastern tip of Cuba helped to assure this primacy. Sometimes referred to as "the Pearl Harbor of the Atlantic," Guantánamo overlooks the Windward Passage, one of the two narrow openings between the Atlantic and the Caribbean. The other opening, the Mona Passage, was controlled by US naval bases in Puerto Rico.

Dismantling of the Soviet missile bases did not restrain the USSR from continuing to pour military and economic aid into Cuba. However, with the exception of Cuban troops who operated in Nicaragua in support of the Sandinistas, direct Cuban military intervention took place outside the Western Hemisphere—in Angola, Ethiopia, and other countries in Africa and the Middle East.

Castro did seek to export Communism to other parts of the Caribbean and South America by supporting revolutionary movements in such countries as Guatemala, El Salvador, Venezuela, Uruguay, and Bolivia. But the support was through arms to guerrilla movements, not through troops. Only in Nicaragua, where the Sandinistas seized power in 1979, and in Grenada, for a limited four-year period, did Cuban and Soviet efforts succeed in helping to sustain Marxist regimes.

While it was clear to most American and international policy makers that Cuba represented no military threat to the United States, Washington's embargo of Cuba continued not just through the Cold War era but into the present. It is an outdated policy that has become increasingly ineffective as international opinion has overwhelmingly favored the lifting of sanctions and foreign investors in Cuba have ignored them.

Stage 4: The Era of the "Benevolent Policeman"

Advancing democracy and human rights became the new US Middle American policy in the early 1980s, as Castro's influence had ebbed. In 1982 Washington pressured the Honduran military government to hold free elections, even as the United States continued to support bases in that country to bolster the Contras in their war against Nicaragua's Sandinista government.

In the 1983 "comic opera war," US troops invaded Grenada to "protect" American medical students there and prevent reestablishment of a Marxist regime. The United States promoted democratic elections rather than permitting the Grenadan army, which had just overthrown the previous revolutionary government and executed Prime Minister Maurice Bishop, to remain in power.

In 1985 Washington withdrew support from the Guatemalan military to permit democratic elections in that country. Four years later, Panama was invaded by twenty-five thousand US troops, who toppled the dictator, Manuel Noriega, and took him to the United States, where he was convicted and jailed for drug trafficking.

The United States continued its "benevolent policeman" policy as the collapse of the Soviet empire in 1989, and the USSR itself in 1991, threw Cuba into an economic tailspin and increased its regional political isolation. With the elimination of the Soviet Union as a factor within Middle America and with the weakening of Cuba, Washington felt free to abandon right-wing military regimes that it had supported on the basis of their anticommunism. When in 1990 Nicaragua's repressive Sandinista government was ousted in democratic elections, the United States hastened to support the new government. The Sandinistas had called the elections in response to widespread unrest and unpopularity, as the national economy had deteriorated under the pressure of the American trade embargo and the reduction in Soviet economic aid.

Ironically, in free elections held in 2006, Daniel Ortega, the revolutionary leader who had been ousted from office, was elected to the presidency by a population fed up with the corruption of parties to both the right and left. He has secured aid from Venezuela and Iran in building the country's first deepwater port, housing, and hydroelectric plants while exporting coffee, meat, and bananas to Iran. A replay did not take place of the 1980s support by Washington of the overthrow of the Sandinistas by the Contra militias. Instead, the United States is encouraging Nicaragua's economic development, promoting its membership in the Dominican Republic-Central America Free Trade Agreement (CAFTA-DR). Free trade alone will not lift Nicaragua and its neighbors out of poverty. It must be accompanied by foreign aid to upgrade physical infrastructure and health and education services and to supplement the incomes of the region's small farmers so that they can compete against highly subsidized US farm imports.

In Guatemala, Washington welcomed the end of the civil war in 1996. The peace accord signed by the government and the leftist rebels opened the way for constitutional reforms. This later prompted President Bill Clinton to apologize for the considerable military aid that previous US administrations had provided the Guatemalan armed forces and the repressive military regimes. During the "dirty war," fought between right-wing oligarchs supported by the United States and left-wing rebels, two hundred thousand were killed or disappeared. Indigenous Mayans, caught in the middle of the conflict, had their villages burned, and many were killed, tortured, or raped. Since the 1996 peace accord, many of the government soldiers, militias, and intelligence agents have morphed into gangs involved in the drug trade and kidnappings for ransom.

In violence-torn Haiti, US intervention restored the ousted Jean-Bertrand Aristide to the presidency in 1994. What followed was an unsuccessful venture in peacekeeping by American troops under the UN banner. The troops were ultimately withdrawn as a result of continual political crises and governmental paralysis. UN peacekeeping intervention was required again in 2004, when Aristide was ousted from power by rebels and fled the country. Gang violence has since abated, and free elections were held in 2006. Nevertheless, this poorest country in the region, where nearly 80 percent of the people live on less than $2.00 a day, continues to lack the foundation for political stability.

GEOPOLITICAL FEATURES

The various states and dependent territories of Middle America have, for the most part, immature geopolitical features. There is no historical core or contemporary political capital that has region-wide influence. The only countries that have well-defined ecumenes with substantial industrial features are Cuba, at its western end around Havana; Venezuela, on its northern coast, from Caracas west to Maracaibo; and Puerto Rico, in greater San Juan. Most of the countries of the region also have limited ENTs, the major exception being the grasslands of Venezuela's Orinoco Valley.

Boundaries

Ironically, boundaries, which had given little cause for dispute in modern times, have again become points of contention in Central America. Honduras and Nicaragua clashed over fishing rights in their Pacific waters in the 1980s and are now engaged in a much wider dispute over their sea border in the Caribbean. Under contention is fifty thousand square miles of water and two tiny islets. The Organization of American States (OAS) is attempting to mediate the dispute.

Another boundary quarrel has erupted between Nicaragua and Costa Rica over the use of the San Juan River, which forms the border between them. Again, the OAS has been asked to intervene.

A third dispute is between Guatemala and Belize, the former British Honduras, which received its independence in 1980.[18] In the negotiations that led up to independence, Guatemala had indicated that it would be satisfied with a more limited area and access to a free port at Belize City. The United Nations affirmed the territorial integrity of Belize, and in 1991 Guatemala dropped most of its claims except for one regarding a section in the far south. However, in 2000, the dispute over that area broke out again, resulting in some minor skirmishing.

Still another boundary issue has to do with Venezuela's claim to all of Guyana west of the Essequibo River—more than half of Guyana's total land area. The claim surfaces from time to time, although recently it has been quiescent. Venezuela is also in contention with Colombia over the maritime boundary between the two countries in the oil-rich waters of the Gulf of Venezuela. Particularly at issue is control of Los Monjes Islands, which lie off the Guajira Peninsula, at the northeastern tip of Venezuela. The islands were occupied by Venezuela in the 1950s, but the issue of Colombia's oil-drilling rights in the surrounding waters of the gulf is unresolved.

A Middle American boundary that is not in political contention yet is probably the most serious of all Central American flash points is Panama's southern border with Colombia. The 170-mile line cuts across the dense tropical rain forests of the Darién Gap (so named because of the gap in the Pan-American Highway system at Panama's southernmost province of Darién). This boundary is readily crossed by drug traffickers heading north from Colombia and smugglers moving arms southward from such Central American countries as Nicaragua and Panama to Colombian left-wing guerrillas.

The Darién Gap has long attracted smuggling, and the unintended consequence of the US-supported Plan Colombia to fight Colombian drug activity is to increase smuggling activities within the province of Darién. While most of the effort under the plan is directed against coca growers and processors in the far south of Colombia (in Putumayo province along the Ecuador border), actions are also directed at another area of production and guerrilla activity, Antioquia, which borders Panama. Narco-guerrillas operating in Antioquia have forced hundreds of refugees to flee across the border into Panama. The guerrillas use Antioquia's jungles as safe havens as well as for arms smuggling routes.

For Panama, which has no army, securing the border is difficult. This security situation has increased the burdens on its police, already heavily engaged in trying to crack down on contraband and drugs that flow through Colón, the second-largest free-trade zone in the world. Without substantial US financial and other aid to secure the border of Panama, the area is likely to become a tinderbox.

GEOPOLITICAL FORCES OF ATTRACTION AND SEPARATION

Overall, the boundaries and other geopolitical features play relatively minor roles in determining geopolitical destinies in Middle America. The determining elements are those geopolitical forces that shape the subregion's relationships with North America.

Geopolitical Forces of Attraction

The most compelling centripetal, or disruptive, force is location, both strategic and economic-demographic. Strategically, the Caribbean islands may be viewed as the northern and eastern sides of a frame that encloses the interior sea, with the Central American coastlands on the west. The northern side of the island frame is of particular significance to the United States. It consists of two "walls"—the Bahamas, which constitute the outer wall, and the Greater Antilles, which are the inner one. Through this part of the frame, traffic is channeled in three major passageways: the Florida Straits and the Windward and Mona Passages. Atlantic-Gulf shipping of the US maritime ring moves via the Florida Straits, while Atlantic-Pacific shipping moves via the Windward Passage and the Panama Canal. Much of the Venezuelan-US traffic uses the Mona Passage, between Puerto Rico and Hispaniola.

The eastern edge of the frame consists of the Lesser Antilles. These smaller and less-populous portions of the Caribbean are mostly European dependencies, although American bases are spotted throughout. Shipping to Europe moves via St. Thomas at the northern end and Trinidad at the southern end of this island string. The US Navy has traditionally guarded the waters of the American Mediterranean from such bases as those at Key West, Florida; Guantánamo Bay, Cuba; Puerto Rico; and Panama. A naval base was established at Chaguaramas, Trinidad, at the onset of World War II, but the lease has been abandoned. So have bases in Panama and Puerto Rico.

The Guantánamo naval base has long been an irritant in US-Cuban relations. Allegations of prison abuses there to those captured in Iraq and Afghanistan have marshaled human rights advocates and opponents of the Iraq War to demand that the prison be closed.

Time and technological change have greatly diminished the strategic importance of these bases. Long-range aircraft operating from the US mainland and self-supporting naval battle fleets can easily dominate the Caribbean Sea. The narrowness of the Panama Canal and its locks structure has eliminated its use as a passageway for aircraft carriers and nuclear submarines. Indeed, the canal itself lost much of its importance to the United States, as it now carries only 12 percent of US waterborne commerce. This has now changed because in 2006, Panama approved construction of a third set of locks, deepening and widening the navigation channels and raising the elevation of Gatun Lake. When completed, this will enable the canal to handle the largest container vessels. Target date for completion is 2014, and the Panama Canal Authority anticipates that the canal will handle substantially increased traffic between the US East and Gulf Coasts and China and the Asia-Pacific Rim.

In 1979, Washington began to anticipate its eventual withdrawal from the Canal Zone when it signed a treaty with Panama that guaranteed the neutrality of the canal. American support of the right-wing regimes of Omar Torrijos and Manuel Noriega (until the latter's drug trafficking became an embarrassment) only served to increase popular anti-US sentiment and turn the country toward neutrality. The US Southern Command headquarters was moved in 1997 from the Canal Zone to an air force station in Miami. By the time the Canal Zone reverted to Panama at the end of 1999, the use of the Howard Air Force Base, located within the zone, had become limited to surveillance efforts seeking to interdict the flow of cocaine and other drugs to the United States. Only a dozen aircraft were permanently stationed there, as it had become a forward-support airfield for fighters, tankers, and surveillance jets that passed through to operate over the skies of Colombia and other Andean countries. To replace this closed US Panama base, alternative sites with only limited military installations and infrastructures are required.

The proximity of much of the Caribbean basin to the US maritime ring is an aspect of its locational attraction. The Florida Straits, between the Florida Keys and Cuba, are only ninety miles wide, while the stretch of water between Grand Bahama and West Palm Beach is only sixty-five miles. New York City is seventeen hundred miles from Puerto Rico, fourteen hundred miles from the Dominican Republic, and one thousand miles from the Bahamas—in each case within two to three hours' flying time. New Orleans is six hundred miles from Cuba and one thousand miles from Jamaica, while South Florida is 750 miles from Honduras and 1,200 miles from the Panama Canal. These distances have made the Caribbean highly accessible to American tourists and business and have facilitated the flow of migrants and visitors from the basin to the mainland United States.

Access cannot be measured solely in miles and time distance, as those who have sought to escape from Cuba will attest, but proximity is a powerful force of attraction. It enables migrants from Middle America to maintain close contacts with families and friends who remain in the homeland. These contacts are the basis for networks that have developed to facilitate additional migration and to direct newcomers to supportive communities on the mainland. They also help to maintain cultural and familial bonds. From cities such as New York, for example, there is an annual exodus of migrants from Puerto Rico, the Dominican Republic, Jamaica, and smaller islands back to their Caribbean homelands for the winter holidays and even longer periods.

Another powerful centripetal force is the complementarity of climate and physiography as well as resources. From a strategic point of view, the petroleum that the United States imports from Canada, Mexico, and Venezuela is a compelling factor in the geopolitical linking of North and Middle America. These three countries provide the United States with its nearest and most secure sources of supplementary supply. The anti-US stance of the Chávez and the successor Nicolás Maduro governments in Venezuela and the nationalization of its oil industry cast some doubt on the reliability of this source. It is likely that the major international oil companies will find ways of continuing to provide technical services and capital investments, as they have in other countries that have either nationalized or taken majority control of their oil industries. However, US oil imports from Venezuela will soon be drastically reduced or eliminated as American oil and gas production continues to expand, supported by alternative energy sources.

Tourism is a major aspect of the Caribbean basin economy and the mainstay of some of the smaller islands. For visitors from the northern parts of the United States and from Canada, the Caribbean winter's warm climate, clear and warm waters, cooling easterly trade winds, and relatively dry weather are welcome relief from northern winters. In addition, the physical landscapes, which range from low-lying reefs, long, sandy beaches, and sheltered coves to volcanic mountains add to the region's attractiveness to visitors. In Central America, tourism has been stimulated by the wealth of archaeological sites and by ecotourism in the zones of tropical forests, with their diversity of plant and animal life.

Complementarity extends also to the agricultural sector. While plantation crops no longer dominate the economy of Middle America as they once did, sugar remains the economic mainstay of Cuba and is a major component of the economies of Barbados, the Dominican Republic, and Jamaica. Honduras is still highly dependent upon bananas, Haiti and Guatemala on coffee, and Belize on lumber. These and other plantation crops, such as cacao, henequen, and tobacco, are also widely grown in neighboring countries and find their markets in the United States and Canada.

Among the most important Middle American minerals for the United States have been petroleum from Venezuela, bauxite from Suriname and Jamaica, and petroleum and natural gas from Trinidad. When ultranationalistic President Hugo Chávez of Venezuela cut oil production to drive up prices in keeping with OPEC guidelines, that country, which had been the single largest petroleum exporter to the United States, dropped to number four, behind Canada, Mexico, and Saudi Arabia. By 2013 Venezuela accounted for only 10 percent of US imports, and they continue to decline. Hugo Chávez's oil policies were politically as well as economically guided. He cemented relations with selected Caribbean and South American countries by supplying them. This was particularly important for Cuba, which was able to barter the exchange of the services of thousands of medical doctors for petroleum.

The dependence of the Caribbean basin on farming, tourism, oil, and bauxite provides an inadequate base to meet the employment needs of its growing population. However, with the exception of Puerto Rico and Venezuela, manufacturing has made little headway in most of the region. There has been some outsourcing of apparel production to Costa Rica, Guatemala, Haiti, and Jamaica—the latter is also a substantial producer of alumina—but these activities have done little to change the economic structure of the region.

Thus much of the Caribbean remains mired in poverty, save areas that specialize in financial services, tourism, or oil exports. Among the pockets of prosperity are the Bahamas (tourism), Barbados (sugar processing and diverse manufactures), Trinidad (oil and gas), and Antigua and Barbuda (tourism). For most of the Caribbean and Central America, however, poverty is endemic and is most acute in Honduras and Haiti.

Venezuela is in the middle-income range, but its oil wealth has yet to raise the standard of living of its depressed classes. Moreover, persistent inflation and shortage of goods has depressed living standards not only for the poor but also for the middle classes. Grinding poverty, poor soils, and lack of land are the "push" factors for migration to the United States. The eighty-five million population of the Caribbean and Central America accounts for a substantial number of the illegals who enter the United States. Of these, the largest number come from five countries—the Dominican Republic, Guatemala, Jamaica, Haiti, and El Salvador. There are special provisions for Cubans. Those who do not secure legal visas and attempt to enter illegally, mostly via Mexico, are allowed to enter provisionally when they reach the US border and are granted legal immigration status after one year. Land pressures in Central America are high, with population density exceeding six hundred persons per square mile in Jamaica, Haiti, and El Salvador. Rural overpopulation and limited arable lands are aggravated by birthrates, which in most of the countries range from just under a 2 percent to a 3 percent increase per annum.

Poverty is not the only basis for the magnet effect of the United States. For Cubans and those who have fled other repressive regimes of both the right and left, strong attractions are opportunities for education and political and economic freedom. So is the desire to generate "migro-dollars" to support kinfolk who remain in the home region.

The drug trade, money laundering, and arms smuggling have also become powerful "pull" factors. While hardly a positive force of attraction, they nevertheless demand a continued US interest and involvement in the region. Interdicting the flow of drugs from the Andean region of South America requires new forward bases for air surveillance. With the closing of the Panama bases, the United States, which has had a military base in Honduras, has developed a facility there for drug surveillance and interdiction missions. Similar air stations have been established in El Salvador and the Dutch Islands of Aruba and Curaçao to aid in the surveillance of traffic from northern Colombia across the Caribbean. For Andes surveillance, an Ecuadorian air force base at the Pacific port city of Manta has provided a US air facility to monitor air and sea activities in southern Colombia. However, the Ecuadorian government refused to extend the lease, which terminated in 2009. The United States also has radar sites, some fixed and some mobile, to monitor drug routes in seventeen countries, including Peru and Colombia.

Honduras plays a pivotal role in this drug trade. Most of the cocaine from Colombia and Peru is transferred by air to the Honduran section of the Mosquito Coast. It is estimated that 40 percent of the cocaine destined for the United States comes through this coast. US counter-narcotic forces which operate clandestinely in Honduras refer to this region as a "battle space." The two hundred thousand Miskito Indians who are the coast's main inhabitants have historically resisted central governmental control. They carve out illegal landing strips for small aircraft that move the drugs and then transfer them by boat or overland to Guatemala and Mexico. From there they are smuggled into the United States. Honduran government efforts to interdict this trade have been fruitless, despite the considerable financial and training support provided by Washington.

The country is by far the most violent of Central American states. It is plagued not only by drug trafficking but also by gang violence and a weak and corrupt government. It has the highest murder rate in the world—double the Central American average—while many members of its small police force are corrupt. As a consequence, civilian militias have arisen to protect Hondurans in their localities, and immigration to the United States has increased. While the country's economic base is supported by foreign-owned factories, call centers, and remittances from abroad, the national government is economically and politically shaky.

The configuration of land and water explains why Jamaica, Haiti, Cuba, the Bahamas, and the Virgin Islands are the chief stepping-stones for the South American drug trade and the reason that the United States is so intent upon building surveillance mechanisms within or surrounding these islands. The Virgin Islands, only one thousand miles from the US mainland, are also take-off points for smuggling illegal immigrants into the United States by plane and ship. Offshore financial service centers have taken advantage of proximity in countries with very permissive tax codes to provide tax havens for investors and centers for laundering money illegally gained. Corporate shells have been established in such centers as the Cayman Islands, Grand Turk, the Bahamas, and Antigua—all close to the United States but also providing ease of air access to Europe and Brazil.

Geopolitical Forces of Separation

Geopolitical unity between North and Middle America is a logical, but not inevitable, consequence of the geographical, strategic, and economic relations between the two regions. Centrifugal forces also characterize these relationships. For the past century, these have been kept in check forcefully by direct or indirect military pressures in addition to having been submerged by the countervailing forces of attraction that have been cited.

Many of the forces for disruption that were latent are now emerging. The resentment against large US corporations that own vast sugar and banana plantations, as well as mineral interests, is based upon the fact that these raw materials are, for the most part, exported for consumption or processing, bringing little value added to the peoples of Middle America. Genuine complementarity would mean that each possesses its fair share of value added. This would be achieved if more food processing were to take place within the region; if some of the bauxite and aluminum from Jamaica and Suriname that is now shipped to the United States were converted to finished products; if Honduran lumber were made into furniture; or if the region's petroleum stores were made into a wider array of petrochemical and plastic products and its hides into shoes and sandals. Most of the apparel making that is now being outsourced from the United States focuses on cheap labor and cheap items. There is a movement by consumer groups to encourage purchase of fair-traded items. Higher-value-added apparel products based on local natural dyes and designs would raise wages for local workers. This is a policy-planning issue for Middle American governments, US economic development aid, and American manufacturers.

While the era of US support of right-wing dictatorships in Middle America is largely over, the question of how to encourage political and economic reform has yet to be adequately addressed. Washington's 1994 military intervention in Haiti went awry because a military presence alone cannot guarantee the transition to democracy. Credible local politicians and a police force free of corruption are necessary to build a full and healthy society. In a country like Haiti, the decade and a half or more that it would have taken to nourish a stable, democratic society proved too long for Washington and the American public. Neither would tolerate keeping forces there indefinitely, as demonstrated by the pullout of US troops in 1999. But Washington must face up to the reality that peacekeeping requires as much energy as waging war. It can and should tolerate a long-range program of aid and investments targeted at building up a middle class, training a governmental bureaucracy, and building a broad educational system.

US support for Middle America's right-wing dictatorships has fostered deep anti-US sentiment in the region. Memories of Washington's support of Venezuela's Marcos Pérez Jiménez, Panama's Torrijos and Noriega, and Cuba's Fulgencio Batista are deeply embedded in the national psyches of those countries. While Venezuela and Cuba embraced leftist ideology, relations with Panama turned positive when US military intervention forced the ouster of General Noriega, whom it had previously backed. Panama now has a bilateral free-trade agreement with the United States, and the only remaining point of contention is Washington's refusal to take direct responsibility for decontaminating military firing ranges left behind when it withdrew from the Panama Canal Zone.

In 2008, Fidel Castro formally handed the reins of power to his brother Raúl. This portended a loosening of state economic controls in favor of a freer market, but the pace of change has been very slow. Under Washington's continuing policies, Cuba is likely to strengthen its economic ties with Europe rather than reengage geopolitically with the United States. If the Cuban American lobby is so powerful that the US Congress is unable to adopt a rational foreign policy, at least planning for the post–Castro brothers era should take into account the opposition of many Cubans to US retention of its Guantánamo Bay naval base. Nestled within the southern basin of Guantánamo Bay, the forty-five-square-mile naval reserve includes airfields and fortifications and is a major training center for the US Atlantic Fleet. It also became the site of a prison encampment for al-Qaeda fighters and other insurgents captured in the wars in Afghanistan and Iraq. The 1903 lease of the land and its 1934 renewal was imposed by the United States. Provisions of the treaty require consent of both governments to revoke it. Since 1960 the Cuban government has rejected these terms and sought return of the land. In 2007 Washington announced plans to move those held in the Guantánamo prison either to the mainland or to other countries. However, there is strong opposition within the United States to moving the prisoners to American soil. The Cubans remain firm in their insistence on a return of the land, but the United States has no plans to abandon the naval base. It is an area for negotiation with some future Cuban government.

Another disruptive military force, the US Navy's use of Puerto Rico's island of Vieques and the naval station of Roosevelt Roads, were major issues for Puerto Rican nationalists, environmentalists, and fishermen. The civil disobedience that in April 1999 prevented the navy from using Vieques as a firing range for the Atlantic Fleet war games became a major political headache for Washington. The storm of opposition to use of the range generated within both Puerto Rico and areas such as New York, Chicago, and Florida that have large Puerto Rican populations finally led to its closing in 2003. Vieques is now being promoted as an ecotourism center, while the Roosevelt Roads airport is to be converted into a civilian airport and its land used for economic development.

The turmoil over the Roosevelt Roads naval reservation led to its closing the following year. It had been founded in 1943 as the central naval and air base commanding the approaches to the Caribbean, at the easternmost tip of the island. The various operational facilities and command structures were transferred to Florida and Texas.

In the 2012 elections for governor of Puerto Rico, the pro-commonwealth party gained 47.7 percent of the vote, the pro-statehood party 47.3 percent, and the independence party only 2.5 percent. With such a razor-thin margin, the statehood forces could prevail in a plebiscite on the future of Puerto Rico. In such an event, reconsideration might be given for relocating military facilities for surveillance and airlift purposes to Puerto Rico. However, given the history of opposition to Vieques and Roosevelt Roads, large-scale installations would not be feasible, considering the island's land needs for tourism, residential, and industrial areas as well as its environmental concerns.

With the loss of its Panamanian bases, the near inevitability of return of Guantánamo to Cuba in a post-Castro era, and the uncertainty that surrounds its Puerto Rican military facilities, the Pentagon needs a long-range strategy for Middle America that is built upon alternative sites.

The surveillance facilities being sought in Honduras, Ecuador, and Peru have only limited functions. For full-scale bases and firing ranges, there may be no alternative, ultimately, but to expand facilities on the US mainland.

CONCLUSION

The integration of Middle America with North America to form a unified geopolitical region is based upon the dependence of the Caribbean basin lands upon the United States and, to some extent, Canada for investment capital, markets, economic aid, tourism, and emigration outlets. Proximity and configuration of its lands and narrow seas combine to make the Caribbean basin strategically vital to the security of the eastern and southern portions of the US maritime ring.

Trade and immigration are major forces of attraction. Washington has forged a free-trade agreement, CAFTA-DR, which includes Guatemala, Honduras, El Salvador, Nicaragua, Costa Rica, and the Dominican Republic. It also has bilateral agreements with other Caribbean states. There is mounting opposition to such agreements, both within the US Congress, which is concerned with the effects of cheap labor on US industry, and in some of the Central American countries, based upon their concerns that subsidized US farm products will even further depress their agriculture. This might be overcome through fiscal and technical support mechanisms that enable Central American farmers to compete with US agriculture.

Mexico has also shown leadership in promoting trade with its Central American neighbors. A free-trade agreement exists among Mexico, El Salvador, Guatemala, and Honduras, while Mexico has separate agreements with both Costa Rica and Nicaragua. The Mexican government has also proposed a "Puebla-to-Panama" plan to integrate efforts at promoting tourism, trade, education, environmental protection, and disaster relief planning among Mexico's nine southern (and poorest) states and their seven Central American neighbors. The projected linking of electric power, telephone, and gas grids within the region would, if implemented, constitute an important geopolitically integrative force.

While the countries of Middle America are too small and poor to attain the partnership levels that Canada and Mexico enjoy with the United States, this does not mean that Washington can ignore their political and cultural sensitivities. The Cold War incentive of US support for right-wing dictatorships is over. It has been replaced by emphasis on economic development as well as actions that encourage democratic government and protection of human rights.

Recent history has demonstrated that heavy-handed military intervention in Middle America does not provide long-range solutions.[19] A more rational policy approach is to expand balanced trade and economic assistance and to use these as leverage when necessary.

The long-term geopolitical status of the Caribbean as part of a unified North and Middle American region is by no means assured. Its strong ties to Maritime Europe and South America, in addition to those that it enjoys with the United States, could develop it into a unique gateway region, tying North and South America with maritime Europe, China, and the Asia-Pacific Rim and serving as an important hinge within the maritime realm. The economic, cultural, and strategic importance of the Caribbean to the United States is indisputable. However, economic ties to Europe are also strong. The fifteen members and five associate members of the Caribbean Community (CARICOM) and ten Caribbean dependencies enjoy preferential entrance to EU markets for bananas, rice, and sugar. In addition, they receive considerable development funds from the EU, by far the leading grant donor to the region, and are recipients of considerable private investment from there.

Cuba and Venezuela represent a different kind of bridge between the Caribbean and South America based upon their commitment to supporting socialist systems within some of the Andean countries. While Brazil has not embraced the radical socialism of these two countries, its commitment is to balancing free-market and social-welfare policies. It is by far the strongest power in South America, and its political influence in the Caribbean is growing.

As its links to Europe, China, and South America strengthen, approaching those with North America, the Caribbean could emerge as a model gateway region due to its geographic location, history, culture, and ethnic mix.

Notes

1. Frederick Jackson Turner, "The Significance of the Frontier in American History" (paper delivered at American Historical Association meeting in Chicago, 1893); reprinted in Turner, *The Frontier in American History* (New York: Henry Holt, 1920), 1–38. The superintendent of the Bureau of the Census had concluded that a frontier line could no longer be traced and that discussions of its extent and westward movement would have no place in future census reports. From this, Turner developed his thesis that with the passing of the frontier the first period in American history was over. It was in the period, Turner held, that free western lands served as the safety valve for the discontented population masses of the East and molded the independent spirit of frontierism.
2. Ellen Churchill Semple, *American History and Its Geographic Conditions* (Boston: Houghton Mifflin, 1903), 397–419; Friedrich Ratzel, *Politische Geographie der Vereinigten Staaten* (Leipzig: Oldenbourg, 1897), 17.
3. Alfred T. Mahan, *The Problem of Asia and Its Effect upon International Policy* (Boston: Little, Brown, 1900), 24–26, 63–65, 84–86.
4. Jon Lee Anderson, "The Commandante's Canal," *New Yorker*, March 10, 2014, 57–60.
5. James Malin, "Space and History: Part 2," *Agricultural History* 18 (July 1944): 65–126.
6. George Cressey, *The Basis of Soviet Strength* (New York: McGraw-Hill, 1945), 245–46.
7. Alexander de Seversky, *Air Power: Key to Survival* (New York: Simon & Schuster, 1950), map facing 312.
8. Richard Lonsdale and J. Clark Archer, "Emptying Areas in the United States, 1990–1995," *Journal of Geography* 96, no. 2 (March/April 1997): 108–22.
9. Fred M. Shelley, J. Clark Archer, Fiona M. Davidson, and Stanley D. Brunn, *Political Geography of the United States* (New York: Guilford, 1996), 235–80.
10. Joel Kotkin, *The New Geography: How the Digital Revolution Is Reshaping the American Landscape* (New York: Random House, 2000), 3–26, 38–51, 130–39.
11. Joseph J. Salvo and Arun Peter Lobo, *The Newest New Yorkers*, 5th ed. (New York: New York City Planning Department, 2013).
12. Shelley et al., *Political Geography of the United States*, 308–35.
13. Derwent Whittlesey, *The Earth and the State* (New York: Holt, 1939), 528–29.
14. Agence France-Presse, *Yahoo! News*, August 10, 2007, http://dailynews.yahoo.com/.
15. Ian MacLachlan and Adrian Guillermo Aguilar, "Maquiladora Myths: Locational and Structural Change in Mexico's Export Manufacturing Industry," *Professional Geographer* 50, no. 3 (1998): 315–31.
16. Semple, *American History and Its Geographic Conditions*, 397–419.
17. Nicholas Spykman, *America's Strategy in World Politics* (New York: Harcourt, Brace, 1942), 51–61.
18. "Central America's Border Order," *Economist*, March 13, 2000, 42.
19. Mattathias Schwarts, "A Mission Gone Wrong," *New Yorker*, January 6, 2014, 44–55.

CHAPTER 6

South America

South America has evolved into an independent geopolitical region that is part of the maritime realm but is no longer the geostrategic satellite of the United States that it was during the Cold War. Soviet penetration of the region during that era through local Communist parties and leftist rebel bands was unsuccessful in overthrowing US-supported governments in such countries as Argentina, Chile, Colombia, Peru, and Uruguay. However, the United States did not promote democracy within the continent, nor did it forge close partnerships with Brazil and Argentina, the two leading powers.

With the collapse of the Soviet Union, South America came to be viewed by the United States as peripheral to its own strategic and economic interests. Along with Sub-Saharan Africa, it became a zone of marginality within the world power structure. This has changed dramatically since the turn of the century with the competition among the United States, maritime Europe, China, and Japan for its resource wealth. Its minerals, timber, agricultural resources, and markets have become greatly sought after. The emergence of Brazil as a dominant regional power on the way to becoming a world power has strengthened South America's role as an independent geopolitical region. Venezuela's support of a "Bolivarian revolution" that would incorporate Bolivia and Ecuador has further separated the continent from the "colossus of the north."

Because it is not geopolitically integrated with North and Middle America, the region is therefore not subject to the same military/strategic influences that the United States can bring to bear on its nearer Latin neighbors in Middle America.

United States–South American Relations

The concept of a unified hemisphere, of Pan-Americanism, was the vision of the Monroe Doctrine, which held that the region was off-limits to European influence and colonization. It was an essentially defensive policy designed to ward off armed intervention or control of those newly established Latin American republics that had revolted from Spain and which the United States considered to be in its own backyard. The objective was to maintain an isolated hemisphere to be shielded from the conflicts of the rest of the world and to protect the republican character of the former Spanish and Portuguese colonies.[1] When Simón Bolívar freed most of the Andean region from Spanish control and created the new Republic of Gran Colombia in 1822, the United States strongly supported its establishment. Initially the countries included were today's Colombia, Venezuela, Ecuador, and Panama. Later, Peru and Alto Peru (now Bolivia) were added to the confederation before it crumbled.

Geography prevented the United States from being able to exercise direct political control in South America—it is too distant, some of the countries are too large, and others are located in terrain too forbidding.

Economics assumed a central role in fostering the concept of the pan-Americanism that was first enunciated by the United States in the Monroe Doctrine—the interventionist policies of Theodore Roosevelt, the control of the Panama Canal, "dollar diplomacy," and Franklin D. Roosevelt's Good Neighbor policy were manifestations of the same objective—to keep Latin America as a strategic reserve for the United States.

The US view of South America's economic importance was strongly influenced by the perceived potential of the Amazon basin (also referred to as "Amazonia" or "Amazonas"). It had long been held to be one of the richest regions of the world, with vast, unexploited mineral, forest, and agricultural resources and access to ocean shipping. This perception was fed by Brazil's rubber boom, which followed Charles Goodyear's invention of vulcanization in 1839. Most of the rubber came from the wild Pará rubber tree in the upper Amazon, which gave Brazil a monopoly on the rubber trade. The boom lasted until the early twentieth century and attracted settlers from the country's northeast, many of whom were put to work under conditions of virtual slavery. With the shift to plantation rubber in Malaya and Sumatra toward the end of the nineteenth century, the Amazonian boom collapsed, as did the African rubber boom. While the Ford Motor Company reintroduced rubber plantations in 1927 and established the town of Fordlândia in the Amazon, it abandoned the scheme after World War II owing to the scarcity of workers.

The idea that the Western Hemisphere could be self-sufficient was as much a fantasy as the concept of a self-sufficient Pan-Eur-Africa. Rather than sustained development, South America's economy has been marked by booms and busts. This was the fate of the mining centers of Peru and, in Brazil, of the brazilwood industry, the sugar plantations of the northeast, the gold of Minas Gerais, the coffee of the Paraíba Valley in eastern São Paulo state, and now the hardwoods of Amazonas. Similar experiences have taken place with the nitrates of northern Chile and the sheep ranches of Patagonia. The economic history of the continent has been one of rapid exploitation and then depletion. Yet the search for quick fortunes continues today with the processing of the coca leaves of Colombia into cocaine and the growing of both sun and shade varieties of Colombian coffee.

The concept of a north-south strategic alignment is not only flawed economically, but it is also misleading spatially. Eastern South America—the most important part of the region—is as near to maritime Europe as it is to the eastern United States. During the 1930s and early 1940s, the idea of a unified hemisphere capable of achieving self-sufficiency was seized upon by American isolationists as a rationale for not intervening in the struggle between Europe's democracies and its Nazi and Fascist regimes.

In many ways, the Cold War struggles between the maritime and Communist powers that took place within the southern continents represented extensions of the panregional concepts. Ironically, much of the struggle took place at a time when it had become generally apparent that these were not the global resource storehouses that they had once been thought to be. Despite Soviet and Cuban efforts to foment Marxist rebellions in various South American countries, they were not able to establish solid footholds within the region, thus sparing the continent from becoming a shatterbelt. Uruguay, Peru, and Colombia were torn by Marxist terrorist activities but did not fall under Moscow's sway. Only Venezuela and Bolivia, through their ties to Cuba, remained Soviet outposts.

In Chile, the Communist Party joined forces with the socialists to enable Salvador Allende to become the first popularly elected Marxist president in Latin America. However, after three years in office, Allende was overthrown by a military coup covertly supported by the United States. Argentina also experienced considerable unrest, first when it was caught between Peronista and Communist forces during the period that followed the first ouster of Juan Perón in the late 1950s and again after he, and then his widow, regained power from 1973 to 1976. The military junta that then took power conducted its "dirty war" against both the Marxists and the Peronistas, thereby keeping the country within the Western orbit. That South America did not become a shatterbelt despite all of this turbulence was because the Soviet Union was too far removed from the region to offset US power.

The Geographical Setting

Cultural geographers find it convenient to divide the Western Hemisphere along the cultural divide of the Rio Grande and to separate Anglo-America from Latin America. This does not apply geopolitically. The strength of the ties between the United States and Middle America, especially Mexico, have overridden the barrier functions of the river as an economic and cultural divide. The unsustainable policy of fencing the entire border between the United States and Mexico in trying to stem the flow of illegal immigrants will not weaken the geopolitical bonds between the two countries. The political power of Hispanics in the US border states, their contributions to the workforce, and cash remittances to their former homelands are far greater centripetal forces.

Another Western Hemispheric divide is framed by the physical environment—the line of the northern Andes-Columbian Cordilleras and the southern Venezuelan-Guiana Highlands that border the Amazon and separate Middle from South America. This is the divide along which the geopolitical boundary has been drawn, assigning the Caribbean countries of Venezuela, Guyana, Suriname, and French Guiana to Middle America. South America is a triangle fronting on two oceans, the Atlantic and Pacific. Two physical features of great magnitude profoundly influence the geopolitical map—the Andes mountains and the Amazon basin. The Andes, with their adjoining forests and deserts, separate western from eastern South America. The Panama Canal has strengthened this condition of separation, making it easier for northwestern South America to communicate with the Caribbean and the North Atlantic than to communicate overland with the rest of South America.

The rain forests, climate, and sparse settlements of Amazonas reinforce the barriers between South and Middle America as well as between the western and eastern parts of South America. Use of the river as a unifying transportation artery between the west coast countries and Brazil has limited value not only because of the Andean barrier but also because of slow and uncertain shipping schedules. From the southern end of Amazonia to Cape Horn, the continent narrows sharply to what is termed the Southern Cone.

Additional forces, other than the Andes and Amazonia, also tend to fragment South America internally. These include the linguistic, cultural, and racial differences that can be traced to many factors, such as sailing directions, local resources, and the rivalry between Spain and Portugal that divided the region in 1493 in accordance with the Partition of Tordesillas. In the sector controlled by Spain, a system of administrative organizations known as viceroyalties formed powerful, quasi-independent political units. These included Peru, New Granada (Colombia, Venezuela, and Panama), and Charcas (whose core was modern Bolivia). The separate river communication systems that these units developed led to the open sea and thence to differing overseas contact points, reinforcing the isolation of the viceroyalties from one another. Finally, several countries were dependent on similar commodities, which limited the possibilities for intraregional trade while spurring national competition for foreign markets.

It is noteworthy that, save between Argentina and Chile, the crests of the Andes do not serve as national boundaries. In the south, where the Andes form a single range, they are sufficiently high, narrow, and unpopulated to warrant a barrier boundary function. To the north, where three distinct ranges are separated by high valleys, and in the center, where there are two ranges and one high valley, they form a wide but habitable zone. There the basins within the Andes serve as zones of unity, not of separatism. The rain-forested areas on the eastern slopes of the mountains serve as the barriers.

An important facet of the geopolitical structure of South America is its population distribution. On the western side of the continent, the populace has historically been highland oriented. The Spanish settled in the mountains for the minerals. They found the Indians already there, and this coincidence of minerals and labor supply kept the European population in the highlands.

Some attempts were made to bring Indians down to the Pacific coast to help develop ports. Most of these efforts ended in disaster. These indigenous peoples were not adapted to rainy lowland conditions, succumbed to tropical diseases, and sought to escape the repressive labor conditions imposed upon them. In the drier parts of the west coast, such as the semitropical savannas and, to the south, the deserts of Peru, the Incas had developed an irrigation culture. But their numbers were small. When the Europeans later sought to develop plantation agriculture along the tropical-forested coasts of the northern Andean countries (and also in coastal Brazil), they imported slaves from Africa or indentured laborers from the East Indies.

Thus the centers of western South American population—the capital cities and business nodes—are in the highlands, in the Bogotá basin, the basin of Quito, the Peruvian highlands, and the Bolivian plateau. Only in central Chile is the population concentrated in the lowland, which here is a broad, moist, and temperate valley bordered by the narrow and high Andes to the east and the low coastal ranges along the Pacific.

The concentration of populations in the highlands of South America is carried over through much of Central America and Mexico, reinforcing the principle that higher altitudes in tropical and subtropical regions cancel out the negative impacts of low latitudes. The process of vertical zonation of climate brings decreasing temperatures with increasing elevation while changing conditions from hot, tropical climates at the lowest elevations to moderate to cool temperatures at the higher ones.

Proximity of the Andean highlands to the coast and improvement of transportation and communications offer considerable potential to those highlands for a seaward orientation and thus for increased urbanization. In modern times, with improved health and medical facilities and air-conditioned buildings, the potential exists for a partial shift of the population to the seacoasts or, in a limited sense, to those lowlands east of the Andes which contain energy resources. The latter interior tramontane areas are either tropical rain forests (selvas) in eastern Ecuador and Peru which contain petroleum or, in Bolivia, savanna lands (Chaco). There, natural gas deposits have spurred urban development in Bolivia's Santa Cruz district at the northern end of the Gran Chaco. However, the shift to the coastlands is likely to occur only after the highland centers become so overcrowded that the states involved have little alternative but to engage in major coastal or interior developments.

In contrast to the population of the western side of the continent, the population of eastern South America is located in Atlantic coastal regions. These include the fertile, drought-prone to well-watered coastal plains that stretch from northeastern Brazil to Bahía Blanca in Argentina. They are backed by the low East Brazilian Highlands, behind which are level, grassland plateaus. In the south, the major population penetration into the interior, along the Paraná estuary and into the Pampas and Gran Chaco, is a strong reflection of the economic orientation of that area to ocean ports and international trade as well as of its moderate, mid-latitude climate.

While most of South America's population lives in western, coastal-rimming mountains or on the eastern coastal plain and accessible plateaus, the interior is a hollow core because of rain forest, dry grassland, and Patagonian desert. The weight of the continent's population and resources is on the eastern side. Brazil, Uruguay, Paraguay, and Argentina have nearly 250 million people, while the western side—Colombia, Ecuador, Peru, Bolivia, and Chile—has only 115 million. In the portions of Colombia that are oriented to the Caribbean, the population is less than 10 percent of the country's total. In Middle America's Venezuela, the reverse is the case—90 percent of its people are oriented to the Caribbean, and no more than 10 percent live in the country's Guiana Highlands and Orinoco regions.

Geopolitical Features

The geopolitical features of South America have remained remarkably immature for a continent that has enjoyed national independence for so long a period. For example, it lacks either historical or contemporary national capitals with sufficient regional reach to unify the eastern or western sections, let alone the entire continent.

ECUMENE

In western South America, the national ecumenes of Colombia, Ecuador, Peru, and Chile are all confined to mountain basins hundreds of miles from one another. Indeed, Peru's ecumene, which is centered at Lima and extends to Callao on the coast, is fifteen hundred miles from Chile's core area, which runs from Santiago southward to Concepción.

On the Atlantic side, the different national ecumenes are closer to one another, but those of Brazil and Paraguay are still substantially removed from the geographically connected ecumenes of Argentina and Uruguay. Brazil's historic core and first ecumene was its northeast. Early settlement had been attracted to the northeast coast because of its suitability for growing sugar. The focus for the development was the zone extending from Salvador (the country's first capital, in the state of Bahia), to Recife in Pernambuco. The sugar plantation culture flourished, based on the large-scale importation of slaves from Africa. When the industry collapsed in the nineteenth century due to soil exhaustion, overseas competition, and the abolition of slavery, the region's economy declined as Brazil's settlement and economic activities shifted southward to where the present ecumene is located. The northeast is now an impoverished, drought-prone region—a far cry from its era of prosperity.

Brazil's present ecumene extends along the coast from Rio de Janeiro to São Paulo and thence to the coastal Santa Catarina and Rio Grande do Sul provinces of the south. The hydropower and minerals (gold, diamonds, and rich iron reserves) of Minas Gerais provided the

Figure 6.1. South America: Major Geopolitical Features

capital and material basis for the late nineteenth- and early twentieth-century industrialization of Rio de Janeiro, where the new ecumene had begun to emerge. Reinforcing Rio's economic growth, Volta Redonda, located within the interior fifty miles from Rio, was developed after World War II into one of the world's largest integrated steel complexes, and it now supplies half of the country's iron and steel.

From Rio, the ecumene then spread southward, as the coffee plantations of São Paulo's hinterland led to the next Brazilian economic boom. Over the years, the plantations, always in need of fresh soils, moved from northeastern São Paulo state to its northern and western sections, as well as southward into the state of Paraná. It was coffee that provided the capital for São Paulo's industrial growth.

By the 1960s São Paulo had become the focus of the Brazilian ecumene, and it remains so to this day. It is the main financial center of South America and the continent's largest, richest, and most urbanized area, with a population of 11.3 million. Its broad industrial base includes electronics, telecommunications equipment, pharmaceuticals, chemicals, food, and textiles.

If the Brazilian ecumene eventually merges with the ecumenes of Argentina and Uruguay, which are located within the Río de la Plata estuary, it will be owing to São Paulo's economic power. However, this expansion is only a long-range prospect because the distance between Porto Alegre in Brazil and Montevideo-Buenos Aires is 450 miles.

EFFECTIVE NATIONAL TERRITORY

The Effective National Territory of Brazil's interior savanna (the Cerrado) and its far south grasslands may someday connect with the Uruguayan and Argentine Pampas—all areas capable of attracting population and economic development—but this, too, is a long-term prospect. The same holds true for vast tracts of fertile, uncultivated lands in eastern Paraguay and eastern Bolivia, whose development would be hastened by improved rail, highway, and air services to the Brazilian coast. Serving as major barriers to the merger of the Brazilian, Bolivian, and Paraguayan ENTs are not only the limited capacity of their ranching-grazing economies to support larger populations but also the location of the Pantanal region between them. The Pantanal, which is a vast wetland that extends across the Paraguay River and is subject to seasonal flooding, is virtually unusable during that period.

BOUNDARY AND TERRITORIAL DISPUTES AND WARS

A number of boundary or territorial issues also inhibit regional cooperation.[2] Chile has territorial claims in Antarctica that partly overlap Argentine and British claims. Bolivia lost the Atacama Desert to Chile through the Wars of the Pacific (1879 to 1883). As a result, Bolivia no longer has a sovereign corridor to the sea, and it continues to harbor the desire for territorial restitution. The two countries also have a dispute over Río Lauca water rights. This relates to a dam and hydroelectric project built by Chile in 1962 that Bolivia charges has caused a reduction of water flow into Bolivia and contributes to the salinity of Coipasa Lake.

Two sections of the boundary between Brazil and Uruguay are in dispute. One is in the area of Río Quaraí (Río Cuareim). The other involves the islands at the confluence of the Río Quaraí and the Uruguay River.

Colombia has a maritime boundary dispute with Venezuela in the Gulf of Venezuela. In addition, Nicaragua challenges Colombia's possession of the Archipelago of San Andrés y

Providencia, which lies off the Mosquito Coast of Nicaragua and is a center for tourism and transshipment of cocaine from Colombia to the United States.

Ecuador and Peru have had a long-standing, bitter conflict over their boundary in the Amazon region. This dates back to the Marañón War of 1942, whereby Peru gained control of the Nor Oriental del Marañón region. This contains the upper Marañón River and the port of Iquitos, thereby providing access to the Amazon River basin. Ecuador accepted that peace settlement only grudgingly. After sporadic fighting in the 1980s and the early 1990s, and again in 1995, the countries finally concluded an agreement in 1999, arbitrated by Argentina, Brazil, Chile, and the United States. This confirmed Peru's claim to the border as running along the high peaks of the Condor Range and provided Ecuador with a patch of Peruvian land in Amazonas (one square mile) to honor its military dead. The accord provides for integrating the economies of the two countries, especially in the border region, and for linking their electrical grid systems. It also gives Ecuador navigation and trading rights on the Amazon River and its tributaries within Peru.

The conflict over territorial sea boundary claims between Peru and Chile was largely resolved in favor of Peru by a ruling of the International Court of Justice. This ruling gave Peru control over fifty thousand square miles of high seas territorial waters, which are important for deep-sea fishing of tuna, swordfish, and squid. On the other hand, it confirmed Chile's right to eight thousand square miles of water in which local fisherman catch mackerel and halibut.

The Falkland Islands (Islas Malvinas) are administered by the United Kingdom but claimed by Argentina, which launched an ill-fated military invasion of the islands in 1982. The citizens of the Falklands, descendants of the island's English settlers, are adamantly opposed to being taken over by Argentina. While Buenos Aires has not renounced its claim, the dispute has been dormant since that war. Argentina also lays claim to the UK-administered South Georgia and South Sandwich Islands, two thousand miles east of Tierra del Fuego in the South Atlantic. During the Falklands conflict, Argentine troops invaded South Georgia but were driven off by the British. Another dispute between the two countries is over territorial sovereignty in Antarctica, where they have overlapping claims.

The Beagle Channel dispute between Chile and Argentina over control of three islands at the Atlantic end of the strait culminated in the award of the islands to Chile. Argentina has never accepted this verdict, but a spirit of cooperation between the two nations now prevails as they engage in joint energy projects in the area.

Geopolitical Forces of Separation and Attraction

FORCES OF SEPARATION

A variety of centrifugal forces—physical, economic, social, and political—divide South America and contribute to its geopolitical fragmentation.[3] These include separate historical orientations and cultures, disputes over territorial expansions and frontiers, and the absence of significant trade links among the countries. (The trade links have increased substantially with the establishment of Mercosur, the east coast free-trade bloc.) The inability or unwillingness of Brazil to exercise a dominating regional role up to now, despite having 60 percent of the population of the region, has been a significant deterrent to regional cohesiveness.

The continent's fragmentation has been exacerbated by the separation of various racial and ethnic groupings on both national and regional levels. Examples are the Afro-Brazilian enclaves of northeastern Brazil; the black populations of Colombia's Pacific and Caribbean coasts; and the Indians of the Andes, the Eastern Andes Piedmont, Amazonas, and the upper Orinoco. Laws perpetuating or protecting the large farm estates known as *latifundia* have helped to keep these populations in situ.

The areas of South America that are favorably endowed physically represent oases of prosperity in otherwise impoverished tropical and semitropical areas that suffer from poor soil, droughts or flooding, distance from the sea, and mountain barriers to efficient land communication. The population that did move onto the fertile highland basins developed surpluses that encouraged the development of commerce and industry. As these prosperous population nodes industrialized, they attracted the rural impoverished. The result was the development of the dominant city, which attracts hundreds of thousands of landless people who cannot be housed or employed within the city because population has outstripped the economic base. Provincial centers, overshadowed by the major urban centers and generally bypassed by highly centralized national governmental structures, tend to wither. The South American experience bears out the comment of Montesquieu that concentration leads to depopulation by depriving local centers of the vigor of being themselves capitals.[4]

Also contributing to geopolitical immaturity has been stop-and-go national economic development and international political attention. Sporadic South American development efforts all too often have been related to crisis politics, such as was brought on by droughts in Brazil or elections and financial crises in Argentina, and then have been put aside as the emergencies have subsided. The situation has been aggravated by the failure of the United States to apply an even, steady flow of political attention, economic aid, and capital investment to the region. Instead, it has usually reacted to crises with programs that rarely outlast the presidential administration that launched them. In recent decades, the influx of immigrants to the United States from such countries as Colombia and Ecuador, as well as the flow of drugs from Colombia and Peru, has commanded much attention from Washington. Inasmuch as these occurrences have long-term impacts, they may stimulate the United States to take a long-range approach to its Colombian development aid, along with its drug interdiction programs.

FORCES OF ATTRACTION

Despite the forces of fragmentation that separate the western and eastern portions of the continent, there are major attractions that connect the two. Most importantly, there is the common Latin culture that binds all of South America, a bond that transcends the differences between Brazil, with its Portuguese history and language, and the rest of the countries of the continent. In addition, the very dominance of eastern South America is a magnet for the western half.

There is some complementarity of economies between the east and west coast countries. Western South America has a relatively stronger mineral base than the east, and this can become a basis for broadening exchange. Air routes currently offer alternatives to the barrier effects of mountains and tropical rain forests. Also, upstream waterways connect Manaus in Brazilian Amazonas to Peru's Iquitos to the west, and to central Ecuador and that country's road system. Southward from Manaus up the Rio Madeira, the water route runs to Porto Velho in Brazil. From there a road extends westward into Peru. These overland connections are still under development.

The feeder of one branch of the Trans-Amazon Highway, the Trans-Oceanic Highway, has been completed to connect with the Bolivian and Peruvian system. It extends from Acre in Brazil for 1,300 miles to Peru's Pacific coast. However, the main highway stops far short of the Colombian border. Similarly, a northern perimeter Amazonian highway does link up with the Venezuelan and Guyanan road systems but does not extend beyond Brazil's Roraima state in the direction of Colombia. In addition, a gas pipeline has been completed from Bolivia's huge gas fields to São Paulo, while another has been completed from interior southern Argentina through Uruguay to Brazil's southern coast at Porto Alegre. Dam building across the Paraná River has proved to be another force of attraction and unified action. The Yacyretá Dam, built across the Paraná River border between Paraguay and Argentina, began to generate electricity in 1994. Another dam is being planned upstream by the two countries at Corpus. Still farther upstream, Brazil and Paraguay collaborated in building the giant Itaipu Dam across their common river border, just above the Iguaçú Falls. The proposed Belo Monte Dam across the Xingu River, a tributary of the lower Amazon, would flood five hundred square miles and displace twenty thousand Amerindians. Planned as Brazil's second-largest hydropower project, the dam has been the focus of lawsuits brought by the natives since 2007. The courts have ruled in favor of the government, and construction began in 2014. This controversy and other environmental conflicts have prompted Brazilian firms to seek new dam sites across the border in Peru.

Regional Economic Organizations

One manifestation of the forces of attraction is regional organization. South America's two major forces of attraction are Mercosur (Mercado Común del Sur, the Southern Cone Common Market) and the Andean Group. The members of Mercosur, the regional free-trade association established in the 1991 Treaty of Asunción, are Brazil, Argentina, Uruguay, and Paraguay. Chile and Bolivia are associate members, having concluded free-trade agreements with Mercosur. The organization's full member states, with their nearly 250 million population, have combined gross domestic products of over $2.5 trillion and a combined annual trade of over $325 billion. Trade within the four states of the bloc has more than tripled since its founding and represents about 12 percent of the foreign trade of all the members. This can be attributed not only to free trade among its members but also to reduced common tariffs on imports from outside the bloc. In addition, foreign investments have soared, attracted by the size of the Mercosur market, especially that of Brazil, which receives ten times as much foreign capital now as it did a decade ago, attracted by its population of over 190 million, which accounts for 40 percent of the region's GDP.

Unfortunately, trade within the bloc has leveled off over the past few years, owing to the failure to implement a genuine common market with a common external tariff and financial crises brought on by currency devaluation and economic stagnation. However, the proportion of trade to countries outside the bloc has experienced increases. Most of the trade of Brazil, Argentina, and Uruguay goes to countries outside Mercosur. Only Paraguay sends half of its exports to Mercosur countries. China is now Brazil's leading trade partner, but trade with the United States, which ranks second, is increasing at a rapid rate. In 2007, Venezuela sought full membership in Mercosur. It was not ratified by Brazil, and given the growing political rift between the two countries, it is unlikely that Venezuela will join the trade bloc in the near future.

While Brazil continues to commit itself to the growth of trade with its Mercosur neighbors and to support of their economic development, other foreign markets offer greater scope for the country's raw materials—soybeans, grains, and minerals. Brazil has become the world leader in the use of ethanol. Since 2003, it has required that every new vehicle use either a blend of regular gasoline and ethanol or 100 percent ethanol. With the oil reserves that it now has and this policy, it has become self-sufficient in motor fuels. Should the United States, with its potential demand for ethanol, drop its tariffs against the sugarcane-based Brazilian product, the growers of the Brazilian northeast would have an even greater boom in exports.

Mercosur's economic clout has enabled it to be used as a vehicle for the development of regional infrastructures. In addition, its political leverage upon member states is substantial. For example, the requirement of democratic government as a condition for entry into the bloc represents a radical break in political history for a continent that has been plagued by dictatorships and corruption for most of the past two centuries. This policy has helped to forestall attempted coups in Paraguay.

For a while, Chile made a strong effort to join Mercosur as a full member. As the year 2000 ended, however, it pulled back from this request, seeking as an alternative a free-trade agreement with the United States. This agreement between the two countries was signed in 2004. Brazil views itself as the key to any Western Hemispheric economic bloc that would embrace all of South America and has opposed the Washington-sponsored Free Trade Area of the Americas because of its fear that the proposal represents the designs of the United States for economic dominance of the hemisphere. In seeking new markets, Brazil has favored negotiations that would lead to a free-trade agreement with the EU.

Brazil and its leaders expect to be treated as equal by the United States since it is South America's largest market by far, with an economy that is the world's seventh largest, rivaling that of Russia. This applies not only to economic negotiations but also to Washington's crafting of political decisions that affect the region, such as its policy toward Colombia.

The Andean group, which was created in 1969, includes Bolivia, Chile, Colombia, Ecuador, Peru, and Venezuela (the latter geopolitically in Middle America). Because, with the exceptions of Chile and Venezuela, it represents economically struggling and unstable countries, it is far less important than Mercosur. Chile's per capita income is nearly twice that of Venezuela, despite the latter's oil wealth, and is second only to Argentina. The function of the Andean group has been largely confined to developing common regulations to control foreign investment. What could give a boost to the association would be an agreement between Chile and Bolivia to guarantee supplies of the latter's gas to energy-poor Chile. However, such an agreement would require that Chile restore Bolivia's lost access to the sea. This is further complicated by the fact that such a corridor would have to traverse Peruvian territory.

For the most part, the trade of the Andean bloc is with the United States and Asia. Venezuela's moves to link leftist governments in Bolivia and Ecuador while offering financial help to these countries weakens their prospects for bilateral free-trade agreements with the United States. The US Congress ratified the free-trade agreement with Peru in December 2007, with Colombia and South Korea in 2011, and with Panama in 2012.

As an associate member of Mercosur and with the prospect for rejoining the Andean Community, which it left in 1976, Chile seeks to keep trade contact with both South American organizations. However, its foreign trade future lies with the United States, China, and the Asia-Pacific Rim. Chile signed a free-trade agreement with the United States in 2005 and is a major exporter of iron ore, nitrates, and precious metals to China.

In May 2008 the twelve members of Mercosur and the Andean bloc formed the South American Union (UNASUR), modeling it after the EU. The union's initial focus is on free trade and economic development, but its impact is likely to be limited until a solid transportation and communication structure is created. Even with such a union, it is unlikely that the Andean bloc would be tightly drawn into Brazil's economic and geopolitical orbit or be able to develop meaningful contacts with Argentina and Uruguay. The US market is far more important to the Andean community than is Brazil or other Mercosur states, and the

Ibero-Indian culture of the Andes is far removed from that of Portuguese-rooted Brazil or the European-Spanish countries to its south.

Prospects for South America's Geopolitical Independence

Full continental geopolitical unity, under the dominance of Brazil, is unlikely because of the deep physical and ethnocultural divisions between Atlantic and Andean South America and because Brazil's economic and political interests focus on the United States, Europe, and China. However, the independence of South America as a geopolitical region is strengthened by Brazil's continued economic growth, political stability, and world influence. It is clearly the dominant political and economic power within South America and one of the major regional powers of the world. The country is linked with Russia, India, China, and South Africa as one of the five BRICS—nations that are expected to grow faster over the next decade than the highly developed countries of the world. It dwarfs the rest of the continent in population (over 190 million out of a total of 360 million), in area (3.3 million square miles out of a total of 6.4 million square miles), and in GDP ($2.25 trillion, or over 55 percent).[5] Possessing common borders with every other South American state with the exceptions of Chile and Ecuador, the South American regional giant is geographically positioned to influence and pressure the other states, especially as various transcontinental transportation and energy projects are brought to completion.

Factors that favor the economic development prospects of Brazil are the attractiveness of its vast market to investment capital and its rich natural resources of bauxite, gold, iron, manganese, nickel, phosphates, uranium, timber, and hydropower. It has made rapid strides in petroleum development.

Discovery of the vast deepwater Tupi oil field (now known as Lula, after the former president) off its southeastern coast in the Santos Basin, was followed by discovery of the even larger offshore Carioca field. These all offer the potential for transforming Brazil into a global energy powerhouse. The country is now almost self-sufficient in oil and gas, meeting its needs mostly from offshore deposits, with the rest coming from the Amazon basin. In addition, all vehicles must use at least a 25 percent ethanol content. The sources of Brazil's newfound petro wealth are the deep Cretaceous salts which trap oil in rocks off the Brazilian coast. This is known as "pre-sal" oil. When this oil eventually comes fully online, the country's reserves will enable it to become an oil exporter second only to Venezuela in South America. Current reserve estimates include fifty billion barrels of pre-sal oil. By 2020, Petrobras, the partly privatized Brazilian oil company, projects an output of five million barrels per day. Now the world's eleventh-largest oil producer, this projection would raise it into fifth place. To exploit this resource fully, considerable capital and sophisticated technology are needed. To this end, in 2010 the Brazilian government invited foreign companies to join in consortia with Petrobras. This will provide Brazil with additional political weight to counter Venezuela's Chávez-Maduro petro-supported foreign policy goals.

Now reliant on Bolivia and Argentina for natural gas, Brazil can develop its large offshore gas deposits in the Santos Basin and move toward national self-sufficiency in gas. This would require major investment to double the country's gas line distribution system, making the timetable for bringing in the gas fields uncertain. Agriculture is also a strength, with farm exports representing over one-third of total exports. The Cerrado has become the site of rapidly growing commercial agribusinesses. With a more reliable climate than the coastal states, these interior savannas have become the major center for soybean, high-quality cotton, and beef production.

The state of Mato Grosso has become the country's leading producer of soybeans, its second-largest rice grower, and its fourth-largest raiser of cattle. Soybeans are now transported by barge down the Madeira River to the Amazon River port of Itacoatiara and then transshipped to oceangoing vessels. Additional links to open the region to further development are a proposed twelve-hundred-mile, all-weather highway north to the port of Santarém on the eastern end of the Amazon and a rail link from southern Mato Grosso to the Ferronorte rail line to São Paulo and the port of Santos. With cheaper shipping and low-cost production on newly cleared land within its ENT, Brazil has passed the United States as the leading soy product exporter, with Argentina ranking third. The three countries collectively account for 90 percent of world soya trade. However, the US share of the market continues to drop as Brazil expands its production to meet demand from China.

Meanwhile, São Paulo state remains the world's largest coffee producer. When these crops are added to sugarcane, oranges, and other fruits, wheat, rice, chicken, and tobacco, Brazil's agricultural future is bright, especially given the prospects for cane-based ethanol. Farm products play an especially important role in balancing trade with Brazil's major commercial partners—the United States, Germany, the Netherlands, and Argentina.

The breadth of the country's industrial economy also contributes to its economic strength. Output includes iron (the country's leading export) and steel products, cement, papers, textiles, fertilizers, electronics, telecommunications equipment, motor vehicle assembly, and civilian aircraft. Brazil competes with Canada as the world's third-largest producer of such airplanes.

While Brazil is clearly the only country capable of protecting South American geopolitical unity from dominance by the "colossus of the north," the degree to which it can fully exercise geopolitical power within its own region is limited by domestic challenges. Widespread poverty, inflation, and the racial divide between the black (6 percent) and "brown" (or mixed, 38 percent) populations and the white population plagues the country. While the racial divide is not overt in interpersonal terms, it is reflected economically, with nonwhites suffering from much higher rates of unemployment and poorer education. The fact that so many of these problems are concentrated in the northeast is evidence of the divide. Global warming presents another major threat to Brazil's long-term stability. The Amazon forests serve as a global storage house for one-fifth of the world's carbon emissions. Drought, fire, logging, and crop clearance have caused massive deforestation in the Amazon, releasing carbon dioxide on such a scale as to account for three-quarters of the country's emissions and making Brazil the fourth-largest producer of greenhouse gases. This is occurring despite Brazil's success in reducing auto emissions through the use of ethanol.

Until recently, Brazil has taken the same position as governments of other major emerging economies—that the wealthiest countries are responsible for gas emissions and must take the lead. As the country's rainfall and vegetation patterns have begun to change, so have the government's attitudes and behavior. Global warming could cause drought to become endemic within Brazil's southeastern breadbasket and reduce rainfall in Amazonas. Currently dams and reservoirs are being planned in Amazonas to pipe water to São Paulo to meet industrial and agricultural needs. It is also feared that the tropical rain forest of the eastern Amazon might suffer soil and water depletion, gradually replacing the trees with savanna. Brasília is now considering market-based strategies such as "cap and trade" and paying farmers and indigenous peoples in the Amazon not to cut forests.

Expansion of its overseas links with maritime Europe and the United States would provide Brazil with additional economic and political power and, if it so desires, enable it to take the lead role in forging an integrated eastern South American geopolitical region. Such a region would include Brazil, Argentina, Uruguay, Paraguay, probably Chile, and possibly Bolivia.

A measure of Brazil's increased importance to the United States as well as its own aspirations for world power is Brazil's April 2000 agreement with the United States. The agreement enables the United States to use the Brazilian air force base at Alcântara, which is located to the east of the Amazon delta, on the Atlantic, and is an ideal location for the launching of spacecraft and communications satellites by the United States. In return, Brazil receives funds to acquire or develop and produce its own rockets and unmanned space vehicles.

While the potential of geopolitical unity for eastern South America is promising, for the western, Andean portion prospects for integration are much weaker. Indeed, with the competition between the US and Venezuelan ideological and economic interests, the Andean region runs the risk of becoming a microshatterbelt. The central and northern Andean countries are torn by internal violence and cross-border conflicts. Moreover, unlike the east, which has recently made strides in solidifying democratic governments, these states remain largely in the grip of authoritarian regimes.

The endemic turmoil in western South America is fueled by drug trade revenues that support both Marxist rebels and right-wing militias. The situation is most acute in Colombia, where large-scale coca production has replaced most of the acreage that had been eradicated in Peru, Ecuador, and Bolivia during the past decade and a half. The bulk of the Colombian production is in the south and southeast, where the largest Marxist guerrilla movement, the Maoist Revolutionary Armed Forces of Colombia (FARC), has waged civil war for half a century. It continues to exercise control over much of this sparsely populated rural region, gaining strength from the taxes that it levies on the growers of coca and poppies and on the drug producers.

This income enabled the rebel movement to maintain a strong force of twelve thousand fighters that has fought the Colombian army to a standstill. A smaller rebel movement—the Cuban-inspired People's Liberation Army (ELN)—operates in the northeast, where it supports itself through kidnappings and extorting money from oil producers. These guerrillas target oil fields and pipelines. Arrayed against both rebel movements have been government troops and right-wing militias and their death squads that have waged terror campaigns against the leftists.

Weakened by internal strife and crushing governmental military blows supported by the United States, the FARC leadership came to an agreement with the government in 2013. The agreement calls for integrating some of the FARC fighters into the country's armed forces, implementation of land reform, and recognition of FARC as a legitimate political party. Fulfillment of the agreement would spell the end of the fifty-year civil war in which over twenty thousand were killed. Equally important, in 2011 the US Congress restored aid which had previously been deeply cut and unfroze the proposed free-trade agreement between the two countries, which had been held in abeyance because of human rights violations by the militias.

Washington's Plan Colombia has channeled more than $5 billion to Colombia to try to eradicate coca production and entice farmers to grow alternative crops, as well as to combat the insurgencies. Nevertheless, as long as cocaine exports continue unabated, the country will continue to be plagued by a narco-economy and narco-society. The alliances between rebels, right-wing militias, and the drug cartels will have to be broken if peace and normalcy are to come to Colombia.

While Colombia still supplies a major share of the world's cocaine as well as much of the heroin that is consumed in the United States, Ecuador and Peru are also now involved in supplying these drugs to the United States. Ecuador provides a rear base for smuggling arms and exporting drugs; the Peruvian Amazon as well as Venezuela are conduits for Colombian drug smugglers. Should the civil war with the FARC be firmly ended, the chances for reducing Colombia's coca growing will be greatly enhanced.

However, even if the campaign against coca growing in Colombia succeeds, there is always the possibility that production might shift back to the neighboring Andean countries, where it had been largely eradicated with US help. Also, other parts of the world would probably take up the slack, such as the Golden Crescent of Afghanistan, Pakistan, and Iran or the Golden Triangle of Myanmar, Thailand, and Laos, which are or have been major producers of opium poppies and heroin. (The Taliban had eradicated opium poppies, but since they were driven out by the United States, Afghanistan now produces more than 90 percent of the world supply.) As long as there is demand in the United States and Europe, there will be sources of supply.

Ecuador has been plagued by political instability, having had eight political governments since 1996. In 2006, Rafael Correa was elected to the presidency. A rabid anti-US leftist, he has moved rapidly to gain control over the country's political institutions and, in close alliance with Venezuela, has become a key participant in the Bolivarian revolution. Tensions with Washington have heightened with the seizure of American oil company assets and the proposed cancellation of the Manta military base lease.

The United States remains the most important market for Ecuador's petroleum exports, which account for 40 percent of the nation's foreign earnings and one-third of its tax revenues. However, Ecuador has shifted more of its oil exports to Japan and other Asian-Pacific markets—markets which are likely to absorb most of its oil exports as the United States moves toward self-sufficiency owing to increased domestic oil production and alternative energy sources. The country's oil production fields are located in the Oriente region and shipped westward, across the Andes, through a three-hundred-mile pipeline to the Pacific port of Esmeraldas. This production has come at a high environmental and political cost. Clearing the tropical rain forests for oil drilling and transportation has encroached upon the traditional homelands of indigenous peoples. This, as well as strikes by oil workers over pay and work conditions, has kept the Oriente in turmoil.

Bolivia, too, has suffered from unrest and political instability. When leftist Evo Morales was elected to the presidency in 2005, he was the fourth to occupy the office since 1995. Former head of the coca workers' union, Morales forced all foreign companies to renegotiate oil and gas contracts in keeping with the Bolivarian revolution, which he also has espoused.

The poorest of the Andean countries, Bolivia, is heavily dependent on trade with Brazil, Colombia, and other South American countries. Much of its economic future depends upon the export of natural gas to Brazil. The gas fields lie in the country's Oriente region, which is known as the Charcas Triangle (formed by the cities of Cochabamba, Sucre, and Santa Cruz). It is described by Lewis Tambs as "the Bolivian heartland power center," and it has, over the years, pressed for greater autonomy.[6] This was reinforced overwhelmingly in a 2008 Santa Cruz province referendum. The economic orientation of the Oriente is to Brazil, and in 2007 its leadership proposed shifting Bolivia's capital from highland La Paz to Sucre, the country's leading commercial center. In 1898, it had lost its capital status to La Paz, the center of the indigenous Indian population, in a bloody war. Anti-Morales sentiment in Oriente and its economic orientation toward Brazil make it difficult for Morales to fully embrace anti-Westernism and a revolutionary stance.

Under the presidency of Alberto Fujimori, the twenty-year civil war that tore Peru apart was ended. In 1992, the Shining Path Maoist leader's capture led to the rebels' defeat. A few years later in the late 1990s, the Túpac Amaru revolt was also crushed. During Fujimori's autocratic rule, free-market reforms were introduced, but the presidency was marred by widespread corruption and bribery. In 2000, Fujimori fled to Japan, from where he tendered his resignation. In 2007, Peru succeeded in extraditing him from Chile to put him on trial for human rights violations during the war against the rebels as well as for bribery and illegal wiretapping. During the six years that followed Fujimori's ousting, the country suffered from considerable political instability.

The president elected in 2006, Alan García, developed strong ties with Washington built on a Peru-US free-trade agreement. The United States is Peru's leading trade partner, based on Peru's minerals, oil, textiles, and food products in exchange for consumer goods and machinery. Garcia was replaced in the election of 2011 by left-leaning Ollanta Humala. He built closer relations with Brazil, Bolivia, and Argentina, in keeping with a policy of strengthening ties with South American neighbors. From a developmental perspective, the South American continent is still in a stage of differentiation. Drives for national self-sufficiency by South America's various countries have promoted this differentiation. The first indications of progress toward specialized integration are the growth of trade and communications links among Brazil, Argentina, and Uruguay. Now that Brazil has turned away from economic isolation as a development strategy, movement toward the higher level of specialized integration is likely to be hastened.

During the nineteenth and first half of the twentieth century, Argentina competed with Brazil as South America's leading regional power. It was rich in natural resources, had a profitable export-oriented agricultural system, and had an ethnically unified population of Spanish and Italian origin. It was a wealthy country with a large, well-educated middle class. Since the end of World War II, economic and political parity with Brazil has been lost. Although Argentina remains a wealthy country, with a population of 43 million, a GDP of $470 billion, and a GDP per capita of nearly $18,000, it has been geopolitically eclipsed by its giant northern neighbor.

The economic and political instability that Juan Perón and succeeding populist Peronista rulers brought to the country led to a decline in its agricultural base, once its chief source of revenue. This was aggravated by the financial crisis of 2001–2, when Argentina defaulted on its foreign debt. At that time, the government raised taxes on grain exports up to one third, and raging inflation pushed farm production costs up exponentially. Many large-scale farming groups drastically reduced their acreage, thereby limiting their exports of soybeans, wheat, corn, and oilseeds. As a result, agriculture now represents less than 10 percent of the country's GDP and only 5 percent of its labor force, while industry now accounts for 25 percent and services 70 percent of the country's gross domestic product.

The decline of agriculture is only one reflection of Argentina's challenges. For years the country has been dogged by military rule and corruption, misguided populist nationalism, economic protectionism, periods of deflation, and fiscal and political mismanagement. Added to this was the "Dirty War," in which thousands of Argentinians "disappeared." Its military defeat in the Falklands War at the hands of the British was an additional humiliation.

The problem has not been economic globalization per se but the rush to embrace it. Fiscal instability rekindled strong nationalistic and antiglobalism sentiments. With the imposition of fiscal restraints by President Néstor Kirchner in 2003 and the refinancing of its debt, Argentina thought it had found the road to recovery and entered into a period of democratic stability. It has increased its trade with traditional partners, such as Brazil, by far its leading source of exports and imports, as well as China, the United States, Chile, and the EU. GDP increases have been fueled by an export boom in soy products, motor vehicles, garments, textiles, and factory production. However, unsustainable borrowing by the federal government led to the country's second declaration of bankruptcy in 2014.

The country has also developed ties with Venezuela, which unsuccessfully sought to draw Argentina into the Bolivarian camp through joint ventures, including a proposed plant to convert Venezuelan liquefied gas. However, there is little likelihood that Argentina will diverge from its course of strong geopolitical ties with Brazil or that it will abandon its market economy. The 2007 election of Cristina Fernández de Kirchner to the presidency has given new focus to relations with Europe, the United States, and Brazil. While remaining committed to the previous president's emphasis on internal economic reforms, Kirchner has sought to strengthen ties with the broader maritime world. On the other hand, the country continues to be plagued by high inflation, and nationalization in 2012 of YPF, the Argentinian oil company formerly controlled by the Spanish oil company Retsol, has strained relations with Spain. In 2014, the peso plunged once again. This was caused by a widening of the foreign debt caused by generous social welfare spending and exacerbated by the need to import energy. Prospects for political stability have dimmed, and along with this, Argentina's geopolitical influence within the continent has weakened.

Conclusion

South America has attained the status of an independent geopolitical region within the maritime realm, with balanced ties to the United States, maritime Europe, and the Asia-Pacific Rim. Brazil's continental preeminence as a regional power has led the way to this independence. While the Mercosur states and Chile have gained a considerable measure of geopolitical stability, this is not the case for the four Andean states. They remain internally fragmented racially, socially, and economically and at odds with one another on territorial issues. They are also caught up in the ideological conflict between the United States and Venezuela.

The dreams of Hugo Chávez of following in Simón Bolívar's footsteps, wherein Bolívar sought to create Gran Colombia, have no likelihood of being resurrected in that form. However, it should be recognized that the Venezuelan government, now led by Nicolás Maduro, controls a highly authoritarian system and is prepared to use the country's oil wealth to influence events within the Andes. The promise of addressing the needs of impoverished, indigenous Andean peasants and the urban poor is appealing. Social, educational, and health reforms that follow the Cuban model are prospects that have an impact that should not be ignored. In 2007, Chávez proposed the establishment of a Bank of the South to finance regional development projects. Seven nations signed off on creating this institution. Brazil, one of the signatories, already had its own development bank but was a participant. The bank was promoted as an alternative to the World Bank and International Monetary Fund and the Interamerican Development Bank, all of which have significant Washington involvement. However, the Bank of the South lacks the capital of the international funds, which remain the major sources for regional investment.

In South America, Washington has focused most of its energies on military aid and drug eradication. To prevent a Caribbean-Andean microshatterbelt from emerging, the United States would have to put considerable resources and sustained attention into promoting widespread economic, social, and political reforms that address the needs of the underserved classes. Brazil is well equipped to partner in this venture.

South America's prospects for developing into a geopolitical region that is well integrated into the maritime realm depends upon the destiny of Brazil, the continent's only regional power. Its central position within this region enables it to influence events in much of the continent's Southern Cone—the geographical triangle that extends from the southern headwaters of the Amazon and the southern Peruvian Andes to Patagonia.

The prospects for the creation of such a region have been improved by the recent turn in relations between Brazil and Argentina. Historically, Brazil's major geopolitical focus has been its rivalry with Argentina for leadership of the La Plata estuary and dominance over the three states that act as buffers between the two countries—Uruguay, Paraguay, and Bolivia. Brazil and Argentina have now achieved a rapprochement that enhances the ability of Brazil to lead the region toward integration and to guarantee peace and stability. Renewal of growth in Argentina's economic recovery is also important to the region's unity prospects. Extending such a region to include the Andean countries of Colombia, Ecuador, Bolivia, and Peru would take considerable time because of the barrier effects of the Amazon region and the Andes. For the near future, these four states are likely to remain isolated and marginal to the mainstream of maritime realm action. This could be changed if the negotiations for a transpacific free-trade agreement led by the United States and including Chile, Peru, and Colombia proves successful.

However, the larger part of South America, led by Brazil, is now poised to reinforce its separate geopolitical identity within the maritime realm through balanced ties with North America, maritime Europe, and the Pacific Rim. It no longer remains within the geopolitical shadow of the "North American colossus" that dominated it for so many decades.

Notes

1. Frederick Merk, *The Monroe Doctrine and American Expansionism, 1843–1849* (New York: Knopf, 1966), preface.
2. Central Intelligence Agency, "Disputes International," in *World Factbook 2007* (Washington, DC: GPO/CIA, 2007).
3. Philip Kelly, *Checkerboards and Shatterbelts: The Geopolitics of South America* (Austin: University of Texas Press, 1987), 48–83.
4. Charles Louis de Montesquieu, *The Spirit of Laws*, Book XIV, trans. Thomas Nugent, Library of the Classics (1906; reprint, New York: Hafner, 1949), 221–34.
5. Central Intelligence Agency, *World Factbook 2007* (Washington, DC: GPO/CIA, 2007), 2, 3, 5.
6. Lewis Tambs, "Geopolitical Factors in Latin America," in *Latin America: Politics, Economic and Hemispheric Security*, ed. Norman Bailey (New York: Praeger, 1965), 36, 42–43.

CHAPTER 7

Maritime Europe and the Maghreb

"Maritime Europe" aptly describes the human habitat that lies within the western peninsular and insular reaches of Eurasia, where European civilization evolved. This civilization is the culmination of over two millennia of development, from the Greek city-state and Roman codes of law, to the eras of feudalism and empires, to the modern nation-state, and now to the European Union. Its human-fashioned landscape has evolved from the system of Roman roads that reached to Scotland and the Rhine to modern expressways and high-speed trains, the Eurotunnel, and Europoort. Once largely agricultural, the landscape morphed into the grimy, soot-covered factory cities of the industrial age and then into today's modern, postindustrial metropolises.

Although torn by nineteenth- and early twentieth-century political and social revolutions, two bloody world wars, and the unspeakable horror of the Holocaust, Europe is now a major global force for peacemaking. The colonialism and imperialism of past centuries has faded into history, and Europe has become a major exponent of the application of "soft" power in its foreign policies. Unlike any other of the world's continents or large regions, Europe is now the laboratory for a "great idea"—the European Union—that can become a model for the rest of the world in creating governance systems that would eliminate much of the intraregional conflict that plagues humanity.

This idea of Europe embraces a geopolitical system that seeks to balance national interests with a unified economic, political, and social framework, propelled by the freedom of movement of people, goods, and expression. The concept of the European Union emerged from the ashes of World War II. Basic philosophical differences among member states are divided between those favoring stronger, centralized federalism and those favoring a system built upon intergovernmental institutions with voting weighted between large and small states. Another difference is between those favoring a strong European defense structure as opposed to relying on NATO.

But these differences are overcome by the fact that regional unity has become Europe's defining concept. This sets it apart from the rest of the world and makes it unique. In many ways, Western Europe is the archetypical maritime region. It is characterized by not only a sea-oriented set of physical and economic conditions but also inhabitants who have developed a distinctive, trade-oriented outlook that stems from their interaction with the sea.

In the past few years, Europe has successfully addressed a major challenge. This was to narrow the economic gap that had developed between its northern and southern nations after the recession of 2008. Eurozone members, such as Greece, Portugal, and Spain, were especially hit by this recession. Their indebtedness mounted from uncontrolled budgets, and unemployment rose to unprecedented levels. The northern countries, especially Germany, Scandinavia, and the Netherlands, as well as central EU financial institutions, bailed them out, demanding austerity measures and economic reform in return. These terms were grudgingly met. While these southern countries (and Ireland) have not returned to their prerecession prosperity, this is a case of the wealthy countries supporting the poor in the interests of unity.

In 2014, the EU achieved greater geopolitical parity with the United States when it resisted efforts by the American administration to apply heavier sanctions on Russia in response to its annexation of Crimea and alleged interference in Ukraine. Heavier sanctions could have set off a new economic cold war in which Europe, not the United States, would have had to bear the major economic burden because of its heavy trade with Russia. That the EU succeeded in resisting US pressures may signal the beginning of a shift in its status from junior to full partner within the maritime realm.

Europe's omnipresent maritime influence is underscored by the fact that most of the region's inhabitants live within 250 miles of open sea and that the region is traversed by major rivers and valleys offering ease of access to the coasts. The physical characteristics of the region are highlighted by temperate, moist, marine forest or Mediterranean-type climates and moderately fertile, humid, midlatitude podzolic or terra rossa soils.

Benjamin Franklin was the first to hypothesize that Western Europe's moderate winter temperatures could be attributed to the warming effects of the Gulf Stream, which originates in the Gulf of Mexico, as it moves northward along the Atlantic coast to Newfoundland and then eastward as the North Atlantic Drift crosses the ocean to Europe's western shores at Norway. However, this is challenged by modern science, which now holds that Europe's winter climate is moderated by solar radiation that warms a vast mass of central tropical Atlantic water which drifts northward by the earth's rotation and then to the northeast. Mediterranean Europe, which is isolated from Western Europe by the east-west trending high Alps, the Pyrenees, and the Carpathians, is open to these warm winds in the winter but also to frequent, brief storms. The Mediterranean stays hot but dry in the summer as it is overlain by a subtropical high-pressure zone that blocks summer's cooling Atlantic winds.

Climates and soils, together with timber, waterpower, coal, iron, and chemical resources, fostered intensive agriculture and facilitated maritime Europe's emergence as the world's leading manufacturing center during the industrial revolution. Toward the end of the twentieth century, the coal reserves were supplemented by North Sea oil and natural gas. The harbors and coves of the well-stocked fishing waters of the submerged Atlantic coastline and the more limited fishing grounds off the jagged Mediterranean coast provided an early basis for a fishing economy as well as for the development of commerce.

It was within this setting that modern national states arose. Most were organized around historic cores nestled within river valleys with access to the seas. The political boundaries that separated them were drawn along such physical barriers as mountains, morainic ridges, marshlands, and open waters. As Western European states developed, they compensated for their relatively limited land bases by trading with far-flung parts of the world and ultimately developing colonial networks. Indeed, the Western European experience demonstrated that a small land area could sometimes be turned to advantage. The land frontiers of the Netherlands needed limited armies, while the nation's fleets had modest manpower requirements. The same holds true for Britain, whose surrounding waters offered considerable protection from outside foes. From their more restricted land bases, both states were able to compete for world power with larger, more populous land powers like France and the German states.

The differences of culture, religion, language, and physical settings that had set European peoples apart from one another during medieval and early modern times intensified with the emergence of the modern national state and the carving out of colonial empires. What these Western European rivals had in common were not only the material conditions of maritimity but also the psychosocial outlooks inherent in the concept of both national state and empire. It was the sea that gave Europeans the opportunity to reach out—to explore and to seek new raw materials, products, and markets in exchange for their manufactured goods. The infinite nature of open-water expanses encouraged a national and regional mindset attuned to opening up new fields of economic activities and pursuing innovations in manufacturing, trade, and services. While from the sixteenth to the twentieth centuries Europe's major powers did indeed divide the world into separate colonial sectors, open systems that depended on exchange were developed within those separate spheres of influence that ultimately would become the basis for intraregional exchange and unity.

The European regional trading system goes back to medieval times and even to the classical Roman era, when traders moved outward with the legions. Thus, a millennium ago, European regional commerce was stimulated by networks of medieval trading centers that linked Anglo-Saxon, Gallic, Germanic, Scandinavian, and Slavic territories. German merchants set up trading houses in London as early as the eleventh century. Two centuries later (1226), the Hanseatic League of north German cities was organized. Over the next four centuries, the league extended its network along the North and Baltic Seas to embrace up to 160 cities and towns before its collapse in the mid-eighteenth century. A similar alliance among the communes of Lombardy, the Lombard League, had been formed in 1167 but lasted for only a century, torn apart by the wars between the papacy and the German rulers of the Holy Roman Empire.

In early modern times, European focus on commerce took on a global range. British, Dutch, and French trading companies operated within Asia and North America from the seventeenth into the nineteenth centuries as they vied for control of international trade. In addition, sophisticated banking and finance systems within Europe spurred the region's economic development. An example was the House of Rothschild, which operated branches in Frankfurt, London, Paris, Vienna, and Naples. This network played a major role in financing the operations of various European governments and providing the capital for railroads, mines, and the Suez Canal.

The global economic and political hegemony of Europe ended with two world wars. The first bled it of youthful manpower; the second left the region too devastated to hang onto its global empires. Despite the Allied victory in 1945, Western Europe could not compete with the American and Soviet superpowers. Its condition of geopolitical inferiority was underscored by dependence upon the United States for its military security as well as its economic recovery.

Four recent forces have enabled the region to overcome its inferior status and take its place as a full geopolitical partner with the United States within the trade-dependent geostrategic realm: (1) political and economic unity as expressed by the European Union and other groupings and agencies; (2) the collapse of the Warsaw Pact and dismantling of the Soviet Union, which eliminated the military and political threats that had absorbed so much of maritime Europe's political energy; (3) the vigor with which European corporate and financial sectors have, in many cases, collectively outstripped US leadership in promoting the global market economy; and (4) the diminution of US power and prestige in world affairs as a result of its unilateral policies and the ensuing military quagmires in Iraq and Afghanistan.

Within a brief half century, maritime Europe has emerged as the world's most and, indeed, its only highly specialized and integrated geopolitical region. The member states of the EU and its neighbors have turned from seeking security exclusively through national economic, political, and military institutions to deriving more and more of this security through common regional agencies and actions, backed by the United States.

This concept of security through regional integration derives strength from the broader geostrategic framework within which Europe is embedded—the maritime realm, the core of which is the Euro-Atlantic alliance. Indeed, absent such a broader framework, Europe's regional unity goals would probably have been far less ambitious and might never have been attained. It was the North Atlantic Treaty Organization, spearheaded by the United States, that provided Western Europe with the military shield against Soviet pressures, especially during the early phases of the Cold War, and enabled it to resist powerful internal Communist parties. Moreover, the presence of the United States as the military mainstay of NATO made it possible for Germany and its neighbors to put aside past enmities in favor of a common regional destiny. NATO protected Western Europe from fears of a revived, militaristic Germany, just as it protected Germany and the rest of the region from the USSR.

It was the economic might of the United States that put Europe on the road to recovery and in the position that it holds today—an economic power, with a population of over five hundred million (including all twenty-eight EU members plus Norway and Switzerland). Its combined wealth and financial centers are on a par with those of the United States. The euro has gained considerable strength against the dollar, and European exports have surged. Europe's engineering, electronic, pharmaceutical, and fashion industries all compete with their American counterparts for global economic markets, though sometimes working in partnership with them.

While maritime Europe has clearly emerged as one of the world's major power centers, it nevertheless lacks some of the geopolitical patterns and features that are found in North and Middle America, heartlandic Russia, and East Asia. First, maritime Europe's core is not a single, unified national state but a federation of such states. Its unity derives from a balance between national and regional interests, and there are constant tensions over the striking of such a balance. Second, the region's land base is limited. It lacks such geopolitical features as a lightly populated and extensively exploited effective regional territory (ERT) and a vast empty area—features that provide the other regions with defensive depth, room for space-age activities, natural resource reserves, and the potential for population absorption.

Incorporating the Maghreb (western North Africa) and the Sahara into the maritime European geopolitical region supplies an empty area. However, the ERT that links the other regions to their empty areas is still missing. The transitional land connection to the Sahara in Morocco, Algeria, and Tunisia consists of a narrow coastal plain backed by the Atlas Mountains. Thus the Maghreb cannot serve as an outlet for European population expansion, as it did during the colonial period. On the contrary, the tide of immigration has been reversed. The overpopulated countries of the Maghreb now provide Europe, especially France, Spain, and Italy, with much of the large pool of migrant labor that forms an unskilled underclass in urban and rural areas and is a source for growing social tensions.

Maritime Europe holds strategic and economic sway over western North Africa. In addition, now that the Russian sphere of action in Eastern Europe and the eastern Mediterranean has been curtailed, Europe has reached eastward through the EU expansion into the eastern Baltic, Poland, Slovakia, Bulgaria, and Romania. Should Turkey enter the EU and Israel arrive at a peace agreement with the Palestinian Arabs, Syria, and Lebanon, Europe's economic aid and investment will be vital to supporting the peace and promoting eastern Mediterranean development. Under such circumstances, the broadening of maritime Europe into a Euro-Mediterranean geopolitical region would become a realistic possibility.

The boundaries that set off maritime Europe and the Maghreb from the rest of the world system are marked by water barriers in three directions—the Atlantic to the west, the Norwegian Sea-Arctic Ocean to the north, and the Mediterranean to the southeast. To the south there are formidable barriers—the Atlas Mountains and the Sahara. The Atlantic water barrier extends from Iceland to the Azores and Canary Islands, excluding Greenland, which is geographically part of North America although it belongs to Europe geopolitically. The northern Norwegian Sea-Arctic Ocean boundary includes the island of Svalbard. The southeastern Mediterranean barrier waters separate Cyprus from the Levant (Israel, Lebanon, Syria, and the Palestinian Authority).

Only in the east does nature play no role in maritime Europe's geopolitical demarcation. There, beyond the Oder River, the northern European plain broadens into Poland, Belarus, Ukraine, and Moldova, which are parts of the Eurasian plain, and where continentality prevails. As a consequence, the geopolitical border between maritime Europe and the Eurasian heartland has fluctuated historically across a broad zone of contention within Central and Eastern Europe. It is not nature but the relative military and economic strengths of competing power cores and the structures of their respective strategic alliances that have fixed the limits of the region.

Soviet power pushed the line westward to the Elbe River in 1945. In the wake of the collapse of the Soviet Union, the boundary has been shifted eastward by Western European economic might and NATO's military power. The ultimate location of the line will depend to a considerable extent on the force that the West can and wishes to bring to bear and on the success with which Eastern European and Balkan countries manage their market economies. However, the boundary will also be fixed by the counterpressures that Russia exercises, especially in Ukraine and Serbia.

Geopolitical Features

The geopolitical features of the maritime Europe and the Maghreb region include its historic cores, political capital(s), ecumene, effective regional territory, immigration patterns, empty area, and boundaries.

HISTORIC CORE

Location of a region's historic core varies with the regional framework that marks a specific era. The nuclear core of Western Europe could be the Plain of Latium, the seat of the Roman Empire. For Eastern Europe and the Mediterranean, the core is Constantinople, capital of the eastern empire. The seat of power of the Carolingian Empire was the North Rhine-Westphalian center of Aachen. Paris was the historic core for Napoleonic Europe, while Brussels is the nucleus for today's unified Europe. It was Brussels that headquartered the first of the European bodies dedicated to the unity of the region—the European Coal and Steel Community (ECSC), which was established in 1952 to create a unified materials and labor market for the coal and steel industries. This supranational regulatory body was originally a community of six—France, West Germany, Italy, and the Benelux countries (Belgium, the Netherlands, and Luxembourg). The ECSC expanded into the European Economic Community (EEC, or the Common Market) to be joined by Great Britain. Later Ireland, Denmark, Greece, Spain, and Portugal became members. The EEC was then consolidated with other European bodies to

Figure 7.1. Maritime Europe and the Maghreb: Major Geopolitical Features

become the European Community (EC), an economic and political federation of European nations that was the forerunner of the European Union (EU).

POLITICAL CAPITALS

Identifying maritime Europe's political capital is equally complex. The capital of a nation is more easily defined than that of a unified region. The former is the seat of centralizing functions that cast their influence upon the various parts of the state. The capital of a geopolitical region, however, must serve a group of nations with disparate interests, zealous in their own prerogatives. In some situations, including that of maritime Europe today, such a capital is seen as "neutral ground," possessing a distinctive political-psychological character that can help regional leaders to mobilize public opinion in support of regional aims and yet not play an overpowering role. At a national level, Ottawa and Canberra fulfill such roles in highly federated states. In other situations, such as that during the Soviet era, Moscow's function and image expressed its regional dominance.

The European solution to the selection of a regional capital eschewed a single, "neutral" site. In the early 1950s, Saarbrücken appealed to many as a possible capital because it was under consideration as an autonomous district within the Western European Union. It fell out of consideration in 1955, when its electorate rejected a Europeanized Saarbrücken, preferring to remain part of West Germany. Geneva, too, was considered as a potential capital, given its location, facilities, history, and tradition as a neutral international center. However, Switzerland remained aloof from the EU and the Western European Union, thereby disqualifying Geneva. The country's strongest concession to formal bonds to a unified Europe are its membership in the European Free Trade Association, along with such other European countries as Norway, Iceland, and the Principality of Liechtenstein.

Rather than one capital being designated for the EU, its political functions were dispersed. Brussels became the seat of the European Commission and the Council of Ministers, Strasbourg of the European Parliament, and Luxembourg City of the European Court of Justice. Of the three centers, Brussels plays the more prominent role because it houses the European Commission, the union's major decision-making body, which is composed of one minister from each member state. The European Parliament in Strasbourg is the popularly elected representative governmental body. However, its legislative powers are largely consultative, save for the fact that it has the final vote on the EU budget. In addition to being the headquarters for the EU Court of Justice, Luxembourg City also houses the European Investment Bank.

The distances between these three "capitals" are short—120 miles separating Brussels from Luxembourg City and 45 miles separating the latter from Strasbourg—thus affording easy communication among the three. Of equal importance is that this "capital corridor" is central to southeastern England, the Paris basin, and the Rhine valley and thus lies within the heart of Europe's ecumene.

The appeal of Brussels to be the "first among equals" of the three centers is not only its central location attributes. The city has a cosmopolitan flavor, a moderate climate, and political and economic stability and has long been a center of culture and the arts. It is multilingual and multicultural, with rich traditions in trade and finance. With a history dating back to the sixth century CE, Brussels can rightly claim that it has been a crossroads of European currents and traditions.

Over and above those cities formally designated as seats of EU functional activities, certain national capitals have strong political or economic influence in determining the destiny of maritime Europe. London, Paris, and Berlin have played the decisive roles in taking Europe to its developmental stage of regional specialized integration and continue to influence the future economic, political, and sociodemographic directions of the region. Frankfurt has become the financial capital of the EU, serving as headquarters for its new Central Bank and the twelve-member eurozone for currency. Architectural and building plans are under way to enhance the city's foundation and image as the modern European capital.

ECUMENE

Outlines of the Western European ecumene are defined by the region's heaviest concentrations of population and economic activity. The area extends from southeastern Ireland, the English Midlands, and the Thames basin through Paris and northern France, the Low Countries, northern Germany, the Rhine valley, and the Swiss plain into northern Italy. Population densities generally exceed three hundred persons per square mile. The ecumene includes such metropolitan centers as London, Paris, Randstad in the Netherlands, the Rhine-Ruhr conurbation, and the Hanover-Bremen-Hamburg triangle. From there, a northern prong extends to Copenhagen and Malmö, an eastern prong to Magdeburg-Braunschweig-Berlin, a southern one along the Rhine to include Frankfurt, Mannheim, and Stuttgart, and a southeastern one from Leipzig to Dresden to Prague. In the Rhine-Ruhr conurbation, Dortmund has become the hub for high-technology firms, which have replaced the declining, older chemical and steel industries. London, Paris, Frankfurt, Geneva, and Milan serve as the driving financial engines.

In the delineation of the ecumene of a nation or a region, small, noncontiguous outliers may also be included. An important outlier is Italy's highly industrialized Po Valley, which extends from Turin through Milan and on to Venice and Trieste. Southeastern Ireland, a thriving center of high-tech industry, and southern Scotland are recent outlier additions, separated from England's portion of the ecumene, despite the physical gaps between them. The addition of southern Scotland reflects its economic revival, owing to the development of high-tech industry. Moreover, offshore oil and gas pumped from North Sea fields have contributed to the economic boom. Indeed, Scottish nationalists argue that an independent Scotland could become a wealthy country, especially if the deeper offshore fields prove to be as extensive as believed. Scotland has voted to remain within the United Kingdom, thus emerging as a northern exclave of Britain's portion of the European ecumene.

The industrial decline of England's Midlands and its northern reaches sets these regions in sharp economic contrast to the high-tech, service-oriented, prosperous southeast, and thus the former are no longer part of the ecumene. The same applies to the "Second England" of the North, where textile and steel mills have closed, the shipbuilding industry has collapsed, and the coal mines no longer operate.

From Bremen-Hamburg, the ecumene extends to the Oresund, where Malmö, Sweden, has been linked to Copenhagen, Denmark, and thence the rest of the continent by a bridge-tunnel system. Copenhagen's airport is a hub for northern European aviation. The dynamic industrial and financial economy of the Oresund is well positioned to reach out to southeastern Norway (Oslo) and southern Finland (Helsinki). Its industrial base includes engineering, motor vehicles and aircraft, pharmaceuticals, shipbuilding, armaments, telecommunications equipment, and a financial sector that has been strengthened by mergers of Nordic banking and insurance firms.

The middle and upper Elbe and Mulde River valleys of southeastern Germany and the Czech Republic branch southeastward from Hanover to extend the ecumene from Leipzig to Halle, to Dresden, and to Prague. This area has a heavy concentration of chemicals, machinery, textiles, transportation, optical instruments, electronics, and armament production besides being a focus for commerce and financial services.

With the growth of the high-tech industry, not only has the European ecumene been revitalized, but also its outer boundaries are being expanded. University centers are playing a key role in attracting venture capital to their cities to support innovations in such fields as software, computer chips, wireless technology, interactive television, and biotechnology. Thus university towns like Cambridge, Leiden, and Louvain have spearheaded developments that have compensated for the decline into rust belts of nearby areas once powered by coal and steel.

In southern Europe, a high-tech industrial arc has developed that extends from the aeronautical factories of Toulouse to the computer chip center of Sophia Antipolis near Nice. This arc is poised to join the Turin-Milan-Venice portion of the current ecumene, which is also a focus for software.

North of the Alps, Munich has become a major center for biotechnology and can be expected to pull prosperous southern Germany into the upper Rhine portion of the ecumene, which now extends to Stuttgart.[1] In northern Europe, Stockholm, Uppsala, and the Finnish university town of Tampere are important for telecommunications. However, they are too geographically removed from southern Sweden to join the expanding European ecumene. The ecumenes of the thirteen states that have joined the EU since 2004—the "New Member States" (NMS) or "New Europe"—are isolated from "Old Europe's" (OMS) ecumenes. The exception is Poland's Silesian ecumene from Krakow to Katowice, which extends along the Upper Oder River to the industrialized Ostrava area on the Czech side of the border.

EFFECTIVE REGIONAL TERRITORY

Europe's effective regional territory (ERT) includes areas that are more lightly populated than the heavily urbanized ecumene but are readily "exploitable" due to their locational relationship to the ecumene, favorable soils or minerals, and an adequate transportation and communication net. From one-quarter to one-third of Old Europe consists of arable lands that constitute the ERT. These lands are mainly in farming or grazing and support substantial rural populations. For example, the rural populace of Portugal is 45 percent, Ireland, 40 percent, Finland, 40 percent, Italy, over 30 percent, France, 25 percent, and Norway and Spain, each over 20 percent. At the same time, these countries, with the exception of Portugal, have highly modern industrial and postindustrial economies to support this farming sector and to speed its modernization.

Under normal conditions of modern development, one could expect the row-crop acreage and pasturelands of these countries to be converted to more intense economic uses and be rapidly absorbed into the ecumene. However, culture, traditions, and politics tend to maintain the status quo and block an urban expansion that could relieve the ecumene from current "piling up." Exceptions are the Upper Garonne (Toulouse to the Mediterranean) and southern Bavaria (Munich to Augsburg).

Without a change in EU farm subsidy policies and national traditions, Old Europe's ecumene is likely to remain contained spatially, burdened by the weight of population and economic activities, rather than expand into the ERT, as is the normal progression of development.

Should there be a change in policy, relatively flexible high-tech, telecommunications, and service industries could readily move into parts of the ERT. Areas with potential for such movement are the Spanish Meseta Central, Italy's Mezzogiorno, and France's Aquitaine basin, which covers the area from the Pyrenees through the Lower Garonne (Bordeaux) and then extends northward along the Bay of Biscay to La Rochelle.

In contrast to the limitations on area expansion of Western Europe's ERT, the region's eastern New Europe has extensive rural areas which house from one-half to one-third of its total populations. As their economies are restructured and West European capital and technology are outsourced to them, the NMS will expand their ecumenes into the present effective regional territory. This is a relatively long-term proposition. EU farm subsidies, migration of younger workers to OMS for factory and service jobs, traditions, and the inertia of an aging farm population are likely to slow economic development. While the NMS receive only about a quarter of the EU's farm subsidies, this may be enough to sustain their farm economies.

As with US agricultural subsidy policies, the EU's has come in for considerable criticism. Its Common Agricultural Policy (CAP) has contradictory policies. Some goals are assuring farmers and fishermen of adequate incomes, making agriculture more competitive and market oriented, stimulating rural development, and furthering environmental protection. However, farm lobbies, especially those in France, Germany, Spain, and Italy, resist lowering subsidies on sugar beets, dairy products, wheat, and poultry. Antisubsidy forces argue that they undermine struggling Third World farmers, especially those in Sub-Saharan Africa, and that the main beneficiaries are large corporations. The antisubsidy struggle has shown some signs of success. The opposition extends beyond Europe, with the World Trade Organization weighing in. In the 1990s, over 60 percent of the EU's budget went to CAP. In 2007, subsidies accounted for 43 percent of the budget, and the goal was to lower the figure to one-third by 2013.[2] This goal was nearly reached that year, as agricultural subsidies represented 38 percent of the budget.

EMPTY AREAS

Maritime Europe has no vast empty spaces, and it is in this connection that the Maghreb is such an important geopolitical adjunct. The empty area for the region is the Maghreb's Sahara, the world's largest desert, which has a population of under two million. Vast oil and gas deposits underlie the desert surface in Algeria. In addition, there are extensive deposits of iron ore in Mauritania and western Algeria, as well as phosphates in northern Morocco and Western Sahara—the former Spanish colony that was annexed by Morocco in 1975. A source of conflict in Western Sahara has been the native Polisaro independence movement, which operates out of Algerian bases and is backed by the Algerian government. While a cease-fire agreement a decade ago muted the conflict between the rebels and Morocco, it has recently heated up again.

Until the end of the 1960s, France was able to use the inaccessible and seemingly endless Sahara Desert tracts for nuclear and rocket-launching activities. Colomb-Béchar and Hamaguir in the Western Sahara, as well as Reggane in southern Algeria, were used for missile testing from the late 1940s through the 1960s. Reggane alone was the scene of seventeen underground and atmospheric nuclear tests conducted by France. However, because of the tensions between Algeria and France, such tests were moved to the Moruroa and Fangataufa atolls of southern French Polynesia in the Pacific Ocean. Inasmuch as use of the Sahara for space-launching sites has also been precluded, France has shifted these activities to Kourou in

French Guiana, where the European Space Agency now maintains an active program. This is a far different function from that played by French Guiana up to the end of World War II. For centuries, this overseas department was used by the French as a site for penal colonies, such as Devil's Island, and for sending political exiles.

When Algeria resolves the long-standing Islamic fundamentalist rebellion that, together with Berber unrest, has destabilized the country, and when it is able to offer Europe a reliable staging area for joint space activities, the Sahara is likely to again become an important world arena for civilian as well as military space-launching purposes.

As previously noted, what differentiates the Saharan empty area from those of the world's other major power centers is that the Atlas Mountains are a major barrier to access from southern Europe to the desert region. In contrast, the settled portions of the United States, Russia, and China have direct land connections with their respective empty areas. In addition, similar to the case of Russia, which has lost most of its midlatitude desert regions to Kazakhstan and the four other former Soviet Central Asian republics, Europe's access to the Sahara is now highly dependent on stable political relations with the Arab western North African states, especially Algeria.

BOUNDARIES

The Eastern Border Zone

The eastern boundary of maritime Europe is the region's only undefined boundary from both a physical geographical and a geopolitical standpoint. Most geographical definitions of the European continent describe its eastern border as running along the Ural Mountains and then southward to the Emba River, which flows into the northwestern Caspian Sea. Within this broad geographical framework, the break between Europe's maritime and continental portions follows a broad zone within which the boundary has oscillated.

The boundaries of this zone, one of the oldest geopolitical features in European history, have fluctuated with the relative power and movements of Germanic and Slavonic peoples. There was, indeed, a boundary between these two, set by the Treaty of Verdun, as early as 843 CE. It ran along the Elbe and Saale Rivers to the Bohemian Forest. For the next five centuries, it was breached by the Germanic peoples, who penetrated into Slavonic territory in a series of forays and invasions.

The deepest early penetration was along the Baltic Sea, where commercial opportunity and large tracts of agricultural lands and forests beckoned. The Hanseatic League created a string of trading centers along the Baltic coastlands in the eleventh century that extended from Lübeck, Copenhagen, and Malmö in the west through Danzig to Riga, Reval (now Tallinn), and Narva in the east.

A more aggressive invasion was that of the Order of the Teutonic Knights, who established control over the whole sweep of the coastal region by the beginning of the fourteenth century. They created large landed estates and strengthened the Germanic hold over these Slavic lands.

In succeeding centuries, the tide turned. The Germans were driven out of the eastern Baltic, which then became a battleground among Poland, Sweden, and Russia. The latter eventually prevailed, gaining control of the region in the eighteenth century. In the western Baltic, however, East Prussia and West Prussia remained German. They joined the Principality of Brandenburg in 1600 and led the eventual unification of the modern German state.

During the first half of the twentieth century, Germany again pressed eastward, invading Russia in World War I and the Soviet Union in World War II. This eastern border zone continued as the meeting point and battleground between Germans and Slavs but now became part of the broader clash between land and sea power.

In 1915, James Fairgrieve described the belt in Europe between the Eurasian heartland and the Western European sea powers as a broad "crush zone" of buffers, extending on the east from Scandinavia and the Baltic countries through Eastern Europe to the Black Sea, and on the west from the Low Countries and Germany to Switzerland.[3] This was a much broader zone than the one presented by Halford Mackinder in 1943, which extended from the Baltic to the Black Seas and represented the contact area between Eurasian land power and European sea power. Fairgrieve postulated that the boundary line within the zone would shift as technological change and political-economic developments gave one side strategic advantage over the other.[4]

In the struggle between maritime and continental Europe that followed World War II, the boundary shifted westward to the Elbe as a result of the extension of Soviet power (see figure 7.1). When the former Third Reich was divided in 1945, West Germany's eastern boundary ran from Lübeck to the lower Elbe and then southward following the Harz Mountains and the Thuringian Forest before swinging eastward to the Ore Mountains. What became East Germany was stripped of its eastern marchlands (the territories of Prussian expansion), which were transferred to Poland and the Soviet Union. The boundary between East Germany and Poland included Szczecin (Stettin) within Poland and then followed the Oder River to the Neisse River to the Sudeten Mountains and the Czech border. This line was recognized by East Germany in 1950; twenty years later it was recognized by Bonn.

The German lands to the east of this boundary were mostly transferred to Poland in compensation for the eastern Polish territory that was annexed by the USSR. This territory covered thirty-nine thousand square miles and included western Prussia (Pomerania, Lower Silesia, and Upper Silesia), the independent state of Danzig, and the southern half of East Prussia. Although the German lands that Poland gained had been highly industrialized, they had been devastated by Allied bombing and the ground warfare between Soviet and German troops.

Offsetting this addition, between World Wars I and II, Poland lost to the Soviet Union an even larger area, totaling sixty-eight thousand square miles, of what had been eastern Poland. These territorial changes left Poland with a total land area of 121,000 square miles, or a net loss of 20 percent of its prewar area.

In addition to the lands that Germany lost to Poland, the northern half of East Prussia (the Königsberg region) was annexed by the USSR. Renamed Kaliningrad, it was directly affixed to the Russian federated republic.

The new post–World War II boundary between Poland and the Soviet Union extended from Kaliningrad and Lithuania south to the Carpathians. This line approximated the proposed Curzon Line, which had been recommended as Poland's border by Lord Curzon at the Versailles Conference following World War I but had been rejected, first by the new Soviet state and then by the Poles. The Soviets demanded only that the line be redrawn to shift several small areas, five to eight kilometers eastward, to Russia that would have gone to Poland.

The Polish territory that was annexed by the USSR had been part of the Jewish Pale of Settlement—that part of czarist Russia to which Jewish settlement was legally restricted. This included such major Jewish population centers as Vilna, Grodno, Baranowice, Brest, Pinsk, Lviv, and Ternopil. Nearly all of the 1.3 million Jews of the Pale and the rest of Poland's total Jewish population of 3.3 million had perished in the Holocaust, as only a handful survived the concentration camps, fled to the USSR, or remained in hiding during the war.

The Soviet Union also seized Bessarabia from Romania to form the bulk of the Moldavian SSR's territory. The southern part of Bessarabia was added to Ukraine, as was North Bukovina, which lay to the west of Bessarabia. In the Soviet far north, strips of land were taken from Finland for the purpose of adding greater defensive depth to Murmansk, the mining centers of the Kola Peninsula, and St. Petersburg. The Baltic countries that had gained their independence in 1919—Lithuania, Latvia, and Estonia—were also reabsorbed as Soviet Socialist Republics.

All told, Soviet land acquisitions in Eastern and Central Europe totaled 265,000 square miles. They contributed substantially to Moscow's ability to keep a firm grip on its Warsaw Pact satellites and to pushing back the eastward reach of maritime Europe.

In the wake of various territorial changes that took place, nearly ten million ethnic German refugees and expellees moved to West Germany. While most came from the lands east of the Oder-Neisse line in Poland and northern East Prussia, 3.5 million came from the Czech Sudetenland and half a million from Hungary, Yugoslavia, and Romania. Territories that had been Germanized for over twelve hundred years were now back in Slavic hands.

Other Boundaries

There are relatively few internal boundary disputes in maritime Europe. The most serious are between Greece and Turkey on the eastern edge of the Mediterranean. One is the conflict over Cyprus and the other revolves around competing claims over territorial waters, airspace, and mineral deposits within the Aegean Sea.

The Greek Cypriot area is controlled by the internationally recognized Cypriot government, which holds 59 percent of the island's land area, and was admitted to the EU in 2004. The Turkish Cypriot area occupies 37 percent of the island, and the two are separated by a UN buffer zone that makes up the remaining 4 percent. Turkey's claims to the continental shelf affect the territorial waters that surround Greece's Aegean islands, like Samothrace, Lesbos, Chios, Nikaria, and Samos. The Turks maintain that these Greek islands, which lie close to the Turkish shores, are entitled to only a six-mile territorial limit beyond their shores, while the Greeks assert that the limit is twelve miles. The dispute affects shipping and airspace rights, and it has been exacerbated by discovery of oil and natural gas in the Aegean seabed.

The sovereignty of Gibraltar remains contested by Britain and Spain, particularly in the encroachment of Britain into what was established in the eighteenth century (in accordance with the 1713 Treaty of Utrecht) as a neutral zone. Gibraltar's airport is within this zone, around which the British have built a wall and fence.

At the northeastern end of maritime Europe, Northern Ireland remains a zone of tension. To be discussed in the section on the Maghreb are the territorial disputes between Spain and Morocco and those among the Arab states of western North Africa.

European Integration

THE MILITARY-STRATEGIC EQUATION

The reunification of Germany, the overthrow of Communist regimes in Central and Eastern Europe, and the collapse of the Soviet Union have made possible the eastward spread of maritime Europe. Since its establishment in 1949, with twelve members, NATO has expanded into a twenty-eight-member body. In 1999, Poland, Hungary, the Czech Republic, Slovakia, and the Baltic States were admitted. They were joined by Slovenia, Bulgaria, and Romania in 2004. All told, twelve of the twenty-eight NATO members are post-Communist countries.

The basic reasons for the initial enlargement of NATO were twofold. One was to strengthen security and democracy within these countries. The other, as expressed by Zbigniew Brzezinski and some leading German officials, was to reduce the overwhelming power of a reunified Germany by enlarging the alliance while at the same time reassuring Poland that Germany would become its strategic partner rather than a threatening neighbor. Macedonia in the Balkans, Ukraine, and Georgia have also sought membership. The former secretary general of NATO, Javier Solana Madariaga, strongly supported this expansion as part of NATO's new strategic concept of protecting Eastern Europe against the possible resurgence of Russia by way of a collective security pact that will have transatlantic links.[5] President George W. Bush vigorously advocated NATO's extension eastward to the borders of Russia, arguing that this would erase the "false" geographic divide between Eastern and Western Europe, protect democracy, and represent no threat to Russia. At the same time, Bush spoke of engaging Russia as a security partner, a goal that the NATO expansion has clearly undermined.

In its efforts to tie Georgia to the West, the Bush administration sent weapons and trainers to Georgia to strengthen its armed forces. American aid amounted to one-third of the country's budget. While this was happening, Abkhazia, a Georgian province on the Black Sea adjoining Russia, declared its independence. The Georgian government mistakenly took US support as a signal that it could attack Abkhazia with impunity. Russia sent troops that crushed the invasion within a few days. Washington was in no strategic position to challenge the dominance of Russia in the Trans-Caucasus, so it stood by.

Admission of the Baltic states to NATO has posed a direct threat to the heart of Russia. If serious tensions were to arise between Russia and the United States, this could lead to the return of short-range nuclear weapons to bases in the Russian enclave of Kaliningrad, which is wedged between Lithuania and Poland and is the headquarters for the Russian navy's Baltic fleet.

Russia has the capacity to destabilize the Baltic states because of their large ethnic Russian populations. Entry of Romania and Bulgaria into NATO has added to Moscow's strategic concerns over its freedom to use the Black Sea. The greatest threat to Russia, however, is posed by the possible inclusion of Ukraine. At present, a vaguely defined "special partnership" status exists between NATO and Russia. Drawing Ukraine directly into the Atlantic Alliance would surely upset the current uneasy strategic balance, for it would represent a significant intrusion into the Eurasian heartland. Moreover, admission of Ukraine would, in all likelihood, influence Moscow to seek to destabilize the Ukrainian government by encouraging the secession of the Russian population in the eastern Ukraine, including heavily industrialized Kharkiv (Kharkov) and the Donets Basin (Donbas).

Even Azerbaijan has sought consideration as a candidate for NATO membership. Should this application be entertained, positive relations between Russia and the West would be in jeopardy. The conflict between Armenia and Azerbaijan would drag NATO into a quagmire.

The proposal of the EU to build an armed force with the capacity for autonomous action in times of regional crises is a related military-strategic policy issue. The motivation is for Europe to be less dependent upon American-dominated NATO in situations that do not require massive involvement but might be brought under control by a robust, mobile force of sixty thousand. The EU rapid reaction force would absorb the military functions of the dormant ten-nation Western European Union. France in particular views such a defense force as a way for Europe to exercise its separate identity and not have to wait on the action or inaction of the US Congress and administration, as well as a counterweight to

US pressures to become embroiled in more distant conflicts. However, no action has been taken because of lukewarm support from some European countries and US opposition. Washington cites duplication of effort, fearing that the EU's defense policy might not be in consonance with that of NATO.

THE EUROPEAN INTEGRATION MODEL

The European integration model differs profoundly from other regional integration models. NAFTA, for example, is concerned almost exclusively with economic integration. The former Soviet bloc, while it represented political, military, and economic unity, was built on a top-down model in which the USSR dominated the regional structures that were established. The European Union is unique in that it is based upon a partnership of states, some with highly centralized and others with federal structures, that have voluntarily turned over many, varied national functions to the regional body.

Three main forces contributed to the emergence of the European Union. First, the EU was conceived as a framework for hastening Europe's economic recovery from the devastation of World War II. It would facilitate the exchange of intraregional raw materials and products and take advantage of economies of scale. Today, half of Europe's international trade is intraregional. Second, it was a response to political pressure groups committed to the concept of federalism with the ultimate goal of achieving a United States of Europe, with democracy as its major political underpinning. And third, it would be an instrument for keeping in check the extreme nationalism that had wreaked such destruction upon Europe's separate states in two world wars and accomplish it without undermining their cultural, historical, and political distinctiveness.

The development of the EU was in stages that reflected these three forces. Fear of Germany's rebirth and the threat posed by the USSR was a prime stimulus for this drive for unity. Western European states recognized that they would need Germany economically but that they had to do this through institutions that would preserve their own national interests while protecting them from future German military resurgence and tie them together to help maintain peace, freedom, and national independence. Economic bonds were the best entry points for achieving this goal.

The other overriding motive was the spreading influence of the Soviet Union and penetration of Communism into Western Europe. To guard against this, rapid economic recovery was critical. European cooperation in production and trade could improve the living conditions of all Europe's citizenry and therefore reduce national tensions that might undermine collective security. Such cooperation would provide a firm economic base on which a strictly military union such as NATO could build.

Between 1948 and 1952, America provided Marshall Plan aid of $22 billion to sixteen European states for their economic reconstruction despite a mild US recession in 1948. This aid made possible the import of capital and consumer goods that gave Europe the breathing space to deal with the economic hardship and high cost of living that had stimulated Communist-led strikes in France, Italy, and Britain in 1947 and 1948.

There were a number of functional organizations that preceded the establishment of the European Union. First came the 1948 Organization of European Economic Cooperation. Its function was to oversee European recovery as called for in the Marshall Plan. This was followed three years later by the 1951 European Coal and Steel Community (ECSC). This was a common market for coal, iron, and steel joined by France, Germany, Italy, and the three

Benelux countries. They expanded this market in 1957 by creating the European Economic Community—the EEC or common market—in which the six countries eliminated tariffs for intraregional trade of manufactured products and imposed a common external tariff. The EEC was subsequently expanded to include the United Kingdom, Denmark, and Ireland, and later Greece, Spain, and Portugal. Note that Spain and Portugal did not enter until the 1980s, when the dictatorships of Franco and his successor and Salazar and his successor were replaced by democratic governments in the mid-1970s.

The situation in Europe changed drastically after 1991, with German reunification, dissolution of the Warsaw Pact, and collapse of the Soviet Union. The following year, the EEC members signed the Treaty of Maastricht to create the actual European Union, which was formed in 1993. Two years later, Austria, Sweden, and Finland joined the EU, to be followed by the ten Eastern European countries, to make a total of twenty-seven members (now increased to twenty-eight with the addition of Croatia). The Eastern European countries had to accept standards of human rights as the best guarantee that they would remain democratic.

Maastricht also called for the adoption of the euro—the common currency. This required common interest rates set by a European Central Bank. Seventeen countries joined the eurozone. Notable exceptions were the United Kingdom, Sweden, and Denmark. The euro replaced individual national currencies, eliminating the need for European travelers to exchange currencies and for businesses to have to deal with different exchange rates.

Achieving European unity is a struggle to find a balance between these national and regional interests at the same time that Europe is striving for a new equilibrium with the United States within the Atlantic Alliance and the maritime geostrategic realm. Within the European Union, the struggle focuses particularly on whether the EU should be a highly centralized body, as advocated by Germany, or a looser federation governed essentially by its member states—a position held by France. Britain is ambivalent. Indeed, Euroskepticism is so far-reaching in that country that a referendum is being promoted by the Conservative government as to whether Britain should remain within the EU.

There have also been differences within the union over such issues as embargoes on British beef by the continent's member states, British opposition to the euro currency, EU farm policies, the pace of enlarging the union, and the suspicion by some members that France is seeking to undermine NATO in its vision of an independent European military capacity. These differences were sharply exposed in 2005, when a proposed constitution was rejected by French and Dutch voters and Britain and Poland expressed strong reservations. Nevertheless, the past decade of substantial economic growth and social advances weighs in favor of greater integration. This is reflected in cross-border corporate mergers; the ascendance of European law over national legislation in such areas as trade, human rights, working conditions, and environmental controls; and the effective loss of sovereign control over monetary policies on the part of those EU members that have joined the euro currency zone—eighteen as of 2014 (Britain, Denmark, and Sweden are among the nonparticipants). Joint customs and tariff policies further strengthened integration. Europeans have a long way to go in developing a sense of regional political European identity, but progress is undeniable.

Although Turkey is now recognized as a formal candidate, its membership application to the EU remains stalled. Consideration has been put off owing to the insistence of Greece that the Cyprus issue and territorial disputes in the Aegean Sea be resolved before admission of Turkey can be discussed. More significantly, the reservations of the Europeans center on inclusion of an Islamic nation. Other candidates for membership are Macedonia, Serbia, and Iceland, although the latter has suspended negotiations owing to strong opposition within the Icelandic parliament.

Even though maritime Europe is not a military superpower in the same sense as the United States, its aims of achieving political parity are well grounded because of its economic strength and historical-cultural bonds and because its national ecumenes, with their dense communications networks, merge into the highly integrated regional ecumene. The twenty-eight EU members constitute the world's largest trading bloc and foreign aid donor. Latvia, the most recent member, joined in 2014. The EU nations' combined wealth of over $16.5 trillion in GDP is greater than that of the United States, and their over five hundred million population is one and three-quarters larger. Wall Street no longer dominates the global capital market. In fact, the combined EU financial markets are as large, and the euro serves to unify these markets by facilitating capital flow and commerce. Globalization of finance has helped Europe to strengthen its world position and prevented US domination of the international economy. London leads the world in investment banking and fund management, and London and Frankfurt both top New York as the leading exporters of financial services. The wave of international corporate mergers that is so feared by Europeans, who decry the American acquisition of European companies, has been far from one-sided. European corporations have been equally aggressive in taking over US concerns so that a transatlantic balance exists in the process of corporate agglomeration.

The operating budget of the EU, which in 2013 was approximately $160 billion, is minuscule compared to Washington's nearly $3.5 trillion and is therefore a far less powerful fiscal instrument for the conduct of foreign policy. Nevertheless, Brussels does use its budget for regional aid to poorer members and, increasingly, for humanitarian assistance to the developing world. The foreign aid component of the budget is already one of the largest in the world. Moreover, the EU has substantial influence upon international financial agencies as well as on the treasuries of its member states, which themselves provide much more humanitarian aid than does the United States.

The major factors that contribute to maritime Europe's march toward political integration are (1) complementary economic and human resources, (2) ease of movement across relatively short distances, and (3) a political commitment to regional unification.

TRADE

Maritime Europe has historically been the world center for international trade, and it continues to be so. The exchange of goods and services that so dominates the economy also has shaped its politics and culture. One measure of the importance of the EU's foreign trade is that it accounts for one-fifth of the world's imports and exports. By contrast, US trade represents one-tenth of the world's total.

The revolutionary change that has taken place over the past half century is that so much of Europe's trade is intraregional, now that the movement of peoples, goods, and ideas is unhampered by Western European national boundaries. Its five largest states conduct over half their foreign trade within the EU; US trade with its NAFTA neighbors comes to 30 percent.

Trading characteristics are linked directly to the region's prosperity as well as to its intensive internal links and its ties to the rest of the world. EU exports amount to approximately three trillion dollars in goods and services, balanced by the same amount for its imports. Exports go mainly to the United States, China, Switzerland, and Russia, while the leading sources of import are China, Russia, and the United States.

Europe's larger countries have broader economic bases but still benefit from specialized roles. Germany's economy is the most varied. It is the largest of maritime Europe's countries,

Table 7.1. Maritime Europe Population and Trade in European Union Key States

Country	*Population (millions)*	*Leading Export Market*	*Leading Import Market*
Belgium	10,449,361	European Union	European Union
France	66,259,012	European Union	European Union
Germany	80,996,685	European Union	European Union
Ireland	4,832,765	European Union	European Union
Italy	61,680,122	European Union	European Union
Netherlands	16,877,351	European Union	European Union
Spain	47,737,941	European Union	European Union
Sweden	9,723,809	European Union	European Union
United Kingdom	63,742,977	European Union	European Union

Sources: Central Intelligence Agency, *World Factbook 2014*, https://www.cia.gov/library/publications/the-world-factbook/rankorder/2119rank.html; Wikipedia, "List of Countries by Leading Trade Partners," *Wikipedia*, updated April 2014, http://en.wikipedia.org/wiki/List_of_countries_by_leading_trade_partners.

with a population of over eighty million and a GDP that ranks fifth among world states. Germany stands out as the world's leading exporter. It is the third-largest manufacturer of motor vehicles as well as a leading producer of metal, engineering products, and chemicals. West Germany successfully met the challenge of absorbing East Germany's aging post-Communist-era economy. The country leads the world in generating wind and solar power. In 2012 this met 22 percent of Germany's electricity needs, and in peak months, winds produced over one-third of these needs. In 2000, the German government announced a phase-out of its nuclear power plants, pledging to close them by 2020.

France is unique among its European peers in that three-quarters of its electricity is produced by nuclear energy. Chemicals, aircraft, and motor vehicles are major industries, along with wines, tourism, and fashions. It is the second-largest maritime European state, with a population of over sixty-six million and an economy which is Europe's second largest. Its reconciliation with Germany after World War II led the way to European integration, including the adoption of the euro.

Italy has retained an important niche in viticulture and the fashion goods industry while its engineering, steel, and chemical industries are economic mainstays. For Spain, machinery, footwear, chemicals, and food are important exports. In its south, a system of intensive vegetable production for export has developed that uses irrigation and plastic sheeting and draws upon a labor pool from nearby Morocco. This complements the region's traditional sales of olives, fruit, and wines.

Great Britain's population of sixty-four million is nearly as large as that of France, and it has a similar GDP. It has offset the decline in its traditional manufactures, such as steel, chemicals, and textiles, to focus on service-related industries, especially finance and information technology. In combination with France, it also rivals the United States for civilian aircraft manufacturing. Britain has played a unique role in linking Europe and the United States geopolitically through the Atlantic Alliance. The auto-rail Channel Tunnel (the "Chunnel") has linked Britain to mainland Europe in both a transportational and psychological sense. However, London still distances itself slightly from the rest of the EU by refusing to join the eurozone. Also, sharing the North Sea oil and gas fields with Norway has given Britain the energy independence that its European neighbors lack. However, this oil peaked at the turn of the century. Output is expected to decline rapidly over the next two decades, changing

Britain's status from exporter to importer. The same applies to Norway, whose economy has benefited even more from the North Sea energy fields.

Sweden's broad manufacturing base provides exports in forest products, machinery, and transport equipment. Its telecommunications products also command a strong market. More than any other country in Europe, and indeed in the world, it has demonstrated that a nation can blend entrepreneurship, work ethic, and improved educational and health systems with a welfare economy that serves those who most need the support of the state.

Complementarity of economies enhances specialization among Europe's smaller countries. Thus, Iceland's electronics industry provides equipment for navigation and exploitation of fisheries to much of Europe's and the world's merchant and fishing fleets. Norway was the major producer of heavy water for nuclear reactors until it ceased production in 1989; but its merchant fleet, the third-largest in the world, continues to carry 10 percent of global trade, and its fish products are widely exported. This is in addition to its chief exports—oil and natural gas. Greece continues to forge ahead as the world's leading shipping nation, with its fleets accounting for over 20 percent of the world's merchant fleet tonnage.

Luxembourg has overcome its depleted iron ores and its declining steel industry to gain prosperity as a world-class center for banking and finance. The economy of the Netherlands, although varied, has a special niche in hothouse flowers and cheese production, while it derives considerable strength from Europoort, which is the westward extension of the port of Rotterdam, located on the southern bank of the Hook of Holland, where the Rhine-Maas-Waal river system enters the North Sea. Europoort is Western Europe's major oil port and handles container traffic and the bulk movement of raw materials destined for interior Europe. Belgium continues to specialize in iron and steel and in textiles while maintaining its position as the world's largest diamond-cutting center and specialization in glass production.

Ireland's economy no longer depends upon fishing and farming, although brewing and food processing remain important industries. Before Europe's deep economic recession of 2008, it had become one of the wealthiest countries in the world, with its prosperity linked to its holding a major share of Europe's PC software and business applications, publishing, teleservicing, and industrial and chemical manufacturing. No longer a country of out-migration, it had attracted back many Irish émigrés and was a destination for East European labor. Then GDP crashed by one-fifth, unemployment rose to 15 percent, and out-migration resumed. It took five years for Ireland to turn the corner, which it did thanks to austerity budgets and tax increases. Foreign investment has begun to flow once again, although as of 2013 unemployment was still 13 percent and GDP was still below the 2007 height.

The products of Finland's telecommunications industry enjoy a wide global market. Denmark has shifted to electrical and electronic equipment and financial services with the decline of its agriculture, fishing, and shipbuilding. Microstates such as Liechtenstein and Andorra specialize in tourism and providing tax havens for trade and headquartering of foreign corporations. To these functions Monaco adds gambling as an important activity.

TRANSPORTATION AND TELECOMMUNICATIONS

The highly integrated transportation and communications systems of maritime Europe have influenced the process of regional unity, which in turn accelerates the continued development of highways, railroads, rivers and canals, pipelines, and telecommunications networks. These are the sinews that bind Europe together. Among the important links in the system are the auto-rail "Chunnel" and the Oresund Bridge and Tunnel between Denmark and Sweden. The latter has already encouraged twenty thousand Danes to take up residence in Sweden's Malmö area, and many Swedes commute daily to Copenhagen, where higher wages beckon.

The oil and gas fields of the North Sea are connected by pipelines to refinery centers along the coasts of the British Isles, Norway, Denmark, the Netherlands, and Germany. From there, a pipeline grid extends across Western Europe. A gas pipeline system also extends from North Africa's fields to southern Europe via Sicily and Italy and to Spain via Gibraltar, while pipelines from Russia reach to the eastern Baltic, Germany, and the head of the Adriatic.

The import of fuels from the North Sea and African fields as well as from the Middle East and other parts of the world is serviced through port installations all along the European coastline. Also, a dense intraregional grid from northern Scandinavia to the shores of the Mediterranean provides for the efficient sale and exchange of electricity, the net exporters of which are Norway, Sweden, France, Switzerland, Austria, and Spain.

Although road transportation now surpasses railways as the leading carrier of people and goods, the European rail system maintains high standards of efficiency, and high-speed railroads are strong long-distance competitors to aircraft. Trains that travel at speeds over two hundred miles per hour link the United Kingdom and France, France and Germany, and Belgium, the Netherlands, and Germany. Similar links are planned between Berlin and Warsaw, France and Italy, and France and Spain.

Canals carry only 5 percent of the goods of Western Europe, but they continue to play an important role for local traffic, especially in northern Germany and the Low Countries. Intricate systems of canals and rivers connect the Seine to the Loire, the Loire to the Rhone, and the Rhine to the Moselle and the Marne. The Rhine-Moselle-Marne water system is especially useful for exchanging bulk materials such as coal, iron ore, and steel.

The spread of modern telecommunications and information systems is also impressive. The region outranks the United States in the development and use of wireless phone systems, although it lags behind the United States in personal computer and Internet technology usage and marketing applications. The heaviest high-technology use centers on Paris, while in much of the rest of France there is cultural resistance to the adoption of home computers. The Netherlands, however, has demonstrated the capacity to develop as a world-class center for software production and e-commerce that is competitive with many US centers. The "Railteam" marketing alliance provides a website that links booking and scheduling information in a network that ties together much of Western Europe.

THE POLITICS OF UNIFICATION

Initially, the driving forces behind the unification of maritime Europe were the devastating effects of World War II and the threat of Soviet-exported Communism. Economic recovery and military defense took precedence in the creation of European regional bodies. In recent years, however, it has become apparent to most Europeans that the region cannot achieve its fullest geopolitical potential without a unity that is reflected in both law and political outlook.

The key legislative institutions that have emerged in furtherance of European unity are the European Court of Justice in Luxembourg and the European Court of Human Rights in Strasbourg. In becoming the world's leading regional regulator, the EU has developed a body of law that addresses nuclear waste disposal regulations, emission controls, trade, fishing quotas, working conditions, human rights, and discrimination in the armed forces. This prescriptive approach also focuses on consumer protection through product standards and environmental and health oversight. The competition between European law and national law is far from resolved, as enforcement of European edicts often encounters resistance from member states. In spite of such resistance, evolution of a supranational body of laws, a sine qua non for regional unity, is progressing steadily.

The two most important issues currently facing the European Union have to do with its governance structure and the management of its expansions. As noted, Germany has been a vigorous proponent of a strong, centralized European federation with a directly elected president and parliament sharing substantial power—in effect, a United States of Europe (as envisaged by Robert Schuman over half a century ago). For their part, Britain, the Scandinavian members, and Poland have long been opposed to any more dilution of national sovereignty and support only limited European parliamentary and executive powers, as in the current situation. It is premature to predict which view will ultimately prevail—a centralized superstate or a union of nation-states. France has now taken a stand against a strong central governance structure.

In 2005 both France and the Netherlands rejected a proposed EU constitution. A new draft treaty was then formulated in Lisbon in October 2007. This would eliminate the trappings of statehood, such as a European flag and anthem that provoked emotional opposition. It would assure retention of national sovereignty over judicial policies and foreign affairs but retain initiatives to streamline decision making. The EU voting system would become simpler and more reflective of a nation's population size. Majority voting would be the rule in many policy areas presently decided by unanimity. The treaty would also create a full-time president of the European Council to be elected for a term of two and a half years, renewable once, and the equivalent of a European foreign minister. This treaty had to be ratified by all members, including the ten East European countries, and is still pending. In 2014 a European parliamentary draft report called for increased cooperation in defense and economic policies. France favors this but opposes a constitution that would create a centralized federation. France also opposes a proposed resolution that calls for strengthening minority regional languages within the EU.

France has slowed reform of Europe's common agricultural policy, while Germany has favored reducing farm subsidies. In addition, Paris fears Berlin's domination of the union and thus opposes the reweighting of votes in the European Council, which would take into account Germany's larger population. For several years these and other differences frayed the relationship between France and Germany. With the election of Nicolas Sarkozy to the presidency in 2007, France sought to rebuild the Franco-German alliance. However, Paris continues to oppose Turkey's admission to the EU, over which Germany has taken no official stand, and has been highly suspicious of Poland's strongly pro-American political stance. Such suspicions were partly allayed by the results of Poland's November 2007 elections, whereby the erratic Jarosław Kaczyński government was ousted by a conservative government headed by Prime Minister Donald Tusk. Germany, for its part, is more interested in promoting the economic weight of the EU, not its political influence.

The Polish government initiated fiscal discipline measures and reduced tax rates, thereby weathering the 2008 fiscal crisis better than most European countries. In 2011 Prime Minister Tusk was reelected. The country continued to promote growth in the auto, pharmaceutical, aircraft, steel, and machinery industries, enabling Poland to emerge as one of the EU's strongest economic performers. In foreign policy, Warsaw has played a leading role in strengthening the "European partnership" between the older western EU members and the eastern newcomers. It has also pursued measures aimed at improving relations with Moscow.

The direction of the EU's political expansion has profound geopolitical implications. A highly centralized EU expanded to include Ukraine at the border of Russia would put

Germany in a central location geographically within the union, in addition to its economic and demographic dominance. It would gain through peaceful politics what it failed to win in two world wars—strategic control of Eastern Europe and a position that could upset the balance between the maritime realm and heartlandic Russia. However, an EU that remains a federation of nation-states would be balanced between England and France, with their Atlantic basin orientations on the one hand and Germany on the other. Under such circumstances, greater equilibrium would be maintained not only within maritime Europe but also within the maritime realm and the world system as a whole.

In 2013–14, EU efforts to tie Ukraine more closely into the union were met by Russian pressures to keep Ukraine within its security belt as part of a common market. The civil strife that broke out over the orientation of Ukraine threatens to divide the country between its western, pro-European half and its eastern, Russian-oriented Donbas region. Both the EU and Russia are treating their links to Ukraine as a zero-sum game. There is little recognition that the country could serve as a bridge between the two regions if it were encouraged into loose partnerships with both powers.

In the expansion of the EU, considerations other than economics come into play. Even when countries are economically weak, their applications have been promoted by Britain and France on the grounds of their having been strong supporters of the West during the Kosovo war. They have also had to conform to Western requirements in cleaning up their environments—a huge challenge for most New Member States, where air and water pollution and unsafe nuclear reactors compromise health and safety standards.

Those countries now seeking membership—Turkey, Croatia, the former Yugoslav Republic of Macedonia, Serbia, and Iceland —must also demonstrate that their political systems are democratic, based on market economies and the legal protection of human rights. Greece also opposes Macedonia's entry on the grounds of its use of the name.

Turkey's application has been put off for its abuse of human rights in putting down the Kurdish rebellion, the opposition of Greece because of the Cyprus conflict, and military control of substantial parts of Turkey's economy. The Turks are convinced that their being a country of Muslims is the fundamental barrier to their membership. The widespread discrimination that Islamic Turks encounter as guest workers in Germany and the similar hostility met by Muslim immigrants from North Africa are cited as evidence of racial and religious bigotry.

Geopolitically, Europe's failure to make a genuine effort to bring Turkey "into the club" could have grave consequences. Turkey is a cornerstone of NATO. If rebuffed by Europe, it could refocus its geopolitical attention toward the Middle East and Central Asia, not only to the detriment of the geostrategic interests of the maritime world but also at the risk of increasing tensions with Greece and undermining the Turkish commitment to a secular state.

Immigration Patterns

Recent immigration has played a key role in the growth of the maritime European ecumene and expansion of its ERT during the past half century. The region that had for so much of the modern age exported its surplus population has in recent decades become an importer of migrant labor from abroad.

There is, as yet, no common European policy on immigrants coming from outside the EU, leaving it to individual governments. Most of those who have migrated to the EU countries and have remained there are guest laborers, seasonal workers, asylum seekers, or illegals who have been smuggled into Europe through a variety of sea and overland routes. The largest number of migrants settle in the major urban centers of the ecumene or in outlying metropolitan regions. Many, however, come as farm laborers, some on a seasonal basis.

The origins and destinations of these foreigners reflect a combination of geographical proximity, former colonial ties, and acquaintance with the language of the host country. Germany has more foreigners than any other European country—over eight million, or 10 percent of its population. From 1960 to 1973, when it terminated the program, the Bonn government heavily recruited guest workers (*gastarbeiters*), the majority of whom came from Turkey. Estimates of its Turkish population vary from 2.5 to 4 million. The higher figure includes a third generation who are German citizens of Turkish origin. They are joined by the hundreds of thousands of immigrants who have come from Eastern Europe—Poland, Hungary, the Czech Republic, Estonia, Romania, Slovenia—and from North Africa.

This flow of immigrants has been augmented by tens of thousands of asylum seekers, especially from the former Yugoslavia and Turkish Kurdistan, but also from the Middle East. The Balkans also serve as a key route for hundreds of thousands of illegals from Asia who seek entry into Europe. While Germany and Austria have been the most generous of the EU member states toward asylum seekers, there is also widespread racial and religious prejudice within these countries toward immigrants on the grounds that their absorption will dilute their host countries' culture and nationalism.

In addition to its foreign immigrants, more than three million ethnic Germans have come to Germany since the collapse of the Soviet empire. The majority of these are the Russland Deutsche, who are descendants of German settlers who were first invited to the lower Volga region by Russian empress Catherine II in 1763. The others have come from Poland, Romania, the Czech Republic, Slovakia, and the Baltic states.

Over the course of time, the Volga German population grew, until it reached 1.8 million by the end of the nineteenth century. The growth was such that farmland became scarce in the Volga region, so in 1890 a program was launched to settle ethnic Germans in western Siberia. In 1924 the German Volga Autonomous Republic was established in recognition of the unique cultural background of the settlers. However, the republic was dissolved in 1941 and the inhabitants were deported to Siberia and Kazakhstan because of Stalin's fears that they were Nazi collaborators. Few of the ethnic Germans who have migrated from Russia are fluent in German, thus their absorption has been not much easier than that of non-German immigrants. This is true also for many of the ethnic Germans who have come from Poland.

France, with nearly eight million foreigners, is the EU's second-largest destination for immigrants. During the Algerian War of Independence (1954–62), one million French colonists returned to the mother country. Since then, they have been followed by five million Muslims from Algeria and Morocco, many via the overnight ferry from Algiers to Marseilles, and another one and a half million Muslim African from French West Africa. Proximity and fluency in the French language facilitate this migration. Employment is primarily in low-paying service and construction jobs in the large cities of France. Italy attracts illegal migrants from Tunisia, Libya, Albania, Ethiopia, and Eritrea, some of whom then move on to northern Europe.

Spain fills most of its farm labor needs from Morocco. The vast majority of workers are illegals who cross into Spain via the Strait of Gibraltar. Some Moroccans use the Gibraltar route to move on to the urban centers of France.

The foreign population of the Netherlands is approximately 10 percent of its total population. The Dutch migrant workers come from widely distributed points of origin—from the former colonies of Indonesia and Suriname, the former Soviet Union, southeastern Europe, and most recently Morocco and Turkey. With a long tradition of tolerance and multiculturalism, the Dutch have recently had to grapple with the resistance to integration of some of its migrants, including some Islamist extremists.

Sweden, too, has a relatively high proportion of foreigners—over half a million, or 6 percent of the populace. Most of them come from Eastern and southeastern Europe.

Many refugees came to Britain from Eastern Europe immediately after World War II. The much larger influx, however, is the result of historic ties with former colonies, which accounts for many of Britain's more than three million immigrants, including over one and a half million Muslims, half from Pakistan. Large numbers of English-speaking South Asians came to Britain to escape the terror of the India-Pakistan War of Partition. They were followed almost immediately by migrants from English-speaking West Africa and the Caribbean countries. West Indies bus drivers and hospital workers were actively recruited in the 1950s and 1960s, before this immigration was closed off in 1971. Expansion of the EU has brought many Eastern Europeans to Western Europe, especially over one million Polish workers into Britain and Ireland, filling skilled jobs as well as becoming construction and service workers. With the economic crisis of 2007 to 2009, most have returned home.

Prior to the recession, Ireland, with an explosive economy short of labor in the fields of information technology and electronics, had succeeded in attracting Irish expatriates from the United States, Canada, and South Africa. In addition, job opportunities for hospital, hotel, and construction workers, as well as farm laborers, brought workers from Eastern European EU countries, especially Poland. The recession put an end to this trend, and most of the migrants returned to their home countries.

Most of maritime Europe's recent migrations have been based on temporary work permits, the granting of asylum, or illegal residence. In many EU countries, the migrants face exploitation, racial bias, and other forms of discrimination. Austria's Jörg Haider and France's Jean-Marie Le Pen have made political capital by opposing Muslim and black immigrants. Their success has encouraged the rise of right-wing, anti-immigrant parties in Italy and the Netherlands and struck receptive chords among groups in Germany, France, Spain, and Greece. Immigration control has now become a mainstream issue in many countries.

Ironically, the anti-immigrant bias coincides with a time of declining population growth within the EU. Recent projections of the UN Population Division suggest that the countries of maritime Europe will need thirty-five million immigrants by 2025 and up to seventy-five million by 2050 simply to maintain the labor force at 1995 levels. The proportion of elderly within the EU is expected to increase to 22 percent by 2025. Without continuing immigration, total EU population may stagnate at today's 500 million, while the United States could increase to 350 million.[6] Because of declining birthrates, some European countries, such as Italy, Portugal, and Poland, face a major decline in population within the next two decades. The rate of natural increase in Western Europe is 0.1 percent, while Eastern Europe is actually experiencing a decline.

The admission of the New Member States has opened a back door to Western Europe. A basic tenet of the EU is free movement of people, goods, and capital among its members. However, the NMS have not yet been able to put in place the controls that the older members apply to external immigrants. Consequently, they have become a route for migrants from the Middle East, southeastern Europe, and elsewhere. Therefore, the treaties that included these new members made provisions, especially for Bulgaria and Romania, for a transitional period of seven years during which restrictions to the free movement of workers from the NMS to the OMS apply.[7] These provisions have now expired.

Mounting opposition within the Netherlands, Britain, and France to the EU policy that permits freedom of movement anywhere within the union is undermining one of its basic principles. This anti-immigration movement is fanned by bias against Muslims as well as Europe's economic crisis. In 2014 a Swiss referendum favoring immigration quotas gave further momentum to those calling for an end of free movement within the EU. Although Switzerland is not a member of the union, it has an agreement with it that includes freedom of trade, capital, and movement of people. This agreement is now in jeopardy.

Terrorist attacks in Western Europe, both foiled and successful, and the resistance to cultural absorption by large blocs of the Muslim immigrants, have led to tightening of immigration controls and made the issue of primary importance in many EU countries. Nevertheless, there is an imperative to continue acceptance of immigrants because of low birthrates, need for labor, and the human impulse to grant asylum.

A major overhaul in immigration policy is required if Europe is to maintain its current living standard. This would involve a systematic approach to instituting a sizable, planned, legal immigration rather than the unordered response to labor needs. There would also have to be a corresponding change in attitude toward foreigners from beyond the EU borders to replace hostility with an understanding of religious and ethnic pluralism and multiculturalism.

Merging of Eastern and Western Europe within the European Union

The EU is trying to reinvent Eastern Europe and pour it into a Western European mold—a policy driven less by sociopolitical and economic realities than by the "soft security" argument of needing to wrench the region permanently out of the Russian orbit.

Prince Klemens von Metternich, a conservative Austrian statesman of the first half of the nineteenth century, sought to balance Central Europe off against a French-Russian alliance. He described Asia as beginning at a street leading out of Vienna called "the Renweg." Translated into modern terms, this suggests that maritime Europe ends with Central Europe—at Vienna, Prague (Germanized Bohemia, the core of today's Czech Republic), and Budapest (the partially German city of Magyar-populated Hungary). From this line eastward, continentality is the regional hallmark.

Vienna and Budapest, the two upstream Danubian cities, served as the twin capitals of the Habsburgs' Austro-Hungarian Empire during the latter part of the nineteenth century. Prague, which is linked to Germany by the Vltava River, a tributary of the Elbe, and by a number of valleys to the south that reached to the Danube and Vienna, was the northern terminus of the Central European axis that extended to Vienna and Budapest. By most cultural, economic, and historical measures, the Czech Republic and Hungary deserve to have been admitted to the EU.

Slovenia, too, once an integral part of the Austrian Empire, has a rich Western heritage. By far the most industrialized, urbanized, and prosperous of the former Yugoslav republics and strongly linked by trade to Germany and Italy, it, too, is organically connected to Western Europe. In the Baltic, Estonia and Latvia, with their rich trading heritage, also have a strong maritime orientation. From these countries eastward, however, the expanded membership becomes problematic. One of the marks of a continental orientation is its heavier dependence upon agriculture compared with maritime trading states. Poland is the largest of the belt of Eastern European countries that border maritime Europe, with a population of nearly forty million, one-third of which is rural, and one-quarter of its entire workforce still dependent upon farming. While the country has made some progress economically through modest market reforms, its agricultural development lags, and its ratio of foreign trade to GDP is low. The same rural and agricultural orientation applies to Bulgaria and Romania.

The eastward advance of the EU represents an enormous challenge—the economic and political-cultural integration of nations that are far less developed than those of Western Europe. This expansion reflects Western Europe's exercise of "soft power" through sharing its wealth and technical know-how—a far cry from the past, when expansion and contraction across Europe were carried out through force of arms.

Political accommodation within the EU is more complex. Many of the post-Communist countries suffer from political turbulence and instability. Switching sides in coalitions is common, as are minority and caretaker governments, and in many the bureaucracy is stifling. An example is Poland, which despite its dependence on EU subsidies and remittances from expatriate workers has refused to conform with certain EU regulations. Poland's national elections of 2007 ousted the strongly pro-US government from control of its parliament, bringing a conservative party to power. Its platform called for withdrawal of all Polish troops from Iraq, reflecting widespread opposition to the war. With the Tusk government, Poland began to take a more cooperative and reliable stance in support of EU policies, taking the lead in bridging differences between Eastern and Western European countries, and in seeking a balanced relationship between the EU and Russia.

State Proliferation

In a geopolitical region, national states are the nodes, and lines of transportation and communications the connectors, that form the regional network. Maritime Europe has the world's densest network of nodes and connectors, enabling it to achieve unmatched levels of specialization and integration. This dense network increases the capacities of the region to maintain a dynamic equilibrium because of the multiplicity of opportunities for feedback and self-correction by its various components. Should a state become destabilized and its connectors to the rest of the region become blocked, the other states have alternative interconnectors to maintain the integrity of the system. Neither civil war in Northern Ireland, nor terrorism in northern Spain, nor the Cyprus conflict has impeded maritime Europe's drive toward regional unity.

The proliferation of nodes within an integrated system accelerates its development because the nodes can become additional centers of specialization. Thus, the proliferation of states, ministates, and national nodes in maritime Europe need not signal fragmentation and anarchy. For example, an independent Slovenia has already carved out its niche as a transit center for goods from Austria and Hungary to southeastern Europe. Should such nodes as Catalonia, the Basque country, Northern Ireland, and Scotland become highly autonomous or even independent, could we not expect them to take advantage of their locations, manpower pools, and resources to add to Europe's economic and political power? This would be possible only if they could turn their full attention to national development rather than dissipate so much of their energies in the struggles for political freedom.

State devolution in Europe does not necessarily mean complete sovereignty, but it does mean granting peoples who live in historically held territories the right to self-determination and the freedom to conduct those functions that they consider crucial to their survival as a people. In general, the interests of peoples struggling to gain their freedom from host countries center on being able to decide on matters of language, religion, culture, and economics. They may well be willing to allow the larger state from which they seek to break away to retain functions that relate to foreign policy and military defense. San Marino, which lays claim to being Europe's oldest state, has renounced such rights as establishing a broadcast station and growing tobacco in return for an annual subsidy from Italy. Liechtenstein, a wealthy country that is joined to Switzerland in a customs union, has no army and is represented abroad through Switzerland but conducts independent taxation and finance policies. Elsewhere, China's recent arrangement with Hong Kong—"two economies, one state"—might be another useful model.

One of the consequences of the creation of the European Union has been to spur these national devolutionary trends through the revival of regional cultures and languages. The charter of the forty-one-member Council of Europe encourages indigenous languages in schools, media, and public life, while the EU's Bureau for Lesser-Used Languages finances projects that promote minority tongues. Moreover, the reduction or elimination of barriers to trade and the movement of peoples throughout the union reduces the significance of current national boundaries.

Table 7.2 identifies national nodes that could emerge through a variety of new territorial entities within maritime Europe, including states, quasi states, confederations, and jointly ruled condominiums.

The Basque country of northern Spain (Vascongadas) extends from the coastal reaches of the Bay of Biscay inland to the Ebro River and into the western Pyrenees, where it overlaps with France. Geographical isolation has enabled the Spanish Basques, who are among Europe's most ancient peoples, to maintain their separate language, traditions, and nationality. During the Spanish Civil War, they established an autonomous state that was then crushed by General Francisco Franco. Over the past three decades, the Basque guerrilla movement (ETA) conducted a fierce battle against Madrid before accepting a cease-fire in 1998. They took up arms once again in 2005, when violent terrorism resumed, and since then peace talks have been on and off. The Basques are divided over their future with Spain. The moderate

Table 7.2. Potential European States and Quasi States

New National Node	*Type*
Azores	Gateway state
Basque region (Euskadi)	Quasi state
Brittany	Quasi state
Canary Islands	Gateway state
Catalonia	Gateway quasi state
Corsica	Quasi state
Crete	Quasi state
Faeroe Islands	Quasi state
Flemish Community (Belgian Flanders)	Quasi state
Galicia	Quasi state
Gibraltar	Gateway UK-Spain condominium
Greenland	State
Madeira Islands	Quasi state
Northern Ireland	UK-Ireland condominium (second-stage independence)
Scotland	Quasi state
Trentino-Alto Adige	Quasi state
United Cyprus	Confederation
Wales	Quasi state
Wallonia (French-speaking Belgium)	Quasi state

Basque right-wing and Socialist parties would accept a high degree of autonomy. The more extreme Basque Independence Party uses terrorism to try to achieve full independence for the Basque Autonomous Region (Euskadi), which has a population of 2.2 million Basques and 700,000 non-Basques. The much smaller Basque population of 250,000 on the French side of the border has shunned calls for linking up with their Spanish kinfolk.

Euskadi is a wealthy region whose per capita income exceeds that of Spain as a whole and which contains the thriving industrial centers of San Sebastian and the port of Bilbao, a major commercial and financial center with a strong industrial base. Although Bilbao's steel and shipbuilding industries have declined in recent years, its modernized industries include motor vehicles, pharmaceuticals, chemicals, textile machinery, and various consumer goods. Its infrastructure has been modified, and its cultural institutions, especially its museum, stimulate tourism. San Sebastian's major seaside resorts have fostered tourism, along with its fishing, metallurgy, and machinery. With peace, the Basque region has the economic potential to become an important gateway linking northern Europe and Iberia.

Catalonia's history of nationhood goes back to its separate political existence from the ninth to the end of the fifteenth centuries. Until the end of the Middle Ages, Barcelona's traders rivaled those of Genoa and Venice for commercial supremacy of the Mediterranean. The region has made consistent attempts to break away from Spain since the seventeenth century. A revolution for independence broke out in 1934 but failed. In the Spanish Civil War of 1936–39, Barcelona became the Loyalist Republican capital before falling to the regime of Francisco Franco, who repressed the Catalan language and culture. In recent years, Catalonia has been bolstered by considerable autonomy from Madrid.

Barcelona, the center of Catalonia, is Spain's chief commercial and industrial center as well as the country's leading port. Its industries include the manufacture of motor vehicles and parts, aircraft, electronics, machinery, and textiles. Catalonia as a whole is the wealthiest of all Spanish regions. With its population of over 7.5 million, its well-trained workforce, and its historic Mediterranean leadership traditions, the region is especially well positioned to become a gateway for the entire western Mediterranean. The Spanish constitution was revised in 2006 to recognize Catalonia as "a national reality." The new status establishes Catalan as the official language, along with Castillian, with the right and duty of every Catalan to know the language. As noted in chapter 3, Catalonia is now a highly autonomous region, with broad jurisdiction over economic, cultural, and policing affairs. With its new political status, Catalonia can retain its own nationality base without undermining Spain's overall economic and political viability.

Galicia is another Spanish province that strives for independence. Located in the northwestern corner of Spain, between the Atlantic Ocean and the Bay of Biscay, the Galicians speak a language akin to Portuguese. Their main pursuit is fishing in the coastal waters. While granted the status of autonomous region in 1981, the separatist spirit remains strong there. The new federal structure for Spain that was shaped by its agreement with Catalonia could and should serve as a model for the Galicians. Gibraltar, another possible gateway state, might emerge as a condominium between Britain and Spain.

In France, the grounds for Breton autonomy demands are essentially cultural and linguistic. Separate sovereignty has had little backing since Paris loosened its centralized grip by granting budgetary power to Brittany.

Corsica, with its distinct language and culture, has been the traditional scene of separatist movements, banditry, and blood feuds from the Middle Ages, when it was ruled by Genoa, up to its transfer to France in 1768. During the 1970s and 1980s, Corsican guerrillas conducted bombing campaigns to advance their independence drives. In recent years, economic development strategies have focused on tourism. At the end of 2001, Corsica was granted limited autonomy, which included the teaching of the Corsican language in schools. This did not halt separatist violence, as Corsicans rejected limited autonomy in a 2003 referendum. A high degree of autonomy and quasi statehood would appear to be a practical solution to the Corsican issue.

Crete was the scene of major separatist unrest against the Turks at the turn of the twentieth century until its incorporation with Greece in 1913. Later, in 1938, independence forces sought freedom from the dictatorship of Greece's Ioannis Metaxas, but the revolt was quashed. During World War II, when Crete fell to the Germans, and then briefly after the war, there was some Communist guerrilla activity on the island, but this did not spur the rise of a strong separatist movement. If the tensions between Greece and Turkey over Cyprus dissipate, and especially if Turkey should enter the EU, Crete's strategic value to Greece will decrease. Under such circumstances, Athens may be inclined to grant the limited powers of a quasi state to this island home of one of the world's earliest civilizations.

Greek Cyprus, with a population of 850,000, has 80 percent of the island's population and nearly 60 percent of its land area. It is internationally recognized and is a member of the EU, but there will be no peace until a solution is found to the fears of Turkish North Cyprus of being absorbed by the larger, more prosperous Greek sector. The Turkish sector has a population of three hundred thousand, of which nearly half are Turkish Cypriots while the rest are settlers from mainland Turkey. Cyprus became independent in 1960 under agreements that forbade either union with Greece (*enosis*) or partition. The 1974 coup by pro-*enosis* forces triggered Turkey's invasion of the northern part of the island to protect its Muslim population. Partition is an option that Greek Cyprus has flatly rejected. A federation of these two bitterly hostile territories, in isolation of their respective ties to Greece and Turkey, is unlikely. An interim solution might be the establishment of a condominium over northern Cyprus by Athens and Ankara.

Belgium is an arena that could divide into two new European national nodes. The political leaders of the Flemish (Dutch-speaking) populace of the prosperous north have expanded their previous demands for the autonomy of Flanders within Belgium to calls for a Greater Flanders, which would include both the Belgian north and the southern part of the Netherlands. Such a "Flemishland" would have a population of twenty-two million and an economy that would rank as the world's tenth largest.

In 2007, Flemish demands for independence reached a high pitch, as radical Flemish separatists created a parliamentary crisis when their party came in first in the national elections. Reflecting the deep divisions in Belgian politics, there were lengthy delays in forming a new government. Since the economies of the two regions are inextricably intertwined and French-speaking Brussels is the headquarters of both NATO and the EU, partition of the country would be complex. Since then, support for Flemish nationalism has waned. France has shown no desire to absorb independence-minded Wallonia, with its declining heavy industry and high unemployment. Neither does the Netherlands evince any interest in annexing Flanders. Neither side has the capacity to exist independently. The most likely alternative is a high degree of cultural and economic autonomy for both, with Brussels as a "corpus separandum" serving both as a federated and EU capital.

Devolution in Northern Ireland has been achieved. The accord that was reached provided for power sharing between the Unionist Protestant majority and Republican Catholic minority. In accordance with its terms, an assembly, executive, and ministerial council were established. With peace, Northern Ireland could emerge first as a condominium, with such powers as defense and foreign affairs being shared by the United Kingdom and Ireland, and ultimately as a separate state.

There are two different territorially and ethnically separatist forces in northern Italy: Trentino-Alto Adige and Padania. Trentino-Alto Adige was once part of the Austrian Tyrol. Its German-speaking populace (now about half of the total population of the province of Bolzano and Trento) has been backed by Austria in its demands for legislative, administrative, and linguistic autonomy. Rome has already granted the region considerable autonomy, but the issue of return to Austria may not remain quiescent without quasi statehood in a condominial relationship to Italy and Austria.

"Padania" is an invention of the Northern League, a north Italian, right-wing party established in 1982. Its leaders speak alternately of secession and federalism. The territory generally viewed as Padania takes its name from the Latin name for the Po River and what is sometimes called the Padana Valley. Geographically, this region covers Lombardia, Piemonte, Liguria, the Veneto, and Emilia (half of Emilia-Romagna). There is no historical territorial basis for a Padanian state, nor is it linguistically distinct from the rest of Italy. What drives the secession goals of the Northern League is the desire to separate the richest part of Italy, the north (sometimes they extend their claim to Tuscany and Rome), from the poorer south. While this political movement cannot be lightly dismissed, the prospects for its dismembering Italy are very poor. There are also separatist movements in Sicily and Sardinia. However, since receiving limited autonomy and because of their economic dependence on Rome, pressures for independence have subsided.

Portugal's Azores and Madeira Islands have already been granted the status of autonomous regions, while the Canary Islands have received greater regional autonomy from Spain—all part of the trend of devolution. Because of their economic dependence on their mother countries, quasi independence would be most realistic for the Madeiras and the Canaries. The more distant Azores could evolve into a gateway state, given their strategic location one thousand miles west of Portugal, one-third of the way across the Atlantic, and one thousand miles off the northwest African coast. The Azores now accommodate NATO air bases and also have popular resort areas.

The establishment of parliaments in Scotland and Wales is an important milestone in their devolution. The Scottish National Party is pledged to seek independence within the EU—a process that would require approval by all members of the EU and therefore be subject to London's veto. The growth of the high-tech industry in Aberdeen and the prospect of control of offshore oil and gas reserves has heightened the nationalist calls for statehood, despite the considerable political autonomy that Scotland now enjoys. Most of Britain's oil fields are located off the Scottish coast, as are 40 percent of the gas fields. In the event that Scotland were to gain its independence, the location of the Anglo-Scottish maritime boundary, which would extend from the River Forth into the North Sea, would become a point of contention. So might the fate of the Orkney and Shetland Islands, which lie off the coast of northeastern Scotland and have their own incipient separatist movements. The situation differs for Wales. The overriding concerns of Welsh nationalists are education, language, and culture. These can be satisfied by greater autonomy as a quasi state, particularly since the depressed economy of Wales makes it dependent upon London for long-term revival. The referendum on Scottish nationalism of September 18, 2014, strongly endorsed continued membership in the United Kingdom.

Greenland already enjoys semiautonomous status under the Danish crown, with foreign policy and defense being handled by Copenhagen. Nevertheless, Greenland continues to pursue self-determination for its more than fifty-five thousand people.[8] In particular, it seeks a stronger voice in the future of the US Thule Air Force Base, which was built during World War II and has been greatly expanded in recent decades. While Denmark has reservations about allowing Thule to be used for the US National Missile Defense system, the Greenlanders appear to favor such an installation and are using the issue as an opportunity to seek Washington's support for gaining a say in the ultimate decision. This ability would represent a form of quasi statehood. In all likelihood, however, statehood may be the only way to satisfy the self-determination goals of most Greenlanders.

Denmark's Faeroe Islands lie between Iceland and the Shetlands. The Faeroes, which first came under Danish rule in 1380, have had a strong nationalist movement since the nineteenth century. In fact, the islanders declared independence in 1946 after a plebiscite but then reversed the proclamation, receiving home rule in its place. This rule has enabled the fifty thousand inhabitants to close their fishing waters to EU members, despite their ties to Denmark. The plebiscite on independence scheduled for May 2001 was canceled after Copenhagen threatened to cut off its subsidies to the Faroes. What may renew impetus for the new independence drive is the possibility of petroleum finds in the surrounding waters. It is likely that a quasi-statehood formula may satisfy the ambitions of the islanders, especially since traditional fishing remains their economic mainstay and the need for annual subsidies from Denmark remains strong. A high degree of autonomy with symbolic ties to the Danish monarchy and close fiscal ties to Denmark seems most likely for the future of the Faeroes.

In summary, territorial devolution of states within maritime Europe can be expected to take different forms. However, rather than serving to fragment and weaken the region, they are likely to enhance its integration and strengthen it by adding specialized parts that will further bind the region together. It is highly unlikely that the members of the EU will allow the union to become the vehicle for facilitating the dismemberment of present national states.

The Maghreb: Maritime Europe's Strategic Annex

The geopolitical relationships between maritime Europe and North Africa are greatly influenced by the shape and structure of the Mediterranean Sea, its branches, and its surrounding coastlands. The present form of the sea is determined by the mountain ranges that make up three-quarters of its shores. The western Mediterranean basin, which extends from Gibraltar to the narrow waters between Tunisia and Sicily, is completely surrounded by mountains. Within the basin, the islands of Corsica and Sardinia form a north-south wall, to the west of which age-old trans-Mediterranean interactions developed between the Iberian Peninsula and France with Morocco and Algeria. The eastern side of this island wall helps to enclose the Tyrrhenian Sea arm of the Mediterranean, directing traffic between the western side of the Italian peninsula and the northern Tunisian shores.

The eastern Mediterranean basin is rimmed by mountains only on its northern and eastern edges. On its southern shores, from Sinai west to Egypt, Libya, and the Gulf of Tunis, the coast is low and straight, with no natural harbors. The transbasin links between the east coast of Italy and Libya cross the Adriatic and Ionian Seas and branch into the Mediterranean. At the eastern end of the basin, the Aegean Sea also branches into the Mediterranean, connecting Greece and Turkey with Egypt and the Levant.

The western Mediterranean basin has experienced a different history of political development than has the eastern end of the sea. The basin extends from its eastern end at the hundred-mile-wide Strait of Sicily, which lies between Cape Bon in northeastern Tunisia and southwestern Sicily, westward to the Strait of Gibraltar, which is only eight miles in width at its narrowest opening, between the Pillars of Hercules. For the most part, the western Mediterranean is encircled by young fold mountains. There are few breaks across them on the European side, save for the Ebro, Garonne, and Rhone valleys. In the Maghreb, the limited openings across the parallel Atlas Mountain chains are blocked from the rest of the African continent by the Sahara Desert. A number of islands lie within the sea and serve as stepping-stones to both northern and southern coasts (the Balearics, Corsica, Sardinia, and Sicily). Settled long ago by Europeans, these islands have been outposts for European states in their strategic relationships with the southern shores, and stepping stones for African asylum seekers in Europe.

The absence of effective breaks across the surrounding mountains has, until modern times, made the issue of control an internal or "family" matter within the western basin. Thus Carthage, Rome, North Africa, Spain, France, and Italy vied for control of all or parts of the basin with little outside interference. Because of their limited North African support base, the Moors (as well as the Carthaginians before them) did not penetrate effectively beyond Spain, Sardinia, and parts of Sicily. During the Middle Ages, Spanish-French-Austrian rivalry over Italy diverted the attention of the European powers from the North African coast.

In modern times came two changes: (1) improvements in land communications across Western Europe to the Mediterranean and (2) the Anglo-French alliance, which controlled both the western entrance to the Mediterranean and the trans-Mediterranean sea-lanes. From the second quarter of the nineteenth century to the beginning of the twentieth, France secured strategic control of most of the Maghreb. It first invaded Algeria in 1830, and in 1844 it defeated the sultan of Morocco, who had aided the Algerians in their continuing resistance. Algeria was formally annexed four years later, and French influence in Morocco grew steadily over the second half of the nineteenth century. Tunisia was invaded and became a French protectorate in 1883.

However, Spanish and Italian interests in the Maghreb, as well as interference from Germany and England, prevented the French from achieving total mastery in western North Africa. Paris had to share power with Madrid when, in 1912, Morocco was divided into a French protectorate over 90 percent of the land and a Spanish protectorate over the rest. In Tunisia, the French met with continuing opposition from Italy, which maintained considerable economic influence in Tunisia and a sizable number of its nationals as residents within the country. Ultimately, the geopolitical patterns of colonial association that France forged with this part of the Muslim world proved incompatible with Muslim demands for equality and political self-determination.

Léon Gambetta, the prime minister of France during the occupation of Tunisia, is quoted as having said in 1880 that the configuration of the French coasts and the establishment of French rule in Algeria had made the Mediterranean, and especially the western Mediterranean, France's "scene of action."[9] History has borne him out, but not in the geopolitical form that he had envisaged. After 170 years of colonization and acculturation, France's political influence in the Maghreb, while still strong, is tenuous.

Since the emergence of the Maghreb from colonialism, its relations with maritime Europe have become ambiguous, despite the reality that France, Italy, Spain, and Germany remain its chief trading partners. The political relationship between France and Algeria still suffers from the legacy of conflict and colonial rule. In addition, with the region's independence, the economic gap that separates western North Africa from Europe has widened, not narrowed, leaving the Maghreb in continued economic dependency. The economy of the Maghreb would be in even greater distress were it not for the safety valve of immigration to Europe by millions of workers, many of them to France, and remittances from these *émigrés*.

What gives rise to the hope that a new, trans-Mediterranean political partnership can be forged is that Europe and the Maghreb are now interdependent and not bound together in the colonial dominant-subordinate mode. The EU needs the Maghreb's oil and gas as well as its labor pool. The Maghreb needs maritime Europe's capital, technology, finished products, and tourists.

Algeria, the world's second-largest exporter of natural gas, has the fifth-largest reserves. Its petroleum exports rank fourteenth in the world. Currently, most of the oil and gas, which accounts for 25 percent of the country's GDP and nearly all of its exports, is sent to the United States and to Italy, France, and other EU countries.

Tunisia is also an oil and gas exporter, mainly to the EU. Strategically located within the central Mediterranean and overlooking Libya, it is the Maghreb's gateway to Italy, southeastern Europe, and the eastern Mediterranean. Oil and natural gas pipelines cross Tunisia from eastern and central Algeria to Mediterranean ports, and the gas line continues across the sea to Sicily and Italy.

The Maghreb is a focus for European capital investment, not only in energy and other minerals and petrochemicals but also in its food industries. In addition, the combined population of seventy-five million for the three countries represents a market with major potential for Europe as well as a major source of its necessary migrant labor. On the negative side, it is also a source of Islamic terrorists.

Algeria, the regional power within the Maghreb, is the key to balanced relations between that area and maritime Europe. With a population of nearly forty million, which is only slightly larger than Morocco's, Algeria's per capita GDP is one and one-half times that of its western neighbor because of Algeria's hydrocarbon resources. Also, Algeria's industrial base is somewhat broader than Morocco's due to the former's petrochemical industries. While the armed forces of the two countries are fairly similar in size, Algeria's is the more battle hardened of the two.

Europe's dealings with Algeria, however, are complicated by the latter's political instability. The thirty-year War of Independence against France, which ended in 1962, left Algeria's economy in ruins and caused half a million military and civilian deaths. In the years that have followed, Algeria has fought border wars with Morocco and has had to cope with political coups and Berber unrest.

The Berbers, who account for one-third of the total population of Algeria, have long struggled to gain cultural autonomy, recognition of their language, and a share of political power through democratization of the regime. Their homeland, known as the Kabylia, extends across the mountains and coastal reaches east of Algiers, from their center of Tizi Ouzou to Skikda. While those living on the coastal plain have become partially Arabized over the centuries, the mountain Berbers have not, having clung to their customs and to the Berber tongue and using French, rather than Arabic, as their second language.

In 2001, a Berber uprising took place against governmental oppression, refusal to recognize the Berber language, and widespread unemployment. This revolt, coupled with a widening Islamic insurgency, continued to keep the country in turmoil. The next year, as a gesture to the Berbers, the Algerian government agreed to make Tamazight, the Berber language, an official language alongside Arabic. This reduced Berber unrest, although resentments over discrimination still are widespread and might be satisfied only by quasi statehood.

After the voiding of 1991 national elections by a military regime, Algeria was also torn by the terror campaign against the government waged by the outlawed Islamic Salvation Front's fundamentalist guerrilla forces, in which up to 200,000 rebels were killed. The war ended in 1999, but the rebellion was fitfully resumed until the two sides came to a formal reconciliation in 2005, followed by the release of thousands of rebels who had been jailed during the 1991–99 war. Because France had sided with the Algerian government, it was subject to a series of terrorist bombings by Algerian Islamic fundamentalists. Political turmoil has stalled economic reform efforts to change one of the most centrally planned economies in the Arab world and to reduce the overdependence on oil and gas resources. Much of the energy wealth has been dissipated through corruption and bureaucratic inefficiencies, while the bloated governmental workforce (30 percent of all workers) impedes the implementation of change. An added burden is the country's heavy foreign debt, built up by its need for continuing capital investment in its energy sector and its efforts to expand other industries.

Morocco, which gained its independence from France in 1956 and Spain in 1958, did so with minor disturbances rather than a full-scale rebellion, as was the case for Algeria. In most of the years that have followed, Morocco has enjoyed domestic political stability under the tight rule of an absolute monarchy. The 1963 border conflict with Algeria was resolved by an agreement in 1970. However, the dispute with Mauritania over control of Western Sahara (formerly Spanish Sahara), which Morocco claims and administers, has yet to be adjudicated. After Morocco seized the entire territory and sent three hundred thousand settlers into the region, Western Sahara guerrillas, backed by Algeria, launched an armed struggle. It lasted throughout the 1980s, ending only when Algeria withdrew its military support. To protect its settlers and beat back the rebels, the Moroccans built a 1,500-mile trench and wall diagonally across the entire territory.

While the cease-fire mediated by the United Nations still holds, the debate continues over the terms of an independence referendum. The Sahrawis (the "Polisaro"), who oppose the granting of voting rights to the Moroccans who have settled in the Western Sahara, maintain a well-organized government-in-exile in the camps of western Algeria. However, poverty is endemic. The economic plight of the Sahrawis, whose thirst for independence is sharpened by the richness of Western Sahara phosphates currently controlled by Morocco, may drive them to break the truce and drag Algeria into the dispute once again. Moroccan offers of West Saharan autonomy were turned down in 2007 by Sahrawi leaders, who would accept nothing less than a referendum on independence. The stalemate continues. The conflict in the Sahara, in which thirty thousand guerrillas were killed, is far removed from where most of the Moroccan populace lives and has had little effect upon day-to-day life, tourism, or foreign investment. Morocco also disputes Spain's control of the coastal enclaves of Ceuta and Melilla and of three small islands, one in the Mediterranean northeast of Melilla, the others off the coast of Western Sahara.

The main challenge for Morocco today is economic. It is the poorest of the Maghrebian states and has the highest percentage of illiteracy. While the country exports phosphates, some iron ore and copper, and food products, the income derived from these products is only one-tenth of what Algeria receives from its oil and gas revenues. On the positive side, proximity to Europe and the cheap Moroccan labor force have attracted considerable foreign investment in industries and services that are rapidly privatizing, while tourism has been growing steadily. A number of bilateral free-trade agreements have been signed between Morocco and the EU since 2000, including those dealing with fisheries and certain goods. In 2013, the two parties announced plans to extend their free trade agreements to include not only goods but also services, agriculture, and investment protection. With continued political stability, prospects for economic improvement are good.

Tunisia is by far the most economically advanced of the three countries of the Maghreb. Its economy is diverse, with agriculture, mining (phosphates), energy (oil and natural gas), tourism, and manufacturing sectors, and its fiscal affairs are in order. The country had already enjoyed a measure of autonomy before it received its independence in 1956 and, under the leadership of Habib Bourguiba, followed a moderate socialist policy that was generally pro-Western and pro-French. Minor boundary disputes with Algeria were settled in 1970, and a 1980 Libyan invasion of a border mining town was repulsed. (A maritime boundary dispute with Libya remains unresolved.) Despite labor unrest during much of that decade, Tunisia has been generally successful in modernizing its economy while providing a moderating influence within the Arab world. Its 1998 association agreement with the EU was the first between the union and one of the western Mediterranean Arab states, and since then, trade barriers have been, and continue to be, gradually removed. With a relatively high economic growth rate and close ties with its European neighbors, Tunisia, already a gateway to trans-Mediterranean European states, can be the linchpin in geopolitically connecting the Maghreb to maritime Europe.

Tunisia was the first country to experience the "Arab Spring," when the Zine ben Ali dictatorship was overthrown in January 2011. The Islamic government that took over gave up power peacefully to a moderate one whose National Constituent Assembly approved a new constitution in January 2014. This constitution calls for recognition of the role of government as protector of Islam but safeguards individual freedom of religious choice.

While most Western European leaders have cast their geopolitical gaze eastward, in their plans to expand the EU and NATO they would do well to look southward with equal, if not greater, intensity. Europe's southern flank—the Maghreb—is already closely linked through history, trade, proximity, and immigrant labor.

Creating a new geopolitical framework that would extend the maritime European region across the Mediterranean is a realistic goal. Regional unity between maritime Europe and the Maghreb is economically feasible. A hurdle that must be overcome, however, is the racial and religious bias that has for so long distorted the European view of North Africa and Islamic extremism that rejects accommodation with the West. Overcoming these obstacles is both an economic necessity and sound geopolitical policy.

A geopolitically unified maritime Europe and the Maghreb has many similarities to North and Middle America. The difference is that the Maghreb is much larger than Middle America and has had a history of hundreds of years of political, economic, and cultural relations with the European lands to its north. Europe enjoys strategic dominance over its southern Arab-state neighbors through its overwhelming military power and control over Atlantic and trans-Mediterranean sea-lanes and Mediterranean islands. In addition, the EU has the economic capacity to support Maghrebian economic development.

When Nicolas Sarkozy assumed the presidency of France in 2007, one of his stated goals was to create a Mediterranean union. While not a new idea, Sarkozy promoted it strongly. The concept is partly defensive in that one of its goals is to stop the flow of Moroccan immigrants to Europe, especially to France, Spain, and Italy, by making heavy investments and promoting free trade with the North African nations. Since France has had difficulty in absorbing Moroccan immigrants, most of whom live in major cities' slums which are breeding grounds for crime and terrorism, the notion is beginning to achieve momentum. Italy, too, has weighed in, viewing Libya as a promising partner. France has large oil and gas interests in North Africa, including Libya, and the Maghreb is a major market for its arms sales. Whether such a policy would stem the flow of North African illegal or legal immigrants is debatable, but a Mediterranean union could be beneficial to both sides of the sea.

Many of the elements involved in unifying the western Mediterranean basin are already in place. The challenge is for maritime Europe to seize the opportunity by developing mechanisms that are not modern versions of the nineteenth- and twentieth-century imperialism that bound the basin together at that time. The requirement today is for institutions based on a mutuality of interests and equality of participation. If, for example, the EU is willing to enlist forces from non-EU-member states in the prospective EU rapid reaction force, it might also consider inviting its neighbors from the Maghreb to supply limited numbers of selected troops, an action that would be largely symbolic. A far more important step would be to forge a strong free trade association with Tunisia, Algeria, and Morocco. Such an association could then be incorporated into a broader free-trade framework, which could also include some Eastern Mediterranean countries.

Conclusion

As the European Union moves toward higher levels of specialized integration, its geopolitical status as full partner with the United States within the maritime realm has led it to take independent initiatives within the global arena. The union has taken a more flexible position on the subject of the sanctions that have been imposed upon Iran and Iraq. It has adopted a different stance from that of Washington on the Arab-Israeli conflict, one which generally exhibits greater sympathy toward the Palestinian Arab position and strongly presses for a two-state solution.

The EU was vigorous in its opposition to the decision of the Bush administration not to ratify the 1997 Kyoto Protocol. This accord, signed by over one hundred countries, called for the reduction in the emission of heat-trapping gases, like carbon dioxide and methane, that contribute to global warming. Since the United States was the source of one-quarter of all greenhouse gasses, its refusal to support the climate accord undermined the agreement's efficacy. At the G-7 plus Russia Summit of 2007, EU leadership strongly opposed the US proposal that a system of voluntary, rather than fixed, quotas be adopted. President Angela Merkel of Germany urged that the new global pact on climate change, scheduled to be formulated by 2009, pledge states to cut their 1990 greenhouse gas emissions in half by the year 2050. For its part, the European Environment Agency has called for efforts to surpass the goal of 10 percent of transportation fuel to be composed of biofuels by 2020. Britain and Germany had met their Kyoto vehicle emissions targets by 2007, demonstrating that industrialized countries can reduce emissions if they have the will to accept the costs. However, the Emissions Trading System (cap and trade) proposed at Kyoto, which is the largest and most comprehensive of its kind in the world, failed to reduce carbon dioxide emissions overall. Instead, they have risen slightly, although the rate of increase did slow down over the past decade. Despite its refusal to accept a binding goal, the United States met the Kyoto Protocol target by 2013. While long the world's leading carbon emitter, the United States has dropped to second place as China, which is heavily dependent on coal-fired electricity generators, has moved into first place.

The 2013 Warsaw Conference on Climate Warming set new targets for curbing emissions, effective as of 2020. The participating countries agreed to seek a path toward an international agreement by 2015 wherein national targets would then be reviewed and subject to approval of the conference. Just as the EU had agreed to nationally determined commitments at the Durban Conference on Climate Warming in 2012, so did the United States agree to this formula at Warsaw. The overall goal of reducing emissions to an annual increase of two degrees Celsius was discussed at the conference but has not yet been embraced.[10]

The Europeans, especially Germany, have expressed strong reservations about Washington's proposed National Missile Defense shield, especially the installations to be placed in the Czech Republic and Poland, on the basis of its flouting the Anti-Ballistic Missile Treaty. Most were also strongly opposed to Washington's invasion of Iraq and its threats to launch war against Iran. While the administration of President George W. Bush drew back from certain foreign involvements such as the International Criminal Court, the EU has taken a more interventionist approach. Other differences between the EU and the United States that are likely to emerge are over operational relationships between NATO and a possible EU rapid reaction force and over the stance to be taken in relations with Russia and Iran. Such differences are neither unexpected nor unhealthy. In a genuine partnership, they can be resolved through a balanced approach to the issues in question. While Germany has played a key role in the EU decision to join the US sanctions against Iran, it has also promoted the 2014 negotiations with Tehran over Iran's nuclear policies.

Within maritime Europe, the reunification of Germany and NATO's expansion into Central Europe and Poland have changed Germany's geographical position from that of border state to one of centrality. The geopolitical consequences of this centrality have a profound bearing on the strategic balance between France and Germany, the states with the two largest economies. With the expansion eastward of the EU, Germany's position has been enhanced because of its central location within Europe as well as its historical ties to the countries to its east and their increasing dependence on the federal republic for trade and economic aid. France's fear of being overshadowed by Germany has increased the pressure for a looser, rather than a more centralized, regional governing body.

It is likely that Britain will overcome its recent Euroskepticism and become more fully engaged in EU affairs. This would maintain the balance among the union's leading members rather than shift it toward German dominance. At the same time, the strength of the historic alliance between the United States and Britain will serve to preserve the partnership of interest between the United States and the EU within the maritime realm.

It is premature to describe Europe as the "United States of Europe," a goal first articulated by Winston Churchill in 1946 and one which T. R. Reid argues has now been attained.[11] While it is correct that Europe is far more than a trading bloc, its political and structural divisions and lack of military capacity prevent it from acting with the same centralized focus that the United States possesses. For example, the rush to war with Iraq could not have happened in Europe because of the strength of its national components.

Europe has taken the lead over the United States in many economic and social areas, such as environmental regulations, aid to developing nations, and social welfare policies. As a global power, it lags in military capacity and in certain areas of technological innovation. Europe's reluctance to become a global military power stems from the devastating experiences of its twentieth-century wars. Emerging from World War II with the total destruction of its military-industrial base, it had neither the capacity nor the will to compete with its American ally or the Soviet Union, relying on a US-dominated NATO to address its defense needs. It could then concentrate its energies and resources on rebuilding its "soft" rather than "hard" power in efforts to resolve international disputes.

One cannot speculate about Europe's future geopolitical place in the world without addressing the military component. However, Europe, as a promoter of soft power and a leader in conflict resolution initiatives, can, in equal partnership with the United States, play a lead role in international affairs. Some have forecast the end of the European dream and the decline of the continent as a result of the EU's current weakened economy, too-lavish welfare states, aging population, and slow GDP growth. This ignores the reality of Europe's inherent economic strength. It remains the world's largest trading block, accounting for one-third of the world's trade in goods and services. Its aggregate GDP of $16.6 trillion is larger than that of either the United States or China. Its members offer models of greater social and economic equality within a democratic framework.

A formal US-European Union partnership would have a combined population of over eight hundred million and a GDP of $32 trillion. With a commitment to democratic liberalism and innovative strength, this partnership of the two great powers can be "first among equals" within the world's major power system. No single superpower can dominate this complex geopolitical structure. However, a strong US-EU alliance would be better equipped than any other single country or group of nations to help maintain global balance in the face of dynamic changes.

The United States and a unifying Europe complement each other. However, Washington has often failed to recognize the geopolitical importance of Europe's economic and moral strength and has resisted treating it as an equal. Such recognition must come as future American administrations recognize the limits of America's global capacities and the hollow appeal to much of the world of "American exceptionalism." Europe and the United States must be partners in dealing with the world's other great powers in pursuit of global equilibrium.

Notes

1. William Drozdiak, "Old World Reinvents Itself as Model for New Economy," *International Herald Tribune*, February 19, 2001, 1, 11.
2. European Commission, *Financial Framework 2007–2013: Investing in Our Future* (Luxembourg: EC Publications Office, April 23, 2008), 3.
3. James Fairgrieve, *Geography and World Power* (London: University of London Press, 1915), 329–30.
4. Halford Mackinder, "The Round World and the Winning of the Peace," *Foreign Affairs* 21, no. 4 (1943): 595–605.
5. Javier Solana Madariaga, "Growing the Alliance," *Economist*, March 13, 1999, 23–28.
6. *2007 World Population Data Sheet* (Washington, DC: Population Reference Bureau, 2007).
7. "Restriction in EU Immigration Policies against the New EU Member States (NMS)," http://www.Europeananalysis.org.uk, 2007.
8. "Denmark and Greenland: Ultima Motives," *Economist*, February 17, 2001, 55.
9. Léon Gambetta, as quoted in Norman Harris, *Intervention and Colonization in Africa* (Boston: Houghton Mifflin, 1914), 238.
10. Rebecca Lefton, Gywnne Taraska, and Jenny Cooper, with Ben Bovarnick, "Warsaw Climate Talks End with a Foundation for a Global Agreement" (issue brief, Center for American Progress, Washington, DC, December 4, 2013).
11. T. R. Reid, *The United States of Europe: The New Superpower and the End of American Supremacy* (London: Penguin, 2004), 1–23, 245–71.

CHAPTER 8

Russia and the Eurasian Convergence Zone

From the centuries of czarist rule, through seven decades of Soviet communism to the current era of authoritarianism headed by Vladimir Putin, Russian history and culture has been shaped by the following forces: highly centralized government and despotism, the pendulum of territorial expansion and contraction, grandiose infrastructure projects, corruption, and isolation from external influences. During the czarist period the Russian Orthodox Church played a central role in unifying the Russian state, rallying the people around the mystical call of "Mother Russia." Ruthlessly repressed by atheistic Communism, the church is now reemerging as an important element in the lives of many Russians.

While Peter the Great sought to modernize Russia by adopting selected aspects of Westernization, most of the impact was superficial. Deeply set Russian values remained unchanged. In molding a new collective society, Soviet Communism gave lip service to granting non-Russian nationalities forms of autonomy. In reality, the goal was to Russify these ethnic and religious groups by applying strict centralized political controls.

When the Soviet Union broke apart in 1991, a major objective of the Yeltsin regime was to eliminate the statist economy, replacing it with a free-market system. Instead, a time of chaos ensued in which private entrepreneurs were able to gain control of state corporations and resources at bargain prices. This was an era of capitalism run amok. A class of oligarchs amassed great wealth but invested much of their capital abroad rather than using it to spearhead domestic development.

Under the leadership of Vladimir Putin, little has changed with respect to the values and strategies that guide the Russian state idea. While Putin is not a declared dictator, he leads a highly centralized authoritarian government and brooks little opposition. Corruption continues to be part of everyday life, and the market system is tightly controlled by the state. Grandiose development schemes continue to be offered to the public as testimony to the government's vision and strength. Hosting the 2014 Olympic Games at Sochi required a capital investment of over $50 billion—most Russians supported this as evidence of the country's international importance. Freedom of expression and deprivation of human rights continue to undermine Russia's claim to have replaced Soviet Communism's repression in favor of democracy. However, for the most part, Russians accept this situation as the price to be paid for the political stability and economic improvements that the Putin era has brought.

In contrast to the era of Soviet territorial expansion, Moscow is now focused on stemming the erosion of its influence over neighboring states. A major challenge facing Putin is maintaining Russian dominance in the Ukraine, or at least keeping the country as a buffer, in the face of European Union efforts to draw that country into its sphere.

When Halford Mackinder delivered his paper "The Geographical Pivot of History" to the Royal Geographical Society in 1904, the czarist Russian empire was in full control of the core of Eurasia—the pivot region, or "Heartland," of the world, which he had deemed impenetrable to maritime powers.[1] The Russians had begun their transcontinental expansion eastward to the Pacific with the crossing of the Urals in 1581. During the subsequent centuries, they pushed settlement across the southern parts of Siberia. The Far Eastern Territory was annexed from China in 1860, when construction began on what was to become the chief Russian port on the Pacific, Vladivostok. Control over all of Siberia was assured in 1905 with the construction of the 5,575-mile Trans-Siberian Railroad from Moscow to Vladivostok. The expansion southward was completed in the late nineteenth century, when the Russians swept over the remainder of the Trans-Caucasus not yet under their control and also seized Central Asia.

Mackinder's 1919 volume, *Democratic Ideals and Realities*, was written after the Bolshevik Revolution had toppled the czar and proclaimed the Soviet state.[2] In it, he voiced the fear that Communism might sweep across Eastern and Central Europe and engulf the seven independent states of the "Middle Tier" between Germany and Russia, which extended from the Adriatic and Black Seas to the Baltic. Not only was the new Soviet state in control of the Eurasian Heartland but also, Mackinder warned, it was now in a position to rule Eastern Europe, the strategic annex of the Heartland. He hypothesized that, in an alternate scenario, Germany might succeed in winning control over a divided Eastern Europe and thus command the Heartland. In either case, control of World-Island and command of the world would follow.

In "The Round World and the Winning of the Peace," written in 1943 at the height of World War II, Mackinder restated the proposition that the Eurasian Heartland was the "greatest natural fortress in the world."[3] This version of the Heartland omitted Lenaland, the region extending from the Yenisey River eastward to the Pacific. Control of this new Heartland of four and a quarter million square miles and 170 million people would, in Mackinder's opinion, provide the Soviet Union with a strategically invulnerable defensive position in its conflict with Nazi Germany. Repudiating his 1919 dictum, Mackinder asserted that rule of the Heartland no longer guaranteed control of World-Island. Instead, the strength of the Heartland was now offset by the inherent power of a unified North Atlantic basin. He predicted that this global balance-of-power system was destined to be strengthened as the monsoonal Asian lands of India and China developed into new geostrategic power centers.

In the wake of its victory in World War II, the USSR gained complete command over its Eastern and Central European "strategic annex." This was accomplished through the direct absorption of the wide swath of territory from southeastern Finland, the Baltic states, and East Prussia to eastern Poland, eastern Czechoslovakia, and northern Romania, as well as by the installation of Communist satellite regimes in the remainder of the region. At the height of the Cold War in the 1960s and 1970s, Soviet-supported Communist regimes further extended the heartland's influence by leapfrogging the ring of containment that the West had established along the perimeter of continental Eurasia. It penetrated the maritime realm in Southeast Asia, the Middle East, Sub-Saharan Africa, and the Caribbean.

The Soviet drive for global command was relatively short-lived. In overreaching its strategic and economic capacities and maintaining a tyrannical and corrupt Communist regime, Moscow hastened the collapse of the Soviet empire and the loss of a considerable part of the heartland. Far from being the strongest land power in the world, Russia found itself strategically exposed to NATO's eastward expansionist policies, the inroads of maritime and fundamentalist Islamic influences into the Trans-Caucasus and Central Asia, and pressures from China along its North Pacific territories.

A realistic depiction of the geographical boundaries of post-Soviet Russia adds Halford Mackinder's 1943 "westward reach of the Heartland" from the Black Sea to the Gulf of Finland to his 1904 "Pivot Area" (see figure 2.4, "Changing Heartland Boundaries"). The new Russia that emerged following the collapse of the Communist Party and the breakaway of the fourteen other Soviet republics suffered economic collapse and was beset by factional political infighting, street violence, and a bitter rebellion in Chechnya. During this period, the West, led by the United States, pushed NATO into the Baltic states in 1995 and the Czech Republic, Hungary, and Poland in 1999, all with the acquiescence of President Boris Yeltsin.

Russia's recovery began with the appointment of Vladimir Putin by an ailing Yeltsin in 1999. Vigorously pursuing a war in Chechnya and recapturing Grozny from the rebels, Putin went on to impose his authority on the government. He reimposed control over the economy in which freewheeling oligarchs had pushed *perestroika* (Mikhail Gorbachev's policy of economic restructuring) beyond limits acceptable to the Russian people.

Russia's political and economic recovery during the first decade of the twenty-first century reflects its inherent strengths. Rich in natural resources, it is the world's largest producer and exporter of natural gas, with 60 percent of world gas reserves. It is the largest oil producer and second leading exporter, with 10 percent of world reserves. It also has the world's second-largest coal reserves and considerable hydroelectric and nuclear power. In addition, Russia has a vast nuclear arsenal, a substantial scientific and engineering population, spatial depth, and a strategically central position within Eurasia. Putin's reforms have swept away much of the crony capitalism of Yeltsin's era, although state-controlled businesses are now in the hands of many of his own favorites. Regaining its self-esteem, Russia's recovery has been accompanied by a revived nationalism, linked to an increasingly influential Russian Orthodox Church, despite the state's secular nature.

The rise in energy prices over the past decade has enabled Russia to build up massive reserves of capital, which it is beginning to invest in modernizing industry, expanding the high-tech sector, and creating a new, consolidated civilian aircraft industry, with the participation of foreign corporations. It is expanding its construction and export of large, state-of-the-art nuclear power plants and is second only to the United States in the export of arms. Problems that plague the country are its shrinking population, unpredictable policies with respect to foreign investment, inefficient state-owned enterprises, high rates of alcoholism, poor health services, and widespread corruption.

The surge in Russian nationalism prompted the Putin government to act heavy-handedly toward some of its former republics and satellites, such as Ukraine, Georgia, and Poland. The reimposition of centralized economic and political controls does not meet Western democratic and free-market standards. However, in taking independent positions, Russia has made it clear that US and Western disapproval is irrelevant.

Loss of the former Soviet republics has left the new Russia with a declining population of approximately 145 million that is 77 percent ethnically Russian and increasingly responsive to the lure of nationalistic slogans and initiatives. The major minorities are the Muslim peoples in the North Caucasus and in Tatarstan in the Middle Volga, Slavic Ukrainians, Moldavians, and Belarussians. Large numbers of geographically concentrated ethnic Russian populations are located in the regions close to Russia's borders in such former Soviet republics as Estonia, Latvia, Ukraine, Moldova, and Kazakhstan. The presence of these Russians is likely to prove a major obstacle to Western efforts to wean the latter three of these formerly constituent republics away from the Russian strategic grasp. A sound maritime realm policy would be to recognize Russia's strategic interests in Eastern Europe and elsewhere within the Eurasian convergence zone. Such a policy would seek partnership with Moscow and, where appropriate, with China and India with the aim of building the zone as a gateway rather than risk its becoming a shatterbelt.

In the Caucasus and Central Asia, international oil interests and some American Cold Warriors have been strong advocates for involvement of the West in a replay of the "Great Game."[4] The Great Game was conducted by Britain a century ago, when it sought to displace Russian influence in Central Asia as well as to penetrate the Black Sea and the Caucasus. An initial step in the new Great Game took place in 1996, when the United States provided modest military aid to Georgia and Azerbaijan when these states joined with Ukraine and Moldova to form a mutual-support group. Uzbekistan was added to the group three years later. Under the acronym GUUAM (from the first initial of each member's name), the organization set the goals of negotiating reduction of Russian troops within or along their borders and promoting the construction of pipelines that would reduce their dependence upon Russia for the supply or transit of oil and gas. The dispatch of American military personnel to Georgia in 2002 to train Georgian troops in antiterrorist tactics and the current strategic partnership between the two countries are examples of US efforts to penetrate the region. So have been the establishment of US and NATO military bases in Romania, Bulgaria, and some Central Asian countries. (When Uzbekistan dropped out in 2005, the organization reverted to GUAM.)

The Great Game strategy has as little likelihood of long-term success today as it had when Britain sought to undermine Russia's strategic interests during the earlier period. Russia has an overwhelming geopolitical advantage in a contest with the West for strategic influence over the Black Sea, the Caucasus, the Caspian Sea, and interior Central Asian areas. It is an advantage similar to that which the United States enjoys in the Caribbean, maritime Europe in the Maghreb, and China in Indochina. Penetration of geopolitically subordinate regions by distant external powers usually turns out to be short-lived and counterproductive.

The Changing National Territory

Present-day Russia, like all territorial states, including the Soviet Union and the czarist empire before it, is the expression of the interaction of a people with the landscape it occupies. The political demarcation of the state produces a national landscape—the arena for its economic, cultural, and political activities. When the political territory changes, national characteristics and objectives change.

A national landscape becomes altered in two ways: vertically, through new internal forms, and horizontally, through the addition of external areas or the loss of existing territory. Vertical changes occur as new sets of environmental conditions emerge or new uses are made of the existing environment. Examples of changed environmental conditions are the Dutch conquest of the sea, climatic desiccation in the African Sahel, and the shrinking of the Aral Sea due to the diversion for irrigation of the waters that feed it. New uses of the existing environment include urbanization, the introduction of new crops, the discovery of new mineral resources, and changing systems of land tenure.

Horizontal change may not immediately affect the existing grain of the national landscape, but it does ultimately. Since West Germany has reabsorbed East Germany, the country's eastern half has begun to change from an older and inefficient heavy manufacturing base in steel and chemicals to a more high-tech, service-oriented economy. After Singapore seceded from Malaysia, it soon became a leading Asian economic power—a global financial center and a leading producer of chemicals, electronics, and refined petroleum products.

Within half a century, Russia has experienced radical horizontal change, first through the direct addition of territory to the Soviet state and domination of the vast belt of surrounding satellite territory, and now through the stripping of much of its former national territory as well as the loss of direct control over its Eastern European strategic annex. The challenge for Russia now is to grow vertically—through modernization of industry, agriculture, and services; application of high technology; and judicious use of its natural resources. The new technical city of Skolkovo—Moscow's version of Silicon Valley—and the Baltic port of Primorsk are examples.

The horizontal expansion of the Russian Empire began in the late sixteenth century, as it proceeded to swallow up dozens of non-Slavic peoples. A century later, the czars embarked also on vertical expansion through modernization. From then on, the two types of change occurred in tandem.

The year after Peter the Great captured Ingermanland (the region drained by the Neva River and the eastern shores of the Gulf of Finland) from Sweden in 1702, he began to build St. Petersburg. In 1712, he moved the capital from Moscow to the new city. For Peter, St. Petersburg was to be more than a "window looking on Europe." It was to be used to spearhead Russia's changeover into a modern industrial state. The port that was built became Russia's leading port on the White Sea, supplanting Archangel (Arkhangelsk), which had to be kept open by icebreakers during much of the year. Peter's modernization plans included the building of a navy, and St. Petersburg's outer port on Kotlin Island provided the site for the Kronstadt naval base.

Other goals of modernization included industrialization, the subordination of the Russian Orthodox Church to the Crown, and an efficient centralized state administration. Diverse manufacturing enterprises, such as shipbuilding, engineering, and textiles, were rapidly introduced into the city so that by the mid-eighteenth century, the new capital had overtaken Moscow as Russia's leading industrial center. Spacious classical buildings and ornamental parks and gardens were designed by French and Italian architects to help make St. Petersburg a world-class cultural center. In a remarkably brief period, the fruits of vertical change had exceeded those of the horizontal expansion.

Peter the Great viewed St. Petersburg as the national engine of change and the instrument of Russia's securing what it needed from Europe to help fulfill its modernization plans. He by no means saw Russia's future as European, however. His goal was for Russia to take what it could from the West and, when it could compete on equal terms, to turn its back on Europe and devote its energies to expanding the czarist empire eastward and southward.

In contrast to the new capital, the country's political center and primary city at the turn of the eighteenth century, Moscow, represented Russia's inward-oriented and landlocked spiritual, as well as geographical, forms and traditions. The city, which had developed from its mid-twelfth-century village origins to become the seat of the Vladimir-Muscovite princes in 1271, lay in a basin at the junction of the Upper Volga plain and the central Russian uplands. It was thus strategically located to enable the rulers of Muscovy to gain dominance over the surrounding Russian lands.

Moscow's built form, as well as the social and military organization of the Muscovite state, reflected an amalgam of influences—Byzantine, Tatar, and Slavic. The dukes of Moscow had to share their power with the Russian Orthodox Church, whose seat had been moved to Moscow in the mid-fourteenth century. Moreover, during the centuries of their struggle with the Tatars, Russian noble families had intermarried with them and adopted many Tatar customs and traditions. Moscow's early public buildings and churches, including the Kremlin, the city's walled center and citadel, were started in the fourteenth century and represented an attempt to create a uniquely Russian architectural version from the amalgam of these influences. The wooden building materials, as well as the bricks of later construction periods, were drawn from locally available sources; the cupolas and towers so characteristic of the city provide a Russian Byzantine form that is derivative but nevertheless *sui generis*.

By the time of Peter's accession to the throne, Moscow had experienced large-scale growth. The market for its products, however, was essentially restricted to the territory embraced by the landlocked Muscovite state, thus limiting continued growth. This commercial consideration weighed heavily in Peter's decision to build St. Petersburg and to try to extend the economic reach of the state beyond its existing territorial bounds.

TERRITORIAL EXPANSION OF CZARIST RUSSIA

The historical development of the Russian state, from the onset of modern times to the present, has been characterized by alternating periods of territorial expansion and contraction. Blocked by the powerful Mongol-Tatar empires in the south, which by the twelfth century had overrun the lands north of the Black and Caspian Seas, and by the Grand Duchy of Lithuania, which had incorporated most of Ukraine and White Russia, the dukes of Moscow expanded their control over territories to their north and eastward to the Volga.

In 1552 Ivan broke the Tatar military power that had confined his predecessors to the territories of Muscovy and Novgorod, sacking Kazan, which had become the capital of the Tatar Khanate of Kazan, one of the four independent khanates to emerge from the 1480 breakup of the Mongol Empire of the "Golden Horde," which was also known as the Kipchak Khanate. Kazan, five hundred kilometers east of Moscow, was the gateway through and around the southern Urals into the central Urals. The central Urals were crossed in 1581 by Yermak Timofeyev and his band of Cossacks, who then took the city of Sibir (near the present city of Tobolsk), capital of the Tatar Khanate of Sibir.

By the end of the reign of Ivan IV, "Czar of All Russia" (1584), the Russian-controlled territory, shaped as an inverted triangle, extended in the north from the Kola Peninsula, the island of Novaya Zemlya, and the frozen waters of the White, Barents, and Kara Seas. Archangel, at the mouth of the Dvina on the White Sea, was founded during the last year of Ivan's reign. Despite being icebound for much of the year, it became Russia's principal port until displaced by St. Petersburg over a century later. The port regained importance after a rail line to Moscow was completed in 1898. However, from the time that Murmansk, on the Barents Sea, was developed as an ice-free port during World War I, Archangel has had to share its role as a port for the north. Murmansk became the major supply base for Allied convoys to the USSR in World War II. It is now a major naval base and home port for the nuclear submarine fleet as well as a leading freight port and fishing center.

The conquest of the Tatar Khanate of Sibir was completed in 1598, after which time the road to all of West Siberia was open. During the seventeenth century, West Siberia was annexed to Russia and the Cossacks moved eastward, building fortresses and trading in furs. The advance of the Cossacks across Siberia was rapid. In short order, they reached the Sea of Okhotsk, an arm of the north Pacific, establishing the fishing and trading settlement of Okhotsk in 1649, although they soon had to abandon the territory, later to be known as the Russian Far East, in the face of Chinese military pressure. The Russians did not return to the Siberian Pacific coastlands for nearly two hundred years, when they occupied all of the territory north of the Amur and east of the Ussuri River (1856–60) and built a military post at Vladivostok (1860). The Siberian fur trade had become a major source of wealth for Russia. When it declined in the early eighteenth century, it was replaced by silver, copper, and lead mining, much of which was carried out by convict labor. In contrast, gold mining, which became Siberia's leading source of wealth in the nineteenth century, was carried out mostly by free laborers.

European Russia's penetration of the lands along its Baltic and Black Sea coasts began more than a century after its push into Siberia. The leading power in the Baltic was Sweden, and it took a coalition of Russia, Denmark, Poland, Saxony, Hanover, and Prussia waging a twenty-one-year conflict (the Northern War of 1700 to 1721) to defeat the forces of Sweden's Charles XII. Early in that war, Peter captured Ingermanland (1702); eight years later, he took Swedish Livonia (present-day Estonia and parts of Latvia). The Peace Treaty of Nystad (1721) confirmed the annexation of these territories, as well as of most of Karelia, but did not give Finland to Russia. Russia conquered and annexed Finland during the Napoleonic Wars a century later (1809). Finland remained under Russian control until the chaotic conditions of the Bolshevik Revolution enabled the Finns to break away and regain their independence.

While the foothold on the Baltic permitted Peter to realize many of his ambitions, Russia still lacked a year-round, open-water port because the Gulf of Finland was icebound three to four months during the year. The Black Sea offered Peter warm-water ports, but the path from there was blocked by the Ottomans.

As early as 1696, Peter conquered the area around the Sea of Azov, the northern arm of the Black Sea, into which the Don River system flowed, although the Ottomans regained it in 1711. Russian control of the western (Derbent and Baku) and southern shores of the Caspian Sea, seized in a war with Persia (1722–23), was also short-lived. While Russia eventually regained the Azov region in 1735, it was not until Catherine the Great's two major wars with the Ottomans that the northern Black Sea coast was conquered and annexed in its entirety. The Crimean Peninsula was gained in 1783, bringing the Khanate of Crimea to an end, and Odessa fell in 1791.

During the first half of the nineteenth century (1806–55), Russia's hold on the Black Sea was extended by its conquest in the Caucasus of Greater Georgia on the eastern shores of the sea. Batum (Batumi), Erevan (Yerevan), Tiflis (Tbilisi), and Baku were now part of the empire. In addition, annexation of much of Bessarabia (1812) provided Odessa with greater defensive depth. In the latter half of the century (1868–84), Russia also succeeded in gaining all of the southeastern shore of the Caspian Sea from Persia as well as the southern part of (Russian) Central Asia (1864–78). The Bukhara and Khiva Khanates, while overrun during this period, remained nominally independent under Russian protection. (The northern half, Kazakhstan, had already been seized from Tatar khanates in wars that had lasted for over a century, from 1730 to 1840.)

Russian control of the Central Asia region was additionally strengthened toward the end of the nineteenth century with the construction of the Trans-Caspian Railroad, which extended from Krasnovodsk on the Caspian Sea eastward through Ashkabad, Bukhara, and Samarkand into Turkestan and then northward to Tashkent in southernmost Kazakhstan. Branches of the system connected to the fertile Fergana Valley and its ancient oasis cities that lay astride the Silk Route between China and the Mediterranean. This line would much later be connected to the Trans-Siberian Railroad by the Turk-Sib Railroad (completed in 1931), which ran from Tashkent to Novosibirsk.

The prize that eluded Russia during these two centuries of conquest and expansion was control of the Bosporus and the Dardanelles—the exits of the Black Sea to the Mediterranean. The Western powers rose to the defense of the Ottomans during the Crimean War (1853–56), putting an end to czarist dreams of breaking the strategic noose that enclosed Russia's warm-water ports.

Nineteenth-Century Expansion into the Far Eastern Territory

The pace of expansion to the east during this period was guided essentially by economic opportunities, the availability of labor, and access. When the Cossacks first conquered Siberia during the seventeenth century, they moved by horse and riverboat, traversing the level portages that linked the east-west Siberian river systems. Native Siberian peoples in the north were few and offered little opposition, as they were incorporated into the fur trade. Agricultural developments were limited and spotty, oriented to the needs of the trading centers, military outposts, and mining communities. In the nineteenth century (1861), emancipated Russian serfs were given free land. This stimulated settlement of the wooded and the black-earth soils in the steppes of the southern part of West Siberia, which were suitable for both row crops and dairying.

From there came the moves across Central Siberia in the mid-nineteenth century to the region later known as the Far Eastern Territory. The Russians took advantage of the weakness of the Chinese empire to gain control of all of the territory north of the Amur and east of the Ussuri, extending from Yakutia and the Lena River eastward to the entire northeast Asian coast.

For the most part, Russian efforts in the Far East were oriented to the Pacific coastlands. The interior section of the region, Yakutia (modern Sakh), extended from the Central Siberian uplands in the west to the Verkhoyansk Range in the east. It covered an area of 1.2 million square miles, or half of the total Far Eastern Territory. Yakutia is one of the coldest inhabited parts of the earth, much of it lying within the Arctic Circle. In the early period of Russian colonization, the small group of settlers was confined to the upper (southern) part of the Lena River valley, where Yakutsk had been established as a fort in 1632. Until the twentieth century, Yakutia remained essentially a region of herding, hunting, lumbering, and gold mining. Today the major source of income is diamond mining. The one million people who now live in a handful of cities and towns are supported by tin, natural gas, oil, coal, and phosphate deposits, along with wood products, paper, and food processing.

The major settlements of the Russian Pacific Far East were oriented to the lower courses of the major rivers and to the Sea of Okhotsk, the Sea of Japan, and the Bering Sea. Their growth into important centers had to await completion of the Trans-Siberian Railroad (1891–1905). Vladivostok, the eastern terminus for both the railroad and the Northern Sea Route, and whose port is kept open in winter by icebreakers, became the chief base of the navy on the Pacific and a center for the fishing and whaling fleet. Vladivostok assumed its importance as a naval base after the Russians lost Port Arthur (the present Chinese port of Lushun) as a result of their defeat in the Russo-Japanese War (1904–5).

The Russians had developed Port Arthur in 1898 as a linchpin of the Chinese-Russian strategic alliance against Japan. Situated at the southern tip of the Liaodong Peninsula in southern Manchuria and overlooking the Yellow Sea, the base was designed to protect the peninsula from the threat of Japanese seizure. For the Russians as well as the Japanese, Manchuria was a major prize. Its vast grasslands provided the potential for large-scale agricultural settlement, and it was rich in mineral resources, especially coal, iron, and timber. Moreover, it was the strategic gateway to North China.

With their victory in the war, the Japanese took control of Port Arthur and southern Manchuria, limiting Russian influence to the northern half of the province and causing Russians to shift their naval operations to Vladivostok. Russia had first begun its penetration of northern Manchuria in the early nineteenth century and continued to retain influence there until World War I.

As early as the seventeenth century, Russians had also explored the island of Sakhalin across the Tatar Strait from their Far Eastern mainland and just to the north of Japan's northern island of Hokkaido. In the following two centuries, Russian and Japanese settlers jointly colonized the island. For a brief period, Russia gained full control, but after its defeat by Japan in 1905 it was forced to limit its sovereignty to that half of the island that lay north of fifty degrees north latitude. After World War II, the USSR regained sovereignty over the entirety of Sakhalin, and the Japanese renounced their claim to it. The current value of Sakhalin to the Russians is enhanced by its oil and offshore gas deposits and by oil pipelines that run from the island under the Tatar Strait to the Russian mainland.

Another strategic objective of both the Russians and the Japanese was the Kuril Islands chain, which extends for 775 miles from the tip of Kamchatka to the north of Hokkaido and encloses the Sea of Okhotsk and Sakhalin. Both countries laid claim to the islands in the eighteenth century. Japan held them from 1875 to the end of World War II, when Soviet forces occupied the islands. Possession of the chain remains a point of diplomatic contention, as Japan demands return of the four southernmost and largest islands. Because of the dispute, no peace treaty was signed between the USSR and Japan following World War II. The Kurils are important for their deepwater, ice-free harbors and the space that they offer for air and naval bases to overlook the North Pacific. In addition, their surrounding waters contain rich fisheries.

Farther north, in the Far Eastern Territory on the Kamchatka Peninsula, is Petropavlovsk, founded by Vitus Jonassen Bering in 1741. Earlier, the Danish explorer had been employed by Peter the Great to explore the eastern part of the Northern Sea Route—the water route sought by the Russians along their northern Arctic coast to connect the Atlantic and the Pacific from Murmansk in the west to Vladivostok in the east. Bering had then discovered Kamchatka when he sailed through the strait that now bears his name in an effort to reach Alaska. The center for a fishing fleet during its early period, Petropavlovsk is now an important Russian naval base and the location of shipyards. It is also the center for the modern-day trawling and factory fishing fleet. Purchased from Russia by the United States in 1867, Alaska had been claimed in 1821 by the czar based on its fur-trading activities.

Another early settlement, Khabarovsk, at the junction of the lower Amur and Ussuri Rivers, was founded as a trading post. Khabarovsk experienced considerable growth and prosperity with the coming of the railroad in 1905 and is now a major industrial center and port with air connections to Alaska and Japan.

Westward Expansion

While the czarist empire was able to expand steadily to the north, south, and east over a period of four centuries, its territorial expansion along its western perimeter was blocked by several power centers, first Lithuania and Poland, then later the German and Habsburg Empires. Kievan Russia, the cradle of Russian nationalism, was captured by the Mongols of the Golden

Horde in the thirteenth century. A century later, rule of Ukraine passed to Lithuania-Poland, although the Crimea remained in Tatar hands. For much of its early modern history, Ukraine was under Polish rule.

Growing interest in Ukraine—the "Land of the Little Russians"—brought Russia into conflict with Poland. The Russo-Polish War of 1667 ended with the partition of Ukraine, Russia obtaining left-bank Ukraine east of the Dnieper River, including Kiev, and Poland retaining the right bank. A century later, the left and right banks were united as Catherine the Great annexed western Ukraine following the partitions of Poland (1772, 1793, 1795). In the twentieth century, eastern Ukraine proved to be of major value to the Russians. They moved large numbers of ethnic Russians into the Donets Basin (Donbas) and Kharkov (Kharkiv) areas, which bordered the Russian centers of Rostov, Belograd, and Kursk. The vast coking coal deposits of the Donbas and the rich iron ores of Krivoy Rog (Kryvyi Rih) became the bases for the emergence of Donbas and Kharkov as two of the most heavily industrialized steel and metallurgical centers of the world.

Belorussia ("White Russia," now Belarus) posed an equally formidable challenge to czarist expansionism. It, too, had been conquered by the dukes of Lithuania and remained under the rule of Lithuania and Poland during the sixteenth- to eighteenth-century wars between Russia and Poland. As with Ukraine, Belorussia finally passed to the czarist empire with the partitions of Poland. After World War I, in 1921, Poland retook western Belorussia, while the eastern, larger part was retained by the USSR. In 1939, the Soviet army moved into the western region and incorporated it into Belorussia, which retains the territory to this day.

Lithuania, which had been one of medieval Europe's largest and most powerful states, gradually came under Polish rule. It joined in a union with Poland in 1569 as a defensive measure against the pressures of Ivan IV and became Polandized. With the partitions of Poland, Lithuania was annexed to Russia. When Russia collapsed after World War I, Lithuania regained its independence but lost its Vilna region to Poland. In 1923 Lithuania seized the Memel Territory (Klaipėda), which had formerly been part of East Prussia. Vilna was passed back to Lithuania as part of the Soviet-German partition of Poland in 1939, while Memel was returned to Germany. Lithuania was occupied by the USSR the following year and forced to become a constituent Soviet republic. After being occupied by Germany during the war with the Soviet Union, Lithuania was regained by the USSR in 1944 and remained a Soviet republic until its independence in 1990.

While Peter the Great had seized eastern Latvia (Livonia) from Sweden, the western part of the country, south of the Western Dvina River and known as Courland, with its Baltic ports of Liepāja and Ventspils, did not pass into Russian hands until the Third Partition of Poland in 1795. Latvia had for centuries been dominated by German merchants who had settled there with the Hanseatic League. Its landowning aristocracy, the "Baltic barons," was also of German origin. The collapse of Russia and Germany made Latvian independence possible in 1918. The country was conquered by the Soviets in 1940 and absorbed into the USSR, but its Lettish population strongly supported the German troops who occupied Latvia during the war.

At the onset of World War I, the czarist empire was at its territorial peak, extending for 5,700 miles from the Baltic to the Pacific and covering a total land area of 8,647,660 square miles (including Bukhara and Khiva). Its population of 145 million was heavily concentrated in European Russia. Despite relatively large-scale movement of settlers into Siberia between 1891 and 1911, the overall population of that region was only eight million, nearly all of whom were Russian. All told, approximately three-quarters of the population of the empire was Slavic, with Turkic as the second-largest ethnic grouping.

By all accounts, Russia had fallen far short of achieving the modernization to which Peter the Great aspired. Its economy was still largely agricultural and underdeveloped. Industry, dependent upon foreign capital, was concentrated in only a few places—St. Petersburg, the leading manufacturing and financial center; Moscow, a major textile and metallurgical center; Baku, the focus of Russia's oil industry; and the Donbas/Kharkov iron and steel region. The rail network was woefully inadequate, with a density of mileage that was only one-tenth that of the United Kingdom, France, or Germany.

The czarist regime was despotic and corrupt, with an ineffective, centralized civilian and military bureaucracy that was ill prepared to lead the nation into World War I. While Russia now extended beyond the bounds of Mackinder's "Pivot Area," it was hardly in a position to be a strategic threat to the maritime reaches of Eurasia that surrounded it. Such a threat would come only after the Bolshevik Revolution, the victory of Soviet forces in World War II, and the spread of Communism into East and Central Europe and East Asia.

TERRITORIAL CHANGES IN THE SOVIET ERA

During the period following the Bolshevik Revolution and its aftermath, the territory that had been embraced by the Russian Empire shrank by 405,740 square miles. The "white" (anti-Bolshevik) republics of Georgia, Armenia, and Azerbaijan in the Caucasus did not long survive and were regained by the Soviet Union. Those territories that were lost to the Soviet Union included Finland, Estonia, Latvia, Lithuania, the Polish provinces that had been held by Russia, Bessarabia (to Romania), and Kars and Ardahan in the far south (which were restored to Turkey). Thus, in 1938 the area of the USSR amounted to 8,340,479 square miles, or approximately 300,000 square miles less than Russia in the czarist period.

Table 8.1. Post-World War II Soviet Land Annexations

Area	*Former Colony*	*Soviet Republic*
Pechenga District	Finland	Murmansk Oblast (RSFSR)
Karelia (Salla)	Finland	Karelian ASSR (RSFSR)
Vyborg District	Finland	Leningrad Oblast
Northern East Prussia and Mernelland	Germany	Kaliningrad Oblast (RSFSR) and Klaipėda Oblast (Lithuanian SSR)
Estonia	Independent	Estonian Union Republic
Latvia	Independent	Latvian Union Republic
Lithuania	Independent	Lithuanian Union Republic
Eastern Estonia and Latvia	Estonia and Latvia	Pskov Oblast (RSFSR)
Eastern Poland (Western Belorussia)	Poland	Four oblasts in Belorussian SSR and Vinla Oblast in Lithuanian SSR
Transcarpathia (Ruthenia)	Czechoslovakia	Transcarpathian Oblast (Ukrainian SSR)
Central Bessarabia	Romania	Moldavian SSR
Southern Bessarabia	Romania	Izmail Oblast (Ukrainian SSR)
Tannu Tuva	Independent	Tuva ASSR (RSFSR)
Southern Sakhalin	Japan	Sakhalin Oblast (RSFSR)
Kuril Islands	Japan	Sakhalin Oblast (RSFSR)

Note: ASSR = Autonomous Soviet Socialist Republic; SSR = Soviet Socialist Republic; RSFSR = Russian Soviet Federal Socialist Republic.

The Soviet state expanded once more, first as a result of the seizure of lands in 1939–40 in accordance with the pact with Nazi Germany and later with the territorial spoils that were confirmed by Soviet victory in World War II. Most of the annexations were in Eastern Europe, although, as previously noted, southern Sakhalin and the four southern Kuril Islands were taken from Japan. In addition, in 1984, nominally independent Tannu Tuva, bordering Mongolia, was formally absorbed.

The basis for Soviet territorial expansion was threefold: strategic, economic, and nationalistic. Historic claims were important only as they related to these factors, as they played an unimportant role within the Soviet propaganda mechanism.

The strategic objective was defensively motivated: to assure command of interior and marginal seas and land gateways. It also served an offensive function in increasing the vulnerability of neighboring states to Soviet pressure.

Economic objectives played a major role in providing the Russian ecumene with improved port facilities in the Baltic for foreign trade. Nationality goals related not only to pan-Slavic ambitions but also to the unity of minority peoples living within the Soviet nationality-based administrative framework. Not only were Russian-inhabited parts of Latvia annexed and combined with the Russian Soviet Federal Socialist Republic (RSFSR) and Ruthenian portions of Poland merged with Ukraine, but also much of the Karelian-inhabited portion of east-central Finland was added to Soviet Karelia.

There were two overriding elements in these territorial annexations—the need for strategic depth in some of the most important cities of the USSR (which had proved vulnerable during the German invasion) and fear of any future invasion from Germany. The principal international ports of the USSR in 1939 were Odessa, Leningrad (St. Petersburg), Murmansk, Archangel, and Vladivostok. Of these ports, all save Archangel were frontier cities. Odessa and Leningrad were twenty and twelve miles, respectively, from the pre–World War II Romanian border. Murmansk was fifty miles from Finnish territory, while Vladivostok was thirty-five miles from Japanese Manchuria. Sovetskaya Gavan (Soviet Harbor), developed during World War II on the Gulf of Tartary as a deepwater naval base and commercial port for the Amur valley, was only seventy miles from Japanese-held southern Sakhalin. With the territorial changes that occurred during and immediately after World War II, Odessa was now fifty, Leningrad ninety, and Murmansk eighty miles from the borders of the Soviet Union, while Vladivostok was shielded by both southern Sakhalin and the North Korean satellite state.

For Moscow, these additional few miles had psychological as well as strategic significance. Leningrad had been besieged for more than two years by the invading Nazi armies, and Odessa had temporarily fallen to the onslaught of combined German and Romanian forces. Murmansk was bombarded by the Germans, who had seized the nearby Norwegian city of Kirkenes in 1940, and the chief Russian supply line was in constant danger of being cut. Moreover, the Soviets well remembered the occupation of Murmansk by Allied troops from 1918 to 1920, during the Russian civil war. They had historical recall also of the vulnerability of Vladivostok, which had been occupied during the revolution by Japanese and other Allied troops, who remained until 1922.

Soviet territorial annexations in the west were designed to provide a buffer against future attack by a revived Germany or by an alliance of hostile Western powers. For example, Hitler's first plans for Operation Barbarossa, the invasion of the Soviet Union during World War II, were to strike the Soviet Union simultaneously through several corridors: (1) northern Finland against Murmansk and Archangel; (2) the Baltic Sea, via southern Finland and the Baltic states toward Leningrad; (3) Belorussia, from along the Warsaw-Bialystok-Minsk land corridor north of the Pripet Marshes and thence northward to Leningrad; (4) southern Poland and the Donets Basin (Donbas); and (5) through Romania to Odessa and the Black Sea.

The post–World War II annexation of the Pechenga District in northern Finland, including the western Rybachyi Peninsula, provided defensive depth for the ice-free port of Murmansk. It also helped to secure the nearby Kola Peninsula's apatite resources, which were the basis for Russia's phosphate industry. South of Pechenga lies Russian Pasvik, which had been annexed by Finland in 1920 to provide access to Pechenga. This corridor and its nickel resources were now in Soviet hands, and, as a consequence of this annexation, the Soviets gained a common border with Norway. The latter's taconite ore mining town of Kirkenes lay exposed, and the population of northern Norway became subject to strong Communist propaganda pressures.

Despite all these territorial additions in the north, the entrances to the Barents Sea were still not in Soviet hands. The Svalbard island group was still owned by Norway, which rejected Soviet claims to this coal-mining Arctic archipelago.

The most important boundary change that occurred was the annexation of the Baltic republics. Soviet geographer Nicholas Baransky offered this apt summary: "Owing to its geographical position, the Soviet Baltic region is of prime importance for the external connections of the U.S.S.R. . . . [It is] a natural harbor which serves the Central U.S.S.R."[5] Although not entirely ice free, Riga in Latvia, the largest city and a major rail terminus, presented the Soviet Union with its best Baltic port. Klaipėda (Memel) and Ventspils (Windau) offered newly developed oil ports, and Tallinn offered a natural gas terminus. Kaliningrad (Königsberg) was an important ice-free addition to the eastern Baltic ports.

The Kaliningrad Oblast, cleared of Germans and populated by Russians, became part of the RSFSR, although separated from it by the Lithuanian and Belorussian republics. Kaliningrad provided direct access to the Polish and East German satellites' ports of Gdansk, Szczecin, and Rostock. Slight internal territorial changes also strengthened the Russian position in the Baltic vis-à-vis both satellite states and non-Russian Soviet republics. A portion of Estonia lying along the right bank of the River Narva was detached to be added directly to the Leningrad Oblast. Finally, Russian-inhabited rural districts of Estonia (Petseri) and Latvia (Abrene and Kacanava), all east of the Gulf of Riga, were detached and added to the Pskov Oblast within the RSFSR. Pskov, at the southern end of Lake Peipus, was important as the land gateway to Leningrad.

Also, following the principle of drawing boundaries based on nationalities, a Lithuanian-inhabited strip of Belorussia was added to the Lithuanian Soviet Socialist Republic (SSR), which had reincorporated Vilna (Vilnius) from Poland. With Vilna and Pskov both in Soviet territory, the Vilna corridor, which follows the high Baltic end-moraine (the ridge that marked the edge of glaciation) northeastward to Leningrad, was more secure. Soviet actions in the Baltic, in a broad sense, can be described as defensively oriented, owing to the exposure of the Russian core to the European lands to the west.

The westward shift of the boundary in Belorussia brought the Pripet Marshes completely within the Soviet fold. This boundary was restored to the Curzon Line of 1919, as the Soviets reclaimed territory lost to Poland after their 1920 war. Return to the Curzon Line completed Russian control over the Vilna Gap, thus blocking the high-ground route to Leningrad and Moscow. In addition, the Curzon Line gave the USSR possession of the most direct route to Moscow, high ground from Brest to Minsk that skirts the northern edge of the Pripet Marshes. Moreover, western Belorussia was claimed on the basis of nationality, White Russians being in the majority over Poles.

Western Ukraine lands taken from Poland included Lviv and Drogobych. The former was a rail hub on the upper Bug River whose industries served the agricultural areas to the east. The latter was a district on the northern slopes of the Carpathians that was once Poland's major petroleum-producing region. Its strategic and economic implications lay in its being denied to Poland as well as in its availability to Kiev. In the case of western Ukraine, unity of the Ukrainian people was an important basis for the claim, although another reason for Soviet interest was the fact that the Soviet border was now but 130 miles from Krakow and just another 50 miles from industrialized Upper Silesia. With the absorption of Transcarpathia, the Russians accomplished much more than the union of Ruthenians with their kindred Ukrainians. This land annexation gave the Soviet Union complete control of the eastern Carpathian Mountains and a base on their southern slopes from which to overlook the Tisa River and all of the Hungarian plain. Czechoslovakia and Hungary now shared common borders with the USSR, and Budapest lay exposed to a Soviet border only 150 miles away. Belgrade and Vienna were also affected by this new Danubian position of the USSR.

The border changes in northern Bukovina and Bessarabia were justified as absorptions of predominantly Ukrainian peoples, but they also served broader Soviet strategic and economic interests. They gave to the Soviets the lands between the Dniester and the Prut as well as the northernmost mouth of the Danube. The Ploieşti oil fields and Bucharest were about 125 miles from the Soviet border—another example of the vulnerability into which a satellite state had been pushed.

Boundary adjustments in Siberia were less important to Moscow strategically than were those in Europe. In the Pacific territories, annexation of Sakhalin and the Kurils (which enclosed the Sea of Okhotsk) pointed a double dagger toward northern Japan. However, these acquisitions did not substantially affect the security of Russia's Sea of Japan coast and Vladivostok because the Sovietization of North Korea provided far greater protection.

In south-central Siberia, annexation of nominally independent Tannu Tuva in 1944 may have been viewed as a precedent for eventual Soviet annexation (which never took place) of the Mongolian People's Republic. A lightly populated and underdeveloped land, the Tuva Autonomous Soviet Socialist Republic (ASSR) is at the headwaters of the Yenisey and overlooks Irkutsk and the Trans-Siberian Railroad from the eastern end of the Western Sayan Mountains.

At the onset of the Cold War, the USSR unsuccessfully revived claims to Ardahan, Kars, and Artvin on the borders of the Middle East in Turkey. These were areas that Russia had once seized from the Ottoman Empire and that the Soviets now wished to add to Georgia and Armenia. Moscow also failed to gain the demilitarization of the Turkish straits. The waterway that connected the Black and Mediterranean Seas had been briefly internationalized and demilitarized in the early 1920s but had been refortified by Turkey in 1936.

Soviet territorial pressures were also mounted against Iran. In 1945 Soviet troops that had been garrisoned in the northern part of the country during World War II supported the establishment of a separatist Communist republic in the oil-rich Iranian Azerbaijan province. Soviet troops also backed a Kurdish separatist republic in the lands to the west and south of Lake Urmia, overlooking Iraq's northern oil fields. The rebellions were quashed the following year, and the USSR had to remove its troops owing to UN Security Council pressures.

Offsetting these failed territorial efforts, however, were later Soviet successes in forging a ring of bases in the Mediterranean and Indian Oceans. From the 1960s to the 1980s, the USSR established naval facilities at Marsah Matruh, Alexandria, and Port Said in Egypt and at Latakia in Syria. South of Suez, along the Red Sea, installations were built at Ras Benas in Egypt, Port Sudan in the Sudan, and Hodeida in Yemen. In addition, the Soviet bases at

Aden (overlooking the Gulf of Aden) and on the island of Socotra provided a strong presence in the waters east of Suez leading to the Indian Ocean.

Since the Suez Canal had been blocked by Egypt as a result of its loss of Sinai to Israel in the 1967 war, leaving the canal out of use until 1975, Moscow's efforts to create a Soviet-controlled Black Sea-Mediterranean-Suez-Indian Ocean route to the Far East came to naught. The peace settlement between Egypt and Israel that was negotiated in 1978 and formally ratified in 1979 ended all Soviet hopes of using Suez as a strategic weapon in the Cold War.

TERRITORIAL CONTRACTION IN POST-SOVIET RUSSIA

The USSR that emerged after World War II had acquired 265,000 additional square miles. This increased its size to 8,600,660 square miles—only 50,000 square miles less than the territories held by the czarist empire at its zenith. When the Soviet Union collapsed forty-five years later, the territorial dissolution stripped the Russian core of fourteen of the FSU's constituent republics. The land that remained to the new Russian Federation was reduced by nearly two million square miles, to 6,592,735. Its 1991 population was reduced to 154 million, as compared with the FSU's 293 million. Since then, Russia's population has dropped to approximately 145 million as a consequence of lower birthrates, higher death rates, and out-migration. The collapse of the health-care system, as well as a number of economic and social factors, is responsible for the continuing population shrinkage. Unless the trend is dramatically reversed, the country could be left with only 135 million people by the end of the present decade, and its economic recovery could be hampered by severe labor shortages.

In contrast to the highly multiethnic character of the USSR, where ethnic Russians were only 53 percent of the total population, Russians now constitute 77 percent of the populace of the Russian Federation. This is not to suggest that Russia is no longer ethnically and religiously diverse. Within its twenty-one republics, forty-eight oblasts, and other political subdivisions, it has over sixty different recognized groups, including large numbers of Ukrainians, Tatars, Yakuts, Ossetians, Buryats, Chechens, Ingush, Bashkiris, Chuvash, Komi, Mari, Jews, Germans, and Armenians. However, forging a new state based on the present multinational profile is far less challenging than the task faced by the Soviet Union, which tried to forge a cohesive state out of 108 distinct nationalities.

IMPLOSION OF THE SOVIET STATE

Implosion of the Soviet Union came after eight decades in which the regime was held together by internal terror and fear of external enemies as well as by the dream of a classless and more just society. The state had been established on the principles of Marxism and the rights of all ethnic groups within the USSR. (There were twenty-two nationalities, each with over one million in population.) However, all were forced into linguistic and cultural assimilation, as tolerance for ethnic equality remained an empty promise. During World War II, millions of minority peoples, including Crimean Tatars, Chechens, Ingush, Volga Germans, and Kalmyks, were deported to Central Asia and Siberia. Economically, the failure of the command economy to provide a better life for the mass of people stood in sharp contrast to the prosperity of the Western world. The Communist system was riddled with inefficiencies and heavy outlays on defense, which sapped the system even further. It was only a matter of time before the implosion took place, as occurred formally in September 1991.

The dissolution was consensual. Eleven of the newly independent states agreed to the establishment of the Commonwealth of Independent States (CIS) on the basis of an expected benefit from a common framework within which disputes could be mediated and trade promoted. Only Georgia and the Baltic states did not join. In fact, however, the CIS remained a hollow organization, as only Russia, Belarus, Kazakhstan, Armenia, and Transnistria (eastern Moldova) have retained substantive ties.

The conflicts that followed the devolution of the FSU were confined mainly to internal strife within the newly independent states. The exception was the bitter war between Armenia and Azerbaijan over the Armenian Christian enclave of Nagorno-Karabakh in southeastern Azerbaijan, which had held the status of an autonomous region. The fighting between the Armenians and the Muslim Azeri had begun even before the breakup of the FSU but peaked after the Armenian population declared the region to be an independent state. Armenian troops entered the conflict and drove out most of the Azeri populace from the enclave and the lands that connect it to Armenia proper. Moscow originally sided with Azerbaijan but then tilted toward Armenia. It now operates air and missile bases in Armenian territory, while Russian troops help guard Armenia's Turkish border. Turkey, meanwhile, has increased its military and economic influence in Azerbaijan and, in 1993, placed Armenia under a trade blockade. This has had little economic effect.

In Georgia, civil war broke out almost immediately after the dissolution of the FSU. In addition, a separatist revolt erupted in Georgia's Muslim Abkhazia, which adjoins Russia's Black Sea coast and its North Caucasus reaches, and sought to make Abkhazia an associated state within Russia. Russian troops aided the separatists, and eventually Moscow settled the conflict, leaving Abkhazia as an autonomous republic within Georgia but under virtual Russian control. Russian intervention imposed a similar solution in South Ossetia. There the Farsi-speaking Ossetians revolted against Georgia in 1992, with the goal of joining North Ossetia, which lies along the northern slopes of the main Caucasus range in Russia. Russian troops intervened on behalf of the Ossetians. The outcome was a South Ossetian autonomous republic in Georgia that remains under Russian protection. While the South Ossetians declared a nominally independent state, Moscow has refrained from recognizing it.

Another separatist region, Muslim Adjara, on the Black Sea in the southwest corner of Georgia, had separated from Georgia in 1992. After the "Rose Revolution" drove the pro-Russian president from power, the Russians agreed to withdraw from Adjara, including its naval base at Batumi, in 2008.

A war of secession broke out also in eastern Moldova, along the eastern bank of the Dniester, adjoining Ukraine. There, toward the end of 1991, the region's majority Russians and Ukrainians declared their independence from Moldova. The separatists established the self-styled pseudostate of the Trans-Dniester Republic (Transnistria) along the Dniester's eastern bank. Its leadership seeks unity of the "republic" with Russia.[6]

Elsewhere, the dissolution of the FSU created considerable tension between Russia and Ukraine over Ukraine's independence and also over the sovereignty of the Crimea. A great deal of the Russian sense of nationhood is derived from Russia's historic and symbolic identification with Kievan Rus (located in the modern Ukraine), the medieval Slavic state that many Russians regard as the historic or nuclear core of Russia. Many consider the Kievan state to be the common heritage of modern Russians, Ukrainians, and Belorussians. Moreover, while only 17 percent of Ukraine's forty-five million population is ethnic Russian, in the eastern Donbas and Kharkiv regions, Russians are nearly half the population. A similar number of Ukrainians who are non-ethnic Russians are also Russian speakers. The Crimea, at that time part of Ukraine, had an approximately 60 percent majority Russian population, and nearly all of the rest is Russian-speaking. When Moscow turned the region over to the Ukrainian SSR in 1954, most of these Russians opposed the exchange. Their grounds were that the Crimean port city of Sevastopol, the home of the former Soviet Black Sea fleet, was indispensable to Russian security.

Both of these issues were peacefully resolved eventually, although the debate was sharp. In 1997 Russia accepted Ukraine's existing national borders and recognized its sovereignty over the Crimea and Sevastopol. Crimea was granted the status of autonomous region—a concession by Ukraine that reflected the region's overwhelmingly ethnic Russian population as well as its strategic importance to Moscow. Ukraine also accorded Russia the right to base its Black Sea fleet in Sevastopol.[7] In 2014, Russia reannexed Crimea.

With the exception of Tajikistan, the former Soviet Central Asian republics were not torn by the kind of conflict experienced by the newly independent Caucasus states. However, in Tajikistan, the poorest of all former Soviet republics, a civil war broke out in 1992 between the Moscow-backed regime led by former Communists and the Islamic United Tajik opposition. Despite a shaky peace that was signed in 1997, the Dushanbe regime has since had to call upon Russian troops to sustain it against attacks from the fundamentalist eastern highlanders. In 2003–4, Russia opened a base there to control terrorism and the drug trade.

Russia itself has not been immune from internal conflict. In the North Caucasus, Muslim Chechen rebels inflicted a humiliating defeat upon the Russian army in their 1994–96 war, at the end of which the rebels announced the creation of an Islamic fundamentalist state. This state was short-lived—its economy collapsed, its territory served as a haven for terrorism, and its central government proved incapable of exercising control over the territory. The war resumed two years later, following Chechen terrorist bombings in Moscow, North Ossetia, and Chechnya, as well as Chechen involvement in a rebellion in Dagestan. The conflict was finally quashed in 2006, when the Chechen leader was killed and replaced by a former rebel who allied himself with Russia and became president of the republic. Since then, Grozny, which had been almost destroyed in 1999–2000, has been largely rebuilt, and the economy of oil-rich Chechnya has been improved. Elsewhere in the North Caucasus, the Russian Republics of Ingushetia, North Ossetia, Dagestan, and Kabardino-Balkaria have suffered Islamic terrorist attacks as well as serving as launching pads for terrorist assaults deep into Russia. These have triggered strong Russian military responses.

From a Russian strategic viewpoint, revolts by Russian North Caucasus territories lying between the Caspian and Black Seas represent a threat to the lines of communication that traverse them, particularly railways and pipelines. Moreover, the fact that the region is located along an international border provides separatist groups with the option of linking up physically with Azerbaijan and Georgia.

Unlike Chechnya, the separatist movement in the interior of the country, in Tatarstan, represents only a minor threat to Russia. Located within the center of European Russia, along the middle Volga and lower Kama Rivers, the oil-rich Tatar Republic, with a strong manufacturing base, is landlocked. It has no access to external support bases. Thus, when in 1991 the leaders of the former Tatar ASSR declared the independent state of Tatarstan (Tataria), the act was strategically irrelevant. Also, the fact that ethnic Russians are aş numerous there as Tatars ruled out any serious threat of conflict. While Tataria was not signatory to the 1992 treaty that established the Russian Federation, it subsequently made its own treaty with Moscow and has the status of a republic.

The establishment of Tuva as an independent entity and of quasi states in Sakh (Yakutia) and the Russian Far East would have little impact upon Russia's power position. Statehood for the sparsely populated republic of Tuva in south Siberia on the border with Mongolia would have no geopolitical impact whatsoever on Russia. The Turkic-speaking, nomadic Tuvans, who practice Tibetan Buddhism, have long sought the independence that Moscow can well afford to grant at no cost to its national self-interest. Quasi statehood for Yakutia and the Far Eastern Province would simply formalize and better regulate the conditions of autonomy that already exist within those areas.

Geopolitical Features

Dismemberment of the Soviet Union has had a substantial impact upon the geopolitical features of the "New Russia," particularly with respect to the contraction of its former ecumene, the loss of some of its mineral-rich effective national territory and empty area, and its changed territorial boundaries. Nevertheless, Russia remains a formidable state, the largest political landmass in the world, extending for five thousand miles from west to east across eleven time zones and for fifteen hundred miles from its Arctic north to the Black Sea, the Caucasus, and the mountains of southern Siberia. No other national state possesses Russia's spatial depth.

This factor is reinforced by the massive nuclear arsenal, which is being modernized at the same time that it is reduced in accordance with US-Russian nuclear arms agreements. An analysis of Russia's geopolitical features identifies the inherent strength that enabled it to recover so quickly from the decade of political and social instability and economic disarray that followed the breakup of the USSR. Regaining its status as a major power that controls the heartlandic center enables Russia to pressure in the heartlandic periphery, especially in Syria, Iran, and Ukraine, thus wielding global influence once more.

HISTORIC CORE

Russia's historic core—the area in which the Russian state originated—is generally considered to be the medieval principality of Kievan Rus, although Novgorod also may lay claim to this status. The origins of Russia may be traced to the arrival of the Varangians, the Scandinavian traders and warriors led by Rurik, who founded his dynasty in Novgorod in 862 CE. Located in northwestern Russia, Novgorod was situated on the Volkhov River, on the major trade route that led from the Baltic to the headwaters of the Volga, then south and southeast to the Black and Caspian Seas. Novgorod's location eventually enabled it to become one of the four chief centers of the Hanseatic League, along with London, Bruges, and Bergen.

Rurik's successor, Oleg, transferred the capital to Kiev, the center of the Kievan Rus state, in 879. However, Novgorod continued to be the main center for foreign trade and ultimately (from the early twelfth to the fifteenth centuries) was capital of all of northern Russia to the Urals.

Vladimir defeated his brother, Oleg, in 880 to become grand duke of Kiev. He then conquered distant Slavic tribes and waged successful wars with Lithuanians, Bulgars, and Byzantines to expand his kingdom. For Russians, the defining moment of their nationhood took place in 988–89, when Vladimir converted to Christianity and made the Greek Orthodox Church the religion of his people, linking secular rule and the church.

Kiev was chosen to become the new seat of the Varangian dynasty because its location along the Dnieper River was better sited for the Scandinavian-Black Sea-Constantinople trade. As the capital of Kievan Rus, Kiev became a leading European commercial and cultural center. Surrounded by the fertile crop- and grasslands of southern Russia, the city had a more

Figure 8.1. Heartlandic Russia and Periphery: Major Geopolitical Features

prosperous agricultural area than Novgorod, which was located within the cool, marshy, and thin-soiled glaciated section of northern Russia.

The name "Russ" initially described the Varangians, who then applied it to the Eastern Slavs who had settled around Kiev and gave their name to the new state—Kievan Rus. Kiev became known to the Russians as the "mother of cities," even after political power shifted to Moscow. Kiev remained the capital until 1169, during which time Eastern Orthodox Christianity consolidated its position among the Slavs and Byzantine culture predominated. It was during this period that the Russian Orthodox Church became an essential part of Russian nationalism and Church Slavonic became the liturgical and literary language of the Russians.

Because the Kievan state was, in effect, a frontier state, exposed to the nomadic attacks of the Mongols who swept out of the Eurasian steppe, it finally succumbed to the invading Mongol armies (1237–40), who established their control over southern and eastern Russia.

POLITICAL CAPITALS

With the breakup of the Kievan Rus state, Russian power shifted northward. The most powerful of the political units to emerge under the Tatar yoke was the principality of Vladimir-Suzdal, which centered on Moscow. Moscow's nodal location in a basin at the juncture of the Volga plain and the central Russian uplands had been advantageous for its development as a medieval trade center and the seat of the Duchy of Vladimir (part of the Kievan dynasty). The city had ease of access in all directions, the surrounding Valday hills, Smolensk ridge, and central uplands serving as the basis for a great watershed system. Moscow was a strategic crossroads for medieval trade routes—the Moskva River runs southeast into the Oka and thence to the Volga River as it flows southward into the Caspian Sea. An arm of the Moskva also flows north into the Upper Volga, which is connected by river systems that flow into the Baltic and White Seas. The Oka River also connects to the Don River immediately to Moscow's south and to the Dnieper to the west; both drain into the Black Sea. Later, canals would effectively link these river systems. The centrality of the city was again reinforced by its radial railway network and by more recent air, electric power, and pipeline links.

In addition to access, Moscow's site had natural defensive advantages. It was protected on the east by the Klyazma-Oka marshy plain, on the north by the marshy plain of the Upper Volga, and on the west and northwest by the Smolensk-Moscow ridge. Farther to the northwest lay the Valday hills. Even though the city was sacked by the Mongols in 1238, it recovered to become the core of the Grand Duchy of Muscovy and the seat of the Russian Orthodox Church. By 1328, it had emerged as the main political and economic center of the duchy, and in 1380 it became the capital of a unified Russian state. By the mid-sixteenth century, the Muscovite rulers took the lead in throwing off the Tatar yoke and began the state's southern and eastern expansion.

Moscow grew as the main manufacturing center of the state and served as the capital of Russia until, in 1712, Peter the Great built the new capital of St. Petersburg on the Baltic Sea to spearhead Russian commercial expansion. For the next two centuries, Moscow remained the religious core and second most important economic center. It resumed its role of political capital in 1918. That shift was both symbolic of Bolshevik rejection of the czarist cultural and economic turn to the West over the previous two centuries and the strategic expression of the Soviet desire for greater defensive depth. St. Petersburg was exposed geographically to invading forces from the west and the north, whereas Moscow had the advantage of being removed from the borders. Moscow is by far the largest metropolis of the country, with a population of over 11.5 million, and the country's financial center. It has begun to modernize its industrial base through establishment of the new "Silicon Valley" technical city in the nearby suburb of Solkovo, which is headquarters for Russia's leading microelectronics firms.

The alternating of the base of political power between Moscow and St. Petersburg represented antithetical points of view. Moscow reflected the inward-turning of medieval and early-modern-age Russia and the Soviet state. St. Petersburg represented czarist efforts to open the state to external technological innovations, cultural influences, and financial capital. It was from St. Petersburg (Petrograd from 1914 to 1924, Leningrad in 1924, and now St. Petersburg once more) that the city's industrial workers, soldiers, and sailors spearheaded the Russian Revolutions of February and October 1917.

ECUMENE

The ecumene of Russia, defined by its highest density of population and economic activities, is shaped like a triangle that lies on its side pointing eastward. Its wide base on the west extends from St. Petersburg to Smolensk (facing Belarus), then to Briansk and Kursk, which adjoin the northeastern Ukraine, and continues southward to Rostov-on-Don at the eastern edge of the Donets Basin (Donbas), which was once a major part of the Soviet ecumene but now lies mostly within Ukraine. St. Petersburg, with a population of five million and long a center of shipbuilding, has reinvented itself as an international financial and business center. It is also the locus for oil and gas trading companies and a modern auto industry.

From the western baseline, the core area extends eastward, embracing Moscow and south-central Russia and then narrowing as it extends to Nizhny Novgorod (Gorky), Kazan, and Perm on its northern edge and Samara (Kuybyshev, on the great bend of the Middle Volga) and Ufa on its southern border. Samara has become a major center for the modern commercial airline industry. Crossing the Urals, the ecumene includes the West Siberian centers of Magnitogorsk, Yekaterinburg (Sverdlovsk), and Chelyabinsk. These cities form a triangular wedge from which the core area then extends eastward to Tyumen, a major center for the oil, natural gas, and chemical industries, and southward to Kurgan, which manufactures agricultural and chemical machinery. Both of these cities are on tributaries of the Ob-Irtysh River, which is the current boundary of the ecumene.

In much of the European portion of the ecumene, the population density ranges between 200 and 330 persons per square mile. From the Urals through West Siberia, peak densities are from 120 to 150 per square mile, while densities on the northern and southern edges of the ecumene range from 60 to 120 per square mile.

Major coal deposits are located in the eastern Donbas and north of Perm, while lignite deposits are in the areas surrounding the Moscow basin. The deposits of petroleum and natural gas in the region that extends from Saratov in the Middle Volga northeastward along the Kama River basin to Perm, in the western Ural foothills, were so extensive that this area was called the "Second Baku." From 1950 to 1975, it was the Soviet Union's largest oil producing and refining center. Since then, it has been overtaken by energy-rich West Siberia. Now described as the "Third Baku," the Tyumen oblast, extending the length of the Ob-Irtysh basin, holds vast natural gas reserves—the largest in the world—and its petroleum deposits have made Russia into the world's second leading oil exporter and largest producer with 10 percent of total output, although the United States production is quickly catching up.

The oil exports go mainly to Europe. Russia also provides Europe with close to one-third of its gas imports, much of which flows through the pipelines that cross Ukraine. The East and

Central European states now receive the major share of this gas. Lines now extend through Belarus, Ukraine, and Poland to coastal and Western Europe. These have been supplemented by a line constructed from Vyborg under the Baltic Sea to northern Germany (the Nord Stream) matched by one (the South Stream) from southern Russia, under the Black Sea to Bulgaria, Greece, Italy, and Austria. This line, now under construction, is scheduled for completion in 2015. These two new routes will bypass the transit countries with respect to pricing policies. A third line (the Green Stream), constructed jointly by Italy's ENI and Libya, extends from Mellitah in Libya under the Mediterranean to Sicily and Italy. In addition, Serbia has an energy pact with Russia that includes the distribution of Gazprom gas exports to adjoining European countries. The expanded system has enabled Russia to more than double its natural gas exports, with most of the increase destined for Western Europe. Such a near-monopoly position has strengthened Russia's geopolitical influence in its relations with the EU. Substantial new oil and gas reserves that will enhance Russia's energy-producing capacities have been found in the Pechora basin north of the Arctic Circle to the immediate west of northern Siberia.

Rich iron ore deposits in western Russia, south of Kursk, and scattered mining centers for molybdenum, copper, lead, zinc, and bauxite are also located within the ecumene. This rich mineral base served as the foundation for the development of Russia's heavy industry—in the eastern Donbas, Moscow, Kursk, and Urals regions.

While the Urals had first developed metallurgical and ironworks in the early eighteenth century, its great industrial spurt occurred during World War II. Then, in the face of invading Nazi armies, much of Soviet industry was transferred from European Russia to the secure reaches of such Ural centers as Sverdlovsk (Yekaterinburg), Chelyabinsk, and Magnitogorsk.

Yekaterinburg today is not only the capital of Sverdlovsk Oblast, with its population of 1.4 million, but it is also the center for a regional grouping of Ural provinces whose populations total 23 million. The city was closed to foreigners until 1992 because of its secret nuclear-weapons-assembly and uranium-enrichment plants. It has now begun to attract foreign investment and modernize its civilian aircraft parts industry and serves as Russia's third-busiest diplomatic center.

Chelyabinsk's initial industrialization steps took place with the building of the Trans-Siberian Railroad; its steel and tractor industries were developed in the 1930s. It, too, was a closed city, serving as a center for the design of nuclear weapons and uranium processing. It now suffers from radioactive contamination due to nuclear waste disposal and nuclear accidents. During the Soviet era, there were ten such closed nuclear cities, with populations totaling seven million. Redirecting their large pool of scientific and technical personnel to civilian projects is an enormous challenge to Moscow but also a major element in its strategy of economic recovery.

Mayak, the largest nuclear complex in the world, is located just north of Chelyabinsk on the Techa River, a headwater of the Ob-Irtysh River system, which drains the West Siberia empty area. The Mayak complex lies within the city of Ozyorsky (formerly the secret city of Chelyabinsk-65). Mayak currently reprocesses fuels from nuclear submarines, icebreakers, and breeder reactors and was the scene of reprocessing accidents in 1949, 1957, and 1967. In 1996, Moscow began construction of a fissile material storage facility there, which has become the world's largest depository of nuclear waste from power plants. The facility serves customers from throughout Europe and Asia, blending down the highly enriched uranium to a level of low enrichment useful for generating electricity.

Safeguarding nuclear wastes is not only a Russian problem—it is a global problem. In 1992, the United States and Russia entered into an agreement to help Russia and other FSU states to destroy nuclear, chemical, and biological materials and delivery weapons. Under this program, approximately 12,000 nuclear warheads have been deactivated and their launching platforms destroyed. This collaborative program has withstood the diplomatic tensions between Moscow and Washington in recent years. It is regarded as a model for dealing jointly with other important issues.[8] The new START (Strategic Arms Reduction Treaty) of 2010 resulted in each country reducing its nuclear warheads to 1,650, and their strategic delivery systems to 850.

The other key Ural center is Magnitogorsk (Magnet Mountain City). It was built in the Stalin era as a factory town around the Magnitogorsk Metal Works. The plant was once the largest steel producer in the FSU and the world's largest milling and shipping complex. Since the collapse of the Soviet state, it produces only half of the raw steel that it once did. The city's ills are representative of those of Russia's rust belt generally—a bloated labor force, antiquated equipment, air pollution, and dependence on a single industry, whose local iron resources have been greatly depleted. With the opening of the country's markets to cheaper foreign steel imports, Russia's steel production has dropped from eighty million tons per annum to seventy million. Magnitogorsk must now find a way to reinvent itself economically.

With Russia's economic recovery and reasserted nationalism, the Putin government has reassumed strong control over the ecumene. During the chaotic conditions of the Yeltsin era, local and regional governments, especially in the Urals, had chipped away at the political and economic power of the center. This disintegrative tendency was stemmed by Putin's success in gathering together all levers of power.

Urbanization and industrialization are the economic mainstays of the ecumene, whose population is three-quarters urban. However, agriculture, the initial support basis of the ecumene, remains a prominent feature of the landscape. In the northern European sections of the ecumene, mixed farming emphasizes potatoes, rice and other grains, sugar beets, livestock, and flax. In addition, a belt of "suburban farming" around the big cities produces vegetables, dairy products, and pork. The fertile chernozem (black-earth) soils at the southerly edge of the European ecumene are major producers of wheat, rye, sugar beets, and sunflowers. The introduction of grains at this edge took place in the 1930s. Over the intervening decades, production has suffered from soil and wind erosion as well as periodic drought.

With the political upheavals of 1991 and the breakup of the USSR, the future of growth of the ecumene lies in its expansion into what remains of Russia's effective national territory.

EFFECTIVE NATIONAL TERRITORY

Just as the dismemberment of the Soviet Union has truncated the Russian ecumene, so has it deprived Russia of vast portions of its former ENT—in eastern Ukraine, the Trans-Caucasus, and northern Kazakhstan. Despite the loss of these territories, Russia's ENT is still large. It includes substantial lands in the North Caucasus and in lands eastward through the Lower Volga and Lower Ural basins, into the southern fringes of West and Central Siberia. Present population densities in the ENT range from twenty-five to sixty persons per square mile; the ENT can support heavier densities through modern urban, industrial, and agricultural development.

Much of this region fell under Nikita Khrushchev's Virgin Lands program, initiated in the 1950s. The aim of the program was to promote large-scale, mechanized grain farming in the belt of long-fallow, chestnut-colored and brown soils that underlay the steppe lands extending from the northern Caucasus through northern Kazakhstan and into West Siberia. Approximately 90 percent of the lands in this development scheme were in Kazakhstan. The plan drew substantial numbers of Russian colonists into the region, as well as engaging the large ethnic German population that was expelled to Kazakhstan during World War II. (Many of the latter have been repatriated to Germany since Kazakhstan's independence.)

In addition to wheat and other grains, livestock farming for dairy and meat products was developed in the northern portions of the steppe, while cattle ranching for beef was the focus in the southern fringe. Irrigated rice, cotton, and fruit were introduced into the Lower Volga, from Stalingrad to the Caspian Sea, and in the North Caucasus.

The Virgin Lands program introduced reforms, such as turning over farm equipment from centralized machine tractor stations to the collective farms and reducing taxation on the private plots of collective farmers. However, low and variable rainfall and susceptibility to drought limited the region's agricultural potential. Much of the newly plowed soil was swept away by dust storms, many of the shelterbelts planted under the plan were in areas too dry to sustain tree growth, and soil erosion was widespread. A gamble because it focused on a climatically marginal region, the program failed to meet expectations.

The larger part of the present ENT lies in the strip of land that extends for eight hundred miles from Omsk in the southern part of the West Siberian lowland to Tomsk, as well as to Krasnoyarsk in Central Siberia. The Trans-Siberian Railroad serves as the spine for this region. Hemmed in on the north by the cold, marshy sector of the West Siberian lowland and on the south by the boundary of Kazakhstan and the Altay and Western Sayan Mountains, the strip varies from 100 to 250 miles in width. Omsk, at the western end of the ENT, at the confluence of the Om and upper Irtysh Rivers, is Siberia's second-largest city, with a population of over a million and the center of its most advanced agroindustrial region. It has also become an important focus of the development of high-tech industry.

Farther east, the main urban centers of the ENT include Tomsk on the Upper Ob and the belt of heavy industrial cities in the coal-rich Kuznetsk Basin (Kuzbas) that cluster around Novosibirsk, Siberia's largest city, with a population of one and a half million and its leading industrial and scientific center. It has emerged as Siberia's "Silicon Valley," where large international companies have invested heavily in high-tech hardware and software industries, supported by state investments in infrastructure. Tomsk, a center for heavy machinery and chemicals, is especially at risk from its nuclear past. Its adjoining city, Seversk, was established to produce materials for the Soviet nuclear weapons program. This nuclear complex—perhaps the largest on earth—contains antiquated nuclear reactors that produce plutonium and have been prone to accidents. In addition, the complex currently contains one of the largest nuclear waste sites. These industrial centers are surrounded by the farmlands of the Baraba steppe.

Still farther to the east, the region terminates at Krasnoyarsk, the capital for the Central Siberian Territory, located along the Yenisey River, which flows twelve hundred miles north to the Arctic. Like Tomsk, Krasnoyarsk was a closed nuclear city with facilities for plutonium production and uranium-enrichment processing. Both cities have begun to transform themselves into modern commercial and industrial centers.

An outlier of the main ENT lies five hundred to six hundred miles deeper into Siberia. It extends from Bratsk, at the northern head of the Bratsk Reservoir, to a cluster of industrial centers that lie between the reservoir's southern end and the westernmost tip of Lake Baikal, the world's largest and deepest lake. This outlier is hemmed in by the cold, barren Siberian Plateau to its north and the Eastern Sayan Mountains to the south. Bratsk is a single-industry city, a major aluminum producer. In contrast, cities such as Cheremkhovo, Angarsk, and Irkutsk, which are at the southern end of the reservoir and form a land bridge with Lake Baikal, have a diverse industrial base, including machinery, aluminum, chemicals, pulp and paper, textiles, and food products. Antiquated pulp plants are a major source of lake pollution, as is expansion of shoreline developments which cater to the fast-growing tourist industry.

A second ENT outlier fifteen hundred miles farther east is located within the Russian Far East in the grassland areas north of the middle Amur and east of the lower Ussuri River. This outlier is an interrupted rather than a continuous strip. The westernmost point is Blagoveshchensk, capital of the Amur region and across the border from the Chinese city of Heihe, an agricultural and gold-mining center. Blagoveshchensk's economy is based on local lignite deposits and food-processing plants. Khabarovsk, on the Amur near its junction with the Ussuri, is a major industrial city and transport hub, with oil refineries, shipyards, lumber-processing plants, and engineering works.

The outlier ends at Vladivostok, where the Ussuri empties into the Sea of Japan. Vladivostok is the chief Russian port and naval base on the Pacific. Kept open by icebreakers in the winter, it is the capital of the Maritime Territory. As terminus of the Trans-Siberian Railroad and the Northern Sea Route, Vladivostok has developed a diverse industrial base, with shipyards, chemical and engineering factories, fish canneries, and food processing factories. The city also serves as the Russian Far Eastern territory's major cultural and education center.

On the east side of the bay, opposite Vladivostok, lies the town of Bolshoi Kamen, a closed city that is home to a naval shipyard that specializes in scrapping nuclear submarines and where the Russian navy has been dumping radioactive waste. Waste-treatment plants have been constructed there with Japanese financing and the assistance of US contractors. Japan's stake in cleaning up contamination in the Sea of Japan reflects the strategically sensitive role of Russia's Far Eastern territory, vis-à-vis not only Japan but also North and South Korea.

Vostochny, a container port on the Sea of Japan sixty miles east of Vladivostok, has modernized its facility with the help of foreign investment. It has begun to attract increasing business from Japan, China, and South Korea. Containers shipped from these countries are loaded directly onto the Trans-Siberian Railroad and moved westward over a six-thousand-mile route to western Russia, Eastern Europe, and Finland.

Areas of modest development are the lower Amur, with its manufacturing center of Komsomolsk-on-Amur, the naval base of Sovetskaya Gavan on the coast southeast of Komsomolsk, and Sakhalin Island across the Tatar Strait from the mouth of the Amur. However, Sakhalin's coal and oil deposits are of growing importance. Promise of larger-scale economic and settlement activities is offered by oil and gas drilling on the northeastern end of the island as well as offshore in the Sea of Okhotsk. In the north, Sakhalin I is operational, shipping oil and gas to the mainland via pipeline. Sakhalin II, under development, is based on shipping oil and LNG to Japan. During the Yeltsin era, foreign oil companies were granted control of the concessions. The Putin government pressured them to divest their controlling interests, turning them over to Russian companies that enjoy Moscow's patronage. The international companies yielded to these pressures, accepting minority shares.

The development of Russia's Siberian ENT, first by farmers, herdsmen, and the military, then by mining and forestry, and in recent times by urbanization and industrialization, has been a centrally organized process. It remains to be seen what effect Russia's turn to a market economy and individual initiative will have on the development of the region. Central government support continues to be important during the transition from military industry and nuclear research and production activities. Moreover, reestablishment of Moscow's political and fiscal oversight of its outlying regions is a prerequisite to the political stability that capital investors require. Therefore, it appears that the future of ENT expansion will depend on a blend of governmental and private initiatives rather than on the free-market forces that have been dominant in the development of similar regions in the West.

The likelihood is that Russia's ecumene will continue to expand into the western and southern portions of the ENT. However, unlike the US West Coast, the Central Siberian and Far Eastern ENT outliers are unlikely to produce separate, secondary ecumenes because they are too constrained by the current rigorous climate, poor soils, and vast distances from the heart of Russia. Global warming might eventually moderate the climate of Siberia's ENT so that it could absorb substantial urban industrial ventures based upon its mineral wealth.

Development of the energy resources of these regions will bring about a surge in population growth in parts of north Siberia and Russian Pacific lower river and valley coastal lands. In the Far East territory, abundant oil and gas will undoubtedly attract industrial expansion, especially in the petrochemical sector. With global warming, Vladivostok's port, now kept open in the winter by icebreakers, is likely to benefit from uninterrupted year-round trade, attracting business from neighboring North Pacific countries. Nevertheless, these areas are too limited to attract the large numbers of people required to create secondary ecumenes.

EMPTY AREA

Siberia occupies most of the empty area of Russia. It is a region of over four million square miles—from Arctic ice fields, tundra, and taiga forests to high- and mid-latitude mountains and plateaus, to the vast marshy West Siberia lowland. Russia's additional former empty spaces of temperate and subtropical steppes and deserts now belong to the independent Central Asian republics.

The empty area is essentially uninhabitable, since it is mostly covered by permafrost and exposed to frigid winters. Therefore, nearly all of Siberia's thirty-two million residents (22 percent of Russia's total population) live within its ecumene or ENT.

In the north, the region's few inhabitants are indigenous Finno-Ugric and other peoples who subsist on hunting, fishing, and reindeer herding. The south is populated by Turkic-speaking and Mongol peoples who raise cattle. Scattered Slavic settlements engage in mining and forestry, while a handful of urban communities serve as processing centers for Siberia's resources.

The rich natural resources of the empty area, including oil and natural gas, nonferrous precious metals, and timber, have been a major support base for the economic development of the ecumene and ENT of Russia. East Siberia remains a storehouse of gold, silver, diamonds, mica, and bauxite. Its giant hydroelectric power stations along the Yenisey and the Angara Rivers, as well as hydropower plants elsewhere, are important components of the national electricity grid.

The empty area's vast West Siberian lowland oil and gas fields, which have been exploited since 1965, enabled the FSU to become the world's largest natural gas producer. They remain Russia's top source of foreign currency. These fields lie within the Middle Ob basin and are served by Surgut, Nefteyugansk, and Nizhnevartovsk, which were constructed in the 1960s and house tens of thousands of energy industry workers. The oil and gas pipelines that radiate from the "Third Baku" serve the West Siberian ENT and its Central Siberian outlier as well as the Urals and European sections of the ecumene.

In addition to these rich gas and oil deposits, Siberia's empty area contains a few cities scattered across Central and East Siberia. Norilsk, Russia's northernmost major city and the second largest located above the Arctic Circle, is linked to the mouth of the Yenisey by the port of Dudinka. Norilsk's local minerals—nickel, copper, cobalt, platinum, and coal—as well as power from nearby hydroelectric plants support diverse metal smelters. Yakutsk, with access to nearby coal and gas deposits, is a major port on the Lena River and has food, textile, and leather goods industries, sawmills, and a shipyard, as well as being the region's cultural and scientific studies center. Magadan, on the Sea of Okhotsk, is the center for the gold-mining region of the upper Kolyma River, manufactures mining machinery, and hosts fish canneries and shipyards.

Siberia has historically served the czars and the Communists not only as a storehouse of minerals to support Russia's settled regions but also as the home to penal colonies and concentration camps. In the air age, its vast, empty space was put to a new use—to serve the FSU's defensive/offensive strategic purposes. During the Cold War, a network of missile and early-warning radar sites were constructed along the Arctic coast, facing the US-Canadian NORAD system. In addition, nuclear-missile-bearing Soviet submarines maintained a constant vigil beneath the Arctic ice cap and waters, facing off against their American submarine opponents in a continuous game of "nuclear tag."

The hilly island archipelago of Novaya Zemlya, five hundred miles east of Murmansk and approximately six degrees north of the Arctic Circle, has been the scene of nuclear testing since 1995. Over one hundred nuclear blasts have been conducted on its snowy and icy wastelands. While the last large explosion took place in 1990, the Russians have continued to use the island for underground experiments that test the reliability of their nuclear arsenal.

With the advent of the space age, the FSU found a new strategic use for its empty area. The region has provided launching pads for space vehicles for both military and commercial operations. The locus of the Soviet/Russian space activity has been, and continues to be, in Kazakhstan. The Baikonur Cosmodrome was developed north of Tyura-Tam, one hundred miles east of the shrinking Aral Sea. Starting with Sputnik in 1957, most of the Soviet Union's and Russia's space and ballistic missiles have been launched from the cosmodrome's three major sites. In addition, the major targeted site for space landings has been nearby at the city of Aral, just to the northeast of the Aral Sea. Vozrozhdeniya Island, which is located within the sea, was the site of the world's largest anthrax burial ground and the Soviet's major open-air biological testing station. Uzbekistan has had to reach out to international agencies for help in cleaning up the sites.

Plesetsk, in northern Russia, 125 miles south of Archangel, has served as a site for a few high-inclination launches, but the Russians have continued to focus their space activities at Baikonur, leasing an area of six thousand square miles from Kazakhstan at an annual rental of $115 million and maintaining ownership of the facilities. They also developed a new launch site at Svobodny in the South Amur Oblast of the Russian Far East, one hundred miles north of the Amur River. In addition, Orsk, in Russia's southern Urals, and Dzhezkazgan, at the western edge of the Kazakh Uplands, are used as supplements to the Aral landing site. It is clear that Russia regards this part of Kazakhstan as a vital part of its empty area and is not prepared to give up its use.

With the end of the Cold War, Siberia's globally central empty area has assumed new and valuable commercial importance. Long-range jet-plane flight routes are being developed across the Arctic and Siberia to connect the major cities of North America directly to such points as Beijing, Bangkok, Shanghai, Hong Kong, and Cairo. Considerable savings in fuel and labor are provided by shortening flight times by up to five hours. Russia and Canada can expect to derive substantial fees from airspace overflight charges. As one dividend of the end of the Cold War, the military air control networks that were developed by both the United States and the Soviet Union across the Arctic space can now be turned to supplementary commercial applications as well.

BOUNDARIES

As previously noted, with the rapid retreat of Arctic ice due to global warming, Russia's territorial claims within the polar region have taken on new political and economic importance. In 2001, Russia laid claim to the Lomonosov Ridge, the 1,240-mile underwater mountain range that extends across its polar ice region across the North Pole. The basis for the claim is that the ridge is part of the Eurasian continent and therefore belongs to Russia's continental shelf under international law. If recognized, the claim would give Russia control of more than four hundred thousand square miles, or nearly half of the Arctic seabed and its vast energy resources. The United Nations rejected the claim for lack of scientific evidence. However, the planting of the Russian flag on the Arctic shelf at the North Pole in 2006 reasserted the claim.

Canada, Denmark, Norway, and the United States also have territorial waters in the Arctic Circle. Their rights to two-hundred-mile exclusive economic zones overlap Russia's claim. In response, Denmark has sent scientific expeditions to study whether the opposite end of the ridge was torn off from the continental shelf north of Greenland. As the technology for extracting oil and gas improves and ice retreat permits cost-efficient transportation, the various parties to the Arctic dispute may conclude that sharing of the resources would be more advantageous than prolonged legal disputes.

Russia's centuries-old land border disputes with China had their roots in much broader territorial conflicts. In the nineteenth century, China was forced to cede 580,000 square miles of territory to czarist Russia. These lands lay in the Tajik and Kyrgyz sectors of the Pamirs; in a large part of southern and eastern Kazakhstan; and in the Soviet Far East, north of the Amur and east of the Ussuri River. The latter territory contains such centers as Vladivostok, Khabarovsk, and Petropavlovsk in the Kamchatka Peninsula. In essence, the claim was against lands in Turkestan, Siberia, and parts of Mongolia that had been colonized by Russians and were the core of what Mackinder described as the Heartland. These lands, which were originally populated by Central or East Asian peoples with no historical racial or linguistic connections to Slavs or Han Chinese, nevertheless became the basis for historical claims between Russia and China.

After the Sino-Soviet split, Beijing reasserted its claims to the section of the Pamirs that adjoined western Xinjiang and an area in southeastern Kazakhstan that is drained by the Ili and Irtysh Rivers, whose headwaters are in northern Xinjiang. Beijing's most strident claims were focused on sections of the border with the Soviet Far East, along the Amur and Ussuri Rivers, involving twelve hundred square miles of territory. It was there that serious military clashes erupted between the two powers in 1969.[9] The Chinese held that the main channel of the Amur ran northeast to Khabarovsk, while the Russians claimed that the channel ran southeast to the Ussuri. The fighting centered on Damansky (Chenpao) Island, a small, uninhabited island in the Ussuri River just south of the Amur River, near Khabarovsk. Both sides sustained heavy casualties, after which inconclusive negotiations took place.

While this border region became heavily militarized in the 1970s, further fighting has not taken place. An agreement was finally reached in 1997 that left in dispute only two small sections of the current 2,300-mile boundary between the two countries and that reduced the border's militarization, and these were resolved in 2004.[10]

In accordance with the 1945 Yalta accord, the USSR occupied the entire Kuril Island chain in the Pacific, which had long been in dispute between Russia and Japan and had been occupied by Japan since 1875. The Kurils overlook Russia's Kamchatka Peninsula—Russia's closest point to the Aleutian Islands and the Bering Sea. However, Japan has continued to demand return of the four southernmost islands, immediately to the north of Hokkaido, which it regards as its Northern Territories. These are the islands of Etorofu, Kunashiri, and Shikotan and the Habomai group. The dispute over these islands has marred the diplomatic relations between the two countries since the end of World War II and is the main sticking point to signing a formal peace treaty. A Russo-Japanese agreement to seek a settlement of the southern Kuril dispute is testimony to the desires of both parties to move toward overall stability in the North Pacific. Another dispute is over the maritime boundary of the Svalbard Archipelago, whose main island is Spitzbergen. The archipelago belongs to Norway and, in accordance with the 1920 Treaty of Paris, is to remain demilitarized. Briefly invaded by the Germans in 1942, the islands were recaptured by Norway, which has since rejected the requests of Moscow that it be allowed to share in their defense. The economic value of Svalbard lies in its minerals, especially coal. The Russian coal-mining concessions represent 60 percent of the island's coal exports, and the Russian miners account for a similar percentage of the small population of 2,665. Russia and Norway have yet to reach agreement on their maritime boundaries within the Barents Sea and on Russia's fishing rights beyond Svalbard's territorial limits.

Since the collapse of the Soviet Union, a number of other issues have remained unresolved along Russia's 12,375-mile border.[11] Russia, Azerbaijan, and Kazakhstan agreed to equidistant boundaries within the Caspian Sea bed. Iran and Turkmenistan have not. There was no consensus on where to draw the boundaries of the surface waters, with their rich fishing resources. Now all five Caspian nations are engaged in negotiations over ownership of both the seabed and surface waters. In the Baltic, Russia's most sensitive boundary issue is with Estonia. The latter claims 770 square miles in the areas of Narva, just west of St. Petersburg, and Petseri, which lies to the west of Pskov. Estonia's boundary with Russia was demarcated and signed by both sides in 2005. However, Moscow then withdrew from the agreement. An accord over the boundary with Latvia was reached in 2011, but again Moscow reneged on its commitment, in this case arguing that ethnic Russians were not receiving fair treatment from the Latvians. In 2003, Russia ratified the 1997 border agreement with Lithuania that reaffirms Lithuania's title to the Klaipėda (Memel) area.

Moscow's strategic boundary concerns in the Baltic are focused on access to its Kaliningrad coastal exclave. Lithuania has implemented a simplified transit process for Russians traveling to and from Kaliningrad. The land boundary between Ukraine and Russia was delimited in 2007, but the maritime boundary between the two, in the Sea of Azov and Kerch Strait, remained unresolved. Both Russia and Kazakhstan ratified their land border delimitation in 2005.

The Eurasian Convergence Zone

The Eurasian periphery of heartlandic Russia has undergone revolutionary geopolitical change since the dissolution of the Warsaw Pact and the breakup of the USSR. This periphery now represents the zone of convergence among the heartland, the maritime realm, South Asia, and East Asia. Once allies of the Soviet Union and bases from which the USSR could control the Eurasian rimland, the former Communist satellites within the periphery have now become a base that can be turned against Russia. In addition, Russia considers the fourteen constituent republics that broke away as its "near abroad" because of their defensive and economic value and because approximately 18 percent of the total ethnic Russian population lives within their borders.

Figure 8.2. Eurasian Convergence Zone

Western policy makers may dismiss as groundless, and even paranoid, Moscow's concerns about NATO's expansion, but memories are indelibly etched of the German invasion during World War II, in which an estimated twenty million Soviets died and many of the nation's cities and industries were devastated.

When Russians look to their western periphery for defensive depth, they recall the wartime vulnerability of the line from Leningrad (St. Petersburg) to Moscow, to Tula, to Stalingrad (Volgograd), to the northeastern shore of the Black Sea at Rostov and Novorossiisk. This line held only because the defensive depth to the west provided the time for the broken Russian armies to regroup. The trauma of the siege of Leningrad, the need to move the capital temporarily to Kuybyshev (Samara) in the face of the failed attack on Moscow, and the near destruction of Stalingrad are all integral parts of Russian history and nationalism.

Russian historic memories of outside invasions reach back well before World War II. In 1812, Napoleon's Grande Armée seized Moscow and burned much of the city before being forced to retreat after one month. During the Crimean War of 1854–56, Anglo-French forces allied with Turkey penetrated the Black Sea and laid siege to Russia's naval base of Sevastopol. In two years of fighting, the invaders won half of the city, and the stalemate bled both sides dry. At the war's end, neither side had accomplished its goals, but all participants were severely weakened. From 1918 to 1920, Archangel, Russia's main White Sea port and the terminus of the Northern Sea Route, and Murmansk were occupied by Allied forces and the Russian White Army in their unsuccessful campaign to overthrow the Bolsheviks. Also during the civil war, Polish troops seized Ukraine in the course of their dispute with the Bolsheviks over the Russo-Polish frontier, while Vladivostok was occupied by Allied forces, including the Japanese, until 1922.

Russia's current security concerns are focused southward as well as westward. Western political and commercial encroachment in the Trans-Caucasus states of Georgia and Azerbaijan have raised suspicions in Moscow. This also applies to Central Asia, where international oil interests have focused investments in the energy resources of the region. These include plans to build oil pipelines that would circumvent existing lines that run through Russia and are regarded as part of a Western strategy to draw the region out of Moscow's strategic sway. US military bases in Central Asia that were developed with the agreement of the Kremlin to support the war in Afghanistan against the Taliban and al-Qaeda, along with US military training missions in Georgia, subsequently added to Russia's disquiet. These bases have now been closed due in part to pressures from Moscow.

Only Mongolia, in the heart of Eurasia, seems safely within Russia's orbit, although China could seek to play a stronger role there. Another of Moscow's worries is the vulnerability to Chinese pressures on Russia's Far East. However, recent tensions there have been reduced, as both countries have become alarmed over US nuclear strategic arms policies.

All of these concerns color Russia's current behavior toward its heartlandic periphery. Resurgent Russian nationalism, reinforced by the renewed strength of the Russian Orthodox Church and by the interests of the military-industrial establishment in regaining past prestige and power, affects policies toward the periphery. These concerns are also linked to the presence of twenty-five million Russians living in the periphery, mostly in areas that border Russia, such as eastern Ukraine, and contain the seeds of a drive for a "Greater Russia." Finally, one cannot discount the importance to Russia of Kazakhstan's empty area or of the Caspian Sea's oil reserves, which Moscow so recently commanded in totality and over which it now seeks to exercise some measure of control.

GEOPOLITICAL FEATURES OF THE EURASIAN CONVERGENCE ZONE

The vulnerability of much of the heartlandic periphery to Moscow's pressures is especially great among the states that adjoin Russia to its west and south. This vulnerability stems from their geopolitical features, especially their political capitals, ecumenes, and boundaries.

Capitals

The proximity of the capitals of most of Russia's nearest neighbors leaves those cities strategically exposed. The following distances to the closest Russian territory illustrate this point: Tallinn (in Estonia), 120 miles (and 200 miles from St. Petersburg); Riga (Latvia), 130 miles; Vilna (Lithuania), 200 miles; Kiev (Ukraine), 170 miles; Tbilisi (Georgia), 70 miles; Yerevan (Armenia), 100 miles; Baku (Azerbaijan), 120 miles; and Ulan Bator (Mongolia), 150 miles. Astana (Akmola), which replaced Almaty as the capital of Kazakhstan in 1997, is located within the Kazakh ecumene in the north-central steppe lands, two hundred miles from the Russian border. Known as Tselinograd when it was the administrative center for the Soviet Virgin Lands agricultural program, it grew rapidly in the 1950s and 1960s, attracting a mainly Russian population. It is now being developed as a special economic zone to generate foreign capital and spur industrial growth as well as to attract more ethnic Kazakhs to the city.

Ecumenes

The ecumenes of these states are equally close to Russian territory and, in some cases, actually merge with those of Russia. Estonia's economic and population core area follows the Baltic coast from Tallinn to Narva, where it joins the Russian core west of St. Petersburg. The Latvian ecumene, which centers on Riga, is only 150 miles from the St. Petersburg core, while the Belarus ecumene, running from Minsk to Vitebsk and Mogilev, merges with Russia's core at Smolensk. Lithuania's economic core region, stretching from Kaunas (Kovno) to Vilna, is only one hundred miles from the western edge of the Belarus ecumene. Ukraine's economic and population core extends from the lower Dnieper (at Dnipropetrovsk) northeastward to Kharkiv at the Russian border and eastward to Donetsk and its associated industrial centers of the Donets Basin, where it merges with the Russian part of the basin at Rostov.

In the Caucasus, Georgia's major economic core area extends northward along the Black Sea at Batumi and northeastward to the Kutaisi area, approximately two hundred to three hundred miles from the southern edges of Russia's ecumene along the Sea of Azov and Rostov. Armenia's industrial centers of Yerevan and Kumayri are 250 to 300 miles from the Russian ecumene, while Azerbaijan's core is farther away—550 miles.

Kazakhstan's ecumene extends from Karaganda and Temirtau northeastward through Astana to the Russian border at Pavlodar, where it is approximately 250 miles from both the Omsk and the Novosibirsk industrialized clusters of West Siberia's ENT. Semey (Semipaltinsk), on the Irtysh River, the manufacturing and transportation center of northeastern Kazakhstan, is an outlier of the ecumene. Mongolia's very limited ecumene extends north from Ulan Bator to the Russian border, where it is less than 150 miles from the Lake Baikal industrial centers of south-central Siberia.

Boundaries

As discussed, Russia now has no active boundary disputes with its neighbors, although the lines with Estonia and Latvia await final ratification and there remains the issue of the Svalbard Archipelago maritime boundary.

Territory and boundary conflicts among the periphery neighbors have been serious obstacles to economic and political development in some of them. Armenia and Azerbaijan went to war over the largely Armenian-populated autonomous region of Nagorno-Karabakh, which lies within Azerbaijan. The fighting led to great losses of life and property and to massive displacement of people. Similarly, Serbia's conflicts over Bosnia and Kosovo have substantially weakened Belgrade. Although Serbia continues to look to Russia for support, it has also indicated a desire to join the EU. In the case of Kosovo, Russia was in a position to help mediate the conflict and by doing so was able to strengthen its influence in part of its periphery.

Russia has played a dual role relative to the separatist revolts that have broken out in Transnistria in Moldova and in the Abkhazia and South Ossetia regions of Georgia. While it provided military support to the separatists, it has at the same time played a moderating and stabilizing role, helping to limit the fighting by placing peacekeepers in Abkhazia and keeping Transnistrian separatism at a de facto level. In 2007, the Moldovan government recognized the legitimacy of Transnistria's Supreme Soviet government. It agreed that the region would have top deputy ministers in the Moldovan national government. Moscow does not officially recognize Transnstria, but it maintains a consulate there. While Russian troops were scheduled to be withdrawn by 2009, they still remain.

Ukraine has a dispute with Romania over the continental shelf of the Black Sea, under which significant oil and gas deposits may exist. This, however, has little relevance for Russia, which has a far greater stake in the Caspian Sea boundaries that have yet to be determined among all the coriparians—Azerbaijan, Iran, Kazakhstan, Turkmenistan, and Russia.

In Tajikistan, the former Communist and now Nationalist government faced an Islamic fundamentalist revolt from 1992 to 1997. Moscow came to the aid of Tajikistan, sending troops to the Tajik border with Afghanistan to try to block assistance to the rebels from fellow Tajiks in Afghanistan. Turkmenistan also has turned to Russia for help in guarding its borders with Iran and Afghanistan, while Moscow has had to keep a watchful eye over Uzbekistan's land disputes with Kazakhstan, Turkmenistan, and Tajikistan.

It is clear that boundary and territorial disputes among the neighbors of Russia's Central Asian periphery have served to strengthen the influence of Russia there. This and the nearness of the political centers and economic core areas of the Central Asian states reinforce Moscow's strategic weight within the region. Tajikistan and Kyrgyzstan have announced that they will join the Russian-led Eurasian Customs Union (scheduled to become the Eurasian Economic Union by 2015).

Eastern Europe

THE BALTIC STATES

During World War I, Halford Mackinder argued that stability in Europe depended upon a "Middle Tier" of independent states between Russia and Germany.[12] After the war, Isaiah Bowman advocated the establishment of such a tier, to be led by an expanded Poland and Romania, as a *cordon sanitaire* between the historically antagonistic Russian and German powers.[13]

What has transpired since then has been quite different. First, the "Middle Tier" was conquered by Germany during World War II, but afterward the states became satellites of the Soviet Union. Now the West has expanded into the region. Should the EU and NATO in combination absorb the entire belt of middle-tier states, the imbalance between the West and Russia will become profound and the situation in Eurasia unstable. As previously discussed, decoupling the military and economic links between Western and Eastern Europe would represent a more viable geopolitical solution.

NATO membership for the Baltic states has profoundly disturbed Moscow. Yeltsin did not formally object to their admission because President Clinton had agreed not to deploy or store nuclear weapons there. Washington withdrew from the ABM Treaty in 2001. The Bush administration then proposed to enhance the advanced US antimissile system by placing radar installations in the Czech Republic and interceptor rockets in Poland, heightening tensions between the United States and Russia.

While NATO membership for the Central European states of Hungary and the Czech Republic represents no threat to long-term stability, the participation of Poland does—particularly since it had agreed to deploy nuclear-based missile interceptors on its territory. In 2010 Warsaw agreed to a US Patriot missile system base and periodic deployment of US war planes. The Czech Republic, on the other hand, in 2011 withdrew from plans to participate in the US missile system.

The Baltic states hold the key to the approaches to St. Petersburg, but also their ports handle a significant share of Russia's foreign trade. Moreover, Lithuania, along with Poland, surrounds Russia's naval base of Baltisk in the Kaliningrad Oblast—home port for Russia's Baltic fleet and for its Eleventh Army. To compensate for its lack of a direct connection to Kaliningrad and as an alternative to the present routes through Lithuania, Moscow has pressed for a secure highway corridor permitting free flow of goods and people to the exclave via Belarus, Lithuania, and Poland. In 2013 Poland agreed to build the road, which extends for 106 kilometers from Elblag near the Polish-Lithuanian corner to Kaliningrad.

Russia has already taken steps to enhance its security interests in the Baltic by constructing a large oil export terminal at Primorsk, one hundred miles northwest of St. Petersburg, at the eastern end of the Gulf of Finland. The facility is connected to a newly completed underwater pipeline that is the first section of the Baltic Pipeline Project, backed by German investment. This project has expanded the present pipeline system to open up large-scale exploitation of the Pechora oil and gas reserves of Russia's Arctic Far North and to better serve the fields of West Siberia and some of Kazakhstan.

A substantial share of Russian oil exports now moves through Baltic Sea terminals in Latvia and Estonia. The largest of these terminals, Ventspils in Latvia, alone takes 15 percent of Russia's petroleum shipments. The Primorsk terminal has facilitated the expansion of the country's overall production and, in an emergency, bypasses the Baltic state transit ways. In addition, Russia has expanded St. Petersburg to become its largest port, with the goal of reducing Russia's dependence on dry cargo ports in Estonia and Latvia.

Added to these strategic concerns are Moscow's interests in the rights of Russians who live in the Baltic states. While Russians now constitute less than 10 percent of Lithuania's populace, they are much more important factors in Estonia, where they are 25 percent, and in Latvia, where they are now 27 percent of the total (having dropped from 40 percent during the Soviet era).

BELARUS AND UKRAINE

Belarus and Ukraine are equally sensitive strategic areas for Russia. Historically, Belarus has been a crossroads for invading armies heading for Moscow along the Smolensk-Moscow plateau. Also known as "White Russians," the Slavic Belorussians never developed a distinct culture, language, or identity apart from the Russians. During the Soviet era, the Belorussian

Republic was developed as an industrial hub for the manufacture of armaments, machinery, motor vehicles, chemicals, textiles, and electrical equipment. However, it remained a relatively poor area, saddled with inefficient, Soviet-era state collective farms and state-owned industries.

The Russians regard Belarus as the key buffer against NATO now that Poland, which adjoins Belarus on its west, has joined the Western alliance. The Communist president of Belarus, Alexander Lukashenko, has pressed for a full reunion with Russia. While the two countries joined in a "Commonwealth of Sovereign Republics" in 1996, this does not provide for the full merger desired by the autocratic Belorussian president. Nevertheless, Minsk is meeting the security aims of Moscow by reintegrating its air defense, intelligence, and arms production, which includes mobile Scud missile launchers. In addition, the Belarus economy is totally dependent upon Russia for its oil and gas supplies, most of which it had received as a gift or at reduced prices. In 2006, a brief dispute erupted over Gazprom's decision to raise its price of delivery to Belarus. This was resolved in a deal whereby Gazprom gained ownership of the transit pipeline westward through Belarus in exchange for continued below-market rates.

Ukraine's importance to Russia is even greater than that of Belarus. The identification of Russians with Ukraine has strong historical, cultural, religious, and economic roots. Russians regard Kiev as the historic core of the Russian state. While later they began referring to Ukrainians as "Little Russians," differentiating them from "the Great Russians of the Muscovite Realm," they still harked back to the common heritage of Kievan Rus. During the Soviet era, Ukraine was far from being the borderland that it had been from the sixteenth through nineteenth centuries. Then it had served as Poland's southeastern frontier against the Crimean Tatars and the Ottomans, and after 1775 it had been added to the Russian Empire. It became crucial to the USSR, as it supplied 30 percent of total industrial production and one-quarter of the food. A study by John O'Loughlin and Paul Talbot in 2005 reported that over 90 percent of Russians surveyed expressed the desire for political and economic unification between Russia and Ukraine. (Nearly the same sentiment for reunification was expressed for Belarus, while Kazakhstan and Moldova also had high percentages.)[14]

The process of "Russification" within Ukraine became so strong that today an independent Ukraine finds itself heavily reliant economically on its ethnic Russian eastern and southern regions. While 17 percent of the country's population is ethnic Russian, the proportion in the east is much higher. In the Donbas it is 53 percent, and in Crimea it rises to nearly 60 percent. The percentage of Russian speakers in these areas is considerably higher, reaching 93 percent in Donbas and 97 percent in Crimea. The Russian-speaking regions of the east and south extend in a scimitar-like shape from the Russian border to Odessa and then northward, embracing Transnistria (figure 8.3). It should be noted that speaking Russian does not necessarily indicate that the speaker wishes to be joined to Russia.

Western Ukraine remains heavily agricultural and poorer; the east produces the bulk of the country's industrial goods, including steel, motor vehicles, and aircraft. Of Ukraine's five largest cities, four are in the east. Kiev, the largest, is in the west but has a population that is about 20 percent ethnic Russian. Moreover, although Ukrainian is the official state language, the first language for over half the population is Russian.

As important as Ukraine is to Russia and despite the weight of its ethnic Russian population, Ukraine is torn between maritime Europe and Russia. Western Ukraine was never part of the Russian empire. It was a province within the Austro-Hungarian Empire with an economy dominated by agriculture and forestry. The division between East and West is evidenced in the fluctuations of power since the "Orange Revolution" of 2004, before which the governments had been led by pro-Russians. The pro-Western Viktor Yushchenko prevailed against the pro-Russian Viktor Yanukovych for the presidency in 2004, but the latter

Figure 8.3. Ukraine Ethnic Divide

became prime minister two years later when his party won a parliamentary election. In 2007, a pro-Western coalition managed to retake the parliament, but in all cases, the margins were very slim. Yanukovych returned to power in 2010. His regime was riddled with corruption. When he rejected EU overtures to become associated with the European Union, he was challenged by pro-European Ukrainians from the eastern part of the country. Protests against the government began as peaceful demonstrations in November 2013 but evolved into bloody violence in February 2014. Yanukovych received financial aid from Russia, which was his steady supporter. The conflict evolved into a rebellion which threatened to tear the country apart, becoming a pawn in the Russian-Western struggle for dominance.

The conflict erupted with the Maidan Square mass protests, which led to the ousting of Yanukovych, who fled to Russia. The government which replaced him issued, and then immediately withdrew, a decree banning Russian as an official language. It also indicated its intention to shorten Russia's lease on Sebastopol and its desire to join the EU and NATO. This sparked a reaction by militant pro-Russians. In Crimea, a referendum was held which overwhelmingly called for the restoration of the region to Russia, which proceeded to annex it. The United States and Europe refused to recognize this annexation,

The Crimea had been a Tatar autonomous republic until the republic was dissolved in 1945. The Tatars were forcibly resettled in Soviet Asia at that time because they had been charged with collaborating with the German occupiers during the war. They were replaced by Russian settlers. Initially, the region was annexed to the Russian SFSR. In 1954 it was transferred to the Ukrainian SSR, but pro-Moscow feelings among its ethnic Russian majority remained strong.

The separation of Crimea from Russia was connected to the negotiations over the disposition of the Soviet fleet. The resolution of this issue was that 80 percent of the ships, as well as 50 percent of the facilities of the naval base at Sevastopol, would remain in Russian hands through a twenty-year lease, with the rest going to the new Ukrainian navy. Sevastopol thus continued to serve the Russian Black Sea fleet, which shared the base with Ukraine's naval vessels. With the reannexation of Crimea by Russia, the Ukrainian ships, mostly in poor repair, became Russian property.

In the eastern and southern parts of Ukraine, pro-Russian militants seized municipal buildings in major cities, such as Donetsk, Lugansk, and Kharkiv. At this writing it remains unclear whether the goal of the uprising is independence, annexation to Russia, or autonomy.

The situation became further confused when President Putin declared that Russian troops massed at the border of Ukraine would be withdrawn and urged that the militants refrain from holding a referendum on breaking away from Ukraine and instead support new national elections. Skeptics question whether this is a true reflection of Putin's goals for Ukraine, but it may well be. Moscow wants to keep Ukraine as a strategic buffer, free from EU and NATO ties. Moscow can't afford to have Ukraine be a divided country, and to have the responsibility for supporting its Donbas southwestern region. Moreover, if Ukraine were to become divided, this would in all likelihood open its western portion to links with the EU and NATO, leading to a rupture in relations between Moscow and the West.

A far better solution would be for Ukraine to remain unified, serving as a bridge between the two geostrategic realms. This would require a guarantee from Europe and the United States that there would be no further attempts to include the Ukraine within the EU and NATO. In addition, establishment of a federal structure of government would provide the Russian-speaking region with linguistic autonomy. Were such a Ukraine to have access to a customs-free agreement with Russia and a trade partnership with the EU, the interests of the country would be best served. This would enable it to become a gateway between the heartlandic and maritime realms.

Moscow's close ties with ethnic Russians outside its borders were also reflected in the establishment of the breakaway Trans-Dniester Republic in Moldova's Transnistria region. Wedged between Moldova and southwestern Ukraine, half of Transnistria's population consists of Russians and Ukrainians. When armed clashes broke out between the secessionist elements and the Moldovan forces, the Russian Fourteenth Army, which has been stationed in the region since World War II, intervened on behalf of the secessionists. Moldova's dependence upon Russia is heightened by its heavy indebtedness to Moscow for the natural gas supplied to it. In 2006, Trans-Dniestria voted overwhelmingly for independence from Moldova and eventual unification with Russia. In 2007, the Moldovan government granted it a form of quasi statehood. The international community, including Russia, has not formally recognized it as a state, but the status quo seems acceptable to all parties.

A second separatist force, the Turkish Gagauzi ethnic group in the far southwest of Moldova, also declared independence at this time, with the support of the Transnistrians. This tiny area, with a population of 150,000 and an economy based on viticulture, overlooks the lower Prut a few miles from where it joins the mouth of the Danube and in between Romania and Ukraine. The conflict was resolved peacefully in 1994 with establishment of the Gagauzi autonomous territory. The Gagauzi were granted the right to conduct their own local affairs and to choose independence should Moldova decide to join another country (presumably Romania).

THE IMPLOSION OF YUGOSLAVIA AND THE BALKANS

Geographically, the Balkan Peninsula includes Albania, most of the former Yugoslavia, Bulgaria, southeastern Romania, northern Greece, and European Turkey. Historically and politically, these six countries have been referred to as "the Balkan states." Geopolitically, Greece and Turkey are now part of maritime Europe, while Romania and Bulgaria are geostrategically vital to Russia. A major concern for Moscow was admission to NATO of Bulgaria and Romania. Membership of these two countries, along with Turkey, in NATO provides the West with control of the western Black Sea littoral. Should Ukraine and Georgia also join the alliance, Russia would then be squeezed into a very small section of the Black Sea's northeastern coast. Naval exercises that NATO has held within the Black Sea, as well as US bases in Bulgaria and Romania, have further heightened Russia's sense of vulnerability and increased its fears of Western containment.

While Russia strongly supports Serbia in a variety of ways, including the Kosovo dispute, it no longer has substantial strategic interests in the other states of former Yugoslavia—Croatia, Bosnia, Macedonia, Slovenia, and Montenegro. Neither does Albania continue to have substantial interests. It is for this reason that this war-torn area has not become a shatterbelt. Dissolution of the Yugoslav federal empire involved far greater conflict than was experienced in the breakup of the Soviet state. The first stages of the breakup were relatively peaceful. Slovenia, the most economically advanced of Yugoslavia's federal republics, was allowed to leave after only limited fighting, while Macedonia declared its independence under the cover of a small UN force. However, Slobodan Milošević's dreams of a "Greater Serbia" included large parts of Croatia plus Bosnia, Montenegro, and the autonomous regions of Vojvodina and Kosovo that lay within Serbia. The wars in Croatia and Bosnia raged for four years. They ended in 1995 with the US-brokered Dayton Agreement for Bosnia and the

Croatian recapture of all Serb-held parts of Croatia. Serbs were then expelled from all parts of Croatia except Eastern Slavonia, where a UN peacekeeping force was installed.

The unrestrained fighting, mass killings, and ethnic cleansings carried out by Serbs, Bosnian Muslims, and Croats in Bosnia and Croatia were followed four years later by similar Serb actions in Kosovo. This was brought to an end by massive NATO air warfare against the Serbs. The peace accords in both Bosnia and Kosovo are maintained through the large-scale intervention of NATO troops, supplemented by Russian forces and UN police units.

The outcome of NATO's military campaign in Bosnia, far from assuring a stable multiethnic independent republic, has reinforced the division of the country into two largely autonomous units—a Serb republic (Republika Srpska) and a federation of Muslims and Croats in which the Muslims dominate in an uneasy alliance. The Dayton Agreement, which was imposed on Bosnia's warring parties, resulted in a highly dysfunctional government with three presidents. The Croats, who are concentrated in southwestern Bosnia, adjoining the Dalmatian coast, seek to break this alliance and rejoin Croatia. The agreement was supposed to have lasted for three years, but the Serbs and Croats have not allowed a unified state to be established. The country is rife with corruption, crime, and unemployment, and industry which was privatized has enabled a few entrepreneurs to sell off old factories for scrap and real estate development. As a result of a 2009 ruling by the European Court of Human Rights, Bosnia is prevented from joining the EU.

The situation in Bosnia brings into question the West's policy of trying to preserve a unified state composed of people who support different sovereignties. In the long run, regional stability may be better served if the Serb part of Bosnia joins Serbia and the Croatian section in western Bosnia is allowed to join Croatia, leaving a smaller but cohesive Muslim Bosnia. The fate of Kosovo, which had been part of Serbia although its population was largely Albanian, has been equally dire. Kosovar rebels broke away from Serbia, resulting in a conflict in which hundreds of thousands of Albanians fled or were expelled by the Serbian army. NATO intervention through bombing brought an end to the conflict, after which most of the Albanians returned, then driving out most of the Serbs. The one hundred thousand Serbs who remain continue to receive political support from Belgrade, but their future is uncertain.

The United Nations report in 2007 called for an independent Kosovo, but Moscow continued to support Serbia in opposing such a solution, although independence was a foregone conclusion. The Serb sector in the northern part of Kosovo centers on Mitrovica in the Ibar River valley, an area with rich copper and zinc deposits. The rivers of the north also supply the waters for Kosovo's main power plant that provides 75 percent of Kosovo's electricity. Recognition of Kosovar demands for independence requires agreement of all of the EU members, the United States, and the UN. If this should come to pass, the northern Serb sector, containing 15 percent of Kosovo's land area, might seek annexation to Serbia or a very high degree of autonomy similar to that enjoyed by the Serb portion of the Bosnian confederation. In either case, Belgrade should also be guaranteed access to key Serbian national and religious shrines located in other parts of the region, especially Kosovo Polje. The Kosovar Albanian provincial government declared an independent state on February 18, 2008, receiving immediate recognition from Britain, Germany, France, Italy, and the United States. Serbia, Russia, and China strongly opposed independence, as did some European states that feared this would encourage separatist movements in their own lands. The rationale for supporting Kosovo's independence is that this would stabilize the region. This may backfire if ethnic minorities in other countries use the same rationale for advancing their independence claims within Eastern Europe, the Caucasus, and even Spain.

Kosovo has special mythic importance to Serbia as the historic core of Serbian nationalism. Slavs initially settled there in the seventh century and fully colonized it by the end of the eighth before converting to Eastern Christianity in the next century. The region was seized by the Turks, who defeated the Serbs in the battle of Kosovo Polje (the Kosovo Plain) in 1389. The battlefield site has since become a shrine and pilgrimage site for Serbian nationalism and the Serbian Orthodox Church.

Under the Ottomans, in the fifteenth and sixteenth centuries, the vast majority of Kosovo's population that was ethnic Albanian was converted to Islam. Thus, the Orthodox Serbs found themselves in a minority when Kosovo was regained from Turkish rule by Serbia and Montenegro during the Balkan War (1913) and after World War I was formally incorporated into Yugoslavia (which was initially named the Kingdom of Serbs, Croats, and Slovenes). Serbs remained as a minority, ranging from a high of 38 percent, owing to a government resettlement policy in the 1920s, to a low of less than 20 percent of the population at the time of the Kosovo War.

What complicates the prospects for a Kosovo agreement is the geographical distribution of the remaining Serbs. While Mitrovica at the northern end of the fifty-mile-long plain is ethnically Serb and adjoins Serbia, the Kosovo Polje battlefield and associated tombs and monasteries are located five miles southwest of Pristina, the regional capital that is now ethnically Albanian. Moreover, Peć, a city of revered churches and shrines on the western edge of Kosovo, is also surrounded by ethnic Albanians, as is Prizren, a town in the far south that has numerous ancient monasteries and churches. Kosovo has unlocked a new set of boundary disputes that are linked to ethnic Albanian populations in southern Serbia and Macedonia. Kosovar guerrilla activity has spread to those areas, despite the efforts of the NATO peacekeeping force to contain them. While Serbia and Macedonia have resolved their border dispute and demarcated the line, Albanian guerrillas continue to threaten to destabilize the situation in their drive to create a Greater Albania.

Approximately 30 percent of the two million Macedonians are ethnic Albanians, including refugees from the Kosovo conflict who were granted entry. Many of the ethnic Albanians have long held grievances against the country's Slavic majority in the areas of job and language discrimination. The bulk of Macedonia's Albanian population lives in three districts along the western border with Albania and adjoining Kosovo and Serbia in the north. Tetovo, the country's second-largest city and the center for Macedonia's Albanians, lies within ten miles of the Kosovo border in the northwestern part of the country. Skopje, Macedonia's capital, is located only ten to twenty miles from the territorial crescent formed by this Albanian population and is therefore highly vulnerable to guerrilla activities.

When Macedonia emerged from the isolation cast upon it by Bulgaria, Serbia, and Greece, Athens challenged its right to call itself by that name, so it is officially known as "the Former Yugoslav Republic of Macedonia." It had developed positive relations with these neighbors when the Kosovar guerrillas violated its territory. For NATO, this was both a political and military setback. The alliance had armed and trained the Kosovars during the war with Serbia and had looked the other way when the Kosovars drove tens of thousands of Serbs out of the province. Now it found itself turning to Serbia to make common cause in containing the Albanians, who also sought control of the ethnic-Albanian-inhabited Preševo Valley in southern Serbia, adjoining Kosovo. NATO permitted the Serbs to send troops into a part of the three-mile buffer zone bordering Macedonia that it had previously established within Serbia to separate Serb from Kosovar forces; Belgrade, rather than the Albanian Kosovars, then became NATO's hope for stabilizing the situation.

Elsewhere within the former Yugoslavia, in 2006 Montenegro voted to secede from its federation with Serbia. The process was peaceful, and the small country (population of slightly over six hundred thousand) is seeking to reinvent itself by becoming part of the EU. In recent years it has become a hub for smuggling, but its location on the Adriatic coast presents opportunities for legitimate trade as well with Western Europe. With an economy based upon aluminum, steel, and a large service sector, its current trade ties are with Switzerland, Greece, and Italy.

In the face of all the turmoil in this portion of the Balkans, Russia continues to be the primary backer of Serbia, supplying it with oil and other commodities. NATO continues to strive for that most elusive of goals—peace and stability. For neither is this imploded area strategically vital.

The Trans-Caucasus and Central Asia

What links the Trans-Caucasus and Central Asia regions is the Caspian Sea. The export of much of the petroleum and natural gas resources of the Central Asian countries of Kazakhstan and Turkmenistan requires pipelines that traverse parts of the Trans-Caucasus.

THE TRANS-CAUCASUS

The extensive Russian military involvement in the affairs of Georgia, Armenia, and Azerbaijan during the 1990s reflects the depth of its strategic interests in the Trans-Caucasus. Russia's relations with Georgia, the only mainly Christian country within the largely Muslim world of the Caucasus, have been especially tense because of Moscow's support of the separatist movement in Abkhazia as well as its ambiguous role in the South Ossetian rebellion.[15]

Abkhazia, the Muslim region within northwestern Georgia, extends from the Black Sea to the south of Russia's Sochi resort area, north to Russia's Karachaevo-Cherkess Republic. The main Abkhazian city, the port of Sukhumi, a resort as well as a manufacturing center, is also the southern terminus of the 120-mile Sukhumi Military Road, which crosses the Greater Caucasus through the Klukhori Pass into Russia. The road provides Russia with an important land link to the Black Sea and, until recently, Moscow kept a military base at Gudauta, north of Sukhumi, as well as three other bases in Georgia.

The rebellion in Abkhazia broke out in 1992 and was supported, according to the Georgian charges, by the Russians. There, at the onset of the fighting, Muslim separatists expelled 260,000 Christian ethnic Georgians, creating a major refugee problem for the Tbilisi government and leaving the territory with a population of only a quarter of a million. Russian and Georgian peacekeepers stabilized the situation by 1994, but in 1999 the pressures for separation mounted and Abkhazia held a referendum on independence, which passed by a large majority. Its political status remains ambiguous today. It continues to operate with quasi independence, and sentiment for reunion with Russia, which has recognized it as a state, remains strong.

In South Ossetia, the rebellion against Georgia broke out in 1992, two years after Tbilisi had taken away the autonomous status that the region, together with North Ossetia, had enjoyed as part of the Mountain Autonomous Republic during the Soviet era. Russian and North Ossetian troops intervened to quell the rioting, and autonomy was restored. In 1995 sporadic fighting erupted once more, as the Christian South Ossetians demanded either independence or to be linked to the Muslim Russian republic of North Ossetia. Again the Russians quieted the unrest, this time stationing troops in the region to guarantee its autonomy. South Ossetia has less strategic importance to the Russians than Abkhazia, although the 170-mile Ossetian Military Road that traverses Ossetia, connecting Alagir in North Ossetia to Georgia's Kutaisi and the Batumi coastal region, is one of the two main routes across the North Caucasus. Although South Ossetia has a small ethnic Russian population, Moscow gave Russian citizenship to all South Ossetians based upon their FSU membership.

Russia has been reluctant to withdraw troops from these separatist regions claimed by Georgia not only because of its strategic interests in Abkhazia and South Ossetia, but also because Georgia has provided safe haven for Chechnyan rebels to mount attacks across the seventy-five-mile border between Chechnya and Georgia. Underscoring the importance of Chechnya to Russia is that a major oil pipeline and railroad from Baku in Azerbaijan to Novorossiisk on the Black Sea runs through Chechnya. (The pipeline from the northeast Caspian shores to Novorossiisk bypasses Chechnya.) Moscow has wished to seal the Chechen-Georgian border by keeping troops in the Pankisi Gorge, a narrow valley that leads to the Shatili Pass across the crest of the mountains and marks the boundary between the two countries. The gorge, long a transit route for drugs and for arms smuggling from Afghanistan to the Chechen Muslim rebels, has also been an escape hatch for the rebels and, according to Moscow, the site for their training camps. Russian troops have not been the only factor that limits the ability of Georgia to ignore pressures from Moscow. The Tbilisi government is also dependent on and in considerable debt to Russia for the natural gas that is the basis for the country's supply of electricity and heating. Moscow has not hesitated to slow down or even temporarily cut off supplies during the winter as political leverage.

Impoverished, riddled by corruption and lawlessness, devastated by the wars of insurrection, and overwhelmed by the collapse of its farm economy, Georgia is caught between the pressures of Russia and the West. In 1998 Moscow removed its troops from Georgia's Black Sea coast and half of Georgia's land border with Turkey. The following year, it agreed to close its base in Abkhazia and an air base near Tbilisi. Nevertheless, tensions persisted as the government of Georgia insisted repeatedly that Georgia's future is with the West and expressed intentions of making application for NATO membership. The United States did not discourage these overtures and made considerable efforts to expand its influence within the country. Its direct foreign aid contribution represents one-third of the Georgian budget, and over the years this aid has amounted to over $3 billion. Adding to Moscow's concerns, in 2002 the Georgian government invited US military forces to train Georgian troops with the objective of clearing the Pankisi Gorge of Chechen and other guerrilla and terrorist bands.

Georgia tried to reclaim South Ossetia in 2008. It had been emboldened to do so by the fact that Moscow had not reacted to Georgia's regaining of Adjara, a breakaway Black Sea territory in the southwestern part of Georgia. Adjara's port city of Batumi is a major oil pipeline terminal and refining center that is economically and strategically important to Georgia—unlike South Ossetia.

Moscow reacted quickly to Georgia's invasion of South Ossetia. Its land, air, and naval forces crushed Georgia in five days and occupied major Georgian cities. Georgia's invasion of South Ossetia was fueled by the assumption of President Mikheil Saakashvili that the United States would protect it from Russian reaction. Washington did not respond, for it was in no position to protect its ally.

The war in Georgia should have been a lesson for Washington—that it lies in Russia's geopolitical sphere. Instead, Washington persists in challenging Moscow on the latter's strategic turf. It continues to promote a US-Georgia strategic partnership while working on a free-trade agreement and supporting Georgian membership in NATO, as well as providing substantial aid.

If the West were to be so reckless as to extend NATO to include Georgia, it would be following a path of serious geopolitical folly. Trying to make a Western-controlled lake of nearly all of the Black Sea would turn the entire region into a shatterbelt, the consequences of which would be a spate of local wars as well as resumption of the Cold War.

Another problem for the Russians has been the 1999 Chechen rebel penetration into the neighboring Russian republic of Dagestan, which lies on the shores of the Caspian, north of Azerbaijan. This incursion, as well as penetration of southern Russia, brought on the Second Chechen War, which was not ended until 2006, although scattered guerrilla bands continue to hide out in mountainous areas. Large-scale Russian air attacks upon Chechnya continued in the fall of 1999 in response to terrorist bombings within Russian cities. Since then, the government of Vladimir Putin has reoccupied most of Chechnya, although the conflict continues with guerrilla hit-and-run tactics.

The Caspian Sea oil and natural gas pipelines that extend through Chechnya to Russia's Black Sea coast or northward into Russia first traverse Dagestan. Control of Dagestan, which is Russia's only land contact with Azerbaijan, also strengthens Moscow's military leverage over the oil-rich Azeris. Dagestan militants, who favor an independent Islamic state, are but a minority. The majority of Dagestanis, who are moderate followers of Sufi Islam, have expressed no desire to leave the Russian federation or forgo Russian economic subsidies. Another reason for the strategic importance of Dagestan to Moscow is that it adjoins northeastern Georgia, placing Russian forces within seventy miles of Tbilisi.

The two other Trans-Caucasus states, Christian Armenia and Muslim Azerbaijan, have been joined in conflict over Nagorno-Karabakh since 1988, blocking the building of pipelines across the Trans-Caucasus to the Black Sea or the Bay of Iskenderun. At that time, Nagorno-Karabakh was an autonomous Soviet region located within Azerbaijan. Its population of 150,000 was more than three-quarters Armenian. When the two countries became independent, Armenian nationalists demanded that the region be included within Armenia. By 1992 Armenian troops, with military support from Russia, had captured the mountainous enclave as well as a corridor of Azerbaijani territory connecting it to Armenia. In the years of fighting, up to 800,000 Azeris and 400,000 Armenians have been displaced, while 35,000 have died in the conflict. A cease-fire was negotiated in 1994, but three years later Nagorno-Karabakh declared independence; although not recognized internationally, it is de facto independent. Armenia, while renouncing its claim to the breakaway territory, continues to occupy it militarily.

Economically, Azerbaijan is of far greater importance to the outside world than is Armenia, although the latter has a considerably higher income, owing to its machinery equipment manufacturing, gold, jewelry, and hydroelectric power as well as investments and remittances from prosperous Armenian communities living abroad. Azerbaijan's significance is its oil production and refining center at Baku on the Apsheron Peninsula. The peninsula and its offshore waters once constituted one of the world's richest oil regions, the main petroleum-producing center of the Soviet Union until World War II. The reserves have declined, but Baku remains important as the primary pipeline terminal for oil coming west from the Central Asian oil-producing countries, as well as for its large refineries.

Azerbaijan has without success sought military and diplomatic aid from the United States in its conflict with Russian-backed Armenia and has offered both the United States and Turkey military bases on Azeri soil. Such propositions place Washington in an awkward position. Although the offers are tempting, the strong Armenian lobby in the United States opposes such a relationship. However, Washington and Moscow have joined in seeking a negotiated peace because of their common interest in the stability of the region. The outcome could be establishment of a self-governing quasi state in Nagorno-Karabakh and in the adjoining Lachin region, which links Nagorno-Karabakh geographically to Armenia. In exchange, Azerbaijan could receive a security corridor to its Nakhichevan enclave in southwest Armenia. Also, Russia and Azerbaijan have signed a ten-year agreement permitting Moscow to continue to operate a Soviet-built missile-tracking station within Azerbaijan that provides coverage of the airspace over South Asia and the Gulf region.

It is Moscow, not Washington, that holds the key to this peace, for the United States is ill equipped to challenge Russia within its Trans-Caucasus backyard. The question looming in the background is whether the West will engage Russia as a full partner in the proposed pipeline developments of the region and acknowledge Russia's interests in protecting the pipelines that now extend from the Caspian Sea through its territories.

THE CENTRAL ASIAN "NEAR-ABROAD" COUNTRIES

The five independent Central Asian states that broke off from the FSU—Kazakhstan, Kyrgyzstan, Tajikistan, Turkmenistan, and Uzbekistan—occupy a vast land area of 1,542,000 square miles, with a combined population of sixty-one million. Landlocked and surrounded by Russia on the north, Iran and Afghanistan on the south, and China on the east, this region of steppe, desert, and mountain is lightly populated and impoverished. It would be of little geopolitical interest to the West were it not for the relatively recent discovery of vast new energy reserves in and around the eastern shores of the Caspian Sea in Kazakhstan and Turkmenistan. As a result of this potential, the Clinton administration embraced the entire Caspian Sea region as a key strategic and commercial objective, thereby asserting a geopolitical interest in the region that has traditionally been Russia's backyard.

Pressured by international oil interests, Washington has taken the position that securing a reliable pipeline system that bypasses Russian territory in bringing the energy exports to market requires aggressive US political and economic support of Central Asian states as well as Azerbaijan and Georgia. Indeed, playing upon the historic role of Central Asia as the locus of the Silk Road, based on the trading of silk and gold between the West and China, American oil interests pressed the Congress to pass, in 1999, the Energy Silk Road Strategy Act, which encouraged US governmental intervention in the affairs of the region.

The geopolitics of oil and pipelines is complex. Russia's involvement in Caspian Sea oil already includes its control of two pipeline routes. One, which taps the Mangyshlak and Tengiz oil fields, runs from Atrau in Kazakhstan northward into Russia to the Baltic Sea. A second line extends westward from Makhachkala in Dagestan on the western shore of the Caspian Sea, through Russia (via Chechnya) to the port of Novorossiisk on the Black Sea. In 2001, this line was supplemented by a much larger new nine-hundred-mile pipeline constructed by Russia, Kazakhstan, and international oil companies. It bypasses Chechnya and moves oil more cheaply than the older lines from the Mangyshlak and Tengiz fields to Novorossiisk. It also carries the initial output of the huge Kashagan oil field, which was discovered under the Caspian Sea in Kazakh waters and opened in 2005.

The Kazakh government, which had granted a concession to a consortium of international oil companies to develop the field, changed the original terms of the contract to increase substantially the royalties of the Kazakh national oil company and give it an ownership share equal to that of each of the consortium partners.

Kaşhagan's reserves have been estimated at up to thirteen billion tons. They could be the biggest petroleum find of the past two decades. These deposits heightened the American interest in the region and prompted Washington to give strong backing to the 1,099-mile BTC pipeline from Baku on the Caspian Sea and thence across Azerbaijan, to Tbilisi in Georgia, through southeastern Turkey to the port of Ceyhan on the northeastern shore of the Mediterranean. The line started operation in May 2006, bypassing the Bosporus shipping route.

Feeders to the line could serve potentially rich oil and natural gas fields in Turkmenistan's Caspian waters, which have also attracted international oil and gas interests. This line bypasses the Bosporus shipping route and therefore is more ecologically sound. However, in the Kurdish homeland of southeastern Turkey, it is vulnerable to being cut by Kurdish rebels. Another line that has been proposed by some international oil companies would run from the Caspian through Iran to its Kharg Island oil terminus on the Persian Gulf. In addition to being more expensive, this route is anathema to Washington because of its tense relations with Iran. Other long-range proposals are lines from Turkmenistan to Afghanistan, Pakistan, and India and, when political conditions permit, through Iran to South and East Asia. These proposals are aimed at ending Russia's domination of Caspian and Central Asian energy resources.

In an exercise of its pipeline politics power, Russia constructed the natural gas pipeline to Turkey. This pipeline extends under the Black Sea at a seven-thousand-foot floor depth, from the Novorossiisk area in Russia to the Turkish Black Sea port of Samsun and thence to Ankara. The pipeline increases to 90 percent Turkey's dependence on Russia for natural gas. Fields in Russia and Kazakhstan, and eventually Turkmenistan, are sources of supply for the line.

Meanwhile, in 2007, Russia signed an agreement with Turkmenistan and Kazakhstan for a natural gas pipeline that would extend along the Caspian shore from Turkmenistan through Kazakhstan into Russia's pipeline system. The project was mothballed two years later.

A realistic US policy would be to support and buy into a mixed set of pipeline routes, including the Turkmenistan-Russian line, perhaps eventually including an agreement to supplement this one with the Iranian route, which Washington has vigorously opposed. Such a line would not be needed for a few years, during which time events in Iran might produce a more favorable climate for restoration of US-Iranian relations. Whatever the direction and timing of the routes, the inclusion of Moscow as a co-owner/shareholder in Western-initiated Caspian pipeline networks would reduce tensions between Russia and the United States while assuring Russia of increased benefits in transit fees from those lines that now cross its territory or may be built in the future. While global geopolitics revolves around Central Asia's oil and gas, hydropower has significant potential. Tajikistan and Kyrgyzstan, both of which have agreed to join Russia's Eurasian Customs Union, have vast untapped water resources that can supply electricity to Afghanistan, Pakistan, and eventually India and China, as envisaged in the CASAREM (Central Asia-South Asia Regional Electricity Market) project. Failure of the West and Russia to cooperate in energy development would ignite another Great Game in Central Asia and bring Russia and Iran even closer together.[16]

Through much of the nineteenth century, the British had maneuvered to prevent Russian control of the region. They failed in their efforts to establish alliances with the emirs of the Silk Road kingdoms and (in the First Afghan War, in 1839) lost in their attempt to gain control of Afghanistan, the rugged approach land to the deserts and steppes of Central Asia. Their military expeditions into Tibet in 1905, southeast of the ancient routes to China, had no lasting effect either. The race for empire ended in the late nineteenth century with Russia controlling Central Asia to the borders of Persia, Afghanistan, and the Tien Shan and Altai Mountains, and to Mongolia.

A new Great Game, this time headed by the United States, has even less chance of long-term Western success than the one played by Britain, which had the Indian subcontinent available as its base. Russia has two major advantages. The first is its strategic location abutting the Caspian Sea and Kazakhstan, by far the largest and most powerful of the Central Asian states and the one with the richest oil reserves. The second is the substantial Russian population located in Kazakhstan and Kyrgyzstan. Slavic organizations in these two countries, playing upon suspicions of China and popular fears of vulnerability to Islamic fundamentalism, have called for a referendum on joining the Belarus-Russian Customs Union. Thus far, these calls have not been acted on, but they cannot be lightly dismissed. The leaders of these two regimes, where Russia has important military installations, are fully aware of their continuing dependence upon the military support of Moscow to maintain the stability of the region.

Over ten million people in Central Asia, or 16 percent of the region's sixty-one million people, are ethnic Russians. Before the collapse of the FSU, ethnic Russians were nearly 40 percent of northern Kazakhstan's population. After the collapse, one million Russians left the country, but Russians still represent nearly one-third of the population of the north. Another eight hundred thousand Germans also left northern Kazakhstan, whose German and Ukrainian population is now 10 percent. The north, which is the center for the country's manufacturing and its major farming area, also houses Russia's space industries and its nuclear testing sites. The Kazakhs are now a slight majority in their country, which has a population of over seventeen million. They hold the key to the country's stability and thus to the prospects for fully exploiting the land and offshore oil deposits. Despite Kazakhstan's energy wealth compared with its impoverished neighbors, any regional integration will depend on Moscow's support.

Eastern Kazakhstan, centering on Ust-Kamenogorsk (Oskemen) on the upper Irtysh near the Russian border, is predominantly Russian. Support there was particularly strong in motivating Kazakhstan to join the Russian-led Eurasian Customs Union. Much of that population is Cossack in origin, their settlement dating back to the late seventeenth century. (Cossacks have also lived in southern Kazakhstan since the early nineteenth century.) Indeed, the northern part of eastern Kazakhstan was part of Siberia until 1936. While separation is currently not a serious issue, an effort to wean the country away from Russia could result in its dismemberment, for the Russians have made it clear that defense of ethnic Russians has a high priority.

Boundaries are another point of possible contention should the Great Game be injected into Kazakh politics. The boundary of northern Kazakhstan, long regarded as an old colonial settlement area by the Russians and a focus for settlement during the Virgin Lands program, is still not fixed. This is true also for the dividing lines within the territorial waters of the northern Caspian Sea, which are underlain by rich energy deposits, and it might even become a problem in the Aral Sea.

Once the fourth-largest sea in the world, the Aral Sea shrank to less than half its original size as Soviet-sponsored irrigation policies diverted over three-quarters of its feeder rivers to cotton fields. Coastal towns became land bound, fisheries were destroyed, and toxic dust storms off the dry lake bed combined to create a major man-made disaster. By the late 1980s, the sea had divided into two. The smaller northern part was wholly in Kazakh territory, and the larger southern part, which in turn was divided into two, was shared by Kazakhstan and Uzbekistan. The Kazakh government, aided by the World Bank, then undertook to restore the northern part of the sea by building a dam to block water from flowing into the southern part of the Aral and regulating use of the Syr Darya River for irrigation. With completion of the dam in 2005, the northern Aral has begun to refill. Uzbekistan, rather than concerning itself with restoration of the southern Aral's highly salty waters, prefers to use the dry seabed to develop natural gas operations. Since it shares this part of the sea with Kazakhstan, the two countries will have to come to an agreement when surplus waters from the northern basin may have to be diverted to the south.

Dividing the Caspian Sea remains a regional challenge. During the Soviet period, Moscow and Tehran had agreed to share the waters and underlying seabed. Now there are five littoral states—Azerbaijan, Kazakhstan, Turkmenistan, Russia, and Iran. Iran has proposed a joint area in the middle of the sea to be shared by the five riparians beyond their coastal zones. Kazakhstan, Azerbaijan, and Turkmenistan have at times argued for using median points to divide the sea into national sectors, while Russia, Kazakhstan, and Azerbaijan have also proposed relating jurisdiction over the waters to length of coast.[17]

In October 2007, the Caspian Sea states held a summit, which concluded with a twenty-five article declaration. They agreed on a number of points: none of their territories will be used as a base by a third party to launch military action against any of the member states; they will respect the pursuit of useful nuclear technology while adhering to the Nuclear Nonproliferation Treaty; only ships carrying flags of littoral states can ply the Caspian; and they will promote Caspian Sea economic development and environmental controls. What the summit did not address was the legal status of the contested body of water and seabed. This was left to future summits.[18]

Russia's second most important area of concern in Central Asia is Kyrgyzstan. As is the case with Kazakhstan, Russia is Kyrgyzstan's chief trading partner. Large numbers of Russians and Ukrainians settled there during World War II. Although many have since left, they still represent a sizable portion of Bishkek (Frunze), by far the largest urban and industrial center of the country. All told, over four hundred thousand of Kyrgyzstan's people, or nearly 7 percent of the population of over six million, are Russian. Their status is of considerable concern to Moscow as well as a strategic asset. Because of its location, bounded by Kazakhstan to the north, Uzbekistan to the south, Tajikistan to the west, and China to the southeast, Kyrgyzstan could prove of importance to future Russian-Chinese relations. Both Kyrgyzstan and Kazakhstan border China's Muslim Xinjiang Uighur Autonomous Region, and each has small Uighur populations living along their borders. The Russian military presence along the borders of the Central Asian countries might be helpful to China should Xinjiang's separatist movement become a serious threat to Beijing, for China and Russia have a common interest in containing the spread of Islamic fundamentalism within Central Asia.

Russia is far better positioned than the West to take a hand militarily in stabilizing Central Asia. The countries of that region are beset with disputes over land and water boundaries and by the threatened spread of Islamic fundamentalism emanating from Afghanistan and Iran. Since helping to quell the civil war in Tajikistan between the government and a fundamentalist Islamic opposition group, Moscow has stationed several thousand troops along the Afghan frontier, across which the Islamic militants received arms from the Taliban. Kyrgyzstan, too, needed Russian help to combat Islamic guerrillas sponsored by Afghanistan, and Russia has been sympathetic to the Uzbek government's repression of Islamic fundamentalism in the wake of 1999 terrorist bombings. A further reflection of Russia's military importance to the region is the agreement signed by Moscow in May 2001 with Kazakhstan, Kyrgyzstan, and Tajikistan to form a joint rapid reaction force based in Bishkek, the capital of Kyrgyzstan, to combat Islamic insurgencies. Uzbekistan, with thirty million people, representing half of Central Asia's total population, claims borderlands in the mountainous section of southern Kazakhstan. In the year 2000, Uzbekistan's border guards seized some stretches of land. The strength of the Uzbek army makes Kazakhstan particularly dependent on the Russian arms provided to it as part of its annual lease payments for the Baikonur space-rocket site. The booming Kazakh energy revenues and market reforms have attracted tens of thousands of illegals from Uzbekistan to work in the cotton and tobacco farms as well as in construction and household services. To control against Islamic militants and smugglers, the Kazakh government is building security fences along the southern border ridges.

In addition to Uzbekistan's claim in southern Kazakhstan, Uzbekistan has claims on the Tajik section of the Fergana Valley, while Turkmenistan and Uzbekistan are at odds over Karakalpakia, the region of western Uzbekistan on the Aral Sea at the delta of the Amu Darya. In 2001, to resolve border disputes and fight Islamic militancy, Kazakhstan, Uzbekistan, Tajikistan, and Kyrgyzstan joined with Russia and China to form the Shanghai Cooperation Council. Turkmenistan joined later. The council called upon the United States to set time lines for withdrawal from Central Asia. Washington rejected this on the grounds that its air bases in southern Uzbekistan and northern Kyrgyzstan were vital for operations in Afghanistan. Russian opposition to a continued military presence in these countries was strong. In 2005 it helped to persuade Uzbekistan to withdraw permission from the United States to operate a large military base at Kanshi-Khanabad. Washington also agreed to withdraw from its air base in Manas, Kyrgyztan, in 2014.

Turkey has sought to extend its influence into Uzbekistan by offering arms and military training to combat the latter's extremist Muslim rebels, but so far the offer has not been accepted. Rigid governmental policies have discouraged foreign investors, who were attracted initially by the country's irrigated cotton production and its substantial natural gas deposits. The uranium that once supplied most of the FSU's needs no longer has the strategic significance that it had during the Cold War.

Mongolia

East of Central Asia lies the Mongolian Republic, covering a vast area of 604,000 square miles, bordered by Russia on the north and China on the south. Mongolia was under Chinese influence during the eighteenth and nineteenth centuries and came under Soviet sway after World War I as the independent People's Republic of Mongolia. The sparse population of approximately three million, which had long followed a nomadic and seminomadic way of life, changed to urban pursuits and settled agriculture under the influence of Communism. With the breakup of the Soviet Union, Mongolia became a multiparty democracy. The country has changed even more with the emergence of China as a major power. Over 70 percent of the populace is now urbanized, and a number of industrial centers have been developed. Nevertheless, the economy remains dependent on the export of livestock, wool, cashmere, copper, tin, gold, and tungsten as well as other minerals.

The landlocked status of Mongolia reinforces its continued dependence upon Russia and China for trade. The Altai Mountains and the Gobi Desert separate Mongolia from China's Inner Mongolia region, while Ulan Bator (Ulaanbaatar), the capital and main industrial city, and most of the other major cities and mining centers of the country are located fifty to two hundred miles from the Russian border, with relatively easy access to the Siberian industrial centers of the Lake Baikal region across high, grassy steppes and low mountains. The strategic vulnerability of this part of Mongolia suggests that the Russian influence of the past century will persist well into the twenty-first century and that Russia's Inner Asian reaches will remain secure from outside penetration.

Halford Mackinder's inspiration for the Heartland theory was the role that the center of what he called "Euro-Asia" had played between the fifth and sixteenth centuries as the source of the waves of nomads sweeping out of its steppes to conquer so much of the continent's ocean-facing margins. Of these groups, the Mongols made the deepest and most lasting impact upon the Eurasian margins, using the horse as the military tank of that era. Superior horsemanship, together with centrality of location and short interior lines, enabled them to move outward in any direction, employing the elements of speed and surprise. This gave them a major geostrategic advantage over the relatively immobile European and East Asian farmers and forest dwellers.

Mackinder viewed the Trans-Siberian Railroad, which was completed the year after he wrote his article "Geographical Pivot of History," as the successor to the horsemen and camel men of the Mongol Empire and the riders of the steppes who followed them. He saw the rail as the key to Russian control of the "Pivot Area" of Eurasia.

Events of the past century have proved that, while Mongolia remains geographically in the center of Eurasia, the center of the heartland lies to the west—in West Siberia. World power is now determined more by where natural and human resources are concentrated than by centrality and mobile lines of transportation. Mongolia is now but a small and strategically marginal country. It has been bypassed by time and technology and is oriented to heartlandic Russia for its modern economic development.

Conclusion

Geopolitical developments of the past century and a half have demonstrated that the centrality of the heartland within the Eurasian continent does not mean command of the Old World or control of the continent in its entirety, and certainly not control of the globe. However, heartlandic Russia's location does enable it to use its centrality to exercise strategic dominance over important parts of its periphery. The bases for such dominance are proximity, short interior lines of transportation and communication, historical/cultural ties, control over militarily and economically important land passageways, energy wealth, and the spread of ethnic Russians and other Slavic peoples into parts of the periphery. These factors provide Moscow with a strategic advantage over outside powers in influencing the course of events in East and Southeast Europe, the Trans-Caucasus, Central Asia, and Mongolia.

This centrality is also a factor in enabling Russia to play a continuing role within the Northern Highlands zone of the Middle East. This geographical advantage has facilitated Russia's sale of arms to Iran, in spite of Washington's efforts to block such sales. At the same time, South Asia is well outside the strategic reach of heartlandic Russia. Moreover, East Siberia, which lies east of Lake Baikal and the Lena River, and especially the Russian Far East are vulnerable to the pressures of China, the Asia-Pacific Rim, and the United States (from its Alaska base). The prevailing physical and geopolitical character of heartlandic Russia is continentality. The vast Eurasian expanses, wealth of mineral resources, and broad agricultural and forestry base have historically focused the energies of the heartland's rulers on development of the interior and not on foreign exchange. In modern times, this continentality was reflected in the czarist and Soviet drives for national self-sufficiency, usually behind closed, authoritarian political-economic systems. Today Russia's economy has fundamentally changed, with its dependence on energy exports, accumulation of massive foreign capital reserves, and shift to a modified market economy. Its political system is a hybrid, combining some elements of democracy with strong authoritarian control. Promotion of Western capitalist ideals of minimizing government interference in the market process has a hollow ring to a people who have seen the rise and fall of a class of corrupt Russian oligarchs who practiced an extreme form of crony capitalism, to be succeeded by state favoritism. For many Russians, the Americanization and globalization of the world economy and culture is seen as a challenge to Russian culture and has fueled nationalism and militarism rather than weakening their impact.

With the exception of international capital investment for the oil and gas industry, most of the investment inflows now are directed toward goods and services for the Russian consumer, not toward building export industries, as was the case for Western investment in the trade-oriented Asia-Pacific Rim countries. Moreover, much of the capital generated by privatization of industry and by energy exports has been sent abroad rather than being reinvested in the domestic economy.

Russia's inherent strengths include its relative ethnic homogeneity, its high degree of urbanization (74 percent) and literacy (98 percent), and its large pool of well-trained scientific, technological, and administrative personnel. These are complemented by the wealth of energy and other mineral resources, abundant forestry and animal products, a strong agricultural base, and the country's advantageous global strategic location. An added source of strength is that the burden on Russia's resources has been greatly reduced because it no longer needs to support its former satellites economically and militarily and the cost of maintaining its huge nuclear arsenal, offensive navy, and massive land force is being greatly reduced.

The election to the presidency in 2000 of Vladimir Putin signaled the restoration of strong central government, with regional governors responsible to Moscow. Nevertheless, developing a cohesive governmental system must take into account the devolutionary forces that are sweeping across Russia. The government will therefore have to find a balance between regional desires and needs and national requirements.

In the North Caucasus, adherence to the Russian Federation by Chechnya, the Ingush Republic, Dagestan, and North Ossetia will depend upon introducing a structure of genuine autonomy that satisfies the Islamic religion, culture, mores, and economic needs of these minority lands. In the Far Eastern territory and Yakutia—so far removed from Moscow and the ecumene—the central government must reinvest much of the regional wealth for local development rather than exploit these resources largely for the benefit of the ecumene.

In this remote Far Eastern territory, the temptation of separatist elements to take an independent economic course is tempered by the strategic vulnerability of the region to China and Japan. This should not lull Moscow into indifference toward separatism.

Moscow's concerns over terrorist attacks and separatist movements within its new borders limit the degree of democracy permitted by the government. Russian democracy cannot be expected to mirror that of the United States or maritime Europe. Western protests of human rights violations in Chechnya were legitimate but have to be balanced with the recognition that Russia will act to preserve its territorial integrity.

Russia has taken important foreign policy initiatives. In the year 2000 Russia approved the START II Treaty as well as the Comprehensive Test Ban Treaty (CTBT). While the United States had approved START II in 1996, the US Senate, along with other holdouts such as China, Pakistan, India, North Korea, and Egypt, has rejected ratification of the CTBT. Moscow sought deeper future reduction of nuclear warheads for START III than was first envisaged by the United States. However, in May 2002, both parties agreed to deep reductions of between 1,700 and 2,200 missiles, representing a cut of approximately two-thirds of the then-existing arsenals. As noted, these were ultimately reduced to 1,650 nuclear warheads and 850 delivery systems in the new START Treaty of 2010. Washington has also reserved the right to store some of the missiles.

Reviving a Cold War atmosphere is in the interest of neither the United States nor Russia. While pressures and blandishments from the United States have succeeded in gaining the grudging approval of Russia to the placing of US antiballistic missiles in Poland, Moscow's residual rancor and mistrust might well undermine cooperation in other areas. Given its massive nuclear arsenal, Russia has little to fear from the national missile defense (NMD) program, the first phase of which includes new radar and missile interceptor systems at Shemya Islands in the westernmost part of the Aleutian chain, 550 miles east of Russia's Kamchatka Peninsula. Russia clearly stands to gain from a strategy that might restrain a possible nuclear strike by an unstable North Korea. However, Moscow has legitimate misgivings that the scrapping of the ABM Treaty by the United States could force it into an unwanted renewal of the arms race.

September 2001 and its aftermath introduced a new era in US-Russian relations. Moscow responded positively when Washington requested support in the war against terrorism in Afghanistan. It consented to the use of air and land bases in Uzbekistan, Tajikistan, and Kyrgyzstan and permitted the overflight of its own territory by US aircraft. However, within a few years, Russia abruptly changed its position and pressured these countries to close the American bases.

A more positive development was the signing of the NATO-Russian Partnership Accord on May 28, 2002—an event heralded as signifying the formal end of the Cold War. Russia was to have been a partner in discussions and actions over such issues as military cooperation and nonproliferation, but this has not been the case. US unilateral action in Iraq was strongly opposed by Russia, and Washington's hard-line approach to negotiations with Iran over its nuclear-weapons-building capacity added tensions to relations between Russia and the United States, as has Moscow's support of the Assad regime in the Syrian rebellion.

While Vladimir Putin's Russia Party's overwhelming victories in the 2007 and 2012 elections were marred by interference with the opposition's electoral campaigning, it seems clear that most Russians want a strong leader. They have accepted the squelching of the pro-democracy forces and violation of their civic rights as the price to be paid for social and political stability as they plunge into the capitalist system. The autocratic Putin regime has brought economic improvements (thanks in no small measure to energy wealth) and restoration of Russia's status as a world power—in sharp contrast to the chaos of the Yeltsin era.

This is the political reality with which US administrations have to deal as the Russian people sort out the mode of governance that best suits them. Preaching American-style democracy only adds to the mistrust that has characterized Moscow's relations with Washington during much of the Bush and Obama administrations' foreign policy initiatives. Under these circumstances, the EU may be better positioned to take the diplomatic lead in creating the West's geopolitical policies toward the heartland.

Russia faces many challenges. Its turn to a market economy in 1991 created an ever-widening income gap between rich and poor. The country is overly dependent on oil and gas, which represent two-thirds of its exports, and upon other extractive commodities for another 15 percent. Military exports, although proportionately small, are very important geopolitically.

The Russian people are living better in terms of availability of goods. However, the costs of education and health have mounted, and while half of the population can now be considered middle class, 20 percent lives below the poverty line. Less than 10 percent of the country's GDP is derived from high-tech industries.

Steps are being taken to meet these challenges. Construction of the Russian version of Silicon Valley, Skolkovo Technical City, located twelve miles west of Moscow, began in 2010. Skolkovo is based upon partnerships between large, foreign high-tech firms and Russian partners that focus on R&D and manufacturing. They are supported by a newly developed technology university. Plans call for a city population of over thirty thousand and over twenty thousand job holders. High-tech developments have also been initiated in the Muslim region of Kazan.

The Russian oil company, Rosneft, and ExxonMobil have partnered in exploiting the oil fields of the Far North, including those in the warming Arctic coastal waters. This Russian Arctic is experiencing the impact of climate change as permafrost melts and the coastal waters are freed of sea ice during the summer. As Laurence Smith points out, by 2050 conditions in Siberia's north may permit the spread of crops and people to the Arctic coast, as well as the use of its coastal waters for east-west shipping across the 2,300 mile route.[19]

Russia still has the capacity to harness its human and resource base in highly productive ways. To do so, it must stanch the outflow of personal wealth, become more friendly to foreign investment, and find ways of encouraging its well-educated scientific and professional class to remain in the country. This will require a radical shake-up in governmental bureaucracy, serious anticorruption measures, and use of sovereign funds to support start-up industries.

The shrinking of population in the country cannot be halted only by making it a more desirable place in which to remain. Russia will have to develop attractive immigration policies that will not only include economic and social benefits but also take stern action against racism. It is estimated that there could be a need for up to twenty-five million immigrants by 2025. While the country has already absorbed ten million immigrants, mostly ethnic Russians from Central Asia, it will have to look to Uzbekistan, Tajikistan, and Kyrgyzstan as well as the South Caucasus for likely immigrants.

The current mood of many Russians is one of resignation. What is missing is the sense of hope and optimism of the Gorbachev era. A country which enjoys the level of science and education on a par with the United States must reach out again to its young adult population, offering the opportunity for professional advancement and entrepreneurial success.

Russian leaders continue to view the heartlandic periphery as their "near-abroad" and a special zone of influence. However, the breakup of the Soviet Union has fundamentally altered the geopolitical nature of this periphery. It has become an arena where the world's three geostrategic realms and the South Asian region meet, and it may therefore be more accurately described as the "Eurasian convergence zone."[20] The zone extends as an inner Eurasian crescent from the eastern Baltic, Eastern Europe, and the Black Sea to Central Asia, Mongolia, to the Korean Peninsula. The Middle East serves as its southwestern hinge and is strategically linked to it. If competition for dominance over Ukraine among major powers, especially the United States and Russia, continues to escalate, if the rebellion in Syria fragments the country, and if Iraq faces a three-fold division, the zone will become a shatterbelt, making it a most unstable part of the world. Given its location, economic resources, and external ties that connect the heartland to the surrounding realms, it has the potential to become a vast gateway. This would require economic consortia, joint military bases and peacekeeping actions, coordination of counterterrorist efforts, and a spirit of cooperation among the major powers.

Notes

1. Halford Mackinder, "The Geographical Pivot of History," *Geographical Journal* 23, no. 4 (1904): 421–44.

2. Halford Mackinder, *Democratic Ideals and Realities* (London: Constable, 1919), 148–66.

3. Halford Mackinder, "The Round World and the Winning of the Peace," *Foreign Affairs* 21, no. 4 (1943): 595–605.

4. Zbigniew Brzezinski, *The Grand Chessboard* (New York: Basic, 1997), 123–50.

5. N. M. Baransky, *Economic Geography of the U.S.S.R.*, trans. S. Belsky (Moscow: Foreign Languages, 1956), 318.

6. Vladimir Kolossov and John O'Loughlin, "Pseudo-States as the Harbingers of a New Geopolitics: The Example of the Trans-Dniester Moldovan Republic," *Geopolitics* 3, no. 1 (Summer 1998): 151–76.

7. Taras Kuzio, "Borders, Symbolism and Nation-State Building," *Geopolitics and International Boundaries* 2, no. 2 (Autumn 1997): 36–56.

8. C. J. Chivers, "Destroying Arms, U.S. and Russia Celebrate Rare Amity," *New York Times*, Sept. 1, 2007, A2.

9. Alan J. Day, ed., *Border and Territorial Disputes* (Harlow, England: Longman, 1982), 264–66.

10. Central Intelligence Agency, *World Factbook 2007* (Washington, DC: GPO/CIA, 2007), 2, 11.

11. Central Intelligence Agency, *World Factbook 2007*, 11.

12. Mackinder, *Democratic Ideals and Realities*, 158–81.

13. Isaiah Bowman, *The New World* (Yonkers-on-Hudson, NY: World Book, 1922), 5–11, 278–94, 328–56.

14. John O'Loughlin and Paul F. Talbot, "Where in the World Is Russia? Geopolitical Perceptions and Preferences of Ordinary Russians," *Eurasian Geography and Economics* 46, no. 1 (2005): 23–50.

15. Andrew Boyd and Joshua Comenetz, *An Atlas of World Affairs* (London: Routledge, 2007), 64–66.

16. Karl E. Meyer and Shareen Blair Brysac, *Tournament of Shadows: The Great Game and Race for Empire in Central Asia* (Washington, DC: Cornelia and Michael Bessie/Counterpoint, 1999), 283–309, 554–73.

17. Elaine Sciolino, "It's a Sea! It's a Lake! No. It's a Pool of Oil," *New York Times*, June 21, 1998, 16.

18. News Central Asia, "Tehran Summit Unites Caspian States on Major Issues," October 17, 2007, http://www.newscentralasia.net/moreNews.php?nID=205.

19. Laurence C. Smith, *The New North: The World in 2050* (London: Profile, 2011), 322.

20. Saul B. Cohen, "The Eurasian Convergence Zone: Gateway or Shatterbelt?" *Eurasian Geography and Economics* 36, no. 1 (2005), 1–22.

CHAPTER 9

The East Asia Geostrategic Realm

The defeat of the United States in the Vietnam War and the collapse of the Soviet Union freed China to enlarge its power base within East Asia, as well as to play an expanded role along the Asia-Pacific Rim and in South and Central Asia. Within a quarter of a century, Beijing has become an acknowledged global power and forged a third geostrategic realm that competes with the Eurasian continental and maritime realms throughout the world, particularly in Sub-Saharan Africa.

The East Asian realm that is dominated by China embraces North Korea and a separate Indochinese geopolitical region that includes Vietnam, Laos, and Cambodia. The strength of Vietnam as the dominant power within Indochina and its historic suspicion of its larger northern neighbor accounts for its being a separate region within the realm. North Korea, once dominated by the USSR, is now within China's orbit. The strengthened position of China within the Yellow, East, and South China Seas presents a serious challenge to Japan as well as to the US western Pacific strategy of the past half-century. That strategy has been to create a geopolitical region within the Asia-Pacific Rim (Asia-Pacifica) as part of the maritime realm and to build up South Korea and Taiwan to both contain China and protect Japan.

The boundaries of Asia-Pacifica are in flux. Were South and North Korea to move toward rapprochement, this could in the long run lead to unification and to geopolitical neutralization of the Korean Peninsula. A unified Korea could become an important North Pacific gateway, linking the three realms. At present, the North Korean dictatorship continues to disdain South Korea, and there is little likelihood that the two states will draw closer to one another. Moreover, China is opposed to unity of the peninsula on the grounds that this would bring US influence and possibly a military presence to its border. Taiwan's current status within the region is problematic, as Taipei vacillates between a "One China" policy and pursuit of independence from Beijing.

China

China has taken its place among the great powers of the world with unprecedented speed in the past decade. With its vast landmass and huge population, its inherent strength and potential has long been recognized by other powers as a dangerous enemy or an advantageous ally. Its centralized Communist government and powerful military machine enables China to dominate the East Asia region, while the country's explosive economic growth in recent years has given it global reach and influence.

Despite its impressive economic achievements, there is little possibility that China will emerge as the world's superpower, leading to a twenty-first-century "Chinese era." Of the four pillars which measure state power, the leadership of Beijing is confined to the economic sphere. Militarily it cannot compete with the West. Its defense expenditures, only 2 percent of GDP, are focused on gaining regional, not global, dominance. Beijing's challenge to the United States is over the control of the waters between the China coast and the Asia-Pacific Rim. With respect to the third pillar, ideological appeal to the outside world is limited. The mixed socialist-capitalist system that the Communist Party has introduced favors state-owned corporations and provides an open door to widespread corruption. With regard to the fourth pillar—governance cohesiveness—the tight controls that the Chinese Communist Party wields provides stability that could prove ephemeral if the lid on freedom of expression and demonstration ultimately blows.

The emergence of China as the center of a new geostrategic realm, with outreach to much of the world, can be attributed not only to the weakening of US and Russian influence in the western and North Pacific but even more to changes that have taken place within China itself. For much of the past half century, China was oriented to the Eurasian continental realm—first as a geopolitical region subordinate to the Soviet heartland and then as its hostile competitor. The country's continentality was expressed by its closed, heavily rural system and Mao Zedong's efforts to shift the locus of economic power, which was in the North and the interior region.

With the end of Maoism and the Vietnam War, China reopened its economic system, enabling forces of maritimity to emerge from the strangling grip of continentality. Farming in the northern and interior rural areas is subject to frequent droughts, while growing urban centers, including Beijing, suffer from chronic water shortages that are aggravated by industrial pollution that makes much of the urban water supply unpotable. This has unleashed the entrepreneurial talents of the peoples of the south and central coasts—from Guangdong (with centers at Guangzhou and Shenzhen), Hong Kong, and Fujian to Zhejiang, Shanghai, and now Jiangsu, north of Shanghai. The Chinese of this region have taken advantage of foreign investment and trade opportunities to make maritime China a world economic powerhouse. This coastal region, sometimes called the "Golden Coast of China," is home to most of China's rapidly growing middle class as well as its wealthy entrepreneurs, and it has the country's highest per capita income and largest share of foreign-funded companies. The focus of these companies is foreign trade.

During the same period, continental China has undergone considerable upheaval. The antiquated, state-owned, large-scale industrial structure in the North, the Northeast, and the interior has shrunk. The system of agricultural communes has been disbanded, leaving hundreds of millions of farmers with small, inefficient plots. This has caused massive displacement of farmers, who have migrated to the cities, where they form a huge underclass. While China's center of economic gravity has now shifted to its maritime-facing "Golden Coast," the great majority of the nation's population and landmass remains in the North and the interior—from Manchuria and North China, where most of the old heavy industry is located, to the country's outer provinces of Inner Mongolia and Xinjiang in the far western area and Tibet in the southwest. The heavily rural middle and upper parts of the Yellow and Yangtze River basins, as well as southwestern China, are parts of this region, which remains caught in the grip of continentality.

The continental-maritime split personality of China distinguishes East Asia from its competing realms. The maritime realm, with its seaman's point of view, is the open-system sector whose outlook is based upon exchange—of peoples, goods, and ideas. Heartlandic Russia, with its landsman's perspective, is inward facing. It has traditionally pursued a closed system based upon internal resources, opened on a limited basis by its large-scale energy exports. China encompasses both of these contrasting world orientations, retaining its repressive, top-down Communist governance apparatus while encouraging a market-oriented economy. The competition is played out within two different geographical arenas—in the North and the interior and in the "Golden Coast"—with varying political, economic, and cultural outlooks. How to reconcile the geopolitical contradictions that grow out of these two outlooks represents China's greatest internal geopolitical challenge. Its outcome will determine whether China will remain united or its destiny is to be divided into two separate states.

CONTINENTALITY VERSUS MARITIMITY

For most of China's four millennia of recorded history, its geopolitical orientation has been continental. It was this landsman's China that shaped the closed culture, religion, dominant language (Mandarin), and imperial bureaucratic system of the nation. This is the culture that nurtured China's high degree of ethnocentrism and its deep-rooted sense of racial superiority. It was a culture that looked down upon foreigners as barbarians and sought to wall itself off from the outside world, psychologically as well as physically. The vastness of the Chinese landmass supported the development of the concept of continental self-sufficiency and isolation.

It was the North that nurtured the regimes that organized China, starting with the Yin dynasty (1523 BCE to 1027 BCE), the first historic dynasty located in modern-day Henan, north of the Huang He (Hwang Ho, or Yellow) River. The North spawned dynasties established by such nomadic invaders as the Huns, Mongols, and Manchus, as well as the Chinese Sung and Ming empires. Much of China's history is represented in the clash between nomadic forces sweeping into China from the north and west and the native Chinese dynasties that emerged out of the middle valley of the Huang He to counter and ultimately overthrow the Central Asian invaders.

Various Chinese rulers from the Qin, who first built the Great Wall of China in the third century BCE, to the Ming (1368–1644 CE), who restored the wall in its present form, sought to protect China from the nomads. The wall extended across the Inner Mongolian plain from the Qilian Shan (mountains) north of the Huang He headwaters for fifteen hundred miles until it reached the Yellow Sea. It embraced Hebei (Hopei) Province, where it was designed to protect Beijing and Tianjin (Tientsin).

While China's geopolitical orientation and development has historically been continental, maritimity has also placed its stamp upon the nation's personality and focus. The locus of the early maritime orientation was the southeastern and central coast, extending from Guangzhou (Canton) on the Pearl River delta northward for six hundred miles to the Ningba flats of the Yangtze Plain, just south of Shanghai. The rocky and highly irregular shoreline, with many offshore islands, was backed by mountains that provided protective defense screens but offered little space for population to spread. Early on the innumerable harbors of the coast became the bases for fishing and exchange of farm products. In modern times this coast became the locus of the great commercial ports and manufacturing centers developed by Western powers that opened South China and its central coastal extension to the outside world. Hong

Kong, on the estuary of the Pearl River, and Shanghai, connected to the Yangtze estuary by the Huangpu River, were the keystones of this development.

Han people, coming from the North, first populated the southern coastal region fifteen hundred years ago, when they displaced the indigenous Thai and Tibetan hill tribes. They crowded into the narrow coastal zones and pushed inland up the narrow river valleys that had cut into the mountains. In these plains and interior valleys, the humid, subtropical climate was favorable for the intensive cultivation on small plots of double-cropped rice, tea, tobacco, mulberry trees for silk, and poppies for opium.

It was this maritime China of the South that produced the fishermen, sailors, traders, and farmers who created the Chinese exchange economy and, in modern times, the great trading cities of Guangzhou and Hong Kong, one of the world's busiest seaports. This was also the overcrowded China from which millions of emigrants—the overseas Chinese—went forth to Southeast Asia and North America. Initially, most the emigrants came from Guangzhou (in Guangdong Province); in recent decades, Fujian Province has been the major source of out-migration. The south and central coasts are where the Cantonese, Fukienese, and Wu (Shanghai) tongues developed, as separate from the Mandarin of the North. The latter, historically the language of the ruling classes, is the official national language of the country and is spoken in most of China, but not in the Southeast.

Guangzhou's port was known to ancient Europe through Arab and Hindu merchants and had extensive political and economic connections with Southeast and offshore Asia for centuries. Nevertheless, it was only in the nineteenth century that China fully entered the global maritime arena. Prior to that time, there had been an initial contact with European trade and political influence when Portugal established the settlement of Macao (Macau) in 1557 on the western side of the Pearl River estuary. However, the antiforeigner policies of the Ming and Qing (Manchu) dynasties kept China relatively closed to modern maritime influences.

Great Britain opened China to the maritime world when it waged the First Opium War (1839–42) because of its dissatisfaction with the limited trade agreements that it had been granted by the Qing emperor. Over the next century, foreign trade zones and footholds were established along the coast. Guangzhou became the first of the treaty ports in 1842. Treaty ports were opened to foreign trade by bilateral treaties between China and foreign governments, and they provided areas available for settlement as well as mercantile activities. Because of the shallowness of Guangzhou's harbor, the British obtained the concession of the twenty-nine-square-mile rocky island of Hong Kong, ninety miles to Guangzhou's southeast, on the eastern side of the Pearl River estuary. A small area on the mainland, Kowloon, was added in 1860. In 1898 the Crown colony of Hong Kong secured a ninety-eight-year lease on the New Territories, 366 square miles of adjoining mainland next to the city of Kowloon, and developed it as a twin city to Hong Kong. The Hong Kong harbor at Victoria is one of the finest natural harbors in the world; thus the Crown colony quickly became the gateway to South China as well as the country's leading link with the maritime world.

While the origins of Shanghai go back to the eleventh century, and while it became a walled city in the sixteenth century, it remained unimportant until it was opened to foreign trade with its establishment as a treaty port the year after Guangzhou. In 1843, Britain received a commercial concession. This was followed by a concession to the United States in 1862, and the two concessions were merged into the International Settlement in 1863, which put the greater part of Shanghai under extraterritorial control. The French maintained a separate concession within the city, which they had first gained in 1849, and substantial numbers of foreigners, including Japanese, Russian, British, and Americans, took up residence there. Subsequently, the international settlements were added in several other Chinese cities. In the

Shanghai and other international settlements, foreigners received deeds to the land within the bounds of the settlement and were permitted to organize themselves into municipal councils governed by their own administrative, judicial, and legislative institutions.[1]

Shanghai was the world's fastest-growing city from the mid-nineteenth to the mid-twentieth centuries and rivaled Hong Kong as a great world port, despite its location five miles from the open ocean on a tidal creek and tributary of the Yangtze. The port extends for fifteen miles along the creek, which is called the Huangpu. Initially built on the opium trade, Shanghai became notorious as a city of sin, gambling, and corruption, but it soon developed into the country's leading industrial center.

Approximately seventy treaty ports were ultimately opened along the China coast, mostly along the south and center but extending as far north as the Liaodong Peninsula on the Bay of Korea in Manchuria. These were ports opened to a foreign trade by treaties, within which large areas were available for foreign trade and settlement. In addition, another twenty-two were designated as open ports, which were opened voluntarily by the Chinese government, although land leases to foreigners were limited in duration. Among the major ports of the South were Shantou (Swatow) at the northern end of Guangdong Province; Amoy (Xiamen), a major port for immigrants to Southeast Asia; and Fuzhou (Foochow), on the central Fujian coast. By 1850 Fuzhou rose to become China's chief port by virtue of its being the world's largest tea export center. Ningbo (Ningpo), just south of Shanghai in central China's Zhejiang Province, which had been an early port of entry for Japanese missions to the Chinese court and a sixteenth-century Portuguese trading settlement, also expanded its commercial activities.

The treaty ports of the North extended to the Yellow Sea and its northern arms, the Gulf of Bohai, and the Bay of Korea. Tianjin, thirty miles upstream on the Hai River and connected to the Huang He by the Grand Canal, was developed by British and French concessions as the major port of the region. Despite its relatively poor harbor, Tianjin became a major international port because it served as the gateway to the North China Plain and the rail terminus for Manchuria. On the southern shore of the Bohai, at the eastern end of the Shandong (Shantung) Peninsula, Britain held a concession at the territory of Weihaiwei. In northeastern Shandong, Germany controlled a major treaty port on the southern coast of the peninsula at Qingdao (Tsingtao) on the Yellow Sea, losing it, along with the surrounding German territory of Jiaozhou, to Japan at the outbreak of World War I.

Dalian (Dairen), the chief commercial port for Manchuria, was at the northern end of the Yellow Sea, at the tip of the Liaodong Peninsula, between the Bay of Korea and the Gulf of Bohai. The city, combined with Port Arthur (Lushun), was administered by the Russians as a naval base and southern terminus of the South Manchurian Railway until its acquisition by Japan as a result of the Russo-Japanese War of 1904–5. In a repetition of history, Dalian was reoccupied by Russian troops at the end of World War II, and it remained a Russian leasehold for a decade, under both the Chinese Nationalists (Kuomintang) and the Chinese Communists.

Some inland centers were also designated as treaty ports. The most notable was Nanjing (Nanking), the largest interior river port of China, located on the Yangtze and connected to Shanghai by the Grand Canal. Much farther inland, along the central Yangtze River, was Hankou (Hankow), which is now part of the urban conurbation of Wuhan. Although six hundred miles from the sea, the port was capable of handling oceangoing vessels. Foreign penetration of the Yangtze valley reached as far inland as the Japanese settlement at Chongqing (Chunking), which became a treaty port in 1891, and in Manchuria at Haerbin (Harbin) on the middle Sungari River. There the Russians obtained a concession in 1896.

The burst of economic development in all of these foreign-controlled treaty ports, concessions, settlements, and territories brought industrialization to China and opened the country to outside capital investment and trade. But this maritime orientation was imposed on China. Nineteen different countries obtained unilateral rights and privileges that were deeply resented by the Chinese. Foreign armed forces and warships were stationed not only along the coasts but also within inland waters. In addition, the imperialist powers mounted intrusions deep into the Chinese periphery—Britain in Tibet, Russia in Xinjiang (Sinkiang) and Outer Mongolia, and Japan in Manchuria.[2]

The Manchu regime of the nineteenth and early twentieth centuries was too corrupt and impotent to loosen the foreign grip on China. When it was overthrown in 1911 and a republic was established under the leadership of Sun Yat-sen, the Chinese government sought to revise or abolish the treaty system but failed. The Chinese had invested great hopes in the Paris Peace Conference of 1919, but these were dashed when the great powers failed to reject Japan's claims in Shandong. This led to the increased strength of the anti-imperialist movement in China, evident when a violent student protest was put down by the Beijing dictatorship, which was backed by warlords who had wrested power from Sun.

Conflict continued in the years that followed. While Sun Yat-sen had sought inspiration from Western ideals, his failure to gain support from the West led him to turn to Russia for help in his struggle against the regime in Beijing. The tangled web of events during this period was marked by the military victories of Chiang Kai-shek and the return of the Kuomintang to power in 1925; the long civil war resulting from the break between the Kuomintang and the Chinese Communist Party; the Japanese invasion of Manchuria (Manchukuo) and establishment of a puppet regime there; and the Japanese attack in 1937, leading to its lengthy and brutal occupation of North China, the Yangtze valley, and the coastal areas.

The Nationalists had moved the capital from Beijing to Nanjing (the "Southern Capital") on the lower Yangtze River, a reflection of their outward orientation. However, a decade later they were forced to flee from the Japanese and move deep into the interior to Chongqing along the upper Yangtze, in the southwestern province of Sichuan (Szechwan). This fertile area is known as the Red Basin for its reddish sandstone-derived soils, which have made it the "rice bowl" of China. There the Nationalists were supplied by the Allies through the Burma Road, which extended from Lashio through Yunnan Province to Chongqing, and in World War II by airlift from India. Several years previously, the interior had provided similar sanctuary to the Communists, who in 1935 had retreated from the Nationalists in their "Long March" to Shaanxi (Shensi) in the Northwest. They made their headquarters in Yan'an (Yenan), at the northern end of the province, which served as their capital until they took power in 1949.

At the height of World War II, the United States and the other Western powers signed treaties with China abolishing the foreign concessions and privileges that had been unilaterally imposed over the previous century. With the defeat of Japan, Germany, and Italy, the Chinese assumed that the era of imperialistic penetration was finally over. To their surprise, Chinese officials learned that the Yalta agreement on the Far East, signed by Roosevelt, Churchill, and Stalin, forced China to grant Moscow territorial and political concessions.

Moscow acquired joint rights to a new railway system, under Soviet control, that would combine the Chinese Eastern and South Manchurian Railways, linking Inner Mongolia and the Soviet Far East to Harbin and Dalian. The USSR was also to enjoy a free lease over the commercial port of Dalian and restoration of the Russian naval base at Port Arthur (Lushun). In addition, China would have to recognize the independence of Outer Mongolia.

These vestiges of nineteenth- and early twentieth-century imperial penetration remained until 1955, when Soviet troops were withdrawn from Manchuria and China regained control of the port, base, and railroad. Moreover, although in the early days under Communist rule China was highly dependent on its Soviet ally and patron, the suspicions of Soviet imperialistic intentions had been fanned by these postwar concessions and would play a role in Beijing's hostility to Moscow, which would lead soon to the Sino-Soviet break.

The Maoist Era (1949–76)

By the end of World War II, the Communists controlled much of interior North and Central China. They quickly took control of Manchuria (the Northeast), turned over to them by the Russian armies that had occupied the region after the defeat of Japan. The ensuing conflict between the Beijing-based Communists and the Nationalists in Nanjing ended in 1949 with the defeat of Chiang Kai-shek's armies and their flight to Taiwan, where they established their seat of government in Taipei.

With the Communist takeover, China's orientation once more shifted inward. For the next three decades, the strategy of the system was continentality, first as subordinate to Moscow and then as an independent geopolitical power in competition with the Soviets. China's goal was self-containment. Its foreign trade with the other continental power, the USSR, under the Sino-Soviet Treaty of Friendship, Alliance, and Mutual Assistance continued until the open split between them in 1960.

For Mao Zedong, maritimity and the opening to the West had degraded and corrupted China. In particular, he had come to despise the social impacts of Western influence as represented by the hedonism and corruption of the wealthy classes of Shanghai and the great gap between those who had been enriched by foreign-supported manufacturing and trade and the millions of the city's poor. Mao was determined to turn away from the world beyond the sea and become self-reliant in food and the products of China's natural resources.

For the most part, China's exports at that time were food, textiles, and minerals, while its imports were heavy industrial products. Trade with Japan and the West, the country's leading trading partners in the 1930s, now became negligible as the focus shifted to the Soviet Union and some of its satellites.

During the Vietnam War, China provided the North Vietnamese with substantial supplies and military equipment. As its foreign policy aim became the spread of Maoist revolutionary philosophy to South America, Africa, and Asia, Beijing extended economic aid to countries that it sought to influence. However, the main emphasis of the Chinese regime was economic development of its own country. In former Manchuria, where the chief coal and iron resources of the country are to be found, the heavy industry base was rapidly expanded with the help of Soviet technicians.

Between 1957 and 1960 Mao Zedong organized the "Great Leap Forward," which sought to focus the nation's attention on the rural areas of the interior. The Communist regime forced millions of people out of the cities into huge farming communes in the countryside. It also promoted the establishment of thousands of small factories that used "backyard" furnaces that produced metals aimed at attaining the revolution's goal of local self-sufficiency. The purpose of locating manufacturing in the interior was to reduce the country's dependence on the heavy industries of the Northeast, which was strategically exposed to the Soviet Union. Most of the metals turned out to be useless.

The social upheaval caused by the communization of agriculture, as well as three successive years of drought, resulted in dramatic crop reductions and widespread famine. Millions of Chinese starved to death during this period. The Great Leap Forward, an outgrowth of Mao's ideological opposition to the de-Stalinization policy introduced in 1956 by Nikita

Khrushchev, became a major factor in China's break with the USSR. The hostility between Beijing and Moscow led to the withdrawal of Soviet economic aid and technicians from the country in 1960. The enmity intensified the following year, when China allied itself with Albania in the wake of the rift between the USSR and the Communist regime in Tirana. The rift increased further in the 1960s, when China's hard-liners objected to Leonid Brezhnev's call for peaceful coexistence with the West. At that point, a simmering border dispute between the two Communist powers erupted into fighting.

The Cultural Revolution of 1966–76 was another great national trauma. Mao swept aside the five-year planning process to focus on the production of staple, high-yield crops at the expense of agricultural diversity. In addition, he initiated a massive antiurban program aimed at building scattered factories throughout the rural parts of the country. The goal was not only to disperse industrial enterprises but also to arrest manufacturing growth in the big cities. Industrial production dropped rapidly during this period. The Cultural Revolution also involved mass mobilization of youth, encouraging them to join the Red Guard, which persecuted technical experts, teachers, and intellectuals and enforced Mao's cult of personality. Universities were closed and thousands were purged. Only Mao's death in 1976 put an end to the excesses of the Cultural Revolution and returned the country to political stability and rational economic development.

REEMERGENCE OF MARITIMITY–ECONOMIC DYNAMISM

Under Mao's successors, Deng Xiaoping and Zhou Enlai, China's farms were decollectivized, industry was modernized, and diplomatic relations were developed with the West. The year that diplomatic relations were established with the United States—1979—was also the year that four coastal cities were declared special economic zones to attract trade, foreign investment, and technology. Fourteen more cities were added to this group in 1984, and eventually Shanghai was added in 1990. Such steps reflected the abandonment of the Soviet-style, centrally planned economy and the move to a market-oriented economic system, although still within the rigid framework of Communist Party control.

Since the 1980s, China has made remarkable progress. GDP has grown tenfold to over $12 trillion in purchasing power parity, accounting for one-quarter of all global economic growth, including demand for oil. It now has the world's second-highest GDP, that of the United States being the highest. If the EU, rather than individual European countries, is included, China's GDP would rank third. Foreign trade has also exploded, reaching $3.6 trillion in 2013. In the words of a Chinese Young Pioneer (one of the urban youth sent to the farming areas): "Chairman Mao founded China, Deng Xiaopeng made us rich, and now Jiang Zemin is leading us into the future."[3]

China is dependent on international trade, which now represents 30 percent of its GDP. It has overtaken the United States as the world's largest exporter of goods, which encompass not only low-value items like clothing and toys but also high-value industrial, transportation, and information technology products. While the United States is China's single largest export market, trade with Asia, followed by trade with the EU, have collectively become China's leading export outlets. Its trade with India, Brazil, and Russia has more than doubled over the past few years, and it rivals the EU as Sub-Saharan Africa's leading trading partner.

China's nearest neighbors, Japan, South Korea, and Taiwan, account for about 20 percent of its total trade and are its major investors. Moreover, China's economic leverage is enhanced by being the world's largest lender, purchasing over one trillion dollars in bonds from the United States as well as making large loans to Ecuador, Venezuela, Turkmenistan, Iran, Sudan, and Angola. Chinese companies are also major investors in European and American corporations as well as supporting infrastructure projects in Africa.

Maritimity involves far more than economics, however. The seafarer's outlook is one of exploration—the search for new places, new ideas, and new contacts. It represents the opening of a system. Land conflict and threats had long been the main concern of China, so its military defense was continentally oriented. The new focus on maritimity has called for a radical rethinking of the role that its navy is to play in the years ahead.

Until recently, China's naval strategy was geared to the waters that separate it from its near neighbors. With a small "brown-water" fleet whose capacity was limited to coastal operations, China was helpless to interfere with the operations of the US and Russian "blue-water" fleets, which were capable of staying in the middle of the ocean for extended periods. Communist China could not prevent the US Seventh Fleet from blocking its planned invasion of Taiwan in 1950 or its threatened invasion of Taiwan in the tense period that followed the intensive shelling of the Nationalist-held islands of Quemoy (Jinmen) and Matsu (Mazu), just off the coast of Fujian. The Vietnam War brought the naval power of the US Third and Seventh Fleets to the South China Sea, where it was applied with impunity against the North Vietnamese and their Chinese allies.

The Chinese naval weakness was further underscored when a Soviet blue-water fleet began to operate in the South China Sea after the withdrawal of American forces from the Indochinese arena. The mounting tensions between China and Vietnam that culminated in the brief border war of 1979 made a stronger alliance with the Soviet Union crucial for Hanoi. As part of the new military agreements between the two, Vietnam turned over the Cam Ranh Bay naval and air bases to the Soviet navy under a lease that extended to 2004. Cam Ranh had been expanded in 1965 as a deepwater port by the United States, which built its main naval base there. When the Soviets took it over in the early 1980s, they made it the largest Soviet naval base outside the USSR. The fleet that they stationed there housed an aircraft carrier and over one hundred submarines, as well as other warships and land-based bombers. An added threat to China was the Soviet development of electronic facilities to monitor Chinese communications in the South China Sea, especially around Hainan.

China's recent history of naval inferiority, in combination with the collapse of the Soviet Union and the end of the land threat to its northern borders, has inspired Beijing to focus on building up its naval forces and expanding its maritime reach. In 1992 Beijing promulgated its Laws of Territorial Waters and Contiguous Zones, which claimed jurisdiction over a two-hundred-mile-wide area beyond its coasts, based upon the extension of its continental shelf. Under these laws, the Chinese claim sovereignty over the waters of the Taiwan Strait in their entirety and therefore could evict the foreign naval vessels and fishermen that use these waters. Those nations that do recognize a two-hundred-mile exclusive economic zone (EEZ) do so only with respect to fishing and underwater mining rights, not air or sea transportation, civilian or military.

In addition, the Chinese claim the Senkaku (Diaoyu) Islands, one hundred miles northeast of Taiwan in Japan's southeastern Ryukyu chain, as well as the Paracel and Spratly Island groups in the South China Sea. Inclusion of the waters surrounding these islands under Chinese jurisdiction would extend Chinese control to the eastern borders of the East China Sea and the southern borders of the South China Sea, near the coasts of southern Vietnam, northern Borneo, and the southern Philippines. In the unlikely event that the Spratlys are recognized as Chinese, the reach of these laws would extend one thousand miles beyond the Chinese mainland. In the East China Sea, Beijing also claims an EEZ of two hundred miles that overlaps with Japan's EEZ. These competing claims have taken on considerable importance with the discovery of a vast underwater natural gas field in the center of the sea. In 2013, China declared an air defense identification zone applying to aircraft flights within most of the East China and South China Seas. Japan rejected this claim, and the United States sent military aircraft into the zone, although it did advise commercial aircraft to notify Beijing in advance of their flights (figure 9.1). The reaction of Japan's prime minister Shinzō Abe was to approve a five-year defense plan expansion to protect Japanese interests in these waters.

As long as China's navy remained a small, obsolete, coastal force, there was little that it could do to enforce its territorial waters laws. Transformation of the navy began in 1994, with the purchase of then state-of-the-art destroyers, submarines, and missiles from Russia and the establishment of a training program for Chinese naval personnel. This new strategic relationship was one of the first products of the entente that had been reached in that year between the two former foes. Since then, China has moved forward with efforts aimed at both purchasing vessels and electronic equipment from abroad and developing its own production capacity in these areas. The purchases have included Russian naval aircraft and, in 2006, a Soviet-era aircraft carrier from Ukraine, which is being completely rebuilt.

In 1999, Chief Vice Admiral Shi Yunsheng announced a ten-year navy modernization program, to include battleships, submarines, aircraft carriers, destroyers, frigates, and missiles.[4] The formal announcement stated the navy's mission, which emphasized near-coast defense rather than blue-water capabilities. However, the very reference to aircraft carriers and subsequent indications of plans to form a fourth Chinese fleet for the Indian and near-Pacific Oceans suggest that the distinction between regional defense and more broadly projected naval power may be a matter of semantics.[5] Because of its increasing dependence on imported oil from the Middle East and Africa, China has a major interest in securing oil shipments that pass through the Arabian Sea, the Indian Ocean, and the Malacca-Singapore Straits. This dependence has become more critical as industrial expansion and consumer demand continue to increase. The threat of terrorist and pirate attacks upon shipping that traverses these narrow waters is also faced by oil importers from Japan and Singapore, as well as exporters from Malaysia and Indonesia. Tokyo and Beijing, so suspicious of each other's naval buildup in their shared coastal waters, have a common interest in securing their oil shipping and other commercial lines from the Middle East and Africa.

The Chinese naval buildup is accompanied by additional measures to strengthen its Indian Ocean presence. It has done so by constructing Chinese-owned or leased deepwater container ports in Chittagong in Bangladesh, Gwadar and Karachi in Pakistan, and Sittwe in Myanmar. It has constructed a twelve-hundred-mile oil and gas pipeline from Sittwe on Myanmar's Bay of Bengal through Myanmar to Kunming in southwest China. In response to these initiatives, India has blocked China from its effort to gain influence in the Seychelles, Mauritius, and the Maldives. To strengthen its influence in Myanmar, India has agreed to develop a deepwater port at Kyaukpyu on Maday Island to serve transit trade for Chittagong, Yangon, and Kolkata. Beijing is also engaged in discussions with Thailand to invest in the construction of a canal cutting across the narrow Kra Isthmus. Such a thirty-mile canal would connect the Andaman Sea to the Gulf of Thailand, bypassing the Malacca Strait. Reflecting the importance of international trade to China, its state firms now own a large world container fleet. Over 40 percent of such vessels were built in China in 2012. Extending beyond the Indian Ocean and the Middle East, Chinese companies have acquired stakes in ports and terminals in what is now termed "a Chinese String of Pearls." Stakes are held in terminals in the ports of Antwerp, Suez, Singapore, Sudan, Piraeus in Greece, Tin Can in Nigeria, Loja in São Tomé, and Djibouti. The Chinese have also agreed to build a new port in Tanzania, and have footholds in Thailand, Burma, Pakistan, Sri Lanka, Bangladesh, the Maldives, and Somalia.

Figure 9.1. China Air Defense Identification Zone

While China now has northern, eastern, and southern fleets to serve its security needs in its adjoining seas, a fleet such as envisaged by Admiral Shi would have considerable striking power, reaching to the Sea of Japan, the Philippine Sea, the Malacca Strait, and the Indian Ocean. In the face of US naval pressure and the growth of the Japanese navy, China's ambition to play a powerful strategic naval role is still limited, even in its regional waters and with one or two small aircraft carriers. This applies to its threats against Taiwan, let alone in the southernmost parts of the South China Sea and the Bay of Bengal, where the Indian navy is the dominant presence. Nevertheless, the buildup of Chinese air, naval, and missile power along the Strait of Taiwan has been of sufficient magnitude to be regarded as a serious threat to Taiwan. Since 2001, Taipei has pressed Washington to sell it state-of-the-art destroyers, antimissile systems, and F-16s. Beijing's objections to such sales have been vigorous, and Washington has urged Taipei to accept its offers of sale of more conventional weapons. While pledged to come to the defense of Taiwan in the event of an attack by China, the United States is reluctant to provide it with the weaponry that would escalate its tensions with the mainland.

Some experts warn that the tilting of naval power in the Pacific as part of the new "Asian century" would be a destabilizing factor.[6] As long as the Asia-Pacific Rim, anchored by Japan and Australia, continues to be integrated within the maritime geostrategic realm, the collective naval power of the maritime states and India will more than counterbalance China's naval growth. The common interests in keeping open the sea-lanes of the Pacific and Indian Oceans offer new opportunities for naval cooperation.

China's emergence as a major economic power and trading nation does not mean that continentality is about to disappear as a geopolitical motif. At best, only about one-third of China's 1.35 trillion people are likely to be significantly affected by the forces of maritimity. Nearly two-thirds of China is rural, with about half of the people living as farmers in the North, the Northeast, and the interior. The Communist Party recognizes the danger to political stability posed by the rural underclass of the interior, where the average family income is $1,600 per annum, in contrast to the coast, where it is over three times as high. China needs to stem the flow to the already overcrowded coastal cities where the rural immigrants are an exploited labor class. Serious riots within the rural interior have become more frequent. Recognizing that its ability to retain control is in jeopardy, the October 2007 Seventeenth National Communist Party Congress announced a national plan to create a new "socialist countryside." It has promised to commit massive investments in rural development, land reform, clean water, and improved transportation. The plan also includes building new urban city-regions, with modernized industries in such interior cities as Chongqing, Chengdu, and Xian. In spite of these investments, the income gap between the coastal and interior regions has actually increased.

In the decades ahead, the forces of continentality and maritimity will continue to compete for dominance. Whether the current regime can successfully resolve the economic, cultural, and political contradictions between them remains the key to China's future geopolitical stability and its very existence as an integrated state.

THE LOCATIONAL PERSPECTIVE

It is not only the geographic setting of a nation but also how it perceives that setting that influences the conduct of foreign policy. Locational "facts" are transmitted by leadership to the public and become embodied in national folklore and myths that drive future generations of leaders to shape foreign policies that conform to that perspective.

Millennia of historic and cultural postures of national egocentrism have led to China's present locational perspective—the perspective of China as the "Middle Kingdom," the center of the world.[7] This perspective evolved from a local to a regional to a global geographical scale. The local sense of space goes back to the period when China was a loose collection of small states that had expanded from the northern part of the country to the Yangtze and then to the South (1500 to 200 BCE). Their Middle Kingdom was differentiated from those around them by agriculture—the essence of the civilized world. What lay beyond the limits of this sown world was of no consequence because it was peopled by uncivilized nomads—"the Barbarians."

The regional sense of space developed when the Han Empire united China through a strongly centralized government in 200 BCE. During the following two millennia, China met other worlds through intermittent foreign trade, the import of Buddhism from India, and nomadic rulers who overthrew their dynasties.

In the early part of this period, the Chinese reached into surrounding areas by conquering and colonizing Korea and the Tonkin delta (618 to 907 CE). They treated these areas as non-Chinese tributary kingdoms, offering protection in return but not absorbing them as provinces within the Chinese space. The exception was Taiwan, which had a small aboriginal populace before it was seized from the Dutch in 1622 CE and settled by Han peoples. (In 1895 the island was acquired by Japan, which called it "Formosa.")

Toward the end of this period, from the eighteenth to the twentieth centuries, the encounter with Europe confronted the Chinese with the challenge of modernity. All contacts, with the exception of the introduction of Buddhism, did little to transform Chinese culture and civilization. A society that had invented the civil service, the wheelbarrow, the compass, and gunpowder had little to learn from "foreigners."

The territorial encroachments and introduction of alien cultures by Europeans, Russians, and Japanese from the mid-nineteenth to the mid-twentieth centuries shook, but did not alter, the Chinese view of themselves as being at the center of the world. The goal became to dislodge the foreigners and restore territorial integrity and regional hegemony. The strength of antiforeigner feeling was evidenced in the Boxer uprising (1898–1900), when the secret society of Boxers, supported by the dowager empress, rebelled against foreign influences, including Christianity, railroad building, and the system of extraterritoriality whereby foreign powers exercised their own economic, diplomatic, judicial, and policing functions over wide areas within China, including the stationing of military forces and warships. The conflict swept over much of North China, although the governors of the southern provinces refused to back it. The rebels occupied Beijing for two months, until the rebellion was finally put down by British, French, Russian, American, and Japanese troops. The failed uprising left foreign spheres of influence entrenched more strongly than ever within the Chinese landscape.

The Chinese Communist revolution, under Mao's autocratic Marxism, introduced the global perspective of a China that continued to be differentiated from the rest of the world but held a central place within it by being the leader of the revolutionary Third World. Norton Ginsburg presented a Chinese model of the world that was formed by four concentric zones. The fourth or outer zone distinguished the underdeveloped rural world from both the capitalist and socialist urban realms.[8] This global view helped the Chinese to reject satellite status vis-à-vis the USSR while providing a defensive strategy against the West. After the Sino-Soviet schism, Lin Pao advanced the concept that China could exploit its position of centrality within the Third World to counterencircle both the West and the Soviet Union from rural bases in Asia, Africa, and Latin America and thus break the ring of containment that had been drawn around it.[9] After 1978, Deng Xiaoping and his successors introduced the hybrid socialist-capitalist economy, which shifted the focus from ideological competition abroad to competing in the world market.

In the light of the sweeping changes that have occurred within the global geopolitical system during the past decades, strategic centrality within the underdeveloped world has little relevance for China's foreign policy. The period of promoting Communist revolution within Sub-Saharan Africa, Latin America, and Southeast Asia is over, and the pursuit of influence within economically and strategically unimportant parts of the world has little appeal to Beijing. For China today, the perspective of centrality is evolving within a new geopolitical order in which China, as the core of the world's third geostrategic realm, holds a position that is centrally located between the heartlandic and maritime realms—independent of them, but interconnected to them in matters of China's choice. The geopolitical regions of greatest strategic concern to Beijing are those bordering Russia and the Asia-Pacific Rim and, increasingly, the Middle East and Sub-Saharan Africa because of their energy resources.

Controlling a geostrategic realm that lies between the continental and maritime worlds, the Chinese can expand their classical perspective of centrality to pursue policies that pit the other realms against one another. In military-strategic terms, China can forge an alliance with Russia without fear of being dominated. Recent examples include Sino-Russian support of Iran and Serbia, expanding Russian oil sales to China via pipeline, and cooperation with Russia in space technology to develop a Chinese-manned spacecraft. In addition, with the upgrading of its armed forces, China has turned to Russia to purchase jet fighters, naval vessels, and other equipment. At the same time, tensions with the maritime realm have increased over Taiwan, the possible development of a national missile defense by Japan, and China's securing of the air over its two-hundred-mile exclusive economic maritime zone—the cause of the "spy plane" incident with the United States in April 2001.

Economically, China has launched an all-out effort to expand its reach to the maritime world. This began with its economic liberalization during the past three decades and the normalizing of trade relations with the United States. China's admission to the World Trade Organization in November 2001 meant the reduction of tariffs and other barriers to trade, foreign investment, and the establishment of foreign company operations in such diverse enterprises as motor vehicles and retail establishments. The trade-off for opening Beijing's markets, including to cheap farm products from US agribusiness, has been the enormous expansion of markets in the West and offshore Asia. This has meant breaking out from economic isolation and decreased self-sufficiency and has brought fundamental changes to the physical and economic landscape of China. The consequences of concentration of manufacturing and services along the coast also means greater strategic vulnerability. This has made the buildup of offensive and defensive coastal air, missile, and sea power a strategic imperative. More recently, China has begun to invest a considerable share of its sovereign funds in developing the continental interior in order to balance the economy territorially and to reduce strategic vulnerability in its west. While failing to achieve its economic objective, it has succeeded in strengthening its strategic position.

The Chinese Communist leadership expresses confidence in its ability to pursue economic reform without losing political control. It remains to be seen whether China's hybrid economic system will destroy or save the current regime. However, it should be recalled that the party survived the massive economic failure of the Great Leap Forward and the social chaos of the Cultural Revolution. It has kept a tight political grip on the country, despite the 1989 massacre of democratic reformers at Tiananmen Square. So far, the party has weathered unrest not only in the impoverished interior but also among the tens of millions of migrants to the coastal cities who remain untouched by the prosperity generated by the export economy.

GEOPOLITICAL FEATURES

Nineteenth- and twentieth-century foreign imperialism, the Communist revolution, and the recent opening to the outside world have contributed substantially to the shaping of the geopolitical features that have characterized China's historic development as an organized state. What follows is a discussion of these features and their evolution, meaning, and trends.

Historic Core

The geopolitical roots of the first historic dynasty of China, the Yin (Shang), which ruled from 1523 BCE to 1027 BCE, were in what is now Henan Province, which is traversed by the Yellow River (Huang He) on the North China Plain. One of the capitals of the Yin, a site near Anyang, at the northern edge of the province, could be described as the historic core of the country—the cradle of the Chinese nation. However, the dynasty of this era was based only upon control of a small city-state that exercised dominance of neighboring city-states of the plains.

A more solid claimant to being the cradle of modern China may be the Wei River valley. The Qin, the first dynasty to unify China (221–206 BCE), gave its name to the country. It extended the limits of China north to the province of Gansu bordering Inner Mongolia, west to Guizhou and the border of the Yunnan Plateau, and south to the Gulf of Tonkin. The seat of the Qin was Xian (Xianyang), the most splendid Chinese city of its time, which was located in North China's current Shaanxi Province on the Wei River. Whichever site one determines to be the cradle of the Chinese state, it is clear that the locus is interior North China near the Huang He and on its tributaries. The continental perspective and inward-turning nature of Chinese civilization may, in great measure, be attributed to the sense of nationhood that evolved from this region.

Capitals

While China has had a number of different capitals, for most of its history they have been located in the North, reflecting the country's continental orientation and concerns. The wide Wei River valley provided capitals for several early dynasties subsequent to the Qin. They were attracted to the valley by its well-watered, fertile, alluvial soils, which supported the cultivation of grain and fruit. The capital of the Zhou (1027–256 BCE), the dynasty that preceded the Qin, was at Chang'an, one of several sites adjoining the modern city of Xian. Chang'an was also the seat of the Han dynasty (202 BCE–220 CE), which followed the Qin and made Confucianism the basis for the bureaucratic state. The city was also the political center for the Tang dynasty (618–906 CE), which introduced the system of civil service exams and brought Confucian culture to a highly developed form. These various capitals sited near Xian were on the major east-west grassy gateway route from the steppes of Mongolia and Turkestan (Xinjiang) to the North China Plain, approximately one hundred miles upstream on the Wei from its junction with the Huang He.

Figure 9.2. East Asia: Major Geopolitical Features

Kaifeng, which lay farther to the east on the Huang He, served as the capital of the Five Dynasties and then the Northern Sung dynasty (906 to 1127 CE). This location commanded the heart of the Yangtze Plain. When the Sung were overthrown and their court fled southward, they established their capital at Hangzhou (Hangchow) on the East China Sea, near the mouth of the Yangtze—the first capital to be located outside the northern interior. The purpose of this move was to remove the seat of government from the Mongol incursions from inner Asia.

Beijing (Chinese for "northern capital") had once been the capital of the Tsin dynasty (265–420 CE) and served as the seat of power for warlords until its capture in 1215 by the Mongol Genghis Khan. The eastward migration of capitals within North China came to an end with this Mongol seizure of power. Kublai Khan (1260–90 CE) constructed Cambuluc, the nucleus of today's Beijing. The Mongol capital was transferred in 1267 from Karakoram in central Mongolia to the Beijing site, which was renamed Khanbaliq. The site lay at the northern edge of the North China Plain and was the gateway to both Mongolia and northeast China. From their new capital, the Mongols gained control over one-third of the then-known world—the largest land empire in history to date.

The Ming dynasty, which overthrew the Mongols in 1368 and unified all of China, had its power base and capital in Nanjing near the Yangtze delta but moved it to Beijing in 1421. The Ming centerpiece, the Forbidden City, remains the largest palace complex in the world. When the Manchus swept into China from the north to establish their dynasty in the seventeenth century, they retained Beijing as their capital.

The city had unique strategic advantages that made it an ideal forward-based capital. Fifty miles to its northwest lay the northern end of Nankou Pass, the chief gateway from Mongolia, which provided a secure route for communication lines from Central Asia. Less than two hundred miles to the east, the Great Wall ended at the sea, and this point served the Manchus as their secure gateway to Manchuria. Another advantage was the absence of physical barriers between Beijing and the rest of North China and the Yangtze delta region of Central China, where Nanjing, the historic "southern capital," is located. After the mid-nineteenth century, Shanghai became connected to North China by a combination of the Grand Canal and riverways. This water route ran northward, crossing the Huang He, and then on to Tianjin, and from there it continued to Beijing or to the sea. Shanghai was also connected to the west via the Yangtze.

The periods during which the capital shifted to the coastal reaches of Central China reflect the pull of maritimity, but they were brief. Nanjing had served as the capital of China from the third to the sixth centuries, as well as being the seat of the Ming from 1368 to 1421. When Sun Yat-sen's revolutionary forces took power in 1912, the city served as Sun's first capital. During the next decade and a half of turmoil, Guangzhou, Beijing, and Hankou also alternated as the country's political centers.

In 1928, Chiang Kai-shek reestablished Nanjing as China's capital, moving it a decade later, after the Japanese conquest, to Chongqing. In 1949 the Republic of China fell to the Communists, who returned the capital to Beijing, where it has remained. So once again, the political center is in the North. While economic modernization and expansion takes place in the coastal provinces of South and Central China, Beijing has not been left behind, as the government has invested heavily in modernizing the city. The blending of the continental and maritime outlooks as reflected in these dual power centers presents China with both pitfalls and opportunities.

Ecumene

The ecumene of China currently stretches from the coastal sectors of the South, a few miles from the Vietnam border, through Guangdong, Hong Kong, and Fujian to Shanghai and the lower Yangtze valley and the great Yangtze delta on the central coast. From there, it extends in two directions—westward, upstream to the middle Yangtze basin, and northward, through Beijing and the North China Plain into Shenyang and southern Manchuria. The total area of this vast Chinese economic and population core region is 580,000 square miles, an area with a population of over seven hundred million.

The Pearl River delta region, propelled by the economic dynamism of its Hong Kong core and Guangzhou's manufactures, accounts for 40 percent of China's exports and 10 percent of total economic output. The official population of the region is estimated at forty-five million. The role of Hong Kong as the center for financial services and magnet for multinational firms and investors has been the major stimulus for the growth and expansion of the ecumene. The legacy of British control, including widespread use of English, a Western-based legal system, and international standards of corporate governance, have made it particularly attractive.[10] In addition to the half-million mainlanders who have taken up residency in the past decade, Hong Kong has attracted an equal number of day workers who cross the border from Guangdong, as well as shoppers and tourists who make their stamp on the city's economic and cultural landscape.

The westward spread of the ecumene extends beyond the middle Yangtze basin's Wuhan urban conurbation and rich, lake-studded agricultural areas until it is blocked by the gorges of the Yangtze. These begin just beyond Yichang, which is the head of navigation of the river, one thousand miles from the sea. It is along this stretch of the river, extending for nearly 120 miles, that construction of the first phase of the Three Gorges (Yangtze) dams and reservoir system, initiated in 1993, was completed in 2006. This mammoth hydroelectric-power, flood-control, navigation, irrigation, and industrial and agricultural land-use project created a lake that displaced nearly one and a half million people and inundated countless historic sites.

Environmentalists have been highly critical of this and other hydro projects, arguing that in addition to the destruction, mudslides, and displacement, China has little need for the capacity that will be added to the country's electricity supply. Nevertheless, construction of twelve smaller dams upstream of the Three Gorges along the Yangtze and its tributaries continues, as China seeks to increase its hydro and nuclear capacities to a goal of 15 percent of total demand by 2020. The counterargument is that the new hydropower will enable the government to retire many coal-burning plants. China now depends on fossil fuels, mostly domestic coal, for 80 percent of its energy. Use of petroleum has also risen rapidly. China now imports nearly five million barrels per day, or more than the 4.5 million barrels per day that are produced domestically. As a result of its dependence on fossil fuels, it has become one of the most highly polluted countries in the world, and air pollution in the big cities is a major health hazard.

With the completion of the Three Gorges project in 2002 and the shifting of another four million people to greater Chongqing,[11] a new ecumene may emerge, embracing the region of Chongqing and northwestward into the Red River basin of Sichuan Province, now a part of the effective national territory. Promoting itself as "China's Chicago," Chongqing is both a city of 4.5 million and a region that has provincial-level status. The region of over forty-five million embraces thousands of towns and villages strung along the Yangtze, the majority of which are rural. The city itself has a population of over four million. With massive governmental investment, Chongqing has developed into a major manufacturing center, attracting farm migrants who retain a rural/urban citizenship status because they do not wish to lose title to their land. Ambitious government plans are to urbanize much of the province. With coal, iron, and oil fields nearby, the city has attracted a large motor vehicle industry, steel industry, oil refineries, and chemical plants. Chongqing is connected by highway and rail to

Chengdu, Sichwan's capital, which is the center for a metropolitan area of over eight million and is in the heart of the main farming area of the province. Chengdu is one of China's ten high-tech free-trade zones. It specializes in electronic information, biochemistry, and precision manufacturing. Such zones are spread throughout the ecumene and the ENT. The largest of them, the Shanghai Free-Trade Zone, focuses on banking, telecommunications, foreign investment services, and travel, as does the Shenzhen Special Economic Zone, which is located near Hong Kong.

Another project that has drawn criticism from environmentalists is located far from the ecumene, in the province of Yunnan in southwest China. There, on the Upper Mekong (Lancang) River, a large hydroelectric power scheme is under way, the second of eight dams having been completed at the end of 2003. A third dam was completed in 2012, and a fourth is under construction. The electricity generated by these dams is scheduled to serve the development needs of Kunming, the capital of Yunnan and the rest of the province. While the project will reduce flooding in the Lower Mekong, it will also threaten Cambodia's fisheries and will reduce the flow of silt to Laos.

North of the Yangtze, the ecumene includes the rest of the lower Yangtze Plain province of Jiangsu and those parts of the province of Anhui that are traversed by the Huai River as it winds its way to the delta. Still farther to the north, the population and economic core grades into the North China Plain, embracing the lower Huang He valley and delta provinces of Henan and Shandong. It then continues northward through the Huang He Plain and Hebei Province to Beijing, Tianjin, and the Gulf of Bohai. From there, it reaches into Liaoning Province of southern Manchuria, focusing on the Shenyang-Fushun-Anshan industrial conurbation.

About half of China's 1.35 billion people live in the ecumene, on a land base that is only about 15 percent of the country's total land area of 3,690,000 square miles. In many places, the densities substantially exceed the average of thirteen hundred per square mile of the economic and population core, not only in its urban portions but also within the highly fertile coastal and interior plains and villages, where thousands of rural villages have attracted the majority of China's farm families. This rural population still accounts for the majority of the ecumene's population.

To slow its rate of population growth, in 1979 China instituted a one-child policy. This has succeeded, but its consequences were not anticipated. Because of the preference for boys over girls, by 2012 there were forty million more men than women, and the Chinese government changed course. It has instituted a new policy whereby a married couple in which one parent is an only child can now have two children. This is expected to encourage fifteen to twenty million couples to expand their families, stem the plummeting birthrates, and correct the gender imbalance. It is also directed at addressing the current crisis wherein an aging population needs more children to care for the elderly. It is not clear whether or not many couples will take advantage of the permission to have more than one child because of the high cost of living, especially housing and education.

As China has promoted a market economy, income distribution within the economic core, as well as between it and other parts of the country, has become increasingly uneven. Per capita income is highest in Guangdong and Zhejiang Provinces and, especially, in such urban centers as Shanghai, Beijing, and Tianjin. The average per capita incomes of Hong Kong and Macau rival those of the most advanced nations and are over five times that of China as a whole.

Economic disparities within the ecumene are considerable, not only between its rural and urban areas but also within and among its urban centers. Many of the estimated one hundred million farmers displaced by the disbanding of the agricultural collectives have moved to the cities from the rural sectors of the ecumene, such as Anhui, Henan, Guangdong, and Shandong. Classified as temporary workers who lack permanent residence certificates, under a household registration system known as "Hukou," they are legally banned from most employment save garbage collection, the building trades, sidewalk vending, household work, or unskilled factory jobs. Living in sprawling shantytowns or illegally built rented rooms, they suffer from poverty and discrimination, have no health care, and lack access to education for their children. Even those children born in the city inherit this second-class status. Yet most are not likely to return to the countryside, where higher-paying jobs are unavailable. This group represents a permanent floating population that could continue to grow with rural overpopulation, agricultural modernization, and China's increasing openness to foreign food imports as the government seeks to open the economy to more foreign trade.

A recent factor that may slow down this flow of immigrants, and in some cases even reverse it, is that the Chinese factory economy is shifting from low-wage, unskilled labor to higher-value products using automation. Just as the temporary workers represent a potential source of urban unrest and political instability, so do the workers in those parts of the ecumene and areas outside of it in the interior, the North, and the Northeast that have become rust belts or are likely to be otherwise affected by the shrinking of state enterprises. Unemployment is widespread in southern Manchuria, the northeastern end of the ecumene, where so many of China's heavy industries were located to take advantage of the rich coal, iron-ore, and petroleum deposits of the province. The industries include massive iron and steel works; aluminum and paper plants; machinery, tractor, locomotive, and aircraft factories; and chemical and petroleum complexes. With these industries now antiquated and inefficient, as much as one-fifth of their labor force has been cut back, as the state-run enterprises have modernized, some owing to privatization. The same fate awaits other large national industries both within and outside of the ecumene, such as the state-owned motor vehicles plants of North China and Sichuan or the big steel and aluminum plants of Shandong.

Beijing, the nation's second-largest city, with a population of nearly twelve million and a metropolis of over eighteen million, also has massive industrial complexes that manufacture steel, chemicals, plastics, machinery, and electronic equipment, many of which have become outdated. Their cutback began as early as the 1970s and 1980s because of concerns over pollution. In recent years, industry has been modernized. The government has dedicated massive resources to making the capital a showpiece of China's economic power. It made special efforts to reduce air pollution in anticipation of the 2008 summer Olympics, but the problems remain because of the heavy dependence of industry upon coal. China accounts for nearly half of the world's coal consumption, causing much of the North to be enveloped with brown and gray soot. The air quality of Beijing is particularly low and dangerous to the health of its citizens. Efforts to combat this pollution include temporary closings of factories, ordering vehicles off the road, and planting trees. These palliatives have had minimal effects, and the region will continue to suffer the pollution until China is able to shake off its dependence on soft coal.

In the interior and those parts of North China that are not part of the ecumene, the state still controls 60 to 80 percent of industrial output, much of it built along the Soviet Communist model. This sector now has to compete with more efficient industries within the ecumene that have been established or modernized by foreign-financed and Chinese entrepreneurial initiatives. These new industries are the basis for China's "Golden Coast"—the locus of the export-driven economy where per capita incomes are five to ten times higher than in the interior.

In provinces such as Guangdong and Fujian, where foreign investments are heaviest, the import of modern industrialization has been most striking. China's version of Silicon Valley, located around Shenzhen, produces a wide array of telecommunications, medical technology, engineering, electronics, and computer hardware and software. In nearby villages and towns, hundreds of small factories produce consumer goods that include toys, lighting fixtures, footwear, apparel, and textiles. This part of the coastal South began to benefit from the shift of Hong Kong's factories and the diffusion of its technological know-how to Guangdong, even before the Crown colony reverted to China in 1997. The process has since accelerated so that much of what is today labeled as "made in Hong Kong" is actually produced outside its borders. The prosperity of Hong Kong, now that it is no longer an important manufacturing center, is based primarily upon its role as the country's premier business and financial center and its container cargo port. The city's financial and commercial power is a major element in the continued industrial growth of the South, while its port, the largest of its kind in the world, now handles nearly half of all China's exports but has lost some of its transfer trade to Chinese ports that benefit from direct importing since China has entered the WTO. Although Taiwan has also joined the WTO, most of its exports to China continue to be transshipped through Hong Kong. The overwhelming financial and commercial weight of Hong Kong, along with its advanced technology, enables it to retain its role as the leading force in the continuing economic growth of China's South.

Northward along the coast, development of manufacturing in Fujian Province, whose coast is 100 to 150 miles from Taiwan, is in great measure owed to Taiwanese capital investment and trade. Most of Taiwan's twenty-four million inhabitants are descendants of Chinese who immigrated from the southern and central coastlands in the eighteenth and nineteenth centuries and speak the Fujianese or Hakka dialects common to Fujian, Guangdong, and Jiangsu. The vast majority of the island's population is concentrated along Taiwan's broad west coastal plain, which faces China and is backed by the heavily forested hills and mountains of the central and eastern parts of the island.

This dense concentration of agricultural and manufacturing activities, as well as its crowded urban centers (Taiwan is over 70 percent urban), constitute Taiwan's ecumene, which functionally is rapidly becoming part of the Chinese mainland ecumene. When and if China and Taiwan enter into some kind of reunification agreement, the two ecumenes will also be fully merged.

Still farther northward, along the coast in Zhejiang Province, the city of Wenzhou has developed as a major center for Chinese private enterprise, producing a variety of items from buttons to electronics. The prosperity of Shanghai, China's largest city and industrial center, with a population of over eighteen million and a total urbanized populace of twenty-two million, depends more and more on its light industry, such as electronics, computer software, and publishing, and major plants developed by such foreign auto firms as Volkswagen and General Motors in partnership with Chinese companies. This growth has benefited from the designation of Shanghai as a free-trade zone. In addition, the city retains its traditional base of large steel, textile, shipbuilding, machinery, and chemical production and oil refining, with a major seaport, including deepwater container facilities, and serves as the country's largest financial and commercial center. A new world-class "Silicon Valley," focusing on information hardware, is developing along a sixty-mile corridor extending westward from Shanghai to Suzhou. It is powered by capital investment and large-scale manufacturing outsourcing from Taiwan, as well as by the engineering and management talents of émigrés who have returned on a temporary or full-time basis.

The economic strength of China's "Golden Coast" was the basis for the country's 8 percent average annual increase in GDP during the 1980s and 1990s and since then has averaged 10 percent. However, this very prosperity contains the seeds of political instability because of the widening gaps between various groups—between the employed and the unemployed; between temporary migrants from the rural areas and the city dwellers with permanent jobs and housing; in terms of wage disparity between high-tech employees and those in the traditional consumer industries; and in terms of living and working conditions.

As previously noted, environmental pollution is another major problem created by the intensification of economic activities within the Chinese ecumene. China is the world's largest producer and user of coal and the world's leading producer of raw steel, which greatly contributes to widespread air and water pollution. Industrial and consumer electricity consumption is now met essentially by soft-coal generating plants, which have increased the amount of acid rain that affects the ecumene's farms, water supply, and urban populace. The rapid increase in motor vehicles as a result of economic prosperity that has made the country the world's leading producer and the construction of thousands of miles of modern highway has also contributed substantially to rising pollution levels, especially in the big cities.

While China is one of the world's major oil producers, imports are required to fill half the country's total needs, which continue to increase. The percentage of petroleum imported from Africa, now one-third of total imports, can be expected to increase in the future, as the various Chinese national oil companies have invested heavily in oil-development projects outside the subcontinent. The major sources for its imports are the Middle East, Sub-Saharan Africa, and Russia. This has resulted in China's becoming more involved in the oil politics of these regions. One example is Beijing's joining Moscow in seeking to negotiate between the West and Iran over the latter's nuclear-weapons-making capacity, since China wants oil and gas from both Iran and Russia. Another has been Beijing's reluctance to apply diplomatic pressure on Sudan in the Darfur conflict and its loans and heavy investments in Angola. So great are its demands for energy that China has overtaken the United States as the world's largest energy consumer and producer (and air polluter).

Oil adds another strategic dimension to Beijing's concerns over the separatist movement in the far western frontier province of Xinjiang, led by the Muslim Turkic Uighurs, who form the province's majority. Critical to China's economy are the vast oil fields of Karamay, near the borders of Kazakhstan, Russia, and Mongolia, and the oil and natural gas reserves of southwestern Xinjiang's Tarim Basin Desert. The need for oil also partly accounts for China's claims to the Spratlys and Paracels. Tensions with Japan over the East China Sea boundary have been sparked by China's growing appetite for natural gas and oil.

In 2014, China became involved in a serious dispute with Vietnam, placing a deep-sea-drilling oil rig (which it later withdrew) in the Paracels, 130 miles off the coast of Vietnam and within the latter's continental shelf. The two countries used fleets of navy and civilian vessels to ram one another, Chinese ships chasing Vietnamese vessels away with water cannons. The Vietnamese are in no position to challenge Beijing's military might. None of their purported allies is willing to risk its own relationship with the Chinese juggernaut.

During a meeting of the ten-country Association of Southeast Asian Nations (ASEAN), Prime Minister Nguyễn Tấn Dũng made a spirited speech asking for support in the dispute. There was no response. They also looked in vain to the United States for leadership in backing Vietnam in what they regard as a violation of their territorial waters. The United States has expressed dismay but is not prepared to disrupt its own relationship with China.

Effective National Territory (ENT)

The areas embraced by China's ENT include the interior provinces that extend from Guanxi and Hainan in the southeast to Guizhou and eastern Yunnan in the southwest. The ENT then stretches northward to the Sichuan (Red) basin in eastern Sichuan Province to Shaanxi's Wei River valley and to the fertile but dry loesslands of the northern part of Sichuan Province, where it is bracketed by eastern Gansu to the west and Shaanxi to the east. Its northern reaches include a narrow fringe of southwestern Inner Mongolia south of the Great Wall (Ningxia Province). The fringe extends eastward along the dry, grassy tablelands that border the wall until it broadens into the grasslands of central and northern Manchuria.

While these regions form a semicircle around the ecumene, their development has for the most part been hampered by topographic barriers, long distances, and poor communication lines with the core. This stands in marked contrast to the ENTs of Russia and the United States, which directly adjoin their ecumenes without intervening physical barriers or lengthy distances. As a consequence, the population and economic cores of these two major powers have been able to expand into the easily developable parts of their countries and thus more easily serve as safety valves for natural growth or as areas of absorption for new immigrant populations.

By contrast, the area that constitutes China's ENT is already heavily settled, crowded along river valleys such as the middle Yangtze and the middle Huang He. Approximately 1.2 million square miles contain a population of 450 million and have an overall density of 430 persons per square mile. Much of the region suitable for farming has long become overpopulated because arable land with available water is so limited. The carrying capacity of the grasslands for pastoralism is also overtaxed, and the urban centers are burdened with inefficient industries.

Government policies are to urbanize and industrialize as much of the ENT as possible, with the hope of raising living standards in the rural interior and stemming the waves of migrants streaming into the ecumene. Supporting this effort is construction of a national high-speed bullet train system that enables owners and managers to build factories in the ENT which they can reach easily from their homes in the ecumene. The rapid growth of domestic airlines, focusing on routes from three hundred to nearly five hundred miles, also supports such access. Conversely, the bullet trains enable workers in the ecumene to return periodically to their distant homes in the ENT, and the world's most ambitious subway system has created thriving suburban districts within the ecumene, which house some of these immigrant workers. This effort to industrialize the ENT has far greater prospects for success than the previous one of the 1960s and 1970s, when Mao moved much of China's heavy and military industry from the strategically vulnerable coast and the Northeast deep into the interior. Fear of nuclear attack from either the United States or the Soviet Union motivated the Communist government to establish a "third line" region of defense in the canyons and caves of Sichuan, Guizhou, Yunnan, and Gansu. This third line was so named to differentiate the region from the "first line" defense region along the coast and the "second line" of the middle Yangtze basin.

During the Cultural Revolution of those two decades, Mao sought to eliminate the educated classes and moved many small factories into the countryside, and the move to the interior took on a revolutionary ideological rationale. Nearly half of the available national investment was spent on relocating hundreds of key industries into these remote provinces. Nuclear weapons and ammunition plants, military research laboratories, steel mills, and truck assembly plants were moved over new highways and railroads, while power plants were constructed to provide industry with the necessary power. History proved the "third line" a colossal waste of manpower and money.

In the past three decades, many of these remote plants have been closed or moved to the valley areas around such interior centers as Chongqing and Chengdu in Sichuan, Guiyang in

Guizhou, Kunming in Yunnan, and Xian in Shaanxi's Wei River valley. For the most part, these were large, state-run factories that produced steel, machinery, chemicals, textiles, aluminum, and motor vehicles. Plagued by antiquated equipment, bureaucratic management, lengthy distance to market, and lack of foreign investment to modernize, most continued to survive only through state subsidies. They are in the process of being privatized, with the aim of attracting foreign investment. New industries, such as electronics and telecommunications equipment, motorcycles, television equipment, and financial services, are thriving, but their employment base is not yet wide enough to absorb workers from factory closures or shrinkage in the older, basic industries. As a result, the provinces of the interior remain among the poorest in China. While Beijing has initiated a "go west" campaign to attract young Chinese to the ENT and the country's empty area beyond, there is little evidence that such a campaign is likely to attract enough settlers to create viable communities.[12]

Empty Area

The empty area of China is vast—nearly two million square miles covering 80 percent of the entire country and with a population of forty million. The provinces included within the area are Tibet (Xizang), Xinjiang, Qinghai, western Sichuan, western Gansu, northern Shaanxi, and most of Inner Mongolia. These are mainly desert or barren highland areas. The overall population density of the empty area, twenty persons per square mile, masks its uneven distribution. For the most part, the densities are two persons per square mile or less. However, a considerable proportion of the population is concentrated in urban oasis centers, especially on the rim of the desert of Xinjiang's Tarim Basin, in the western half of the province and on the steppes and semidesert lands of the Dzungarian (Junggar) Basin in the northern part of the province.

The relative geographical location of China's empty area is quite different from those of the United States and Russia. The empty area of the continental United States is bordered on the east by the country's ENT and on the west by the Pacific coast ecumene. Only to its south and along the Rockies to its north does it adjoin the foreign countries of Mexico and Canada. The separate empty area of Alaska borders Canada and Russia. Russia's empty area is also quite isolated from these neighboring countries. With the exception of the lands that adjoin the Bering Strait across from Alaska, the region lies to the north and northeast of Russia's ecumene and ENT, extending to the Arctic.

In contrast, the Chinese empty area adjoins eleven different countries, which provides the heavily populated core regions of the country with a deep, protective, strategic spatial screen against a hostile military land invasion. It also offers Beijing advanced forward bases from which to threaten its neighbors.

This strategic advantage, however, is offset by two factors. Much of the empty area is populated by minority, non-Han people—Tibetans, Tibeto-Burmans, Turkics, and Mongols. Some of these minorities have long sought to break away from the rule of Beijing. In addition, China faces the strategic liability of having its main population centers far removed from the outer edges of its empty area, while the centers of South Asia, Central Asia, and Russia are closer to this Chinese region.

The geopolitical consequence of these factors is that political separation sentiment finds support from contact with adjoining countries. Tibet (Xizang) was made a nominally national autonomous region under the control of the Dalai Lama, according to a 1951 agreement. Today it is in reality ruled by a Chinese Communist Commission. Land reforms and the sharp curtailing of the powers of the monasteries led to full-scale revolt in 1959.

The Tibetans were ruthlessly suppressed, and the Dalai Lama fled to India. It is estimated that a million Tibetans were killed and thousands of monasteries were burned during the years that followed. Establishing his government-in-exile at Dharamsala at the base of the Himalayas in northern India, the Tibetan leader still commands the allegiance of most of the 2.5 million Tibetans as he continues to try to mobilize worldwide support to regain autonomy for a "Greater Tibet" that would include the Tibet Autonomous Region and Tibetan parts of neighboring provinces. While China's crackdowns on protesters in 2008 and again in 2011 and 2012 are not to be compared with the 1959 revolt, the worldwide response to the repression brought home to Beijing the need to engage in dialogue with the Dalai Lama lest its trade ties be harmed. The Dalai Lama seeks a level of freedom within which the Buddhist religion and Tibetan language, tradition, and culture can be sustained, making it clear that the goal is cultural autonomy, not independence. The issue is urgent for the Tibetans because government-supported migration of Han people into eastern Tibet and Lhasa will soon make the Tibetans a minority within their own homeland. The Han migrants already number over two and a half million and continue to increase.

In Xinjiang, the Turkic-speaking Uighur tribesmen have waged a half-century struggle for independence since 1950. The Chinese had crushed the sovereign state of East Turkestan, which the Muslim Uighurs had managed to establish in 1944 during the wartime chaos that engulfed China. The creation of the independent Muslim states of Central Asia following the breakup of the Soviet Union gave new hope to the seven million Uighurs. In addition, rising Islamic fundamentalism among these Muslim tribesmen has been fanned by the growing influence of the fundamentalists of neighboring Pakistan and Afghanistan (which has a twenty-mile border with Xinjiang) and by the strength of the fundamentalist rebels who have been seeking to overthrow the government of adjoining Tajikistan. However, the major force behind Uighur separatism is the nationalism that grows out of language, culture, history, and ties to the land, as well as the desire to control the province's newly found oil reserves. Terrorist attacks continue to plague China's control of the region. To link the Autonomous Region of Xinjiang more closely to China, Beijing has sponsored the move of Chinese to Xinjiang on a very large scale. Han migrants now represent over 40 percent of the population and threaten to overtake in numbers the Uighur tribesmen and other smaller minorities, such as Kazakhs, Mongols, Hui, and Kirghizi. Many of these new settlers have been organized in paramilitary fashion within a string of agricultural colonies along the border.

Transportation lines are being constructed or improved to bind the empty area to eastern China. They include the rebuilding of the Beijing to Lhasa highway and the construction of a 680-mile railroad from Golmud in Qinghai Province to Lhasa, Tibet. From Golmud, the line connects to the railway in Xining, and from there to the main Chinese high-speed rail system. Most of the railroad in Tibet is more than thirteen thousand feet above sea level. It must cross a pass in the province that is over sixteen thousand feet in elevation, making it the highest railroad in the world. Economic justification for the project was that it would permit the development of Tibet's oil and gold resources as well as greatly increase the export of meat to the rest of China.

In northern Xinjiang, the Karamay oil fields near the border with Kazakhstan are connected to the provincial capital and oil refining center of Urumqi. In southern Xinjiang, where Chinese presence has been slight, a highway has been built across the Taklamakan Desert to spur the development of oil fields. A one-thousand-mile railroad was completed along the northern edge of the desert to connect Urumqi with the southwestern oasis town of Kashi (Kashgar), a bastion of Uighur culture near the border with Kyrgyzstan and Tajikistan. Kashi, in turn, is connected to Rawalpindi in Pakistan by the eight-hundred-mile

Karakoram Highway (the Great Pakistan-China Friendship Highway). A natural gas pipeline from the Tarim Basin to Shanghai is also planned. These developments serve the dual purpose of exploiting the empty area's riches and stimulating the settlement of Han peoples to offset the separatist drives of restive minorities.

Despite the efforts of China, the drives for independence in both provinces remain active. In the long run, a workable solution in both Tibet and Xinjiang might be a high degree of autonomy and guarantees of noninterference in the political, religious, and economic affairs of these regions, but with the treaty arrangements that provide for Beijing to maintain defense forces there and conduct foreign affairs.

The empty area is of importance to China in other ways. The Dzungarian Basin of northern Xinjiang contains coal, iron, tin, gold, silver, and uranium, as well as the vast oil fields already noted. These have been the basis for the industrialization of the region. In Urumqi, Xinjiang's main manufacturing and service center, the developments have included steelworks, oil refineries, machinery, chemicals, and motor vehicle plants. Another industrial center, Yumen in northwestern Gansu, is China's oldest and still one of its leading oil centers, based on rich oil deposits to its northwest. The area's minerals also support light, nonferrous metal smelting works. In addition, as previously mentioned, extensive deposits of oil and natural gas lie beneath the Tarim Basin Desert of Xinjiang.

Still another strategic value of the empty area lies in the sites that it provides for space launchings and nuclear testing. Jiuquan, in northern Gansu east of Yumen, and Xichang, in southwest Sichuan south of Kangding, are China's main space satellite launch centers. Secret sites until the 1990s, they have since been opened to foreign tourists. Another launch site is near Taiyuan in northern Shaanxi. The country's nuclear test sites are also located deep within the interior—in central Xinjiang within the Tarim Desert, near the town of Yuli in eastern Tibet, and in Inner Mongolia.

China has signed the Nuclear Non-Proliferation Pact and the Comprehensive Test Ban Treaty (CTBT). Moreover, as one of the five major nuclear powers, it has joined with the others in agreeing to the eventual elimination of all nuclear weapons. However, Beijing signed the CTBT only grudgingly, and it continues to seek an amendment that will permit nuclear testing for peaceful purposes. In the light of this policy objective, the nuclear test sites of the empty area may well not have outlived their usefulness. Certainly the importance of the space launch sites for commercial satellites will continue to grow as the demand for telecommunications increases.

Boundaries

The concerns of China over its international boundaries have brought it into conflict with India and the FSU over land borders and with several countries over the Spratly and Paracel Islands in the South China Sea. Most recently, friction with Japan has arisen over the sovereignty of the Japanese-held Senkaku (Diaoyu) Islands in the East China Sea (Sea of Japan).

Disputes over the forty-five-hundred-mile Sino-Soviet border led to conflict between China and the Soviet Union in 1969. Serious fighting broke out over control of Damansky Island in the Ussuri River north of Vladivostok, while conflict also erupted over the border between Xinjiang and the USSR in Kazakhstan.

Since the Soviet divestiture of Kazakhstan and Kyrgyzstan, the Sino-Russian boundary has been reduced to twenty-three hundred miles in length. With the improvement in recent years of relations between Russia and China, tension over this boundary has eased, and there have been substantial troop reductions all along the border. The line that demarcates the once-disputed islands at the confluence of the Amur and Ussuri Rivers and in the Argun River was settled in 2004. The border between China's Xinjiang Province and Tajikistan remains to be settled but is not a cause for tension.

The most serious of the boundary controversies have been with India.[13] These have led to two wars and, until 1999, the closing of border trade between the two countries. At that time the two nations also agreed to partial demilitarization of their borders. The first conflict broke out in 1959 over the Longju incident, when the Chinese seized control of a small garrison in India's North-East Frontier Agency (Arunachal Pradesh) at the southeastern edge of the Tibetan Plateau, which they continue to occupy.

The second and more major war erupted in 1962, not only over this eastern Himalayan border but also over the western end. There the Chinese territorial claim embraced the Ladakh region of northernmost India, in Jammu and Kashmir state, and northeasternmost Pakistan. Ladakh is sometimes referred to as "Little Tibet" or the "India Tibet" and is ethnically and geographically allied with Tibet. Its population is predominantly Lamaist Buddhist. The region was a dependency of Tibet until annexed by Britain and attached to Kashmir in the nineteenth century. It was divided between India and Pakistan during the partition of India. There had been some skirmishing over the region in 1959, and the 1962 full-scale war broke out over the strategic Karakoram Highway that the Chinese had built across the barren and uninhabited Aksai Chin high plain in northern Ladakh to connect western Tibet with Xinjiang. For China, this was a war over regional security. For India, Chinese control of the territory meant the strategic exposure of the northern Indian plain to Chinese forces via passes cutting through and around the Karakoram range. The area is also the transit way for China to the Pakistani-held sector of Kashmir and northern Pakistan.

China's victory in the 1962 war has left its troops in control of 5,985 square miles, or over 40 percent, of Ladakh. To complicate the situation, a Sino-Pakistani protocol of 1987 recognized the boundary as terminating at the Karakoram Pass, thus accepting Chinese sovereignty over three thousand square miles of the disputed area. In addition, Chinese troops continue to occupy the area west of Aksai Chin and two small pockets on the southwest Tibet border that were at issue in the 1959 conflict. In 2005, the two countries agreed to defuse tension over Aksai Chin and the parts of northern Kashmir that Pakistan had ceded to China in 1964.

During the 1962 war, China also launched an offensive that overran India's North-East Frontier Agency (Arunachal Pradesh). After a cease-fire, it withdrew its troops to a line of control that approximated the border between India and Tibet, known as the McMahon Line, that had been established by Britain in 1914. However, Beijing continues to maintain its claim to the region. Chinese and Indian troops clashed once again in Arunachal in 1986–87. A decade later, the two countries agreed to a no-fly zone and partial demilitarization over the line of control, but this did not prevent subsequent Chinese incursions in Arunachal and in the southwestern Tibet area bordering India's Uttar Pradesh.

Still another focus of contention in the Himalayan region has to do with Sikkim. India absorbed the mountain kingdom in 1975, but Beijing continues to insist upon the independence of this Buddhist land, which was ruled by Tibet for two centuries and in the nineteenth century came under nominal Chinese suzerainty. In addition, the boundary between northwestern Bhutan and Tibet remains to be demarcated.

Two other boundaries are in dispute between China and its land neighbors. One is over the sovereignty of the islands in the Yalu and Tumen Rivers that form the boundary between China and North Korea. Another revolves around sections of the land border with Vietnam, where the line is indefinite. There, clashes over disputed areas broke out as early as 1974, and in 1979 they culminated in China's invasion across the seven-hundred-mile frontier. This was a counterinvasion to that mounted by Vietnam against the Cambodian Khmer Rouge regime of Pol Pot, which resulted in his ouster in favor of a Vietnamese-supported government.[14]

China is involved also in a number of maritime boundary conflicts. The dispute between China and Vietnam in the Gulf of Tonkin stemmed from Vietnamese fears that China intends to control the "East" (South China) Sea and thus the Indochinese peninsula, as a springboard to the rest of Southeast Asia. The issue was resolved by two agreements—one an accord over the Vietnam-China land boundary in 1999 and the second an agreement in 2000 to the demarcation of territorial waters and fishing rights in Beipu Bay.

Elsewhere, China's territorial claims to South China Sea waters off the shoals of Sarawak and Indonesia's Natuna Islands have increased the tensions in that region. Both of these areas are rich in natural gas, and Beijing has announced its rights to award exploration concessions there. The Natuna offshore gas field, one of the largest in the world, is a particularly tempting prize. The island lies 130 miles off the northern tip of the Indonesian province of Kalimantan, but the field extends northeast of Natuna, within waters that lie in part within two hundred miles of the Spratlys, which are claimed by China, Vietnam, Taiwan, Malaysia, and the Philippines. These islands have considerable offshore oil potential. In 2005, they were the subject of a joint accord on oil exploration by China, Vietnam, and the Philippines, and both China and Vietnam have expanded construction facilities there.

Beijing's claim to the uninhabited Senkaku Islands, off the coast of southwestern Japan, is on the basis that they once belonged to China's Fujian Province before being captured by Japan in 1895. The Chinese argued unsuccessfully for the return of these islands after the defeat of Japan in 1945. Japan contends that these tiny islands are part of the Sakishima group, which are located at the southern end of the Ryukyus and are part of Japan's Okinawa Prefecture. Thus far China supported these claims with only an occasional coast guard and fishing boat presence. This could change as its navy acquires a greater long-range capacity. To complicate matters, Taiwan also has a claim to these islands.

Another important maritime conflict involves ownership of the Paracel Islands, located far off China's mainland coast in the South China Sea. Some of the Paracels, which are also claimed by Taiwan and Vietnam, have been occupied by China. As noted, China's 2014 oil-drilling activities resulted in open conflict between Chinese and Vietnamese vessels. This issue, as well as the boundary between China and Japan in the East China Sea, will be discussed in the chapter that deals with the Asia-Pacific Rim. As previously discussed, the Chinese declaration of an air defense identification zone covering much of the East and South China Seas has prompted the United States to seek to mediate the dispute and keep the waters open to all shipping destined for its Asia-Pacific Rim allies and China.

The above-mentioned boundary issues, as well as the overriding goals of China to re-establish control over Taiwan, must be kept in mind as Washington pursues its hopes for a strategic alliance with China. Beijing is quite capable of separating its economic policies from its geostrategic aims, and the assumption that the latter will be abandoned as the price for expanded international trade is probably wishful thinking.

The East Asia Rim Periphery

The waters that border mainland China are partially enclosed to their east by a peninsular-insular rim. This rim is formed by the Korean Peninsula, Taiwan, the Philippines, and the Indochinese peninsula. Since South Korea and the Philippines are parts of the Asia-Pacific

Rim geopolitical region and thus under the military shield of the United States, the focus of China's strategic aims are, at least for the present, North Korea; the Indochinese peninsular states of Vietnam, Laos, and Cambodia; and Taiwan.

For much of the past half-century, the Soviet Union acted either in partnership or as a competitor with China in support of North Korea and the Indochinese countries in their wars against the United States and France. While Russia's influence has waned, it is by no means negligible. In North Korea it has assumed the role of mediator rather than intervener, as it has become active in promoting negotiations over the unification of the two Koreas. In Vietnam, it is seeking to reinforce its former strategic partnership by selling advanced weapons to Hanoi. In spite of Moscow's activism, China clearly has a much stronger geopolitical hand in the relations with North Korea and Indochina than was the case before the collapse of the Soviet Union. It was China that took the lead in moving North Korea to the negotiations table, leading to the 2007 agreement to dismantle its nuclear weapons facilities. The new reality is that the two geostrategic realms that now clash directly in this contact zone are the maritime and East Asian, not the heartlandic.

In both North Korea and Indochina, China must exercise its strategic superiority judiciously in dealing with these battle-hardened nations that jealously guard their independence of action. To draw them firmly into the East Asian orbit, Beijing will have to develop partnerships based on fulfilling mutual strategic needs rather than seeking to create a dominant-subordinate relationship.

TAIWAN

The situation with Taiwan presents China with both dangers and opportunities. In the face of United States opposition, China currently lacks the sea power and air power to reunify the mainland and the island militarily. Both the Beijing and Taipei regimes have, until recently, been in agreement that Taiwan is politically indivisible from the mainland. Its increasing capital investments in China are an important element in the development of the Golden Coast. However, Taiwan is economically and geopolitically a member of the Asia-Pacific Rim region and the maritime world as a whole. Only if a geopolitical structure is developed that would enable the island to serve as a bridge, or gateway, between the two realms will China be likely to fulfill its strategic and historic territorial ambitions.

The need to find a solution to the Taiwan issue became more acute with the rise of the independence movement in 2000. The Democratic Progressive Party, which ousted the Kuomintang Party in 2000, redefined its relationship with the mainland as "state to state." This came at a time when the Taiwanese economy benefited greatly from close economic ties with China. Nearly 40 percent of all Taiwanese exports now go to the mainland, and China has become the island's second-largest source of imports, after Japan. Taiwanese capital investment and outsourcing of industrial parts has been a major force in China's emergence as an economic powerhouse. All of this has led to a very high standard of living for twenty-four million Taiwanese.

In 2007, the new government of Taiwan became more strident in its calls for independence. However, polls show that a substantial majority of the population is satisfied with the status quo that has made the island one of East Asia's economic "tigers," with a GDP of $475 billion and foreign reserves that are among the world's largest. What might be acceptable to the disputing parties is a "Hong Kong Plus" model, which would provide Taiwan with greater freedom than the "two economies, one state" system that characterizes Hong Kong's current status within the framework of Chinese sovereignty. Taiwan can hardly be satisfied with less than complete economic, cultural, and political freedom, including retaining its own elected legislature, whereas China's 1997 agreement with Hong Kong guarantees the retention of the latter's present economic system for only half a century. A confederated political framework that would permit Taiwan to retain special trading ties with closely related neighbors, such as in the Asia-Pacific Economic Cooperation Forum (APEC), or to join the Association of Southeast Asian Nations (ASEAN), might satisfy Taipei.

From China's standpoint, maintaining and increasing the flow of investment capital from Taiwan is essential. Nearly half of all the foreign investments in China are in the electronics area, and Taiwanese computer companies account for over half of these investments. Using the formula that permitted Ukraine and Belarus to hold membership in the United Nations when they were part of the Soviet Union, it might be possible for China to agree to the restoration of a seat for Taiwan within the UN General Assembly, from which it was expelled in 1971. China would have little to lose, owing to its own role as a permanent member of the Security Council, which would guarantee Beijing's dominance within the United Nations of a China Federation, were it to be created. Such an agreement could include Taiwan's control of its own internal police force while assuring China of strategic oversight of the Taiwan and Luzon Straits.

A small but possibly significant step toward an eventual political agreement is the accord signed by Taipei and Beijing to permit limited exchanges between the heavily fortified Taiwanese Islands of Jinmen (Quemoy) and Mazu (Matsu) and the province of Fujian. Passengers and goods now may cross the narrow Taiwan Strait rather than travel via third countries, as Taipei long required. There is also discussion of developing a commercial port on Jinmen as another step in expanding the direct trade, transport, and postal exchanges that Beijing has long desired not merely with the tiny offshore islands but between the mainland and Taiwan.

NORTH KOREA

North Korea, the last of the Stalinist states and heir to the tradition of the "Hermit Kingdom" of seventeenth- to nineteenth-century Korea, lies within the geostrategic orbit of China. This dependence is relatively recent, stemming from the collapse of the Soviet Union and the disappearance of Moscow's military and economic aid. Previously, Pyongyang was able to call upon both the Soviet Union and China for strategic support, playing its patrons off against each other and thereby maintaining a degree of independence.

Russia has continued to provide North Korea with international diplomatic backing in support of the coexistence of two Korean states. Together with Beijing, Moscow has used its influence to counter the US-inspired image of North Korea as a "rogue state" and a member of the "axis of evil." This has not deterred Washington from initiating the development of its new national missile defense system in the North Pacific. Moscow can and does sell weaponry to North Korea, but it cannot offer Pyongyang the military support that Beijing can provide in times of crisis.

That North Korea has had little alternative but to seek the strategic patronage of Beijing is evidenced in the international negotiations that have taken place sporadically during the past decade. These have been over nuclear weapons policy issues, tensions in the demilitarized zone (DMZ) between North Korea and South Korea at the thirty-eighth parallel, terrorist attacks, and on-and-off unification talks between the Koreas. Negotiations over North Korea's nuclear weapons complex evolved from a four-party structure, including South Korea and the

United States on one side and North Korea and China on the other, to one that was joined by Russia and Japan. These culminated with the 2007 agreement that dismantled the North Korean facility in exchange for oil, food, and financial incentives. The lead role in the negotiations was taken by China. That agreement was subsequently broken by the North Koreans, who successfully conducted a nuclear missile test in 2013.

When Korea emerged from World War II, it was the North that had the bulk of the peninsula's industry and its mineral resources. In this part of the country were 90 percent of Korea's minerals (coal, iron, copper, lead, uranium, manganese), its hydroelectric power resources, and its forest products. The industrial base included steel and chemicals, and the North was by far wealthier than the South. Although devastated during the Korean War, North Korea was able to recover quickly with massive Soviet and Chinese aid. The state-owned industrial base was rebuilt and expanded by the addition of armament and aircraft as well as machinery and petrochemicals plants and by the modernization of the steel, chemical, and textile industries.

The Achilles' heel of the North is agriculture. Little farmland was available because of the rocky and mountainous terrain, poor soils, and a short growing season. The peninsula in its entirety is only 20 percent arable land because of the terrain, but there is even less land proportionally available in the North, where the mountainous landscape gives way to the broad floodplains formed by the Taidong, Chongchon, and Yalu Rivers, which face Korea Bay at northeast China. Farms were collectivized and mechanized while irrigation facilities were expanded in pursuit of agricultural self-sufficiency, but the climate is too cold for paddy rice, the staple of the South, and grain supplies have been erratic owing to the vicissitudes of climate.

Since the postwar recovery period, North Korea has become the poor neighbor of the South. Its economy has been weighed down by the cost of seeking food and industrial self-sufficiency and by extraordinarily heavy military expenditures, including its nuclear and ballistic missiles program and a million-man army. As North Korea has struggled with the inefficiencies of its Soviet-style, state-run economic system, the previously poorer South Korea has by far surpassed it economically.

With the collapse of the Soviet Union and the attendant loss of heavy Soviet aid, North Korea has been ill equipped to cope with the series of natural disasters that have come upon it in recent years—floods and droughts that have brought famine and disease and taken hundreds of thousands of lives. Grain production has dropped by 40 percent. Plagued by food, fertilizer, and fuel shortages, the country must depend upon foreign aid from Japan, China, South Korea, the United States, and international agencies in order to cope with the crises.

Thanks to massive US aid after the Korean War, South Korea rebuilt its economy, changing from an impoverished, heavily populated, agricultural country into a prosperous, highly industrialized one. Agriculture was surpassed in importance by manufacturing as early as the 1960s, and today farm output represents only 6 percent of GDP, while industry accounts for 43 percent and services 51 percent. The South Korean economy is fully integrated within the global economy. It exports such products as electronics, electrical equipment, steel, machinery, autos, ships, and textiles, and its total foreign trade in goods represents nearly half of its GDP of over one trillion dollars. The fifty million South Koreans, 85 percent of whom are urban, enjoy a standard of living, with a per capita GDP of $32,000 and a total GDP of over one trillion dollars, in stark contrast to the standards of the twenty-five million North Koreans (over 60 percent of whom are urban), whose per capita GDP is less than $2,000.

North Korea is still the world's most centrally planned industrial economy. State-owned industries provide 60 percent of the GDP of $12.5 billion, and collectivized agriculture 25 percent, while the service sector is minuscule—only 15 percent of GDP. International trade represents only 10 percent of GDP, reflecting the isolated nature of the economy and the burden of military expenditures. This burden is overwhelming, accounting for approximately 30 percent of GDP, in contrast with South Korea's 3 percent. Recently, China has been encouraging the North Korean leadership to initiate economic reforms by moving in part toward a market economy, thus emulating the reforms that Beijing has undertaken in recent years.

In addition to this grim economic picture, North Korea has been cast as a pariah nation by the United States and much of the rest of the world over its nuclear threat and sponsorship of international terrorism. This makes it even more dependent on the patronage of Communist China, which has evolved as the main power broker on the North Pacific mainland. There have been some recent tensions between Beijing and Pyongyang over the expansion of the latter's economic ties with South Korea—a position contradicted by the fact that China itself is now the largest importer of South Korean goods and a recipient of substantial capital investment from that country. The explanation for this position lies in the opposition of Beijing to Korean unification.

The dependence of Communist Korea upon China has its roots in the Korean War. At that time, three hundred thousand Chinese "volunteers" joined the North Korean troops that had been driven back to the Yalu River to push the American-led UN forces back below the thirty-eighth parallel. The line had been arbitrarily established at the end of World War II as a temporary means of separating the northern, Soviet-occupied zone of the country from the southern, US-occupied zone. The thirty-eighth parallel became a formal boundary in 1948, when the two separate regimes—the northern Democratic People's Republic of Korea and the southern Republic of Korea—were established, and the Soviet and American troops were withdrawn. The sudden invasion by the North Korean army in 1950 breached the boundary and pushed back the South Koreans and the American troops who had been rushed to their aid, to the small pocket around Pusan at the southeastern tip of the peninsula.

The subsequent US counterattack, initiated by the landing at Inchon on the west-central coast near Seoul, drove the North Koreans back to the Yalu River border with China. This brought China directly into the war, as they pushed the UN forces back. Ultimately, up to one million Chinese troops became engaged, and their casualties were estimated at up to a half million. The bitter fighting ended with the armistice in 1953 and the establishment of the DMZ, which ran from the Han Estuary northeast across the thirty-eighth parallel. The boundary does not follow the parallel precisely but cuts across it diagonally. In actuality, North Korea has 850 square miles south of the parallel along the west coast, including Kaesong, a commercial and industrial center, which from the tenth century to the end of the fourteenth century had served as the capital for Korean dynasties. As the gateway for rail and road traffic to the Korean south from Manchuria and North Korea, Kaesong was a major battleground during the war. South Korea holds 2,350 square miles north of the parallel in the center and along the east coast. This area includes the fishing port of Sokcho, on the Sea of Japan and backed by the Taibak Mountains.

For China, the exact location of the boundary between North and South was not the issue. Of crucial importance to Beijing was the preservation of the boundary zone as buffer and, indeed, all of North Korea as a security screen for Manchuria. In this sense, China perceived the Yalu River as its final line of defense, not its first line. General Douglas MacArthur had taken as saber rattling the Chinese warnings against his pushing north of the thirty-eighth parallel. He underestimated Beijing's resolve. Under the urging of Stalin and with his military support, the Chinese attacked and overwhelmed the much smaller UN force that had reached the Yalu.

China had a genuine fear of an attack by the United States in support of a Kuomintang effort to return to the mainland. Moreover, the Chinese entered the war because Stalin's request that they do so included the promise of air cover; the training of pilots for the MIGs that were given to them, which would enable the Chinese to participate with the Russians in the air war; and the massive supply of military equipment. Despite their heavy casualties, the Chinese armed forces emerged from the war with far more effectiveness and power than they possessed before the war, while the Chinese air force became the third largest in the world.

For the same security reasons that prompted its military response half a century ago, Beijing continues to prop up the Pyongyang regime economically and politically. China is North Korea's main trading partner, and the two countries share the enormous quantity of hydroelectric power supplied by waters impounded by the Supung Dam on the Yalu River, one of the largest dams in Asia. In fact, China has electric power facilities on the North Korean side of the Yalu.

After the war, China helped North Korea on the manpower front. The flight of several million people to the South had caused serious worker shortages. These were partly offset by Chinese colonists from Manchuria as well as repatriated Koreans from Manchuria and Japan. On this score, however, there has been an ironic turnabout since the mid-1990s. Seeking to escape the famine that has raged in the North since 1995, tens of thousands of North Korean refugees have crossed the border to China seeking food and jobs. Approximately one hundred thousand to three hundred thousand of these migrants, who have fled mostly to the border provinces, are to be found seeking shelter among China's ethnic Koreans, who constitute up to 40 percent of the population of some of the districts of northeast China. Some are sent onward by underground networks into Mongolia and then by circuitous routes into Thailand and, eventually, South Korea. The majority, however, are trapped in these border provinces, where they live and work under most difficult conditions and in constant fear of being sent back by Chinese authorities. Initially Beijing turned a blind eye toward their presence. Now, however, considerable numbers are being returned, both because of Beijing's concern that the area will be overrun by the refugees and out of deference to the North Korean regime's policy of trying to prevent such flight. When caught by the police, the refugees are handed over to border guards to face possible punishment in North Korea for having left the country illegally.

The agreement of June 14, 2000, between Presidents Kim Jong-il of North Korea and Kim Dae-jung of South Korea was heralded as a historic breakthrough and dubbed "the Sunshine Policy." The two leaders agreed to seek reconciliation and unification, the establishment of peace, furtherance of family visitations, cultural exchange, and restoration of railroad and road links between the two countries. This policy led to the establishment in 2003 of the South Korean–financed Kaesong Free Trade Industrial Zone (KIZ), located on the northern side of the DMZ on North Korea's west coast. Employing over fifty thousand workers in 2013, the goal of the South Korean factory owners for the KIZ is to increase exponentially the number of plants to the point where they can employ seven hundred thousand workers. As a result of increased tensions with South Korea and the international community over North Korea's nuclear missile test in 2013, North Korea briefly shut down the zone but opened it four months later. At the eastern end of the DMZ, the much smaller Mount Kumgang Tourism Project is a South Korean–sponsored resort with duty-free stores that is also expected to grow.

The 2000 accord has profound implications for both China and the United States as well as for the Koreans. The North Koreans are adamant in seeking the withdrawal of US troops from South Korea, while China's interests require guarantees that a merged Korea not be drawn into the maritime realm strategic alliance. Moreover, the North Korean leadership is hardly prepared to jeopardize Communist control of its country, while the South Koreans will in no way take any steps that would undermine their economic system and weaken their ties with Japan, the broader Asia-Pacific region, and the maritime realm.

The signing of this accord had an immediate effect upon US relations with North Korea. Washington eased trade sanctions and softened the rhetoric it had long used to describe North Korea. "Rogue state" was dropped from the lexicon of the US State Department in favor of "state of concern." (This new terminology applies as well to Cuba, Iran, Sudan, and Syria.) The easing of the sanctions reflected an important policy change, moving toward greater emphasis on negotiating differences rather than on punishment. Moscow seized upon the changing relations between North and South Korea to assume a mediating role between them. The negotiations that followed between the two Koreas have enabled Moscow to expand its influence with both countries. The South Koreans have sided with Moscow in seeking a diplomatic approach to the resolution of the North Korean missile threat, rather than supporting the American national missile defense project. In addition, in an effort to draw Seoul and Pyongyang more closely together, the Russians have proposed linking the Pacific coast railroad systems of the two Koreas to the Trans-Siberian Railroad terminal at Vladivostok. This overland rail system would cut to twelve days the time required for goods from Korea's ports to reach Russia and Europe, as compared with the current twenty-four-day sea route. China is also interested in the North and South Korean link, which would provide it with access to South Korea via the existing rail line between Pyongyang and Manchuria. Another desire of Russia is to develop a pipeline network from its border through North Korea to the South, to open the Korean market to its new East Siberian natural gas fields. The North Koreans have requested that Moscow sell them weapons and military, especially naval, equipment. Both Koreas seem to be open to improved relations with Russia.

When and if Korea does unite, the United States, China, Japan, and Russia will have to find a formula that neutralizes the country militarily and encourages it to serve as a bridge between the three geostrategic realms. At present, reunification is a dim hope unlikely to be realized. For a few years, reduction of tensions and peace along the world's most heavily militarized border seemed close at hand, given South Korea's promotion of the Sunshine Policy and the nuclear dismantling agreement of 2007. North Korea's breaking of this nuclear agreement and its strident anti-United States and South Korean vituperation in recent years has raised the tension once again.

Perhaps the current atmosphere can breathe life into a proposal long discussed by peace seekers, who have sought to persuade the two Koreas to convert the 150-mile-long, 2.5-mile-wide DMZ into a nature reserve. The zone is currently ringed by hundreds of thousands of troops and studded with military installations. Environmentalists have emphasized its ecological uniqueness. Because of disuse by humans, it has evolved over the years into a nature sanctuary. Such use could serve as a basis for ecotourism that could benefit both states and help to reinforce the current efforts to bring stability and greater openness to the relations between North and South. Converting the Korean Peninsula to a gateway region that would link all three realms is an important goal in the quest for global geopolitical equilibrium.

INDOCHINA

Vietnam

The geopolitical relations between China and Vietnam have followed a highly tortuous course. The depth of China's involvement in the Vietnam War was evidence of the strategic importance it gives to the Indochinese peninsula. South China's coastal provinces are directly exposed to the threat of hostile forces in the Gulf of Tonkin and coastal Vietnam. Moreover,

Yunnan, in southwest China, is open to land invasion from forces moving up North Vietnam's Red River Valley or up the Mekong from Saigon (Ho Chi Minh City) through Laos and Cambodia. Having American troops on China's doorstep was a strategic nightmare to the Chinese leadership, which explains China's vigorous support of North Vietnam during the Vietnam War.

Following the withdrawal of France from Vietnam in 1954 and the division of the country into North and South along the seventeenth parallel, both China and the Soviet Union provided the Ho Chi Minh regime with enormous amounts of economic and military aid. Even after the Sino-Soviet split, the two Communist powers continued to finance the development of industry and agriculture. Focus of industrial development was in the Red River delta, coastal areas of the Gulf of Tonkin, and the port city of Haiphong, which brought the ecumene of the country to the doorstep of South China.

As the Viet Minh launched their guerrilla warfare against South Vietnam, the Chinese supplied them with the bulk of their military equipment. The flow increased when the United States entered the war directly in 1964 and the North became exposed to systematic bombing from US land bases in the South and aircraft carriers in the Gulf of Tonkin. Much of the Chinese equipment was moved southward by the Viet Minh along the Ho Chi Minh trail—a network of jungle-covered mountain tracks that extended along the eastern border of Laos to South Vietnam and Cambodia.

The United States effectively withdrew from the war in 1973, two years before its official termination. While North Korea's alliance with both China and the Soviet Union had held during the war there, the first break between China and the now united Socialist Republic of Vietnam came quickly, precipitated by China's seizure of some of the Paracels in 1974, which they continue to administer to the present day. The schism widened in the late 1970s and early 1980s. Vietnamese forces invaded Cambodia in 1978 and drove Pol Pot's Khmer Rouge from power after the excesses of that regime had caused the deaths of three million people and emptied out the cities. Pol Pot, who had seized control of the government in 1975, had exiled most Cambodians to the countryside in an action reminiscent of Mao's Cultural Revolution of 1966–76, which had similarly devastated China.

The presence of Vietnamese troops in Cambodia triggered a brief Chinese invasion of Vietnam's border provinces in 1979, during which China captured several border towns. Minor clashes had broken out between China and Vietnam as early as 1974 along their 750-mile disputed border, which had never been clearly delineated.

The primary factors that led to the war were the installation of a Vietnamese-sponsored government in Cambodia, which displaced the Chinese-supported regime, and the discriminatory treatment by the Vietnamese of their ethnic Chinese, highlighted by Hanoi's clampdown on the large body of Chinese private businessmen. During this period, over a quarter million ethnic Chinese fled Vietnam. Most of those living in the Vietnamese provinces that bordered China made their way to the People's Republic or to Hong Kong. The Chinese troops withdrew from Vietnam after two months, having suffered heavy casualties. The two countries then entered into years of negotiations over their land-border dispute, which was not formally concluded until an agreement signed in December 1999. The rift with China gave great urgency to Hanoi for seeking the patronage of Russia as a counterbalancing force. In 1978, just before the Chinese invasion, Vietnam had joined the Soviet-led Council for Mutual Economic Assistance (COMECON) and concluded a treaty of friendship with the Soviet Union. Now, with Beijing ending its economic aid program, Soviet assistance became crucial. From the signing of the friendship treaty until its collapse a decade later, the Soviet Union was the major supporter of Vietnam, supplying arms, economic aid, and fuel. In return, Moscow received the rights to operate and expand the Cam Ranh Bay naval and air bases, which had been abandoned by the United States, thus strengthening its strategic position in both the South China Sea and the Indian Ocean. Adding to the Chinese-Vietnamese friction in the 1980s, China foiled Vietnamese incursion into the Paracels.

In the 1990s, tensions between China and Vietnam lessened as a result of a series of economic and political agreements between the two. Since normalization of relations in 1991, China has become a major importer of Vietnamese products and a major source for capital investment. The countries share similar approaches to their market reforms, following "open door" economic policies while clinging to their Communist governing structures. Vietnam's withdrawal of its troops from Cambodia in 1988 and its recognition of China's rule over Taiwan eased tensions and paved the way for a joint declaration of friendship between the two countries. The agreement committed the two countries to resolving their land and maritime border disputes and to opening the land border fully, save for a military intelligence station that monitors shipping in the South China Sea. This helped to ease China's security concerns and led to the final border accords.

Vietnam's strategic vulnerability to Chinese pressure partly relates to the location of its northern ecumene. As previously noted, the center of North Vietnamese industry and agriculture is the Tonkin delta, especially around Hanoi and Haiphong, whose development was fostered by both China and the USSR from the 1960s to the 1980s. This region merges geographically into the southern end of the Chinese ecumene's densely populated industrial and agricultural centers in the province of Guangxi Zhuangzu, such as the coastal cities of Beihai and Hepu and the inland cities of Nanning and Wuzhou. Nanning has played a singular role in Chinese-Vietnamese relations as the gateway for Chinese supplies to North Vietnam during the war. Beijing has strengthened its strategic influence over the region by sponsoring the construction of a highway system from South China through the Indochinese peninsula as well as Thailand and Myanmar (the North-South Economic Corridor).

China has the surplus capital but is too absorbed with its own development needs to provide Vietnam with the level of economic aid and investment that is required to be a major factor in the country's economic advancement. Alternatively, Vietnam has looked to Singapore, Japan, South Korea, Australia, the EU, and the United States for most of its capital investment and trade. After Washington reestablished diplomatic ties with Hanoi, the two countries signed a far-reaching trade agreement in 2000. Since the trade agreement, the United States has become Vietnam's leading export market and overall trading partner. US investment is also on the increase, as high-tech firms have taken advantage of the country's skilled labor supply and tax reforms. Recognizing its need to look to the Asia-Pacific Rim for economic links, Vietnam joined ASEAN in 1995. In 2006, it was admitted to the World Trade Organization. While foreign trade represents over 30 percent of its GDP, the country still has a long way to go before it can reach parity with its more prosperous Asia-Pacific Rim neighbors. Over half its population of ninety million remains agricultural, and per capita income remains at $3,800 per annum.

Vietnamese economic development has benefited from the fact that its labor costs are even lower than those of China. As a consequence, some foreign outsourcing of low-value goods has moved from China to Vietnam. This is not a dependable road to prosperity, since improvement in overall economic conditions will eventually raise wages, closing the gap. Vietnam will have to eventually move into higher-value exports. A major challenge facing Vietnam's Communist regime is the economic disparity between the North and the South. Foreign investments have been attracted to the freewheeling capitalist atmosphere of Ho Chi Minh City (formerly Saigon), not to the centrally planned, antiquated industrial zones of the North. Thus the country that was officially reunified in 1975 remains far from unified economically. The South is the source of two-thirds of Vietnam's wealth, sends 90 percent of its tax revenues to Hanoi, and is the recipient of most of the cash remittances from families abroad. This economic gap is hardly a recipe for healthy political relations between the two parts of the country.

As the bitter memories of the Vietnam War, in which three million Vietnamese lost their lives, has faded, Hanoi has turned to the maritime realm to offset the reality of China's growing strategic power in East Asia. In 2006, the United States and Vietnam agreed to strengthen defense ties. Although this may be mostly a symbolic gesture, it makes it clear that Vietnam is far from being a satellite of China. Having struggled against Chinese domination for two thousand years, Hanoi has crafted economic policies that enable it to deal with Beijing as a partner—neither an opponent nor a satellite. A sign of China's recognition of Vietnam's geopolitical independence within the East Asian realm was its settlement of the land and coastal water boundary disputes that had marred relations between the two countries for so many years. From the standpoint of Beijing, eliminating the vestiges of territorial conflicts with Vietnam is the most direct way of rebuilding a strategic alliance. Additional steps that could be taken, such as agreeing to a condominium over the Paracels and joint sponsorship of claims and energy concessions in the Spratlys, would reassure Hanoi of Beijing's intentions as it seeks to develop a strategic partnership with its neighbor to the south. For its part, Hanoi might open its doors to the return of ethnic Chinese who fled, not only to redress an old wrong but also to benefit from the economic dividends that come from strengthened familial ties with overseas Chinese and mainlanders.

In 2002, Russia's military strategic relationship with Vietnam formally ended when it withdrew from the Cam Ranh Bay naval base. One of the finest deepwater shelters in Southeast Asia, Cam Ranh had served as the Soviet Union's major military beachhead within the region and as its largest naval and staging area outside the USSR. The warships and aircraft based there, as well as electronic listening facilities, facilitated surveillance over both the South China Sea and the Indian Ocean.

As the Soviet empire began to crumble at the end of the 1980s, Moscow withdrew from most of Cam Ranh Bay, leaving only a few auxiliary vessels and a small military force there to maintain the intelligence station and using the port for occasional merchant ship repairs.[15] At the same time, it drastically lowered its economic support of Vietnam—a factor that influenced Hanoi's decision to seek repair of its relations with China.

Vladimir Putin's visit to Hanoi early in 2001 signaled Russia's interest in reengaging Vietnam. The two countries signed a "strategic partnership" accord that awarded Moscow exploration rights in a thirty-eight-square-mile tract of Vietnam's oil-rich continental shelf. In addition, it provided for Russia's sale to Hanoi of advanced arms, especially naval weapons, and promised help in constructing Vietnam's first nuclear power plant. The Russians also agreed to forgive nearly all of the $11 billion debt owed to them. The two parties used the signing of the agreement as an occasion to voice their common objection to the proposed US national missile defense (NMD) system.

The Russian actions in Vietnam are in keeping with the "Orient Policy" enunciated by former prime minister Yevgeny Primakov, who advocated regaining political influence in North Korea, Vietnam, and India through military assistance programs.[16] In recent years, however, Moscow's military sales to Vietnam have been modest as the strategic interests of both countries focus on oil development and expanding trade. Washington's efforts to forge a new partnership with Vietnam were highlighted by the visit of President Clinton in December 2000. While the focus of the visit and of US policy initiatives was trade and free markets, the

American initiative also had the objectives of offsetting Chinese pressures on Vietnam and containing China's southward expansion. Whatever directions the relations between Beijing and Hanoi may take, the United States has neither the capacity nor the will to try to affect the basic strategic relationships between these Asian powers. The 2006 strategic agreement between the United States and Vietnam has resulted in visits by US naval vessels, but little more. To suggest to the Vietnamese leadership that the United States might help them to break off China's geostrategic embrace might encourage them to challenge China only to discover that there is no American safety net. Hanoi's refusal to lease Cam Ranh Bay to such interested parties as the United States, China, and India reaffirms its strategy of trying to keep a low military profile and not upset its independent regional posture within the East Asian Realm.

Laos and Cambodia

Vietnam is the dominant state among the nations of Indochina. The economy of Cambodia (Kampuchea) is depressed—the country's per capita income of $2,400 is two-thirds that of Vietnam—and based largely on agriculture. A trade agreement between the United States and Cambodia in 1996 led to the rapid expansion of the country's garment industry, with most of its exports destined for the United States. The low US tariff on Cambodian goods has attracted dozens of investors from Taiwan, Singapore, Hong Kong, and China, as garments have become the country's biggest export earner. Nevertheless, the number of these factory workers (under two hundred thousand) does little to reduce Cambodia's rural poverty, inasmuch as 80 percent of the population of thirteen million lives as farmers or farm laborers. For imports, such as construction materials, petroleum products, and consumer goods, the country turns to Thailand, China, and Singapore.

Cambodia's domestic politics remain unstable, despite the efforts of the United Nations to bring stability to the country. From 1991 to 1993 Cambodia was virtually a UN protectorate under the UN Transitional Authority in Cambodia (UNTAC), as twenty thousand peacekeeping troops sought to pacify the country. UNTAC withdrew after elections were held, but the Khmer Rouge continued their activities until the movement split in 1996. Pol Pot was captured the following year, and he died in captivity. A coup in 1998 brought the Communist Party, led by Hun Sen, to power. The party remains in power.

The country's military vulnerability to Vietnam remains a powerful element in the political relations between the two countries. Unlike in Laos, which is separated from Vietnam by heavily forested mountains, Cambodia's border with its larger neighbor is completely open. Most of its people are concentrated in the lower Mekong and are geographically connected with the river's delta area and Ho Chi Minh City.

Laos is lightly settled, with a population of 6.5 million and one-third the population density of Cambodia's. Its per capita income of $2,800 is slightly higher than that of Cambodia. Laos, too, has suffered from its landlocked position and from years of warfare. Ruled by the Communist Pathet Lao, which came to power with the help of the Vietnamese, its economy remains underdeveloped, with Vietnam as its largest trading partner. Mountains cover most of the country. The rapids of the Mekong River, along which half of the Laotian population lives, impede movement along this, the nation's main communications artery, while land and air connections are limited.

The result of this isolation is that most Laotians are subsistence farmers, with rice as the main crop. Exports to Thailand and Vietnam are mainly tin, timber, and coffee. Most of the surplus electric power goes to Thailand. The controversial Nam Theun River dam in Central Laos, which has flooded one-fourth of the Nakay Plateau, has displaced four thousand villagers and caused considerable ecological damage. The hydropower project has enabled the Laotians to export even more surplus electricity to Thailand and some to Viet Nam. With support from the World Bank, construction of the dam began in 2007 and was completed in 2010.

Viangchan (Vientiane), the capital and largest city of Laos, is located on the Mekong River on the border with northeastern Thailand and is a center for trade with that country. However, there is at present little possibility that Communist Laos will move out of the geopolitical orbit of Vietnam. In addition to the strategic advantage that Vietnam holds over Laos, the contrast between the democratic political system of Thailand and that of Communist Laos makes it even more unlikely that Laos would move away from Vietnam and toward Thailand.

Conclusion

A clear geopolitical hierarchy in the East Asian realm has evolved over many years of turbulence. Indochina is dominated by Vietnam, the second-order power of its geopolitical region. The region, in turn, is under the strategic sway of China, the primary geopolitical force of the East Asian realm. While China has major differences with Vietnam, especially over territorial waters that hold gas and oil reserves, it is unlikely to plunge into conflict with its battle-hardened neighbor. On the contrary, the two nations have strengthened their ties since resuming diplomatic relations in 1991 and, in 1999, they resolved all outstanding disputes along their common 740-mile land border. However, Vietnam, Laos, and Cambodia are scarcely in a position to challenge their northern neighbor's strategic pressures, and China's claims to South China Sea waters are likely to persist and eventually prevail.

China is indisputably a world power, given its economic and technological growth. From a geostrategic point of view, China's unique regional reach to so many important parts of the world has made it a strong global power with direct geographical impact upon much of Eurasia. China has land boundaries with fourteen countries and sea borders with three others—South Korea, Japan, and the Philippines—as well as with Taiwan. Altogether, the seventeen neighbors have a combined population of two billion. Adding China's own populace brings the total to well over three billion, or slightly more than half of the people of the world, who are affected by the actions of Beijing.

In geospatial terms, the East Asian geostrategic realm that is led by China impinges upon the heartlandic geostrategic realm, the maritime realm's Asia-Pacific Rim, the South Asian geopolitical region, and the Central Asian arena. This is a position of centrality that, in some ways, competes with the centrality of Russia. The latter has eleven landward neighbors and four with which it shares intermediate water or frozen waste spaces (Iran, Japan, the United States, and Canada). Heartlandic Russia lies between the maritime realm to its west, north, and east (where it faces maritime Europe, North America, and offshore Asia, respectively), East Asia to its southeast, and Central Asia to its south. US centrality is more limited. The United States holds an intermediate position within the maritime realm between maritime Europe and the Asia-Pacific Rim while overlooking Middle America to its south. Surely a Chinese paradigm based on global centrality has as much of a spatial claim as those of its two major competitors.

At present, China cannot compete with the United States or Russia in the sophistication of its armaments. Given its economic strength, however, there is little doubt that China can ultimately achieve parity in the armaments area should it choose to use its resources for that purpose. In the interim, its military power is felt by many of its neighbors, which are in geographical settings that are more removed from the security umbrella of the US superpower.

The end of the Cold War has seen efforts by both Moscow and Washington to strike up strategic alliances with China. Indeed, both President Boris Yeltsin and President Bill Clinton agreed with President Jiang Zemin to develop separate "strategic partnerships." In this burst of enthusiasm for partnerships, Prime Minister Yevgeny Primakov of Russia went so far as to advocate a Russian-Chinese-Indian strategic triangle (as distinct from the previously mentioned Orient Policy, which would have linked North Korea, Vietnam, and India to Russia). The goal of such a triangular relationship would be to maintain Russia's Cold War alliance with India while rebuilding its strategic ties with China. The prospects for such a triangular partnership, however, are dim now that the Cold War is over. The United States and India have drawn closer in recent years. The need for Washington to aid Pakistan militarily and economically has lost its strategic rationale because the war in Afghanistan has reached its end, and Pakistan is at risk of implosion. Given India's growing strength in South Asia and the Indian Ocean, the United States is likely to seek a stronger alliance with India, although India is unlikely to relinquish its traditional posture of geostrategic independence.

China and India normalized their relationships in 1993 and opened cross-border trade six years later. Their outstanding territorial disputes are no longer cause for tension between them. Instead, the competition between China and India to gain influence over Myanmar has grown. The unsettled political scene in Myanmar casts uncertainty over the lasting impact of the economic and strategic initiatives of either suitor. China made headway by supporting the former Burmese military junta. Now that the military has given up power and Myanmar has taken a road toward democracy, India is gaining greater influence.

In the long run, India is geographically better positioned than China to strategically dominate the Indian Ocean, on which the ecumene of Myanmar is located. In Central Asia, the two powers have more to gain from partnership than from competition. Until the issues of the status of Taiwan and the possible reunification of Korea are settled, a strategic partnership between the United States and China represents essentially a public relations slogan designed by Washington to justify its desire for increased trade links with Beijing, now its largest source of imports. Indeed, it would be more accurate for American leadership to speak of economic, not strategic, partnership.

Japan, the anchor of US geostrategic policy in the Western Pacific, has yet to sort out its long-range strategic relations with China. It is China's leading source of investments as well as being one its major trading partners. Tokyo values its own security arrangement with the United States. However, one of its concerns is that US sales of sophisticated weapons systems to Taiwan could raise the level of Chinese antagonism toward Japan, which provides the major bases for US forces in the Pacific. While uneasy about China's growing military presence in the East China Sea, Japan is loath to jeopardize its economic ties with China. Japan's strategic relationship with China also may be affected by events that unfold within the Korean Peninsula. Should the status quo change and the two Koreas become unified, Korea might shift toward neutrality and the American military screen in South Korea would be eliminated. Given these uncertainties, Washington would do well to recall that no strategic partnership between China and the United States would offer America geopolitical security in the western Pacific unless it were to safeguard the strategic interests of Japan.

The water boundary between the East Asian realm and the maritime realm's Asia-Pacific Rim region has become a source of renewed tensions with the rise of China as an economic and military power. Washington cannot accept any limitation on its use of international waters to oversee Chinese military activities and communications. Without this surveillance, the US shield over Taiwan would be greatly weakened, as would the defenses of South Korea and Japan. In addition, such limitation could be used as a precedent to foreclose the airspace and waters around the Paracel Islands, two hundred miles off the coast of Hainan, to Vietnam and Taiwan, which also lay claim to them.

The arena of sharpest economic and political competition between China and the United States is Sub-Saharan Africa, with its abundance of oil and minerals. The Chinese posture is to offer investment with no strings—political, human rights, or counterterrorist related. It is promoting a model of commercial relations and open markets without an ideological agenda. China's trade with Africa is growing faster than with any other region besides the Middle East, with Angola becoming China's largest source of oil. Chinese merchants, managers, workers, and arms merchants are a highly visible presence in many African countries. While the United States and the EU are still Sub-Saharan Africa's larger trading partners, China is climbing fast.[17]

This visible Chinese presence in Africa has a downside for China. Its activities have engendered widespread African resentment and accusations that the Chinese are following a colonial path of settling merchants in Africa, robbing the continent of its mineral and forest products, and accumulating a huge trade surplus that contributes to the loss of local job opportunities because of the influx of low-priced Chinese goods. China's state oil companies are being accused by African governments of polluting the environment, price gouging, and corruption. Chad claims that the poverty level of its people has not risen despite the oil production, while Chinese workers have built roads and public buildings in that country. In Gabon, new permits for oil concessions have been withdrawn. Resentment in Niger focuses on high oil costs and the fact that refinery workers, who are ethnic Chinese, return home for holidays rather than spending their time and money in the country.

In Central Asia, China is drawing equal to Russia in economic influence, although it cannot compete on a military-strategic level. The China National Oil Company holds a share of Kazakhstan's huge North Caspian Sea oil fields. In Turkmenistan, the company opened a new onshore gas field, the largest in the world, which sends gas to Shanghai via an eleven-hundred-mile pipeline which was built in 2009. China has become Uzbekistan's second-largest trade partner.

China's influence in South Asia is also expanding. This is evidenced by the ports that China has built or leased in Sri Lanka, Bangladesh, and Myanmar. The port of Colombo in Sri Lanka has one of the world's largest terminals and handles the transshipment of 13 percent of all of India's container traffic.

Two realities stand out in the relationship between China and the United States. The first is the strategic vulnerability to American air and sea power of the coastal regions containing China's most important economic centers. The second is the economic interdependence of the two countries, which acts as a restraint on the behavior of both during crises. China cannot afford to have US restraints imposed on trade and capital investment. The stake held by US corporations in Chinese manufacturing operations is too large, and the thirst of US consumers for low-cost imports too great, for the United States to impose trade sanctions—a weapon of last resort.

Mutual economic dependence (MED) has become as powerful a balancing force as mutual strategic dependence (MSD). The strategic equilibrium that has developed between Washington and Moscow stems from mutual nuclear deterrence; the balance between Washington and Beijing has grown from their increasing economic interdependence.

A more likely scenario than a US-China strategic partnership is the renewal of the former strategic alliance between heartlandic Russia and China. Moscow's interest is in offsetting US expansion into the Baltic countries via NATO and keeping Ukraine from joining the alliance, as well as in warding off Western geopolitical penetration of Central Asia through control of energy resources and pipelines. China's interest is in curbing the extension of US power into the Southeast Asian mainland. China and Russia share the goal of keeping a unified Korean Peninsula from becoming absorbed within the Asia-Pacific Rim and thus the maritime realm. This would weaken the North Pacific positions of both countries. Together, therefore, the two neighboring continental Asian powers have a stake in putting their decades of feuding behind them and seeking jointly to counterbalance the American superpower.

The fruits of the new strategic partnership are already evident. China's substantial purchase of Russian fighter jets, a reconditioned aircraft carrier, submarines, and other weapons has been accompanied by a border agreement. Nearly all of the twenty-three-hundred-mile boundary between the two countries, which was the site of conflicts in the 1960s, has been demarcated. Expanding trade, especially in oil and gas, and the 1997 agreement between the two countries to settle all border disputes is recognition of this mutual interest. It reflects the perception in both regimes that they are in danger of being penetrated from various directions because of their vulnerability to American-led strategic pressures. This perception motivated the two countries to form the Shanghai Council that included the Central Asian states. However, the council has not evolved into the hoped-for "NATO of the East." Its sponsors remain wary of one another, and Moscow is suspicious of Beijing's rising influence in Central Asia.

For Russians, the threat is Western military and economic intrusion into its periphery, the Eurasian convergence zone. For China, the maritime military threat is exacerbated by the economic muscle of its Asia-Pacific Rim neighbors and the growing dependence of its own industrial base upon Western capital, technology, and trade. Notwithstanding its global trade reach and interests, China's military-strategic focus remains regional. It is the seas between the Chinese mainland and the Asia-Pacific Rim of the maritime realm that Beijing seeks to dominate, not far-flung areas in which competitors maintain the competitive advantage. In addition to its focus on its coastal waters, consolidation of its hold on its western territories of Tibet and Xinjiang remain the geopolitical priority of Beijing.

Any look into China's geopolitical future should take into account the possibility that its entry into the global market and attendant domestic economic and social influences and strains might undermine Chinese Communism. What could follow? Highly unlikely would be a smooth transition to a cohesive, market-oriented, liberal democratic state. This did not take place in the wake of the collapse of the Soviet Union. It is even less likely to happen in China. The failure of current efforts to close the gap between the heavily rural and antiquated industrial continental North and interior and the more prosperous, modern maritime south and central coasts could lead to collapse of the Communist regime. The resultant chaos would strengthen the independence ambitions of Far Western China, especially the Uighurs in Xinjiang.

The East Asian realm has evolved into a formidable competitor to the maritime and heartlandic Russian realms. Global equilibrium now rests not on a bipolar power balance but on a triangular base.

Notes

1. William L. Tung, *China and the Foreign Powers* (Dobbs Ferry, NY: Oceana, 1970), 69–89.
2. Tung, *China and the Foreign Powers*, 69–89.
3. Erik Eckholm, "After 50 Years, China Youth Remain Mao's Pioneers," *New York Times*, September 26, 1999, A12.
4. Oliver Chou, "Navy Boss Outlines Force of the Future," *South China Morning Post*, April 22, 1999.
5. Anthony Davis, "Blue Water Ambitions," *Asia Week* 26, no. 11 (March 24, 2000): 1.

6. Robert D. Kaplan, "Lost at Sea," *New York Times* , Sept. 21, 2007, A19.

7. C. P. Fitzgerald, *The Chinese View of Their Place in the World* (London: Oxford University Press, 1964), 68–72; Andrew L. March, *The Idea of China* (New York: Praeger, 1974), 7–22; Benjamin I. Schwartz, "The Maoist Image of World Order," in *Image and Reality in World Politics*, ed. John C. Farrell and Asa P. Smith (New York: Columbia University Press, 1968), 92–102; and Derwent Whittlesey, "The Horizon of Geography," *Annals of the Association of American Geographers* 35, no. 1 (March 1945): 1–36.

8. Norton Ginsburg, "On the Chinese Perception of World Order," in *China's Policies in Asia and America's Alternatives*, ed. Tang Tsou (Chicago: University of Chicago Press, 1968), 73–96.

9. Lin Pao, Excerpts from "Peking Declaration Urging 'People's War' to Destroy U.S.," *New York Times*, Sept. 4, 1965, 2.

10. "A Special Report on Financial Centres," *Economist*, September 15, 2007, 10–13.

11. Antoaneta Bezlova, "Environment-China: Three Gorges Dam May Displace Millions More," Inter Press Service, October 12, 2007.

12. "Go West Young Han," *Economist*, December 23, 2000, 45–46.

13. Alan J. Day, ed., *Border and Territorial Disputes* (Harlow, England: Longman, 1982), 252–57.

14. Day, *Border and Territorial Disputes*, 276–80.

15. Nayan Chanda, "Cam Ranh Bay Manoeuvres," *Far Eastern Economic Review* 163, no. 52 (Dec. 28, 2000): 21–23.

16. Gerald Segal, "Does China Matter?" *Foreign Affairs* 78, no. 5 (June 1999): 24–36.

17. Padraig R. Carmody and Francis Y. Owuse, "Competing Hegemons? Chinese vs. American Geo-economic Strategies in Africa," *Political Geography* 26 (2007): 504–24.

CHAPTER 10

The Asia-Pacific Rim

The Asia-Pacific Rim, or Asia Pacifica, is the third major geopolitical power center of the maritime realm. This region extends for over six thousand miles in an arc from South Korea, Japan, and Taiwan (at least for the present) through the Philippines, Singapore, Malaysia, Thailand, Indonesia, Brunei, Timor-Leste, and Papua New Guinea to Australia and New Zealand. The region also includes a number of western Pacific island states, such as Palau, the Federated States of Micronesia, the Solomons, Vanuatu, and the Marshalls, as well as such US dependencies as Guam and the Northern Marianas (Saipan). Thus it embraces the string of island states of offshore Asia that border the China seas and reach into the southwest Pacific and the peninsular lands that adjoin this string on both its northern and southwestern ends. The countries of the Indochinese peninsula—Vietnam, Laos, and Cambodia—plus North Korea are excluded from the region on the grounds that they lie within China's geostrategic orbit.

Unlike North America and maritime Europe, the other two regions of the maritime realm, the Asia-Pacific rim is not integrated by intraregional political, economic, or sociocultural forces. The economies of many of its component states are more closely linked to China rather than to Japan, its weak regional core. What unifies the rim geopolitically is its dependence upon the American strategic military umbrella. In reaching out economically to China to its west and militarily to the United States to its east, Asia Pacifica holds out the long-term prospect of becoming an independent gateway between the two great powers rather than remaining part of the maritime realm.

A striking characteristic of the region is the absence of a strong core to bind its states together. While Japan plays an important role in intraregional trade, its leading commercial ties are with China, the United States, and Australia (table 10.1). Only South Korea is an important rim trading partner. The dream of a Greater East Asia Co-Prosperity Sphere, which a resource-poor Japan pursued through its bloody occupation not only of the Asia-Pacific Rim but also elsewhere in Manchuria, coastal China, and Southeast Asia, was shattered by the war against the United States and its allies that culminated in Japan's defeat.

Even though Japan has experienced a phenomenal economic growth since its recovery from the nuclear ashes of that war, this recovery is not dependent upon the natural resources and labor of the Asia-Pacific countries that loomed so important to its leaders when they launched their war to create the Co-Prosperity Sphere. Instead, Japan has used its technological and scientific advances to develop a highly sophisticated industrial base that fuels its role as the world's fourth-largest economy. While Tokyo does carry on trade with some of its Asia-Pacific Rim neighbors, the political impact of this trade is negligible and is offset by the bitter memories of the Japanese occupation during World War II. This is especially the case in Japan's relations with South Korea, which continue to be clouded by the lukewarm apologies that the Japanese government has made over the use of Korean women as slave laborers in brothels that served the Japanese military during World War II.

The importance that Washington attaches to the Asia-Pacific Rim was reflected in President Barack Obama's speech to the Australian parliament on November 17, 2011. His focus was that, with the US drawdown in Iraq and prospectively Afghanistan, it was now turning its attention to the Asia-Pacific Rim. He emphasized that, as a Pacific nation, the United States would not cut defense spending in Asia Pacifica as it was being forced to do elsewhere. He singled out Japan, South Korea, Malaysia, and Singapore (along with Vietnam and Cambodia) as partners, balancing the need to provide them with security in the South and East China Seas while building cooperation with China.

This strategic pivot to the Asia-Pacific is in keeping with Washington's efforts to create a transpacific partnership. While negotiations for such an agreement began during the George W. Bush administration in 2008, they have taken on much greater urgency as Washington seeks to forge a twelve-nation free-trade agreement. This would link the rim states of Japan, Australia, New Zealand, Singapore, Brunei, and Malaysia (as well as Vietnam) with the United States, Canada, Mexico, Chile, and Peru. Such a partnership would account for 40 percent of the total world GDP. These negotiations have been slowed down by the opposition of American trade unions and their congressional supporters but is likely to be overcome by the country's long-standing commitment to free trade.

The overriding geopolitical characteristic of Asia Pacifica is its maritimity. Its island and peninsular states are well positioned to engage in international trade because of the comparative advantages of sea transportation over movement of goods by land. The strategic downside of this dependence upon trade is that sea-lanes are vulnerable to interdiction, especially since so much of the traffic that moves within the region and to and from other parts of the world must pass through a substantial number of straits and narrow seas. The rim depends heavily upon US naval power and air power to secure these shipping lanes. At the developmental level, it is a geopolitically specialized region that lacks integration because the trade and political links of many of its states are externally oriented.

Another aspect of this maritimity is the region's climatic patterns. They grade southward from the humid, moderate climates of the continental, temperate, and subtropical zones of the northern parts to the tropical, rainy areas straddling the equator. The zones then reverse to Australia's humid subtropical east and southwest coasts and New Zealand's humid temperate clime. Only Australia's interior is desert and semiarid. The initial stimulus for the early dense settlement of much of the region was the favorable conditions for agriculture within its temperate and tropical zones. Modern colonial economic development was based on significant trade in plantation and forest products.

In preliterate and ancient times, the region's narrow and shallow seas facilitated the diffusion of races, languages, religion, crops, cultures, and technologies from mainland Asia. Colonizing European powers were able to use their naval superiority to secure the territories that they ruled and to control access to them. Today's independent states continue to use the seas to their advantage through control of coastal waters and airspace. In effect, the waters on the one hand have become isolating screens behind which diverse national cultures have been able to strengthen themselves, while on the other they connect the various countries by trade.

A most striking example of the advantage of naval and air power over land power has been the case of Taiwan. Taiwan occupies the island of Jinmen (Quemoy), which is only four miles from China's coastal port of Xiamen (Amoy). Nevertheless, China has been unwilling to risk deployment of its massive military manpower across this water to seize that island from Taiwan in the face of the US-Taiwan security pact, backed by naval and air power. It has also refrained from invading Mazu (Matsu), which lies immediately off the coast from Fuzhou (Foochow), let alone to sweep across the ninety-mile-wide Taiwan Strait to "liberate" Taiwan.

Beijing was able to exploit its manpower advantages to help the North Koreans fight the US superpower and its allies to a standstill in the Korean War and to use its land connections to Vietnam to contribute substantially to the US defeat in the Vietnam War. However, it could not cope with American naval and air superiority within the waters of its own geographical backyard when it tried to seize the Chinese Nationalist-held islands. The buildup of Chinese air, naval, and missile forces along the Taiwan Strait and the efforts of Taipei to counter this by purchasing state-of-the-art destroyers, aircraft, and antimissile radar from the United States represent another phase in the conflict. Over the years, Washington has sought to dampen the arms competition in an effort to assuage China's objections. It has continued sales of patrol boats and air-defense systems to Taiwan but refused to sell advanced fighter jets, agreeing only to upgrade older F-16s.

Evolution of the Region

The Asia-Pacific Rim geopolitical region has emerged during the past half century, having overcome the effects of the Japanese occupation, the devastation of World War II bombing, and postwar Communist rebellions supported by the USSR and China. Asia Pacifica lacks the politically integrative structures and concomitant economic and social institutions that have forged maritime European unity. The region has attained a very modest degree of integration through its intraregional economic ties, but its unity is based upon a security framework backed by US military power. While Japan is clearly the core of the rim, its regional influence is limited. The political and geographic framework that has evolved in Asia Pacifica is a far cry from the "Co-Prosperity Sphere" that Tokyo imposed upon conquered nations during the 1930s and 1940s. At that time, political unity was enforced by arms, and the greatest part of the region was the East Asian mainland.

In Japan the seeds of modern Pan-Asianism were planted after the Meiji restoration of 1868. Japanese imperialists at that time promoted the spiritual bond of Asian brotherhood as their rationale for leading a unified Asia that would be morally and culturally superior to the materialistic world of the West. Panregionalism envisaged a three- or fourfold division of the world, based upon great or panregions arranged along a north-south axis and organized around a dominant northern core. Karl Haushofer, the father of German *geopolitik*, knew Japan well. He had served as Germany's military observer in Japan from 1908 to 1910 and wrote his PhD thesis on the geographic foundations of Japanese power. He saw Japan as the core of the Pan-East Asia region, with its industrial and military center drawing food and raw materials from the resources of the periphery in exchange for finished goods.

The region that he anticipated included not only Japan, Southeast Asia, and Australia but also China and East Siberia. While Haushofer viewed Japan as the leader, he also believed that China, and possibly Russia, had to be embraced as its partners. The influence of Haushofer and his school of *geopolitik* on Japanese military and industrial leaders was profound, and many of the basic ideas of German geopolitics were incorporated within Japanese politics. Thus, Tokyo's concept of a "Greater Asia Co-Prosperity Sphere" was the outcome of Japanese studies of the German "Great Space Economy."[1]

The Japanese failed, however, to heed Haushofer's warning not to be drawn into war with China but rather to seek a partnership with it. Tokyo's taste for territorial spoils had been whetted by its seizure of Formosa (Taiwan) and the Pescadores Islands from China after the Sino-Japanese War of 1894–95. Following Japan's victory in the Russo-Japanese War (1904–5), during which China allied itself with Russia, Japan created a protectorate in Korea, which it formally annexed five years later. It also gained economic control over southern Manchuria in 1905, built the southern Manchurian Railroad, and developed the economy of the region. However, Chinese warlords continued to exercise military control over the province, a situation ultimately unacceptable to the Japanese militants. They invaded the province in 1931, occupied it, and established the puppet state of Manchukuo the following year. Through this action, the Japanese eliminated Russian influence from northern Manchuria, building up the province as a base for initiating the second Sino-Japanese War in 1937, during which they overran northern and eastern coastal China during the next three years.

After the fall of France in 1940, the Japanese moved southward to conquer Vietnam, where they allowed Vichy France to maintain a puppet administration until 1945. This was the next step in the creation of the Greater East Asia Co-Prosperity Sphere. Following the Japanese attacks upon Pearl Harbor and Singapore, which marked Tokyo's entry into World War II, its troops quickly overran Southeast Asia, from Burma, the Malay Peninsula, and Singapore to the Philippines, Indonesia, and the islands of the western Pacific.

Thailand was spared an invasion because it was already a satellite of Japan. The military regime that seized power in Bangkok in 1938 turned to Japan for support in advancing Thai territorial claims in Cambodia, Laos, northern Malaya, and the Shan states of northeastern Burma.

The Thai alliance was strategically important to Tokyo for it permitted the stationing of Japanese military forces at bases on the eastern and southern Thai coasts. These bases became launching sites for the invasions of the Malay Peninsula and the Dutch East Indies that began on December 8, 1941, when the Thai government permitted Japanese forces to enter the country. The oil resources of the Indies were especially crucial to the Japanese, whose US supply had been cut off by Washington's embargo. That embargo, as well as the neutrality treaty signed with the Soviet Union, were major factors behind the attacks upon Pearl Harbor and Singapore, which initiated the war in the Pacific.

By the 1930s, Australia had become an important trading partner of Japan—a valuable source of wool, wheat, and pig iron in return for finished goods. While Australia had long been included in Tokyo's Pan-Asian plans, the Japanese failed to invade Australia during World War II. They did manage to bomb and shell Darwin, in the far north on the Timor Sea, the industrialized port city of Newcastle, northeast of Sydney, and Port Jackson (Sydney Harbor). However, their plans to invade the island continent were dashed by the 1942 battle of the Coral Sea, in which US naval and air power defeated the Japanese fleet, stopping its southward advance.

The Japanese envisioned the Co-Prosperity Sphere fashioned by their conquests as an East Asian mercantile system, within which their *zaibatsu*, the great trading enterprises, were to play pivotal roles. Japan's World War II defeat and its devastation by US bombing, including the atom bombs that were dropped on Hiroshima and Nagasaki, put a conclusive end to the Japanese dream of creating such a sphere. Replacing this framework was the geopolitical region that first emerged as offshore Asia. With the end of the Vietnam War, Southeast Asia's shatterbelt status came to an end. The Indochinese peninsula now clearly lay within the Eurasian continental framework, while the peninsular and insular parts of Southeast Asia (Thailand, Malaysia, Singapore, and Indonesia) just as clearly belonged to what now could be called the Asia-Pacific Rim region.

Linking Australia to Asia Pacifica

When the Japanese threat to Australian security became overwhelming, Australia's strategic fate (and that of New Zealand) became inextricably linked to the island-peninsular region to its north. Until then, Australians had accepted the traditional British view of Australia as the "end of the line," as belonging to the peripheral portion of South Asia. In such a view, Australia was located on the "farther" side of Asia and part of "Further India" or the "Farther East."

The threatened invasion of their country in World War II and the United Kingdom's divestiture of its South Asian empire gave Australians a new perspective on their place in the world. Offshore Asia and peninsular Southeast Asia had become meaningful neighbors.

The shift in Australia's geopolitical orientation brought about a change in its attitude toward immigration. Immediately after World War II, large numbers of Eastern Europeans were admitted, but Canberra continued to practice an Asian exclusion policy that was discordant with the new geopolitical realities. This policy was officially discarded in 1973. By 1998, about 40 percent of all immigrants to Australia had been born in Asia, as the total number of Asians exceeded 1.4 million, or 7 percent of the population. New Zealand favored immigrants from Britain, other European countries, and North America until 1987, when it instituted a system based upon skills and potential economic contribution. India, China, the United Kingdom, and the Philippines are now the sources for skilled-worker resident and family visas. Combined, these quotas add up to about sixty thousand newcomers per annum.

A very special issue in New Zealand has to do with the struggle of the Maori, the indigenous inhabitants, to regain their historic rights. They now represent 15 percent of the country's population of 4.5 million. From 1840 to 1890 they fought bitter wars with white settlers and lost nearly half the territory of the country. In recent years they have created political movements to regain some of their lost lands, protect their native language and culture, and improve their economic conditions. Although they are now mainly urbanized, they have persisted in the pursuit of the lost lands. The government recognized these claims in 1996, providing the Maoris with a land and cash compensation package. What the Maori now seek is the right to manage their own communal resources and local governing responsibilities. They have received the government's support for these aims, although the details have yet to be worked out in law.

The orientation of the two countries is reflected in international trade. Whereas before the 1950s half of Australia's imports and exports went to Britain and much of the remainder went to other European countries and the United States, the main flow shifted to the rest of the Asia-Pacific Rim. A major factor in the redirection was the elimination of the imperial trade system, which accorded tariff preferences to the territories of the British Empire and then to the members of the commonwealth, such as Australia. The elimination of this system was a condition for the admission of Britain to the European Community in 1973—the same year that Australia opened its gates to Asian immigrants.[2]

Today the major share of Australia's international trade—over half of its imports and three-quarters of its exports—is with other Asia-Pacific members, especially Japan. China is its largest trading partner, accounting for one-fourth of total trade, and the United States is the source for 15 percent of its imports. This is a powerful illustration of the importance of its regional links. New Zealand's trade patterns are also strongly oriented to the Asia-Pacific Rim. Australia is by far its largest trading partner, with China as its second, followed by Japan and the United States.

Politically, Australia's ties with the United Kingdom were not formally severed until 1986, when Britain passed the Australia Act, which terminated the power of the United Kingdom's

Parliament to legislate for Australia. However, Canberra's loss of its British security umbrella occurred much earlier. In 1951 the Australia, New Zealand, United States (ANZUS) Treaty was concluded as a substitute for the vanishing British military presence. This pact committed Australia and New Zealand to serving as forward bases to support US strategic interests in the Pacific and Indian Oceans, with the focus on securing Japan's sea-lanes.[3]

Three years later, Australia became increasingly involved in military ties with the countries to its north. Together with three of its Pacific Rim neighbors—Thailand, the Philippines, and New Zealand—Canberra joined the United States, Britain, France, and Pakistan in the Southeast Asia Treaty Organization (SEATO). The purpose of SEATO was to oppose the advance of Communism in Vietnam and other parts of Southeast Asia, especially Indonesia and Malaysia. The organization became redundant, as the Communist threat weakened in Indonesia with the 1966 massacre of hundreds of thousands of alleged Communists (many of whom were ethnic Chinese) and the ousting of pro-Chinese president Sukarno the following year. In addition, Communist rebellions were put down in the Philippines in the late 1960s and early 1970s. South Vietnam fell to the North Vietnamese in 1976, and SEATO was formally disbanded the following year.

Australia and New Zealand contributed troops to the Korean and Vietnam Wars, although New Zealand sent only token forces. However, the two countries diverged over US policy when New Zealand refused port access to US nuclear-armed ships in the mid-1980s and was effectively suspended from ANZUS. The gap in policy between the two increased when Australia sent forces to the Iraq War while New Zealand did not participate. However, it has contributed development aid.

The creation of another regional organization, the Association of Southeast Asian Nations (ASEAN), in 1967 did not directly involve Australia. However, the regional economic growth that ASEAN fostered provided considerable market opportunities for Australia. Another political mechanism that helped to bind Australia to its near north was UNTAC, which was established in 1991. This peacekeeping and civilian administrative body included not only the five permanent members of the UN Security Council but also Japan, Australia, Indonesia, and Thailand in recognition of the important role that could be played by these regional states in helping to stabilize the Cambodian situation. When order was restored in the country and free elections were held in 1993, the Cambodians who had fled to Thailand as a result of Khmer Rouge actions began to return.

A Region of Trading States

Three decades ago the region that now embraces the Asia-Pacific Rim included only offshore Asia. South Korea, Japan, Taiwan, the Philippines, Australia, and New Zealand were already closely linked by trade, by their military treaties with the United States, and by their common experiences in war. Southeast Asia, however, was a shatterbelt, within which external powers—the United States, the Soviet Union, and China—exploited intraregional differences to further both Cold War and "hot" war aims.

Thailand, Malaysia, Singapore, and Indonesia began to see that their strategic interests lay within the maritime realm. Similarly, the offshore Asian nations and their Western supporters came to the conclusion that these Southeast Asian nations were vital to maritime geostrategic security because they could assure control of the links between the Indian and Pacific Ocean. Moreover, by the mid-1970s one-third of the trade of Japan and Taiwan and 15 percent of

Australia's international trade were already with Southeast Asia, and the potential for its increase was considerable.

Since then, the geopolitical status of Southeast Asia has fundamentally changed. Most of the Southeast Asian shatterbelt has merged with the Asia-Pacific Rim, as Russian influence has all but disappeared and China's strategic concerns have focused on relations with the former Indochinese countries. Australia and Japan have emerged as the northern and southern strategic cornerstones of the new Asia-Pacific Rim region. This flies in the face of geopolitical analyses offered by some scholars who discount Japan's regional power role within the western Pacific and hold that the fate of Southeast Asia and Australia rests exclusively with a US-China accord.[4] Asia Pacifica is now an integral part of the maritime realm, and its future geopolitical status rests to a considerable extent on the strength and prospects of its own member states, particularly Japan, rather than on outside powers.

As suggested at the beginning of this chapter, trade is the lifeblood of Asia Pacifica, providing the region with a distinct maritime stamp. Table 10.1 presents the leading trading partners of each of the countries of the region. Unlike in other parts of the former colonial world or other Third World countries, which are also dependent upon trade, a high proportion of the Asia-Pacific Rim's exports are in manufactured goods and therefore possess a high value-added dimension.

The Chinese populations of several of the countries of the region have played a very important role in the region's industrial and commercial development and in its intraregional trade. Singapore has a large majority of Chinese (77 percent) and Malaysia a substantial number (30 percent). Elsewhere, the proportions drop to 14 percent in Thailand, 3 to 4 percent in Indonesia, and 3 percent in the Philippines. However, they provide a significant share of the wealth and market capitalization of their host countries. The large transnational conglomerates that are controlled by Chinese entrepreneurs are linked by informal networks that facilitate trade and capital investments among them.

Another characteristic of the region is its high proportion of urban population and the fact that so many of its member states have high or medium income levels. This reflects the extraordinary economic progress of the region over the past half-century from an underdeveloped, essentially colonial and shattered set of countries to the thriving economies of today. Maritime Europe also made a remarkable recovery during this period, but it was able to build

Table 10.1. The Asia-Pacific Rim: A Region of Trading States

Country	*Leading Export Market*	*Leading Import Market*
Singapore	Hong Kong	European Union
Brunei	Japan	Malaysia
South Korea	China	China
Taiwan	China	Japan
New Zealand	Australia	Australia
Thailand	European Union	Japan
Papua New Guinea	European Union	Australia
Australia	China	European Union
Japan	China	China
Philippines	European Union	Japan
Indonesia	China	China

Source: Wikipedia, "List of Countries by Leading Trade Partners," *Wikipedia*, updated April 2014, http://en.wikipedia.org/wiki/List_of_countries_by_leading_trade_partners.

Table 10.2. Asia-Pacific Rim Population and GDP

Country	Population (millions, est 2014)	GDP (nominal $ Million US dollars, est 2012)
Australia	22,507,617	1,542,000
Brunei*	422,675	16,630
Fiji	903,207	3,996
Indonesia*	253,609,643	878,200
Japan	127,103,388	5,964,000
Malaysia*	30,073,353	303,500
New Zealand	4,401,916	169,700
Papua New Guinea*	6,552,730	15,790
Philippines*	107,668,231	250,400
Singapore*	5,567,301	276,500
South Korea	49,039,986	1,156,000
Taiwan	23,359,928	474,000
Thailand*	67,741,401	365,600
Timor-Leste	1,201,542	4,173

Sources: Central Intelligence Agency, *World Factbook 2012* (Washington, DC: GPO/CIA, 2012); Central Intelligence Agency, *World Factbook 2014* (Washington, DC: GPO/CIA, 2014), https://www.cia.gov/library/publications/the-world-factbook/rankorder/2119rank.html.

*Members of ASEAN (Other ASEAN states are Cambodia, Laos, and Vietnam, which belong to the East Asia realm.)

on an advanced human and natural resource base. In addition, it called on unprecedented financial, technological, and political support from the United States not only in restoring its economy but also in establishing innovative, regional political and economic institutions that have taken it to unprecedented levels of prosperity.

What is remarkable about Asia Pacifica is that its recent development has not followed traditional colonial and neocolonial lines of economic complementarity, whereby the underdeveloped portions of the region provided the low-value-added raw materials in exchange for the developed sector's high-value-added finished goods. The tropical monsoonal areas do, indeed, possess such raw materials as rubber, timber, rice, sugar, palm oil, copra, petroleum, iron, chrome, and manganese. And Japan and Australia do have advanced manufacturing bases, which draw on these resources to a considerable extent. But early on, the Japanese organized a complementary manufacturing strategy that built upon the market potential as well as the large, cheap labor supply of the rest of the region to export its products and services to countries outside the rim. Japanese multinational auto companies established factories that built components in various countries, such as engines in Thailand and batteries in Indonesia, and established motor vehicle assembly plants in the United States. Computer companies outsourced electrical components to Singapore and assembled fax machines and microcomputers in Malaysia.

The South Korean steel, semiconductor, and automotive industries gained their start by depending upon Japan for technology and parts. Its investments in China are broad and deep, with particular focus on high-tech industries. Together with Japan, South Korea created shipping cartels that built three-quarters of the world's ships during this period. Today, Japan ranks second only to Greece in its ownership of merchant fleets, while South Korea, the world's leading shipbuilding country and noted for its highly engineered vessels, is the eighth-leading owner.

Japan was not alone in pursuing this complementary manufacturing strategy within the region. US and European companies did so also. Dutch and British oil interests built refineries in Singapore based on petroleum from nearby Indonesia, while Singapore's shipbuilding industry purchased steel from South Korea. In South Korea, much of the textile, apparel, shoe, and later the electronics industries were developed by the outsourcing of production from the United States and Japan. The same was the case for Taiwan and, to a lesser extent, Thailand. Indonesia exports nearly half of the world's hardwood but also engages in wood processing and a variety of outsourced computer products.

Japan's economic ties with China have blossomed, despite prickly political relations between them over Japan's brutal occupation of China before and during World War II and a current boundary dispute in the East China Sea. This adds up to a region of increasingly balanced exchange, powered by the great financial centers of Tokyo and Singapore. The regional trend is for the most advanced countries to shift more and more of their manufacturing abroad and concentrate on the service aspects of their economies, such as Tokyo's focus on telecommunications, software development, and financial services. Singapore reexports half of what the country imports.

The Philippines, with a large, technologically literate labor pool, has become one of the fastest-growing importers of high-tech parts from the United States as well as one of the fastest-growing exporters of high-tech goods to the United States. While agriculture still accounts for over 40 percent of the country's GDP, industry and services are on the increase. Philippine specialties include the assembly of computer hardware and the development of software. The progression has been from the subcontracting of parts and finished products by American and Japanese multinational firms to the creation of Internet ventures and global customer-support services.

The Japanese and Australian economies remain the strongest in the region. However, although it exports machinery, motor vehicles, and consumer electronics and imports most of its raw materials, Japan also imports manufactured goods. While Japan's main trading partners are now China, the United States, and South Korea, it has also expanded its trade with Australia, New Zealand, and Singapore. It has free-trade agreements with all these countries except the United States and China.

Australia, with the most balanced of the region's economies, is an exporter of wheat, wool, coal and ores, aluminum, machinery, and transportation equipment, but it also imports these last two items as well as telecommunications products and computers. New Zealand also has transformed its economy over the past two decades from what was largely agricultural to one that has broadened and deepened the technological base of its industrialized economy. Its foreign trade is now approximately one-quarter of GDP and on the increase. It spans sectors from food processing and paper and pulp to machinery, finance, and tourism. The United States refused to sign a free-trade accord with New Zealand until the ban is lifted on the use of its ports by the US Navy. The ban was lifted in 2012, and the two countries are negotiating the free-trade accord that has eluded them for several years.

Political Stability and Instability

A geopolitical region is more than an economic or strategic unit. Its character is also defined by the political conditions that prevail among its constituent parts. In this regard, the Asia-Pacific Rim is divided between politically stable states and states plagued by instability.

POLITICALLY STABLE COUNTRIES

Japan and Australia, the regional anchors, are highly stable politically, as is New Zealand. Malaysia has prospered within an atmosphere of political calm as its ruling coalition, dominated by Malays with the support of Chinese and Indian parties, has provided a framework for ethnic harmony. This is despite long-standing tensions between the Malay Muslim (60 percent of the population), Chinese (30 percent), and South Asian (10 percent) communities. Singapore has enjoyed political stability since its split from the Federation of Malaysia in 1965. It has flourished economically within an authoritarian political environment, attracting considerable foreign investment and becoming a world leader in high-technology manufacturing.

South Korea and Taiwan

South Korea and Taiwan have also benefited from internal political stability, even as their relations with their Communist neighbors have kept both countries in states of continuing international tension. Seoul responded to its financial crisis of 1997–98 by electing a reform government that not only guided economic recovery but also succeeded in reducing frictions with North Korea.

Taiwan, one of the great economic successes of modern times, has matured politically. Its new generation of native Taiwanese leaders has thrown off the lengthy rule of the authoritarian Kuomintang (Nationalist Party) of the mainlanders to establish a democracy. The current government, led by the Independence Party, had taken a cautious approach to its relations with China, not forcing the issue of independence, until 2007, when it unsuccessfully sought UN recognition as an independent state. With the 2008 election of a government favorable to closer ties with China, trade and tourism between the two countries has doubled. Economic ties have been further strengthened by large-scale investments in China by Taiwanese entrepreneurs, who have also increased their outsourcing of industrial production to the mainland. For example, Foxconn, the world's largest design manufacturer, is based in China but owned by a Taiwanese billionaire. Patient negotiations could ultimately find a confederated formula that might satisfy mainland China's claim to sovereignty over the island nation without Taiwan's sacrificing most of its current freedom of action.

The Philippines and Thailand

The Philippines and Thailand are still beset by the political uncertainties of countries that have thrown off dictatorships and military rule. However, they have gained in political stability in two ways: they have weathered the transition to democracy under popularly elected (if not always corruption-free) governments, and they have kept in check the insurgency movements that have menaced their countries.

With a population of nearly one hundred million, the Philippines have enjoyed political stability under three popularly elected governments, even though Joseph Estrada, who won the presidency in 1998, was driven from office by popular protest in the wake of a bribery scandal and impeachment proceedings. He was replaced by the vice president, in accordance with Filipino law.

A developing country by most standards, the economic growth of the Philippines, especially in the high-tech area, can be attributed to the political stability that has followed the overthrow in 1986 of the corrupt dictatorship of Ferdinand Marcos. A further factor was the removal of US military bases in the early 1990s, which defused tensions between Manila and

Washington and paved the way for a new and healthier era of cooperation between the two countries, including the flow of considerable aid from Washington. The former US Clark Air Force Base and Subic Bay Naval Base, to the west and north of Manila, respectively, have since been transformed into special economic zones, with seaport, international air, and manufacturing facilities. These zones complement the industrial and financial centers of Manila and areas to the south of the capital, where the country's high-tech electronics industry is rapidly growing. Industry now accounts for over one-third of the country's GDP of $450 billion and per capita income of $4,700.

Internal unrest continues to plague the country. However, the scale of violence is far lower than in the past, and on-and-off peace negotiations reflect the substantial weakening of guerrilla groups. The Communist (Huk) insurgency that dragged on for decades on Luzon suffered heavy casualties in the 1980s and has been virtually eliminated as the government waged a vigorous counterinsurgency campaign after 1992. The Muslim rebellion in Mindanao does not threaten the stability of the Philippines. That conflict, which erupted in 1971, was precipitated in great measure by large-scale resettlement projects initiated by the Philippine government after World War II that brought tens of thousands of Christians from Luzon to Mindanao. By the early 1980s, the island had become 80 percent Christian, and the threatened Moro (Muslim) minority increased its separatist demands and the scope of the conflict. In response to a raging insurgency in 1990, Manila established an autonomous region for Muslim Mindanao that included the adjoining Sulu Archipelago, where the islands of Basilan and Jolo served as centers for the separatist movement. This was followed six years later by a formal peace with the main Moro group. Terrorist attacks and kidnappings by the small breakaway Abu Sayyaf faction continue to cause turmoil. Prompted by fears that al-Qaeda members might move a base to the southern Philippines and by the seizure of two American hostages, Washington accepted the government of the Philippines' request to send US military forces to work with Filipino soldiers in efforts to destroy the terrorist band. Although the Abu Sayyaf leader was killed in 2002, occasional terrorist bombings still plague the country.

In 2014, the Moro Islamic Liberation Front came to an agreement with the Philippine government to end the decades of conflict. The accord calls for the establishment by 2016 of an autonomous political territory named Bangsamoro in parts of Mindanao, thus assuring the Muslims of self-rule. In exchange for giving up their arms, the Moro are to have the right to their own police force and to keep control of three-quarters of the revenues derived from their mineral resources.

Thailand, a nation of almost seventy million, has made progress toward achieving political stability as well as economic vitality. The only Southeast Asian country to have escaped colonialism, Thailand emerged from its World War II alliance with Japan to become strongly allied with the United States during the Vietnam War. Until 1988 the internal political climate was highly unstable, as a succession of military rulers quashed efforts to maintain civilian government. In that year, the first prime minister not imposed by the army was popularly elected. The new system survived a bloody military revolt four years later. The country was governed by a series of multiparty coalitions in an unwieldy, but nevertheless democratic, system until 2006. At that time, a military junta took control of the country in a bloodless coup, which was in response to widespread corruption and election fraud. Free elections are promised. Various attempts have been made to introduce economic reforms and to clean up widespread political corruption. The former have met with greater success than the latter. The largely rural northeast, with one-third of the total population, remains impoverished, while the center of the country is thriving. In 2014, the friction between the two regions caused political turmoil as the middle and elite classes of the center vigorously objected to the subsidies offered by the government to the farmers of the northeast.

Political stability requires that this economic gap be narrowed. The long-running "Free Thai" Communist rebellion based in the north that had derived support from bases in China and Vietnam was stamped out. However, the Islamic separatist movement in southern Thailand, adjoining Malaysia, where Malaysian Communists had established bases for operations in that country, has taken many lives and continues to spread. With the closing of US bases in Thailand after the Vietnam War, Bangkok has been able to improve its relations with both China and Vietnam while remaining allied with the West. The changed relationships have been helpful in Bangkok's successful campaign against the Thai Communists.

With peace along the Cambodian border, Thailand has recently begun to invest in tourism and gambling in Cambodia. Angkor Wat's temples have stimulated Thai investment in hotels close to that world-class archaeological site, while gambling resorts have been developed in towns directly across Cambodia's western boundary with Thailand as well as on Cambodian islands in the Gulf of Thailand. The country has improved its infrastructure, which supports an industrial economy now based on the development of electronics, motor vehicles, and appliances. Its GDP of $675 billion generates a per capita income of nearly $10,000, propelled by a strong market-oriented system.

Singapore and Malaysia

The city-state of Singapore is, literally, an island of stability. It became independent of Malaysia in 1965. It is an economic powerhouse, and its citizens enjoy one of the world's highest per capita incomes of over $62,000. It owes much of its prosperity to its role as a world-class financial center and major port. Manufacturing still accounts for one-quarter of all jobs and has shifted to high-value products in the marine engineering and biotechnical fields. With a population of only 4.5 million, the country has considerable need for immigrant labor. It has attracted so many immigrants that approximately one-third of its residents were born in other countries, mainly India and China. The country's overall ethnic mix is over three-quarters Chinese, the rest being mostly Malays and Indians. The government is dominated by a single party, dedicated to prosperity and order, with high standards for education, health care, and public services.

Malaysia has been transformed from a land that produced raw materials for export to one with a multisector economy. The country has enjoyed stability since gaining its independence from Britain. Rich natural resources have spurred industrial development and economic growth, generating a GDP of over $500 billion and a per capita income of $17,500. While in colonial times it was dependent on plantation crops such as rubber and palm oil, as well as on tin mining, it now is a mainly urban and industrial country, focusing on rubber and palm oil processing, oil and gas production, and electronics. It conducts much of its trade with China, Japan, and Singapore. Its large Chinese and Indian minority (one-third of the thirty million population) was brought into the country in the colonial period to work the plantations and mines. They now dominate the country's business and professions.

The Malaysian government keeps tight control over its three million foreign workers, the majority of whom come from Indonesia. Estimates are that half of these migratory laborers are illegal, and they have become the targets of a government-organized volunteer force with powers to detain and deport illegal migrants.

POLITICALLY UNSTABLE COUNTRIES

The exceptions to the general trend toward political stability within the Asia-Pacific Rim are Indonesia, Timor-Leste, and the small Pacific Island countries of Fiji and the Solomons.

Fiji

Fiji, the most populous of the South Pacific island countries, consisting of over three hundred mainly volcanic islands, has been torn by ethnic tensions and army coups since gaining its independence in 1970. Many of the inhabitants of Fiji had come there over the previous century as indentured plantation workers from India. These migrants became a majority until the unrest of the postindependence period prompted many of them to emigrate, leaving the native Fijians as the majority. The exodus was especially heavy after the adoption of the 1990 constitution, which favored native Fijian control of the government. Nevertheless, those of Indian stock still account for slightly over half of the population of 840,000.

The main struggle is carried on by the traditional Fijian tribal chiefs, who refuse to yield to the authority of elected governments when led by Indo-Fijians and who resent the long-term land leases held by the Indian sugarcane farmers. The overthrow of a government in 2000 that had been led by Indo-Fijians who had been elected the previous year has been followed by continuing turmoil. The all-Fijian military government that overthrew the Indian-led one in 2007 continues to dominate the country, and ethnic tensions remain high. This coup resulted in the suspension of the country from the Commonwealth of Nations. The turmoil has exacerbated the country's economic difficulties stemming from a severe drop in the world price of sugarcane, Fiji's main export, as well as a drop in tourism.

The Solomon Islands

The situation in the Solomon Islands has been equally turbulent. Since the islands gained their independence in 1978, militias representing immigrants from different island communities have fought with each other, keeping the country in chronic turmoil. Guadalcanal, the largest and most important of the islands in the archipelago, contains the town of Honiara, the capital. The country's economy, based essentially on the export of timber, fisheries, gold, and tourism, is depressed. The per capita income is now $3,200.

The population of the islands, numbering approximately 525,000, is mainly Melanesian but is divided into over eighty different language and cultural groups. In addition, there is a small but influential Chinese business community. Conflicts over landownership and bias against immigrants from neighboring islands led to the overthrow of the government of the Solomons by immigrants to Guadalcanal from Malaita. The counteraction of Guadalcanal's ruling Istabu ethnic group forced twenty thousand Malaitans out of their homes. Factional fighting reached such a high level that an Australian-led force, sanctioned by the Pacific Islands Forum, had to intervene in 2003 to restore civil order, which was accomplished in 2005. With restoration of order, the force was withdrawn and civil government reestablished. The Solomon Islanders continue to resent the Australian intervention as an example of colonialism. In both Fiji and the Solomons, the political chasm between traditional leadership and those seeking governmental reform shows little sign of narrowing.

Indonesia

Indonesia is widely recognized as an "Arc of Instability."[5] The Suharto regime (1966–98) clamped down on many of the separatist groups that had threatened to tear the archipelago state apart in the 1950s and 1960s. However, Indonesian politics has been tranquil neither during that period nor since. The regime took power in a coup that saw the killing of hundreds of thousands of Communists and their sympathizers. The so-called stability during the Suharto era was based upon ruthless repression, corruption, and the self-enrichment of a small military and political elite.

The difficulty of forging a unified state out of the Dutch East Indies was manifest from the time that Indonesia proclaimed itself independent, shortly after the Japanese surrender in 1945. The highly centralized government in Java had to impose its sovereign control on a region extending for over three thousand miles, from the Indian Ocean into the western Pacific. The island republic includes over 13,600 islands (3,000 of which are inhabited), the most important culturally and economically being Java, Sumatra, and Bali. Moreover, it must fashion a nation out of over 300 diverse ethnic groups and 350 indigenous languages. The national slogan may be "One Country, One People, One Language," but the reality is such overwhelming diversity that national unity remains highly elusive. As a consequence, economic growth has suffered. The GDP of $1.3 billion yields a per capita income of $5,200, and the service sector of the economy remains poorly developed.

The core of the country consists of the very densely populated and developed islands of Java and Madura, whose linguistic stock is Deutero-Malay. They are ringed by the great arc of islands to their west, north, and east that are commonly referred to as the "Outer Islands."

Separatism is encouraged by the combination of the sheer size of the country (752,410 square miles), the poor transportation and communications, and the resentment against the Javanese, who constitute over half of Indonesia's more than 250 million people. The Ambonese Christians of the Moluccas (Malaku) Islands, once called the "Spice Islands," established the short-lived South Molucca Republic at the southwestern end of the archipelago. The republic was annexed by Indonesia in 1950 but remained in open rebellion until 1956.

In 1958 rebellions also broke out in Sumatra, Sulawesi (the Celebes), and Kalimantan (Borneo), where Islamic parties had strong bases and were in opposition to the secular state program of President Sukarno's Nationalist Party. The Sumatra rebellion was the most serious, fanned by general dislike of the Javanese and the fact that most of the country's exports came from Sumatra's petroleum and natural gas (Indonesia is the world's largest exporter of liquefied natural gas), palm oil, rubber, and tropical hardwoods, while most of the national expenditures went to Java. Although the rebellion ended three years later with reassertion of full authority by the government, the resentment has continued.

Aceh, the northernmost province of Sumatra, which had been a Muslim sultanate since the sixteenth century, has also been the scene of unrest and rebellion. The Dutch gained control in the nineteenth and twentieth centuries, but the Acehnese waged guerrilla war for decades. This devoutly Islamic province set up an independent Muslim state in 1848 that remained formally independent from the Dutch until 1903 and maintained a quasi-independent status until the Acehnese rebels were crushed at the end of the Sumatra war in 1961. The province was then designated a special territory with autonomy in religion, culture, and education, but it remained a powder keg for Jakarta.

Sukarno, the country's first president and a leader of the independence movement against the Dutch, had created a "guided democracy" in 1956, as he skillfully balanced the competing interests of the army and the rapidly growing Communist Party. As convener of the Bandung

Conference the previous year, he had gained a position of leadership within the Asian-African world with his anticolonial rhetoric and his call for Third World economic cooperation and independence from Western influences.

In the late 1950s Sukarno began to lean toward the powerful Indonesian Communist Party and toward China. He launched undeclared war against Malaysia in 1962 in opposition to the creation of the independent Malaysian Federation, which he considered a British imperialist subterfuge. Indonesian military raids were mounted against Malaysia's North Borneo territory from Kalimantan, the southern two-thirds of the island of Borneo, and part of Indonesia. In addition, Jakarta withdrew from the United Nations in 1965, a gesture of opposition to Malaysia's having been granted a seat on the Security Council.

Indonesia's course of direction changed abruptly during that year, when an attempted Communist coup against the military was repulsed by the army, led by the pro-Western General Suharto. In this operation, half a million Chinese and Indonesians were killed, and two hundred thousand were imprisoned on political grounds. Suharto, in effect, replaced Sukarno in that year, and two years later he became president, ushering in what many Western statesmen considered an era of stability.

In fact, while the highly centralized Jakarta regime kept the lid on most of the separatist movements during this period, it could not eliminate them. Although crushed in 1961, the Acehnese declared their independence once again in 1976 and established a government-in-exile as they continued their conflict. The South Moluccans, who had created a government-in-exile in 1966, persisted in their resistance.

Western (Dutch) New Guinea, which had been seized by Indonesian troops in 1962 and formally annexed in 1969, remained a source of unrest. The Free Papua movement rebels, who declared an independent state in 1961, have waged guerrilla warfare from their jungle refuges for four decades. The settlement of over sixty thousand Javanese families as part of Jakarta's voluntary resettlement program (known as "transmigration") further aggravated the situation in the province (first called West Irian and now Irian Jaya). The clashes were particularly intense in 1977 and 1984.

East Timor was also a focus of major unrest during the Suharto era. The Indonesians seized the former Portuguese colony in 1975, touching off a war with the Timorese that devastated much of the country. Washington gave unwavering support to General Suharto for this annexation, ignoring the fact that he used American arms in the invasion and subsequent slaughter of two hundred thousand East Timorese. The US rationale was Indonesia's strategic importance in terms of its location, size, resources, and market potential. Nevertheless, the Timorese persisted in their drive for independence.

Although it had also originally supported Indonesia's annexation, by the 1990s Australia had changed its position owing to popular outrage over the abuses perpetrated by the Indonesians on the East Timorese. This outrage was coupled with the growing geopolitical importance of East Timor to Australia based on the proximity of the territory—less than three hundred miles away—the oil and gas potential of the Timor Sea, and fear of a flood of Timorese refugees.

Suharto was ousted in 1998, and the president to follow him, B. J. Habibie, agreed in 1999 to a referendum in which the Timorese voted overwhelmingly for independence. This touched off an even worse bloodbath by progovernment militia and some Indonesian troops that ended with the intervention of Australian armed forces, but only after much of the territory had been destroyed and fifty thousand Timorese had been killed.

The events that centered on East Timor reflected contrasting strategic priorities for the United States and Australia. Unlike Australia, the United States did not have a primary geopolitical interest in East Timor. Its concern was the oil of Indonesia located far to the west, in Sumatra. As a result, Washington procrastinated while Australia took the lead in the intervention.

East Timor became independent in May 2002, changing its name to Timor-Leste. It made the transition from UN tutelage, rebuilding its devastated country and developing the frameworks of statehood. While most of the one million Timorese are impoverished and depend largely on agriculture, their hopes for a brighter economic future rest on the proven oil and gas reserves that underlie the Timor Sea. This area, called the Timor Gap, lies midway between Australia and East Timor. Australia initially claimed half of the reserves based upon a boundary agreement it had made with Indonesia in 1972. The Timor Gap is less than four hundred miles wide; therefore, drawing a boundary based upon an international standard of two hundred miles would result in overlapping claims. Australia agreed to accept the consequences of a median line boundary, placing 90 percent of the Timor Gap under Timor-Leste's sovereignty. The fields are still treated as a single, shared entity, without formally fixing the new boundary along this median line.[6] By 2007, Timor-Leste had realized about $1 billion from oil and gas revenues, but political instability has stalled the use of these funds for economic development. Gang violence had engulfed the capital, Dili, to the point that in 2006, Australia and other nations had to send peacekeepers to quell the violence.

In Indonesia, the "stability" of the Suharto era was based on repression. Little wonder that with the end of the military regime, many of the rebellions that had been repressed or brutally contained again rose to the surface. The strongest separatist movements remain in the northernmost and easternmost sections of the archipelago, far removed from Jakarta.

Aceh has constituted the most serious military challenge to Jakarta's rule and has been the most important of the separatist movements. Adjoining the northwestern entrance to the Strait of Malacca, the world's busiest shipping lane, the province lies eleven hundred miles northwest of Jakarta. The population is about 4.5 million (out of Sumatra's total of approximately 40 million) in an area of 21,000 square miles. Aceh accounts for 15 percent of Indonesia's oil and natural gas exports and also produces coffee, pepper, rice, tobacco, rubber, and timber.

The Acehnese rebel movement was well supported financially and powerfully motivated by the history of the region as an independent principality. The Indonesian government and the military opposed Aceh's claims for independence not only for economic reasons and on the grounds of the province's being an integral part of the national territory, but also for its strategic location along the Strait of Malacca. The rebellion disrupted production from onshore and offshore gas fields around Arun, where a liquefaction plant is located that ships its products to Japan and South Korea—a matter of concern not only to the international companies operating in the area but also to Indonesia and its international customers.

Indonesian insistence on holding onto the territory ignored the centuries of Acehnese history as an independent Muslim sultanate. Its economic importance to Jakarta, albeit substantial, needs to be considered within the broader economic context. Aceh's oil and gas contribute only 3 percent of Indonesia's energy revenues and a small fraction of the national GDP of nearly $1 trillion. Aceh's energy reserves are dwindling owing to the depletion of its fields. Indeed, so rapidly has all of Indonesia's oil output decreased and local demand increased that it is no longer a net oil exporter; it left OPEC in 2008. While the Indonesian government was unable to crush the rebellion of the devout Acehnese in nearly thirty years of fighting and with the loss of fifteen thousand lives, nature intervened to bring the two sides to an agreement. The devastating tsunami of 2004 washed over the province, killing up to 170,000 people and leaving more than half a million homeless. This took the fire out of the conflict. The rebels laid down their arms in exchange for the right to form a political party, to receive 55 percent of the oil and 45 percent of the natural gas revenues, and to apply strict Shariah law within Aceh. Their rebel party won the special provincial election held in 2006 prior to provincial parliamentary elections in 2009. To the benefit of both the Acehnese and the rest of Indonesia, the focus turned from conflict to recovery from the devastation wrought by the tidal wave.

Separatism in the remote South Moluccas (the islands of Ambon, Buru, and Seram) is focused on Ambon, the provincial capital and largest town, which is fourteen hundred miles from Jakarta. The basis for the separatist drive is historical and religious, for half of the one million population of the South Moluccas (an area of 10,500 square miles) is Christian. Five hundred years ago, the Spice Islands were important because they were the only source of nutmeg and cloves; Dutch traders in these items brought Christianity to the islands. Today the islands are unimportant agriculturally and economically in general. The Christian-based separatist movement is not propelled by concerns of economic discrimination but by fear of being swamped by Muslim immigrants who have settled on the island as part of the "transmigration" program. If a small, Christian-dominated state or quasi state were to be established in these islands, which lie just to the west of Irian Jaya, it would have little negative strategic or economic consequence for Indonesia. Christian communities in Halmahera in the North Moluccas, where communal strife is widespread, might then choose to relocate to a new South Moluccan Republic.

Irian Jaya is the locus of the third major separatist conflict. This western half of the island of New Guinea has a population of under two million in a land area of 163,000 square miles. Most of the Irianese (also known as Papuans) are indigenous Melanesian tribespeople who live on subsistence farming in the jungle areas and have little in common with the Javanese.

These native Papuan rebels have continued a struggle for independence that first broke out over four decades ago and has lasted into the post-Suharto era. Their resentment over loss of lands to timber interests that have overexploited the province's tropical hardwoods is intensified by their failure to derive any benefits from the large-scale copper, gold, and silver mining operations that are conducted by foreign corporations under lease from Jakarta, or from the island's oil deposits. One of the corporations operating in Irian Jaya is the single largest in Indonesia.

Offers of special autonomy by the Indonesian government have been spurned by the Free Papua Congress, which has declared independence for the country. The Papuans are armed with only bows and arrows, in contrast to the rebels in wealthy Aceh province, who were well equipped with modern weapons with which to conduct full-scale operations against the Indonesian army. Nevertheless, the Papuans have attacked and killed non-Papuan migrant settlers in the towns of Merauke and Fafak and have stepped up guerrilla warfare within the entire province. In response, Indonesia has poured troops into Irian Jaya's capital of Jayapura and cracked down heavily on the native population, committing widespread human rights abuses.

The West Papuans might well seek a federation with Papua New Guinea, the independent state that covers the eastern half of the island. With a population of over seven million, or nearly three times the population of Irian Jaya, Papua New Guinea is part of the (British) Commonwealth of Nations. It has a relatively strong agricultural base, with important oil and natural gas, mineral, and forestry resources. Under Australian administration for most of the twentieth century, until it gained independence in 1975, its major trading partner remains Australia. Its capital, Port Moresby, is located on the Coral Sea, three hundred miles from northeastern Australia and within the Australian security umbrella. Papua New Guinea itself has had to deal with a separatist movement on its island of Bougainville, which is rich in copper and has extensive natural gas reserves. Since it depends on Australian economic aid and police protection, it might be receptive to a federation with Irian Jaya, which is also much closer to Australia than it is to most of Indonesia.

These three areas—Aceh, Irian Jaya, and the South Moluccas—have been the main, but not the only, trouble spots in Indonesia. There is major unrest in Kalimantan, the southern 70 percent of the island of Borneo. (North Borneo contains the Malaysian states of Sabah and Sarawak and the independent, oil-rich Sultanate of Brunei.) Although sparsely populated by indigenous native tribes, Kalimantan is wealthy in oil, gold, natural gas, and valuable tropical hardwoods. A government transmigration program that brought tens of thousands of Madurese farmers to the island has provoked violence by the Dayaks in West Kalimantan against the Madurese, forcing many to flee back to their island of origin. The unrest has stimulated calls for independence, especially in East Kalimantan, where the oil resources are located. In addition, in the Indonesian waters, especially those north of Borneo leading to the South China Sea and the Pacific, piracy is rampant. Over 50 percent of the world incidence of piracy occurs in these waters or those of the Strait of Malacca.

Separatist movements also exist in Christian North Sulawesi (the northern Celebes) and in the Muslim-populated Ujung Pandang (Makasar), the capital and largest city of South Sulawesi. The latter, at the juncture of the Makasar Strait and the Flores Sea, was a historic center for the spice trade and is now a major distribution and transshipment point for goods from Europe and Asia. It had a long history as an independent sultanate until it was conquered by the Dutch in the mid-seventeenth century.

Potentially the most serious breakaway threat besides those in Irian Jaya and the South Moluccas lies in the province of Riau in west-central Sumatra, opposite Singapore at the southeastern end of the Strait of Malacca. Riau's vast oil and gas reserves rival those of Aceh. These include the huge gas fields that lie under the territorial waters surrounding the province's Natuna Islands, in the shallow waters of the South China Sea. The islands are closer to the Malay Peninsula and eastern Malaysia (on the Island of Borneo) than to Riau's mainland, and proposals have been made to tap the West Natuna gas field by pipelines to Singapore and possibly the southern tip of the Malay Peninsula. Bintan Island in the Riau Archipelago has extensive bauxite and tin mines. The great threat to Indonesia of Riau's separatist movement is that its success could trigger breakaway sentiments within the rest of Sumatra and lead to a repeat of the island's rebellion of 1958–61. The Indonesian military has been adamant about retaining all of these rebellious regions. However, there is not a strong case for holding onto remote Irian Jaya, which is over two thousand miles from Jakarta and populated by Melanesians. That region has been exploited by Indonesian military leaders for self-enrichment through control of coffee plantations and the awarding of mining concessions, but its economic importance to the country as a whole is minor.

Indonesia is a state waiting to implode. If an agreement can be reached with the South Moluccas and the province of Riau, its prospects are favorable for surviving as a strong and influential power. However, should all of the island of Sumatra, with its wealth of natural resources, break away, those prospects would be considerably diminished.

Java is overpopulated, with a density of more than two thousand persons per square mile—one of the highest in the world. While agricultural productivity on the island has increased in recent years, and while most of Indonesia's industry is located within the island's centers of Jakarta, Surabaya, and Sandung, Java would be hard-pressed without access to part of Sumatra. Java's land area is one-tenth that of Sumatra, while the population is three times as large (Sumatra has a population of approximately forty million). Sumatra has been an outlet for modest transmigration from its crowded neighboring island in addition to being valued for its natural resources. The wealth of its oil, gas, minerals, timber, and crops produces the major share of Indonesia's GDP. Without Sumatra, Indonesia would be impoverished.

Transmigration cannot solve the problems of overcrowded Java, Madura, and Bali. During the Suharto-initiated program, six million settlers were transferred, mainly to the Outer

Islands, but this did not compensate for the natural increase in population of the overcrowded islands. However, settlement in Sumatra has not stirred the ethnic passions that have torn the rest of the Outer Islands.

The challenge to Jakarta is to reorganize its political structure to satisfy the needs of its Outer Islands. With approximately 60 percent of the population of the country, Java need not fear losing its leadership within a reconstituted state, provided that it changes its current hegemonic rule to one based upon partnership with federated units. Such a policy would be especially reassuring to Bali, with its unique Hindu/Buddhist culture and rituals that are akin to the ancient Javanese Hindu culture, and would make this small island of three million people a major attraction for international tourism.

An Indonesia at peace and without remote breakaway territories could become a genuine keystone of Asia Pacifica and a fitting partner of Japan and Australia in the continued development of the region. It would remain the most populous Muslim country in the world and the fourth most populous national state. An Indonesia in continuing strife, with unwilling and unassimilated parts, will fall far short of realizing its national potential and will be a drag on prospects for regional unity.

Democracy alone is no guarantee of Indonesian stability. Although the Indonesian parliament was democratically elected after the ouster of General Suharto in 1998, the country has suffered from considerable political instability. Within a three-year period (1998–2001), it had three presidents—B. J. Habibie, Abdurrahman Wahid, and Megawati Sukarnoputri. The latter, a daughter of Indonesia's founding father, Sukarno, was replaced by Susilo Bambang Yudhoyono in the election of 2004. However, even if political transitions continue to follow free and open elections, Indonesia's secular government remains heavily dependent on the military for support in stabilizing the country. This is because of the threat of radical Islam to Indonesian democracy.

This most populous of Muslim nations has had, from the introduction of Islam in the twelfth century, a tradition of religious moderation and tolerance. It embraced elements of the Hinduism, Buddhism, and animism that characterized the islands' earlier cultures and societies. In recent years, however, conservative Islamic forces have gained strength, and a number of hard-line Islamic parties have emerged. Some observers attribute the trend toward more extreme religiosity as a response to the desire to escape from poverty and minimize the threat to Indonesian democracy.[7]

Sporadic attacks against Christians and foreigners have been carried out by Islamic militant groups, the most prominent of which is Jemaah Islamiya, whose goal is a Southeast Asian Islamic caliphate. The Indonesian military has been successful in capturing many of the terrorists, including their leadership. Containing political separatism and radical Islam will continue to require a strong partnership between the secular parties and the military while furthering local autonomy and respecting the religious values of the citizenry.

Geopolitical Features

HISTORIC CORE

The Asia-Pacific Rim has no regional historic core, inasmuch as there was no single defining political event to initiate the process of regional geopolitical cohesion. National and subregional historic cores include Kyoto, seat of Japanese dynasties in central Honchu; Songdo, seat of the Koryo dynasty in western Korea; Sukothai, capital of the Khmer Empire in northern Thailand; and Borobudur, temple compound center for the Srivijaya Empire in central Java.

Figure 10.1. Asia-Pacific Rim: Major Geopolitical Features

POLITICAL CAPITALS

The Asia-Pacific Rim has no single, formal political capital. Bangkok served as the capital of the now-defunct military alliance, SEATO. ASEAN, the current economic, social, and cultural alliance, is headquartered in Jakarta, while the seat of the Asia-Pacific Economic Cooperation Forum (APEC) is Singapore. However, neither ASEAN nor APEC is coterminous with the boundaries of Asia Pacifica.

The political capitals with the greatest political-economic impact upon Asia Pacifica are Tokyo and Singapore. Tokyo represents the region's leading economic, political, and military power (although constitutionally the military can be applied only for self-defense). Singapore, Asia Pacifica's leading international trading center, lies at the convergence of some of the world's major sea-lanes between Europe and East Asia. It is a major center for international finance, vying with Tokyo in this respect, and is regional headquarters for many world-class multinational corporations.

ECUMENE

The map of the Asia-Pacific Rim displays a geopolitical region of mostly island states separated by narrow waters and broader seas and nearby mainland peninsular countries. For most purposes, an ecumene is defined as a contiguous area of densest populations, transportation and communications networks, and clustering of economic activities. Contiguity can include narrow seas as well as land, and in a water-oriented region, where seas are connectors rather than barriers, a chain of national ecumenes that link up with one another form a regional ecumene.

The most important of such ecumenes in Asia Pacifica extends along the east coast of Japan's island of Honshu, from metropolitan Tokyo-Yokohama southward through Nagoya, Osaka, and Kobe, to Hiroshima and Shimonoseki at the southern tip of the island. From there, it is connected by a railroad tunnel and bridge southward across the very narrow Shimonoseki Strait to Kitakyushu, along the northwestern coast of Kyushu to Fukuoko and Nagasaki, as well as into the north-central part of the island to Kurume and along its northeastern coast.

This water-connected national ecumene is the economic powerhouse of the Asia-Pacific Rim. It contains approximately 80 percent of Japan's 127 million people and the vast majority of Japan's electronics, metallurgical, motor vehicle, ship, chemical, and textile production. Together with commerce, finance, and services, this concentration of population and economic activity has made the modern economy of Japan second only to that of the United States in productivity. Population densities within the ecumene range from ten thousand per square mile in the Kanto Plain (Tokyo-Yokohama) to three thousand per square mile in Nagoya.

The Honshu ecumene also extends westward across the hundred-mile-wide Korean Strait into South Korea. This South Korean extension forms the other part of the regional ecumene. It is a major independent global economic force, formed in great measure by Japanese investment and supplemented by US aid. The Japanese outsourcing of manufactures and export of capital investment and technology that followed the Korean War provided the spur for what has become a varied and cutting-edge economy.

Most of South Korea's manufacturing takes place within its ecumene, which contains thirty million people, representing 60 percent of the nation's total of fifty million. Population densities of the ecumene average three thousand persons per square mile and continue to increase because so much of the eastern half of the peninsula is mountainous and unsuitable for the spread of population.

The Korean and Japanese ecumenes are linked at Pusan, Korea's second-largest city (population 3.6 million) and its largest port, which handles most of the country's foreign trade and serves as the gateway to Japan. South Korea's economic core area then runs inland through Taigu, the third-largest city, and on to Taijon on the west coast. It then follows the coast northward to Seoul, the capital and the most important urban and industrial center of the country, with a city population of nearly ten million. The city, which is located on the broad plain of the Han, the largest river in the country, is backed by a rim of mountains. Historically, it served as a junction for routes connecting the entire peninsula, extending northward along the west coast, via Kaesong, to Pyongyang, northeastward across the mountains to Wonsan (all now in North Korea), and southeastward across the peninsula to Pusan. As large as it is, Seoul has not been able to absorb all of the population that its industrial base supports, and a megalopolis has grown up within an approximately thirty-mile radius. Over fifteen million people now live in these outer centers, including the industrial port of Incheon and the city of Suwon. Incheon has a population of nearly 3 million, and Suwon has 1.2 million. Both are connected by subway to the capital.[8]

The Seoul megalopolis of over twenty-five million now both dominates the country and mirrors its remarkable industrial growth. Its motor vehicle, shipping, steel, chemical, machinery, and textile industries have pushed into the outer periphery of the region. Electronics, including semiconductors, computer, and telecommunications equipment, and financial, insurance, and information services are more concentrated within the central city.

The South Korean ecumene extends to the northern suburbs of Seoul, only twenty miles from the Demilitarized Zone (DMZ), which marks the border between the two Koreas. While Seoul is now a frontier city, it does not stretch the imagination to envisage its eventual reemergence as the center of the peninsula—if not of a united Korea, then at least as a link between two Koreas that are open to economic and social interchange. The current distance between the northern edge of the South Korean ecumene and the North Korean economic core area, centering on Pyongyang-Nampo, is only sixty miles. This gap has been filled by the spillover of Seoul's industries, across the 2.5-mile DMZ to the Kaesong. There, South Korean small and medium-sized firms employ thousands of North Korean workers, with the output designed for export. These exports take advantage of South Korea's free-trade agreement with the United States. In anticipation of a united Korea, South Korean land adjoining the DMZ has escalated in value.

With political unity, one could expect the Korean ecumene eventually to expand northward from Pyongyang along the Yellow Sea to the Yalu River and link up with the industrial complexes of southern Manchuria. At such time, the vision could well be realized of Seoul as the hub of northeast Asia, linking Japan, Korea, and northeast China. A unified ecumene would then extend from Honshu and northern Kyushu across the Korean Strait and then along the full length of Korea's west coast. From there it would connect northwestward to Manchuria's Liaodong Peninsula and then into the industrial heart of Liaoning Province from Shenyang to Bohai Bay (Gulf of Chili) at the northern end of the Yellow Sea. Russia's southern Maritime Territory, centering on Vladivostok and the Upper Ussuri valley, could become an important outlier.

The Asia-Pacific Rim also includes several significant but scattered secondary ecumenes: southwestern Malaysia-Singapore; the northwest coast of Java; the southeast coast of Australia, with one cluster extending from Newcastle through Sydney and Wollongong to Canberra and the other extending from Melbourne to Geelong; and western Taiwan.

Taiwan is the most important of these secondary core areas, extending from the northern tip of the island at Taipei along the length of the western coast through Taoyuan, Taichung, and Tainan, to the southernmost end at Gaoxiong. While Formosa, as the Japanese called Taiwan, had undergone modest modernization under the Japanese occupation (1905 until the end of World War II), it was still largely agricultural when the Chinese Nationalists gained control of the island in 1949, after being driven from the mainland. Most of the population during that period lived, as it still does, on the semitropical, broad, fertile west coast plain, since the central and eastern parts of the island are heavily forested hills and high mountains.

Over the next half-century, massive US aid spurred industrial development, mainly in light industry, producing consumer and food products. The development shifted to heavy industry at the start and then to high technology and services. Chemicals, steel, motor vehicles, pharmaceuticals, electronics, electrical goods, telecommunications, and transport equipment now are spread throughout the Taiwanese ecumene.

An example of Taiwan's economic strength is Hsinchu Science Park, located outside Taipei. Known as Silicon Valley East, this center is the core of the world's third-largest high-tech industry concentration and accounts for one-third of Taiwan's manufacturing exports and a large share of the world's computer production.

An outstanding characteristic of Taiwan's industry is that small and medium-sized companies predominate. These companies are flexibly structured and have shown an aptitude for developing innovative technologies and organizational systems. When China's reforms in the 1990s provided an opening for Taiwanese investment, Taiwan was prepared. Since that time, thousands of businesses have been set up in China as well as in Southeast Asia. In a massive shift, many of Taiwan's labor-intensive manufacturing enterprises have been relocated to the Chinese ecumene in Hong Kong and the provinces of Guangdong and Fujian, just one hundred miles across the Taiwan Strait from Taiwan's ecumene. Recently, a considerable amount of Taiwan's high-tech computer hardware and software production has been outsourced to jointly owned Chinese coastal industries; up to one-third of all Chinese exports are now estimated to be made by Taiwanese-owned manufacturing firms. China and Japan are now the leading trade partners of Taiwan.

There are profound geopolitical consequences of what is becoming, in effect, a merged Taiwan-China ecumene. As Taiwan's economic success becomes increasingly bound up with that of maritime China, its role as a gateway to the mainland increases. Despite serious political differences between the two countries, the reality of a merged economy may lead to a peaceful unification more quickly than many currently anticipate. This is despite occasional aggressive actions by mainland China toward Taiwan and native Taiwanese leadership's continuing affirmation of the goal of independence.

EFFECTIVE NATIONAL TERRITORY

Lack of regional land contiguity mitigates against the delineation of a coherent effective regional territory. National immigration laws also work against the possibility of settlement on a regional basis of less densely populated areas possessing favorable climatic and terrain features.

Only Australia has vast amounts of effective national territory (ENT). These developable lands form an arc that borders the ecumene from Brisbane west to Adelaide and the Murray River valley. In addition, they include areas that lie in Perth's interior in southwest Australia. The ranching and commercial farming areas of the semitropical northeast (the coastal sectors of Queensland), where pockets of urbanization already exist, also belong to the ENT.

Australia's extensive coal deposits extend along the coast northward from Sydney through Queensland and Cape York. Coal, together with western Australia's rich iron ore, have found an important export market in China, as have its wheat, beef, and wool, such that China now vies with Japan as Australia's leading trade partner. Despite the elimination in 2007 of the Asian exclusion laws, the numbers of legally admitted immigrants from within and outside the region remain limited to 190,000 skilled workers per annum, with another 60,000 allotted to family members. This does little to relieve the population pressures of Asia Pacifica, especially since only about one-quarter of the immigrants come from within the region.

The extent and proportion of ENT in other countries within the region are much more restricted. Japan's ENT includes much of western and southern Hokkaido and Shikoku as well as parts of northern Honshu and the southern island of Kyushu. The economy of Kyushu is mixed. The area along the north coast has a sizable motor vehicle industry, with most of the exports destined for China. The west coast, however, is not as prosperous, since its textile and garment industry has collapsed, and Nagasaki's shipbuilding industry is losing its competitive edge because of the high cost of steel.

In the Philippines, there is development potential in Mindanao, some parts of Leyte, and the smaller islands that all lie to the south of Luzon. So is there potential in portions of tropical peninsular southern Thailand and areas within its semiarid savannah northeast. The lowland and upland jungles of much of Malaysia are unfavorable for human settlement, although the northwest around George Town and the northeast coast do offer some room for expansion.

Indonesia's ENT includes southern Sumatra and that island's west-central and northeast coast. In addition, there are expansion prospects in some of the Outer Islands east of Java, such as Lombok, western Sumbawa in the Lesser Sundas, southern Flores, and southern Sulawesi.

Most of New Zealand's population is concentrated in the urban centers of the North Island, as is the bulk of its agricultural production. The plains on the eastern side of the South Island, the larger of the country's two main islands, represent New Zealand's ENT.

Singapore has no ENT, being completely filled by its ecumene. Likewise, there is very little ENT in South Korea or Taiwan because most of the land outside their ecumenes is mountainous.

What blocks the development of some of these ENTs is political unrest as well as lack of development capital. This is reflected especially in Indonesia. Past efforts to resettle Javanese, Balinese, and Madurese in developable parts of Irian Jaya, the South Moluccas, and Kalimantan have contributed to political unrest and turmoil, which in turn inhibits such development.

EMPTY AREA

Many of the countries of the Asia-Pacific Rim have empty areas in their mountainous and jungle sectors. Very sparsely inhabited, the jungles serve as bases or places of refuge for guerrilla groups, support indigenous cultures and tribal ways of life, or provide a basis for large-scale timber operations and the destruction of the ecological balance. But only one part of the rim has a vast empty area—Australia.

Most of the interior of Australia, especially the western and central portions, is desert that covers about one-third of the continental landmass of nearly three million square miles. This interior is a flat, dry, and uninhabited plateau with no permanent rivers or lakes. The country's population of over twenty-three million hugs the eastern and southwestern coasts, while the rainy tropical northern coasts are also virtually uninhabited.

The deserts of the interior include the Great Sandy, Gibson, Great Victoria, Tanami, and Simpson. In the east-central portion of Australia's deserts, the monotony of the landscape is broken by the MacDonnell Ranges (which overlook the town of Alice Springs) and the Musgrave Ranges. North of the latter is the sandstone monolith of Ayers Rock (Uluru), which rises boldly above the plain and is, like Alice Springs, a tourist attraction.

The empty interior holds considerable mineral wealth—gold, copper, molybdenum, oil, and natural gas—and in the Kimberley Plateau in northwest Australia is the world's largest diamond mine. In addition, it supplies a quarter of the world's uranium oxide exports. These currently go only to countries that have signed the Nuclear Non-Proliferation Treaty. In 2007, Australia made an exception for India as part of its policy of building a solid relationship with India similar to that which it has with Japan and China.

The interior's greatest strategic value is in the realm of space rocketry and stellar observation. Woomera, on the fringe of the desert in South Australia near the usually dry saltwater Lake Torrens, is the site of the major missile testing range used by Australia and its allies. This testing range extends deep into Western Australia and was once the biggest land rocket range in the world. It was from here that Australia's only space satellite was launched in 1967 and here that the British multiple reentry nuclear warhead testing program was conducted in the early 1970s. The town of Woomera now has a population of fifteen hundred, or one-quarter of its size during the height of rocketry activities.

In addition to the range, the interior provides tracking stations in Western Australia and Queensland. Geraldton, two hundred miles north of Perth on the desert's coastal edge, is part of a network of ground stations that monitor North Korea and Pakistan and are operated by the United States, Britain, Canada, Australia, and New Zealand. The clear, dark skies and excellent viewing conditions have also attracted important observatories to east-central New South Wales, at Siding Spring and Trunkey Creek, in the semiarid grasslands that lie to the east of the desert.

The Pine Gap Joint Defense Space facility in a remote part of central Australia is an electronic spying base operated jointly by Australia and the United States. Its large antennae, which pick up signals from US space satellites, have the potential of playing a key role in an early warning system for the proposed American NMD system. This use of Pine Gap has become highly controversial within Australia, provoking demonstrations and protests. The Labor Party is opposed for fear of the impact of such use on the relations between Canberra and both China and some of the Asia-Pacific states.

BOUNDARIES

The important boundary disputes involving Asia Pacifica are not intraregional but involve issues with nations that border the region. These are strategic boundaries because of their substantial impact upon the relation of Asia Pacifica with its neighboring geostrategic realms. The boundary controversies among Asia-Pacific state members have only tactical or local impacts.

The dispute between Japan and Russia over four islands held by Russia—Etorofu and Kunashiri, the southernmost of the Kuril Islands chain, and, to its south, the geographically distinct islands of Habomai and Shikotan. The dispute involves definition of the boundary between the heartlandic Russian and maritime realms as well as the border between the two countries. In the light of Japan's expanding trade and economic assistance to Russia since 1997, there may be a possibility of ending what has been a bitter dispute since the end of

World War II. In 2006, Russia offered to return Habomai and Shikotan, provided that Tokyo renounce its claim to the much larger Etorofu and Kunashiri. This has not been accepted. Also, while Japan renounced its claim to southern Sakhalin in 1952, it has left the issue in limbo because it has not approved Russia's sovereignty over it. Unless some compromise on these islands can be reached, a peace treaty between Russia and Japan will remain elusive.

The North-South Korea and China-Taiwan conflicts over unification of their territories are disputes not about the drawing of boundary lines but about territorial sovereignty. As such, these relate to the boundary between the East Asia and maritime geostrategic realms. There is also controversy over the line of demarcation between North and South Korea. The North Koreans never accepted the "northern limit line" unilaterally drawn by the UN Command at the end of the Korean War and assert their title to five small islands in the Yellow Sea off Panmunjon that are occupied by South Korea. This has resulted in naval clashes between the two countries. North Korea also claims a two-hundred-mile economic zone in the waters of the Sea of Japan off its east coast, and this has precipitated armed clashes over the rights of South Korean and Japanese fishing boats.

Both China and Taiwan have sought to exercise sovereignty over Japan's Senkaku (Diaoku) Island group in the Ryukyu (Nansei) archipelago south of Okinawa—the Senkaku Islands are five uninhabited coral islands that lie only one hundred miles off the east coast of Taiwan. Japan and South Korea dispute ownership over Tsuhima/Dogdo—the islands that lie between them in the Sea of Japan. The geopolitical impacts of these disputes are minor because of the relative insignificance of the areas that are involved.

The major disputes over the strategic boundary between East Asia and Asia-Pacific Rim countries revolve around the Spratly and Paracel Island groupings and the demarcation line between Japan and China in the East China Sea. The Spratlys are located at the southern end of the South China Sea, midway between Vietnam, Malaysia, and the Philippines and 650 miles southeast of Hainan. They were held in the 1930s by France and during World War II by Japan, which built a submarine base on Spratly (Storm) Island, the largest in the chain. In 1946, the Chinese Nationalists declared sovereignty over the islands and left a garrison on one of them.

Called the Nansha Islands by the Chinese and the Kalayaan Islands by the Philippines, this archipelago consists of nearly two hundred islands, scattered coral reefs, and sandbars that lie astride the sea passage between Singapore and Japan and guard the southern entrance to the South China Sea.

Both historical and strategic arguments were the basis for the initial claims to the Spratlys by China, the Philippines, Taiwan, Vietnam, Malaysia, and Brunei. These claims took on greater urgency when in 1976 oil was discovered at Reed Bank, midway between the Spratly group and the Philippine island of Palawan. Oil production began there in 1979 by a consortium to which the Philippine government granted the concession. Since then, natural gas reserves have been discovered that are potentially richer than even the petroleum deposits.

The overlapping claims by the various parties have led to a series of naval and troop clashes in the Spratlys between China and the Philippines, the Philippines and Vietnam, and China and Vietnam. The clashes between China and Vietnam were one of several factors in the deterioration of their relations after the unification of Vietnam.[9] Incidents occurred as early as 1974, but the most serious clashes took place in 1988, when the Chinese navy sank several Vietnamese naval vessels.

The dispute between China and the Philippines has been sparked by facilities constructed by the Chinese on Mischief Reef, which lies west of Palawan and falls within the two-hundred-mile exclusive economic maritime zone of the Philippines. The Chinese claim them to be fishing shelters, but Manila insists that they are military installations. In addition, Brunei established an exclusive fishing zone around Louisa Reef in the southern Spratly Islands but does not formally claim the island. Despite the attempts of ASEAN to develop a regional code of conduct to prevent the use of force, China refuses to recognize the dispute as a multilateral one. It is unlikely that Beijing will yield on the Spratlys because of their oil and gas potential and China's growing dependence upon imported energy supplies.

In the northern part of the South China Sea, the Paracel (Xisha) Islands are also in dispute. These 130 barren coral islands and reefs lie 175 miles southeast of China's Hainan Island and 230 miles off the Vietnam coast. Chinese armed forces seized the Paracels from the Vietnamese in 1974, following Saigon's announced intention of conducting oil surveys there. The Chinese continue to administer them in the face of Vietnamese claims to the chain. Although the waters of the island are now used by fishermen, their economic significance is in the oil reserves that underlie them. While the boundary controversy is essentially between the two East Asian mainland powers, Taiwan still formally claims them on the basis of being the legitimate government of China, adding a strategic dimension to the dispute. As with the Spratlys, the oil potential of the Paracels is likely to block a speedy resolution of the dispute, though both countries have agreed to negotiate their differences. The Chinese claim is reinforced by the fact that the Paracels are close, not only to Hainan, but also to Hong Kong and Guangzhou, which are only 450 miles away.

Japan and China are at loggerheads over the international boundary in the East China Sea. Their claims to exclusive economic zones (EEZ) overlap where an important natural gas field exists under the seabed. China began to drill in this area close to Japan's two-hundred-mile boundary, and Japan claims that the field should be shared because of the overlap of the EEZ.

The outstanding intraregional boundary disputes are relatively minor. One has to do with conflicting claims between Japan and South Korea over the uninhabited, volcanic Tok Do islets (Liancourt Rocks), which lie between the coasts of southwestern Honshu and east-central Korea. Claimed by Japan in 1905, they called the islands the Takeshimas. Although the islets are worthless, the dispute over ownership still arouses passionate nationalist sentiments in both countries.[10]

Another dispute is over two small coral islands off the coast of Sabah that have been developed as resorts by Malaysia but are claimed by Indonesia. Both sides have agreed to submit this dispute to international arbitration. Malaysia and Singapore also have conflicting claims to two small islands.

A more significant territorial issue between Malaysia and Indonesia was resolved in 1974. Then, thanks to the reduction in tension between the two countries that occurred after Indonesia joined ASEAN (Malaysia, Thailand, and the Philippines had been its founding members), Jakarta recognized the incorporation of Sabah (northern Borneo) into the federation of Malaysia. The Philippines renounced its claim to the former British protectorate three years later as its contribution to ASEAN unity, although it has not formally revoked its rights.[11]

On the landward western side of the Asia-Pacific Rim, alignment of Thailand's border with Burma is in dispute and has occasioned sporadic conflict. Tensions between the two countries have recently increased, as Bangkok has tried to seal its borders against the flow of illicit drugs from eastern Myanmar's processing factories. Parts of Thailand's borders with Laos and Cambodia are also indefinite, but this has occasioned only minor friction. Thailand and Vietnam came to an agreement over their border in 1997.

Conclusion

Japan and Australia remain the linchpins of the Asia-Pacific Rim. Each has developed increasingly important links with China. However, their security interests as well as trade ties with the United States and the rest of the maritime realm place them squarely within that geostrategic sphere. Singapore, Malaysia, and Thailand are also tightly linked with Japan. All of these nations have strong trade ties with China. However, they depend on the US security shield to maintain their national integrity in face of looming Chinese pressures. Papua New Guinea, Timor-Leste, and the Solomons lie within Australia's security and economic orbit, while Brunei is linked to Japan, Singapore, Malaysia, and Australia. In 2007, Australian national elections brought Labor to power, Kevin Rudd defeating the Liberal Party's long-serving John Howard, who had fostered close military ties with the United States. Rudd announced Australia's economic relations with China, and he has reaffirmed Canberra's commitment to the ANZUS treaty. Rudd also ratified the Kyoto Protocol, leaving the United States as the only developed nation not to have signed it.

While Indonesia has important trade links with China, it is located outside Beijing's geostrategic reach. The historical prejudice of this Muslim nation against its Chinese mercantile-class citizens and its global trading links to the United States, Europe, and Japan are likely to keep it within the Pacific Rim maritime sphere.

The future geostrategic status of South Korea and Taiwan, currently important Pacific Rim members, is uncertain. The political unification of the Korean peninsula and integration of Taiwan within a "One China" framework, although not imminent, are likely to be realized at some future time. When this does take place, the geostrategic status of the two countries will be altered.

Developmentally, the Asia-Pacific Rim, which has achieved an economically specialized level, is still a less geopolitically mature region than the others within the American and maritime European realms. Before it can achieve parity with those regions as an integrated geopolitical force, it needs to establish a stronger regional political, economic, and military framework and to reduce its dependence on the US military-strategic umbrella.

The frameworks that presently bind the region are either too narrowly or too broadly drawn. ASEAN, which includes five of the Asia-Pacific Rim countries, excludes South Korea, Japan, Taiwan, Australia, and New Zealand—the most economically advanced portions of the region. ASEAN's ten-member group (Myanmar, Thailand, the three Indochina states, Malaysia, Singapore, the Philippines, Indonesia, and Brunei), with a combined population of six hundred million, has developed an ASEAN Free Trade Area, in which tariffs and customs duties have been radically lowered or eliminated. India, Australia, New Zealand, South Korea, Japan, and China have forged free-trade agreements with ASEAN but are not incorporated within its framework. ASEAN's tariff reduction policies are designed to stimulate trade, investment, and currency exchange and to facilitate economic specialization among its members. Another drawback of ASEAN is that it includes Vietnam, Cambodia, and Laos, which lie within the East Asia geostrategic orbit and have very different strategic interests from their Asia-Pacific Rim neighbors. It also includes Myanmar, which is caught between East and South Asia. Under such circumstances, the poorer Southeast Asian states are dependent upon ad hoc aid from their more affluent neighbors. What they lack is a structural form within a regional body, such as the EU, whose policies they could help to shape while being helped to develop.

The Asia-Pacific Economic Community (APEC) is far too broad a framework to meet the direct economic needs of Asia Pacifica. Established under the leadership of the United

States in 1989, APEC was founded to liberalize transpacific trade. In addition to the ASEAN states, Japan, South Korea, Australia, and New Zealand, the organization's members include countries with very divergent strategic interests—China, Russia, the United States, Canada, Mexico, Peru, and Chile. While APEC can serve the important purpose of binding the Asia-Pacific Rim to the entire Pacific world, including the Western hemispheric portions and the north Eurasian Pacific, it is an inadequate forum for addressing such regional issues as intraregional migration, short-term labor exchanges, smuggling of drugs and other goods, and narrowing the economic gap.

Regional geopolitical unity is the outgrowth of political, social, and military/strategic bonds, as well as economic linkages. Such bonds are still in an incipient stage within the Asia-Pacific Rim. Instead, bilateral agreements, especially those between the region's member states and the United States, characterize the region. An Asia-Pacific Rim economic framework is needed whereby the region's stronger states can take the lead in reducing regional economic inequalities.

In military affairs, the American military shield protects South Korea, Japan, Taiwan, the Philippines, Thailand, Australia, and New Zealand. A common regional strategic framework would strengthen the geopolitical unity of Asia Pacifica. A major step in building such a framework would be the creation of an Asia-Pacific rapid-response regional defense force by those six states. Such a force could play a vital role in heading off local conflicts or minimizing the impact of wars that erupt.

The regional approach to peacemaking and peacekeeping would be politically more effective than the efforts of individual countries or of international agencies. Moreover, a regional military command would help to build a spirit of confidence and cooperation among countries that have long harbored suspicions about one another over boundary issues or support of separatist groups. Such a regional defense arm would not diminish the need for the American strategic air and naval forces that help to secure the Asia-Pacific Rim from Chinese and Russian geostrategic pressures. It could, however, substantially reduce the number of US armed forces now stationed in South Korea (twenty-eight thousand) and Japan (fifty thousand), which represent nearly 80 percent of all American troops that are "forward-deployed" in Asia and the Pacific.

Asia-Pacific security cooperation will depend heavily upon Japan's agreement to assume a major regional defense role and upon the willingness of its neighbors to accept such a role. The present Japanese constitution, which renounces war but does not rule out self-defense, was adopted in part to reassure those countries that had suffered under Japanese militarism. Just as Germany has become militarily integrated with its former Western European enemies, so may Japan's Asia-Pacific neighbors come to see that the twenty-first century requires a regional security architecture that parallels regional economic ties.

The major debate that is now taking place in Japan over the future of its armed forces has to do with a proposed constitutional change that would enable Japan to exercise military power in an unhampered way. This reflects the struggle between the resurgent Japanese nationalism of President Shinzō Abe's government and those who remain committed to pacifism. Part of the nationalist argument is that greater military might, combined with Japan's status as the world's fourth-largest economic power, would strengthen Japan's case to become the sixth permanent member of the UN Security Council. It would also enable Japan to extend its naval mission to include the South China Sea, the Strait of Malacca, and the Indian Ocean, helping secure its supply lines from the Middle East and Europe.

Article 9 of the Japanese constitution, which renounced Japan's sovereign rights to the use of force in settling international disputes, would have to be revoked. This is the position favored by Abe, who has provoked the anger of China over his 2013 visit to the Yasukuni Shrine that honors Japanese war dead, including war criminals. However, a remilitarized Japan is favored by Washington. During the Afghan and Iraq Wars, it called upon Tokyo to use its naval vessels to help refuel US and Allied naval forces operating in the Indian Ocean. Owing to an interpretation of the limits set by Japan's current constitution, Tokyo announced withdrawal of its vessels at the end of 2007 but rescinded the decision the following year. This reflected its concerns over Middle East instability and Japan's interests in keeping the sea-lanes of the Indian Ocean open to oil and other shipments. China has strategic concerns that are raised by the possibility that a militarily powerful Japan, freed from restraints, might be tempted to take an interventionist position in conflicts within the Asia-Pacific Rim. Russia might have the same concerns, which could conceivably move Moscow and Beijing closer together.

A broadened security role for Japan requires more than a constitutional change. Expanding its armed forces would require a substantial increase from its current defense spending of $80 billion, or approximately 1.4 percent of Japan's $5 trillion GDP. Japan currently has no long-range bombers, missiles, or carriers since its defense strategy is confined to the home islands. Its navy consists mainly of submarines and destroyers. Instead, it relies on the United States to keep its sea-lanes open or to deal with territorial disputes that might destabilize the region. Such expansion would satisfy those in Japan, as well as many Europeans, who call for less military dependence on the United States in military affairs.

A more assertive Japanese Self-Defense Forces (SDF) role in regional affairs would enable the United States to reduce substantially the number of its troops stationed in Okinawa. This small, agricultural, tourist-oriented island in the southern part of the Ryukyu (Nansei) chain south of the main Japanese islands is strategically important because it lies midway between Taiwan and South Korea. When Okinawa was returned to Japan in 1972, the United States retained 30 percent of the densely populated southern part of Okinawa for military facilities. Half of the fifty thousand US personnel stationed in Japan are crowded into Okinawa. These include two large air bases, a helicopter base, and the infrastructure that supports a full US Marine division. Opposition to this US presence has added fuel to the deeply rooted Okinawan independence drive.

In 2007, Tokyo and Washington agreed to reconfigure their military alliance. By 2014, the marine division and its families were to be relocated to Guam. Also, the large Futenma Air Force Base in southern Okinawa was to be relocated to Henoko on the east central coast and its land returned to local farmers. Other facilities were to be relocated to Guam and Hawaii. A naval air wing based outside Tokyo was to be located in a sparsely populated area near Hiroshima.[12] Japan was to pay all costs involved. These changes have yet to take place due to strong opposition of many Japanese who have little desire to house American military facilities. The issue of closing Futenma became more problematic in 2014 when Henoko's newly elected mayor refused to permit the base to be built there. The issue is still unresolved.

After half a century of shouldering the security burdens of the region, Washington inevitably will wish to reduce its defense responsibilities, especially in view of the heavy financial and political costs of the wars in the Middle East. Under such circumstances, the need for an Asia-Pacific regional defense force becomes even more urgent. This urgency will be reinforced by fear of China's pursuit of its strategic goals toward which it is modernizing its armed forces and creating a blue-water navy. Another force that can further regional integration is a planned approach to immigration. Japan and Australia can benefit from large-scale immigration. Japanese demographic projections suggest a major decline in its current population of 127 million, based upon a rapidly declining birthrate and an aging populace. This is an unexpected reversal for a nation that, during the first half of the twentieth century, sought to create a Pacific empire that would be able to absorb colonists from the overcrowded Japanese islands. However, it is not surprising in light of Japan's shift from an essentially rural nation to a highly urbanized one based on industry and services. A United Nations study has suggested that six hundred thousand immigrants per year will be needed to maintain the present workforce.[13] The population of the country is aging more rapidly than that of any other country in the world, making immigration a pressing need.

To develop an open and coherent immigration policy will require a fundamental change in Japanese attitude. Historically, the country is more hostile to immigration than any other industrialized nation. It is the most homogeneous nation in world, with Japanese constituting 98.5 percent of its population. The largest immigrant group, approximately one million Koreans, is descended from those who were brought to Japan as laborers or military conscripts between Japan's annexation of Korea in 1910 and the end of World War II in 1945. They have never been fully accepted into Japanese society. Neither have the tens of thousands of Chinese who have entered illegally in recent years to take on menial jobs or the handful of Southeast Asian refugees who have been given entry by Tokyo. As difficult as it will be for Japan to open its society to outsiders, the alternative of economic decline is even less acceptable. Both economic necessity and the fostering of regional ties with its Asia-Pacific neighbors are likely to force the Japanese to face up to the challenge.

While Australia has become open to immigration during the past half-century—first from Eastern Europe and then from Asia—the numbers of legal immigrants remain low. Recently, illegal immigrants, many seeking refuge from war-torn Middle Eastern and southeastern European counties, have entered Australia via Southeast Asia; while their numbers are small, the government has begun to crack down on asylum seekers.

As the Australian economy continues to mature, shifting from farming, extractive industries, and manufacturing to high-tech and information-age industries and services, the current labor pool that can be drawn from its population of twenty-three million needs to be augmented. Recognizing this, the Australian government, led by Prime Minister Tony Abbott, head of the Liberal Party who was elected in 2013, has increased its skilled-worker immigration quota from 60,000 in the mid-1990s to over 190,000 in 2014. The Philippines, Malaysia, Thailand, Indonesia, Taiwan, India, and China are sources for such immigration. Working against this long-term manpower need is a growing fear among white Australians of being swamped by Asians. This has given rise to racist and anti-immigrant sentiment and precipitated a national debate on immigration policy.

Japan is the major economic and political core of the Asia-Pacific Rim. The fortunes of its neighbors are tied to its fortunes. When Tokyo experienced the breathtaking economic and technological development that propelled it into becoming the world's second-largest economy in the 1970s and 1980s, its Asian neighbors benefited from Japanese capital and outsourcing. The demand-side stagnation that engulfed the Japanese economy in the 1990s brought on financial crises and economic slumps among its neighbors also. The economy has since recovered but is burdened by a large government debt and its lack of domestic fossil energy resources. To compensate for the latter, Japan had turned to nuclear power, building forty-eight reactors. In 2011, meltdown of the Fukushima reactor led to the mothballing of all of these reactors, causing the national trade deficit to mushroom. Conventional power plants cannot fill the void. As a result, Japan's Nuclear Regulation Authority is inspecting the closed reactors with the goal of resuming operations at many of the nuclear power plants.

While Japan enjoyed annual trade surpluses for the past two decades, it has recorded trade deficits since 2011. This trade imbalance is especially heavy with respect to China, and has evoked calls for more restrictive trade policies. The strongest protectionist voices come from the Japanese farm lobby, which fears being inundated by cheaper Chinese vegetables, which in recent years have won nearly half the Japanese market. However, most of the trade deficit comes from the import of consumer products, many of which are made by Japanese manufacturing plants that have been established in China. This makes it unlikely that Tokyo will reverse its trade policies. However, rising economic tensions could spill over into the political area.

With a GDP of nearly of $5 trillion and per capita income of nearly $40,000, Japan remains by far the richest and most advanced state in Asia Pacifica and, indeed, in all of East and South Asia. Its leadership role is solidly based. It has been, and will doubtless continue to be, a generous provider of development aid to its poorer Pacific Rim neighbors. Indeed, since the end of the twentieth century, Japan has been a leader among the world's nations as a donor of overseas development aid, ranking it second only to the EU and ahead of the United States. It is also likely to maintain its role as a primary generator of capital investment, outsourcing of manufacturing, and trade.

Since the mid-1990s, Japan has lessened its overwhelming dependence upon trade with the United States. Confronted by high wages and labor shortages, Japanese manufacturers are shifting their production operations to other Asia-Pacific Rim countries and to China. Earnings from overseas investments exceed merchandise export earnings, and manufacturing's share of Japan's GDP has dropped to 25 percent. Continuation of this trend, with increasing focus on design and marketing of high-technology, high-quality products and financial services, mirrors US economic structural trends, where manufacturing now accounts for approximately 10 percent of the GDP. An important difference between the two economies is that the United States will continue to have a powerful agricultural sector, while Japan depends upon food imports.

As Japan's economy has become more similar to that of the United States, it becomes more competitive in the search for manufacturing outsourcing and financial investment opportunities. Geopolitically, economic competition might encourage Tokyo to adopt a more independent course in international affairs, especially with issues that concern the Korean Peninsula, China, Indonesia, and the Middle East—the latter being Japan's major oil supplier.

While China has become Japan's largest trading partner by far, followed by the United States and South Korea, Tokyo remains firmly linked geopolitically to the maritime realm. Together with its Asia-Pacific Rim neighbors, it continues to look to the American military shield as the guarantor of its national and regional independence and to the maritime world for the largest share of its market opportunities.

A more independent international political and economic course for Japan will not weaken the maritime realm geopolitically. Rather, in tandem with maritime Europe's increasingly independent posture, this will lead to a more balanced, multipolar geostrategic realm within which Washington's propensity to take political and military initiatives without consulting its allies is likely to be curbed.

Geopolitical regions are dynamic. Their nature and orientation may change as their geographic and economic landscapes are altered or as the political/ideological, religious, and social forces that shape these landscapes undergo change. Through time, peripheral parts of a region may become detached and added to an adjoining region. At present, the center of the Korean Peninsula and the Strait of Taiwan form boundaries of tension between the Asia-Pacific Rim and the East Asia realm. This could change. Future negotiations could find an accommodation whereby Taipei accepts Beijing's political sovereignty while China permits Taiwan to pursue a "Hong Kong plus" arrangement that includes an independent economic and domestic political path, with control over its own police force, but as a demilitarized entity.

The on-and-off opening of relations between North and South Korea, along with the "Sunshine Policy" being pursued by the South, are not aimed at reunification in the near future. Each country belongs to a different geostrategic realm, and the economic and ideological gap between them is too great. However, a formal peace between the North and the South is a long-range prospect. With peace would come open borders, the exchange of people, and the flow of capital and technology from the South in exchange for low-cost goods from the North. North Korea at one point agreed to dismantle its nuclear weapons facilities in exchange for South Korea's agreement to open the rail link between the two countries and expanded economic investments in the North, starting with the Kaesong Free Trade Industrial Zone located within the North. When North Korea broke the agreement with its resumed nuclear missile testing, the Sunshine Policy was shaken. In a modest effort to rebuild its relations with South Korea, North Korea has permitted some family visits and reopened the Kaesong Zone for its North Korean workers. However, it opens and closes these doors capriciously. As North Korea's economic plight becomes increasingly dire, it is likely to embrace South Korea's Sunshine initiative more wholeheartedly. Were there to be a permanent peace, the North Pacific boundary between Asia Pacifica and the East Asian and heartlandic Russian realms could become a boundary of accommodation, with the Korean Peninsula and Taiwan serving as gateways. Under such circumstances, the reduction of the US strategic presence would inevitably follow, and Japan's leadership role as economic, political, and military core of the Asia-Pacific Rim would be enhanced within a regional framework of cooperative action.

Notes

1. Hans Weigert, *Generals and Geographers* (New York: Oxford University Press, 1942), 167–91.
2. Bruce Ryan, "Australia's Place in the World," in *The Australian Experience*, ed. R. L. Heathcote (Melbourne: Longman, 1988), 305–17.
3. Robert O'Neill, "Australia and the Indian Ocean," in *The Southern Ocean and the Security of the Free World*, ed. Patrick Wall (London: Stacey International, 1977), 177–89.
4. Zbigniew Brzezinski, *The Grand Chessboard* (New York: Basic, 1977), 151–93.
5. Thomas Friedman, "The Mean Season," *New York Times*, September 9, 1999, A23.
6. Seth Mydans, "East Timor's Dream of Oil," *New York Times*, October 20, 2000, A13.
7. Seth Mydans, "Religiosity, Not Radicalism, Is New Wave in Indonesia," *New York Times*, July 2, 2007, A7.
8. Wook-ik Yu, "Seoul: The City of Vitality," *I.G.U. Bulletin* 50, no. 1 (2000): 5–19.
9. Alan J. Day, ed., *Border and Territorial Disputes* (Harlow, England: Longman, 1982), 327.
10. "South Korea and Japan—Rocky Relationships," *Economist*, March 26, 2005, 42–43.
11. Day, *Border and Territorial Disputes*, 330–31.
12. "Japan and Its Neighbors," *Economist*, May12, 2006, 25–26.
13. Howard W. French, "Still Wary of Outsiders, Japan Expects Immigration Boom," *New York Times*, March 14, 2000, A1, A14.

CHAPTER 11

South Asia

South Asia embraces some of the world's most volatile, impoverished, conflict-ridden countries. It has both deep and persistent problems and untapped potential. The Eurasian heartland, the maritime, and the East Asian geostrategic realms form a crescent around the region, which abuts and influences lands rimming the Indian Ocean. The countries included within South Asia are India, Pakistan, Bangladesh, Sri Lanka, the Maldives, Nepal, and Bhutan. Myanmar, ruled by the British as part of India until 1937, lies on the margins of the region and is also tied to both East Asia and the Asia-Pacific Rim.

The South Asian subcontinent is not a shatterbelt, even though much of it is internally fragmented, wracked by rebellions within states and conflicts among them. What distinguishes it from a shatterbelt is the dominance of India that keeps the major powers from establishing positions of influence within the region and the absence of natural resources which diminishes their interest.

South Asia and the Middle East are geographically connected by Pakistan and Afghanistan. Pakistan, which is organically part of South Asia, has been in conflict with India since its independence. It has become increasingly involved in Middle Eastern affairs through its ties to Afghanistan via the Pashtun lands that straddle the border between South Asia and the Middle East. India's interests in Afghanistan are aimed at preventing Pakistan from expanding its base of power by drawing Afghan Pashtuns into its orbit.

To the north, the Himalayas block China from India. While its towering peaks and high altitudes provide India with a substantial defensive screen, these harsh mountain conditions did not prevent China from overrunning Aksai Chin, at the western end of the border, and Arunachal Pradesh, at its eastern end, in the Sino-Indian War of 1962. China withdrew from the eastern end but retains full control of Aksai Chin.

India, the core of the region, while not yet a major power, is overwhelmingly the regional power. It has the potential to join the ranks of the world's major powers but has not lived up to its potential. Using our four pillars of major powerdom, India is a major military and economic force. It has the third-largest GDP in the world as well as a formidable blue-water navy. However, it falls short with respect to the ideological and political cohesiveness pillars. Ideologically, India has offered itself as a model of nonviolent democracy and neutrality. In reality, India is beset with internal and external conflicts, many of a violent nature. The stubborn social stratification of the caste system, although officially banned, remains a barrier to political cohesiveness as well as economic mobility and ethnolinguistic diversity. Even during the Cold War, many nations which responded to Jawaharlal Nehru's call for nonalignment developed political and military ties with the United States or the USSR and engaged in conflicts among themselves. This included India, which turned to Moscow for weapons needed for its wars with Pakistan.

Historical Background

Under the British Raj, most of South Asia was a unified geopolitical region. Only Nepal and part of Bhutan lay outside the boundaries of British India. Since the end of British rule and the emergence of the subcontinent's independent states, a divided South Asia has known little but conflict. India and Pakistan have fought three wars. The 1947–48 War of Partition resulted in anywhere from one to two million people killed and fourteen million refugees—8.6 million of whom were Muslims and 5.3 million of whom were Hindus. Myanmar (then Burma) had split off from British India in 1937 and gained its independence in 1948. From that time, it was torn by civil war until 1962, when unstable and repressive military juntas took control. For nearly two decades, Sri Lanka (formerly Ceylon), which also became independent in 1948, was in the grip of a bloody separatist rebellion by Tamils against the ruling majority Buddhist Sinhalese. Peace was finally achieved in 2009. The Tamils live in the north and east of the country and are Hindu. The independent state of Bangladesh was created when East Bengal, which was then East Pakistan, split off from West Pakistan, with the help of Indian troops, in the war of 1971–72, in which five hundred thousand were killed.

Thus, the unity which the Mughal (Mogul) and British Empires imposed on South Asia has been shattered by the political divisions and religious and sectarian strife of the past half-century. While neither of those empires fully encompassed all parts of the region, their rules embraced most of its territories and brought administrative order. The Muslim Mughal Empire reached its greatest territorial expanse by the end of the seventeenth century, when it extended from its base in Afghanistan east to Orissa on the Bay of Bengal and south through nearly all of the Deccan. Only the island of Ceylon, the northern Himalayas, and Burma lay outside its bounds.

As Mughal rule crumbled in the eighteenth and nineteenth centuries, British power began to extend over the subcontinent. The British Raj, too, never succeeded in fully encompassing all of South Asia. It failed to conquer Nepal and much of Bhutan, and while Burma proper had become a British colony, the rebellious Shan states of eastern Burma had only protectorate status, their local chiefs exercising political controls. At that time, the Government of India Act established the All-India Federation, and a framework of unity was put firmly into place. In accordance with this act, the native states were given freedom in domestic policies in exchange for British control of foreign affairs, defense, and communications.[1] Britain tried to extend its rule to Afghanistan, engaging in two wars during the nineteenth century before the border of British India was fixed by the Durand Line in 1893. The third Afghan war in 1919 ended with Afghanistan freeing itself from British influence by getting full control of its own foreign affairs.

While South Asia is not, and never was, a completely unified geopolitical region, it is a distinct geographical region, possessing many cultural and human similarities and separated from the rest of Asia. The Indian subcontinent stands aloof from its neighbors, behind a barrier of rimming deserts, mountains, and monsoonal forests. Its best connections to the outside are via the Indian Ocean.

Within South Asia, the population is most heavily concentrated along the Brahmaputra, Ganges, and Indus River valleys in the north and along the east and west coasts. It thereby forms an almost continuous population ring around the Deccan—the highly dissected southern half of the Indian subcontinent whose center is semiarid. While population densities in the rural Deccan are high—over six hundred persons per square mile—they do not begin to compare with the densities of the great northern interior valleys that form the Plains of Hindustan, nor with the densities of the east and west coastal plains, which contain most of the big cities, industries, and transportation networks. There the mixed rural and urban populations range from twelve hundred to over five thousand persons per square mile. The populations of the Plains of Hindustan cross national boundaries in both the Punjab and Bengal to further intertwine the geopolitical fates of Pakistan and Bangladesh with that of India.

South Asia's geopolitical distinctiveness is influenced by its dependence upon agriculture and its inward economic orientation, as well as its geographical isolation caused by its rimming mountains. Over half of the workforce of the region is dependent upon agriculture (table 11.1). Much of this agriculture is traditional farming, although significant strides in modernization have been made in parts of India, Pakistan, and Sri Lanka. For the most part, the region feeds itself, the exception being Bangladesh, one of the world's poorest countries. Bangladesh's agricultural production is subject to the vicissitudes of disastrous floods, droughts, and monsoonal storms, making it dependent on food aid imports.

Exchange with other nations is of secondary concern to many South Asian countries, whose trade in goods and services as a percentage of GDP averages a little over 5 percent. Three exceptions are Sri Lanka, whose exports of textiles, clothing, tea, gems, and rubber and imports of machinery, transportation equipment, petroleum, and sugar represent over 20 percent of its GDP; the Maldives, whose economy is based on tourism, shipping, and fishing; and India.

Although India's foreign trade is only 17 percent of its GDP, its offshore software and outsourcing business-processing industries command over half the world market, and its market economy is growing rapidly. Because of its large pool of scientists and skilled technology workers, India has considerable potential for expanding its high-tech industry. Software exports, mostly to the United States, continue to increase, as have exports of pharmaceuticals.

The concept of South Asia as an independent geopolitical region separated from surrounding geostrategic realms and their regional subdivisions was first advanced by this writer in 1963.[2] It diverged from the worldview of Halford Mackinder, who had considered India, the Southeast Asian peninsula, and China to be a unified monsoonal coastland. In

Table 11.1. South Asia Population and Trade

Country	*Population (millions)*	*Leading Export Market*	*Leading Import Market*
India	1,236,344,631	European Union	European Union
Pakistan	196,174,380	European Union	European Union
Bangladesh	166,280,712	European Union	China
Myanmar	55,746,253	Thailand	China
Nepal	30,986,975	India	India
Sri Lanka	21,866,445	European Union	India
Bhutan	733,643	India	India
Maldives*	393,595	Thailand	Singapore

Sources: Central Intelligence Agency, *World Factbook 2014*, https://www.cia.gov/library/publications/the-world-factbook/rankorder/2119rank.html; list of countries by leading trade partners, *Wikipedia*, http://en.wikipedia.org/wiki/List_of_countries_by_leading_trade_partners, updated April 2014.

* 2.5 percent of the Maldivian labor force engages in fishing and, minimally, in agriculture because of the infertility of its coral soils.

his 1919 volume, he depicted this region as one of the six "natural" regions of the world.[3] In continued support of this thesis, he argued in 1943 that "a thousand million people of ancient oriental civilization inhabit the lands of India and China. They must grow to prosperity. . . . Then they will balance the other thousand million who live between the Missouri and the Yenisei."[4] The latter reference is to the heartland and North Atlantic units working in cooperation with one another.

What this worldview failed to appreciate was that the geopolitical destinies of India and China could not be shared because of their unique geographical and cultural-historical settings. Even in Mackinder's time, as today, the two had different demographic and resource bases and different sets of strategic concerns. China was an essentially homogeneous nation caught between the Eurasian heartland and Asia Pacifica, with much of its space belonging to the continental interior. In contrast, India's populace was highly diverse racially, ethnically, linguistically, and religiously. Its Indian Ocean strategic orientation was reflected in the historic reach of its sailors and merchants to Southeast Asia's islands and to the eastern and southern coasts of Africa—the two major regions where the Indian diaspora first took root. In addition, the ecumenes of the two great civilizations were too far removed from each other geographically to develop significant interaction or to enable one power to dominate the other militarily.

Although the historic buffer zone of Tibet and the Himalayas that lies between East and South Asia has been breached by China in recent decades, India holds the dominant position within its region. In general, the towering Himalayan mountain ranges continue to bar the route to northern India. They wall off Tibet from the lands to the south and, while the northern part of Azad Kashmir, which Pakistan ceded to China, now connects China's Xinjiang to Pakistan, it is too remote an outpost to serve the Chinese as a serious military threat to northern India.

During the course of the Cold War, the USSR was able to gain some influence in India, while at various times China and the United States became important military backers of Pakistan. However, these inroads did not fundamentally alter the geopolitical status of South Asia. It remained a separate and inwardly oriented geopolitical region, most of which took a neutralist posture in the struggle between the Western and Communist realms. Pakistan's ties to the West and China's rise as a major power did not alter Pakistan's fundamental geostrategic orientation, which remained South Asian. Its major concern was its struggle with India over Kashmir, but it also felt threatened by the Soviet inroads into Afghanistan.

South Asia was spared from becoming another Cold War shatterbelt by the combination of physical vastness, a huge population that has now reached 1.7 billion, an inward economic and cultural orientation, a common political history, and India's dominant role. However, while it stands apart from adjoining geostrategic realms and maintains independent geopolitical regional status, the unity that the Indian subcontinent once enjoyed eludes it today.

Regional Geopolitical Overview

INDIA AND PAKISTAN

India gained its independence in 1947. It adopted a policy of nonalignment or neutralism in the Cold War, based in part on what Jawaharlal Nehru described as its geographical position: "India is big and India is happily situated. . . . [A]n invasion or attack on India . . . will give [other countries] no profit."[5] The main preoccupation of India's leadership was its disputes with Pakistan over Kashmir, water rights, and East Pakistan.

India did have a broader view that extended beyond the region. This was reflected in its leadership role within the "third force"—the grouping of Asian and African states initially assembled in 1955 at Bandung, Indonesia, where Nehru expressed his opposition to military alliances and called for a moratorium on nuclear testing. However, he had doubts as to whether the Asian-African conference could ever develop into a cohesive group.[6] In this, he was being realistic. India was so preoccupied with its conflict with Muslim Pakistan and binding together the union of India that it had little surplus energy, beyond moral exhortations, to look beyond the subcontinent. The partition of British India left one hundred million Muslims within India, out of its then total population of four hundred million. Muslims now number nearly 220 million, or 14 percent, of India's population of over 1.2 billion, including heavy concentrations in Mumbai and Bangalore. They are heavily urbanized, with a high poverty rate. Intercommunal strife between the Hindus and the Muslims remains a serious threat to India's unity, particularly since Hindu militants have gained political influence with the rise of the Bharatiya Janata Party in competition with the Congress Party.

The response of Washington to India's neutralism was to draw Pakistan into a military alliance, first in 1955 through the short-lived Central Treaty Organization (CENTO), which also included Turkey, Iraq, and Iran, and later through bilateral arrangements. Also in 1955 Pakistan joined the now-defunct SEATO, which together with its involvement with CENTO reflected both westward and eastward strategic pulls.

Hindsight teaches us that the Cold War policy of tolerating no neutrals pursued by US Secretary of State John Foster Dulles was a major blunder. For Dulles, the nonalignment of India was "immoral," regardless of the fact that India was the world's largest democracy. He therefore turned to the alliance with Pakistan, which was to be plagued by corrupt and often dictatorial military rule and chronic political instability throughout the Cold War and beyond.

India's hopes for nonalignment were severely shaken by the intrusion into the region of both the United States and China. With its mortal enemy, Pakistan, in alliance with the United States and its relations with China deteriorating because of border disputes, New Delhi had to open itself to Soviet military, economic, and political support to gain Moscow's backing for its position on Kashmir.

In the 1959 Longju incident, China occupied a garrison post in India's North-East Frontier Agency (which in 1987 was renamed Arunachal Pradesh State). Khrushchev sought unsuccessfully to mediate the dispute, as he tried to balance Soviet-Indian ties with the ideological and strategic Sino-Soviet bonds. However, just before the 1962 war broke out between India and China, the Soviets agreed to build and deliver jets for India. Moreover, rather than backing Beijing, Moscow remained neutral when the war broke out. All of this contributed to the eventual Sino-Soviet schism, for it fanned Mao's fears that the USSR was seeking to outflank China through an alliance with India. As noted previously, Beijing has remained in control of over 40 percent of Aksai Chin—that cold, high desert plain in the northeasternmost part of Jammu and Kashmir that is bordered by Xinjiang on its northeast and Tibet on its southeast. The Chinese also invaded India's North-East Frontier Agency, which lies north of Assam, but withdrew at the end of the war.

Beijing's speedy reaction to the Soviet-Indian ties was to settle outstanding differences with Pakistan over their common border in northern Kashmir in 1963. At that time, Pakistan ceded to China 2,050 square miles of the northern Azad Kashmir territory also claimed by India. Beijing, in turn, became Pakistan's major arms supplier during the next two decades. The two countries agreed to build the Karakoram Peace Highway—a 750-mile, all-weather road over the Karakoram Range from Rawalpindi, Pakistan, to Kashi (Kashgar) in Xinjiang that crossed the mountains at the 15,420-foot Khunjerab Pass. (It was completed only in 1978.) The road is the sole paved section of the historic Silk Route from the Mediterranean to China.

By 1971, when the Bangladesh rebellion broke out in East Pakistan (which is separated from the western half of Pakistan by eleven hundred miles), China openly supported Pakistan, while Moscow backed India. Washington supported neither its Pakistani ally nor India, whose troops quickly triumphed over those of Pakistan. In the months of civil war that had preceded India's intervention, estimates vary widely on the number of native Bengalis killed in East Pakistan, ranging from three hundred thousand to three million. Several million fled into exile in India.

Beijing subsequently supplied Islamabad with nuclear technology. At the same time, while the United States was decrying the spread of nuclear weapons in South Asia, it was building up Pakistan militarily to support the Afghan rebels in their war against the Soviet Union.

The second war between India and Pakistan was over Kashmir. It took place in 1965 and caused the United States and Britain to impose an embargo on the sale of arms to both countries. This further strengthened the bonds that India and Pakistan had, respectively, with the USSR and China. The embargo was lifted in 1975, but in the meantime India had turned to Moscow for new and major infusions of weapons, as part of a 1973 aid agreement that Prime Minister Indira Gandhi had forged with Moscow. New Delhi abandoned its antinuclear policy the following year, when it exploded an underground nuclear test device in the Thar Desert.

When the Soviet Union invaded Afghanistan in 1979 to prop up its Marxist governmental ally in Kabul against Islamic fundamentalist rebels, Washington called upon Islamabad to help foil the Russian move. Pakistan became the main arms conduit from the United States to the rebels and provided the Afghan mujahideen and volunteers from other Islamic countries with major training and supply bases. Also, since this period, it has sheltered well over two million Afghan refugees. Saudi Arabia, which was also enlisted in the effort in Afghanistan, provided considerable financial support to the rebels. The magnitude of US military and economic aid to Pakistan during the 1980s—$600 million per annum—made Pakistan the third-largest recipient of US aid, after Israel and Egypt. Adding to India's fears over the resurrected US-Pakistan alliance was the continuing thaw in the relations between Washington and Beijing. For India, this raised the specter of encirclement and provided additional justification for its drawing closer to the Soviet Union.

The sudden pullout of Soviet troops from Afghanistan in 1989 and US suspension the following year of all military and economic aid to Pakistan because of its nuclear weapons program appeared to set the scene for a radical restructuring of alliances in South Asia. India had become far more attractive to Washington as a potential ally on several grounds: (1) its significance as a potential market (from 2002 to 2011, India's economy grew by over 7 percent per annum, only to drop to 4.4 percent the following year), (2) its pool of technological brainpower, (3) its role as a leader of developing countries in bridging the differences between the Third World and the World Trade Organization, and (4) its importance as the world's largest democracy.

The convergence of US and Indian interests also related to the deterioration of ties between Washington and Islamabad, until the exigencies of the US war in Afghanistan restored these relations. The collapse of the Soviet Union had undercut the strategic rationale for the US-Pakistani military alliance of the 1980s. Tensions then increased between the two countries because of Pakistan's role in supporting the Taliban and Osama bin Laden's terrorist base in Afghanistan and because of its 1998 testing of nuclear weapons. The unintended consequences of the American effort to support the Afghan mujahideen against the Soviet forces and their Afghan allies was the rise to power of the fundamentalist Sunni Taliban. There are strong bonds based on Pashtun lineage between the Taliban of Afghanistan and the twenty million Pashtuns who live within Pakistan's western borderlands, from Peshawar to Quetta. Pakistan harbored many Islamic fundamentalist guerrillas who had been redirected from the Soviet Afghan war to support Muslim militants in the Indian-held part of Kashmir. A strong Pakistani Pashtun Taliban movement has arisen to make common cause with its Afghan compatriots.

After the invasion of Afghanistan in 2001 by the United States and its allies, the alliance between the United States and Pakistan was resumed. With the rout of the Taliban, Pakistan's Pashtun border region became the safe haven for both al-Qaeda and the Taliban. Despite billions of dollars' military aid provided by Washington, Pervez Musharraf's military regime had been unwilling or unable to eliminate these bases. The Pakistani army's Interservice Intelligence (ISI) has played a shadowy role in the battle against Islamic militants, using much of the military aid to continue to train and supply militants to operate against India in Kashmir while maintaining links with the Taliban.

While Pakistan's military commitment has been weak and its political scene highly volatile, the United States saw little choice but to stay the course. It tried to balance support of Musharraf with the restoration of civilian government amid the rising tide of Islamic extremism. Pressured by failure to rein in the militants, opposition from lawyers and judiciary, and widespread public demand for free elections, Musharraf abandoned military rule for civilian government in 2007. The ensuing political campaign, punctuated by Benazir Bhutto's assassination, culminated in the February 2008 victory of the Pakistan Peoples Party and the Pakistan Muslim League-N, marginalizing Musharraf. Meanwhile the country remains torn among the elected political parties, the military, and Islamic militants. Pakistan's future stability depends on whether partnership between civilian government and the military can contain the militants and whether widespread corruption and one of the highest illiteracy rates in the world can be successfully overcome. In an effort to restore peace in the Tribal Areas, the new civilian government agreed to withdraw all army forces in return for Pashtun withholding of support to the Taliban and al-Qaeda. The agreement was made in the face of opposition by the United States, which feared a weakening of the government's commitment to eliminating terrorist bases within Pakistan's border areas. This agreement has not held. Within a few years, Pakistan returned troops to the border. The current Pakistani government, led by Prime Minister Nawaz Sharif, which has had on-and-off peace talks with the Taliban, launched air strikes against them in their strongholds within the tribal region of North Waziristan along the Afghan border.

With the end of the Cold War, the estrangement between India and the United States was repaired. In recognition of India's economic and strategic importance, Washington sought stronger ties. In 2007, the United States and India began negotiations for a strategic partnership, wherein India would be able to acquire US nuclear technology and materials for energy use. While initially these negotiations encountered strong opposition from their respective legislatures, the accord was formally signed in 2010. It provides for joint military and naval exercises and missile defense coordination as well as nuclear energy cooperation. For decades Russia had accounted for nearly 80 percent of India's weapons imports, but in 2011 New Delhi, the world's largest importer of arms, turned to the United States as its major weapons supplier.

SRI LANKA

Sri Lanka is a largely rural and agricultural country with a population of over twenty million that is deeply divided ethnically, linguistically, and religiously. The Tamils, Hindu descendants of immigrants from southern India, live mainly in the northern and eastern coastal parts of the island and represent slightly over 10 percent of the country's population. The majority Sinhalese, three-quarters of the populace, are Buddhist. Civil war broke out in full force in 1986 between the Sinhalese government and the independence-seeking Tamil Eelam "Liberation Tigers," who felt discriminated against economically and linguistically. It continues to rage despite sporadic cease-fires. In the early 1980s, Indira Gandhi had ordered the covert arming and training of the Tamil rebels, seeking to court the political support of India's then fifty million Tamils (they now number over seventy million) in the southern state of Tamil Nadu by allowing the Sri Lankan "Tigers" to set up bases on Indian soil.

However, growing concern that the creation of an independent Tamil state in northern and eastern Sri Lanka might encourage separatism among the Tamils of Tamil Nadu in India caused the Indian government of Rajiv Gandhi to do a policy about-face in 1987. An added complication for India was that Tamil Nadu adjoins Kerala—long a bastion of Communist Party strength and plagued by a separatist movement. Accepting the Sri Lankan government's request for assistance in securing a peace with the separatists, New Delhi sent over forty thousand troops to help quell the rebellion and broker a peace. The effort failed, and India pulled out its forces in 1990 at the request of Sri Lanka. Nevertheless, the ties between Sri Lanka and India have continued to be strong, especially since the Sinhalese-dominated government in Colombo has sentenced to death the Tamil Tiger leader held responsible for the revenge assassination of Rajiv Gandhi in 1991, when he was already out of office. New Delhi continued its support of the Sri Lankan government in the quest for peace. Meanwhile, the conflict, which had taken well over sixty thousand lives and caused the displacement of one million Tamils, continued to rage as truces were signed and broken. In 2009, the Sri Lankan government declared military victory over the rebels and granted the Tamils control over a semiautonomous province.

The Muslim population of the country, numbering about 1.8 million, has tried to stay neutral but has been caught up in the war because the Tamils see them as a barrier to full control of the north and east, where both groups live. In the east, in particular, this has spurred the growth of Islamic fundamentalism as the Muslims seek a distinct identity. Tamil oppression has led some of them to seek an autonomous Muslim region.[7]

MYANMAR (BURMA)

The political relations of Myanmar with India and the rest of South Asia have become more tenuous since the Burmese gained their independence in 1948. During much of the nineteenth century, most of the country was controlled by British India. While Burma was given a new constitution in 1935 (effective in 1937), separating it from the rest of British India, the Japanese invasion during World War II gave Burma little opportunity to exercise its newly won freedom.

Since its postwar independence, the country has been torn geopolitically by pressures from both India and China. Indian strategic interests lie in Myanmar's location overlooking the Bay of Bengal and economically in the offshore gas deposits in the bay, as well as in the oil and gas fields of Lower Burma. Another strategic consideration for New Delhi is that its provinces of Assam, Nagaland, and Arunachal Pradesh adjoin the northwestern part of Upper Burma, which is exposed to the Chinese military threat. Were Myanmar allied with India, it could be a helpful buffer.

Beijing's interests in Upper Burma stem from the geographical proximity of the region to Yunnan Province and Tibet. If Myanmar were drawn into Beijing's orbit, it would also enable China to exercise greater leverage upon Laos and northern Thailand, which adjoin Myanmar along its northeastern and eastern border.

Shortly after the Union of Burma was established, its government sought to loosen ties it had developed with India during the British Raj. To offset India's pressures, the Burmese government cautiously reached out to the new Communist regime in Beijing, looking for help in ousting the Chinese Nationalists who had been driven across the border into Burma, where they had quickly organized the drug trade. The Nationalist troops did leave Burma in 1953, although in response to the orders of the United Nations, not because of actions by Beijing.

Myanmar-China-India Relations

Trying to maintain a balancing act between India and China, Burma's Socialist government of U Nu adopted an approach that fit a broader ideological position of nonalignment and orientation to the Third World—a policy that paralleled that of Nehru's India. In keeping with this spirit of nonalignment, and to further relations with China, Yangon refused to join SEATO.

In 1960 China and Burma signed the Treaty of Friendship and Mutual Non-aggression in which China relinquished claims upon Burma for territories in the far north (Kachin State) and the northeast (Nam Wan and the Wa states). In return, Beijing received five small villages in these border areas.[8] With these provisos, Beijing accepted on a de facto (but not a de jure) basis the Sino-Burmese section of the McMahon Line, which had been drawn in 1900 by a joint Anglo-Chinese boundary commission.

In 1962, beset by insurgencies in the north, east, and southeast, Burma plunged into chaos, and a military junta seized power. The pro-Chinese "White Flag" majority Communist Party of Burma (the minority "Red Flag" Communists had split off and operated in the south) gained control of much of the northeast, along the border with China. Elsewhere in the north, Shans and Kachins captured considerable territory. The Chinese provided the insurgents with arms and even sent Red Guard volunteers to the "White Flag" Communists. Despite the fact that at one point the various rebel groups had seized control of nearly one-third of the country, they failed to overthrow the government, and China's efforts to penetrate Burma came to naught. The junta drove its ethnic Indian civil servants and Chinese merchants out of the country, as it shifted from nonalignment to isolationism, autarchy, and socialism. In the years that followed the military takeover, two million Burmese took refuge in Thailand. Many fled after economic unrest sparked an antigovernment uprising in 1988, which was put down by the military at the cost of thousands of lives.

With the disintegration of the Communist Party in the 1980s and after making peace agreements with other rebel movements, Burma (renamed Myanmar in 1989) appreciably improved its relationship with China, which became its main arms supplier, while trade links were established that opened Burma's market to a flood of Chinese consumer goods. In addition, China permitted its territory to become the conduit by which heroin is transported from the poppy-growing areas of eastern Burma's "Golden Triangle" to Hong Kong, and thence to the United States, Australia, Southeast Asia, and Europe. Since much of the heroin was controlled by Myanmar's military junta, China's cooperation in shipping the drug to Western markets was eagerly sought.[9] In recent years, its opium trade has shrunk considerably, as 80 percent of the world's opium production and heroin trade has shifted to Afghanistan. Government and isolated rebel bands continue to clash in the north and east, both using child soldiers, but this poses little threat to the country's stability.

The relations between India and Myanmar were strained since the military junta overthrew the U Nu government in 1962, despite the fact that India was the largest market for Myanmar's exports. A major issue between the two countries was the aid provided by Burma to the Naga rebels, who have fought for nearly half a century for Nagaland's independence from India. Nagaland is a small state in northeastern India, wedged in between Bangladesh and Myanmar. When driven out of India in the mid-1970s, the Naga army took refuge in the Burmese Naga hill lands and used the transborder sanctuaries as bases from which to mount raids against Indian forces. While for many years the Indian government failed in its attempts to enlist Yangon's support against the Naga rebels, in 1999 India and Myanmar signed an agreement to promote joint action against the Nagas (the Burmese Naga tribesmen had risen up against the Yangon regime) and against the drug traders operating along their mutual border. This cooperation has helped India to quell that rebellion.

Another cause of friction between the two countries was India's firm support of the prodemocracy forces in Myanmar in the face of their persecution by the ruling junta. Thousands of Burmese dissidents were given refuge in India when they fled Yangon's repression of antigovernment riots that followed the junta's invalidation of the 1990 democratic elections. At that time, the arrest of the leaders of the victorious democratic party led by Aung San Suu Kyi evoked strong criticism from New Delhi, while Beijing backed the crackdown against the dissidents.

The military junta also cracked down violently on student and monk demonstrations which called for the restoration of democracy. So intent was the junta on retaining power through isolating the country from foreign pressure that it severely restricted entry of international aid workers and materials during the critical days following the May 2008 cyclone and flood surge that devastated the Irrawaddy delta.

Economically, the generals began to allow private investors to buy into the industrial and farm businesses that the government had expropriated and mismanaged and enabled international energy corporations to obtain oil and gas development concessions. This was seen as a desperate attempt to save an economy that is in grave difficulties, with rampant inflation and collapsing government services. Once one of the world's largest rice producers and exporters and South Asia's wealthiest nation, Myanmar now ranks among the world's poorest.

What began to improve the economy has been the development of oil and gas reserves in the Bay of Bengal waters and the expansion of older inland fields. Both China and India are competing for access to these energy reserves. Natural gas, which accounts for 90 percent of energy revenues, is being exported in significant quantities via a five-hundred-mile pipeline to Thailand. China has built oil and gas pipelines from Myanmar's Indian Ocean ports to southwest China, thereby bypassing the sea route through the pirate-infested waters of the Strait of Malacca. India, for its part, has constructed a natural gas pipeline from Myanmar's western coast through Bangladesh to India.

Over the years, economic sanctions by the EU over the human rights abuses of the junta (known as the State Law and Order Restoration Council, SLORC) had little effect. China openly supported the junta, and India drew back from its past vigorous support of Myanmar's democratic movement in the interests of protecting its stakes in energy development there.

All of this changed when the military gave up much of its power, paving the way for general elections in 2011. While key cabinet posts are retained by the generals in the new constitution, Myanmar is no longer a pariah state. Aung Sang Suu Kyi returned from exile to lead the parliamentary opposition, and foreign investments began to strengthen the economy of the country. Myanmar has also benefited from a Chinese-brokered agreement in 2013 with the Karen, Shan, and Kachin rebels of the northeast. However, the country is still plagued by fighting between its Buddhist majority and the Muslim Rohingya, who have long been subject to widespread discrimination and denied citizenship. The 1.3 million Rohingya live in the northern part of the west coast state of Rakhine. Recently they have been deprived of basic medical services caused by the governmental ban on the operations of Doctors without Borders, which had provided most of their medical services. Persecuted by extremist Buddhists, tens of thousands of Rohingya have fled to Malaysia via Thailand. Here they are prey to Thai smugglers who abuse them, often with the connivance of Thai officials who have refused them temporary shelter within the country.

THE MALDIVES REPUBLIC AND DIEGO GARCIA

The Maldives Republic, within the Indian Ocean extension of South Asia, has a tiny population (approximately four hundred thousand Muslims) that depends upon tourism, fishing, coconut products, shipping, and apparel. It consists of 1,200 low-lying coral islands, which are at risk of flooding in a period of global warming. It enjoyed strategic importance until Britain withdrew from the naval base in the southernmost island of Gan in 1976, replacing it with facilities on the island of Diego Garcia, which lies eight hundred miles to the south of the Maldives. Diego Garcia is part of the Chagos Archipelago, a series of tiny coral atolls that were part of Mauritius until they were detached from that former British colony in 1965, at the height of the Vietnam War. The central location of Diego Garcia within the Indian Ocean, twelve hundred miles northeast of Mauritius, made it an ideal site for a strategic "floating" base that would be secured from attack by its distance and isolation. Britain later leased the base to the United States, which developed it as a base for long-range strategic bombers and for refueling naval vessels. The island proved its worth as part of the maritime realm's global security network, not only during the Vietnam and Gulf Wars but also in the war against terrorism in Afghanistan.

For many years India had a hands-off policy toward the Maldives. This has now changed. New Delhi is pushing for fair elections there, has expanded its commercial activities, and is solidifying its strategic interests in the island republic by placing Indian radar installations on some of its atolls.

A complicating political factor is that now-independent Mauritius continues to claim the Chagos chain, while Diego Garcia's native islanders, who were moved to Mauritius when the American base was built, have lodged legal proceedings to be allowed to return to Diego Garcia or to go to other parts of the Chagos chain.

Geopolitical Features

HISTORIC CORE

An area that might be considered South Asia's historic political core is Rajputana, the center of the historical region within the northwestern part of the Indian subcontinent that is coextensive with the modern Indian state of Rajasthan. It was there that the ancient Hindu warrior caste came to power in the seventh century and held sway for nearly a millennium, until the several Rajput Princely Territories were conquered by the Mughals in the late sixteenth century. Tribal divisiveness during that Hindu era prevented the establishment of a single, great political capital. Today, Rajasthan remains the bastion of conservative Hinduism, as the region plays a major role in the shift of India's politics toward right-wing religious nationalism.

Delhi's historic function as the site for the capitals of both the Mughal and British empires gives it a more clear-cut claim to being South Asia's historic core. For both empires, it was the nerve center that unified most of the subcontinent during the periods in which they held power. As the crossroads of routes leading to all parts of India, the Delhi area had been strategically important to early Hindu and Rajput dynasties. The site of the present city is the head of the two great sections of the Hindustan Plains (the valleys of the Ganga [Ganges] and upper Indus), on the Yamuna River, a major tributary of the Ganges, the Hindu holy river where dipping into its waters is held to wash away one's sins. Delhi dates back to the twelfth century, when it became the capital of Turko-Afghan rulers. In the seventeenth century, the Mughals built the city of Old Delhi (1658) to serve their empire, moving the capital from nearby Agra, which they had founded a century before (1556) as the seat of the Mughal court. These Muslim overlords merged the various parts of their empire with an effective administrative system that laid the groundwork for the idea of Indian nationhood. When the British Raj embraced the subcontinent in its entirety, Old Delhi served as the capital until it was replaced by Calcutta (Kolkata).

CAPITALS

The modern political capital of India is New Delhi, but Kolkata played a unifying role as the earlier capital of British India. The rise of Kolkata is related to the centralization of the activities of the British East India Company. During the seventeenth and eighteenth centuries, the company established three settlements or "presidencies," in Bombay (Mumbai), Madras (Chennai), and Kolkata. The latter is located on the Hooghly River at the delta formed by the confluence of the Ganges and the Brahmaputra on the Bay of Bengal. It was from Kolkata, which Robert Clive had made the main center of British commercial power and rule, that Britain was able to establish dominance over the Bengal region and oust its French East India Company rivals.

Kolkata's port and its role as the center or *entrepôt* for jute production and milling, textiles, and tea exports were the bases for the city's preeminence. Boats could move from Delhi, at the head of navigation of the Yamuna River, downstream to Kolkata, thus traversing the entire Gangetic Plain. The formal shift of British India's capital from Old Delhi to Kolkata did not take place until 1833, but the political center of gravity had shifted there decades before. By the time Britain moved the capital back to Old Delhi in 1912 to strengthen its position in the Hindustan Plains against the Russian threat from Central Asia, Kolkata had already become South Asia's largest city and port.

New Delhi, the current capital of India, was inaugurated in 1931, the Delhi Cantonment serving as interim capital while New Delhi was under construction. Designed as a resplendent city whose architecture would express the grandeur and power of British India, the capital was expanded over the years from administrative center to the home of commercial and modern industrial functions.

Two hundred miles to the north of New Delhi, at an elevation of over seven thousand feet on the Himalayan ridge, was Shimla (Simla)—the hot-weather seat of government, to which the British annually migrated. When the British shifted their capital back to Delhi, they

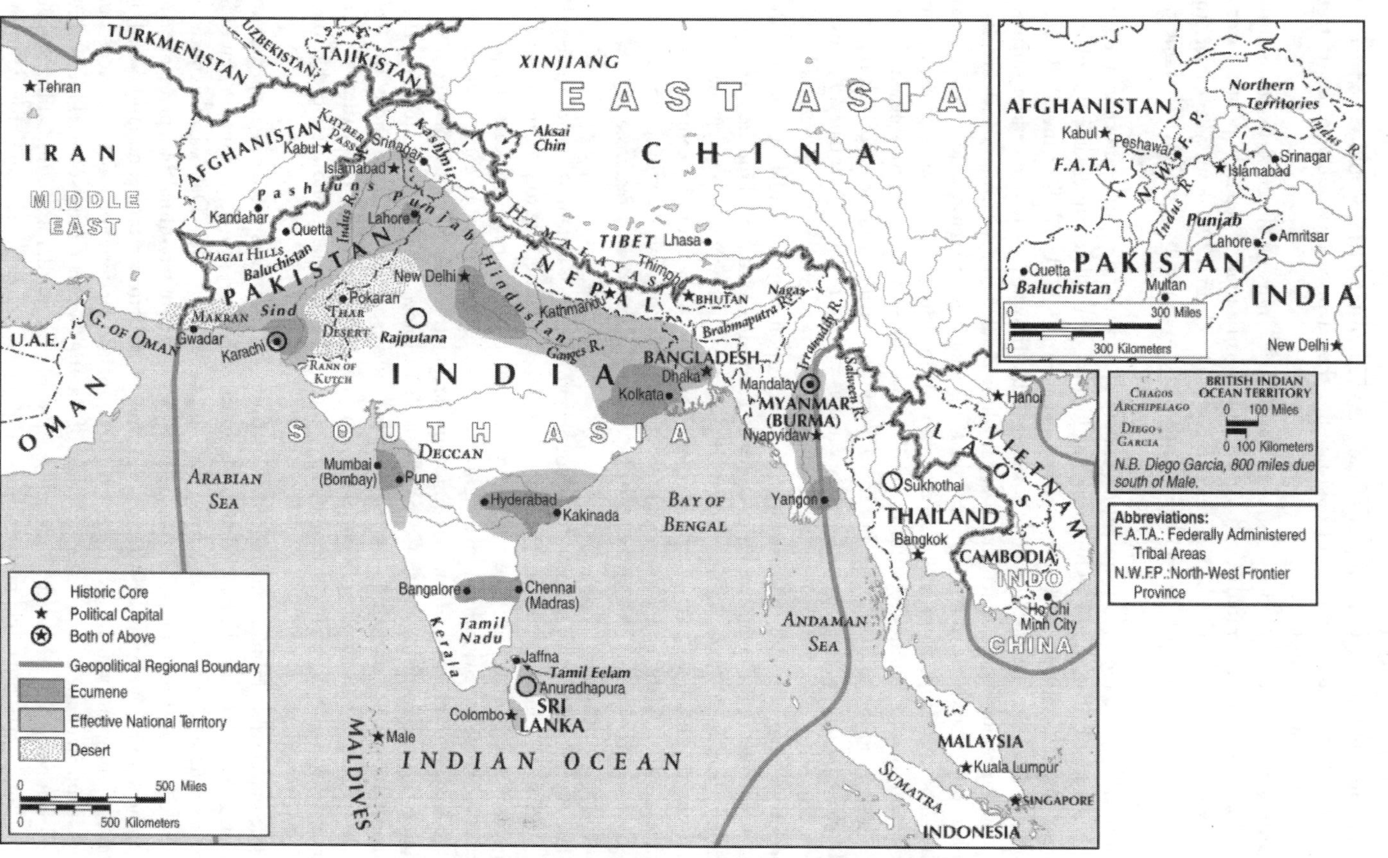

Figure 11.1. South Asia: Major Geopolitical Features

did not anticipate that the western part of the great Hindustan Plains would someday break away to form the separate country of Pakistan and thus deprive New Delhi of its strategic continental bridging position.

During the period of British control of South Asia, India's political impact upon the region's outer parts was limited. Ceylon (Sri Lanka) had acquired separate political status as a Crown colony when the British displaced the Dutch in 1798. Four years later, the ancient city of Colombo, which had been modernized as a port by the Dutch, became the capital of the colony.

Burma, too, was removed from British India's administration during much of the time that it was under British rule. The Burmese kingdom was not fully conquered by Britain until 1887 and, unlike India, enjoyed no self-government until 1923. Until this time, all Burmese capitals had been sited in the "dry zone" of the middle Irrawaddy valley in central Burma, a scrub-covered region where agriculture is essentially restricted to dry farming, with emphasis on millet, pulses, and beans, and minimal land is available for irrigation. There, Mandalay, which had been the capital of the Burmese kingdom from 1860 to 1885, reflected the historic geographical focus of Burmese culture and civilization that was distinctly non-Indian. Britain finally recognized the cultural difference in 1937 and separated Burma from British India.

In 1923 Rangoon (Yangon) had been selected as capital, replacing Mandalay, because of its location on the Bay of Bengal in the south-central part of the country. It was built up as the country's chief port and relied for its labor force upon the large Indian population that had earlier settled in the lower Irrawaddy valley and served as a labor pool for the surrounding plantation areas. In 2005, the military junta abruptly moved the capital to Naypyidaw, a new military city that has been built in an underpopulated part of the country's central heartland, 150 miles south of Mandalay. This military fortress capital represents an effort by the secretive junta to isolate itself from civil unrest in its heavily populated coastal regions and to ease its paranoid fears of invasion.

The capital of Nepal, Kathmandu, is connected by a sixty-mile highway to the border of the Indian Hindustan Plains and therefore is especially vulnerable to pressure from New Delhi. However, Indian influence never fully penetrated the country politically, despite the fact that Nepalese royalty, whose sovereignty had been recognized in 1923, is Hindu. During the Cold War, Nepal's monarchs sought to distance themselves from Indian control by balancing their relationships with China, the Soviet Union, the United States, and India and maintaining a nonaligned policy. Nevertheless, and especially since the end of the Cold War, India remains the most influential foreign power in Nepal because of the countries' geographical proximity, their cultural affinity, and the substantial economic aid that India renders to Nepal.

The inaccessible Himalayan Buddhist kingdom of Bhutan was more heavily penetrated than was Nepal by British India, which took control of Bhutan's foreign affairs. When India gained its independence, London turned over this function to New Delhi. India continues to oversee Bhutan's diplomatic affairs, despite the kingdom's nominal independence and its membership in the United Nations. Even though Bhutan is remote and landlocked, its capital of Thimphu, which lies along a tributary of the Brahmaputra River, is accessible to Indian military forces from the province of Assam. When China seized Tibet, which borders Bhutan from the north, India closed the Bhutan border and built military roads into the kingdom. China's claim that Bhutan is part of Greater Tibet has reinforced India's commitment to asserting its dominance in Bhutan's military affairs. In a sign of the times in the Himalayan kingdoms, Bhutan announced its conversion from an absolute to a constitutional monarchy.

Buddhist Sikkim, another Himalayan land, which lies wedged between Nepal and Bhutan, became an Indian protectorate in 1950. Its capital and only town, Gangtok, was relegated to the status of a state capital when, in 1975, the kingdom was formally annexed to India. At that time, New Delhi deposed Sikkim's traditional chogyal leader and converted the country into India's twenty-second state.

Pakistan's current capital, Islamabad, lies in the western Punjab within the Himalayan foothills, only forty miles west of the border with Indian-held Kashmir. It is also only ninety miles east of the Khyber Pass and the Afghan border and thus very much a "frontier" capital. Located on the main highway and railway route from Afghanistan and Pakistan's North-West Frontier Province, Islamabad was completed as a planned city adjoining Rawalpindi, the chief urban center of the northern Punjab. Rawalpindi had served as the country's interim capital from 1959, when the capital was moved there from Karachi, to 1970.

Siting Islamabad in the northern Punjab was not only a statement designed to emphasize the strategic importance of the region to Pakistan vis-à-vis its Kashmir and Afghanistan interests. It was also a move to reinforce Pakistan's commitment to securing its North-West Frontier Province and the Tribal Areas against the separatist ambitions of its Pashtun (Pathan) tribespeople. With its capital now located in the Punjab, which contains half of the country's total population as well as the army headquarters in Rawalpindi, the country's political-military center of gravity lies firmly in the northwest.

ECUMENE

South Asia lacks the semblance of a regional ecumene, and India itself has no unified population or economic core area. Instead, it possesses three widely separated ecumenes: West Bengal-Bihar, focusing on Kolkata (Calcutta) at the northern end of the Bay of Bengal; Mumbai (Bombay), with an extension inland across the Western Ghats onto the western edge of the Deccan in the Mumbai-Pune (Poona) district; and a zone that extends from the south central Deccan at Bangalore eastward across the Deccan to the coast at Chennai (Madras) on the Bay of Bengal. As a historical note, these areas include the same locales that were the seats of the East India Company presidencies. Delhi, the center of the northwestern part of the Hindustan Plains, with a dense city population of eleven million and an urban region of twenty-two million, is located in an essentially agricultural region lacking the depth of industrial activity that a modern-day ecumene requires.

Kolkata, with a city population of 4.5 million and a metropolitan population of over 14 million, is India's second-largest port and is served by a major network of rail, highway, river, and ocean transport facilities. Its dense population concentration ranges between fifteen hundred and two thousand persons per square mile. The major industries are the older, traditional light and heavy ones—textiles, food processing, shoes, paper, steel, chemicals, aluminum, transportation equipment, and shipbuilding. The region is the focus for traffic from eastern India and Nepal. Kolkata itself, teeming with refugees from Bangladesh, has become overwhelmingly crowded.

Mumbai, the only deepwater harbor on the west coast and the country's leading port, is India's largest city with a population of 12.5 million and a total urban region of approximately 18 million. In addition to its industries, it owes much of its preeminence to being the center of India's finance and banking as well as of its film and other media production industries. Pune is the country's center for chemicals, oil refining, motor vehicle and machinery manufactures, textiles, fish products, pharmaceuticals, and electronics.

The Bangalore-Chennai ecumene is a mixture of old and new industrial India. Chennai, with a city population of 4.7 million and a metropolis of over 8.7 million, is the capital of the state of Tamil Nadu. It is a focus for chemicals, machinery, textiles, motor vehicles, and tanneries. Its harbor on the Bay of Bengal is the node for transportation links that radiate outward across peninsular India. Bangalore, with a population of 8.5 million, is the inland hub for this southern part of India and has become the core of the country's high-tech industry. It is known as the "Silicon Valley of India" and its "science capital." As the newest and fastest-growing sector of an Indian ecumene, it plays a prominent role in India's plans for becoming a world software power. Its computer, electronics, telecommunications, and aircraft industries are likely to spill out and fill the corridor that now connects the Bangalore district to Chennai (population seven million) on the coast.

The seeds of a fourth ecumene are to be found in Hyderabad, which is situated in the central Deccan in Andhra Pradesh. The city of nearly six million in population has become India's newest software center, benefiting from the presence of several scientific and technological institutions, and competes with Bangalore for the "Silicon Valley" title. Hyderabad is three hundred miles from the heavily populated east coastal centers of Andhra Pradesh, which are surrounded by intensively cultivated areas of rice, sugar, cotton, and palm-oil production. One can envisage the development over the next few decades of a corridor of modern industry cutting eastward to the coast through this agricultural zone that will serve as the basis for a new ecumene.

It is only in the Ganges delta that a major Indian ecumene merges with that of a heavily populated neighboring country. The international boundary between India and Bangladesh divides Hindu West Bengal, which is economically dominated by Kolkata, from Muslim East Bengal. Dhaka, the Bangladeshi capital, with a city population of over 6.6 million and a metropolis of over 15 million, has its country's greatest concentration of industry—textiles, apparel, jute products, and handicrafts. Moreover, it is the heart of a densely populated and fertile agricultural region that is the world's largest producer of jute. However, it is an area subject to severe flooding from monsoonal rains, cyclones, and tidal waves, and land connections from Kolkata are poor and unreliable. Bangladesh is overwhelmingly poor and overpopulated, its 2,250-persons-per-square-mile population density being the highest in the world except for some small island states, and it is also lacking in mineral resources. Unfortunately, Dhaka is notorious for the poor safety of its garment factories, in which low-paid workers toil in unsafe buildings, some of which have actually collapsed, burying the workers. Although the distance between Dhaka and Kolkata is only 150 miles, there is little prospect that the limited ecumene of Bangladesh will ever benefit from and merge with that of Kolkata.

Pakistan's ecumene is bifurcated. One is centered on Lahore, the industrial and commercial core in the northern Indus valley. The second is the lower Indus valley of Sind focused on Karachi, the country's largest city and seaport, with a population of thirteen million. Its commercial and industrial area, extending one hundred miles to Hyderabad, is an important trade and manufacturing center. Despite these two heavily populated areas, only a little over one-third of Pakistan is urbanized.

The economy of Sri Lanka is based essentially upon the export of plantation crops. The country's small and underdeveloped ecumene, which centers on Colombo in the southeastern part of the island, has made progress in expanding the manufacture of textiles, clothing, rubber, and food products. However, it remains a minor economic core in comparison with those of India.

Elsewhere in the region, neither Nepal nor Bhutan possesses a population and economic core area of any magnitude. The growth of Myanmar's limited ecumene, which focuses on

Yangon and the Irrawaddy delta, was stunted by the military government's closing of the country's economy to outside contacts.

India's ecumenes completely dominate those of its neighbors. The prospects for the development of a regionwide ecumene are negligible. While India is an important trading partner for Bangladesh, Sri Lanka, Nepal, Bhutan, and Myanmar, these heavily agricultural countries are only marginal markets for New Delhi. With the exception of Bangladesh, they are self-sufficient in food, but because of their widespread poverty they can import few finished goods and services.

Thus, India's main economic links lie outside South Asia. Its leading trading partners are the United Arab Republic, the United States, and China. Moreover, the Indian market itself, rather than international trade, is the main catalyst for the growth of its ecumenes. The country's middle class, estimated at two hundred million people, is potentially one of the world's largest consumer markets and accounts for a disproportionate share of the nation's $5 trillion GDP. Even though India now has the world's third-largest national GDP, its per capita income of $4,000 is less than half that of China, while its ratio of trade to GDP is approximately 15 percent.

The modernized sector of the Indian economy is the engine of growth that offers the greatest long-range hope for pulling the impoverished rural portions of the country and the urban poor out of their present miseries. But, for the foreseeable future, the middle class will remain a relatively self-contained segment of relative prosperity with all too little impact upon the impoverished classes. India therefore remains vulnerable to social upheavals as the poor flock to the great cities, where only a small proportion of them succeed in securing employment, housing, and adequate health services. So pervasive is poverty that nearly one-third of all Indians live on less than one dollar per day, infant mortality is thirty-five per one thousand, and adult illiteracy is over 50 percent.

EFFECTIVE REGIONAL/NATIONAL TERRITORY

South Asia's countries possess few lands that are now only moderately settled and that therefore could attract substantial new population growth. (See table 11.1 for population densities.) Most of Pakistan is mountain or desert. The mountainous region is the North-West Frontier Province and the Federally Administered Tribal Areas (FATA). Baluchistan is mainly desert basin or nonarable hills and uplands. Most of the country's population is crowded onto the Indus Plain in Punjab and Sind.

Bangladesh, one of the world's most densely populated nations, is one great floodplain with no room for expansion. With climatic warming, half of Bangladesh could be inundated, causing massive death, suffering, and displacement.

Mountainous Nepal and Bhutan have limited narrow valleys that hold nearly all of their populations.

Sri Lanka's landscape is characterized by a central mass of mountains surrounded by wide coastal plains that are very densely populated in the wet western and southern portions of the island. The "dry zone" of the northeast has for decades been heralded by Colombo governments as a resettlement area that could absorb the overpopulated reaches of the country. In historic times, this region was heavily populated through the use of "tanks," or basins that could store water for irrigation. However, diseases and wars caused it to become deserted over the centuries, and it is now largely covered with swamps and dense jungles.

Converting the dry zone, where populations are under fifty persons per square mile, to effective national territory has been a slow process. Malarial swamps have been cleared and irrigation schemes have been initiated, including the diversion of waters from the Mahaweli dam in the moist central highlands. However, settlement efforts have lagged behind the country's population growth for political reasons that have hampered the development of infrastructure. The zone is largely in the poor, Tamil-inhabited regions, and the Tamils oppose the large-scale movement of Sinhalese farmers from the overcrowded "wet zones," where population densities range from six hundred to three thousand persons per square mile.

Extreme nationalists among the Sinhalese majority were opposed to regional autonomy for the Tamils, which the Sri Lanka government had proposed in order to end the rebellion. As the reason for their opposition, the nationalists cited the need for continuing central governmental controls of the dry zone. With the creation of a semiautonomous Tamil province as a price for the end of the Sinhalese-Tamil civil war, Sinhalese resettlement plans within the dry zone were dashed. The solution for Sinhalese overcrowding within the wet zone now depends upon the rapid growth of industry and services there that will promote the urbanization of small subsistence farmers.

Myanmar, with its central core of forests and mountains running from the northern borders to the delta of the Irrawaddy, has little expansion room. The dry belt is the central Irrawaddy valley, which is already densely populated. It contains such former capitals as Mandalay and two cities that lie immediately to the south of Mandalay, Amarapura and Ava, as well as the new capital of Naypyidaw. For reasons of politics and terrain, the northern and western hills and the eastern Shan plateau also hold little promise of absorbing large numbers of additional people. Instead, the crowding is likely to continue within the lower Irrawaddy valley and delta, the Arakan coast facing the Bay of Bengal, and the Tenasserim coastal region that fronts the Andaman Sea.

India, too, has little available land for agricultural expansion. Whatever areas might be described as effective national territory are the already densely populated farm regions, where the replacement of agriculture by urban industrial activities is serving to expand existing ecumenes. These areas include the western portion of Bihar in the lower Gangetic Plain, the Western Ghats to the east of Mumbai, and the Hyderabad-Chennai corridor.

EMPTY AREAS

South Asia possesses four main empty areas: (1) the Thar (Great Indian) Desert of western India, which extends into Pakistan's southeastern Sind Province; (2) the Rann of Kutch, which is the vast salt waste and swamp that lies mostly in India's Gujarat State south of the Thar Desert but extends into southern Sind; (3) the Kharan and Makran Deserts of Pakistan's southwestern Balochistan; and (4) the Himalayas.

The value of the Thar Desert to India is essentially strategic. It was at Pokaran, in the east-central Thar, that India exploded its first nuclear device in 1974 and conducted its underground nuclear tests in 1998. The Chagai Hills, along the northern rim of the Kharan Desert in Balochistan, straddle the Afghan border and provide Islamabad with its nuclear testing sites, including those where the 1998 tests took place.

The Rann of Kutch, originally an arm of the Arabian Sea, is now a vast salt waste and swamp depression. The dispute over its boundary was one of the causes of the 1965 India-Pakistan war. In a 1968 international arbitration, India was awarded more than 95 percent of the Rann's eighty-four hundred square miles. The area's sole economic resource is salt, which can be extracted only in the dry season. As pointed out by Govind Singh, it was hardly worth fighting for, but both sides saw this as an issue of historic territorial rights and were willing to go to war over what each regarded as its territorial integrity.[10]

The Himalayas, Asia's great mountain system, extend for fifteen hundred miles from northern Pakistan across northern India, Tibet, and Nepal to eastern India, Bhutan, and Nepal. A series of parallel ranges, the towering southern (Great) Himalayas are snow covered year-round. Little of the region is inhabited, save the southern foothills. Its main geopolitical function is as a frontier barrier between India and China. The Himalayas also serve as the source of the largest rivers of the Indian subcontinent, on which Pakistan, India, and Bangladesh are so dependent. The Karakoram, the major pass across the Karakoram Mountains, enables traffic to skirt the western end of the Himalayas. The Diphu Pass, at the eastern end of the Himalayan range, serves as the main crossing point there. Both passes have been important objectives in the competing Indian and Chinese territorial claims. Control of the Karakoram Pass by China affords Pakistan direct access to Xinjiang Province. India's control of the Diphu Pass blocks China's access to Assam.

BOUNDARIES

The major conflict over boundaries between South Asia and an adjoining geopolitical realm was the one between China and India over the territories at the western and eastern edges of the Himalayas, as previously discussed. Elsewhere, along the region's outer rim, there is a minor dispute that has caused sporadic conflict between Myanmar and Thailand over alignment of the border.

The most serious and widespread border disputes, however, are intraregional. The territorial dispute between India and Pakistan over the status of Kashmir has not only triggered three wars, but it also has brought the two nations into the dangerous nuclear confrontation that threatens to destabilize the entire region. "Liberation" of Indian-held Jammu and Kashmir—India's only heavily Muslim state—has been the consistent objective of Pakistani military and civilian rulers. At the time of the partition of India, Kashmir was ruled by a Hindu prince who, despite the region's mainly Muslim population, placed Kashmir under India. A Muslim revolt ousted the prince, but he was reinstalled by Indian troops who were flown to Kashmir to repulse the Pakistani-supported rebels.

The present cease-fire has been maintained since 2004. The line divides the region in two—the lightly populated, half-Muslim and half-Buddhist northern and western portion in Pakistan known as Azad Kashmir, and the southern and more populous region, the Indian state of Jammu and Kashmir. The latter contains the heavily Muslim-populated Vale of Kashmir, including Srinagar, capital of the state. The Vale of Kashmir is the most populous part of the region and its economic heart. Jammu, in the south, is two-thirds Hindu.

The emotional and ideological pull of Kashmir on both Indians and Pakistanis has been the major stumbling block to mediation of the dispute. However, over the years the strategic issue has intensified. The part of Aksai Chin that China occupies is in eastern Ladakh, one of Kashmir's subregions, and forms an important link between Tibet and Xinjiang. In addition, the Pakistani-Chinese boundary agreement of 1962, whereby China was granted 2,050 square miles of northern Azad Kashmir that had been in dispute between India and China, provided for highway links between Pakistan and Xinjiang (the Karakoram Highway and an earlier one built through the Mintaka Pass in 1968).[11] The Pakistani shift of this territory to China was a strategic gain for Pakistan as well as for China, while it was viewed by India as a strategic setback.

The economic cost of the Kashmir conflict has been enormous. For example, the Kargil campaign caused a 28 percent increase in India's 1999 military budget, or in other words, over one-fifth of total federal expenditures. India now spends $48 billion per annum on defense, while Pakistan's expenditures are $7 billion. Proportionately, this represents 2.5 percent of India's GDP and 2.7 percent of Pakistan's.[12]

The waters of the Indus River basin are also an issue in the Kashmir conflict. The Indus, Jhelum, and Chenab Rivers flow through the state of Jammu and Kashmir before entering Pakistan. They are crucial to agriculture in Pakistan's Punjab and Sind. The 1960 Indus Water Basin Treaty did not provide for integrated water development but rather for each country to develop and manage its own water resources. Construction of upstream dams for power and irrigation by India remains a point of contention for its potential impact on downstream Pakistani users.

Another river boundary controversy between the two countries revolves around Sir Creek—the stream that separates India and Pakistan at the southwestern edge of the Rann of Kutch. India claims that the boundary is midchannel of the creek where it enters the Arabian Sea, just below the mouths of the Indus; Pakistan claims the right bank, thus the stream exit in its entirety. The precise location of the boundary here is important in fixing its maritime extension. What is at stake for Pakistan is that its claim would permit the seaward extension of its exclusive economic zone to include another 250 square miles of water whose seabed holds promise of oil and gas reserves.

Two minor disputes, one between India and Bangladesh and one between India and Nepal, are worthy of mention because of the broader principles that are involved. The first dispute is over a small island that was formed in 1979 after a cyclone and tidal wave in the Bay of Bengal. The island lies in the estuary of the Hariabhanga River, the main channel of which forms the boundary between India and Bangladesh. The bank of the river on the Indian side is three miles west of the island, while the Bangladeshi bank is five miles to the island's east.[13] The island—"New Moore" to India and "South Talpatty" to Bangladesh—has no intrinsic value. The dispute relates to control of the maritime zone of the continental shelf that extends out from the island. The shelf possesses rich oil and gas reserves—an extension of the delta's resources. While there have been no military incidents since the navies of the two countries skirmished in 1981, the definition of the maritime zone remains an important issue to both countries.

India and Nepal were in dispute over control of thirty square miles at the source of the Mahakali (Sharda) River along the border between the two countries, where India constructed the Sharda dam on the river despite Nepal's objections. In 1996 the two countries came to an agreement on sharing the dam's water and hydroelectric supplies and established the Mahakali River Commission to adjudicate future disputes. The principle of the agreement was that the India-built dam did not prejudice Nepal's sovereign rights. The agreement permitted both parties to cooperate while continuing to disagree on the boundary location.

China considers its forty-three-mile border with Afghanistan to be a strategic problem, although it is not in dispute. This boundary is at the eastern end of Afghanistan's Wakhan salient, which cuts between the Pamirs in Tajikistan and the Hindu Kush in Pakistan and adjoins China's Xinjiang Province. The Taliban and al-Qaeda were able to smuggle arms via the Wakhan to the province's Muslim Uighur rebels and to bring them to Afghanistan's terrorist training bases. This is one of the factors in China's cooperation with the United States in the war against terrorism.

Challenges to National and Regional Unity

South Asia is a distinct geopolitical region, separated from surrounding realms and regions by nature, culture, social difference, politics, and, to a considerable extent, religion. It can be neither dominated by major powers nor absorbed into adjoining geopolitical frameworks, although Pakistan and Myanmar, on the region's western and eastern margins, respectively, have strong links with bordering geopolitical regions.

As a geopolitical region, South Asia lacks internal unity because of its deep divisions—religious, racial, ethnic, linguistic, and social. The depth of these divisions is such that significant regional frameworks of cooperation have yet to evolve. The Colombo Plan for Cooperative Regional Development, aimed at strengthening the economies of various members through economic and technical assistance, was signed in 1951. It then embraced Southeast and South Asia as well as the United Kingdom. The United States, which joined later, became the largest donor among its twenty-six members. The plan, which has been extended indefinitely, provides for educational, health, and technical aid; grants and loans; and food supplies. However, it has had marginal impact on the economy of South Asia.

Equally ineffective in attaining the stated goals has been the South Asian Association for Regional Cooperation (SAARC). Established in 1985 with a membership that included all of the region's states (save Pakistan, which joined later), SAARC's goals include cooperation in such areas as easing poverty, environment, education, controlling drug trafficking, and trade liberalization. It has created the South Asia Preferential Trade Association to stimulate regional trade and development and founded a regional development fund, which has almost no money available for stimulating the economies of the region's least developed countries. SAARC's main achievement lies within the realm of publishing studies, but it falls far short of being an instrument for furthering regional unity.

The divisiveness of South Asia has been a major factor in its development lag over the past half-century. Looming above the other regional conflicts is that between India and Pakistan over Kashmir. The dispute has led the two countries into an expensive arms race and a dangerous nuclear weapons competition. In addition to the full-scale wars waged between the two countries, Muslim guerrillas supported by Pakistan have mounted actions within India's Jammu and Kashmir State that have caused twenty-five thousand deaths since 1989. Fighting broke out between India and Pakistan over Islamabad's support of these guerrillas, although this conflict did not erupt into a full-scale war between the two countries.

Prospects for resolution of the conflict through outside mediation have shown little evidence of improvement since the end of the Cold War. The web of foreign power entanglement continues to complicate the dispute. India is the world's largest arms importer, amounting to nearly $6 billion in 2012. While Russia was long its major supplier, accounting for 80 percent of its imports, the United States has now become its leading supplier, with sales reaching $2 billion in 2013. The shift from Russia to the United States represents a need on the part of India to acquire high-end equipment to catch up with better-equipped Chinese armed forces as well as to buttress its troops against its Pakistani rivals. This dependence on imports relates to India's failure to create a domestic arms industry. Efforts to manufacture its own high-tech weapons have faltered due to high costs, poor quality control, and inefficiencies.

The situation is now further complicated by the fact that while the United States is giving economic and military aid to Islamabad, it has also forged a strategic partnership with New Delhi for the sale of civilian nuclear power and advanced fighter aircraft. When the former Musharraf regime joined the coalition against the Taliban, it was in the face of enormous opposition by Pakistan's Islamic fundamentalists. Recent Pakistani military pressures against the Taliban have served to strengthen the extremists, who are also opposed to a compromise over Kashmir. Washington's acknowledgment of the legitimacy of India's goal to become a nuclear power has paved the way for a new role of balanced engagement in world affairs for India in place of past nonalignment policies. A stronger India would not only counterbalance the weight of China in Asia and further strengthen the foundations of global geopolitical equilibrium but also secure India's dominance within South Asia.

Changes in South Asia's regional boundary contours depend upon the geopolitical directions that Pakistan and Myanmar may take. Pakistan, together with Afghanistan, may become a shatterbelt, internally divided and torn by pressures from the United States, Iran, India, China, and Russia. The positions of Afghanistan and Pakistan are already very shaky, as represented in their respective high rankings in the Index of Failed States—Afghanistan is listed as number 7 and Pakistan is number 13.[14] As Pakistan's Pashtuns have strengthened their ties with the Pashtuns of Afghanistan and Islamic fundamentalism has gathered momentum within Pakistan, Islamabad's Middle Eastern orientation has become stronger.

One possibility is that a postwar Pashtun-controlled Afghan government, based in Kabul and hostile to Pakistan, might revive historical claims within Afghanistan for the unification of all Pashtun peoples. These tribespeople had been divided by the 1893 Durand Line, when Afghanistan was separated from British India. Alternatively, should Afghanistan break apart, its Pashtuns might mount a drive for reestablishment of an independent state that includes western Pakistan in an area that has been called Pakhtunistan. The cause of an independent Pakhtunistan was pursued by Kabul at the time of the creation of Pakistan and clouded relations between the two countries from the 1950s to the 1970s.[15]

Also, Afghanistan supported guerrilla activities in Pakistan's central and southern Balochistan Province during this earlier period on the grounds of the tribal links between its inhabitants and those of Balochistan. Absorption of the province would provide landlocked Afghanistan with an outlet to the Arabian Sea through the newly constructed Balochi port of Gwadar. The Balochi guerrilla separatist movement has been quiescent since the rapprochement between Afghanistan and Pakistan that took place at the time of the Soviet-Afghan War. However, since 2005 bloody conflict has again broken out. The Balochis, who number 13 million out of Pakistan's over 182 million population, are the least economically developed and have the highest rate of poverty. They claim to have been marginalized in Pakistan's development planning.

Pakistan might well become dismembered through the loss of its North-West Frontier, the Tribal Areas, and Balochistan, and through changes in the status of Kashmir. What would remain of Pakistan would be a much more cohesive state extending across the Indus Plain to include the provinces of (West) Punjab and Sind. Such a state would include more than 80 percent of the country's current population and its two ecumenes and would be a far more stable entity than present-day Pakistan.

Elsewhere within the region, additional proliferation of states could take place in the wake of new strife and conflict. This proliferation could take two forms—statehood or quasi statehood. For example, one option for resolving the Kashmir dispute would be for Kashmir to become a quasi-independent state through the joining of Azad Kashmir, which Pakistan now controls, with Indian-held Jammu and Kashmir in a condominium administered by India and Pakistan. The conflict has been costly in lives, resources, and energy. India could benefit from independence of a unified Kashmir, first as a condominium with Pakistan and then, possibly, as a separate, sovereign state. The cease-fire signed in 2004 by the two countries has held. The other dispute over water sharing of the Indus River and its tributaries has yet to be addressed.

India's progress toward becoming a world power is unlikely to be affected by such territorial changes. Indeed, its prospects would be enhanced by making accommodations with areas that drain it economically and militarily.

Emergence of a quasi-independent Sikh state (which the Sikhs call "Khalistan") would resolve another conflict that has bedeviled India. New Delhi can ill afford to lose control over security and foreign affairs of the Sikh homeland. It is a vital part of the Hindustan Plains, its economy having national significance as the country's granary, and it serves as a frontier province vis-à-vis Pakistan's western half of the Punjab region.

The militant Sikhs, whose religion is a combination of Hinduism and Sufism, had terrorized the Indian states of Punjab (East) and Haryana in their quest for independence. The Punjab was the historic center for Sikh kingdoms, and Amritsar is their sacred city. It was the seizure of the Golden Temple in that city by militant Sikhs and the subsequent storming of the temple by the Indian army troops that led to the assassination of Prime Minister Indira Gandhi by her Sikh bodyguards in 1984. The insurgency was then quashed, but the Sikhs continue to seek independence by nonviolent means. India would benefit considerably from satisfying the Sikh desire for independence in religious, economic, and local political affairs in order to resolve this bitter conflict.

An independent Nagaland, the home of Naga tribespeople living in the forested hill country east of India's state of Assam in the far northeast, would have no impact upon India's economy. It proved too small and weak to win its insurgency, and the rebellion was quelled. India then promised to fund economic development in Nagaland, including highway improvement and plans for a railroad that would extend to Thailand. However, New Delhi could go beyond this promise and satisfy the mostly Christian Nagas by offering a Bhutan-like sovereignty whereby India would retain responsibility for diplomatic relations and have assured military access to the country, while the Nagas would preserve their traditional culture, tribal modes of governance, and religion. The same solution could be applicable to other separatist movements within Assam, where unrest has been reduced by the heavy out-migration of tea plantation workers to India's urban centers.

By satisfying these separatist sentiments, India could become a more cohesive nation, better able to modernize its economy and human services by reducing its current heavy defense expenditures.

Elsewhere within the region, conditions have stabilized. The conflict in Sri Lanka has ended, and the Tamils there have gained provincial autonomy. Peace has also returned to Nepal, which had been plagued by Maoist rebels seeking to overthrow the constitutional monarchy and establish a parliamentary democracy. In 2006, they forced the two-hundred-year-old monarchy to yield to parliament, giving up its absolute power and paving the way to the end of the civil war. In 2007, after six years of fighting, the Maoists signed a peace agreement with the Nepalese government, joining an interim parliament and storing their weapons. The government subsequently agreed to the Maoist demand that the monarchy be eliminated and replaced by a constitutional democracy. They now have the third-largest party in the Constituent Assembly. A remaining threat to Nepal's territorial integrity is ethnic strife in the Terai, the southern plains region that adjoins India. Culturally and ethnically indistinguishable from the Indians, many of the Madhesis, who dominate the Terai and may represent up to 40 percent of Nepal's total population, lack Nepalese citizenship and voting rights. Their campaign for rights and autonomy has turned violent and is a problem which the Nepalese government must face sooner rather than later.

In another sign of the times in the Himalayan kingdoms, Bhutan announced its conversion from an absolute to a constitutional monarchy.

The restoration of democracy in Myanmar presents it with the opportunity to escape from the geopolitical grasp of China. Granted, China has a strategic stake in northern Myanmar bordering the Chinese provinces of Yunan and Tibet and has played an important role in mediating Yangon's conflict with its restless northeastern provinces. However, Myanmar's strategic importance is even greater to India. It is the gateway to Thailand and Southeast Asia. India has been active in strengthening this land bridge by renewing the Burmese port of Sittwe and constructing a highway through Myanmar which is to be extended to Thailand and ultimately to Laos and Cambodia. While currently China and India rank equally as trading partners of Yangon (Thailand is its leading trade partner), India has forged a bilateral trade agreement with Myanmar which has set a $3 billion trade target by 2015, with emphasis on India's import of natural gas, timber, jade, and gems.

The support that India gave to Burmese refugees who fled Myanmar's military regime and the democratic values that the two countries share are likely to be the decisive forces in drawing Myanmar back into the South Asian political region.

The number of possible new South Asian states or pseudostates is limited by the strengths of the central governments involved, particularly that of India. However, proliferation of states has not run its course in this subcontinent of 1.65 billion people—22 percent of the world's population living in only 4 percent of the world's states. It cannot be predicted whether separatism can be guided into constructive frameworks of negotiation or violence will continue to prevail. Nevertheless, in assessing the geopolitical near future of South Asia, it is fairly safe to predict that some devolution can be anticipated.

Conclusion

India's overwhelming economic and military strength can be the driving force for regional integration. However, it cannot currently be classed as a major power because of its social and political fragmentation, widespread corruption, crippling bureaucracy, and loss of too much professional and scientific talent to emigration. Although it has considerable energy reserves, it is dependent upon oil, gas, and coal imports because of lack of investments in this sector. Fiscally it continues to suffer from huge budgetary and trade deficits. Its manufacturing base is constrained by poor infrastructure, inadequate transportation networks, and its inflexible labor laws that inhibit its taking advantage of its pool of cheap, unskilled labor.

India has the potential to correct these deficits. The large Indian middle class generates a pool of well-trained scientific and technological personnel who use English to communicate with one another. This manpower pool has already made a global impact through the Indian émigrés, who play so important a role in the United States and other Western high-technology worlds. These émigrés have been helpful in stimulating India's rapidly growing software and pharmaceutical industries, as more and more outsourcing of software activities and services has been directed toward India. The high-technology industry alone cannot directly solve the country's massive unemployment problem. It can, however, generate billions of dollars in exports that can then be plowed back into the nation's inadequate physical and social infrastructure—roads, water, electricity, communications, wiring, education, and health. Its application to older manufacturing industries can also bring about dramatic productivity increases there and help to modernize India's agriculture.

All of this would expand the domestic and foreign market for Indian goods and services, which would, in turn, further stimulate the flow of outside capital investment. Manufacturing and information services that are outsourced to India could eventually raise India to the level of China as one of the great trading nations of the world. India has a long way to go before it can close the current gap with China. However, it has the human and material resources to do so within a democratic system that can energize these resources through political consensus rather than coercion.

Should India remain unified in the face of the various devolutionary currents that may sweep across the region and should it resolve the Kashmir conflict, its regional dominance will be reinforced. With its large and efficient armed forces and nuclear capacity, its high-tech industrial leadership, and a population that is likely to overtake that of China in size, it could become a major power and serve as the core of a new Indian Ocean geostrategic realm.

Such a realm would embrace eastern coastal Africa, especially Tanzania (with its islands of Zanzibar and Pemba) and Kenya. It would also include Myanmar, which borders the eastern Bay of Bengal and the Andaman Sea. In addition, the realm would include the Indian Ocean island states of the Maldives, the Seychelles, the Comoros, Madagascar, and Mauritius, as well as the French dependencies of Réunion, Mayotte, and Iles Glorieuses, and the British Indian Ocean territory of the Chagos Archipelago that contains Diego Garcia.

Traders and settlers from India have long influenced the lands around the Indian Ocean. Two millennia ago, Hindu civilization spread to Sumatra and much of Java and Bali, as well as to the Malay Peninsula, and Indian traders were active in Zanzibar. Over the centuries, small but influential Indian populations have settled along the fringes of the ocean, including South Africa, where they have engaged in commerce and, in some instances, plantation agriculture. These communities could play an important role in reconstructing the trading networks that linked the basin a millennium ago and thereby reinforce the geostrategic influence of the prospective realm upon neighboring realms.

In forging an Indian Ocean realm, India can build upon its balanced set of relationships with the other three realms. The geographical settings and boundaries of those realms brings them into direct geostrategic contact with one another in Europe and the western Pacific. By contrast, India is spatially removed from such direct contact. Its location, therefore, enhances its capacity to serve as a link rather than as a competitor.

India maintains strategic ties to heartlandic Russia through cooperative missile and space research projects, arms imports, Indian oil development investments in Russia, and Russia's construction of nuclear power reactors in India.

While there is keen competition between New Delhi and Beijing for sources of raw materials and world markets, there are also substantial economic ties. China is the leading source of imports for India. The two countries are engaged in joint information technology ventures, based upon the complementary nature of India's software and China's hardware industries. In Sudan, India and China are engaged in joint energy activities. Both have a common strategic interest in keeping open the lanes of oil supply from the Middle East and in opposing US efforts to control some of Central Asia's energy.

Washington's interests in developing a strategic partnership with New Delhi are reflected in the nuclear materials and technology agreement, and the sale of advanced US aircraft and missiles to India. Equally important is the outsourcing of large-scale information technology projects to India and the close ties between the scientific personnel of the two nations. The prospect of Pakistan's implosion and the expansion of Iranian influence in the Middle East makes it strategically imperative to the maritime realm that the Indian Ocean lanes remain open to world trade. This can best be accomplished by Washington's support of New Delhi's expansion of its political and economic influence within the Indian Ocean Basin, backed by Indian naval and air power.

Emergence of an Indian Ocean realm led by a major power such as India, with balanced relations to the three other realms of the world, can strengthen global geopolitical equilibrium.

It would also further the goals of India's founding fathers, who envisaged their country's role as a major contributor to world peace.

Notes

1. Percival Spear, *Modern India* (Ann Arbor: University of Michigan Press, 1961), 386–406.
2. Saul B. Cohen, *Geography and Politics in a World Divided* (New York: Random House, 1963), 280–84.
3. Halford Mackinder, *Democratic Ideals and Reality* (London: Constable, 1919), map facing 77, 83–104.
4. Halford Mackinder, "The Round World and the Winning of the Peace," *Foreign Affairs* 21, no. 4 (1943): 278.
5. Michael Brecher, *The New States of Asia* (New York: Oxford University Press, 1966), 205.
6. Brecher, *New States of Asia*, 210.
7. "Sri Lanka's Muslims: Homeless and Homesick," *Economist*, October 13, 2007, 45–46.
8. Bertil Lintner, *Cross-Border Trade in the Golden Triangle* (Durham, England: Boundaries Research Press–University of Durham, 1991), 13–22.
9. Lintner, *Cross-Border Trade*, 1, 25–26.
10. Govand Singh, *A Political Geography of India* (Allahabad, India: Central Book Deposit, 1969), 134–37.
11. Alan J. Day, *Border and Territorial Disputes* (Harlow, England: Longman, 1982), 255–57.
12. Central Intelligence Agency, *World Factbook 2013* (Washington, DC: GPO/CIA, 2013), 9, 10.
13. Day, *Border and Territorial Disputes*, 251.
14. Fund for Peace, *The Failed States Index 2013*, *Foreign Policy Magazine*, http://www.foreignpolicy.com/failedstates2013.
15. Day, *Border and Territorial Disputes*, 236–50.

CHAPTER 12

The Middle East Shatterbelt

The Middle East is a shatterbelt, rent by the deep divisions within and between its sovereign states and peoples and further magnified by great power competition. Fragmentation of shatterbelts is a dynamic, not a static, process. Internal divisions are deep and widespread. When some rifts are healed, others open up to keep the region in turmoil. Thus Egypt and Israel forged a peace agreement, but withdrawal of Israel from Gaza continued the conflict between Israel and Arabs in this part of the region. The shifting of alliances between external powers and states within the region is common. When Iran's Khomeini broke with the United States, Washington found an ally in Saddam Hussein's Iraq. When the links between the USSR and Egypt were broken after Nasser's death, Moscow found a toehold in Syria.

Sunni and Shia Muslims, Jews, and Christians; Arabs, Turks, and Persians; Azeris, Kurds, and Druze; Uzbeks, Tajiks, and Pashtuns; Alawites and Maronites; Nilotic blacks and Sudanese Arabs; Bedouins and farmers; religious fundamentalists and secularists—all are part of the human landscape of the Middle East. Rather than forming a coherent mosaic, however, the parts overlap and rub against one another, fitting poorly into the national frameworks that are the region's political overlay. The ethnic, religious, and racial strife engendered by these schisms is further intensified by disputes over the scarce commodities of water and arable land and by conflicting claims over oil and natural gas resources.

As fragmented as it was during the Cold War, the Middle East has become even more shattered. The Afghan and Iraq conflicts waged by the United States and some of its allies have unleashed internecine struggles within Islam between Sunni and Shia and have provided an opportunity for Iran to penetrate the Arab world. These wars have pulled Pakistan into the Afghan maelstrom, have expanded the operational bases of international terrorism from the Afghan-Pakistan borderlands into Iraq, and from Iraq into Syria. The geopolitical fallout from America's poorly planned and incompetently waged war in Iraq has had an impact that extends far beyond the region. It has diminished the US status as a superpower, fanning anti-American sentiments not only throughout the Muslim world but also much more widely, even among its staunchest allies. The same applies to the US invasion of Afghanistan to topple the Taliban, which triggered thirteen years of warfare. When al-Qaeda militants were driven from their bases there and largely dislodged from their Pakistan hideouts, they shifted their operations to other parts of the region.

The "Arab Spring" of December 2010 has not brought peace and democracy to the region. Instead, the dictatorships that were toppled were replaced by regimes that were fragmented and chaotic, especially in Egypt, Libya, and Syria, followed by the rise of ISIS.

The location of the Middle East at the junction of the Old World's three continents has long given global strategic importance to its water and land transit ways. These transit ways, as well as the vast petroleum and natural gas reserves of the region, are the magnets that now draw outside powers to the region. In their efforts to gain competitive advantages, outside powers build upon and reinforce the internal divisions. All of these factors have blocked the geopolitical integration of the region, as most of its parts have turned to external powers for military support and exchange of capital and resources. This was not always the case in the Middle East. Indeed, it has experienced lengthy periods of unification imposed by imperial powers interspersed with periods of political fragmentation. The fall of Constantinople to the Ottoman Turks in 1453 signaled the rise of the Ottoman Empire and an era of regional unity that would last for four centuries. Weakened by military defeats at the hands of European powers and Russia and sapped by the "capitulations" system, which awarded commercial rights to the Europeans, the empire began to decline in the mid-nineteenth century. By the end of World War I, it had formally dissolved. In its stead came the European imperial rule that segmented the Middle East into spheres of influence. This was followed by the Cold War, during which the United States and the USSR carved the region into zones of influence and, in the present era, a multiplicity of outside powers, which include not only the United States and Russia but also the EU, China, and India.

Modern Colonial Penetration

Throughout the nineteenth and twentieth centuries, Western European powers and Russia jockeyed for bases and influence within the region. Even before the collapse of the Ottoman Empire, Britain, the most powerful colonial force, had a number of strategic goals, the most important of which was securing the sea-lanes to India. The acquisition of bases in Suez, at the southern entrance of the Red Sea, and along the Persian/Arab Gulf provided control over this route. The opening of the Suez Canal in 1869 enabled Britain to expand its trade with South and East Asia, making it the dominant commercial power in the world.

Cyprus provided Britain with the forward base for the occupation of Egypt in 1882 and for command of the canal. Defeat of the Mahdists, who had wrested control of the Sudan from Egypt by Anglo-Egyptian forces, enabled the British to establish the Anglo-Egyptian Sudan condominium in 1879. This gave Britain oversight of the western shores of the Red Sea to complement the base on the other side at Aden, which commanded the Strait of Bab el-Mandeb, the exit to the Indian Ocean. Rule over Sudan also assured control of the waters of the upper Nile, thus strengthening Britain's hold on Egypt.

Another British goal was to eliminate piracy in the Arabian Sea and the Indian Ocean and to halt the slave trade from East Africa that moved along these waters.[1] British protectorates were established over Bahrain (1867), the Trucial States (1892), and Kuwait (1899), which became bases from which to pursue this struggle. Afghanistan was the land gateway to India, and fear of Russian and Persian penetration of Afghan territory led the British to take preemptive steps. They became embroiled in a series of wars with the Afghans, who were forced to cede the Khyber Pass and other border areas in the east to British India. Later the situation was stabilized when the Afghans signed formal border agreements with Russia and Persia as well as with Britain.

Other European powers also actively engaged within the region. France sent troops to Christian Mount Lebanon to put a halt to the massacres by the Druze of the area's Catholic population. This became the foothold within the Levant from which Paris ultimately gained control over all of Lebanon and Syria. The French also seized Djibouti on the African shore of the Gulf of Aden, where they developed the port into a commercial and strategic rival to British Aden. Italy seized Eritrea, along the southwestern shores of the Red Sea. The Eritrean ports of Assab and Massawa commanded the access to landlocked Ethiopia, which was to become the main focus for Italy's imperial ambitions in northeastern Africa.

Russian penetration of the region during the nineteenth century was confined to securing territories around the Caspian Sea. This brought the czars into conflict with both the Ottoman Empire and Persia. The lands on the eastern shores of the Caspian were taken from Persia, while on the western shore the Ottomans ceded northern Azerbaijan to Russia.

At the dawn of the twentieth century, Britain, out of fear of German and Russian designs on the region, felt obliged to strengthen its position in the Persian Gulf through control of overland routes leading there. Turkey and Germany had signed an accord in 1896 to extend the German-owned Anatolian Railway from Konya in southeastern Anatolia to Baghdad and Basra and then to the open waters. Russia also put forward claims for concessions in the Gulf. For London, such moves represented a threat to vital communication lines needed for the defense of India.[2] British and French opposition held up the line to Baghdad until construction was resumed in 1911 and completed by the end of World War I.

However, none of the above considerations were to become as important to Britain's Persian Gulf strategy as its twentieth-century efforts to exploit and safeguard the oil resources of the region. William D'Arcy had been granted a concession by Persia to drill for oil in 1901. By 1908, the oil fields of Khuzestan, Persia's Arab-populated southwestern province, were revealed to be among the richest in the world.

Meanwhile, Russia sought to penetrate Persia from its Caspian Sea bases. In 1907, it carved out a sphere of influence in northern Persia that extended in the west from Tabriz (nominally under Ottoman control) through Tehran to Mashhad in the east, and that reached south to Esfahan. This coincided with the establishment of a British zone of influence covering the southwestern part of the country, extending from the Persian Gulf port of Bandar Abbas northeastward to the borders of British India and Afghanistan and backed by British bases along the western coast of the Gulf.

The Anglo-Iranian oil company then commissioned the building of a refinery at Abadan, whose production was to prove of great importance to the Allied war effort during World War I. It was the defense of the oil fields and facilities that prompted the British to attack the Turks in Iraq, seizing Baghdad in 1917 and then moving on to Mosul. (Abadan was to be expanded into the world's largest oil refinery in the 1970s.)

Britain reinforced its grip on the Gulf by becoming the protector of Ibn Saud, ruler of the Nejd in the center of Arabia, against the Turks. This close relationship between Britain and Saudi Arabia was later affirmed in a 1924 treaty that recognized Britain's special status in Kuwait, Bahrain, Qatar, and the Oman coast. The accord was, in part, a quid pro quo for Britain's acceptance of Ibn Saud's conquest of the Hejaz, which had been ruled by Husayn ibn Ali, sherif of Makka and head of the Hashemite family—a branch of the tribe to which Muhammad the Prophet had belonged. This paved the way for a unified state from the Red Sea to the Gulf. Even though driven out of Arabia, the Hashemite dynasty retained a prominent role within the region, as in 1921 the British had put one of Husayn's sons, Faisal, on the throne of Iraq and installed another, Abdullah, as head of Trans-Jordan.

From the end of World War I through World War II, much of the region was divided among European colonial powers into fairly coherent subunits—the British in Palestine, Trans-Jordan, Iraq, Southern Yemen (the Aden Protectorate), Egypt, and Sudan; the French in Lebanon and Syria; and the Italians in Libya (which they had conquered in 1912).

Modern Turkey, now limited territorially to Anatolia and Turkish Thrace in Europe, took the path of detachment from the region and initiated a drive toward Westernization, secularization, and self-sufficiency under the leadership of Kemal Atatürk. Saudi Arabia, Yemen, and Iran also remained independent of colonial rule. While Britain remained the major Western supporter of the Saudi Wahhabite dynasty during the 1920s and 1930s, the United States entered the Saudi Arabian scene in 1936 with the discovery of oil by an American oil company, which eventually became the Arab-American Oil Company (ARAMCO). Commercial production began two years later at Dammam on the Al-Ahsa coastal plain, although it was not until 1951 that a gusher was brought in at nearby Al-Hofuf that, three years later, would prove to be part of the Ghawar structure—the world's largest oil field. The new Pahlavi dynasty in Persia, meanwhile, managed to free itself of the British and Soviet spheres of influence that had been established in the north and south of the country.

While the Middle East had become a highly divided region from the end of World War I to the mid-twentieth century, it also had enjoyed a degree of geopolitical stability. The European powers had struck a balance of power within the territories under their control and had limited the spread of Soviet influence. It was during the Cold War that the deep divisions and instability that have come to be associated with the Middle East converted the region into today's shatterbelt.

The end of the mandate system and of colonial rule in general following World War II produced a multiplicity of national states within the region—stretching from Turkey, Cyprus, Iran, and Afghanistan in the north, south through Israel and a politically divided Arab Levant and Mesopotamia, and into Africa, from Libya and Egypt down through Sudan. The conflicts within and among the twenty-four diverse sovereign states of the region were inflamed and expanded by Cold War competition. This struggle between the maritime realm democracies and the Eurasian heartland Soviet Union for influence and control of strategically important spaces and for access to oil and gas reserves tore the Middle East asunder. Alliances forged by the outside powers with states and opposition groups removed all semblance of the geopolitical unity that had been achieved within the region in previous eras.

Great Power Rivalry: Cold War Period

The Cold War competition within the Middle East between the West and the Soviet Union was initiated by Soviet efforts to detach northern Iran from the rest of the country in 1945–46. At that time, Moscow supported breakaway Communist republics in the Iranian portions of Azerbaijan and Kurdistan. The seeds of this intervention had been planted in the early years of World War II, when Soviet troops had occupied Iranian Azerbaijan to establish a supply line for Allied military aid being transshipped to the USSR via the Persian Gulf.

Toward the end of the war, Moscow asked for a concession to explore the northern region for oil but was put off by Tehran. A major worry for the Soviets was that their Baku oil fields were aging.

The Soviets also resurrected historic Russian ambitions for a corridor to the Persian/Arab Gulf, their appetite now whetted by the region's oil deposits that extended along the flanks of the Zagros and from there along the coast to Qatar and the Arab emirates. When the USSR agreed to withdraw from Iran, it did so with the promise that oil concessions would be granted, subject to parliamentary approval. However, the Iranian parliament resoundingly rejected the proposal the following year, further worsening the relations between the two countries.

Moscow then sought to penetrate Iran through support of the Iranian Tudeh (Communist) Party and the Iranian National Front, headed by Mohammad Mosaddegh. Mosaddegh came to power in 1951, when the front gained enough seats within the parliament to pass an oil nationalization act. He was opposed both to foreign oil interests and to the Shah's rule. The Shah then fled but was returned to power in 1953 when Mosaddegh was forced from office (with covert help from the CIA). A firm military alliance with the United States then emerged, foreclosing Iran to penetration by Moscow.

Another Soviet attempt to inject itself into the region failed when Ankara refused to revise the Montreux Convention and give the USSR joint control of the Turkish straits—the entranceway to the Black Sea. Turkey countered the Soviet threat by turning strongly to the West and becoming a full member of NATO in 1952.

In the meantime, the position of the West within the Middle East was undergoing rapid change. In the Levant (Lebanon, Palestine, and Syria), France gave up its mandate over Lebanon in 1945 and over Syria the following year. Britain, which had split off Trans-Jordan from Palestine in 1922, granted the kingdom its independence in 1946, although Britain maintained its influence there by continuing to subsidize and train the Jordanian armed forces.

A year later, London gave up its mandate over Palestine, leading to the November 29, 1947, resolution of the United Nations which called for division of Palestine into a Jewish and an Arab state, with an internationalized Jerusalem. This triggered the first Arab-Israeli war. France and the Soviet Union were the sources for arms for the fledgling Jewish state in these formative years. Israel won this War of Independence in 1948. The military and economic alliance that subsequently developed between Israel and the United States helped the former to develop a powerful military machine and a strong modern economy. Washington gained an important strategic military and intelligence asset within the region, but at the cost of bitter and enduring Arab opposition.

British military influence in Iraq, where it had relinquished its mandate in 1934, weakened in 1948 as the Iraqi parliament refused London's request for modifications in the treaty of alliance between the two countries. Libya, which had been placed under joint Anglo-French military government after the Allied victory over German and Italian forces in North Africa in 1943, became independent in 1951. Libya subsequently signed military treaties with Britain and the United States, permitting the establishment of military bases on its soil, including the large American Wheelus Air Base. Sudan gained its independence from Britain in 1956.

With the passing of the European colonial era, the United States moved onto the Middle Eastern scene, replacing Britain and France as the primary Western external power. Because war-torn Europe was in economic shambles, it was left to Washington to apply its military and financial leverage to defend the interests of the maritime realm within the region. This it did by placing large NATO bases in Turkey and providing it with massive economic aid, developing strong military and economic ties with Saudi Arabia, forging close relations with Israel, and giving powerful support to the monarchy in Iran.

In response to the West's policy of containment along the Middle East's Northern Tier, which included formation of the Baghdad Pact in 1955, Moscow developed a strategy of alliances that leapfrogged the ring that had been drawn along its borders. The situation in Egypt offered the Soviet Union its first major opportunity to gain a strong foothold within the heart of the Middle East. When British troops completed their evacuation of the Suez Canal Zone in 1956, Colonel Gamal Abdel Nasser nationalized the Suez Canal and broke relations with London.

Three months after the canal had been nationalized, Britain and France moved to regain control of the waterway in tandem with Israeli land forces. Israel's motives were to block Palestinian guerrilla attacks from Egyptian-controlled Gaza and Sinai and to regain access to the canal, which had been denied to it by Cairo since 1950. An additional goal was to break the Arab blockade of the Strait of Tiran at the southern end of the Gulf of Aqaba, Israel's only alternative access to oil supplies from Iran and trade with the Far East. The campaign to seize the canal was foiled by UN intervention, led by the United States and the Soviet Union. The war ended with an armistice whose terms included the withdrawal of the attacking forces. Israel's principal military supplier had been France, which in the late 1950s provided Israel with the nuclear know-how and technology that has enabled it to acquire a nuclear arsenal. Jerusalem has never publicly admitted that it possesses such weapons.

Moscow then emerged as Egypt's major patron, providing the funds for the Aswan Dam, supplying massive military and economic aid, and establishing military and air bases within the country. The Egyptians pursued economic development in the Soviet style, nationalizing their industries. This relationship lasted until Anwar Sadat suddenly expelled the Soviet military personnel from Egypt as a prelude to the October 1973 attack upon Israel by Cairo and Damascus—a conflict that the USSR had been reluctant to support.

The ties between Egypt, the Arab world leader, and the Soviet Union had facilitated the rapid spread of Soviet influence within the region. When Cairo signed a military accord with Moscow in 1956, Damascus followed suit. These alliances were designed to counter the Baghdad Pact. Led by the Baath Party, which combined socialism and nationalism, Syria formed a union with Egypt in 1958 called the United Arab Republic. Yemen soon joined the union, which was renamed the United Arab States. The merger lasted only three years, until a military coup against the Baathists led to Syria's withdrawal. In 1966 the radical wing of the Baathists regained power with support from the Soviet Union, which then equipped the Syrian army with modern weapons.

The Arab strategy of dual attacks upon Israel from the north, south, and east was the cornerstone of the 1967 and 1973 wars. Despite the purchase of substantial arms from the USSR and modernization of their armed forces by the Soviets during this period, the Syrians, Jordanians, and Egyptians together proved no more of a match for Israel than had Egypt and Jordan in 1956. It was after the 1967 war that the United States came to view Israel as a powerful military ally that offered it a stable foothold in the Middle East. In 1968 Washington began to supply Israel with advanced aircraft and in 1987 granted it the stature of a "major non-NATO ally."

During the Cold War, many of the West's efforts to maintain its position in the Middle East were undermined by changes of regimes and shifting alliances. In 1955 Iraq joined Turkey and Iran in the Baghdad Pact but withdrew in 1959 after a coup that overthrew its monarchy. It then turned toward Moscow. In subsequent years, the Iraqi Baath Party came to power. With its nationalist and socialist ideology, the Baathists were, for quite some time, wary of Moscow but in 1972 signed a fifteen-year friendship treaty with the USSR, legalized the Iraqi Communist Party, and thus expanded the sphere of Soviet influence.

Gaining independence from Britain in 1967, South Yemen formed the Democratic People's Republic of Yemen, the only official Marxist state in the region. Aden, the historic British naval base, became available to Moscow's naval forces, which continued to operate from this base until South Yemen merged with North Yemen in 1990.

Afghanistan steered a neutral role in the Cold War until the 1970s, receiving aid from both the United States and the Soviet Union. After the king was deposed in 1973, however, a Marxist government emerged and oriented the country toward Moscow. Guerrilla opposition to the Kabul regime ultimately led to the Soviet invasion and the decade-long Afghan war

(1979–89), which not only devastated the country but also sapped Moscow's military forces to the point that they had to withdraw.

The Soviet position within the region during much of the Cold War also benefited from the wave of nationalist revolutions that swept Libya, Sudan, and Iran. In Libya, Muammar al-Gaddafi ousted King Idris in 1969. He forced Britain and the United States to evacuate their military bases in Libya, thus strengthening Moscow, and allowed the Soviets access to naval shore bases.

Colonel Mohammed al-Nimeiry seized power in Sudan during the same year, banned all political parties, and nationalized much of the country's industry and the banks. Nimeiry forged strong ties with Cairo, which had broken with the West, and later instituted strict Islamic law, further isolating the country from its former Western supporters. Successor Sudanese regimes reinforced this isolation as Khartoum strengthened ties with Libya and supported Iraq in the Gulf War.

The Iranian revolution of 1979, which was led by the Ayatollah Ruhollah Khomeini, toppled the Shah, one of the closest allies of the West. Khomeini exploited the widespread resentment against the Shah's autocratic regime, which had become repressive and corrupt. This was the most severe blow to US interests in the Middle East. While the fundamentalist Iranian regime was far removed ideologically from Moscow, its virulent anti-Americanism served the strategic interests of the USSR by breaking the ring of containment in the northeastern part of the region. Tensions between Washington and Tehran rose to a fever pitch in late 1979, when militants seized the US embassy and held Americans there hostage for 444 days.

In sum, Moscow's various Middle East alliances made possible the deployment of powerful naval forces in the eastern Mediterranean, the Gulf of Aden, and the Indian Ocean. At different periods, the Soviet navy had access to bases in Libya, Egypt, Syria, Aden, and across the Red Sea and Gulf of Aden waters, in Ethiopia's Eritrean province and Somalia. In addition, it maintained several permanent anchorages in the Mediterranean and the Indian Ocean.

The extensive Soviet penetration of the region required major strategic realignments on the part of the maritime realm powers. The most important anchors in this strategy were Turkey, Saudi Arabia, Israel, and after 1976, Egypt. These countries provided stable bases from which the United States and maritime Europe could respond to the upheavals that brought Soviet military power into much of the Arab world, Iran, and Afghanistan. In addition, on the margins of the Middle East, the competition between the superpowers extended into the Horn of Africa.

Israel played a pivotal role in two dramatic episodes that affected great power strategic relationships in the region during the Cold War. During the 1967 Arab-Israeli war, Israel invaded the Sinai, seizing control of the entire peninsula and reaching the east bank of the Suez Canal. During the course of the fighting, the canal was blocked by sunken ships and became the boundary between the two countries. The Egyptians refused to clear the wreckage, so the waterway remained closed to all shipping. For the USSR, this closure represented a strategic gain in that it forced vessels that normally used the canal to link Europe and the North Atlantic with the Persian Gulf, Indian Ocean, and Asia-Pacifica to take the longer and more costly route around the Cape of Good Hope. The canal remained closed until 1975, when it was cleared with the help of the US Navy, after Egypt and Israel had signed an agreement for military disengagement and withdrawal of Israeli troops from Sinai.

The second episode had to do with the consequences of the October 1973 war. Israel emerged victorious after warding off surprise attacks by Egypt and Syria on its southern and northern fronts. Given the debacle of that war, President Anwar Sadat concluded that Egypt had no prospect of defeating Israel militarily. Moreover, the alliance with Moscow that had provided so much military and economic aid had ended when Sadat ousted Soviet personnel before the outbreak of the war. A 1976 US agreement to provide Egypt with aid in developing nuclear technology for peaceful purposes, as well as the prospect of peace with Israel, pointed to a reorientation of Cairo's foreign policy back toward the West.

The Camp David Accords of 1978, brokered by US president James Earl Carter, was followed by a formal peace between Egypt and Israel the next year. President Sadat was then free to pursue a full military and economic alliance with the United States. When he was assassinated in 1981, his successor, President Hosni Mubarak, greatly expanded these ties. The relationship was strengthened by Cairo's participation as a full-fledged member of the Allied coalition during the First Gulf War against Iraq in 1991. As a result of its return to the Western camp, Egypt was rewarded by being made the second-highest recipient of annual US aid, Israel being the first.

The Geographical Setting

A unique geographical characteristic of the Middle East is that its landmass is almost completely surrounded and interpenetrated by major water bodies. It is rimmed by five seas—the Caspian, Black, eastern Mediterranean, Red Sea/Gulf of Aden, and Arabian/Persian Gulf. These water bodies not only define the Middle East but also are strategically important to external powers that have historically sought to gain full control over them. With a population of nearly 450 million, the region extends from Turkey and Iran in the north to the Levant, Iraq, and the Arabian Peninsula in the center, to Tunisia, Libya, Egypt, and Sudan in the south.

The region is divisible into three east-west trending structural zones—the Northern Highlands, Intermediate, and Southern Desert. Each of the zones has distinct physical and resource characteristics that have influenced its economic, cultural, and political development.

THE NORTHERN HIGHLANDS ZONE

The Northern Highlands Zone consists of high, folded, earthquake-prone mountains that are part of the Alpine-Himalayan system and rim high interior plateaus. A good deal of this mountainous area is subject to widespread tectonic activity, thus earthquakes are a major hazard. Most of Turkey and Iran and all of Afghanistan lie within the zone, as does Iraq's northeastern highlands, which are home to the country's Kurdish populace. The parts of Turkey that lie outside the Northern Highlands Zone are its narrow Aegean and Mediterranean coastal fringes and its southeastern Mesopotamian plains, the latter being part of the Intermediate Zone.

The Highlands region is vast, extending over nearly 1.5 million square miles, and has a population of well over one hundred million in parts of Turkey, Iraq, Afghanistan, and Iran.

While Turks and Persians form the preponderance of the populations of their nations, all four of these countries haves large ethnic minorities that have long sought independence within their remote highland territorial bases. The ancient homeland of Kurdistan extends in an arc from the plateaus and mountains of southeastern Anatolia, where an estimated fifteen million Kurds live, through northeastern Iraq and northwestern Iran, where Kurds number six to eight million in each area. This homeland has smaller outliers in northeast Syria and parts of Armenia. Kurdish independence aspirations date back to the nineteenth century. In 1946, a revolt whose goal was a Soviet-supported Kurdish Communist state was crushed by Tehran. In Turkey, the Kurds have been in rebellion for decades, using terrorism as an instrument of war. At the end of the First Gulf War, the Iraqi Kurds, encouraged by the United States, launched a rebellion that was ruthlessly quashed by Saddam Hussein. Washington stood by as three hundred thousand Kurds were killed.

The other large minority within the zone is the more than fifteen million Azeris of northwestern Iran. Their rebellion, also in 1946, led to a short-lived Communist state supported by the USSR, but it was quickly put down by the Iranian military.

Afghanistan is divided into towering mountainous highland, inland valley, and desert regions. Within each, various ethnic groups have developed separate linguistic and cultural characteristics. The Pashtuns (Pathans), the largest regional ethnic group, constituting 45 percent of the population, live in the east along the Pakistan border and in the south; the Tajiks, making up 25 percent of the total, live in the west and northeast; the Uzbeks, 8 percent, live in the north; and the Shiite Hazaras, about 10 percent, are in the central mountains. While most Afghans are Sunni Muslim, the ethnic divisions have long been a basis for civil strife, compounded by the civil war between the Communists and the mujahideen during the 1980s, the former supported by the USSR and the latter receiving weapons and training from the United States. Some of the mujahideen formed the Northern Alliance, which was composed largely of Tajiks, Uzbeks, and other non-Pashtun ethnic groups, and took control of the government following the Soviet defeat. The extreme Sunni fundamentalist Taliban, who are mostly Pashtuns, imposed their rule upon most of the country in the civil war of 1996, after defeating the Northern Alliance forces. Afghanistan's ethnic and tribal divisions are reinforced by nature, as the core areas for these different groups have developed within river valleys that are separated by mountains and deserts. The Kabul River valley is the focus for the Pashtun core around the city of Kabul—the gateway to the Khyber Pass and South Asia. The focus for the Pashtuns of Kandahar in the southeastern part of the country is the middle portion of the Helmand River, which originates in the Hindu Kush and flows southwest to Iran. They are separated from the nomadic Balochis of Rejistan's semiarid and desert lands to their southwest.

The Tajiks of western Afghanistan are concentrated around Herat, a large oasis within the Harirud valley. The north, where the Amu Darya River forms the border with Uzbekistan and part of Turkmenistan, is the homeland of the Uzbeks, who are centered on Mazar-e-Sharif, which is located on the Balkh River, a tributary of the Amu Darya. The Tajiks of the northeast also are concentrated along the Amu Darya plain. The Hazaras have maintained their separate Shiite religion from their mountain bastions within the center of the country.

The political organization of the country is deeply rooted in a system based on fiercely independent tribal chiefs and warlords. This system is strongly reinforced not only by nature but also by the poor transportation and communications that inhibit the interconnections among the country's different parts. The nation building that has been envisaged for the post-Taliban era by the United States and its allies has yet to find strategies that can incorporate this cultural-physical mosaic that has endured for so many centuries. Indeed, as Washington and its allies prepare to withdraw most of their troops from the country by the end of 2014, prospects are dim for a stable and cohesive Afghanistan that does not depend on continued American financial support and military reinforcements.

After coming to power, the Taliban provided sanctuary and training bases for networks of Islamic extremists, the most prominent of which was Osama bin Laden's al-Qaeda group. These groups are dedicated to exporting terror to many parts of the world in order to further their fundamentalist aims. Afghan-trained guerrillas, including veterans of the Afghan war, have targeted Chechnya, Xinjiang, Uzbekistan, and Kashmir, as well as the Middle East, North Africa, and, most dramatically, the United States. While bin Laden was killed on May 2, 2011, by US Special Forces in his Abbottabad, Pakistan, hiding place, al-Qaeda and allied extremist groups continue to operate from bases throughout the Middle East. To compound the problems of Afghanistan, the country has suffered from a lengthy period of drought and famine that has caused millions of its rural poor to leave their villages in an effort to avoid war and starvation. As many as five million Afghans have fled across the border into Pakistan or Iran, where they are gathered in refugee camps, or have flocked to Afghanistan's larger cities, which lack the means to sustain them. The flow of refugees was renewed when the United States began its heavy bombing campaign in October 2001. Both Pakistan and Iran sought to close their borders but were only partially successful.

Tensions between Shiite Iran and the Sunni Taliban, long strained over religious differences, were exacerbated in 1998 by the murder of Iranian consular officials in Mazar-e-Sharif, the major center of northern Afghanistan. This nearly led to war between the two countries.

While the population of the Northern Highlands Zone is engaged mainly in farming, grazing, and handicrafts, the country's nonferrous and ferrous minerals have been important to the industrialization of Turkey and Iran. In the first half of the twentieth century, coal and iron ore became the basis for heavy industry, especially steel, enabling Mustafa Kemal Atatürk, the founding father of modern Turkey, to pursue the policy of self-sufficiency under state ownership without dependence upon foreign capital and influence. The economy broadened as oil was discovered in southern Turkey (part of the Intermediate Zone) and came to support a petrochemical and chemical fertilizer industry.

Turkey's situation changed after World War II, when it abandoned its policy of neutrality and moved toward democracy and alignment with the West. Massive aid from the United States began to flow into the country with the Marshall Plan recovery program, and state capitalism was relaxed in favor of private enterprise. These conditions attracted foreign investment that, combined with continued large-scale American aid, considerably expanded industrialization and moved Turkey into an international exchange economy.

A more recent stimulus for growth in both industry and agriculture has been the Guneydogu Anadolu Project (GAP) in southeast Anatolia—the giant Atatürk Dam and Reservoir, supplemented by a string of smaller dams and hydroelectric plants that draw on the waters of the upper Euphrates and upper Tigris Rivers. The project had been bitterly opposed by Syria and Iraq, the downstream riparians of these rivers, and plagued by the conflict between Ankara and the Kurdish separatists, punctuated by terrorist attacks launched by the outlawed Turkish Workers Party (PKK). Nevertheless, it has begun to bring industrial and agricultural prosperity to the southern and southeastern parts of the country. In the past, most of Turkey's farm areas were located in the wetter, western part of the plateau, with grazing taking place in the semiarid interior. Today, irrigated cotton, fruit, vegetables, and tobacco have been rapidly expanded into the areas affected by the project, as has manufacturing. Tourism along the southern coast and in Istanbul and remittances from Kurds living abroad in Europe have also become important economic mainstays.

Iran, too, possesses a variety of minerals, such as iron, coal, copper, chromium, and zinc, and it has developed the manufacturing of steel, carpets, textiles, chemicals, and food products. However, it has not felt the pressure to industrialize as keenly as has Turkey because of its wealth of oil and natural gas resources. The country has been the world's fourth-largest oil producer. It remains dependent upon petroleum for over 80 percent of its exports, and its economy is therefore subject to the wild swings of the world oil market prices. Despite Iran's oil wealth, refining capacity is so limited that it has had to import 40 percent of its refined oil needs. Since sanctions have been imposed by the West upon Iran's oil exports because of its nuclear development policies, the country's economy has suffered gravely.

During the first three decades of the Cold War, Turkey and Iran served as the Middle Eastern mainstays of the West. With their Turkish and Aryan/Persian populations and long histories of conflict with the Russians to the north and Arabs to the south, they were logical allies for Washington, especially since so much of the Arab world had been convulsed by upheavals in the 1950s and 1960s and some Arab countries had aligned themselves with the Soviet Union.

Since 1979, the orientation of the zone has changed drastically. After the takeover of the American embassy in Tehran in that year and the ensuing hostage crisis, Washington became so obsessively anti-Iranian, matching Iran's virulent anti-Americanism, that it had no compunctions about supporting the ruthless dictatorship of Saddam Hussein in Iraq's war against Ayatollah Khomeini's Iran. The arms supplied to Iraq would later be turned against Kuwait and the West in the First Gulf War and were later used by Saddam's forces against the invading US-led forces in 2003. With the defeat of the Iraqi army, many of these weapons were looted from unguarded storage depots by the Iraqi insurgents. While Iran had dropped out of the Western strategic fold in 1979, Turkey has remained a cornerstone of the Western alliance as a member of NATO. US air and missile bases in that country, especially the large air base at Incirlik, played a significant role in the First Gulf War. They supported the aircraft that then imposed the no-fly zones over Iraq. In addition, these bases have played an important role in the war in Afghanistan as well as in the antiterrorism struggle. Incirlik and the port of Iskenderun (Alexandretta) continue to permit the large-scale transfer of supplies to American and allied troops in the second Iraq war.

The once highly secularized Turkish society is feeling the influence of a growing Islamic movement that is making considerable inroads within the Sunni Muslim populace. Moreover, the fate of Ankara's application for EU membership may affect its overall relationship with the West. Now that it no longer needs the NATO shield for protection from Moscow, Turkey's attention is focused on prospects for economic improvement through economic integration with maritime Europe. Turkey might turn to a more neutral geopolitical orientation should it be spurned by the EU because of its human rights abuses, the Kurdish problem, differing economic policies, and widespread European fears of admitting an Islamic country into the union.

THE INTERMEDIATE ZONE

This zone, with a population of over 150 million, stands apart from the Northern Highlands Zone to its north and the Desert Zone to its south. The Levant (Israel, Lebanon, Syria, and the Palestinian areas of the West Bank and Gaza) and Mesopotamia (the ancient "Fertile Crescent"), which includes the northern and western shores of the Persian/Arab Gulf, are a physical unit. Structurally, all of this area, save the eastern Mediterranean coast, is part of the Arabian tectonic plate. (The Northern Highlands have been formed from the Turkish and Iranian plates.) Most of the Intermediate Zone is exposed to the influence of the eastern Mediterranean Sea or the Persian/Arab Gulf. Low coastal mountains and adjoining plateaus along the more moist western half of the zone in Lebanon, Syria, Israel, and the West Bank of Palestine provide ease of land access to the drier eastern half of the zone in Jordan, Iraq, Kuwait, eastern Saudi Arabia, Bahrain, Qatar, and the United Arab Emirates (UAE).

The gentle geological downward warp of Mesopotamia, from northeastern Syria to the head of the Persian Gulf, as well as the western and northeastern shores of that body of water, are overlain by tertiary- and quaternary-age sedimentary layers. Their porous limestones and sandstones have trapped oil in their slight structural foldings to create storage places for the world's richest petroleum reserves. While the bulk of these deposits lie in the semicircle that runs on and off the Gulf shore from Khuzestan in southwestern Iran through southern Iraq, Kuwait, Saudi Arabia, Qatar, the UAE, and Oman, substantial oil is also produced in the fields of northern Mesopotamia—in northern Iraq, northeastern Syria, and the southern edge of southeastern Turkey.

The Persian Gulf-Mesopotamian countries possess two-thirds of the world's currently proven petroleum reserves and 40 percent of its natural gas deposits. Over half of the latter are located within Qatar, Saudi Arabia, and the United Arab Emirates. Iran, with the world's largest known gas reserves, has over 35 percent. Not only does Saudi Arabia presently have the world's largest onshore oil field (Ghawar), but it also possesses the largest offshore field (Safaniya). The Burgan field in Kuwait ranks second only to Ghawar.

As important as Middle Eastern oil fields are today, accounting for over one-third of the world's production, their future role may be even greater if new finds elsewhere fail to keep up with rising demand worldwide or if stringent conservation methods are not adopted by the United States, China, and emerging countries. An early estimate was that, by the year 2040, only the Middle East would be a petroleum exporting region.[3] This estimate has since been proved to be off the mark, as it did not anticipate the large-scale petroleum developments in Russia, the United States, the oil reserves of Venezuela, the expanding production in Africa, and prospects that substantial oil and gas reserves in the Arctic may become exploitable with global warming. The United States and Russia now match Saudi Arabia as the world's leading oil producers. US production has increased thanks to the technological advances in extracting oil (as well as natural gas) from shale rock through the "fracking" process.

The states of the Levant are well situated to serve as gateways to Iraq and the northern gulf. This applies not only to their potential for transferring goods and serving as communication links from the eastern Mediterranean. It also refers to the agricultural and consumer products and services that they can generate to be exchanged with Mesopotamia and the gulf. Regrettably, in the recent years of war and terrorist attacks, such transfers have consisted heavily of smuggled weapons, drugs, oil, and other goods.

As wealthy as this Intermediate Zone is in oil and natural gas, it is poor in water resources. Water scarcity has been a traditional source of tribal disputes and armed conflicts in the Middle East, as well as a stimulus for technological innovations in water reuse and desalinization. Half of Israel's water supply now comes from desalination and reclaimed wastewater, while most of the rest is provided by the rainfall of the north and the fresh waters of the Sea of Galilee. Those natural waters are routed to the rest of the country by the National Water Carrier, which extends from the Sea of Galilee through the Valley of Jezreel and the coastal ecumene to the northern Negev. Some water is also drawn from a rapidly depleting coastal aquifer and the mountain aquifer of the West Bank. Recycled sewerage water accounts for nearly half of Israel's agricultural needs, while large-scale desalination plants now supply 80 percent of the urban domestic water.

So rapidly has desalination succeeded in meeting Israel's water needs that plans have been shelved for importing freshwater from Turkey's Manavgat River in southeastern Anatolia by ships and pipelines. This does not mean that they may not be revived in the future. Israel currently supplies some freshwater to the West Bank and Jordan—water-deficient areas whose needs are likely to grow to the point where they cannot be filled by Israel. At such time, Turkey's role as a source for water that can be transferred through Israel can become important. In 2013, Israel, Jordan, and the Palestinians signed an agreement to build a desalination plant on the Gulf of Aqaba.

There are limitations to how widely Lebanon can increase its production of fruit and vegetables because of the restricted amount of available flatlands and the country's continuing civil strife. However, additional irrigated waters in the semiarid Beqa'a Valley could raise this output. The specialized agricultural crops of Israel and Gaza, much of which are under greenhouse cultivation, cannot be greatly expanded under current irrigation water restrictions. Since Hamas has gained political control of Gaza, agricultural production has declined greatly because the Israeli market has been closed by blockade in response to rocket attacks on Israeli territory. With peace and the implementation of a rational water-sharing scheme for the Jordan-Yarmuk River and Lebanon's Litani River, production from these countries could become an important source of exports to Saudi Arabia and neighboring Gulf states. The greatest potential for agricultural growth within the region is in Syria. Thirty percent of Syrian land is arable, but this land requires irrigation for its optimal development. Measures to expand irrigation works have been taken for the past three decades in the following areas: (1) the northern part of the Ghab (an extension of the Beqa'a) that parallels the coast within the Mediterranean climate belt and through which the Orontes River flows before emptying into the Mediterranean at the southwest corner of Turkey; (2) the northern steppe zone, from Homs to Halab (Aleppo), where the dry farming of these grasslands for grain is now marginal because of variable rainfall; and (3) the arid lands of the northeast.

For agriculture to become fully developed in the Intermediate Zone, a radical change is required in the political relations of the three Euphrates riparian states: Turkey, Syria, and Iraq. Damascus and Baghdad came close to war in 1974 as a result of their dispute over Syria's building of the Tabqa Dam on the Euphrates to form Lake Assad. In addition, Turkey's control of the river's headwaters leaves Damascus vulnerable to Ankara's major long-range plans for exploiting the headwaters. Politics further complicates possibilities for water sharing. Syria backed Iran in its war with Iraq, then supported the Allies in the First Gulf War, and most recently has developed a close anti-US alliance with Iran. Both Syria and northern Iraq have also provided safe havens for Kurdish Workers Party guerrillas in their struggle for independence from Ankara.

In the far southwest of Syria, the Yarmuk River, whose main headwaters rise in Syrian territory, forms the border between Syria and Jordan. It also serves as the boundary between Israel and Jordan south of the Sea of Galilee, before entering the Jordan Rift Valley. Most of the waters of the Yarmuk between Syria and Jordan are used for irrigation. Jordan has built a dam across the river and diverted some of the flow to the East Ghor Canal. Before Syria can exploit more of the Yarmuk waters, it would have to invest substantially in irrigation works. By the same token, Damascus would have to expend considerable sums of money were Syria to develop an agreement with Lebanon to enable it to exploit waters of the Litani River that flow through the Lebanese part of the Beqa'a Valley and then into the Mediterranean at Tyre. Syria's attempt to divert the headwaters of the Jordan River by constructing a diversionary canal was foiled by Israeli military actions between 1964 and 1967. This was a major factor in Israel's initiation of the June 1967 war against Egypt and Syria.

Therefore, both politics and capital are involved in Syria's agricultural expansion. Syria will be unable to realize its fullest agricultural potential without agreements with Turkey and Iraq and without a resolution of the conflict with Israel. Syria's most important source of income is petroleum, which represents two-thirds of its exports. The capacity of Damascus to invest these petroleum revenues in agriculture is constrained by the emphasis on expanding its civilian industrial base, its heavy investments in the development of a domestic military industry, and its purchase of armaments from abroad. Moreover, Syria faces a reduction in its oil revenues as a result of depletion of its fields. Most of all, the rebellion that has torn Syria apart since 2011 has resulted in massive relocations of refugees within the country as well as flight to neighboring lands. To speak of economics under these circumstances is to address the impact of de-development, not development.

Economic development within the Intermediate Zone is frustrated not only by inter-Arab and inter-Islamic disputes but also by the Arab-Israeli conflict. The peace between Jordan and Israel helped to expand tourism in both countries, while Jordan has benefited from water transfers when it has experienced shortages. An end to the Arab-Israeli conflict through West Bank Palestinian independence might stimulate exchanges that would be of mutual benefit to Saudi Arabia, the Gulf countries, and Israel.

For the present, however, there is little prospect that such peaceful economic relations will soon be realized. Instead, the Intermediate Zone remains conflict ridden and highly unstable. Particularly intractable are the conflicts in Lebanon, Iraq, and Afghanistan and between Israel and the Palestinians. These affect the region in its entirety and contribute heavily to its shatterbelt status.

THE SOUTHERN DESERT ZONE

Structurally, this zone extends across the African plate from Libya through Egypt and Sudan and then eastward along the Arabian plate that underlies the Arabian Peninsula. It is an essentially desert region, with under ten inches of annual rainfall. The population of the zone is concentrated along the Nile, in parts of the Red Sea and southeastern Mediterranean coasts, and in interior desert oases. In northeast Africa, exceptions to the area's desert character include the northern coastal tip of Cyrenaica in northeastern Libya, which has a Mediterranean-type climate and vegetation in an area backed by a narrow, semiarid belt, and Libya's coastal northwestern Tripolitania, which borders Tunisia and is also characterized by semiaridity.

For the most part, however, Egypt and Libya are northern and eastern extensions of the Sahara, as is northern Sudan. In Sudan, the twelve degrees north latitude line, which runs to the south of Khartoum, is the boundary between the desert of the north and the semiarid savanna region of the center that grades into the south. There, the landscape changes into the permanent and seasonally flooded swamplands of the Sudd, a semitropical region with higher rainfall rates that is subject to flooding from the Nile headwaters and covered with thick, aquatic vegetation.

From the very onset of Sudan's independence in 1955, the rebel southerners were able to sustain their war against Arab Muslim northern regimes from within the inaccessible reaches of South Sudan's negroid Sudanic, Nilotic, and Nubian animists and Christians. The intensity of the conflict sharpened with Khartoum's attempt to impose Islamic law upon the south. In 2005, a peace agreement was signed between the north and the south. Two separate states, Sudan and South Sudan, ultimately emerged in 2011, only for South Sudan to become torn by civil war.

In 2003, the province of Darfur in western Sudan erupted in conflict. Although they are Muslims, Darfur's farming and pastoral tribes began a rebellion that prompted the Sudanese government to mobilize Janjaweed Arab militias to support the Sudanese army in the campaign to put down the rebellion. As of 2007, two hundred thousand Darfurian blacks had been killed and two million displaced. Many had fled across the border to Chad and the Central African Republic, destabilizing those countries. Efforts to bring an end to the human toll and suffering have failed, in part because the rebels themselves are bitterly divided. The major problem, however, has been the Sudanese government's resistance to stationing of substantial UN forces to enforce a cease-fire. The small African Union (AU) force that was allowed into the region was inadequately equipped to stop the carnage. China's diplomatic support, motivated by its oil development interests, allowed the Khartoum government to stave off UN intervention. Beijing's grudging agreement in 2007 to an enlarged UN-AU force has raised some hope for an eventual resolution of the conflict.

In the adjoining Sub-Saharan compression zone of the Horn of Africa, deserts also cover Eritrea, most of Somalia, and southeastern Ethiopia, which shares the Ogaden with Somalia.

Most of Saudi Arabia is situated within the Southern Desert Zone. However, the country belongs to both the Southern Desert and Intermediate Zones because its important oil resources lie along its northeastern Gulf coast in the Intermediate Zone, while its major population concentrations, as well as Makka (Mecca) and Medina, are located on or close to the coast in the Southern Desert Zone.

The portion of Saudi Arabia that lies in the Desert Zone is a plateau of ancient crystalline rocks, parts of which are desert and parts of which are semiarid. Nafud, to the north of the sparse grasslands of the Nejd, is desert. So is Rub' al Khali in the southeastern corner of the country—one of the world's largest sand deserts and an uninhabited area known as the "Empty Quarter."

The climatic and vegetational exceptions to this desert pattern are the southwest coast of Saudi Arabia—the province of Asir—and northern Yemen, where lofty coastal mountains rise up from the Red Sea to intercept summer monsoon winds. These well-watered areas support dense human settlement and traditional production of coffee, grains, and fruit.

Farther north from Asir, along the Red Sea coast, lies the Hejaz, which consists of a narrow coast backed by highlands with steep slopes dissected by narrow valleys that have been shaped by water and wind. The region's leading city, Jeddah (population of 2.7 million), is the country's historic seaport and trading center. Jeddah is the main port for imports and for pilgrims to nearby Makka and Medina and the country's commercial and business center. Makka (Mecca), Islam's holiest city, has a population of over 1.5 million and is the destination for two million Muslims who make the annual hajj. However, it also represents a flash point for Muslim fundamentalists, both Saudi and foreign, who have clashed with Saudi troops. Medina, with nearly a million people, is Islam's second-holiest city. An ancient oasis, it lies inland from the Red Sea and is generally visited by those who make the pilgrimage to Makka.

While the Hejaz contained the older Saudi ecumene because of its farming oases, livestock grazing lands, and access for Muslim pilgrims via the Red Sea, in recent decades it has been eclipsed in political and economic importance by the new ecumene that extends from Riyadh (population four million) to the Gulf countries. This is not to minimize the continued rapid growth of Jeddah, Makka, and the city of Yanbu, whose Red Sea port was modernized and expanded in 1885. It is the terminal for oil and gas pipelines from Jubail and Bahrain on the Persian/Arab Gulf and a focus for the petrochemical and other industries.

The geographical shift of power from the Hejaz to the interior and the Gulf coast is not without its liabilities. Up to one-half of the Eastern Province's population of over four million is Shia, whose discontent with Riyadh's Wahhabi Sunni regime has been fanned since the Iranian revolution. Moreover, the majority of the country's 7.5 million foreign workers are located in the Gulf area. Since they outnumber the Saudi labor force by over two to one and are one-quarter of the country's total population of twenty-seven million, they are potentially a highly destabilizing force. During the Arab Spring, the Iranians stepped up their efforts to create unrest in the Eastern Province, but the Saudi government quickly clamped down.

Saudi Arabia's split geopolitical personality could become the basis for political divisiveness in times of domestic stress. Thus far the Saudi government has maintained the military and political power that it needs to strengthen the unity of the kingdom through petroleum wealth, repression, US military support, and an alliance with the country's fundamentalist religious leadership.

In the African sector of the Southern Desert Zone, major petroleum and natural gas deposits lie at Egypt's portion of the northern end of the Red Sea trough, where the African and Arabian plates meet. There the sedimentary strata that overlie the ancient rock base of most of the zone yield petroleum within the fields of the Gulf of Suez waters and natural gas deposits that extend along the coast from the Nile delta westward.

One of the dividends to Israel of its peace with Egypt is that it is able to purchase energy from Egypt. An agreement has been signed to construct a joint Egyptian-Israeli underwater pipeline to carry natural gas from the Egyptian gas fields to Israel, where the gas will replace imported oil as the main fuel for Israel's power plants.

Petroleum and petroleum products have become Egypt's single largest export, but agriculture remains an economic mainstay, with over half the population being rural. The country's fairly broad economic base includes tourism, chemicals, textiles, cement, steel, and foodstuffs. However, Egypt's population of eighty-five million is crowded onto 4 percent of the land—not enough to support the vast farm labor force. Therefore, Cairo is heavily dependent for its financial stability on foreign aid, mainly from the United States and Qatar, on Suez Canal revenues, and on cash remittances from Egyptians working abroad. This state of dependency results in Egypt's need for close relations with the maritime world as well as for firm alliances with Saudi Arabia and the Gulf States.

Geopolitical Features

The geopolitical immaturity of the Middle East shatterbelt is reflected in the absence of significant regional geopolitical features. The region lacks either a historic or a current political core to serve as a unifying force, and its national ecumenes and effective national territories are, in most cases, so physically distant from one another that they inhibit even subregional unity. Those features that do have a regional impact are boundaries and empty areas, and they have served as barriers to interaction rather than as facilitators.

HISTORIC CORE

The Middle East lacks a single, unifying historic regional core. This is because the capitals of the empires that had ruled the region in various eras—from Nineveh, Memphis, Babylon, and Persepolis to Alexandria, Antioch, Constantinople, and Baghdad—do not serve as rallying points today for the concept of a unified Middle East. Jerusalem is a unique world religious core, while serving as the capital of modern Israel, and its eastern Arab sector is potentially the capital of a modern Palestinian state.

REGIONAL POLITICAL CAPITALS

A modern, Middle Eastern regional political capital is an equally remote concept. There is no regional organization whose seat might be viewed as the forerunner of a political core. In

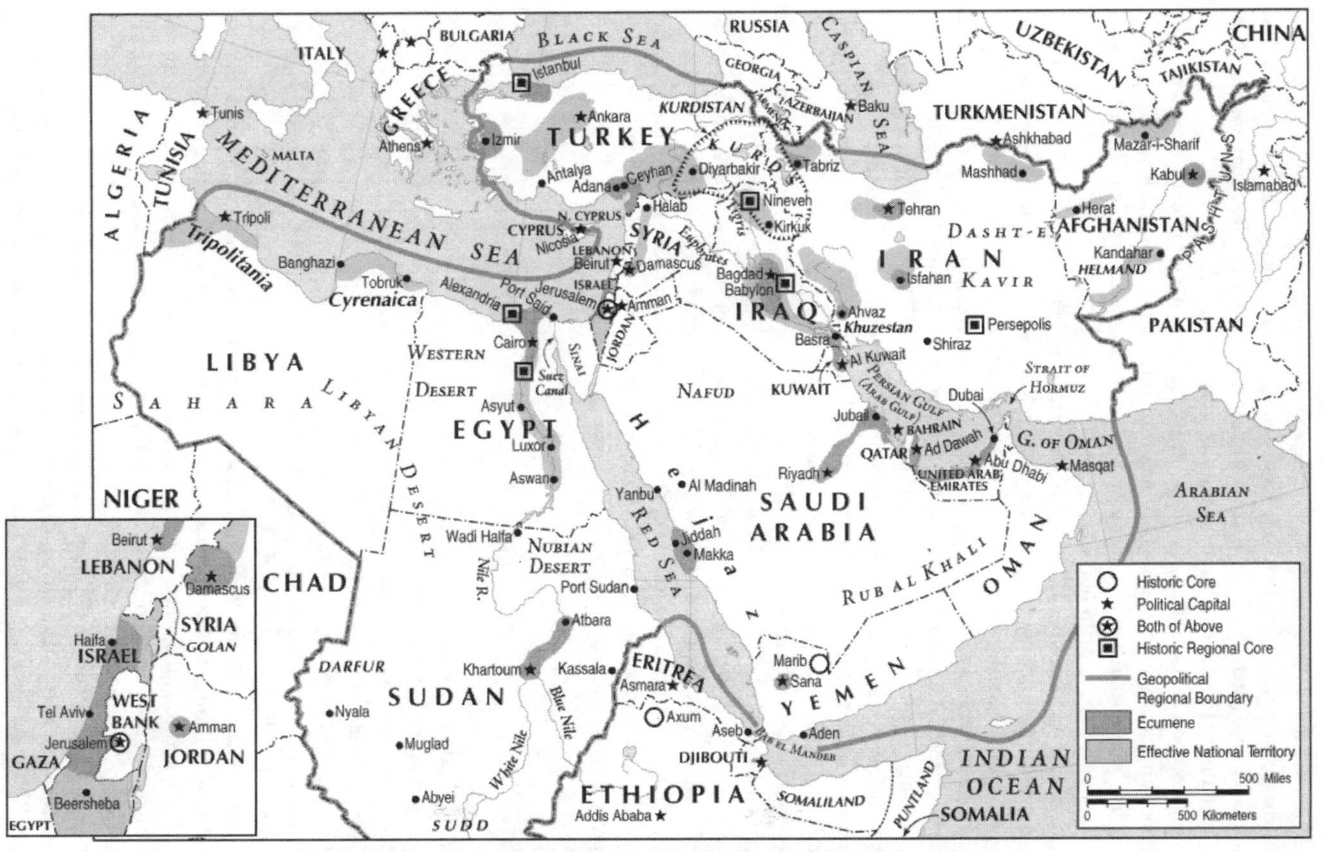

Figure 12.1. Middle East Shatterbelt: Major Geopolitical Features

fact, there are only two frameworks that make a pretense of serving the goal of regional unity. One is the geographically limited Gulf Cooperation Council, which includes Saudi Arabia, Kuwait, Bahrain, Qatar, the United Arab Emirates, and Oman. Headquartered in Riyadh, the council promotes cooperation in economics, agriculture, industry, education, and culture; sponsors free trade in the exchange of agricultural, industrial, and mineral products; and has established an investment corporation. One of its functions is the settlement of disputes, but while it has been effective in this area among its own members, it has not been successful in avoiding war in disputes with outsiders.

The twenty-two-member League of Arab States (the Arab League), which was formed in 1945, now includes not only the Arab states of the Middle East but also those of North Africa, Somalia, Sudan, Djibouti, Comoros, and one nonstate, the Palestinian Authority. The non-Arab Middle Eastern states of Turkey, Iran, and Israel are excluded. Cairo is the league's headquarters, but inter-Arab conflicts have thus far prevented it from being accepted as a regional capital. (When Egypt's membership was suspended from 1979 to 1989, the seat was moved to Tunis.) Moreover, the stated functions of the league—promotion of economic, social, political, and military cooperation and the mediation of disputes—have rarely been implemented.

Efforts to unify even parts of the region have generally ended poorly. The merger between Egypt and Syria, with the later addition of Yemen, fell apart. So did attempts to form a federation of Arab republics by Egypt, Syria, and Libya and a unified state between Libya and Egypt. The federation never became operational. Still another short-lived effort at unified political action was the Arab Cooperation Council, which was formed by Egypt, Iraq, Jordan, and Yemen in 1989 but broke up the following year when Iraq invaded Kuwait. The merged states of North and South Yemen have been torn by civil war since they joined together in 1990. The sole example of a successful merger is the United Arab Emirates, which was established in 1971–72.

ECUMENES

Geography and politics have conspired to separate the national ecumenes of the Middle East from one another. The areas of densest population concentration and economic activity are generally removed from one another by mountains, plateaus, or deserts. There are three exceptions, where ecumenes cut across national boundaries.

The largest of these transnational convergence areas is located at the head of the Persian/Arab Gulf. It extends along the coast from Kuwait to Basra, Iraq's second-largest city, on the Shatt al-Arab; to the Iranian centers of Abadan, on an island in the delta of the Shatt al-Arab; and to Khorramshahr, at the confluence of the Karun River and the Shatt. Rather than serving as a unifying force, this convergence has been the focus of two intraregional wars—one between Iraq and Iran, the other between Iraq and Kuwait. The economies of these adjoining core areas are based upon the oil fields of Kuwait, southern Iraq, and southwestern Iran. However, their pipelines, ports, refineries, petrochemical industries, and cities have no connections with one another because of the deep hostilities among the three countries.

Another transnational convergence cluster rims the Bay of Iskenderun. There, where the Orontes River flows into the sea, Syria and Turkey meet. Latakia, Syria's leading port, and Halab, the country's second-largest city and leading manufacturing center, adjoin the Turkish province of Hatay, whose possession was long disputed by Syria. Antakya (Antioch) and Iskenderun are the major urban centers of Hatay; from here, the population concentration continues westward along the coast to the large Turkish manufacturing center of Adana, capital of Adana Province.

Under different political circumstances, this region might have developed as a unified ecumene. It is served by a nexus of ports, highways, and railroads that radiate outward to Turkey, Syria, and Iraq. However, the hostility between Turkey and Syria has limited the region's development. Instead, Turkey's economic and population core areas center on Ankara (population of five million) in the interior of the country, Izmir (population of 2.3 million) along the Aegean coast, and the area from Istanbul (with a metropolitan population of over fourteen million) to Izmit along the Bosporus and the Sea of Marmara. Syria's ecumene is focused on Damascus, with an outlier at Homs (Hims) to its north.

The third transnational ecumene, linking Saudi Arabia to Bahrain, straddles the Intermediate and Southern Desert Zones. It extends for 240 miles from Riyadh in the desert interior to the Saudi shore of the Persian/Arab Gulf centers of Dammam and Jubail, and from there across narrow waters to include the archipelago of Bahrain.

Riyadh, the capital and fastest-growing urban center of Saudi Arabia, has nearly 15 percent of the country's total population of twenty-eight million. It is expected to double from its current populace of 3.6 million to 8 million in a little over a decade. As the nation's political, cultural, financial, and transportation center, the capital played a special geopolitical role in the creation of Saudi Arabia. It is the center of the Nejd, the peninsula's ancient heartland, which never fell to the Ottomans but remained under the control of its desert tribes. From their Riyadh oasis base, the Saudi rulers have drawn upon the desert's culture, its strict Wahhabite religious system, and its social traditions to adapt Bedouin life, first to the sedentary oasis world, and now to the modern urban era. Fanning out from the Nejd, the Saudis developed highway, rail, and air links to the Gulf and the wealth generated by its coastal and offshore oil resources.

The Gulf region, which is the coastal portion of this third ecumene, contains the major industrial center of Dammam and its associated towns, with a population of over two million. Dammam was developed as a deepwater port and the eastern terminal of the railway from Riyadh. Adjoining it is the oil center of Dhahran, which is also an international air hub and, until 2003, the site of a large US air base. At that time, Saudi Arabia denied the United States use of its bases because of its opposition to the invasion of Iraq. The Pentagon then moved its regional air command center to Al Udeid Air Base in Qatar.

Jubail, to the north, is the largest of Saudi Arabia's two planned industrial cities and a major petrochemical center. Backing these coastal urban concentrations is the Al-Ahsa coastal plain (the Eastern Province), which includes some of the country's most fertile agricultural oases and is its chief oil-producing center.

The Saudi ecumene also extends directly across a narrow stretch of water to Bahrain, one of the most important banking and financial centers of the Middle East. While Bahrain's oil reserves are modest, the refineries that were built there after the discovery of oil in 1931 have become important for processing Saudi crude. Britain also developed a major naval base and refueling station at the Bahraini port of Manama. Since 1948, Bahrain has served as the US Navy's key strategic base during the Cold War, the First Gulf War, and the wars in Afghanistan and Iraq. Its port city of Manama is presently headquarters for the navy's Fifth Fleet. Elsewhere, national ecumenes are geographically removed from those of their neighbors. During the Arab Spring, widespread protests by the majority Shiite population of Bahrain broke out against the ruling Sunni monarchy. This spread to Saudi Arabia's adjoining Eastern Province. The Saudi reaction was swift. Its military crossed the King Fahd fifty-mile causeway that connects Bahrain to the Saudi mainland and crushed the incipient rebellion.

Iraq's ecumene centers on its capital and largest city, Baghdad, which, at the start of the US invasion that toppled Saddam Hussein, had six million people, nearly 20 percent of the country's then total population of nearly thirty million, and most of Iraq's manufacturing and service industries. Over five million were refugees in other countries, and a similar number were displaced by sectarian conflict. Although Iraq is still beset by Kurdish separatism and loss of territory to ISIS, its population has now risen to thirty-six million, with metropolitan Bagdad's urban populace numbering 6.5 million. From Baghdad, the ecumene extends southward for approximately one hundred miles, through the densely populated agricultural Mesopotamian plain and the Shia holy cities of Karbala and Najaf.

In Iran, no single ecumene dominates the country. The capital, Tehran, in the north, is a city of 7.7 million with an urbanized area of 11 million out of the country's total population of 77 million. It is the major economic and population core area of the country, accounting for half of its industrial output. Other important clusters center on Tabriz, the capital of Iranian Azerbaijan in the northwest; oil-rich Khuzestan in the southwest; and the manufacturing city of Esfahan in the center. The spread of the Tehran ecumene is limited by the Elburz Mountains to its north and the semiarid to arid lands to its south and west, so it does not connect to the country's other industrial and population clusters.

The Egyptian economic and population core area extends southward from the Nile delta, upstream through Cairo to Faiyum, a distance of approximately 150 miles. It also extends for one hundred miles along the delta's coast from Port Said, at the entrance to the Suez Canal, to Alexandria. The latter, Egypt's great ancient metropolis, now has nearly 4.5 million people and is the country's leading port; a major industrial center for petroleum products, textiles, food, and consumer goods; and home to a naval base. However, it is dwarfed in importance by Cairo, the largest city, with a population of over nine million and a total metropolitan populace of over seventeen million. As the capital of the country's highly centralized political system, it is Egypt's chief financial and industrial center and the major focus for tourism, one of Egypt's most important economic resources.

The Israeli ecumene extends along two-thirds of its coastal plain for approximately eighty miles, from the port of Ashdod in the south, through the metropolitan Tel Aviv region, to the northern end of the coastal plain. Its width, only between six and fifteen miles, was constricted by the Green Line, the pre-1967 division between Israel and the Jordanian-held West Bank. It now extends beyond the line, into the West Bank of Palestine in several population clusters. The population density of the Israeli ecumene is over two thousand per square mile, its over 4.5 million people accounting for over 60 percent of the nation's total population of over 8 million. The overall population density of the country, which is nearly one thousand persons per square mile, is an unusually high figure for a country and is exceeded only by the Netherlands and Belgium among comparably advanced states. In the Tel Aviv district, the density runs to over four thousand persons per square mile. The country's Jewish population represents 75 percent of the total, and Arabs are another 20 percent. The remainder are non-Arab Christians and those who choose not to be classified. The Arab populace is mainly located in three areas—the north, the "Arab Triangle" at the eastern edge of the Sharon Plain, spilling onto the Samarian foothills, and the northern Negev.

The ecumene contains most of Israel's manufacturing and services, including cut diamonds, military industry, pharmaceuticals, finance, tourism, and high technology. The latter is the fastest-growing part of the economy, with emphasis on computers, software, telecommunications, biotechnology, medical technology, and avionics. Research and development centers that belong to the world's leading computer hardware and software companies help to drive the high-technology industry, which accounts for 60 percent of the country's total exports and is the largest sector of the Israeli economy.

The rest of the national ecumenes of the Middle East are small and underdeveloped. The larger among them are the landlocked core areas of Sudan and Sana'a. Sudan's ecumene is limited to a narrow strip along the Nile, extending from the capital, Khartoum (five million population) and its environs, northward for two hundred miles to Atbara and Berbera near the river's fifth cataract. In 2011, Sudan was formally divided into an Arab Muslim north called Sudan and the Christian and animist African south called South Sudan. Sudan, which contains the ecumene, has a population of thirty-four million, and South Sudan has twelve million. Yemen's ecumene is centered on its capital and largest city, Sana'a, which is located in the center of the country's high plateau and has a population of about one million of the country's twenty-five million.

EFFECTIVE REGIONAL/NATIONAL TERRITORY

Just as there is no unified regional ecumene within the Middle East, so is it lacking in an effective regional territory. For the most part, the effective national territories of the individual countries are both limited and separated from one another by desert conditions. The only point where ENTs meet is in the grasslands of Upper Mesopotamia, where Syria and Iraq converge. In ancient times, this was the main contact zone of the Fertile Crescent. The depth of the political rift between the two states has barred the cooperative ventures that might unify these two ENTs.

EMPTY AREAS

For the most part, the empty areas of the region are the deserts across which national boundaries run and which serve as barriers. Vast, barren reaches separate Egypt from Libya, Israel, and Jordan; Saudi Arabia from Jordan; Syria, Iraq, the Gulf States, and Yemen from one another; and Iran from Afghanistan. Only Iran, Turkey, Syria, and Iraq are not blocked from one another by empty areas. However, the mountains and hills of Kurdistan do inhibit ease of east-west communication in the Kurdish region that extends from eastern Turkey and northeastern Syria through northern Iraq and into northwestern Iran.

BOUNDARIES

Boundaries are important geopolitical features within the Middle East, and disputes over their locations, as well as over territorial sovereignty, have been major forces in creating and maintaining the shatterbelt character of the region.

Table 12.1 is a summary of the region's current boundary disputes and disputed areas. Table 12.2 lists recent dispute resolutions, and table 12.3 lists the major irredentist areas.[4] The most prominent of these disputes have been the ones over the Shatt al-Arab, Kuwait, Israel's border with the West Bank of Palestine and Syria, and the boundary between North and South Sudan. These last two disputes will be discussed in the section dealing with the Israeli and Sudanese conflicts.

Table 12.1. Current Middle East Boundary Disputes

Countries	*Disputed Boundaries*	*Disputed Areas*
Iraq-Iran	Shatt al-Arab	
Saudi Arabia-Kuwait		Qaresh and Umm al Maradim Island
Iran-UAE		Lesser and Greater Tunb Island, Abu Musa Island (jointly administered)
Israel-Palestinian Authority	Future boundary of Palestinian state	West Bank, Gaza
Israel-Syria	Golan boundary along the Sea of Galilee's northeast coast	Golan Heights, Shaba Farm (ownership also claimed by Lebanon)
Cyprus	Land boundary	Division into Greek and Turkish sectors
Turkey-Greece		Sea, air, and territorial claims in Aegean Sea, width of Turkish continental shelf
Libya-Tunisia	Maritime boundary	
Libya-Algeria		Libya claims part of southeast Algeria
Libya-Niger	Land boundary	Libya claims part of northern Niger
Egypt-Sudan	Red Sea coast boundary	Halaib Triangle occupied by Sudan
Sudan-S. Sudan	Land boundary	Abyei, North Kordofan, and Blue Nile provinces
Caspian Sea	Indeterminate surface and seabed boundaries	Azerbaijan, Iran, Kazakhstan, Russia, Turkmenistan
Latent Disputes		
Iran-Bahrain		Iran claim to Bahrain
Iraq-Iran		Iran claim to Khuzestan

Table 12.2. Recent Middle East Dispute Territorial Resolutions

Countries	*Disputed Boundaries*	*Disputed Areas*
Iraq-Kuwait	Land boundary	Warba and Bubiyan Islands; Iraq renounced claim in favor of Kuwait, 1994
Israel-Lebanon	Land boundary demarcated, 2000 (save one very small segment)	South Lebanese Zone, Israel withdrew
Yemen-Oman	Land boundary resolved, 1992	Delimitation of desert area that lies between them
Yemen-Saudi Arabia	Land boundary delimited, 2000	All of Najran and most of Rub' al Khali are within Saudi Arabia
Yemen-Eritrea		Hanish al Kabir Island awarded to Yemen; rest of Hanish Islands divided between the two, 1998
Libya-Chad		Aouzou Strip returned to Chad, 1994
Bahrain-Qatar	Maritime boundary resolved, 2001	Larger Hawar Island awarded to Bahrain, smaller island to Qatar

Table 12.3. Middle East Irredentism

Country	*Irredentist Movements and Areas*
Afghanistan/Pakistan borderlands	Pashtuns, Pakhtunistan
Iran	Azeris, northwestern Iran (Azerbaijan provinces); PJAK Kurds, northwestern Iran
Iraq	Kurds, northern Iraq; Arabs, southwestern Iran (Khuzestan)
Israel	Palestinian Arabs, Occupied West Bank, Gaza, East Jerusalem
Sudan	Darfurians
Syria	PKK Kurds, northeast Syria
Turkey	PKK Kurds, southeast Turkey

Iraq and Iran: The Shatt al-Arab Dispute

The eight-year war between Iraq and Iran, which cost over a million lives, was fought over control of the Shatt al-Arab, the tidal waterway formed by the confluence of the Tigris and Euphrates Rivers and flowing into the Persian/Arab Gulf. The river supplies freshwater to southern Iraq. After decades of dispute over the boundary, the two countries signed an agreement in 1975 establishing the line as following the thalweg—the deepest channel of the river—thus assuring Iran access to Abadan at the head of the estuary.[5] In exchange, Tehran agreed to end its support of the Iraqi Kurdish rebellion.

With the Islamic revolution in Iran in early 1979, relations between the two countries deteriorated. Saddam Hussein, who had seized power in Iraq that same year, abrogated the treaty and proclaimed Iraqi sovereignty over both banks of the Shatt. His assumption was that, since Iran was then in turmoil, it would offer little resistance. This was not the case, and an eight-year war ensued. Iraq invaded Iran through oil-rich Khuzestan, the southwesternmost province of Iran, capturing Khorramshahr on the east bank and surrounding the Abadan refinery. While Baghdad asserted its historic right to Khuzestan, it promised that it would support an independent state should its irredentist Arab inhabitants so wish. However, within two years, the Iraqis were driven from the east bank, bringing the war to a stalemate. With its conclusion in 1988, the status quo ante was restored, thus the thalweg remains the boundary today. Although the dispute has not been fully resolved, the Algiers accord of September 30, 2000, signed by Baghdad and Tehran, reinstituted the 1975 agreement.

Iraq-Kuwait Border

The invasion of Kuwait by Iraq in 1990 that precipitated the First Gulf War was essentially over a long-standing border dispute, although contributing factors were Kuwait's refusal to forgive a $30 billion debt incurred by Baghdad during its war with Iran and Kuwait's exceeding OPEC export quotas. The roots of the controversy lay in Britain's post–World War I territorial policies. In the early 1920s London created Kuwait by carving out a portion of Iraq's desert on the Gulf coast. When oil was discovered in Kuwait in 1936, the Iraqis revived their claim that the kingdom was part of their southern province of Basra.

The British-drawn boundary, which had been validated by the United Nations after World War II, included the large island of Bubiyan and the smaller Warba to its north. These islands commanded the approach to the new Iraqi port of Umm Qasr, which had been built in 1961 as an alternative to Basra. Baghdad became more assertive in its claims to the islands after it initiated the war with Iran.[6]

In addition, the Iraqis held that the Kuwaitis had extended their part of the Rumaila oil fields into Iraqi territory during the Iraq-Iran war and that they were stealing oil through slant drilling into the Iraqi portion of the field. The resulting invasion of Kuwait and its devastation, as well as the ensuing First Gulf War, is well known. However, even in defeat Iraq continued to cling to its claims and, at one point in 1994, moved Republican Guards toward the Kuwait border. As pressures mounted, Iraq reconsidered its stance and shortly afterward agreed to recognize Kuwait's independence and its borders.

The victory over Iraq by the American-led coalition of twenty-five nations (including the Soviet Union) was followed by a series of economic sanctions and inspection requirements to assure that Iraq was not secretly engaged in the research and manufacturing of nuclear and biological weapons. For the most part, the Iraqis evaded the inspection efforts and, toward the end of the decade, Saddam Hussein ousted the UN inspectors. A low-level conflict simmered, as US and British planes countered Iraqi attempts to impede their coverage of the "no-fly" zones in the north and the south. All of this changed with the US invasion of Iraq in 2003.

Major Conflicts

ARAB-ISRAELI CONFLICT

At the beginning of the 1990s and after five wars, the Arab-Israeli conflict shifted in emphasis a decade ago from the Arab challenge to Israel's right to exist to Arab demands for an independent Palestinian Arab state within part of the Holy Land. Arab extremists still refused to recognize the Zionist state, and Jewish extremists clung to the concept of an undivided land of Israel. At the Madrid Conference of 1991, both sides moved toward territorial compromise as a basis for resolving the conflict.

This was followed by the Oslo I (1993) and Oslo II (1995) agreements between Israel and the Palestine Liberation Organization, which were endorsed by the two Arab states—Egypt and Jordan—that were formally at peace with Israel. Oslo called for the Palestinian Authority to gain military and/or civilian control of up to 42 percent of the total area held by Israel in the West Bank and 60 percent of Gaza, including all of the larger cities and towns, in a step-by-step process that would lead to an eventual peace. However, Oslo promised only autonomy—statehood was to come with a permanent peace and after most of the Palestinian areas had been returned to an elected Palestinian government. During this interim period, the two parties agreed to take joint security actions to prevent violence by extremists on either side.

The lagging pace of the Oslo process influenced Prime Minister Ehud Barak of Israel to drop the step-by-step strategy and seek a speedy, comprehensive peace. President Clinton then assumed a proactive role in the negotiations between the Israelis and the Palestinians, following up the Camp David Summit of July 2000 with continued participation. Barak offered far-reaching terms at the subsequent Wye Plantation Summit and negotiations that followed at Taba. These were rejected by Palestinian chairman Yasser Arafat, thus derailing the peace process.

The total breakdown of negotiations was followed in 2000 by the outbreak of the Palestinian uprising known as the "Al-Aqsa Intifada" and the election as Israel's prime minister of Ariel Sharon, leader of the populist-nationalist Likud Party. Sharon had long been opposed to withdrawal from the occupied Palestinian territories. In 2005 he did an about-face by withdrawing completely from Gaza and promising to reduce the number of Jewish settlements on the West Bank. To do so politically, he left the Likud to found a new Centrist party, Kadimah, which, in coalition with Labor and some religious parties, viewed the unilateral withdrawal from Gaza as the first step toward peace. At the end of 2005, Sharon suffered a major stroke and was replaced as prime minister by Ehud Olmert. In 2006, Israel became entangled in a war in South Lebanon. The war ended with the help of UN mediation and the stationing of UN peacekeepers and Lebanese army forces in South Lebanon. However, it left the Hezbollah in a greatly strengthened position. The Olmert government was weakened by its failure to destroy the Shiite Hezbollah and to prevent the continuous rocket attacks launched from Gaza upon southern Israel. The result was a resurgence of support for the right wing.

In 2007 the Bush administration abandoned its earlier hands-off policy and put pressure on both sides to agree to a cease-fire and to resume negotiations that would lead to peace and a "two-state" solution. This was partly in response to Arab demands for progress and the US need to enlist their support of the war in Iraq and the battle against terrorism. Such a solution had been recommended in 2004 by the "Quartet" (United States, EU, Russia, and the UN) but had been shelved. This was put back on the diplomatic table. In addition, Egypt, Jordan, and Saudi Arabia have proposed full peace between Israel and all Arab states in exchange for Israel's withdrawal from the Occupied Territories to the 1967 boundary lines. To complicate matters, the 2006 elections in Gaza brought the Hamas Party to power there. It has refused to recognize Israel, renounce terrorism, or join the peace process and drove the Fatah militia out of Gaza. This has left peace negotiation to Israel and the Fatah-controlled Palestinian Authority, which controls the West Bank and is led by Mahmoud Abbas, successor to Yasser Arafat.

At the end of 2007, President Bush held a "peace summit" at Annapolis, Maryland, which resulted only in commitments by Israel and the Palestinian Authority to further negotiation. Saudi Arabia and Syria were among the countries present. Summits, conferences, high-level visits, and external pressures are all useful prods toward peace. However, any final accord must be reached by the parties to the conflict.

Since then, Washington has sought to promote a two-state solution. In 2013–14, Secretary of State John Kerry held extensive talks with each side, seeking that they accept an agreement framework as a prelude to final negotiations. The West Bank leadership, led by Abbas, has demonstrated a desire to forge such an agreement. The Israeli government, headed by Prime Minister Benjamin Netanyahu has encountered considerable opposition from its right-wing coalition partners to abandoning control of the West Bank.

In any negotiations that take place, knotty geopolitical issues have to be faced. First is Gaza's viability. This would require land concessions by both Israel and Egypt from the northwest Negev and North Sinai to help alleviate Gaza's population pressures.[7] However, as long as Gaza is controlled by the religious extremist Hamas, which is opposed to peace with Israel, negotiations are focused on the West Bank.

In 2014, the PLO and Hamas agreed to unite in a government headed by technicians. Israel's reaction was to break off US-brokered negotiations for a two-state solution between themselves and the West Bankers. Past agreements forged between Hamas and the PLO have been broken. Abbas insisted that bringing Hamas into the Palestinian fold means that it will have to accept a PLO-led two-state solution. Whether the agreement holds and whether Hamas would agree to be part of a government which recognizes Israel remains to be seen. Indeed, the war between Hamas and Israel that broke out in the summer of 2014 suggests that the agreement has no currency. The fighting led to the destruction of vast parts of Gaza and hundreds of Gazan fatalities—both civilians and militants. While Hamas launched hundreds of rockets against Israel, nearly all were intercepted by Israel's "Iron Dome" antimissile system. A major surprise in the conflict was the network of tunnels developed by Hamas that extended from Gaza into Israel. They were destroyed during the fighting. For the present, the breaking of negotiations plays into the hands of Israel's right-wing parties, and especially the Israeli West Bank settlers who seem committed to holding onto the West Bank at any price.

Second, the sharing of the Temple Mount will have to be addressed. One option is to create a horizontal international boundary that awards the top of the Mount to the Arabs and its base to Israel. Third, the contradiction between the pressures for separate Israeli and Arab sovereignties and the advantages of functional unity in Jerusalem must be faced. East Jerusalem has three hundred thousand Palestinian Arab and two hundred thousand Jewish residents. Jerusalem's Arabs would have to be territorially linked to a West Bank state. The Israeli Jews of East Jerusalem would have to be territorially linked to the three hundred thousand Israeli Jews already living in West Jerusalem as well as more than fifty thousand who live in Greater Jerusalem beyond the Green Line. A possible approach might be a federation of the two municipalities for infrastructure operations and a metropolitan government that combines city-region functions through special authorities. East Jerusalem would serve as the capital of the Palestinian state, while West Jerusalem would remain Israel's capital.

Fourth is the development of joint Israeli-Palestinian mechanisms to ensure the equitable sharing of the water resources of the mountain and coastal plain aquifers that underlie the West Bank, Israel, and Gaza. Fifth, a mechanism for arbitrating the right of return for Arab refugees displaced in Israel's War of Independence must be developed. United Nations estimates are that over seven hundred thousand fled from Israeli-controlled territory in the war of 1948–49; they and their descendants now number over four million. The original displacement is balanced by the 850,000 Jews who fled from Arab League countries after 1948. Sixth, Israel's demands for security, which include demilitarization of the West Bank, military overflight rights, stationing Israeli troops along the Jordan River for a number of years, and naval patrol of Gaza's coastal waters, will have to be balanced by Palestinian territorial sovereignty rights.

And seventh, Israel would have to withdraw from the scattered settlements and one hundred illegal outposts that it has built in the West Bank. These settlements are connected to one another by specially built, modern roads that bypass Arab cities, towns, and villages. In effect, the road, electric, and water infrastructure that supports the Jewish settlements in the West Bank represents a separate, superimposed network. If a peace agreement is signed, the West Bank Palestinians would benefit from grafting this network onto their present inadequate infrastructures. Those West Bank Jewish settlements that adjoin the Green Line are likely to be retained by Israel for security, as well as political, reasons. They contain about three-quarters of the nearly three hundred thousand Jewish population of the West Bank. Responsible Jewish leaders have made it clear that they are prepared to compensate for the annexation of such lands by providing a Palestinian state with equivalent Israeli territory in the Negev.

Any permanent solution will require the territorial contiguity of the Palestinian West Bank. Creating land hinges between the northern, central, and southern West Bank sectors will necessitate the uprooting of nearly all the Israeli settlements along the north-south axis. Another territorial challenge will be linking Gaza to the rest of Palestine. The shortest distance between northeastern Gaza and the southwestern West Bank is approximately twenty-five miles. If neither a tunnel road nor an elevated highway is feasible, an alternative may be a land corridor under joint Israeli-Palestinian control, which would permit free north-south movement within Israel as well as east-west movement within a Palestinian state.

Peace between Israel and Arab Palestine is unlikely to be achieved without both sides enduring a measure of civil war. Within the Arab camp, this began in 2007, when Hamas fought with and drove out the Palestinian Fatah militia. The Abbas government, with Israel's support, then began to disarm Hamas supporters located within the West Bank and other militias opposed to peace. Israel, too, has to contend with the powerful nationalist/fundamentalist settler movements in the West Bank and their supporters in Israel proper. Well over 200,000 Jewish settlers live in blocs just to the east of the Green Line and are now enclosed by parts of the 450-mile security fence/wall that has been built to ward off terrorist attacks and theft. The wall section cuts through densely urban areas, while most of the barrier consists of a wide swath of electronic fence, ditches, and security roads.

The barrier has created bulges into the West Bank that include Arab villages as well as the Jewish settlements and has cut off other West Bank villages from some of their farmlands. The Israeli government has made clear that inclusion of these bulges within Israel's formal boundaries are a prerequisite to any agreement. In exchange, an equal amount of territory would be added to the Palestinian state from Israeli lands that adjoin the West Bank. The fate of the Arab villages and farmlands within the bulges would be open to negotiation. Some might prefer to remain within the borders of Israel because of better economic opportunities. Those outside the line but with farmlands within it would need far freer access than is now available to them.

Confrontation would come from many of the eighty thousand Jewish settlers who live in the heart of the West Bank and are bitterly opposed to territorial compromise. Well over half are religious nationalists and ultraorthodox who insist that Samaria and Judea (the West Bank) is holy territory that cannot be traded away, even for peace. The major opposition to giving up the settlements would be the political struggle within Israel based upon ideological and strategic differences. There might also be armed, rather than passive, resistance to withdrawal from the extremist wing among the settlers.

Another obstacle to peace negotiations is that the Arabs view Israel as a client state of the United States, and many Israelis view Europe as having a pro-Palestinian bias. Israel's alliance with the United States has thus far enabled it to ignore European mediation efforts. This is not a viable long-term policy for Israel. American strategic interests within the Middle East are waning, especially since the US is nearing self-sufficiency in oil and gas. Should the negotiations with Iran initiated by Washington in concert with other powers prove successful, Washington would have even less of a stake in the Middle East, permitting it to turn greater attention on East Asia as well as shoring up the Western position in Eastern Europe.

The European partnership has become increasingly important to the United States, both because the two powers are on a par economically and because European political support is essential to US foreign policy objectives. Washington will have to take European positions into account in the negotiations and will depend upon Europe to provide much of the financial assistance that a new Palestinian state would require for its economic development.

Germany has led the effort within the EU to grant both Israel and a Palestinian state a "special privilege partnership"—the highest form of association short of full membership—should the parties agree to a two-state solution. Conditions would include generous free trade, financial, and investment opportunities. Thus far, this incentive has not changed the opposition of the right-wing Israeli government to a two-state solution, but greater pressure from Washington could be persuasive.

The fragility of Saudi Arabia's monarchy and concern for its strategic position in the Gulf as a whole has also made the United States more responsive to the pressures of the Arab states in finding a solution to the conflict. In the long run, an Israeli policy that builds on European links rather than relying exclusively on Washington's protection could be a first step in expanding maritime Europe into a broader Euromediterranean region.

LEBANON

Since winning its independence in 1945, Lebanon has been torn by religious, factional conflict and outside pressures and invasions. Its governing structure, as outlined in the National Covenant of 1943, was designed to balance the interests of the country's three major religious groups—the Christians based in Mount Lebanon and East Beirut, the Sunni Muslims in the north and the Beqa'a, and the Shia Muslims in the south. Each of these areas is dominated by prominent families and clans who control their territories almost as ministates. In this "confessional" system, the presidency is held by a Maronite Christian, the prime ministry by a Sunni, and the speakership of the parliament by a Shia. This arrangement was sponsored by France, which held the mandate over Lebanon from 1920 to 1941. In order to secure the position of the country's Christian population, it gave considerable powers to the president. Demographic changes, civil wars, and external interference have made this structure untenable. The Christian numbers have fallen from 53 percent when the last official census was taken in 1932 to an estimated 35 percent due to emigration and lower birthrates. The Shia now outnumber both Christian and Sunni communities

The once-prosperous country of the Ottoman and mandatory periods and through the 1960s has been devastated by four decades of conflict. Lebanon was a magnet for banking and other financial services and a major distribution center for the entire Middle East, and it had a healthy local economy based upon food processing, apparel, jewelry, and carpet industries.

Civil wars have erupted between Christians and Muslims, Christians and Druse, and the government and militant Palestinian refugees. Other conflicts have been with Syria and Israel. Peacekeeping efforts by the United States in 1958 and then by French, Italian, and US forces (1982–84) ended with their withdrawals and resumption of warfare. UN troops, together with Lebanese army forces stationed along the border with Israel in the wake of Israel's 2006 invasion of South Lebanon, maintain an uneasy cease-fire. Meanwhile, Hezbollah, which controls the south, grows in strength with the help of Syria and Iran.

The infrastructure of the country, its national economy, and tourism have long suffered from the ravages of conflict and divisions over Syria's ambitions to regain its influence over Lebanon. In view of their numerical growth and military power, the Lebanese Shiites succeeded in gaining a leading role in the government. However, power remains divided, government is frequently paralyzed, and political parties controlled by powerful families keep the country in turmoil. The long, raging rebellion in Syria, which erupted in 2011, has added to Lebanon's woes. Hezbollah troops from South Lebanon and the Beqa'a have taken a leading role in support of the Assad government, and Sunni refugees from Syria have placed a heavy economic burden on Lebanon while attracting many Lebanese to support the Syrian Sunni rebels.

Selected Countries

IRAQ

The misguided US invasion of Iraq in 2003 has proved a major geopolitical blunder. Initiated on the false premise that Saddam Hussein was developing a nuclear arsenal, a genuine widely based alliance was never developed. Rationale for the war shifted to bringing democracy to Iraq and the Middle East and preventing the spread of terrorism. In fact, the Saddam secular and despotic regime was a bulwark against terrorist infiltration, keeping al-Qaeda pinned down in its Afghan and Pakistani bases. It also posed a major military threat to Iran's efforts to expand its influence within the Middle East. Removal of the Saddam Hussein regime by the US invasion unleashed sectarian civil war within Iraq, opened the borders to terrorists, and facilitated the penetration of Iranian influence into much of the Middle East, especially Syria and South Lebanon. Elections promoted by Washington have also brought the Iraqi Shia into power, many of whom have close political ties to Iran.

Now that American troops have been withdrawn from Iraq, fierce conflict rages there between the Shiite-controlled Iraqi government and Sunni of the western province of Anbar, as well as in the central part of the country. Suicide bombing and terrorist attacks, especially in Baghdad and Fallujah, occur almost daily. Three possible outcomes face Iraq—a strong, centralized state controlled by a Shia majority, a loose confederation of highly autonomous Kurdish north, Sunni west, and Shia south, or a division into three mutually hostile separate states. For any of these, pullout of US troops is likely to bring on a period of continuing, if not increased, violence. The drawback of the first solution is that Iraq might well become an Iranian client state and a base for the spreading of Shia control throughout the Gulf states.

Confederation, the most constructive resolution, is not as clean as it appears on paper. While each of the three regions has a majority population as outlined, the country's major cities that are located along the borders between them are mixed. This is especially true for Baghdad, which used to be a thoroughly mixed city. It is now divided as a result of sectarian warfare, with the Shia to the east of the Tigris River and the Sunni to the west. In a confederated state, Baghdad would have to serve for a period of time as a federal capital under UN peacekeeping units. It might eventually be able to regain some measure of ethnic integration.

Kirkuk and Mosul lie along physiographic and ethnic fault lines, which separate the Kurdish north from the Arab populace. Kirkuk's mixed population of Arabs, Kurds, and Turkomen lies within Iraq's northern, oil-rich region, where the plains of the Upper Tigris valley meet the northern uplands. It has been an ethnic battleground, as Saddam replaced its Kurdish residents with Arabs, and the Kurds are now expelling Arabs to reclaim the city and its oil. Mosul, now under ISIS control, is divided between Sunni Arabs on the west side of the Tigris and Kurds on the east. Each group has pockets on the other side of the river.

As a confederated country, the western Sunni province, which lacks oil resources, might become an economic and strategic ward of Saudi Arabia if the issue of oil revenue sharing is not resolved. The Kurdish North can fend for itself economically, especially if its claims to Mosul and Kirkuk are upheld. Its main lines of communication currently run through Turkey. If it does not help to clear its northwestern Qandil Mountain borderlands of the PKK safe havens from which they mount transborder terrorist operations against Turkey, it could find itself completely isolated.

IRAN

The end of the US military presence in Iraq and its imminent withdrawal from Afghanistan has provided an opening for Iran to enhance its standing as a regional power. In addition to arming and training Shia militias, Iran is also investing in power plants in southern Iraq and the Shia holy cities of Najaf and Karbala, and in small projects in Baghdad's Shia Sadr City sector. Tehran's influence in Syria extends beyond its military support to significant investments in Syria's economy. It has used Damascus for transshipment of missiles to the Hezbollah of South Lebanon. The attraction of hundreds of thousands of Iranian pilgrims to sacred Shia shrines in both Iraq and Syria is another force behind the extension of Iran's regional power.

If not checked, the prospect of Iran's development of nuclear weapons capacity could elicit reactions from Saudi Arabia and Egypt in the direction of developing their own nuclear weapons as well as invite the air attack that Israel has threatened. Since Israel already has a nuclear arsenal, these additions would further destabilize the region. In January 2014, the P5 + 1 nations (United States, Britain, France, Russia, and China, plus Germany) began negotiations with Iran aimed at defining the terms of a permanent agreement over the latter's nuclear program. The goal of the negotiations is to ensure that Iran cannot develop nuclear weapons, which it claims it does not intend to do, while assuring Tehran that it can pursue a strictly civilian nuclear energy program. During the six-month negotiation period, existing economic sanctions on Iran were lightened. The agreement to seek a solution encountered considerable opposition from the US Congress and Israel. They contended that Iran is not to be trusted and that sanctions should be increased, not slowed down. President Obama resisted this opposition, and European leadership expressed satisfaction with the direction of the negotiations.

Tensions between the United States and Iran have spilled over to the Gulf states. Washington has sought to enlist them in confronting Iran over the nuclear weapons issue and Iran's support of terrorism. The Gulf states are in an awkward position. They are dependent for their security on their military alliances with the United States and fearful of the threat posed by Iran to their internal stability. These Sunni regimes are rapidly modernizing in the Western style and are encouraging tourism and building Western-style educational and cultural institutions. However, they are vulnerable to their large Shia populations and their dependence on the overseas workers who constitute over a quarter of the population of the Gulf Cooperation Council states.

The council was formed in 1981 with the goal of containing Iran, and some of its member states now house large American military bases (Saudi Arabia is the only exception). However, their economic links with Iran have become increasingly important. Bahrain imports its natural gas from Iran, and Iran is the main destination of trade with the United Arab Emirates, especially Dubai. These emirates are home to tens of thousands of Iranian expatriates, and several thousand firms partly owned by Iranians contribute greatly to economic modernization.

With the exception of Bahrain, which houses the large American naval base at Manama, and Qatar, the site of a major US air base, the Gulf states have been reluctant to ally themselves openly with Washington against Tehran. All of their governments opposed the US invasion of Iraq on the grounds that it would destabilize the region. They view a possible conflict between the United States and Iran as an even greater threat to their stability. While Washington continues to sell them billions of dollars' worth of arms, their main interest lies in calming, not inflaming, US-Iranian relationships.

While not underestimating Iran's growing clout within the Middle East, it is important to keep in mind its limitations. Iran and Iraq are both Shia, and strong ties developed with the Iraqi political and religious leaders who were provided shelter in Iran during Saddam's reign. However, the Iraqi are Arabs and the Iranians Persian. For historic, linguistic, and strategic reasons, the Iraqi Shia are likely to be wary of becoming an Iranian dependency. Moreover, Iran is beset by many internal problems. Despite its energy wealth, the state-dominated economy is poorly managed and corrupt, joblessness is widespread, and the country suffers from a serious "brain drain" of its university graduates. Refinery capacity is so limited that Iran must import finished products despite its own oil wealth. Foreign investors shy away from an unpredictable government, and there is considerable social dissatisfaction with the oppressive theocratic regime.

In addition, Iran is far from a monolithic Persian country. Only about half of the population is Persian. The remainder are Azeri Turks (nearly one-quarter of the total population), Arabs, Kurds, Balochis, and Turkomen. As a consequence, the country is vulnerable to unrest and terrorist threats from its minority areas. In the southeast, Sistan, home to many ethnic Balochis, who are Sunni with ties to the Balochis of Pakistan, is a gateway for drug smuggling. In the southwest, oil-rich Khuzestan is populated by Arab Iranians, who have long represented a separatist threat. The northwest Kurdish and Azeri regions of Iran have been targets of antiregime attacks by the Party for Freedom and Life in Kurdistan (PJAK), which has close ties to the PKK. Some PJAK guerrilla bands operate from safe havens in Iraq's northeastern Kurdish mountains. Washington has denied Tehran's charges that it is aiding the PJAK, but they operate from Iraqi territory that is under US patronage—a parallel situation to the safe havens close to the Turkish border offered the PKK by Iraqi Kurds.

In view of Iran's internal problems, "soft diplomacy" may yield better results than the threat of military power. Washington should recognize that Tehran's suspicions of its intentions are partly rooted in US support of the despotic shah Mohammad Reza Pahlavi and then the assistance it gave Saddam Hussein in the war he initiated against Iran. The 2014 negotiation process, which was initiated by the United States and its Western allies, involves recognizing mutual interests. The United States needs guarantees on the nuclear issue as well as formal assurance that Iran will respect Iraq's integrity. In addition to backing Iran's admission to the WTO and providing Tehran with a security guarantee, the United States could support Iran's sovereignty claims over Abu Musa and the two Tunbs islands, which both Iran and the United Arab Emirates claim. These islands control the western approaches to the Strait of Hormuz. To reassure both parties, the United States and NATO could guarantee that the strait would be open to all shipping. Another positive step would be international guarantees that the navigation channel of the Shatt al-Arab would be shared by Iran and Iraq and Iraq's renunciation of all past claims to Arab Iranian Khuzestan.

AFGHANISTAN

Afghanistan was a far bigger threat than Iraq to the United States and the West because it harbored al-Qaeda under the protective rule of the Taliban. Instead of concentrating on eliminating al-Qaeda after the Taliban were driven out of Afghanistan, Washington diverted its energies by invading Iraq. Implementation of the Afghan invasion was botched when the United States relied upon Pakistani troops to close the trap on the fleeing Osama bin Laden, who had been cornered in the Tora Bora mountains. Since that time, US and NATO troops in Afghanistan have been unable to control much of the countryside south of Kabul.

The political structure and ethnic traditions of Afghanistan are not wedded to the ideal of a unified democratic state. Pashtun leaders, including the last king of Afghanistan, never abandoned their dreams of a greater Pakhtunistan, which would unite the Pashtun peoples of eastern and southern Afghanistan with their fellow tribespeople in the mountainous regions of western Pakistan. The country is deeply divided ethnically. Over 40 percent of its thirty million people are Pashtuns, whose lands form a crescent-shaped belt from the Pakistan border on the east and south to the Iranian border on the west. The Tajiks, with over one-quarter of the population, and the Uzbeks, with 10 percent, occupy the mountainous regions to the north. They form the Northern Alliance that helped US-NATO forces expel the Taliban. The Tajiks also live in the western plains adjoining Iran. The Hazaras, with another 10 percent of the population, live in the central, mountainous core of the country and are a Shia people who are a long-depressed class that suffered persecution under the Taliban. All of these peoples still live in a culture of tribalism and warlordism. The Taliban imposed unity by the brutal force of extremist Islam.

Washington's state-building goal for a democratic Afghanistan ignores the strength of this culture. As of 2014, the Taliban had regained control of much of the east and the south, intimidating the populace and supporting themselves through the opium trade, taxing the poppy growers, and kidnappings. Only the north, where Tajiks and Uzbeks predominate, is stable, and there, too, stability depends upon accords among its warlords.

The United States has abandoned its policy of "staying the course" in Afghanistan, withdrawing from its substantial air and ground bases in the country by the end of 2014. The Soviet experience in Afghanistan is not analogous to that faced by the United States and NATO in that the allies have the capacity to retain a small military contingent to train and support the large Afghan army. The North and Kabul offer a receptive setting for absorbing outside foreign economic development projects and housing small Western military detachments. While the former Afghan president Hamid Karzai rejected an agreement to retain such a presence, his successors have all expressed support for it. Meanwhile, the Bagram military prison was turned over to Afghanistan, and arrangements have been made to close the major American bases in the country. However, the costs of remaining in the South, whether it becomes part of a greater Pakhtunistan or remains a separate Pashtun country, outweigh the benefits of trying to rebuild Afghanistan as a unified state.

TURKEY

Turkey is at a crossroads in terms of its geopolitical orientation. Its major concern now is whether or not it will be accepted into the EU. Well over half of its foreign trade is with EU nations. Membership would lead to trade expansion, provide Turkey's agricultural sector with support, and increase the capital investments that are vital to the country's future.

Europeans are weighing the degree to which Turkey's geopolitical interests outside the European framework are likely to be consistent with European policies. Turkey had been a strategic forward point for NATO and the West during the Cold War with respect to containment of Soviet penetration of the Mediterranean. European focus now has shifted to the Middle East, the Trans-Caucasus, and Central Asia. Access to oil and natural gas, counterterrorism, and the threat of Iran are major concerns. Turkey's role as a sea and land transit for Russian and Central Asian energy resources and its religious, historical, and racial ties with many of the peoples of these regions would seem to weigh strongly for admission. Those Europeans who oppose admission do so on the basis of fear of inclusion of an Islamic nation, opening the doors to mass immigration, and Turkey's human rights record in regard to its Kurdish citizens. In response to this fear, Turkey can offer the EU countries a model of a modern, secular Muslim republic, many of whose citizens maintain a deep commitment to Islam without undermining the state's secular character, and can interact with the West on equal terms.

Until recently, Ankara's economic, legal, and humanitarian strides in bringing Turkey closer to EU standards have been made under the reform leadership of a moderate Islamic party headed by Recep Tayyip Erdoğan. The government has significantly improved health care, roads, electricity, and the general economy of Kurdish southeastern Turkey and recognized Kurdish language rights. However, concerns have been raised among the secular sectors of the populations by revelations of widespread corruption within the Erdoğan administration as well as measures aimed at strengthening the Islamic nature of the state, such as lifting the ban on wearing the hijab (female head scarf). Moreover, Erdoğan has become more authoritarian in his leadership style. His standing was bolstered by the victories of his Justice and Development Party (AKP) over the secular Republican People's Party (CPF) in nationwide mayoral elections in 2014. The increasing polarization in the country could influence Turkey's ability to pursue a wider regional role.

Turkey aspired to be influential in bringing peace to the Middle East. Thus far its efforts have come to naught. Once the Syrian rebellion is resolved, however, Turkey could be helpful in stabilizing parts of the Middle East. It could take steps to reassure Syria and Iraq that the Guneydogu Anadolu Project (GAP) will not affect their use of Tigris and Euphrates waters. It can also help stabilize the region by directing unused freshwater from rivers such as the Seyhan and Ceyhan that now discharges into the Mediterranean to the "peace pipeline" to the Levant and the Arabian Peninsula. This was proposed by Turkish leaders years ago but did not come to pass. As a member of the EU and with its financial assistance, the project would be feasible. Another asset would be Turkey's armed forces of over one million well-trained and equipped personnel, including six hundred thousand on active service and a history of extensive involvement in UN and other peacekeeping missions. The integration of Turkish troops would strengthen the EU's rapid reaction force and enhance Europe's influence as a global peacekeeper.

Turkey could also establish formal ties with Armenia by admitting Turkey's role in the Armenian genocide and ending its blockade of that country in exchange for Armenia's acceptance of the present border and renunciation of historical territorial claims. Another geopolitical issue of concern to the EU is Cyprus. As sole protector of the North Cyprus Turks, Ankara has been resistant to resolving the Cyprus dispute with Greece. This is one of the EU bargaining chips in the issue of Turkish admission.

Until recently, Turkey has been the suitor in its effort to join the union. This eagerness could be jeopardized by actions taking place in northwestern Iraqi Kurdistan. Turkey greatly resents the lack of support by the United States and the West for its demands that PKK rebels operating from their safe havens in Iraq be expelled. The pressure on Ankara is not to invade. Without concrete measures by the United States, the Iraqi Kurds, and the Iraqi government to eliminate the PKK incursions, a break between Turkey and the West would be a strong possibility.

The 2004 decision of the EU to recommend admission negotiations represents the start of a process that has dragged on for over a decade. Part of Europe's reluctance to move the process forward can be attributed to suspicions as to the depth of commitment of Turkey's Islamic political parties to the concept of a secular, democratic Muslim republic. Another issue is European fear of being overwhelmed by waves of Turkish immigrants. This can be allayed by time restraints upon freedom to take up residence and work anywhere within the union, as was applied to Romania and Bulgaria over a limited number of years. In the long run, Turkey's membership could not only strengthen the EU but also contribute to greater global geopolitical equilibrium.

QATAR

Qatar is a very small country, with a population of only two million, that has an influence greatly disproportionate to its size. Governed by the progressive Emir Tamim bin Hamad Al

Thani, its homogeneous Sunni population is free of sectarian disputes, leaving Qatar free to act as mediator in a variety of conflicts, including those in Lebanon, Sudan, Yemen, and Eritrea. Thanks to its natural gas wealth, it can play the role of honest broker between conflicting Middle Eastern parties. Qatar is the world's fourth-largest gas producer, possessing its third-largest gas reserves. Most of the production is exported as LNG, whose proceeds represent two-thirds of all of its exports as well as nearly half of its GDP.

As a mediator of regional disputes, it supports the Muslim Brotherhood while maintaining economic relations with Israel and has gained Jerusalem's permission to supply construction materials to Gaza. It houses al-Jazeera, the Pan-Arab media channel, which is free of government censorship, and projects a progressive voice within the Middle East and beyond.

The Qatar Foundation has provided generous foreign aid to many Middle Eastern states and even to victims of Hurricane Katrina in the United States. Qatar hosted the US Central Command in the wars in Iraq and Afghanistan while maintaining relations with Iran, refusing to support sanctions against that country. While Qatar's natural gas wealth enables it to play these roles (it has quadrupled its output from 2008 to 2013), it is the vision and creativity of its leadership that has enabled it to become such an influential international player.

EGYPT

Egypt has long been the undisputed power of the Arab Middle East, with its population of over eighty million, nearly half of which is urbanized. It has the Arab world's largest and most skilled workforce and is the center of Islamic learning. Most of the population is concentrated along the Lower Nile and within the delta and contains Cairo, with a population of eighteen million.

The country has the third-largest natural gas reserves in the region, which it exports by pipeline to Jordan, Syria, and Lebanon, with a branch to Israel. It also has liquid natural gas (LNG) plants in Damietta in the Nile delta and near Alexandria, most of which is exported to France and Italy. The country also has substantial oil reserves, which have attracted foreign investment, and tourism is its single largest industry.

The 110-mile Suez Canal is Egypt's most important strategic asset. Completed in 1869, it has been enlarged several times, the most recent in 2010 to permit the transit of large container carriers. Four percent of the world's oil supply is transshipped through the canal or via a pipeline extending through the isthmus that parallels it. The transit fees are a major contribution to Egypt's budget. The Red Sea port of Sokhna, at the southern end of the canal, is a free-trade zone which facilitates commerce with the Middle East, Asia, and Africa. On August 5, 2014, Egypt began the widening of the forty-five-mile Suez Canal. The goal is to double the number of ships that can be accommodated during this transit, as well as to reduce the time of passage. New ports and industrial and economic zones will be constructed along the enlarged waterway.

A high point in Egypt's modern history was completion of the Aswan High Dam in 1970, with the help of Soviet engineering and financing. Backed up by Lake Aswan, the dam served as a symbol of national pride and unity, controlling the headwaters of the Nile. On the negative side, the dam has caused environmental damage in the delta, reducing the rate of sediments and nutrients that are so important to agriculture in enriching the soil as well as increasing water salinity.

Abdel Nasser's populist, anti-imperialist, and Pan-Arab agenda placed Egypt as the unchallenged leader of the Arab world against the conservative, pro-Western Arab regimes of

Arabia. With the death of Nasser in 1970 and the peace treaty with Israel signed by Anwar Sadat, in 1976 this phase of Egypt's dominant influence in the region came to an end. The United States became Egypt's major economic and military supporter, providing it with more than $2 billion per annum for many years. Even as late as 2013–14, support from Washington remained at $1.3 billion with another $200 million in economic assistance.

When the Arab Spring broke out in Egypt in 2011, Hosni Mubarak was overthrown. The elections that followed brought the Muslim Brotherhood, led by Mohamed Morsi, to power. Morsi overreached in seeking to impose Islamic law and practices, bringing on a second revolution in 2013 led by the Egyptian military. While Washington has been faced with the quandary as to how to deal with the overthrow of a popularly elected government, it has been reluctant to halt aid to Egypt. Meanwhile, Saudi Arabia, Qatar, the UAE, and Kuwait have supplanted the United States as the primary source of support, providing Egypt with $15 billion in grants and loans. They are motivated by Egypt's heavy crackdown on the Muslim Brotherhood. The 2014 elections consolidated the power of Abdel Fattah el-Sisi, the retired head of the Egyptian Armed Forces, as president of the country. Egypt will probably regain the imposed stability that prevailed during the Mubarak style of authoritarian leadership.

However, Egypt's regional geopolitical influence is now far less than it was during Nasser's time. This influence was substantially reduced when Egypt became perceived as a satellite of the United States and will be further diminished as it becomes economically dependent upon Saudi Arabia and its neighbors.

SYRIA

A shattered Syria is the image of a shatterbelt region and represents the elements that constitute this condition. The socialist Baath party, led first by Hafez al-Assad and then by his son Bashar al-Assad, long held sway over the country. Internal rifts were stifled, and for much of this period the Soviet Union exercised considerable influence on domestic affairs. Neither Syria's ongoing conflict with Israel nor serious on-and-off efforts to extend its power into Lebanon affected the rule of the Assad clan. The country's internal religious, ethnic, and socioeconomic divisions were papered over by the despotic regime.

This all changed with the outbreak of civil war in March 2011, as the impact of the Arab Spring spread to Syria. First only an uprising of secular and Sunni opponents of the regime, the rebellion quickly became a fratricidal conflict that engulfed all of its religious-ethnic factions and drew a wide variety of external forces into the fray. The Syrian factions in this land of twenty-three million were divided as follows: Arab Sunnis, 60 percent; the ruling Alawite Shiites, 12 percent; Kurdish Sunni, 9 percent; Greek Orthodox Christians, 9 percent; Armenians, 4 percent; and Druse, 3 percent.

The fighting has drawn outside countries as well as foreign Islamic militants into the fray. Rebel supporters include the jihadists of ISIS (Islamic State in Iraq and Syria) and several thousand militants from Europe and the Maghreb. Foreign supporters of the government involved in the fighting are the Hezbollah from Lebanon's South and the Beqa'a. Iran and Russia have provided the Assad government financial, technological, and military aid, while the rebel Free Syrian Army is sheltered by Turkey and receives weapons and diplomatic support from Qatar, Saudi Arabia, and the United States. Iraqi Kurds back their Syrian Kurdish kin. Adding to the complexity of the rebellion, some of the rebels have been drawn into conflict with one another—the Kurds of the northeast have engaged in battle with the jihadist al-Nusra, and the moderate Free Syrian Army with ISIS.

The lone example of cooperation among the external interveners was the joint Russian-US initiative on eliminating chemical weapons. Reports of governmental use of nerve gas against the rebels prompted Washington to threaten to attack the Syrian government-controlled stores. This brought Moscow into the picture, and the Russians persuaded the Assad government to give up its chemical weapons stockpile—a drawn-out and difficult process wherein the gas is transported to the coast to be treated and dumped into the ocean by foreign vessels.

By 2014, Syria was a ravaged land. Approximately 2.5 million Syrians have taken refuge mainly in Lebanon, Jordan, and Turkey, where many live in squalid camps. Some found refuge in Iraq and Europe. An estimated six to seven million Syrians are internal refugees—displaced from their homes and lacking jobs as well as access to education and health facilities. They amount to nearly 40 percent of the country's 2011 population. Up to an estimated 150,000 persons have been killed in the fight. Syria has become the nightmare that faces so many of its neighbors in the Middle East shatterbelt. Will Iraq or Lebanon be next?

Oil, Pipeline Routes, and Politics

Nothing better reflects the instability and unpredictability of the Middle East than its system of oil and gas pipelines and the impact of politics and wars upon their use. The region's first major pipeline from Kirkuk in Iraq to the Mediterranean at Haifa in Palestine was built in 1934. It was closed during the Arab-Israeli war, never to be opened again. Alternative lines to the Mediterranean at Tripoli in Lebanon and Baniyas in Syria have been opened and closed with the winds of politics and war.

Other examples abound of how conflicts in the Middle East affect pipelines. The two Kirkuk-Dortyol-Ceyhan lines from Iraq to Turkey skirt Syria. They were closed during the First Gulf War and not opened again until six years later. The Iraq-Saudi pipeline from the Rumaila fields in southern Iraq to Yanbu on the Red Sea was closed in 1990, when UN sanctions embargoed Iraq's oil exports. While the line was reopened six years later, it has been subject to frequent closures, the most recent in 2012. The Baku-Tbilisi-Ceyhan oil pipeline, which transports crude from Azerbaijan to the Mediterranean, has had its operations interrupted several times by PKK Kurdish rebel actions. Most recently, the semiautonomous region of North Kurdistan in Iraq built a pipeline from Kirkuk to Ceyhan because the Iraqi government denied it the use of the Kirkuk-Dortyol-Ceyhan line, objecting to the unilateral agreement that the Kurdish leadership had made with international oil companies and Turkey. The huge trans-Arabian pipeline—Tapline, completed in 1950—extends for 1,040 miles from Dammam through Jordan and Syria to Sidon (Saida) in Lebanon. It was closed during the Arab-Israeli war of 1967, when Syria lost the Golan Heights to Israel, and has remained mothballed ever since. To replace Tapline, an even larger line with three times the throughput capacity was built by Saudi Arabia. Called "Petroline," it extends from Saudi Arabia's Gulf coastal fields to the country's western provinces and the Red Sea oil terminus and refining center of Yanbu.

The American stake in Saudi Arabia's oil quickly led to a major military and economic alliance between the two countries. For the United States, this was a commitment of strategic necessity. By the middle of World War II, the center of gravity of world oil reserves had shifted from the US Gulf of Mexico/Caribbean region to the Middle East. Middle Eastern reserves, which were then estimated at nearly half of the world's total, then climbed to two-thirds by the turn of the century.[8] Currently the region accounts for 56 percent of the global reserves, of which Saudi Arabia alone accounts for 18 percent and Iran, Iraq, Kuwait, and the UAE constitute another 40 percent. While the United States has recently become the world's leading oil producer, closely followed by Russia and Saudi Arabia, its domestic output is still outstripped by demand. The gap has greatly narrowed, and US imports of crude from Canada and Mexico are becoming increasingly important, as they are refined for export in the Gulf of Mexico.

Although still a minor oil exporter, South Sudan has also been caught up in oil pipeline politics as its production and reserves rapidly increased. The country gained its independence from Sudan in 2011, inheriting major oil fields located in its territory. While peace was achieved in 2005 after twenty-two years of civil war between the Arab North and the black African South, the boundaries between the two remained a point of contention. They are in dispute over control of Abyei, which contains the oil-rich Muglad Basin. South Sudan is landlocked, and the oil must be transported by a 930-mile pipeline from Muglad to Port Sudan on the Red Sea. While the agreement that led to South Sudanese independence called for oil revenue generated in the South to be shared equally, South Sudan now seeks to revise its share upward. Sudan, in turn, threatens to close the pipeline. This had stimulated South Sudan to enter into negotiations with Kenya to build an alternative pipeline to Kenya's port of Lamu. The question of sovereignty over these oil-bearing areas, the use of the pipeline to Port Sudan, and the division of royalties will most assuredly continue to be major issues.

The Turkish Straits continue to present international political problems, although they no longer are the focus of the historic struggle for strategic control that had embroiled them in wars and international controversies. Instead, it is Ankara's fear of oil spills that now pervades the politics of the straits. The completion of the pipeline from the Tenghiz oil fields in Kazakhstan to Russia's Novorossiisk on the Black Sea has aggravated Turkey's fears of oil leaks and spills from large tankers traversing the Bosporus. However, the Montreux Convention limits Turkey's ability to restrict the movement of civilian shipping or to require the use of local ship pilots in navigating the narrow waters. It is the environmental concern that so strongly motivated Turkey to support the 1,080-mile pipeline from Baku through Georgia and Turkey to its Mediterranean port of Ceyhan, the construction of which was completed in 2006.

Closure of the Suez Canal between 1967 and 1975 was a blow to the export of oil from the Middle East. This closure and cutoffs of some of the overland pipeline routes made it imperative to develop a new system for moving the Gulf's oil. One solution was the building of supertankers. These vessels, which are too big to transit the Suez Canal, proved themselves capable of transporting petroleum around South Africa's Cape of Good Hope more efficiently and cheaply than it could be transported via Suez, even after the reopened canal was deepened in 1980. Supertankers continue to play an important role, although the majority of Middle Eastern oil exports go eastward to Asia rather than to Europe and the United States.

This shift in the Middle East oil transportation pattern relates to the remarkable growth of the Japanese, Chinese, and Indian economies, with their huge demand for oil. Direct shipments to that region from the Gulf via the Indian Ocean have no need for Suez and Mediterranean pipeline systems. Ensuring an uninterrupted flow requires the securing of the Straits of Hormuz and Malacca and is now an international strategic imperative.

Conclusion

The fractured nature of the Middle East as a geopolitical arena and its polynodal regional power structure inhibit the establishment of stable regional or subregional geopolitical units. Their absence limits the more effective use of human and material resources through sharing and transfer mechanisms. Rather than presenting a regional mosaic whose diverse parts complement one another, the Middle East is an assortment of competing states and interest groups. In this competition, Turkey, Egypt, Syria, Iran, Saudi Arabia, and Israel are all important power centers. Iraq could regain its status as a power center should it rebuild itself as a unified state, although that prospect currently seems remote.

Intraregional trade remains relatively limited, inasmuch as the chief trading partners of the Middle Eastern states with the largest economies lie outside the region. There are a few exceptions. Saudi Arabia serves as an important market for products from smaller, economically weak states, such as those that lie across its Red Sea waters, and some of its Arabian Peninsula neighbors. Lebanon also, because of its gateway or exchange functions, transships some of its imports to other Middle Eastern states and provides them with financial services and food and textile products. Bahrain has long served as a banking and financial service center for the Arabian Peninsula countries. Now oil-rich Dubai and Qatar are competing to be regional, and possibly global, financial hubs.

Aside from the close links among the six states of the Gulf Cooperation Council, which have expanded their functions to include a free-trade agreement among the members, political ties among the region's states are fragile. Various attempts to achieve full-scale political mergers ended in failure, save the United Arab Emirates and Yemen, although the latter remains deeply divided along its former north-south lines.

More promising than attempts at full-blown mergers of countries are functional ties that have limited objectives. Egypt, Jordan, and Syria have an electricity line that links their electrical grids. Other examples include: the international airport at Aqaba in Jordan, which also serves Israel, Saudi Arabia, and Egypt; the desalination plant at Aqaba, which provides freshwater to Jordan, Israel, and the West Bank; and the agreements between Egypt and Sudan on defense and Nile navigation.

Water remains a major cause for tension and dispute, since as much as 90 percent of the region's major streams and many of its aquifers cut across international boundaries. Thus not only is Turkey's diversion of the Tigris-Euphrates headwaters opposed by Syria and Iraq, but also control of the Southeast Anatolian Water Project could become a major issue in the negotiations between Ankara and the Turkish Kurds in their demands for independence or greater autonomy.

Agreement between Syria and Israel over the Golan Heights is hampered by Syrian insistence that peace depends on Israel's withdrawal not only from the Golan Heights and the Shaba Farms area but also from a ten-meter strip along the northeastern shore of the Sea of Galilee, Israel's main reservoir. It lay within the bounds of the former Palestine Mandate. Israel and the Palestinian Authority are at odds over Israeli control of the mountain aquifer under the West Bank, which is rapidly being depleted.

In the Persian/Arab Gulf, the Shatt al-Arab and maritime boundaries remain sources of contention. Conservation practices, recycling, desalination, the sale of freshwater, and establishing water pricing policies are measures that need to be taken to address the region's water problems, but political fragmentation is a major obstacle to their implementation.

While the region has abundant petroleum and natural gas, many of the disputes over these energy resources occur in connection with land or maritime boundaries that are in areas populated by minorities who seek independence or autonomy. This is the case with Iraq's petroleum fields located at the edge of the Kurdish North and the Shia South, which stiffens the opposition of a centralized Iraqi government to a loose confederation of highly autonomous provinces. The western Sunni province, which lacks oil, also has more to gain from a unified state in which it could have a strong claim to a share of the nation's oil revenue. Iran's major oil lies within its heavily Arabic province of Khuzestan. In the north of the country, Iranian Azerbaijan has important potential reserves of both oil and gas. Its boundary within the Caspian Sea, with its vast oil and gas reserves, has yet to be determined. This complicates the search for solutions to that country's irredentist conflicts.

The dispute between Sudan and South Sudan over the location of the boundary in the oil-rich Abyei region remains unresolved. Tension over demarcation of the boundary has been increased by the demands of two states in North Sudan—South Kordofan and Blue Nile—to join South Sudan (fig. 12.2). The ethnic Nubians of mountainous South Kordofan fought beside the South Sudanese in their civil war and have little in common with Sudan's majority Arabs. In the state of Blue Nile, which has a sizable Nubian population, clashes are ongoing between African Nubians and local Arab nomadic tribes backed by the Sudanese military. In addition, the Blue Nile state contains the river's Roseires Dam, an important source of hydropower and irrigation for the lands to its north. Adding to the complexity in South Sudan is the civil war that broke out between the Dinka, the country's largest tribe, and the Nuer, its second largest. The issue is a power struggle between the Dinka president and the Nuer vice president whom he ousted. In the course of the fighting, eight hundred thousand South Sudanese have been displaced, and one-quarter million have fled the country. Efforts by the United States and international organizations to mediate the conflict have failed to bring the two sides together.

Other obstacles to regional stability are the massive numbers of foreign workers in Saudi Arabia and the Gulf states; use by terrorist groups operating in one country of bases in neighboring countries for training and supply purposes; Iran's possible development of weapons of mass destruction; transborder nomadic migrations; and the presence of refugees from war and civil strife. Sudan, Eritrea, Somalia, Kenya, Turkey, Lebanon, Jordan, Iraq, Kuwait, Iran, and Afghanistan have large numbers of refugees. Of the nearly four million Palestinian refugees, one-third have languished in camps in Lebanon, Jordan, Syria, Gaza, and the West Bank for well over half a century, enduring hardship and creating instability in those lands. Refugees from Syria constitute a major economic burden and threat to the stability of Jordan, Lebanon, and Turkey.

All of these obstacles plus disparities of wealth, land degradation and other environmental problems, and agricultural production deficits present formidable challenges that are more difficult to tackle owing to the political fragmentation of the shatterbelt.

The magnet of the circumterral seas of the Middle East continues to attract major external powers, even as their comparative influence has changed. Russia retains some influence over the course of events in the Persian Gulf through its contacts with Iran and in the eastern Mediterranean, where it continues to back Syria.

Although the United States remains the prime military force in the Gulf and maintains strategic supremacy there, its interest in the region is waning. Its failures in Iraq and Afghanistan have weakened public support for continued involvement in the Middle East, particularly since oil from that region is no longer strategically critical to the United States.

America's relations with Israel and Saudi Arabia continue to be significant. Washington's alliance with Israel is based on that country's military power and the strength of its intelligence system as well as strong domestic support from American Jewry, fundamentalist Christians, and the US Congress. Arms sales to Riyadh, the largest customer for US military hardware, is a measure of the importance of the relations between the two countries. The economic ties between the two have broadened as Saudi Arabia has become the fifth-largest trading partner of the United States and the recipient of the largest share of US investments in the Middle East. As long as Iran remains a potential nuclear threat, the strengthening of Saudi Arabia is within Washington's strategic interests.

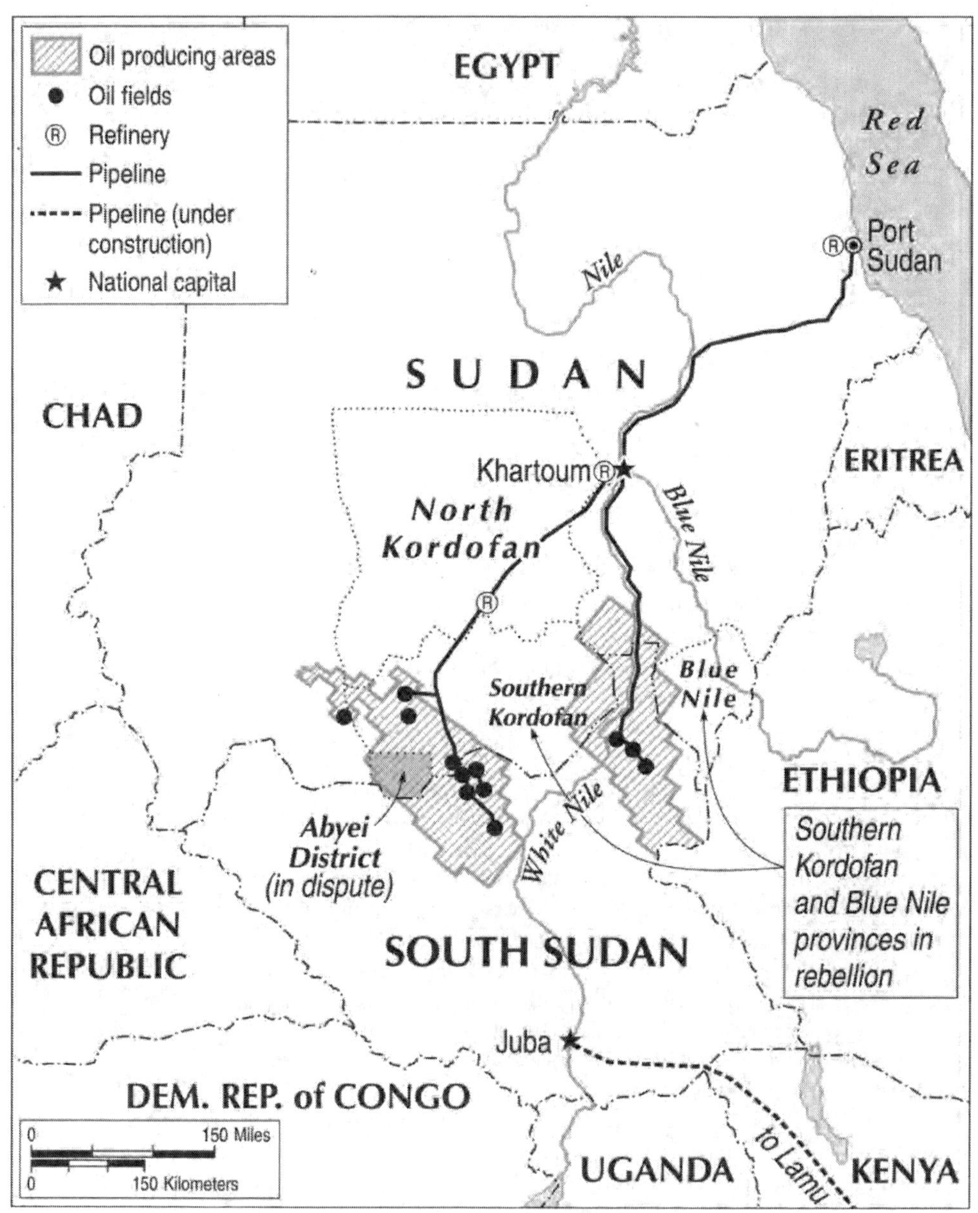

Figure 12.2. Sudan/South Sudan Boundary Dispute

Shifting alliances among the Arab states of the Middle East are an ongoing aspect of the geopolitical scene. Ideology, economics, personalities, successful coups, and big-power interests and support all play a part in the swings between friendship and hostility among Middle Eastern states. In a region as unstable as the Middle East, geopolitical forecasts are risky. With this caveat, it can be noted that present trends suggest that the current geopolitical atomization may diminish as new subregional blocs emerge. However, there are significant "ifs"—if the Arab-Israeli dispute is finally resolved, and if Turkey is admitted to the EU, the western half of the Middle East might become part of a Euro-Mediterranean expansion of maritime Europe and the Maghreb. Egypt is already strongly oriented to Europe and the United States, both militarily and economically. Libya, now searching for unity, with a weak government that lacks specific foreign policy objectives, would probably gravitate more strongly into the Egyptian orbit in a strategic sense while becoming part of an economically focused Mediterranean union.

Israel is part of the "Western Europe and Others" regional grouping in the United Nations because it has been banned by Arab states from the Asian regional group. As a leading high-technology economy and society, an Israel at peace with its neighbors could provide a bridge to high-tech maritime Europe. As it is, Israel is the leader among non-EU members participating in EU programs. Membership in the EU and NATO would guarantee Israel's security far more that its current diplomatic and military dependence on the United States. Meaningful geopolitical links between the rest of the Levant and maritime Europe depend upon Lebanon's resolution of its deep internal divisions and the reorientation of a post–civil war Syria to the West.

On the eastern border of the Middle East, Iran has yet to emerge from the international isolation that it has imposed on itself and that has been reinforced by Western sanctions in reaction to Tehran's nuclear policies and sponsorship of international terrorism, including support of Syria and the Hezbollah in southern Lebanon. Its geopolitical position within the region has been greatly strengthened by the rise to power of the Shia in Iraq and Tehran's consequent ability to affect the stability of Iraq. Tehran has also sought to offset Washington's strategic primacy within the Middle East by developing closer ties to Russia and China. Iran has been aided by Moscow in developing medium-range strategic missiles aimed at putting it on a par with Pakistan and Israel. Russia completed construction of a nuclear energy plant for Iran at Bushehr on the Persian Gulf in 2013 and signed an agreement to construct two more such plants.

Iran seeks to play an independent geopolitical role and link itself to the world's diverse geostrategic realms without joining any of them. It could become the core of a powerful independent geopolitical subregion with considerable influence over Shia-controlled Iraq. Parts of Central Asia, which historically have been exposed to Persian culture, might gravitate toward Tehran if its regime were to move toward a balanced relationship between religion and politics while abandoning its support of international terrorism. However, Iran's Shia religion continues to be an obstacle to closer ties with Sunni neighbors in both the Arab world and Muslim lands to the east of Iran.

Were the Levantine western parts of the Middle East to become absorbed within the maritime European orbit and Iran to maintain its separate geopolitical stance, the remainder of the region—Iraq, Saudi Arabia, the Gulf states, Afghanistan, and Sudan—would continue to constitute a shatterbelt, albeit considerably smaller than the present one. Polarization within such a reduced shatterbelt region might be intensified if the United States continues to maintain a strong presence in Saudi Arabia and the Gulf States and Russia succeeds in building closer ties with Iran. Afghanistan could well break up under pressures from Pakistan and

Iran, while Pakistan itself might crumble, with one or more of its parts becoming oriented to the Middle East.

What can be predicted with some certainty about the Middle East shatterbelt is that it will continue to be a region of conflict and shifting alliances. What cannot be predicted with any measure of confidence is how these alliances may regroup and what the region's internal and external borders may be.

Notes

1. Reader Bullard, *Britain and the Middle East* (London: Hutchinson's University Library, 1951), 28–47.
2. Bullard, *Britain and the Middle East*, 48–65.
3. Richard C. Duncan and Walter Youngquist, "The World Petroleum Life-Cycle" (paper presented at Petroleum Technology Transfer Council Workshop at the University of Southern California, Los Angeles, October 22, 1998).
4. Central Intelligence Agency, "The World Factbook: Field Listing—Disputes—International," https://www.cia.gov/library/publications/the-world-factbook/fields/2070.html.
5. Alan J. Day, *Border and Territorial Disputes* (Harlow, England: Longman, 1982), 214–19.
6. Day, *Border and Territorial Disputes*, 222–25.
7. Saul B. Cohen, "Gaza Now! Prospects for a Gaza Microstate," *Mediterranean Quarterly* (Spring 1992): 60–80.
8. US Department of Energy, Energy Information Administration, "Annual Energy Review," in *World Almanac and Book of Facts 2007* (New York: World Almanac Education Group, 2007), 113.

CHAPTER 13

The Sub-Saharan African Shatterbelt

Sub-Saharan Africa, the poorest region in the world, has been a shatterbelt since the outbreak of the Cold War—its internal fragmentation magnified by the ideological, military, and economic pressure and intervention of external powers. While outside powers had acquired colonial footholds as early as the fifteenth century, they did not subdivide the region into separate spheres of influence until the modern imperialist era of the late nineteenth century. Only Ethiopia and Liberia retained their independence during this period. However, the region did not become a shatterbelt because internal divisions were stifled by the outside rulers.

Following World War II, Sub-Saharan African states gained their independence only to be caught up in the Cold War as arenas of conflict between the United States and the Soviet Union. The two superpowers offered military and economic aid to ideologically minded groups within these states, opening up the fissures which had been dormant during the imperialist era. This was the process that created modern shatterbelts, and Sub-Saharan Africa has stood out as the most highly atomized of such fragmented regions. Today the main goals of external interveners are no longer ideological, they are economic, and it is China, not the Soviet Union, that vies with Europe and the United States for influence within the region. Not only is this economic competition over supplies of raw material, but it also reflects the quest for markets and investment.

So intense is Washington's concern over China's growing influence in Sub-Saharan Africa that the Pentagon decided to establish a new US Command (AFRICOM). The original intent was to locate it somewhere on the Gulf of Guinea coast, since the major objective of the command was to secure access to the oil riches of the Gulf of Guinea in the face of increasing Chinese competition, although humanitarian aid was, and remains part of, its mission. Because of logistical problems, AFRICOM was located instead in Stuttgart, Germany. For many Africans, the competition between the United States and China is welcome as a spur to economic development, although it also stirs memories of centuries of colonial exploitation as well as the resentment of being plundered for raw materials without being provided with commensurate job opportunities. Where military assistance is made available by the United States or European countries, it is not designed against China. Rather, it is offered as part of an antiterrorist campaign or as a means of securing a government against internal rebellion. The background to this colonial/imperial period follows.

Colonial/Imperial Background

The race for the anticipated riches of Sub-Saharan Africa resulted in the fierce European colonial struggles of the late nineteenth and early twentieth centuries. After World War I, German *geopolitik* promoted the doctrine of a Pan-Eur-Africa as part of a north-south panregional theory.[1] This was rooted in the proposition that the southern continents were the "exploitable worlds" and vital to the progress of northern, industrialized societies.

European penetration of Africa dates back to the discovery period of the fifteenth century and to the era of the slave trade that flourished in the seventeenth and eighteenth centuries. However, it began in earnest with the explorations and footholds that were established in the late eighteenth and nineteenth centuries. This is conveyed in the names accorded to the West African coast—"Grain and Pepper Coast," "Slave Coast," "Gold Coast," "Ivory Coast." The "Copperbelt" of Northern Rhodesia/Zambia and southeastern Congo (Katanga) is another example.

A rationale offered for European intervention in Africa during the nineteenth century was assumption of the "white man's burden" as the duty of Christian powers to stop the slave trade and "civilize the natives." However, the main motive was economic exploitation. The rapid industrialization of Europe between 1870 and 1890 stimulated the search for new markets, not only within Europe and North America but also in Africa and Asia. In addition, it produced the capital surpluses that were required to exploit the mineral riches and agricultural potential of these tropical regions. Population growth in Europe resulted in massive overseas emigration after 1880, not just to the United States but also to the African colonies, where white immigrants could help their mother countries retain political control.[2]

Congo is a most egregious example of the ruthlessness with which native Africans were exploited in the search for riches. Britain's colonial interest was not sparked by Henry Stanley's three explorations of the great Congo river during 1871–84, following those of David Livingstone. However, these explorations did prod Belgian king Leopold to establish the Independent State of the Congo as his private preserve. His pursuit of the "wonderful natural wealth" that Stanley ascribed to the Congo led to the exploitation, first of rubber and ivory, and then of the copper resources of the river's upper basin. All of the concessions that were awarded by Leopold utilized forced labor, and the brutality of this system sparked widespread outrage. In response, the government of Belgium eventually annexed the territory from Leopold in 1908, establishing the Belgian Congo and ameliorating the conditions somewhat.

While the African rubber trade declined steeply with the shift of the industry to the plantations of Southeast Asia, copper remained a significant export, although today it is exceeded in importance by diamonds. Other minerals (such as cobalt, zinc, tin, and uranium), petroleum (from offshore deposits at the mouth of the Congo), tropical hardwoods, and plantation crops remain the backbone of the modern Congo (Zaire) economy. In addition, some of the substantial hydroelectric potential of the great river has been harnessed, although most of it remains untapped. However, the Congo basin never proved to be as rich as the early explorers and exploiters assumed. Poverty of soils, climatic rigor, disease, labor force instability, and competition from crops and minerals of other parts of the world prevented the region from attaining its perceived potential.

Since the collapse of the European colonial system, Sub-Saharan Africa has sunk into a state of de-development. The world's poorest region, it is geopolitically atomized, torn by recurrent conflicts among and within its fifty national states. These states essentially follow the territorial frameworks that were established during the colonial period. There is growing consensus that these national frameworks are flawed because they have failed to account for many of the drives for territorial sovereignty of ethnic, tribal, and religious groups that are subsumed within them.

One recipe for reducing conflict is a larger number of smaller, more homogeneous states. Another school of thought takes the opposite view, holding that substantially larger states are the answer to the African crisis. For example, A. S. Gakwandi proposed a new political map of Africa with only seven states as a way to resolve the current problems of border disputes, refugees who have been separated from their homelands, and the liabilities of landlocked states. The rationale is that a balance among a handful of states that are ethnically and religiously diverse but economically viable would promote political stability.[3]

The position of the Organization of African Unity (now the African Union—AU), however, is that all member states should respect the borders existing at the time of their independence and that to attempt to redraw them would be an invitation to the spread of conflict in a region already torn by widespread violence.

Postcolonial Political Frameworks

Postcolonial Africa has experienced many efforts to break up existing states or to forge unions among them. Separation has often led to bitter warfare, heavy loss of life, devastation of the countryside and cities, and massive flows of refugees. The most prominent have been secession attempts in Nigeria and the recurrent attempts in Congo/Zaire. The Ibo of oil-rich southeast Nigeria established the independent state of Biafra in 1967, seven years after the country gained its freedom from Great Britain. In a war that lasted three years before the defeat of Biafra, more than one million Biafrans are said to have died of starvation.

Shortly after Zaire (now the Democratic Republic of Congo, DRC) became independent in 1960, Katanga (Shaba), the mineral-rich province in the southeastern plateau portion of the country, seceded. The Katangese waged a civil war for three years before the rebellion was put down by UN and Belgian troops, whose aim was to save Zaire from anarchy and maintain the stability of the copper industry. Patrice Lumumba, the leftist prime minister, failed to secure UN intervention when the rebellion broke out and turned for help to the Soviet Union. He was dismissed by President Joseph Kasa-Vubu and was subsequently murdered by the troops of Colonel Joseph Mobutu Sese Seko, head of the army. Mobutu eventually succeeded in crushing the rebellion and seized power in 1966 with the help of Belgian troops and the US Central Intelligence Agency, initiating a dictatorial and exploitative regime that lasted until 1997, when it was overthrown by General Laurent Kabila. Since then, however, Congo has known little peace.

Five years after Uganda was established as an independent republic in 1962, its southern province of Buganda sought to secede. Buganda had a long history as an independent kingdom before becoming a British protectorate. It rebelled against the abolition by the central government of the high degree of autonomy that had been guaranteed to it when Uganda became independent. The rebellion was quashed, although in 1993 Uganda and other traditional monarchies were restored for ceremonial purposes only. Over the years the country has suffered from intermittent civil wars, coups, and dictatorships.

Shortly after Angola won its independence from Portugal in 1975, the Kongo people in the oil-rich Cabinda exclave, the main source of the country's petroleum, were unsuccessful in their struggle to establish a separate state. However, a major rebellion broke out in Angola that year between the Marxist MPLA government, headed by José Eduardo dos Santos, and the

UNITA rebels. The conflict raged continuously until Jonas Savimbi, UNITA's founder and leader, died in battle in 2002, resulting in peace. The rebels' diamond-rich highland base, plus US and South African military support, had enabled them to maintain a "state within a state" throughout the fight that displaced one-quarter of the country's inhabitants. Since then, the country has changed from a one-party, Marxist-Leninist system to a multiparty democracy. Dos Santos was reelected president in 2008 and again in 2012. Angola is now Sub-Saharan Africa's second-largest oil producer, challenging Nigeria for the lead.

Thanks to its oil reserves, Angola's population of eighteen million has a per capita income of nearly $6,500, with oil accounting for 45 percent of its GDP and 90 percent of exports. China is the main market for these exports, followed by the United States and Europe, although the American share is rapidly declining thanks to US production increases.

One example of a successful separatist struggle has been the experience of Southwest Africa (Namibia), which rebelled against South African rule and gained its independence in 1989. The territory had had a history separate from that of South Africa. A German protectorate in the late nineteenth century, it was occupied in World War I by South Africa, which administered it under a League of Nations mandate. The South Africans refused to surrender this mandate to the UN trusteeship system in 1945. In the 1970s a nationalist guerrilla movement, the South West Africa People's Organization (SWAPO), based largely in Angola, organized a guerrilla war against Pretoria's rule that culminated eventually in the establishment of the separate state of Namibia.

Secessions have also occurred in the Horn of Africa. The Arabic-speaking, Muslim Eritreans are oriented toward trade and fishing, unlike the highland Christian Ethiopian farmers. The coastal territory, which had first been occupied by Italy in the 1880s, was administered as a separate colony until merged with Ethiopia when the Italians conquered that country in 1935–36. From the 1960s onward, the Eritreans fought for their freedom. In the late 1970s they forged an alliance with the Tigrinya-speaking Ethiopian rebels in a struggle to overthrow Ethiopia's Amharic-controlled Marxist regime. After three decades, and at the cost of 100,000 to 150,000 fatalities, the regime was overthrown, and shortly thereafter Eritrea was able to become an independent, secular republic. While Eritrea separated from Ethiopia peacefully in 1993, the two countries waged war from 1998 to 2000 over a border dispute that was ultimately resolved through UN intervention. Nevertheless, tensions over that border have remained because Ethiopia refused to accept an adjusted line that included Badma in Eritrea. Eritrea opposed Ethiopia's 2006 intervention in Somalia, but the two parties came to a final agreement in 2009. Both Ethiopia and Eritrea are internally divided along religious lines, but the Amharic Ethiopian Orthodox Christians generally dominate Ethiopian politics, while Eritrea is Muslim led.

On the Somali coast, Britain, France, and Italy had all established colonies during the previous century, each centering on a strategic port. Britain created a protectorate around the port of Berbera on the Gulf of Aden. London's objective was to have a presence on the Somali coast to counter French-controlled Djibouti, which had been developed in 1862 as a commercial and strategic rival to Aden. In addition, Britain was interested in securing a food supply for Aden, especially mutton, from the Somali herdsmen. Italy followed suit in 1889 by establishing a protectorate along the central coast, focusing on the port of Mogadishu, which overlooked both the Gulf of Aden and the Indian Ocean. Italy expanded the territory southward in the years that followed.

The British and Italian colonies merged to become the independent Republic of Somalia in 1960. (French Somaliland did not join and gained its own independence, as did Djibouti, in 1977.) Torn by clan fighting, Somalia splintered into a number of unstable parts in the civil war of 1991. The conflict that broke out after the separation of Eritrea from Ethiopia and the dismemberment of Somalia will be discussed in the section on compression zones.

Attempts to create larger African states through federations or mergers have, for the most part, been unsuccessful. In 1959, Mali and Senegal formed the Mali federation only to have it dissolved the next year. Guinea and Ghana, which had joined in a symbolic union in 1958, expanded that union to include Mali in 1961. This merger had no practical effect and ended in 1966, when Ghana's Kwame Nkrumah was deposed.

The East African experience with regional unions was similarly disappointing. While Uganda, Kenya, and Tanganyika were still under British rule, the idea of an East African federation was promoted. A royal commission (1953–55) proposed that the three territories establish a federated framework with functions that would include transportation, communications, and taxation. The proposal was not implemented at that time because it called for eventual control by native Africans, and it was therefore strongly opposed by the white settlers. An East African Community (EAC) was formed by the three countries after independence (1967), but it made little headway because of conflict between Uganda and Tanzania over Tanzanian control of the Kagera Region in northwest Tanzania, on the southwestern shore of Lake Victoria. The EAC was formally dissolved in 1977, but it was revived in February 2001 as an economic bloc.

In Southern Africa, Southern Rhodesia became a member of the Federation of Rhodesia and Nyasaland. The federation was broken up in 1963. A year later, Northern Rhodesia (Zambia) and Nyasaland (Malawi) became independent. In 1965 the white minority government of Southern Rhodesia (Zimbabwe) declared itself independent of Britain—it later renamed itself the Republic of Rhodesia—and instituted complete separation of the voting franchise along racial lines. UN economic sanctions and African nationalist guerrilla warfare ultimately led, in 1980, to the independence of Zimbabwe under black majority rule. An attempt to unite the Portuguese colonies of Cape Verde and Guinea-Bissau failed in 1980, and a confederal arrangement between Senegal and the Gambia (called "Senegambia") was dismantled the following year.

There were a few limited successes in merging former colonies. The Gold Coast and British Togoland were united in 1957, when the two colonies gained their independence, to form Ghana. In 1961 the southern part of the British Cameroons joined the French Cameroons to form Cameroon, while the northern British Cameroons passed to Nigeria. Three years later the island of Zanzibar, a sultanate that had gained independence only to be overthrown in a bloody revolution, merged with Tanganyika to form Tanzania—a poor country of forty-six million people with a GDP of $75 billion and per capita income of only about $1,500.

Julius Nyerere, Tanzania's first president, created TANU, a heavy-handed socialist party which collectivized the land and nationalized most of its economic institutions. Nyerere, strongly influenced by Maoism, aligned the country with China, which built the Tazara Railway, linking Tanzania's port of Dar es Salaam with Zambia. While a multiparty system has developed over the years to replace the oppressive single-party regime, the country's economy continues to languish. Agriculture, its mainstay, accounts for 85 percent of its exports, 80 percent of its work force, and 25 percent of its GDP. The main crops are maize, casaba, millet, rice, sorghum, and coffee. Gold, diamonds, and natural gas make a modest contribution.

Religious and economic differences between the two territories introduced friction early on. Zanzibar, for centuries the center for Arab slave traders, is almost completely Muslim, and the large majority of Tanganyikans are Christian or of traditional faiths. In addition, the impoverishment of the island of Zanzibar as a result of the collapse of the world clove market and the erosion of its autonomy in recent decades has given rise to a modest Zanzibari secessionist movement. Cloves had been the mainstay of Zanzibar and the nearby island of Pemba. With the steep drop in prices and demand, these offshore islands have sought to shift to a tourist economy, but this industry's development has not yet had the desired impact.

Continental and regional African economic frameworks have also had limited impacts.[4] In its 1980 Lagos Plan of Action, the Organization of African Unity (OAU), which had been established in 1963, set forth the goal of creating a single Pan-African Common Market by the year 2000. The African Union (AU) now includes not only the fifty Sub-Saharan African states but also four of the five North African countries. Also in 1963, at the Yaounde Convention, eighteen French-speaking African states and Madagascar formed the Economic Community of West and Central Africa, to whose exports the Common Market accorded tariff-free access. The organization made little coordinated progress, save sharing a common currency tied to the French franc. A European development fund was also established in connection with the agreement, which did prove a valuable source of aid.

The successor to the Yaounde Convention was the Lomé Agreement of 1975, which called for free movement of goods and people among and between the African signatories and the European Community (EC).[5] The African members at Lomé also formed a new geographical regional community—the Economic Community of West African States (ECOWAS), which now includes sixteen states, both French-speaking nations and Nigeria and other former British colonies.

The Lomé Agreement was initially sponsored by both France and Britain, reflecting a European decision not to disengage from Africa despite widespread tensions over decolonization. By 1999 the Lomé Agreement had been expanded to include a total of seventy-one states, including fifteen from the Caribbean, eight from the Pacific, and forty-eight from Africa. The EU members now provide the African Union with nearly half of the region's development aid and facilitate the access of African products to European markets.

Headquartered in Addis Ababa, the AU member countries total over one billion people. Agricultural development and food security continue to be the focus of AU-EU negotiations, as Europe's Common Agricultural Policy protects European farming, limiting the export of African agricultural commodities. Thus the goal of a free-trade area between the two regions remains unrealized, although there has been an agreement to establish a customs union by 2014.

Expanding its function, ECOWAS has become a political cover for the troops of Nigeria and other West African states to send peacekeeping forces to Liberia and Sierra Leone. The EU has sent peacekeepers to Burundi, Somalia, and Darfur, and France has independently dispatched peacekeeping troops to Mauritania, Togo, Mali, and Chad.

Another regional economic grouping, the fourteen-member Southern African Development Community (SADC), which intervened in the Democratic Republic of Congo, has also sought to turn itself into a regional security force. In effect, the civil war there was expanded into a regional conflict. Angola, Zimbabwe, and Namibia, acting on behalf of SADC, sent peacekeeping troops into Congo to save the Laurent Kabila regime from being toppled by rebels. The rebels were supported by forces from Rwanda, Uganda, and Burundi. Thus, three Southern African states became arrayed against three East African Nilotic countries.

South Africa, by far the largest and most economically powerful of the SADC members, has opposed this intervention. Without South African support, SADC has little political or economic power.

ECOWAS and SADC are the most important of the present regional groups. There are others, such as the Common Market for Eastern and Southern Africa (COMESA) and the Economic Community of Central African States. All of these organizations, however, have made little progress in furthering regional economic integration, in part because of the protectionist policies of the various states.

Geographical Background

Sub-Saharan Africa has a population of over 900 million that is widely scattered for several reasons. One is the broad spread of arable lands throughout the higher areas of the tropical and subtropical parts of the continent. Another is the limited extent of the various coastlines. A third is the multiplicity of widely separated river systems, each of which tends to attract denser settlements to the lower and middle courses.

No single coastal area in Sub-Saharan Africa possesses the population and economic concentrations that are necessary for a dominant regional power to arise. The region's largest country, Nigeria, has 175 million people, or nearly 18 percent of the population of the African subcontinent. However, Nigeria is torn by regional and religious factionalism.

The region is predominantly black racially, with Europeans, Indians, and Arabs combined representing under 5 percent of the total. However, Africa is subdivided into over one thousand ethnolinguistic groups, contributing to its atomization. Much of Sub-Saharan Africa's 7,800,000 square miles is unsuited to absorbing the rapidly increasing population. Tropical rain forests, poor and dry savanna soils, and deserts are all impediments to agriculture and settlement. Most of the subcontinent consists of high plateau that has experienced successive geologic uplifts, and much of it is inaccessible to the coast. The smooth, emerged coastal plains are narrow, covering a much smaller proportion of the land area than do coastal plains in other continents, and they afford few good, natural harbors. Where these plains do occur, they frequently are too dry and therefore are lightly populated or quite narrow and blocked off from the interior by highlands. Some coastal areas were also depopulated by slaving activities.

Development of modern urban economies has been inhibited by lack of such large, coastal populations in much of the region. There are important exceptions, however. These include the mouths of the Niger and the coastal lands along the Gulf of Guinea to the west and east, the lower Congo, the southwestern and eastern coasts of South Africa, coastal Tanzania, and eastern Madagascar. The rich oil and gas reserves of the Niger delta and the Gulf of Guinea waters, as well as Angola's offshore deposits, have played the key role in the developments of their coastal lands. Much of the revenues that have been generated by the energy resources have been squandered by corrupt regimes rather than applied to basic development purposes.

TRANSPORTATION

The railroad has not played the pioneering nation-building and economic development role in Sub-Saharan Africa that it has played elsewhere in the world, especially in the United States, Western Europe, the Eurasian heartland, southern Brazil, and the Pampas of Argentina. In those cases, railways served to attract large-scale settlement, first agricultural and then urban, and became the backbones of national ecumenes. On the African subcontinent, the role of railroads has been limited to transporting minerals and commercial crops to the sea for export rather than serving as frameworks for dense population and economic activities. Not only are fifteen of the Sub-Saharan states landlocked, but also in many other of the region's countries, mineral and timber resources are located in remote regions with sparse populations.

Indeed, instead of becoming nation-building agents, most of the railroads have been centrifugal forces. The Katanga (Shaba) railway in southeastern Congo runs to Benguela on the Atlantic coast of Angola rather than to the political capital of the DRC in Kinshasa, which is located on the lower course of the River Congo. Another rail line from Shaba connects with the Zambian and Zimbabwean systems to the port of Maputo on Mozambique's Indian Ocean coast. While the Katanga secession movement of the early 1960s was ultimately quashed, the separatist tendencies of the Katangese have been reinforced by geographical isolation and continue to simmer. This is despite the fact that Shaba's land connections to the rest of Congo have been improved in recent years.

Another important railway that has failed to attract broad economic development is the Tazara (Tan-Zam) Railway. It was built in the 1970s by China (fifteen thousand Chinese workers were involved in the construction) in its efforts to gain influence in East Africa. The line extends for eleven hundred miles and connects landlocked Zambia to the sea via Tanzania's port of Dar es Salaam. The railway's geopolitical significance is that it has freed Zambia from having to export its major copper resources through the Zimbabwean rail system to either the Mozambique ports of Beira and Maputo or the ports of South Africa. In recent years the railroad has been paralleled by a highway and an oil pipeline. While the Tazara line has been economically important to Zambia, it has not appreciably helped to broaden the country's economy, nor has it served as the spine of a corridor of major settlement and economic activity for either Zambia or Tanzania.

In general, transportation remains the Achilles heel of Africa's economic development efforts. Rail freight rates are much higher than in other parts of the developing world—50 percent higher than in Latin America and twice as high as in Asia. Road systems are even more problematic, as they suffer from continuing deterioration due to inadequate maintenance that is exacerbated by unfavorable conditions relating to climate, vegetation, and terrain.

ECONOMY

Sub-Saharan Africa is the poorest region in the world, with an average per capita income of slightly over $2,300. Even more alarming, 70 percent of the region's working poor earn less than two dollars per day. The pervasive poverty is aggravated by an international debt to foreign governments and international lenders. While at the end of the year 2000, the industrial nations of the world agreed to provide debt relief to the twenty-two poorest countries—eighteen of which were located within Sub-Saharan Africa (the other four were in Latin America), this has done little to ameliorate the region's poverty. Today nineteen of the twenty poorest countries in the world are located within Sub-Saharan Africa. While direct foreign investments have tripled since 2000, they still represent only 7 percent of total world investment in developing countries. In addition, much of this investment is in oil development that does not benefit most of the poor.[6] Over the past few years, the GDPs of Sub-Saharan Africa's countries have increased at an annual rate of 5 to 6 percent. While this offers a ray of hope for lifting the region out of poverty, this growth has only brought the regional economy back to where it was more than a decade ago. Sub-Saharan Africa continues to remain in a condition of economic and therefore geopolitical dependence upon the outside world—a reality underscored by the acrimony that was evinced in the rejection by most African nations of the EU's proposal for a Euro-African Free Trade Agreement at the December 2007 Lisbon Conference. In addition to inadequate capital investment, the region is plagued by HIV-AIDS and other diseases, such as Ebola, civil strife, and war.

While minerals, including petroleum, and commercial crops and fibers are important generators of export currency and have expanded the region's GDP by over 5 percent per annum in recent years, they cannot support the continent's vast subsistence agricultural and urban population. Swings in international mineral prices and high foreign tariffs on agricultural products contribute to economic instability. In addition, corruption siphons off much of the export income into the pockets of the political and economic elite. Periodic crop failures brought on by drought and plant disease devastate the rural countryside, forcing waves of hunger-stricken subsistence farmers to abandon their homes for crime-ridden urban slums in the major cities that cannot support existing populations, let alone absorb these newcomers. The refugees from famine, as well as those fleeing war-torn areas, gain some measure of security and access to food from international relief agencies but remain rootless in their cities of refuge. The flight from countryside to city is also accelerated by the land consolidation that goes hand in hand with agricultural development efforts to increase farm productivity.

The tragic consequences of this massive flight are reflected painfully in the urban anarchy that prevails in Lagos. This Nigerian megacity has grown from a peaceful center of two hundred thousand half a century ago to a metropolis of over twenty-one million, the largest in all of Africa. It lacks any semblance of an urban infrastructure, as the continuing streams of newcomers take shelter in shantytowns and in the devastated areas, amid open sewers and with limited access to potable water. Disease is rife, children are unschooled, and crime is endemic. Yet Nigerian migrants keep fleeing the drought-stricken Sahel to the cities. Unless a major international effort is made to stabilize Lagos and the other megacities of the Third World, there is little prospect that the urban tragedy can be ameliorated.

A major challenge for Sub-Saharan Africa, as in so many parts of the developing world, is to find ways of increasing farm output and incomes of small farmers. In the region as a whole, less than 40 percent of the population is urban. In many African countries, 60 to 80 percent of the population consists of an impoverished rural peasantry. Estimates for oil-rich Nigeria and Angola, for example, are over 50 and over 60 percent, respectively. Even in South Africa, which has the most advanced economy of the region, the rural populace is 40 percent.

The role of manufacturing in the region's economy remains very limited except in South Africa. An indicator of Africa's lag in this sector is its minimal participation in world merchandise trade. While developing nations as a whole now account for more than one-third of the world's total merchandise exports, Sub-Saharan Africa's share of world trade is minuscule, and less than 10 percent of its trade is intraregional. While the EU is the region's largest trade partner, China is by far the leading single trading source for imports and exports. This lack of exchange contributes to the atmosphere of isolation and atomization and feeds long-held antagonisms and hostilities among the member states of the region.

Under these woeful human and economic conditions, it is clear that Sub-Saharan Africa lacks the capacity to advance without massive economic and technical aid and capital investment from the developed world. Ameliorating the plight of the rural and urban poor by improving health, fighting disease, providing safe water and sanitation, and reducing illiteracy will require far greater investment than has heretofore been provided. The aid that the region has been receiving in the form of grants and loans has amounted to billions of dollars over the decades, and it annually accounts for 10 percent of the economic activity of the subcontinent. However, it has proven to be insufficient and has not been used effectively. Since the region has the world's most rapid population growth, with a median age of fifteen in ten of its countries, birth control measures are necessary to balance the population growth that would accompany improvements in health and other living conditions.[7]

Even with increased aid and additional loan forgiveness packages, there will not be significant economic progress for the region without elimination of corruption and the encouragement of interstate cooperative projects. However, such steps will have limited impact unless the conflicts that sap the human and economic development capacities of Sub-Saharan Africa can be radically reduced. Regrettably, regional geopolitical structural trends provide little evidence that the atomization that is both cause and effect of Africa's current economic and political plight will soon run its course.

Geopolitical Features

In its geopolitical features and patterns, Sub-Saharan Africa is the least mature region of the world's geopolitical system, and there is little likelihood that it will soon evolve coherent geopolitical structures that could overcome the current regional atomization.

HISTORIC REGIONAL CORE

No single place can lay claim to have planted the seed of Sub-Saharan African unity and thus fulfill the role of historic political core. The leading early proponent of Pan-Africanism, Kwame Nkrumah, led Ghana to independence from his base in Accra. Although Ghana received considerable economic and technical aid from both the United States and the Soviet Union, falling world cocoa prices and ill-conceived large-scale development projects led to economic chaos and the overthrow of Nkrumah in 1966. Ghana then lost its role as a Third World ideological leader, the country being plagued with political instability and military rule that depressed it for more than three decades. Since then, it has recovered from its impoverishment of that period. Democracy has been restored through a multiparty system, and Ghana is on the verge of becoming middle income, adding the manufacturing of clothing and the expansion of service industries to its traditional economic base of cocoa and timber exports. This is supplemented by exports of such minerals such as gold, bauxite, diamonds, and manganese.

Lomé, the capital of Togo and the founding site for ECOWAS, has also failed to become a rallying point for regional unity. The same applies to Arusha in Tanzania, which was the site for President Julius Nyerere's 1967 Arusha Declaration, in which he called for African socialism, egalitarianism, hard work, and self-reliance. The declaration had a powerful influence within Africa during this period, and the city became the headquarters of the East African Community. However, the EAC was later disbanded because of intraregional conflict. Thus, Arusha did not sustain the spirit of Pan-Africanism in changing political and economic times, and it became merely an interesting historical footnote.

The African Union (AU) is modeled after the European Union. The AU has a much broader mandate than its predecessor, the OAU. Its lofty goals include achieving political and economic integration among its members, promotion of democratic institutions, and good governance. A common parliament, central bank, court of justice, and a single currency are also envisaged.[8] The organization is also authorized to intervene in stopping genocide, war crimes, and human rights abuses. Under this mandate, it has been enlisted in attempts to halt the bloodletting in Darfur, but with little success. For the most part, peacekeeping within Sub-Saharan Africa continues to depend on UN-organized troops or those of individual states, especially France.

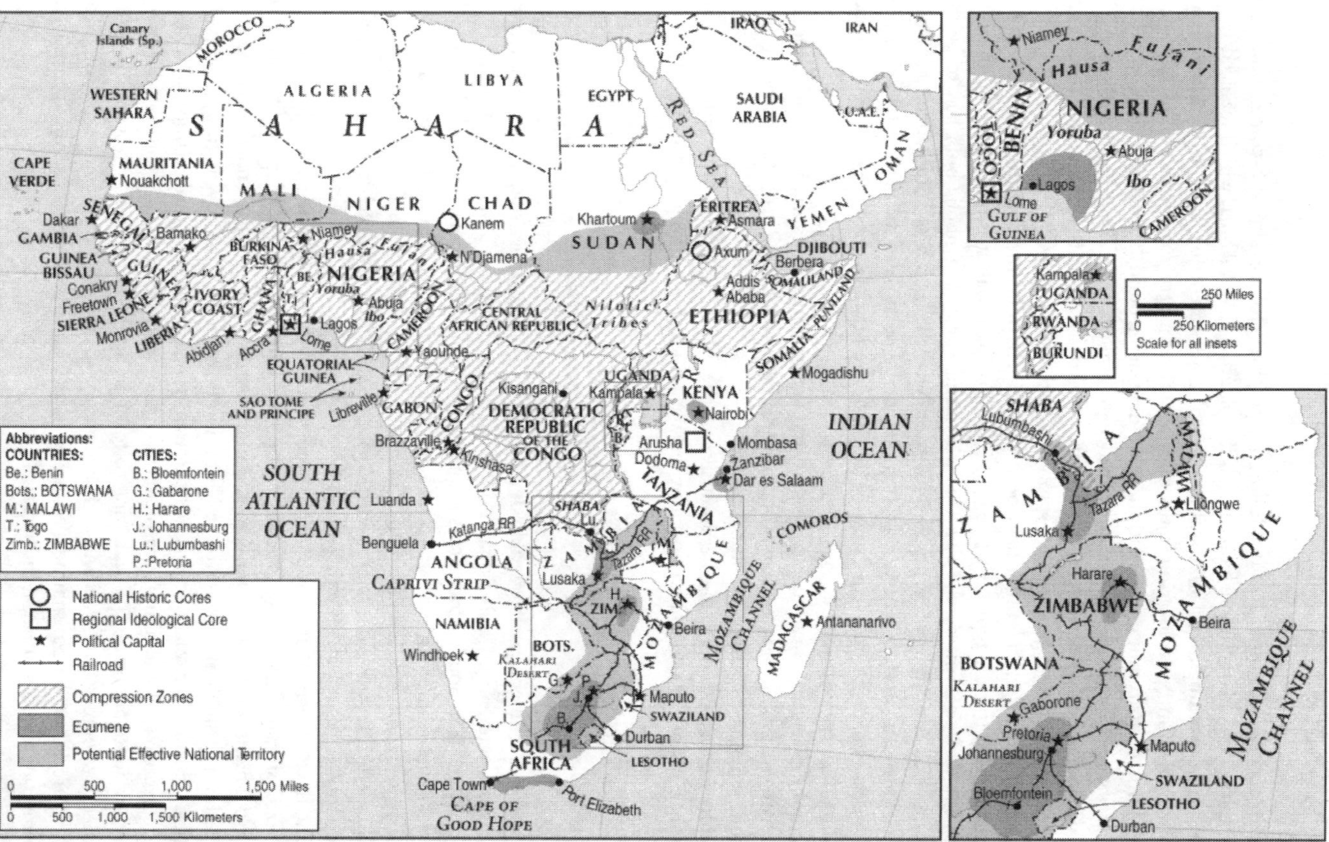

Figure 13.1. Sub-Saharan African Shatterbelt: Major Geopolitical Features

POLITICAL CAPITALS

Similarly, no current political center holds the potential for becoming a contemporary regional political core. Nigeria's federal capital, the planned city of Abuja, which replaced Lagos as the seat of government in 1991, is the center of government for West Africa's largest and most powerful country. Its location in the middle of the country was selected for its salubrious climate, limited surrounding population, and "neutral" ground between North and South. However, Nigeria's cohesiveness is undermined by political strife and violence. Lagos, the largest urban center, has been the scene of unrestrained ethnic strife between the Yoruba and Hausa and has become a geographical symbol of national disunity.

South Africa's Pretoria might have been a candidate to become Southern Africa's political capital, but it is more representative of the colonial past than it is of future African unity. Built by the white colonizers, the city has little in the way of a symbolic built landscape that can evoke black African political aspirations. Moreover, the leaders of South Africa have only recently evinced interest in seeking regional influence. For most of the period following Nelson Mandela's ascension to the presidency in 1994, the new black regime has been absorbed in national, not regional, affairs.

Nairobi, Kenya, is headquarters for several international organizations, including the UN's environmental programs. It was the historical capital of the British East Africa Protectorate but remains essentially a regional center.

Addis Ababa, Ethiopia, the headquarters of the AU, is located in the Horn of Africa on the margins of the region and does not serve as an ideological rallying point for the Sub-Saharan continent.

ECUMENE

Since national ecumenes are so weakly developed, it is little wonder that there are few traces of a regional ecumene in Sub-Saharan Africa. The subcontinent's only well-developed national ecumene is in South Africa. This economic and population core area extends across the Transvaal from its hub in greater Johannesburg, northward toward the border of Zambia and southeastward across the Drakensburg Mountains to the coast, from Durban southward to Port Elizabeth. However, the main South African ecumene has no physical connection with the economic core area of adjoining Zimbabwe.

One development that may someday lead to a Southern Africa regional core is the potential extension of South Africa's ecumene into Mozambique via the Maputo Development Corridor. This is an improved rail and toll highway corridor that runs northeastward from Johannesburg through Swaziland to the Mozambique coast at Maputo. A natural gas pipeline from fields in the Transvaal also extends through the corridor. Maputo's economy has been strengthened by steel and aluminum plants anchoring the eastern end of the corridor, while a ribbon of dense population is beginning to form along the transit way. However, intensive industrial development in Swaziland and the interior sections of Mozambique are still in the distant future. A smaller transnational ecumene—the Copperbelt—extends from northeastern Zambia into Congo's southeastern Shaba.

EFFECTIVE REGIONAL TERRITORY

Two vast grassland areas—the Southern African savanna, which extends from the Transvaal through Zimbabwe and Zambia, and the West African Sahel and Savanna grasslands have the potential for becoming effective regional territories. However, the obstacles to the mergers of the effective national territories in these areas are formidable. Scarcity of rainfall, disease (both cattle and human), and distance from open seas thwart the potential for oceanic trade. The semiarid Sahel, which extends from Senegal through Mauritania, Mali, Burkina Faso, Niger, and northern Nigeria and thence into Sudan and Ethiopia, suffered disastrous droughts and famines in the 1970s and 1990s. This brought devastation to the region and resulted in the depopulation of vast areas rather than absorption of the additional populations that effective national and regional territories must be able to attract.

BOUNDARIES

Another major geopolitical feature—boundaries—also reflects the geopolitical immaturity of the region. Some of Sub-Saharan Africa's borders have never been clearly demarcated and remain in dispute. Others, while demarcated, separate territories that are claimed by two or more states and are the sources of often bitter conflict. These boundaries cut across ethnotribal, linguistic, or religious groupings, leaving substantial minorities on one side of the border who seek to reunite with transborder kinfolk (see table 13.1).[9] Tables 13.1 and 13.2 present current and latent boundary and territorial disputes and note their status.[10]

Table 13.1. Sub-Saharan Africa: Current Boundary and Territorial Disputes

Countries	*Disputed Boundary*	*Disputed Territory*
Cameroon	International boundary—delimitation in Lake Chad (involves Chad, Niger, Nigeria)	
Comoros		Claim Mayotte Ile from France; Iles of Mwali and Nzwani secessionists seek return to France
Congo/DRC-Congo/Brazzaville	Most of Congo River boundary indefinite except in Stanley Pool area	
Eritrea-Djibouti	Ras Doumeira Red Sea headland and island	
Ethiopia-Somalia		Somalia claims southern half of Ethiopia's Ogaden Desert region
Gabon-Equatorial Guinea	Maritime boundary—oil-rich waters of Gulf of Corisco Bay	
Gabon-Nigeria	Maritime boundary—oil-rich waters of Gulf of Guinea	
Gambia-Senegal	Short section of boundary indefinite	
Madagascar		Glorioso Iles and Juan de Nova Island, from France
Niger		12,000 square miles of northern Niger claimed by Libya
Somalia		Divisions between Somaliland, "Puntland," and rest of Somalia
Swaziland		Claims territory held by South Africa

Table 13.2. Sub-Saharan Africa: Latent Boundary and Territorial Disputes

Countries	*Disputes*
Cameroon-Niger	Bakassi Peninsula and nearby island divided between the two countries. Military clashes in 1990s. Rich offshore oil deposits.
Chad-Libya	43,000 sq. mi. Aozou Strip in northern Chad claimed by Libya. War in 1980s. Awarded to Chad by ICJ in 1993. Rich in uranium.
Ghana-Togo	Pan-Ewe secessionist movement in southern Togo. Quiescent since 1980s.
Kenya-Somalia	Dormant dispute in Kenya's northeastern province over rights of Somalian majority to join Somalia.
Lesotho-South Africa	South Africa sovereignty over Transkei, which received independence in 1976 and was absorbed by South Africa in 1994.
Namibia-Botswana	Sovereignty over Kasikili Island in Linyanti River resolved in favor of Botswana by ICJ in 1999.
Senegal-Mauritania	Dispute over grazing rights in southern Mauritania. Clashes in 1989.
Tanzania-Malawi	Dispute over Lake Malawi.

Note: ICJ = International Court of Justice.

Many of the boundary conflicts cannot be separated from broader disputes over control of natural resources, access to the sea, and reunification of peoples. Nor can they be disentangled from civil strife and governmental instability in a particular country, which may lead to the porousness of its borders—a major contributor to conflict in Sub-Saharan Africa. Uncontrolled borders permit guerrilla groups to operate from bases outside a country and to make transborder strikes, drawing adjoining states into the conflict. Congo/DRC and Zambia were used as bases for Angolan rebels in their battle for independence against the Portuguese. Later Angola served as the organizing center for Namibian rebels in their campaign to gain freedom from South Africa. Zambia was accused by the Angolan government of permitting the UNITA rebel movement to maintain itself by selling diamonds across the porous Zambian border and bringing back military supplies. As another example, Mozambique provided a secure headquarters for the leadership of the Zimbabwean rebel guerrillas in their fight for independence.

Guinean rebels operating from Sierra Leone and Liberia have launched transborder attacks against Guinea's army, devastating parts of the country's southwestern and southeastern border regions. Botswana shelters Lozi tribesmen from Namibia, who use bases there to attempt to create a separate Lozi state in Namibia's Caprivi Strip and parts of southwest Zambia. The narrow Caprivi Strip, fifty miles wide and three hundred miles in length, juts into Botswana and Zambia several hundreds of miles from Namibia's major centers and is highly vulnerable to border incursions by the Lozi rebels.

The civil war in Sierra Leone, which raged from 1992 to 2002, was fueled by support from Charles Taylor, the Liberian dictator, who enabled the rebels to purchase their arms. The rebels controlled the southeastern part of the country, the heart of the diamond mining and trading industry. It was only with Taylor's resignation and exile that Sierra Leone was able to achieve peace and hold elections in 2002 and 2007, with the participation of the former rebels. Taylor, the warlord who kept his own country in turmoil for years, had plundered Liberia, leaving the country in abject poverty from which it is only beginning to emerge owing to revenues from its international shipping fleet and rubber. In 2012, Taylor was found guilty by a Special Court at The Hague for his brutal crimes and sentenced to life in prison in Britain.

One of the most volatile of recent conflicts has raged along the border between Congo/DRC and Rwanda. Rwandan Hutu guerrillas who had fled into eastern Congo have used bases there to launch transborder raids against the Tutsi-controlled government in Rwanda. Burundi rebels, also operating from Congo territory, have mounted raids against Burundi's Tutsi regime. It was because of the inability, or lack of desire, of Congo's president, the late Laurent Kabila, to put an end to the Rwandan Hutu raids that the Rwandan government, joined by Uganda, sided with the Congolese rebels seeking to overthrow Kabila. Ironically, the Tutsi president of Rwanda, Paul Kagame, had initially sided with the Kabila insurgency, which overthrew the Congolese dictator Mobutu Sese Seko in 1997 because Mobutu had permitted the Rwandan Hutus to take refuge in eastern Congo.

The Central African Republic has been torn by civil war between its Muslim and Christian populations. In 2012 Muslim rebels from the North, who are mainly herders and nomads, encroached upon the lands of Christian farmers to their south, overthrowing the government. With the help of two thousand French troops, the Muslims were ousted the following year and the government restored. Christian militias then took vengeance with wanton killings of Muslims, causing thousands of Muslims to flee the country. The AU then sent in six thousand troops as peacekeepers, including detachments from Chad, some of which were accused of siding with the Muslims. This became a controversial issue, leading to withdrawal of the Chadians from the peacekeeping force. In an effort to stabilize the country, the French troops remained, and the EU has promised to augment them with another one thousand soldiers.

In the Horn of Africa, the long-running rebellion of the Eritreans against Amharic Ethiopian rule spanned the regimes of both Emperor Haile Selassie and Mengistu Haile Mariam, who overthrew Selassie in 1974. In the 1980s the Eritreans joined forces with Ethiopian rebels from the province of Tigre, and together they eventually overthrew the Soviet-supported Marxist government of Mengistu, spelling the end of centuries of Amharic domination. In 1993 the new Ethiopian government, now controlled by the leader of the former rebels, Meles Zenawi, agreed to the independence of Eritrea. Inasmuch as the separation left Ethiopia landlocked, the Eritreans granted it a free port at Aseb, which is connected to Ethiopia by highway. It appeared that peace had finally come.

However, the former allies soon stumbled into war with each other over parts of the 625-mile boundary that had never been delineated. The focus of the fighting was possession of the Badme (Yirga) Triangle. With large numbers of battle-hardened troops on both sides, what started as minor skirmishes in 1998 developed into full-scale war. A cease-fire brokered by the OAU in the summer of 1999 was broken a year later, when the Ethiopians pushed into Eritrea, displacing upward of a million Eritreans. A second cease-fire was signed in September 2000, with both sides agreeing to return to the line that existed before the initial Eritrean invasion.

A small UN peacekeeping force was deployed within a sixteen-mile buffer zone along this line, and both countries have agreed to the demarcation of the border by the United Nations. An Independent Boundary Commission completed the demarcation in April 2002, awarding the disputed town of Badme to Eritrea. While Addis Ababa initially rejected this decision, it has since accepted outside mediation, which confirmed the placement of the boundary. The cost of the conflict between these former allies has been one hundred thousand soldiers killed, widespread devastation of the landscape, and massive displacement of Eritrean refugees. The economic development of two of the world's poorest countries has been pushed backward even further.

As a result of the conflict and despite the peace accord, landlocked Ethiopia has shifted from using the Eritrean port of Aseb as its main outlet for trade to using Djibouti and Berbera.

A large share of the country's imports and exports now move via the 487-mile railroad from Djibouti to Addis Ababa. This slow and antiquated line, completed in 1929, must climb a tortuous mountain route to reach the capital on the Ethiopian plateau, eight thousand feet above sea level. The smaller port of Berbera in Somalia's breakaway state of Somaliland, has become increasingly important as an *entrepôt* for Ethiopia. The former British Somaliland has become politically stable through the establishment of a representative, clan-based government. While Berbera has no railway, its highway connection to Addis Ababa via the Ethiopian commercial center of Harar is the easiest and fastest of the transit ways. Large food shipments for famine relief entered through Berbera in 2000, and the Ethiopian government has cautiously developed other economic relationships with Somaliland.[11] Following the terrorist destruction of the World Trade Center on September 11, 2001, Washington established a US Naval Expeditionary Base at Djibouti, which remains a centerpiece for US strategic oversight of the region.

Most of Sub-Saharan Africa's border disputes are the legacy of colonial boundary making, just as so much of the civil strife within the region's various states is a product of dividing up territories to suit European colonial aims or to accommodate competing aims. As noted earlier, there is a difference of opinion about whether to tamper with these borders to make states more ethnically cohesive or to enlarge them to create more economically feasible states.

LANDLOCKED AREAS

The especially large number of landlocked countries, sixteen in all, is a unique geopolitical feature of Sub-Saharan Africa. These countries are Mali, Burkina Faso, Niger, Chad, South Sudan, the Central African Republic, Uganda, Rwanda, Burundi, Zambia, Malawi, Zimbabwe, Botswana, Swaziland, Lesotho, and Ethiopia. Their populations represent 40 percent of the total population of the region. The only other region that begins to approximate such a density of landlocked states is Central Asia, Afghanistan, and the Caucasus, which in combination have eight such national units.

Sub-Saharan Africa's landlocked states are among the poorest in the world, possessing lower per capita incomes than even their own coastal neighbors, most of whom rank among the world's least developed countries. These landlocked countries are dependent upon costly, slow, and often unreliable land and river corridors to the open seas. Rising oil costs and plunging prices of commodities play havoc with already fragile economies, while transit fees levied by coastal states add to the costs of imports and exports. Lack of direct access to the oceans also inhibits economic specialization and thus adds to the economic weakness of these states.

In the center of the region, Lake Chad has shrunk to 5 percent of its 1963 size because of the construction of large-scale irrigation projects that have diverted the waters from the feeder streams. What is left of the lake is a series of small ponds and islands. The problem has been compounded by less-than-normal monsoon rains during this period, exacerbated by the encroachment of the Sahara due to climate change. The ecological damage that has been done to the lake's fisheries and the impact of shoreline retreat are causes of considerable political tension among the four states that border the water body—Nigeria, Niger, Cameroon, and Chad—as well as affecting the lives of twenty million farmers.[12]

In Rwanda, the genocide of up to eight hundred thousand minority Tutsis and moderate Hutus was perpetrated by extremist Hutus after the airplane carrying Hutu president Juvénal Habyarimana was shot down and he was killed. Paul Kagame, leader of the rebel Tutsis, put an end to the killings. He then became president, stabilizing and uniting the country. Kagame has raised living standards, attracted investments, reduced corruption, and improved women's rights. Today, the official policy of the country is "No Tutsis and no Hutus, only Rwandans"—it is working.

Without secure access to the sea, the sovereignty of landlocked states is often compromised and they are subject to military as well as economic pressures from their neighbors. A driving force behind the various attempts to establish federations in both East and West Africa has been the incentive for their landlocked countries to link up with coastal states to gain such access. This was also a major factor in the establishment of the Southern African Development Community (SADC), for it offers the landlocked states of Zambia, Zimbabwe, Malawi, Botswana, Swaziland, and Lesotho not only the promise of lower common tariffs but also cheaper and more efficient transportation to the sea.

Even the coastal states have landlocked interior sections, and these are the least-developed parts within those countries. The southern coastal parts of the West African countries that adjoin the Atlantic Ocean were developed by the European colonial powers for their agricultural, forest, and mineral resources. In the process, these sea-oriented regions were also Christianized. However, the Europeans had little interest in developing the northern grassland portions of their colonies and allowed them to languish economically. The fact that the populations of these interior regions were Muslim added a religious dimension to the schism. The current bitter struggles between northern and southern Nigeria are a reflection of this economic/religious rift.

Ironically, the northern belt was once the locus of great medieval Muslim kingdoms (the Mali, Sengali, and Kitari) founded by Arab traders who had drawn their wealth from the trans-Saharan trade in gold, salt, and slaves. However, the mobility of the desert- and grassland-based camel men and horsemen lost its effectiveness when they tried to penetrate the coastal equatorial rain forests. This left these areas open to sea power and allowed the Portuguese, at the end of the fifteenth century, and the other European powers who followed to establish coastal bases. From there, European imperialism eventually took control of the interior. The Europeans created the trade that led to the control of mineral and slave wealth and to the establishment of cities and commercial agriculture. This shifted the economic balance from the interior to the coast, a condition that continues to this day. With the discovery of coastal and offshore oil and gas deposits in recent decades, the gap between coast and interior has widened.

Regional Subdivisions

While Sub-Saharan Africa is divided into six subregions—East, West, Central, Northern, Southern, and the Horn of Africa—only two of them, West and Southern Africa, have the potential to become cohesive geopolitical units led by a regional power.

Central and Northern Africa are the most geopolitically problematic of the subregions, now that Congo has imploded as an organized state. Central Africa constitutes a compression zone that extends from East Africa and the African Horn to West Africa.

A second compression zone, Northern Africa, has developed along the northern fringe of Sub-Saharan Africa. It embraces the short-grass Sahel and the tall-grass savanna belts that are bordered by the Sahara to the north and the rain forest to the south. The zone extends from Mauritania on the Atlantic eastward through the Sudan. Muslim herders and nomads occupy the northern part of the zone, and Christians the southern part. Jihadists and other Muslim extremist groups operating from northern bases wage civil war against the governments of the more populous south. Their ranks are reinforced by extremists from the Sahara and lands to the north, such as Algeria, Libya, and Tunisia. These rebels have fostered rebellions in Mali, Niger, Chad, and northern Nigeria, supporting themselves through smuggling cigarettes, weapons, and drugs to Europe via coastal countries like Guinea-Bissau.

The governments of this zone are too weak to quash the rebels and depend upon outside troops to retain control. ECOWAS has sent troops to help, but they are dependent upon Western logistics and intelligence. It is essentially French military intervention, especially in Chad and Mali, which has kept the Muslim extremists in check. Of all of the Sub-Sahara African shatterbelts, this zone is the most highly fragmented.

Several factors prevent East Africa from developing a cohesive core. One is the fairly even balance in population and resources among its three large states—Kenya, Uganda, and Tanzania. Another is the civil strife between the Hutu and Tutsi populations that tore Rwanda and Burundi apart and spilled over to eastern Congo. Historically cool relations between Uganda and Tanzania have also played a role. In 1978 Uganda invaded Kagera, the tin-mining and coffee-producing region of northwest Tanzania, seeking to annex it. The Tanzanians counterattacked the following year, liberating Kagera and then capturing Kampala, Uganda's capital. They drove Idi Amin from office and kept their occupation forces in Uganda until 1981.

It was Uganda's 1998 invasion of eastern Congo, where Ugandan rebels had found safe haven, which helped precipitate the war within Congo that has cost over five million lives. While a formal peace was signed between the government and the rebels in 2004, the conflict between the Congolese Tutsi and the central government continued to rage. Another peace agreement was reached with the rebels in 2008, but the fighting continues to simmer. Another point of contention between Uganda and Congo is their water boundary within Lake Albert, and particularly the ownership of Rukwanzi Island at the southern end of the lake, where oil was discovered in 2006.

PROSPECTS FOR REGIONAL POWER CENTERS

It is in the remaining two regions—Southern Africa and West Africa—that prospects for regional cohesion are greatest, because each has a large and relatively powerful leading state, with Nigeria in West Africa and South Africa in Southern Africa. However, even though these countries are much stronger than their neighbors militarily and economically, each has internal weaknesses that will have to be overcome before it can play a successful regional power role. Moreover, the fragmentation in West Africa is so great that regional integration there is highly elusive.

No single state within Sub-Saharan Africa has the potential to become a major, or first-order, power that can gain ascendancy over the subcontinent. At best, the prospects are for regional, or second-order, powers to emerge that will be able to dominate the subregions within which they are located.

Southern Africa

South Africa is, by far, the most powerful state economically, not only in Southern Africa but also within the subcontinent as a whole. With its population of fifty million, or half of the subregion's total, it has an economy that is three times as large as the combined economies of the thirteen other members of the SADC and accounts for 40 percent of the GNP of all of Sub-Saharan Africa. Nevertheless, the South African government throughout the 1990s was unwilling to influence SADC with respect to the war in Congo. It opposed sending troops there to help the Kabila regime and has failed in its aim of having SADC act by consensus on security matters or in developing common tariff and banking arrangements.

In only one instance in the 1990s did South Africa turn from diplomacy and economics to influence affairs within SADC countries. This was in 1998, when it sent troops into Lesotho to reinstate the elected government of Ntsu Mokhehle, which had been toppled in a coup. The reason for intervention in this case was strategic, because Lesotho is totally enclosed within South African territory. Most recently, South Africa has modified its position with respect to involvement in regional conflicts. While it remains reluctant to impose its will upon warring states and peoples, it has adopted a proactive role as mediator and peacekeeper. Thus it has become involved in mediating the Congo civil war and has dispatched peacekeeping troops to Burundi, Congo, Ethiopia, Eritrea, and the Comoros. However, in 2008 it reverted to previous disengagement when it refused to press openly for the removal of Robert Mugabe, whose dictatorial rule brought Zimbabwe to the brink of economic collapse, reverting instead to ineffective diplomacy.

South Africa is far closer to becoming a regional power than is Nigeria. Economically, its per capita income is twice that of Nigeria and its manufacturing sector seven times as large. Unique among African states, it ranks as a middle-income, developed country, blessed with abundant natural resources, such as gold, diamonds, chromium, platinum, coal, iron, uranium, and copper. South African corporations have invested heavily in Southern Africa. In addition, it has a broad agricultural base that includes maize, wheat, sugarcane, fruit, vegetables, beef, poultry, dairy, and fish products.

South Africa not only has by far the strongest industrial manufacturing and service base of any African country but also is a major manufacturer of military arms and possesses excellent transportation and financial service networks. Moreover, the vicious apartheid system was dismantled through peaceful means when Nelson Mandela was elected president, replacing white with black rule and sparing South Africa the violence that has torn apart so many other African nations in their quests for independence. And stability has been maintained since Mandela's retirement from the presidency in 1999.

Despite the breadth of its human and material assets, South Africa contends with major problems. The diversified economy continues to be controlled by whites, who constitute under 15 percent of the country's population of fifty million people. There is an enormous income gap between blacks (who are 75 percent of the population) and others ("coloureds" and Asians, as well as whites), as 10 percent of the population owns half the wealth. Other serious problems are unemployment (30 percent of the workforce), poverty, crime, and HIV-AIDS. (This disease has spread so widely that the country's population has the highest infection rate in the world.) Because manufacturing is so advanced and employs only 15 percent of the workforce, opportunities for the black majority are limited. Another problem is that 90 percent of the arable land requires irrigation, while periodic droughts reduce employment opportunities in commercial agriculture. This marginalizes the many subsistence farmers who still make up a sizable portion of the rural populace, which is half of the country's total.

In the regional arena, the very fact that the economy of South Africa is so much more highly developed than that of the rest of Southern Africa, and indeed the entire subcontinent, means that South Africa has little reason to pursue intraregional trade. Its remoteness from the geographical center of Sub-Saharan Africa and poor continental transportation links make a significant increase in such trade unlikely, except for the growth of trade with nearby countries. This growth has been promoted through establishment of the Southern African Customs Union (SACU) in 2011. Led by South Africa, the union includes Botswana, Lesotho, Namibia, and Swaziland.

Most of the country's foreign trade is with China, maritime Europe, the United States, and Japan, but trade with China is rapidly increasing. The EU countries collectively are the largest trading partner, drawing 40 percent of total South African trade. Commerce is facilitated by a free-trade agreement between the EU and South Africa. South Africa also receives $600 million in annual economic aid from the EU as well as $300 million in military assistance. The fear of many African states is that South African manufactures would overwhelm their incipient industries were SADC to become a vehicle for reducing tariffs. They also perceive the strength and sophistication of South Africa's armed forces as a source of possible political and economic pressure against them. These considerations, in addition to South Africa's domestic racial and economic disparities, suggest that it will be many years before South Africa is able to exercise fully its capacities as a regional power. Without an improvement in the economic status of the black population of South Africa, internal political and economic turmoil is always a possibility.

With so much of the South African economy being white controlled, the potential for interracial strife remains. In their relations with their former masters, the black majority has thus far adhered to the nonviolent philosophies of such leaders as the late Nelson Mandela, Bishop Desmond Tutu, and Thabo Mbeki. However, a more radicalized generation of younger black South African leaders could try to redress current economic disparities by seeking to gain partial control of large industries or through large-scale land expropriations, as has occurred in Zimbabwe under the authoritarian regime of Robert Mugabe. There, the large landholders, who are mostly whites, owned 75 percent of the Zimbabwean farmland, although they number only 4.5 percent of the farmers. Mugabe encouraged black squatters to seize white-owned properties, adding to the turmoil in a country whose economy is in a state of near collapse.

In 2007, Zimbabwe's economy reached hyperinflation heights. This moved Mugabe to impose price controls, only to cause shopkeepers to remove goods from their shelves. Despite the dire circumstance of the country and despite the flawed elections of 2008 in which the opposition outpolled him, so far Mugabe has managed to hold onto power. Zambia, on the other hand, is relatively prosperous, owing to its rich Copperbelt deposits. Copper production continues to increase, finding a ready global market, especially in China. The country benefits from a strong infrastructure of railways, roads, and modern airports, which are supported by these exports.

Next to South Africa, the two largest countries in Southern Africa are Angola and Mozambique. Both have been torn by major civil wars, and both were deeply impoverished. Of the two, Angola has succeeded in strengthening its economy and becoming a strong force within the region. It has rich natural resources, including its leading exports of petroleum and natural gas as well as diamonds, timber, and foodstuffs. In fact, it is Sub-Saharan Africa's second-largest oil producer.

What undermined both its economy and society was the bitter civil war that raged after its independence from Portugal in 1975. The Marxist government that then gained control with the help of the Soviet Union and its Cuban surrogate maintained its position against the rebels, even after its patrons withdrew at the end of the Cold War. At the same time, South Africa and the United States ceased their support of the UNITA rebels, led by Jonas Savimbi, who are essentially drawn from the Ovimbindu, Angola's largest ethnic group, with 40 percent of the total population. Nevertheless, peace remained elusive, as a UN-sponsored peace initiative broke down in 1999. The struggle continued between the government based in Luanda and UNITA, with the latter financed by its illegal sale of diamonds from the areas under its control. The economic development of the country remained stalled; the United Nations peacekeepers left; the rebels controlled the countryside; the government controlled the cities; and the stalemate continued. Savimbi's death in battle in February 2002 brought dramatic change. The stalemate was broken, and peace was achieved.

Recovering from its civil war, which devastated the country and caused the loss of half a million lives, a now prosperous Angola now plays a role as a regional intervener. Not only has it participated in the SADC-Congo/DRC military venture but also, in 1997, it dispatched troops to the Republic of Congo (Congo-Brazzaville) to intervene in a civil war there. Its interest in the Congo was twofold: (1) during the Cold War, the "People's" Republic of the Congo was ruled by a Marxist party that had signed a treaty of friendship with the Soviet Union and looked to Angola as a model and (2) the Republic of the Congo adjoins the northern border of Angola's Cabinda exclave (Congo/DRC surrounds it from the south). Securing Cabinda from internal separatist movements as well as from threats from both Congo/DRC and the Congo-Brazzaville is of the highest priority for Angola. The exclave accounts for two-thirds of Angola's petroleum, while its rich offshore fields have considerable development potential.

Oil has catapulted Angola into geopolitical prominence as the world's tenth-largest oil producer, as well as the second-largest producer in Sub-Saharan Africa. International oil companies have invested heavily in its offshore oil fields, increasing annual production to two millions barrels per day in 2007 with increased production targets. Although Angola joined OPEC in 2007, the country has given little indication that it accepts quotas that might slow production growth. Since half of the offshore South Atlantic oil reserves lie within Angola's territorial waters, which also contain rich natural gas deposits, it is likely that it will reach its long-term targets.

Given political uncertainties in the Middle East, the United States expanded its oil imports from West Africa, mainly from Nigeria and Angola. This has proved to be only a transitional measure, as US domestic production, combined with imports from Canada and Mexico, has made African imports far less important. China, for its part, is now investing heavily in the development of Angola's offshore fields. It imports one-third of its oil from Africa, mainly from Angola, which is China's single largest supplier.

Mozambique, which had also gained independence from Portugal in 1975 under the leadership of a Marxist party, the Frelimo, was torn apart by civil war as well. The new Marxist regime was backed by the Soviet Union and Cuba, while the main supporter of the rebel Renamo movement was South Africa. A lengthy campaign of guerrilla warfare devastated the country, and the struggle continued throughout the decade. Frelimo formally abandoned Marxism, adopting a free-market economy, but the civil war did not end until 1992. The country continues to struggle with the return of more than one million war refugees and ravages from the worst droughts of the century. With a resource base far more limited than that of Angola, prospects are that Mozambique will continue to be mired in poverty and torn by civil strife.

West Africa

NIGERIA

Nigeria, by far the most populous of African states (175 million and climbing), has the highest GDP, nearly 40 percent greater than that of South Africa. Rich in resources, especially oil, its economy has grown by 7 percent per annum over the past decade. Nevertheless, most of this wealth has not trickled down to the bulk of the inhabitants, whose per capita income averages only $2,700 per annum, or half that of South Africans.

While telecommunications, banking, filmmaking, and construction are fast-growing industries, the rest of the economy languishes. Development is stymied by poor infrastructure, including an unreliable electrical grid system and widespread corruption. The country is also weakened by rebellion of the militant Islamic Boko Haram in the northeast. While Nigeria has the resource base and oil wealth to be the core state of West Africa, it falls short of being able to realize its geopolitical power potential.

This has not prevented Nigeria from aggressively intervening in the affairs of other West African states. As the region's military giant, it has organized and led military interventions in Liberia and Sierra Leone and has been the major contributor to the AU's peacekeeping forces in Darfur. In other displays of regional power, it maintains military advisers in Gambia and Chad and has used trade as a weapon to secure the compliance of the regimes of Benin and Niger.

Nigeria's entry into the Liberian conflict started with the rebellion by Charles Taylor in 1989. Nigerian jets and gunboats sought to stop Taylor's invasion and keep President Samuel Doe in office. The conflict raged until 1997, when Nigeria shifted its support to Taylor, enabling him to get the upper hand, impose a cease-fire, and gain the presidency through an election. While the cost of the Nigerian involvement was estimated at $2 billion, the Nigerian military has profited richly from control of Liberia's diamond and hardwood trade.

Sierra Leone, long torn by unrest, became a battleground when a military coup overthrew President Joseph Mobutu in 1992. The Nigerian intervention was mounted that year, when the Sierra Leone government requested help in defending itself against rebels based in Liberia and aided by arms that funnel through that country. In the ensuing year, the Nigerians succeeded in preventing the rebels from gaining control of Sierra Leone's various governments. However, they could not quell the rebel campaign of terror, maimings, and kidnappings that devastated the country.

Wearying of the continuous support of the conflict, Nigeria brought the two sides together in 1999 and forced the government to share power with the rebels. The truce was soon broken, as the rebels took five hundred UN peacekeepers hostage and attacked Freetown. The Nigerians, the core of the UN's single largest peacekeeping force, withdrew their troops in June 2000 in response to the disenchantment of the Nigerian populace with the costly and unproductive nine-year intervention. However, the war weariness of the Sierra Leoneans brought about peace in 2002, and national elections followed.

Despite these displays of regional power, the Nigerian domestic scene has been in turmoil because of corruption and mismanagement and has been fragmented by ethnic and religious strife. While a civilian government was established in 1999 after years of Muslim military rule, the regime remains unstable. The country has been divided nearly evenly between Muslims and Christians, but the former are becoming the majority due to higher birthrates. The Muslim Hausa and Fulani of the North, who make up nearly 30 percent of the population, are perennially at odds with the Christian Yoruba of the southwest and the Ibo of the southeast, each of which makes up approximately 20 percent of the populace. The massacres of the Ibo that touched off the Biafra civil war continue to haunt the country, and rebel activities in the Niger delta region continue to cause stoppages and reduction in the country's oil production. Introduction of Shariah (Islamic law) in a dozen of the northern Muslim states has sharpened the divide between north and south. This divide could eventually lead to the breakaway of the south, which remains impoverished despite its vast oil resources.

The north-south division is compounded by the volatility of the "Middle Belt"—the "breadbasket" of central Nigeria, which lies between the middle courses of the Niger and Benue Rivers. There the region is torn apart by ethnic, religious, and intercommunal fighting aggravated by drought, starvation, and poverty. While the Niger dams projects that were begun in the 1960s have helped to develop farming in the Middle Belt, the friction among the different tribes and clans, many of which have migrated from the north, keeps the region in continuing turmoil at a local communal level and is the source of increasing numbers of refugee camps within the belt. Massacres of Muslims by Christian militias in 2004 sharpened the sectarian conflict in the country. The reverse situation now occurs as Christians in the north are subject to widespread killings and kidnappings.

Revenues from vast petroleum resources in the Niger delta in southeastern Nigeria and in the Gulf of Guinea (the Bights of Guinea and Biafra) have done little to allay the poverty that grips nearly half of the region's population or to reduce the nearly 25 percent unemployment rate. Oil production is falling because of turbulence, and oil revenues are looted or squandered by governmental leaders, who are responsible for Nigeria's reputation as one the world's most corrupt countries.

Prolonged droughts in the Sahel of northern Nigeria, as well as the collapse of fishing in Lake Chad, which has shrunk as a result of the droughts, have pushed hundreds of thousands of migrants to the cities of the south. They cannot be readily absorbed there, and their presence further exacerbates the civil strife.

With the decline of agriculture, especially at the subsistence level, Nigeria, once a food exporter, must now import food. While the democratically elected regime in the federal capital of Abuja may be able to take the lead in mounting major peacekeeping efforts among its strife-torn neighbors, as it did in Liberia and Sierra Leone, its political and economic staying power as a regional influential state remains tenuous. Civilian governments that have led the country since 1999 have raised hopes among Nigerians that internal conflict will fade, but thus far it is still a hope, and the violence has continued. Until Nigeria coalesces around widely accepted national goals, stabilizes its government, and learns to use its oil revenues wisely, its role as a regional power is likely to be limited and its regional policies unpredictable.

The greatest danger facing the country is that the current wave of rebellion and terrorism will develop into full-scale war between the Islamic north and Christian south. Samuel P. Huntington's "Clash of Civilizations" may well be played out in Nigeria and extended into the rest of West Africa, which is also divided between Muslims and Christians.

OTHER WEST AFRICAN COUNTRIES

Elsewhere in West Africa, civil wars in Liberia, Sierra Leone, and Guinea have ended. However, much of the rest of the region continues to be caught up in civil strife and border wars. Côte d'Ivoire (Ivory Coast) was West Africa's most stable and prosperous nation from its independence until 1993, when its founding father, Félix Houphouët-Boigny, died. At that time, the impoverished, mainly Muslim Sahelian northern half of the country broke away from the south, claiming that its people were discriminated against by the Christian and traditional animist believers. Many of those living in the north come from neighboring Sahelian lands and lack citizenship. A UN "confidence zone" divides the rebel and government-held zones, manned largely by French peacekeepers. In 2007 an accord was reached by the two sides. Elections were then held, only to be challenged once again in 2011 by rebels. French troops intervened to restore democracy. The fundamental problem is that the country's wealth is in the south, where its main export crops, coffee and cocoa, and light industries are located in the coastal zones and nearby forests. Most of these economic activities center on Abidjan, the main port and former capital, which enjoys growth and prosperity. However, the Muslim north remains mired in poverty.

Senegal also has suffered from instability, as separatists from the Cassamance Province in South Senegal waged a twenty-two-year insurgency for independence. The secession ended in 2004 with a peace agreement that maintained the unity of the country. The rebel movement was both geographically and economically inspired. Cassamance is nearly isolated from the rest of the country by being wedged between Gambia and Guinea-Bissau and thus cut off from the main economic centers of northern Senegal and major investment opportunities.

Only three countries stand out as having gained stability since their early years of turmoil and strife—Ghana, Benin, and Gabon.

Ghana was led by Jerry Rawlings, who first seized power in a military coup and then assumed the presidency in 1982. The country overcame its period of disunity and economic distress to stabilize its economy and expand it through free-market innovations. Subsequent elections have confirmed the country's political stability through peaceful transfer of power by free elections. Agriculture remains Ghana's economic base, but its mineral and forest products, clothing industries, software development, and aluminum smelting have been expanded with the help of outside investment. Revenues from a recently discovered, vast oil field have stimulated the country's GDP. All of this has moved Ghana closer to being a middle-income country, and its ties to the West appear firm.

Benin abandoned its Marxist system in favor of private enterprise a decade ago. Since that time it has moved to popular elections and a multiparty system that has made it a model of an open society in West Africa. While Benin, with a population of nine million, is dependent on subsistence agriculture and cotton, its prospects for economic development have improved with the discovery of oil off its shores. Tiny Gabon (population 1.5 million), with a GDP per capita of $8,000, enjoys stability thanks to a sturdy economy. Oil accounts for 40 percent of its budget, and the rest is derived from other abundant natural and food resources and foreign investments.

However, these three countries, as well as South Africa, do not mirror the dismal conditions that characterize the region as a whole. There are works, exemplified by Dayo Olopade's *The Bright Continent*,[13] that try to put an optimistic gloss on the prospects for the region based on Ghana's success. But Ghana is not representative of the violence, poverty, and corruption that hampers development in so much of Sub-Saharan Africa.

Important oil reserves have also been found in tiny Equatorial Guinea and Chad. The former, with a population of just over half a million, has doubled its per capita income in the past decade. Landlocked Chad, with a population of ten million, is one of the world's poorest countries, but it has vast reserves in its south. A large pipeline was completed in 2003 to transport oil from the fields near Kome to Douala on the Cameroon coast. However, little of the oil revenue reaches the general population. Instead, it flows from governmental coffers to the political, military, and business elite, as has been the case in much of Africa and the Middle East. The upheavals in Darfur have spread across the border to Chad as Darfurian refugees have fled into southwestern Chad, where they are preyed upon by both Darfurian rebels and Janjaweed militias. France has had to intervene with military force to stabilize the situation.

Central Africa

The bellwether of Central Africa is Democratic Republic of the Congo—the largest country of the region. Its population of seventy-five million is 70 percent of Central Africa's total, and its land area of nine hundred thousand square miles represents 60 percent of the total.

The conflict in Congo/DRC resumed in 1998, the year after Laurent Kabila had toppled the dictatorial regime of President Mobutu Sese Seko, with the strong support of Rwandan Tutsi government troops as well as forces from Burundi and Angola. Although Congo's neighbors claim that their interests lie in bringing peace to the country, their main motives seem to be gaining access to its rich resources and cutting off the bases of rebels who operate against their own countries from different parts of Congo.

Domestic dissatisfaction with the Kabila regime soon led to the outbreak of civil war in the eastern part of the country. Many of the rebels were Banyamulenge Tutsi, born in Congo but denied citizenship by both Mobutu and Kabila. Kabila's army was then backed by Hutu refugees who had been driven out of Rwanda in 1994 and had been using Congo as a base for cross-border incursions aimed at destabilizing Rwanda's Tutsi government.

Aided by mass defections from the Congolese army, the rebels swept across eastern Congo to the gates of Kinshasa and also seized the port of Matadi, the capital's lifeline for food, arms, and electric power. Kabila was saved by the military forces from Zimbabwe, Angola, and Namibia, acting in the name of SADC, which were then joined by troops from Chad and Sudan. The rebels were pushed back to their eastern bases. Fighting continued until September 1999, when a tentative peace accord, brokered by Zambia, was reached, but the accord was soon breached, and fighting resumed. A large UN force has remained in Congo since then, helping to oversee elections.

Despite the strengthening of the central government in recent years, upheavals continue to plague the eastern part of the country. Congolese Tutsis have maintained a separate army and administration in North Kivu, clashing with the Rwandan Hutu rebels, who have found refuge within the province. The 2008 peace agreement between the government and the Congolese Tutsis calls for the Tutsis to turn in their arms and for some units to be integrated within the Congolese army, but as with the 2004 agreement, this proved ephemeral. Currently a number of armed rebel groups operate around Lake Kivu, which lies between Rwanda and eastern Congo. The largest of these groups, M23, kills and harasses the local Congolese inhabitants with impunity while forcibly recruiting child soldiers. The Congolese military has been unable to control the rebels, and peacekeepers from the AU, led by South African troops, have unsuccessfully sought to quell the mayhem.

Centrality of location often offers strategic advantages to a country, but for Congo it is a serious handicap. Its government has been unable to form a cohesive unit because its threefold physical divisions—east, west, and south—are separated by an impassable interior. This leaves Congo prey to outside pressures, especially from well-armed states to the east and south lured by Congo's rich resource base, which includes gold, copper, diamonds, other minerals, and timber.

East Africa and the Horn of Africa

The Horn of Africa, consisting of Somalia, Djibouti, Ethiopia, and Eritrea, has been drawn into the great power struggle. Somalia and Ethiopia have fought over the Ogaden, Ethiopia and Eritrea plunged into a bloody war, and Somalia has broken apart. In Somalia, the United States and the United Nations failed in their efforts during the early 1990s to quell the interclan and intertribal fighting. Since then, no central government has existed, and Somalia has frequently been cited as a failed state.

Rebels in northern Somalia (the former British Somaliland) seceded in 1991 and established the independent, although not internationally recognized, state of Somaliland. This country fronts on the Gulf of Aden and contains Berbera, the former Soviet naval and missile base that is one of the few pieces of real estate in Sub-Saharan Africa with geostrategic importance. Together with Djibouti (former French Somaliland) and Aden (on the opposite shore), it commands the southern gateway to the Red Sea.

Along the northeastern coast of the Horn, another rebel group broke away to create "Puntland," taking its name from the Red Sea coastland called "Punt" by the ancient Egyptians. The new territory, a buffer between Somaliland and Somalia, centers on the port and commercial center of Bossasso, where the Gulf of Aden enters the Indian Ocean, and trades in food and frankincense. The separatist leaders there have not declared independence but resist control by a central government. Meanwhile, they have brought stability to Puntland, as have the Somaliland rulers to their land, where they have been able to create a modicum of harmony among the mainly nomadic clans and bring basic services to their people. They have done so through a complex system of government that balances strong clan leaders in an upper house of parliament with an elected house of representatives.

In 1992 the United States had unsuccessfully intervened in the civil war in Somalia, sending troops to protect food deliveries to a starving population caught by war and famine. The killing of eighteen US troops, along with several hundred Somalis, resulted in a speedy withdrawal and Washington's abandonment of peacekeeping efforts. Its return to this scene in 2006 was prompted by the seizure of the government by Islamic militants who drove out the secular warlords backed by the United States. The concern of the United States was that, under an Islamic regime, Somalia would become a haven for terrorists, posing a threat to the security of shipping through the Gulf of Aden as well as providing a base for al-Qaeda.

The large, well-armed troops of America's military ally, Ethiopia, then intervened with US support. They quickly drove the Islamists out of the country, reestablishing the secular provisional government that had been ousted by the rebels from Mogadishu, the capital. The conflict is far from over. The Islamists have forged new alliances with some of the warlords, promoting unrest in Mogadishu, and have supported the Somalian Oromo Liberation Front rebels in Ethiopia's Ogaden desert region.

Ethiopia, an impoverished country of over ninety million people, with a GDP of $1,300 per capita, is an ally of the United States. The United States backed Addis Ababa in a war launched in 2007 against the Oromo rebels. In a replay of its Cold War policy of alliances with right-wing dictators, the United States continued to expand its strategic alliance with the dictator of Ethiopia, Prime Minister Meles Zenawi—a policy that evoked considerable African and international criticism. He died in 2012 and was replaced by Hailemariam Desalegn. Ethiopia plays an important role in America's war against global terrorism, receiving considerable economic and military aid, despite its poor record on human rights.

The leading nation in East Africa is Kenya, which enjoys political stability and steady economic growth. The country has enjoyed significant economic aid from its close ally, the United States. It has provided bases for US forces, cooperating in the war on terrorism and in joint military exercises. Kenya's port of Mombassa also serves as the gateway to landlocked Uganda, South Sudan, Rwanda, and parts of northern Tanzania via combinations of rail and road. This is a significant support to the economies of these countries. South Sudan has negotiated with Kenya to build an oil pipeline from its productive fields to the Kenyan port of Lamu, where a refinery is planned.

Kenya's stability was disrupted in 2007 by the dispute that arose over the presidential elections late that year. Charges of electoral fraud by incumbent Kikuyu president Mwai Kibaki, who declared himself the victor, caused the followers of his Luo opponent, Raila Odinga, to go on a rampage. Hundreds of Kikuyu living in the Luo and Kalenja tribal areas in the western Rift

Valley and in the southern slums of Nairobi were killed, as were many opposing tribal peoples living in Kikuyu. Kibaki served as president until 2013, when he was replaced in a peaceful election by Uhuru Kenyatta, the son of Kenya's founding father, Jomo Kenyatta.

The Kikuyu, who are the largest of Kenya's forty-two tribes, with 22 percent of the population, have dominated the country from its independence, controlling its politics and commerce. While their tribal base is in the verdant, rolling hills of the Central Highland district and in Nairobi, they also gained control of substantial farmlands in the Rift's grassy plains. These lands were cut from large plantations formerly owned by colonialists and were distributed to Kikuyu by the government. The outburst of violence was as much over land as over tribal politics.

Kenya has been distinguished from its neighbors by its sense of nationhood despite its many tribes. The Kikuyu overreached in their refusal to share not only political control but also the fruits of economic development. The quick response of the international bodies and the United States in efforts to mediate the dispute attested to the importance of Kenya as an island of stability within the shatterbelt. A measure of democracy survived the crisis, as demonstrated by the election and seating of the parliament with a majority of opposition members. This suggests that prospects for emergence of a political power-sharing system between prime minister and president may overcome the tribalism that has atomized so much of Sub-Saharan Africa. The displacement of over three hundred thousand persons in the wake of the violence has created more homogeneous ethnic provinces and districts and could well lead to the emergence of a federal system of governance replacing the centralized national system that vested so much power in the presidency.

Conclusion

During the Cold War, Sub-Saharan Africa was the scene of intense competition for influence between the Soviet Union and the United States and its European allies. In seeking to gain or retain geopolitical control, these outside powers exploited the deep tribal, religious, racial, and ideological differences within most of the region. Both sides ignored the violence and corruption of client states. With the collapse of the USSR, the United States and its European allies concluded that Sub-Saharan Africa was no longer a geostrategic asset and reduced their economic and military assistance accordingly. Within the world geopolitical system, Africa (as well as South America) had become a zone of geostrategic marginality.[14]

With the turn of the century, great power interests in the region were rekindled, and Sub-Saharan Africa has reemerged as a shatterbelt. Now the major competitors are China and the United States in partnership with Europe. This is a competition for economic and political influence rather than the Marxist-capitalist struggle that characterized the Cold War shatterbelt era. Washington's strategic attention in Africa is now focused on Islamic terrorist groups that recruit and train followers who infiltrate Iraq, Afghanistan, and the Gulf states, as well as Europe. Securing the shipping lanes that link the Suez Canal and the Middle East, especially against pirate attacks in Bab el Mandeb and the Gulf of Aden, is a key strategic goal. Its other interest lies in expanding and securing access to Angola's oil and gas resources, which are fast outstripping America's declining and unstable oil imports from Nigeria.

China has made strong headway in Sub-Saharan Africa, negotiating substantial energy, mineral development, and construction contracts and more than tripling its trade with the region. Beijing has become the region's single largest trade partner, even though the EU as a whole exceeds it substantially. China's trade amounts to over $170 billion per annum. Its imports are mainly petroleum and agricultural products, while its exports are largely manufactured goods. As noted, nearly one-third of its oil now comes from Africa, mainly Angola. While there is a modest amount of military sales, the main relations that Beijing has forged with the region are based neither on arms nor on ideology, but on economics. Chinese companies are engaged in building ports and railway networks, mining coal and iron ore in Tanzania, leasing farmland in Sudan, and investing in the port of Djibouti.

The competition between China and the West for Sub-Saharan Africa is asymmetrical. Both seek raw materials and investment opportunities and offer development assistance. However, while Europe, especially France, and the United States provide military aid to selective countries, China's arms sales are minimal. The strategic partnership that the Chinese have with the region is strongly based on loan and debt relief programs, with few of the strings that the West imposes, particularly in terms of the latter's demand for political and economic reform. As it floods Africa with cheap consumer goods, the Chinese presence is highly visible owing to a market-based labor migration organized by Chinese overseas companies. Anywhere from half a million to a million Chinese workers, managers, and technicians engage directly with Africans in construction projects, while Chinese merchants are active throughout the region.

China has surplus labor as well as capital to forge its strategic partnership, using these resources to extend its influence across the subcontinent. Its construction projects, which are organized both by the Chinese state and increasingly by private companies, use cheap construction materials from China. An essential element in this partnership involves training of local labor and management working side by side with the Chinese.

Ding Fei points out that the strategy of partnering through construction projects can, if successful, lead to the building of a well-trained and experienced African workforce and therefore provide a sustainable contribution to African development. She emphasizes the need for African states to develop effective regulatory and legal mechanisms to protect labor rights—not an easy challenge under the current system, which focuses on maximizing profits and minimizing labor costs.[15] Nevertheless, this kind of egalitarian partnership between China and Sub-Saharan Africa strengthens Beijing's hand in its competition with the West for geopolitical influence.

Washington's strategies in Sub-Saharan Africa face other challenges as well. The United States is viewed with suspicion by many Africans, especially Muslims, for its intervention in Somalia and Iraq. Its reluctance to use its political power to halt bloodletting within the region, as in Rwanda, Congo, and Darfur, is widely criticized. The US quagmire in Iraq and its failure to have eliminated Taliban and al-Qaeda operations in Afghanistan have undermined Washington's ability to be an effective peacemaker and peacekeeper in Africa.

Despite a surge in US aid, the high prices of commodities exports to Europe, China, India, and Brazil, as well as to the United States, have contributed more to Africa's economic development than does direct aid. This by no means suggests that continuing development aid is not a critical necessity. However, over the past forty years, well over $700 billion in such aid went to Africa, much of which was lost to corruption or poorly conceived and managed. It does point to the need for using development aid to build cooperative regional and subregional infrastructures that can stimulate economic exchange and move Sub-Saharan Africa into a differentiated stage.

Sub-Saharan Africa remains a highly atomized shatterbelt, but geopolitical structures are not immutable. Looking into the distant future, we can anticipate geopolitical changes coming to Sub-Saharan Africa partially as a result of political developments in neighboring regions. Also, global warming is likely to have a severe impact on Africa because its farm and fishing economies are so highly dependent on natural resources whose biodiversity would be greatly affected by climate change. The region is already suffering from drought, high prices of imported food, and declining food production. Increasing drought in the interior and flooding in such coastal areas as the Niger delta would upset the current fragile biodiversity balance that now sustains most Africans. Resultant forced migrations in search of grazing and farmlands, as well as water, would intensify conflict in this already war-torn shatterbelt.

The coastal countries and offshore islands of eastern Africa, especially Tanzania, Zanzibar, Madagascar, the Seychelles, Comoros, Maldives, and Mauritius, might be drawn into a new Indian Ocean geostrategic realm. Such a realm would be dominated by India, as discussed in the chapter on South Asia. The Horn of Africa is likely to remain under the shadow of events in the Middle East. The southern and western half of Sub-Saharan Africa might also, in the long run, emerge from its current shatterbelt status to become a new geopolitical region linked to the maritime realm. This would depend upon the abilitiy of South Africa to achieve strong internal cohesiveness and take the lead in making ECOWAS and SADC tightly knit economic and political subunits that could then be linked within a broader geopolitical region and the ability of Nigeria to stave off disintegration from its religious and ethnic conflicts. Such a unified region might also be strengthened by the addition of new states in the lower Congo and Shaba, in the eventuality that Congo/DRC either federates or divides into three states. These would consist of one centering on Kinshasa and western Congo, a second centering on Lubumbashi and Shaba in the southeast (Katanga), and a third in eastern Congo or the upper Congo basin that would probably be oriented to East Africa and the Indian Ocean realm. South Africa signed a free-trade pact with Mercosur in December 2000 with the express goal of decreasing its trade dependence on Europe and the United States. However, it is highly unlikely that this accord could lead to a set of strong economic and geopolitical links between Africa and South America.

Notes

1. John O'Loughlin and Herman Van der Wusten, "Political Geography of Panregions," *Geographical Review* 80 (1990): 1–20.
2. Norman Harris, *Intervention and Colonization in Africa, 1884–1914* (Boston: Houghton Mifflin, 1914), 3–19.
3. A. S. Gakwandi, "Towards a New Political Map of Africa," in *Politics, Economy and Social Change in the Twenty-First Century*, ed. A. I. Asiwaju (London: Hurst, 1996), 252–59.
4. Peter J. Taylor, ed., *World Government* (New York: Oxford University Press, 1990), 188–201.
5. Morag Bell, *Contemporary Africa: Development, Culture and the State* (London: Longman, 1986), 98–111.
6. World Bank, *Global Development Finance* (Washington, DC: World Bank, 2006).
7. Population Reference Bureau, *2007 Population Data Sheet* (Washington, DC: Population Reference Bureau, 2007).
8. Norimitsu Onishi, "African Bloc Hoping to Do Better as the 'African Union,'" *New York Times*, July 12, 2001, A3.
9. J. V. R. Prescott, "Africa's Boundary Problems," *Optima* 28 (1980): 3–21.
10. Central Intelligence Agency, "Disputes International," in *World Factbook 2007* (Washington, DC: GPO/CIA, 2007); and Alan J. Day, ed., *Border and Territorial Disputes* (Longman, 1982), 95–178.
11. "Somaliland, the Nation Nobody Knows," *Economist*, April 14, 2001, 42.
12. Andrew C. Revkin, "Lake's Rapid Retreat Heightens Troubles in North Africa," *New York Times*, May 27, 2001, F4.
13. Dayo Olopade, *The Bright Continent: Breaking Rules and Making Change in Modern Africa* (New York: Houghton Mifflin Harcourt, 2014), 272.
14. Saul B. Cohen, "Global Change in the Post–Cold War Era," *Annals of the Association of American Geographers* 81, no. 4 (1991): 551–80.
15. Ding Fei, *Labor Relations with Chinese Construction Projects in Sub-Saharan Africa* (paper presented at Association of American Geographers annual meeting, Tampa, FL, April 2014), 18.

CHAPTER 14

Epilogue

The international system is in transition from the global geopolitical order that was imposed, first by two superpowers, the United States and the Soviet Union, and then by the United States alone, to a system in which a number of major powers dominate the world system. This comes as a shock to many in the United States and elsewhere who still believe that America is the world's superpower. The right wing within the United States calls for military action to impose stability, whereas the left wing expects Washington to promote peacekeeping and provide economic aid to quell turbulence throughout the globe. In fact, the United States is not free to intervene in all parts of the world and finds it productive to cooperate with unfriendly states as well as allies in order to exercise influence.

The United States is no longer the world's superpower, nor is any other nation. While US military power continues to be unrivaled in a traditional sense, the nature of warfare has changed. Enemies are no longer massed armed forces which can be overwhelmed by a stronger army but are elusive guerrilla bands. Drones, rather than heavy bombers or aircraft carriers, are the weapons of choice in modern warfare. For the United States, this means acquiring and maintaining bases close to zones of conflict in areas that may themselves be unstable. Economically it is no longer the wealthiest country in the world, a status now held by Gulf states and Canada. High debt and debt service costs as well as heavy defense expenditures are a brake on US ability to continue to be as generous a promoter of foreign economic and military aid as has been the case until now.

In this period of geopolitical transition, global stability is dependent upon the policies of the world's major powers—the United States, the European Union, Russia, China, and Japan, with India and Brazil on the verge of joining them—and on such regional powers as Turkey, Australia, Vietnam, Iran, Israel, and South Africa. The geopolitical destinies of the major powers are so entwined that they are unlikely to risk direct conflict with one another or through surrogates. While economic rivalry marks their relationships, mutual economic dependence (MED) binds them together through the benefits of economic specialization, trade, technology transfer, and investment flows. They also share the common threats posed by international terrorism and the spread of nuclear weapons. These mutual concerns led to multipower cooperation in the US-initiated war against the Taliban and al-Qaeda in Afghanistan. The five UN Security Council members plus Germany are also cooperating in negotiating with Iran to forestall its development of nuclear weapons while recognizing its right to nuclear energy.

The most unstable parts of the world are still the two geostrategically located shatterbelts—the Middle East and Sub-Saharan Africa, which are geographically joined at the Horn of Africa. The boundaries of these shatterbelts may expand or contract. In the Middle East, unchecked major power rivalry for oil, gas, and pipeline control could result in the extension of its boundaries northward into the Central Asian portion of the Eurasian convergence zone. Implosion of Pakistan could expand the shatterbelt into western Pakistan's Pashtun and Balochi borderlands. Membership of Turkey within the EU would draw it more closely toward Europe and away from the Middle East. It could prove to be an important bridge between the Euromediterranean region and the Middle East.

Since 2011, when Syria's majority Sunnis rebelled against the Arab socialist Baath Party, led by Bashar al-Assad and his Alawite followers, fighting has been constant. It has involved both Sunni moderates and extremists frequently engaging in conflict with each other as well as with the Syrian government. The battle has spread to Iraq, as the Sunni extremists ISIS—Islamic State in Iraq and Syria (sometimes known as ISIL—Islamic State in Iraq and the Levant) seek to create a caliphate over both countries. ISIS has gained control over much of eastern Syria and pushed Iraqi government forces out of northern (including Mosul) and western Iraq but has not secured the backing of moderate Sunnis. Defeat of Iraqi government military forces in this region has also provided an opportunity for the Kurds of northern Iraq to seize the oil center of Kirkuk and to strengthen their drive for an independent Iraqi Kurdestan.

The Shia-controlled government of Iraqi prime minister al-Maliki has been reluctant to give up its power monopoly and share political power with the Sunnis and Kurds. Should it persist in this policy, Iraq's future as a unified state is in jeopardy. Iraq could well split into an independent southern "Shiistan," a western and central "Sunnistan," and a northern Kurdistan. The Iraqi Sunni state might then well merge with Syria's Sunni center and east. This would leave the current Alawite Syrian government with control over only the coastal highland region east of the Orontes River and the Ghab, known as Jabal al-Sahiliyah, which is the homeland of Syria's Alawites.

In the Sub-Saharan African shatterbelt, southern Africa from Angola through Mozambique and south to the Cape of Good Hope could become an independent geopolitical region, escaping the instability of the present shatterbelt. This would depend upon the rising fortunes of South Africa as a regional power and the revitalization of a Zimbabwe freed from the tyrannical rule of the late Mobutu Sese Seko.

Individual countries are also unstable, torn by separatist conflict, sectarian violence, and displacement of large numbers of people. Examples of countries where recent civil wars have been resolved are Colombia, Sri Lanka, Algeria, Indonesia, and the Philippines. Civil wars now rage in Syria, Afghanistan, Pakistan, Iraq, South Sudan, the Democratic Republic of Congo, the Central African Republic, Mali, and Somalia, as well as elsewhere. While they are serious internal threats, they pose little danger to regional or global equilibrium, as the shatterbelts do. An exception is Nigeria. Should its current rebellion erupt into full-scale war between the Muslim North and Christian South, all of West Africa is likely to be swept up in conflict.

Global equilibrium is based upon a multipolar world system. The failure of the United States to recognize this geopolitical reality in the second Iraq War has led to the greatest crisis that the world has faced since the end of the Cold War. The conflict was launched despite the opposition from most of the world and has resulted in the devastation of Iraq and expansion of the base for international terrorism. In trying to impose "democracy" on a country riven by religious sectarianism and tribal enmities, Washington has paved the way for the Shia majority, led by an authoritarian ruler, to gain control of the government, army, and police and facilitated the spread of Iranian influence within the country, as well as providing Iran with access to Syria and South Lebanon. US plans for controlling Iraq's oil and establishing a permanent military presence there gave way to a search for a way to extricate American forces with the hope that sectarian bloodshed could be contained through some Iraqi political compromise. This has not happened, and conflict rages between the country's Sunni Arab minority and the Shia majority, with the semi-independent Kurdish North as bystander.

America's failed effort in Iraq has not only weakened US influence in the Arab and wider Muslim sphere but also severely undermined its stature throughout the world, including among its closest allies. Future Washington administrations will have much to overcome in regaining international confidence and credibility. The Iraq War laid to rest any assumption that the United States is the world's sole superpower and that it can secure global equilibrium.

The promise of multipower cooperation that characterized the first phase of the war in Afghanistan was squandered by the diversion of most US military forces and aid to Iraq. The limited American and NATO troops in Afghanistan have been unable to check the return of the Taliban to much of the country's Pashtun southern and eastern provinces. In addition, failure to capture bin Laden and the fleeing al-Qaeda bands in the early days of the war can be attributed to the Pentagon decision not to pursue them into the Tora Bora Mountains that straddle the boundary with Pakistan but to leave their elimination to the Pakistani military. The "domino" effect of this miscalculation has resonated throughout both countries. Islamic militants based in Pakistan's Federally Administered Tribal Areas, in league with the Taliban and al-Qaeda, have fought the Pakistani military to a standstill. Indeed, there is some basis for believing that Pakistan's Inter-Services Intelligence (ISI) actually collaborates with the Taliban.[1] Terrorist attacks have spread to Rawalpindi, Pakistan's military garrison city in its northern Punjab province, where the assassination of Benazir Bhutto took place, and to Karachi. With withdrawal of American and Allied troops scheduled for the end of 2014, Afghanistan's future as a stable, unified country, free of Taliban influence, is highly doubtful.

The United States is not the only power to ignore global stability in its unilateral conduct of foreign policy, disregarding the interests of others. Russia's heavy-handed energy policies toward Eastern Europe have created serious tensions with the EU, especially in light of its annexation of Crimea from Ukraine. China's escalating military threats against Taiwan and unwillingness to reach a compromise over the political status of the island is another potential flash point. So are its claims to sovereignty over most of the waters of the East China (Sea of Japan) and South China Seas. Military steps against Taiwan would jeopardize China's relations with the United States and Japan and destabilize the Asia-Pacific Rim. The Japanese government has responded to China's claims to the Senkaku/Diaoyu Islands, which they also claim, by interpreting the constitution of the country to permit Japanese action in collective self-defense operations. Iranian actions to stir unrest among the Shia populations of the Gulf Cooperation Council countries and Saudi Arabia's Eastern Province would assuredly evoke a strong military response from the West.

The progress toward greater global equilibrium continues. However, events of the year 2014 posed heavy challenges to this advance. There were major upheavals within the world's two shatterbelts—the Middle East and Sub-Saharan Africa, These included the continued rebellion in Syria; the expansion of ISIS into western and central Iraq and the flight of Iraq's Christian populace northward into Iraqi Kurdistan; the Israeli/Hamas war in Gaza; intervention by France to contain rebellions in the Sahel; the military success of the Islamic extremist Boko Haram in northern Nigeria, spreading into eastern Cameroon; the civil war in South Sudan; and penetration of Islamic extremist Al-Shabab from Somalia into Kenya.

Elsewhere, China's aggressive policies over its territorial water claims in the South China Sea and its oil exploration activities provoked tension with Vietnam and the Philippines. Japan took steps designed to strengthen its defense capacities against China.

Even more threatening to global stability were the events in Eastern Europe, where conflict broke out between the Russian-supported eastern Ukraine and the Ukrainian government backed by the European Union and the United States. The sanctions that the latter imposed upon Moscow for its annexation of Crimea and its military aid to the Russian-oriented east Ukrainian separatists fractured what had been a balanced relationship between East and West. Mitigating these tensions is the mutual economic dependence of the two sides. Russia needs continuing access to Western credit sources and energy technology as well as the European market for its oil and gas. W.estern Europe, and especially Germany, is not only dependent on this oil and gas but also on Russia as a market for its goods and services.

Mapping the Future

Projecting the outlines of the world geopolitical map of the future is a questionable proposition. Figure 14.1 should therefore be taken as a "guesstimate," not a prediction. The regional structural changes depicted on the map are based upon an analysis of how global forces are likely to impact geopolitical fault lines, which may cause some shifting of today's structural plates that are depicted in figure 3.1. In a dynamic geopolitical world, some unexpected changes will take place. However, some can be anticipated, and these are the ones shown on the map.

In anticipation of India's becoming a full member of the major power "club," a new Indian Ocean realm is likely to emerge. The relative weakening of Pakistan would enable India to focus more of its economic and political energies on the Indian Ocean Basin. This realm would embrace the coastlands of East Africa on the western side of the Indian Ocean Basin and Myanmar on the Basin's Bay of Bengal-Andaman Sea eastern side. It could act as a counterbalance to Chinese pressures against the Asia-Pacific Rim and have a strong influence upon the rim and upon East and South Africa.

A distinct possibility is the implosion of Pakistan, with its Pashtun borderlands that lie between the Durand Line and the Indus, joining the Pashtun eastern and southern parts of Afghanistan. Another is the creation of an independent Pakhtunistan in a confederation with Balochistan. Afghanistan has claimed the Pashtun areas of Pakistan as far back as 1893, renewing the claim in 1949. Landlocked Afghanistan has also been interested in annexing Balochistan, thereby gaining access to the Arabian Sea.[2] Should the Pashtuns break away and join their kindred Afghan tribesmen, the Tajiks of the west and the Tajiks and Uzbeks of the north might seek independence or, at the least, a very loose confederation.

In the Eurasian convergence zone, Eastern Europe, the Trans-Caucasus, and Central Asia could emerge either as gateway or shatterbelt regions. The geostrategic importance to Moscow of these regions, located along Russia's western and southern borders, cannot be overstated. Russia's vital interests are based on its strategic vulnerability to a potentially hostile presence, such as NATO would represent if it expanded into the northern and eastern shores of the Black Sea; the stationing of US troops in the Caucasus or Central Asia; the discrimination by neighboring countries toward their ethnic Russian and Slavic Russophile groups who look to Moscow for physical security and cultural support; and the spread of Islamic fundamentalism from seven republics in southern Russia (such as Chechnya) should they fall into the hands of radical Islamic regimes. Russian interests also include the maintenance of access for Russian investment to the rich oil and gas reserves of Central Asia and the Trans-Caucasus and, above all, strategic control over the regions mentioned above for directing transit of their new energy pipeline infrastructures across Russian territory.

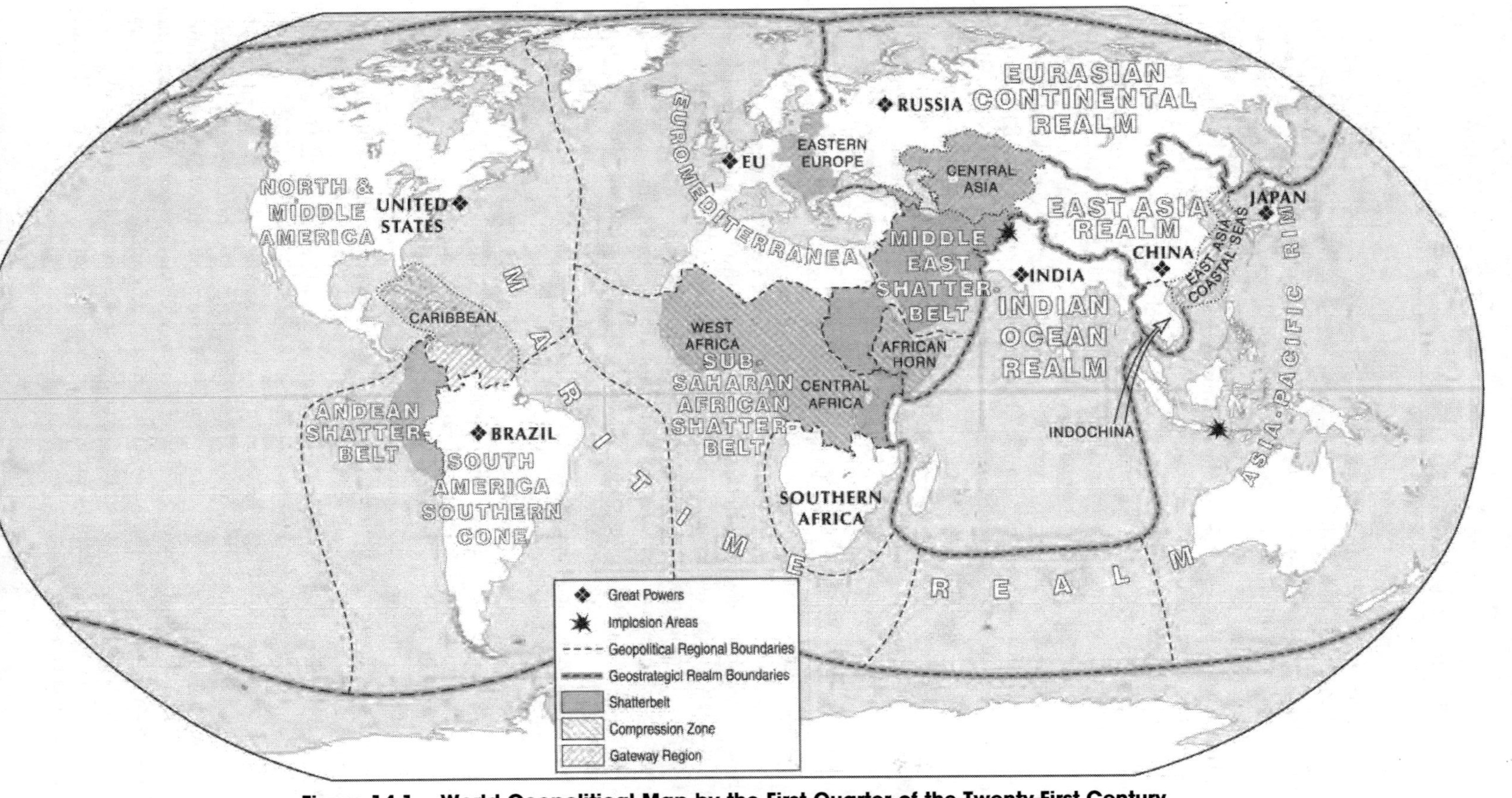

Figure 14.1. World Geopolitical Map by the First Quarter of the Twenty-First Century

It was the fear that NATO and the EU would draw Ukraine into their orbits that prompted Moscow to regain control of Crimea. Reassurance over these concerns could encourage Moscow to work together with the West in converting the Eurasian convergence zone's Eastern European, Trans-Caucasus, and Central Asian regions into a broad gateway zone. Otherwise, they would become shatterbelts. In the latter case, geographical proximity and other features would give Russia a strategic advantage in countering Western penetration efforts. Unless Russia and the West come to terms over Ukraine's role as a bridge between them rather than a focus of conflict, the country could well split apart and become the source of a new "cool" war between Russia and the West. This requires European and US guarantees that NATO would not seek to admit Ukraine, as well as assurances that the eastern and southern Russian-speaking regions of the country enjoy full linguistic, and a measure of economic, autonomy through a new federal governmental structure.

No geopolitical discussion of any part of the Russian periphery can take place without reference to oil and natural gas. The future development of these resources in both the Trans-Caucasus and Central Asia is of great interest to the West as well as to China and India. To Russia, this zone is important in terms of both its energy resources and its strategic military value. In 2014, Europe's concerns that it is overly dependent on oil and gas from Russia led the EU to force Bulgaria to block the extension of the South Stream Pipeline that is planned to extend from Russia under the Black Sea, through Bulgaria and southeastern Europe, and terminating in Austria.

The extensive Russian military involvement in the affairs of Georgia and Armenia during the past decade reflects the depth of Moscow's strategic interest in the Trans-Caucasus. For its part, Washington made considerable efforts to expand its influence within Georgia through its support of Western oil interests which built the BTC pipeline from Baku in Azerbaijan across Georgia, through Turkey, to Ceyhan on its Mediterranean coast. The United States also provided Georgia with military trainers and weaponry and dangled before the Tbilisi government the prospect of admission to NATO. Georgia reciprocated by sending the third-largest, after Britain, contingent of Coalition troops to Iraq. These American efforts to draw Georgia into its sphere of influence sparked the Russo-Georgian war of 2008. The result was the speedy defeat of Georgia while the United States was helpless to intervene. Moscow then stationed troops in breakaway Abkhazia and South Ossetia.

Any move to sponsor admission of Georgia or Ukraine to NATO would spark a movement toward the region's becoming a shatterbelt, with dire consequences for global stability. In all likelihood, Russia would formally annex Abkhazia and South Ossetia. Ukraine's admission to NATO would encourage eastern and southern Ukraine to seek unification with Russia. Either or both such events would throw the region into turmoil and might well result in a policy rift between Europe and the United States that would undermine maritime realm unity.

Within the maritime realm, the present region of maritime Europe and the Maghreb could expand into a new region, Euromediterranea, which would encompass Turkey, Israel, Lebanon, and northeastern Africa. The creation of such a region would hold profound geopolitical implications for the United States. The major burden for maritime realm strategic and economic responsibilities in these lands would shift from the United States to maritime Europe or should be equally shared by both. Emergence of the new region hinges upon a number of eventualities. The most important is Turkey's admission to the EU and its continuing market-oriented economic reforms, which would link it more closely to the global economy. This is being jeopardized by Erdogan's increasingly authoritarian rule and accusations of governmental corruption.

Resolution of the Arab-Israeli conflict through establishment of a Palestinian state in nearly all of the West Bank and in Gaza is also a key requirement. Since Jerusalem is so important to both parties, it might be accorded special federated status that unifies the city and its metropolitan Israeli and Palestinian sectors functionally but leaves West Jerusalem in Israel and Arab East Jerusalem in Palestine politically. Prospects presently appear quite dim for resolution of that conflict. However, a convergence of elements might ultimately bring the warring sides to the negotiating table. These include the escalation of bloodletting, the suffering and economic privation of the Palestinian Arabs, and international pressures on Israel to implement a two-state solution. Additional forces for peace are generated by the West's concerns that continuation of the conflict will increasingly undermine its relationship with Arab oil states and the Muslim world as a whole.

In the immediate future, Israel's military-technological superiority over the Arabs will continue to depend heavily upon its strategic alliance with the United States. This guarantees security in war but does not bring peace closer—indeed, it lulls many Israelis into a false sense of security. In the long run, resolution of the conflict more likely depends upon the integration of Israel and a Palestinian state within a Euromediterranean structure that provides both parties with political, economic, and security benefits, drawing them more closely to Europe.

Resolution of the Cyprus dispute is another prerequisite. If the island is to be reunified, a Greco-Turkish quasi condominium over a bizonal, bicommunal confederated Cyprus/North Cyprus state may have to be established as the first step if United Nations confederation peacekeeping oversight is rejected by either or both parties.

A further requirement is modernization of the Egyptian economy and democratization of its governance structure to address Europe's concerns. This would strengthen Cairo's leadership role within the Arab lands of the Levant and northeast Africa. The restoration of military rule in Egypt following the ousting of elected president Mohamed Morsi and the subsequent crackdown on the Muslim Brotherhood is a setback on the road to this goal.

The rationale for the emergence of Euromediterranea is geopolitically compelling. If it gains the military capacity to match its economic power, maritime Europe will be well positioned to replace American leadership within the western rim of the present Middle East or at least share equally in the diplomatic, strategic, and economic burdens. For Washington, a Euromediterranea could mean substantial reduction of its current military and economic aid programs to Israel, Egypt, and Jordan. At the same time, the United States would be relieved of a good many political entanglements that would be assumed by Europe.

Should the western rim of the Middle East become geopolitically reoriented to Europe, the Middle East shatterbelt would be reconstituted. It would then consist of the Arabian Peninsula, the Persian/Arab Gulf, Iraq, Iran, and Afghanistan. In addition, the region's eastern border would probably be extended to include Pakistan's Pashtun areas, because neither Afghanistan nor Pakistan are cohesive national units. There is a strong likelihood that, despite the extraordinary efforts by the Allied powers to rebuild Afghanistan as a unified state, it will not be possible to overcome the ethnic, tribal, and spatial divisions that have torn the country apart.

In Iraq, if a satisfactory resolution of competing Sunni-Shia-Kurdish demands are not fulfilled, the western Sunni part of the country could well gravitate toward the Arab Sunni world while the southern and eastern Shia provinces seek an alliance with Iran. This would present an opportunity for the Kurds, who now enjoy quasi independence, to achieve full independence. In the past, Turkey has made it clear that it would not accept an independent Iraqi Kurdish state because this might jeopardize its control over its restive Kurdish province in eastern Turkey. Ankara has recently moderated its position because it views an Iraqi Kurdistan as an island of stability within the volatile Iraqi state.

The US army's recruitment of Sunni "Awakening Council" militias to fight al-Qaeda and other insurgents as part of the military "surge" in 2007–8 has boomeranged. These seventy thousand militiamen, most of whom had served in Saddam Hussein's army, have turned their American-supplied arms against the ruling Shia in the wake of withdrawal of US troops from Iraq and in response to the Shiite government's discriminatory practices against the Sunni. The concept of "my enemy's enemy is my friend" also did not work in Afghanistan. There, the United States armed the Taliban against the pro-Soviet Afghan regime and then the Soviet army, only to have these weapons turned against the Northern Alliance and eventually the United States.

The Caribbean is likely to emerge as a gateway region. It could become a bridge connecting the countries of a new South American Southern Cone region (see cone shape, fig. 14.1), North and Middle America, and Euromediterranea. In the post-Castro era, Cuba, along with Venezuela, could play a key role in creating this gateway. Much would depend upon the durability of Venezuela's post-Chávez regime. The successor Maduro government is facing serious unrest, fueled by roaring inflation, lack of consumer goods, and authoritarian rule. Should it succeed in holding onto power and sponsoring the Chávez goal of a socialist Bolivarian revolution to include Nicaragua, Cuba, Ecuador, and Bolivia, a mini-shatterbelt would emerge within the Caribbean and the Andes.

Prospects of the creation of a strong, unified South American geopolitical region are based upon Brazil's emergence as a major power in the world system. Its sheer size, resource base, and military power relative to its neighbors should enable it to dominate all of the Amazon basin. Argentina no longer rivals its northern neighbor economically, militarily, and in size of population. The Southern Cone would also include Uruguay, Paraguay, Chile, Bolivia, and the Amazonian sectors that now belong to Colombia, Ecuador, and Peru—states threatened by implosion. As a stable democracy, Brazil has become one of the world's leading food exporters, with vast undeveloped farming areas still available for expansion. It is the world leader in ethanol derived from sugarcane, it is a major exporter of iron ore, and it has in process of development huge oil deposits off its southeastern shore. It currently meets its own domestic energy needs through its vast hydroelectric resources, its ethanol, existing local oil deposits, and natural gas from Bolivia. When it develops its offshore oil fields, it will become a major oil exporter.

Brazil faces the problem of vast numbers of impoverished urban and rural dwellers and the challenge of developing a sustainable program to protect its biodiverse tropical rain forests while permitting controlled logging and land clearing for ranching. However, a balanced program for development can overcome these challenges. The emergence of Brazil as a major power will give stability to South America and the world as a whole.

Perhaps the most far-reaching potential geopolitical change is the prospective East Asia Coastal Seas gateway region that would link much of the present East Asia realm to the Asia-Pacific Rim. It would also link the Asia-Pacific Rim to the Russian Far East. The new gateway, composed of China's "Golden Coast," Taiwan, and a unified Korea, would serve as a buffer between continental East Asia and the Asia-Pacific Rim. In all likelihood, the Golden Coast would not break away from north and interior continental China as an independent state but would be a quasi-independent one in confederation with the rest of China. Confederation could also be the path taken by Taiwan. In both cases, a "Hong Kong Plus" model might be the vehicle whereby they could enjoy economic and a modicum of political independence, such as UN membership and worldwide diplomatic representation. At the same time, as demilitarized states, they would come under China's protection and be junior partners in the political confederation. Whether or not a division of China takes place, Tibet and Xinjiang are likely to become quasi states, if not independent ones.

The Asia-Pacific Rim would contract geographically as a result of the change in political status of Korea, the possible implosion of Indonesia, and the expansion of the Indian Ocean realm. Nevertheless, under the leadership of Japan in partnership with Australia, the rim would remain a cornerstone of the US maritime realm and derive strength from the East Asia Coastal Seas gateway.

The world envisaged on the map in figure 14.1 is one of an interdependent geopolitical structure with the promise of greater equilibrium than exists at the turn of the twenty-first century. The continuing evolution of such a world system will put great pressure on the United Nations to effect major institutional changes that would reflect the system's increased hierarchical specialization and complexity. Within the Security Council, the current group of five permanent members is likely to be expanded to include Japan, Germany, India, and Brazil—all existing or potential major powers.

Readjustments within the UN structure might also give greater voice to the rising number of regional powers and limited voting weight to those in the quasi-state category. Regional bodies, such as the EU, NAFTA, Mercosur, and ASEAN, will develop into major political-economic forces within the world system, and thus some means of formal accommodation for them should be worked out. While a radical reorganization of the UN would no doubt meet considerable opposition from those states that benefit from the status quo, without institutional innovations that reflect the sweeping global geopolitical changes ahead, the world body will run the risk of becoming ineffective and irrelevant.

As the number of national states and quasi states continues to increase, it could reach 225 by the end of the first half of this century. Such proliferation is taking place at the same time that globalization is making it more of a challenge for states to control their national economies and preserve certain valued aspects of their national cultures in the face of continued large-scale immigration. Especially in Europe, Russia, Japan, and Australia, declining populations with longer life spans will require immigration to fulfill essential services. Countries that have long been monocultural are already facing the challenge of absorbing immigrants, many of whom wish to live in a bicultural milieu. By mid-century, decolonization and the division of states will have run its course, and some states may find it in their best interests to federate with their neighbors.

Globalization exerts contradictory forces in many countries. While it has facilitated economic and sociocultural ties, irredentist and terrorist movements take advantage of global telecommunications, travel, currency, and eased restrictions on trade to secure weaponry and manpower in support of their struggles for national freedom or governmental overthrow. Global institutional religious ties are also increasingly important, as they reinforce faiths that have become the driving forces of nationalism in so many parts of the world.

The increase in the number of major and regional powers and the strengthening of regional organizations will not eliminate disturbances in the system. These will persist as new states join the international community and unresolved conflicts between existing states continue to rage. However, such disturbances will be more easily contained by an international system that has more nodes at different geospatial levels and more links between and among those nodes. This will build a more diverse and dense global network that is more capable of withstanding the shocks to the system from various disturbances.

A most profound shock to the world system may well be climate change. Global warming is a reality. The Arctic is warming twice as fast as the rest of the planet. The retreat of its glaciers has made possible summer shipping routes from Norway to the Bering Sea (the Northern Sea Route) and from the Bering Sea to Baffin Bay (the Northwest Passage). However, the melting of the Arctic ice cap and Greenland glaciers is raising seawater levels—an indicator of how broad global warming is likely to impact coastal areas in much of the world. Forecasts that warming may cause seas to rise by two feet by the year 2100 are a warning to the world. Such a rise would displace millions of people in such low-level countries as Bangladesh and low-lying Indian and Pacific Ocean atoll states and inundate much of the East Coast of the United States from Florida to Manhattan, as well as low-lying areas from San Francisco to Seattle. In the Pacific island of Kiribati, which consists of thirty-three scattered atolls, some of which rise only two feet above sea level, a number of villages have been swept away by rising tides. The government has purchased land in Fiji where the displaced settlers can grow food and eventually settle. The Marshalls, Tuvalu, and Maldives are also threatened by rising sea levels.

Flood walls and other barriers like those built to protect the Netherlands are unlikely to be able to protect vast coastal reaches. Nor is the solution of removing or forbidding the building of structures on these stretches politically feasible. Reducing greenhouse gas emissions globally is the only secure way to combat rising sea levels and climate extremes that are produced by increased world temperatures. The United States has made substantial strides in reducing carbon dioxide emissions from coal-fired power plants and motor vehicles, but this progress is undercut by the rise in methane gases which are a by-product of fracking shale for oil and gas.

The major powers can no longer shirk their responsibility for reducing emissions and pollution on the grounds of economic necessity. At the Intergovernmental Conference on Climate Change in December 2007, the EU and other developed countries proposed specific quotas and other remedial steps.[3]

The United States, China, and India—together responsible for over 60 percent of global pollution—refused to commit to a specified quota system. The US stand was that it would not do so as long as China and India opted out. China and India argue that, as emerging countries, they must first catch up with the developed world. At Durban, South Africa, in 2001, the UN-sponsored conference agreed to adopt a global treaty by 2015 which would be implemented by 2020. Industrial countries led by the EU are likely to meet global warming reduction policies. Indeed, the EU has proposed an emission reduction target of 40 percent below the 1990 level before the year 2030. However, the prospects that China and India will do so are dim, and less developed nations are unlikely to be able to take significant steps without large-scale outside funding. The United States could show leadership by offering technological help to the emerging economies in pollution control and development of alternative energy sources, as well as negotiating a longer time line for them to fulfill their quotas. It is to be hoped that the intensifying weight of scientific evidence[4] and the increasing pressure of public opinion will propel the recalcitrant major powers to recognize the urgency of this worldwide threat. Without concrete and systematic steps now, the result will be global destabilization from the turmoil caused by flooding, drought, famine, and uncontrolled migrations.

In an increasingly complex geopolitical world, pervaded by the influence of globalism, power will be even more widely dispersed and hierarchy weaker so that no single state or realm can expect to be dominant. The twenty-first century has become the "Global Century," not the "American," the "Chinese," or the "Pacific" one. The very complexity of the system requires the leadership of all the major and regional powers to keep the world in balance in the face of dynamic changes. As "first among equals" of the major powers, the United States, in partnership with the European Union, will have ample opportunity to apply its power in international affairs with wisdom, determination, and consistency while remaining mindful of the limitations, as well as the responsibilities, inherent in the exercise of power.

Notes

1. Carlotta Gali, *The Wrong Enemy: America in Afghanistan, 2001–2014* (New York: Houghton Mifflin Harcourt, 2014), 329.

2. Alan J. Day, ed., *Border and Territorial Disputes* (Harlow, England: Longman, 1982), 236–50.

3. Brian Walsh, "Who Won and Lost at Bali," *Time*, Dec. 16, 2007.

4. Intergovernmental Panel on Climate Change, *Fourth Assessment Report, Climate Change 2007*. Synthesis Report, 23 pp. (Geneva, Switzerland: Intergovernmental Panel on Climate Change, 2008).

Bibliography

Agnew, John. *Geopolitics: Re-visioning World Politics*. London: Routledge, 1998.

———. *Mastering Space: Hegemony, Territory and the International Economy*. London: Routledge, 1995.

———. *Place and Politics*. London: Allen and Unwin, 1987.

———. *Western Geopolitical Thought in the Twentieth Century*. New York: St. Martin's, 1985.

Amin, Ash, and Nigel Thrift. "What's Left? Just the Future." *Antipode* 37 (2005): 220–38.

Anderson, Jon Lee. "The Commandante's Canal." *New Yorker*, March 10, 2014, 57–60.

Ardrey, Robert. *The Territorial Imperative*. New York: Atheneum, 1966.

Aslund, Anders. *How Capitalism Was Built: The Transformation of Central and Eastern Europe, Russia and Central Asia*. New York: Cambridge University Press, 2007.

Baransky, N. M. *Economic Geography of the U.S.S.R.* Preface and translation by S. Belsky. Moscow: Foreign Languages, 1956.

Barrionuevo, Alexei. "Chavez's Plan for Development Bank Moves Ahead." *New York Times*, October 22, 2007, A3.

Bell, Morag. *Contemporary Africa: Development, Culture and the State*. London: Longman, 1986.

Bertalanffy, Ludwig von. *General System Theory*. New York: Braziller, 1968.

Bezlova, Antoaneta. "Environment-China: Three Gorges Dam May Displace Millions More." Inter Press Service, October 12, 2007.

Blouet, Brian. *Halford Mackinder: A Biography*. College Station: Texas A&M University Press, 1987.

Bowman, Isaiah. *The New World*. Yonkers-on-Hudson, NY: World Book, 1922.

Boyd, Andrew. *An Atlas of World Affairs*. 10th ed. London: Routledge, 1998.

Boyd, Andrew, and Joshua Comenetz. *An Atlas of World Affairs*. London: Routledge, 2007.

Bracken, Paul. *Fire in the East*. New York: HarperCollins, 1999.

Brandt, Willy. *North-South: A Programme for Survival*. London: Pan, 1980.

Braudel, Ferdinand. *The Mediterranean and the Mediterranean World in the Age of Philip II*. 2 vols. Translated by Sian Reynolds. New York: Harper & Row, 1973.

Brecher, Michael. *The New States of Asia*. New York: Oxford University Press, 1966.

Brigham, Albert Perry. *Geographic Influences in American History*. New York: Chautauqua, 1903.

Brown, Seyom. "Inherited Geopolitics and Emergent Global Realities." In *America's Global Interests*, edited by Edward K. Hamilton, 166–97. New York: Norton, 1989.

Brunn, Stanley D., Jeffrey A. Jones, and Shannon O'Lear. "Geopolitical Information and Communications in the Twenty-First Century." In *Reordering the World*, edited by George J. Demko and William B. Wood. Boulder, CO: Westview, 1999.

Brzezinski, Zbigniew. *The Choice—Global Domination or Global Leadership*. New York: Basic, 2004.

———. *Game Plan*. New York: Atlantic Monthly Press, 1986.

———. *The Grand Chessboard*. New York: Basic, 1997.

———. *Out of Control: Global Turmoil on the Eve of the Twenty-First Century*. New York: Scribner's, Macmillan, 1993.

———. *Three Presidents and the Crisis of American Superpower*. New York: Basic, 2007.

Bullard, Reader. *Britain and the Middle East*. London: Hutchinson's University Library, 1951.

Bush, George H. W. "Toward a New World Order." September 11, 1990. *Public Papers of the Presidents of the United States, George H. W. Bush, 1990.* Washington, DC: Government Printing Office, 1991. Reprinted in Ó Tuathail, Gearóid. *Critical Geopolitics: The Politics of Writing Global Space*, 131–34. Minneapolis: University of Minnesota Press, 1996.

Carmody, Padraig R., and Francis Y. Owuse. "Competing Hegemons? Chinese vs. American Geo-economic Strategies in Africa." *Political Geography* 26 (2007): 504–24.

Central Intelligence Agency. "Disputes International." In *World Factbook 2007.* Washington, DC: GPO/CIA, 2007.

———. "The World Factbook: Field Listing—Disputes—International." https://www.cia.gov/library/publications/the-world-factbook/fields/2070.html.

———. *World Factbook 2000.* Washington, DC: GPO/CIA, 2000.

———. *World Factbook 2007.* Washington, DC: GPO/CIA, 2007.

———. *World Factbook 2013.* Washington, DC: GPO/CIA, 2013.

———. *World Factbook 2014.* Washington, DC: GPO/CIA, 2014.

Chanda, Nayan. "Cam Ranh Bay Manoeuvres." *Far Eastern Economic Review* 163, no. 52 (Dec. 28, 2000): 21–23.

Chivers, C. J. "Destroying Arms, U.S. and Russia Celebrate Rare Amity." *New York Times*, Sept. 1, 2007, A2.

Chou, Oliver. "Navy Boss Outlines Force of the Future." *South China Morning Post*, April 22, 1999.

Chrone, G. R. *Background to Political Geography.* London: Pittman, 1969.

Churchill, Winston. "Iron Curtain" speech. Graduation address, Westminster College, Fulton, MO, March 5, 1946. Excerpted in *Internet Modern History Sourcebook*, August 1977.

Cohen, Roger, David E. Singer, and Steven R. Weisman. "Challenging Rest of the World with a New Order." *New York Times*, October 12, 2004, A1, A22.

Cohen, Saul B. "Asymmetrical States and Geopolitical Equilibrium." *SAIS Review* 4, no. 2 (Summer/Fall 1984): 193–212.

———. "The Eurasian Convergence Zone: Gateway or Shatterbelt?" *Eurasian Geography and Economics* 46, no. 1 (2005): 1–22.

———. "Gaza Now! Prospects for a Gaza Microstate." *Mediterranean Quarterly* (Spring 1992): 60–80.

———. *Geography and Politics in a World Divided.* New York: Random House, 1963; 2nd ed. New York: Oxford University Press, 1973.

———. "Global Change in the Post–Cold War Era." *Annals of the Association of American Geographers* 81, no. 4 (1991): 551–80.

———. "A New Map of Geopolitical Equilibrium: A Developmental Approach." *Political Geography Quarterly* 1, no. 3 (1982): 223–42.

Cohen, Saul B., and Lewis D. Rosenthal. "A Geographical Model for Political Systems Analysis." *Geographical Review* 61, no. 1 (1971): 5–31.

Collier, Paul. *The Bottom Billion: Why the Poorest Countries Are Failing and What Can Be Done about It.* New York: Oxford University Press, 2007.

Collingwood, Robin George. *The Idea of Nature.* Oxford: Oxford University Press, 1993.

Cressey, George. *The Basis of Soviet Strength.* New York: McGraw-Hill, 1945.

Crossette, Barbara. "Europe Stares at a Future Built by Immigrants." *New York Times Week in Review*, January 2, 2000, 1, 4.

Cutter, Susan, Douglas Richardson, and Thomas Wilbanks, eds. *The Geographical Dimensions of Terrorism.* New York: Routledge, 2003.

Davis, Anthony. "Blue Water Ambitions." *Asia Week* 26, no. 11 (March 24, 2000): 1.

Day, Alan J., ed. *Border and Territorial Disputes.* Harlow, England: Longman, 1982.

De Seversky, Alexander. *Air Power: Key to Survival.* New York: Simon & Schuster, 1950.

Diehl, Paul F., ed. *A Road Map to War.* Nashville: Vanderbilt University Press, 1999.

Dorpalen, A. *The World of General Haushofer: Geopolitics in Action.* New York: Farrar and Rinehart, 1948.

Drozdiak, William. "Old World Reinvents Itself as Model for New Economy." *International Herald Tribune*, February 19, 2001, 1, 11.

Drucker, Peter. *The New Realities.* New York: Harper & Row, 1989.

———. *Post Capitalist Society.* New York: Harper Business, 1983.

Dunbar, Gary. *Élisée Reclus, Historian of Nature.* Hamden, CT: Archon, 1978.

Duncan, Richard C., and Walter Youngquist. "The World Petroleum Life-Cycle." Paper presented at Petroleum Technology Transfer Council Workshop, University of Southern California, Los Angeles, October 22, 1998.

Eckholm, Erik. "After 50 Years, China Youth Remain Mao's Pioneers." *New York Times*, September 26, 1999, A12.

Economist. "Central America's Border Order." March 13, 2000, 42.

———. "China Survey." April 8, 2000, 13.

———. "Denmark and Greenland: Ultima Motives." February 17, 2001, 55.

———. "France and Germany: Scenes from a Marriage." March 24, 2001, 27–30.
———. "Go West Young Han." December 23, 2000, 45–46.
———. "Japan and Its Neighbors." May 12, 2006, 25–26.
———. "Russia's World." May 9, 1998, 21.
———. "Somaliland, the Nation Nobody Knows." April 14, 2001, 42.
———. "A Special Report on Financial Centres." September 15, 2007, 10–13.
———. "Sri Lanka's Muslims: Homeless and Homesick." October 13, 2007, 45–46.
———. "Survey Taiwan." November 7, 1998, 14.
Elau, Heinz. "H. D. Lasswell's Developmental Hypothesis." *Western Political Quarterly* 21 (June 1958): 229–42.
European Commission. *Financial Framework 2007–2013: Investing in Our Future.* Luxembourg: EC Publications Office, April 23, 2008, 3.
Fairgrieve, James. *Geography and World Power.* London: University of London Press, 1915.
Fei, Ding. *Labor Relations with Chinese Construction Projects in Sub-Saharan Africa.* Paper presented at Association of American Geographers annual meeting, Tampa, FL, April 2014, 18.
Fitzgerald, C. P. *The Chinese View of Their Place in the World.* London: Oxford University Press, 1964.
French, Howard W. "Still Wary of Outsiders, Japan Expects Immigration Boom." *New York Times*, March 14, 2000, A1, A14.
Friedman, Thomas. *The Lexus and the Olive Tree.* New York: Farrar, Straus & Giroux, 1999.
———. "The Mean Season." *New York Times*, September 9, 1999, A23.
Fromkin, David. *A Peace to End All Peace.* New York: Henry Holt, 1989.
Fukuyama, Francis. "After Neoconservatism." *New York Times Magazine*, February 19, 2006.
———. *The End of History and the Last Man.* New York: Free Press, 1992.
———. *The Great Disruption: Human Nature and the Reconstitution of Social Order.* New York: Free Press, 1999.
Fund for Peace. *The Failed States Index 2013. Foreign Policy Magazine.* http://www.foreignpolicy.com/failed states2013.
Gakwandi, A. S. "Towards a New Political Map of Africa." In *Politics, Economy and Social Change in the Twenty-First Century*, edited by A. I. Asiwaju, 252–59. London: Hurst, 1996.
Gali, Carlotta. *The Wrong Enemy: America in Afghanistan, 2001–2014.* New York: Houghton Mifflin Harcourt, 2014.
Garton Ash, Timothy. *Free World: America, Europe and the Surprising Future of the West.* New York: Random House, 2004.
Giblin, B. "Élisée Reclus, 1830–1905." In *Geographers Bibliographical Studies*, edited by T. W. Freeman, 125–32. London: Mansell, 1979.
Ginsburg, Norton. "On the Chinese Perception of World Order." In *China's Policies in Asia and America's Alternatives*, edited by Tang Tsou, 73–96. Chicago: University of Chicago Press, 1968.
Gyorgy, Andrew. *Geopolitics.* Berkeley: University of California Press, 1944.
Hardt, Michael, and Antonio Negri. *Empire.* Cambridge, MA: Harvard University Press, 2000.
Harris, Norman. *Intervention and Colonization in Africa, 1884–1914.* Boston: Houghton Mifflin, 1914.
Hart, B. Liddell. "The Russo-German Campaign." In *The Red Army*, edited by B. Liddell Hart, 100–126. New York: Harcourt, Brace, 1956.
Hartshorne, Richard. *The Nature of Geography.* Lancaster, PA: Association of American Geographers, 1939.
———. "The United States and the 'Shatter Zone' in Europe." In *Compass of the World*, edited by H. Weigert and V. Stefannson, 203–14. New York: Macmillan, 1944.
Hennig, Richard. *Geopolitik: Die Lehre vom Staat als Lebewesen.* Leipzig: Hirzel, 1931.
Henrikson, Alan K. "Diplomacy for the 21st Century: 'Re-crafting the Old Guild.'" Paper presented at the 503rd Wilton Park Conference, "Diplomacy: Profession in Peril?" Published in *Current Issues in International Diplomacy and Foreign Policy.* Wilton Park Papers, Vol. 1. London: H.M. Stationery Office, 1998.
Hepple, Leslie. "Geopolitics, Generals and the State in Brazil." *Political Geography Quarterly* 5 (Supplement 1986): S79–S90.
Herb, Guntram H., and David H. Kaplan, eds. *Nested Identities.* Lanham, MD: Rowman & Littlefield, 1999.
Hooson, David, ed. *Geography and National Identity.* Oxford: Blackwell, 1994.
Huntington, Samuel P. "The Clash of Civilizations?" *Foreign Affairs* 72 (1993): 22–49.
———. *The Clash of Civilizations? The Debate.* New York: Council on Foreign Relations, Simon and Schuster, 1996.
———. *Political Order in Changing Societies.* New Haven, CT: Yale University Press, 1968.
Hutton, Will. *The Writing on the Wall: Why We Must Embrace China as a Partner or Face It as an Enemy.* New York: Free Press, 2007.
Intergovernmental Panel on Climate Change. *Fourth Assessment Report, Climate Change 2007.* Synthesis Report, 23 pp. Geneva, Switzerland: Intergovernmental Panel on Climate Change, 2008.

———. *Fifth Assessment Report, Climate Change 2013*. 1,535 pp. Geneva, Switzerland: Intergovernmental Panel on Climate Change, 2014.

Jefferson, Mark. "The Civilizing Rails." *Economic Geography* 4 (1928): 217–31.

Johnson, Chalmers. *The Sorrows of Empire: Militarism, Secrecy and the End of the Republic*. New York: Henry Holt, 2004.

Jones, Stephen B. "Global Strategic Views." *Geographical Review* 45, no. 4 (1955): 492–508.

———. "The Power Inventory and National Strategy." *World Politics* 1, no. 4 (July 1954): 421–52.

———. "A Unified Field Theory of Political Geography." *Annals of the Association of American Geographers* 44, no. 2: 111–23.

———. "Views of the Political World." *Geographical Review* 45, no. 3 (1955): 492–508.

Kahn, Joseph. "World Bank Cites Itself in Study of Africa's Bleak Performance." *New York Times*, June 1, 2000, 6.

Kaplan, Robert D. "The Coming Anarchy." *Atlantic Monthly* 273, no. 2 (1994): 44–46.

———. *The Coming Anarchy: Shattering the Dreams of the Cold War*. New York: Random House, 2000.

———. "Lost at Sea." *New York Times*, Sept. 21, 2007, A19.

———. *The Revenge of Geography*. New York: Random House, 2012.

Kaufman, D., A. Kraay, and M. Mastruzzi. *Governance Matters, 2007: Worldwide Governance Indicators 1996–2006*. www.worldwidebank.org, www.govindicators.org.

Kelly, Philip. *Checkerboards and Shatterbelts: The Geopolitics of South America*. Austin: University of Texas Press, 1987.

———. "Escalation of Regional Conflict: Testing the Shatterbelt Concept." *Political Geography Quarterly* 5, no. 2 (1986): 161–86.

Kennan, George. "The Sources of Soviet Conduct." *Foreign Affairs* 25 (1947): 566–82.

Kennedy, Paul. *Preparing for the Twenty-First Century*. New York: Random House, 1993.

———. *The Rise and Fall of the Great Powers*. New York: Random House, 1987.

Kissinger, Henry A. *Does America Need a Foreign Policy? Towards a Diplomacy for the 21st Century*. New York: Simon & Schuster, 2001.

———. *The White House Years*. Boston: Little, Brown, 1979.

Kjellén, Rudolf. *Staten som Lifsform*. 1916. Published in German as *Der Staat also Lebenform*. Leipzig: Hirzel, 1917.

Kliot, Nurit, and Stanley Waterman, eds. *The Political Geography of Conflict and Peace*. London: Belhaven, 1991.

Kolossov, Vladimir, and John O'Loughlin. "Pseudo-States as the Harbingers of a New Geopolitics: The Example of the Trans-Dniester Moldovan Republic." *Geopolitics* 3, no. 1 (Summer 1998): 151–76.

Korn, Daniel A. *Ethiopia, the United States and the Soviet Union, 1974–1985*. London: Croom Helm, 1986.

Kotkin, Joel. *The New Geography: How the Digital Revolution Is Reshaping the American Landscape*. New York: Random House, 2000.

Kuzio, Taras. "Borders, Symbolism and Nation-State Building." *Geopolitics and International Boundaries* 2, no. 2 (Autumn 1997): 36–56.

Lacoste, Yves. "Editorial: Les Géographes, l'Action et la Politique." *Hérodite* 33 (1984): 3–32.

———. *La Géographie Ça Sert, d'Abord, à Faire le Guerre*. Paris: Maspero, 1976.

Langewiesche, William. *The Atomic Bazaar: The Rise of the Nuclear Poor*. New York: Farrar, Straus & Giroux, 2007.

Lefton, Rebecca, Gywnne Taraska, and Jenny Cooper, with Ben Bovarnick. "Warsaw Climate Talks End with a Foundation for a Global Agreement." Issue brief, Center for American Progress, Washington, DC, December 4, 2013.

Levins, Steve. *Oil and the Pursuit of Empire in the Caspian Sea*. New York: Random House, 2007.

Lieven, Anatol, and John Hulsman. *Ethical Realism: A Vision for America's Role in the World*. New York: Pantheon, 2006.

Lin Pao. Excerpts from "Peking Declaration Urging 'People's War' to Destroy U.S." *New York Times*, Sept. 4, 1965, 2.

Lintner, Bertil. *Cross-Border Trade in the Golden Triangle*. Durham, England: Boundaries Research Press–University of Durham, 1991.

Lonsdale, Richard, and J. Clark Archer. "Empty Areas in the United States, 1990–1995." *Journal of Geography* 96, no. 2 (March/April 1997): 108–22.

Lukacs, John. *The End of the Twentieth Century and the End of the Modern Age*. New York: Ticknor and Fields, 1993.

Mackinder, Halford. *Democratic Ideals and Reality*. London: Constable, 1919. Reprint, New York: Norton, 1962.

———. "The Geographical Pivot of History." *Geographical Journal* 23, no. 4 (1904), 421–44. Reprinted in Mackinder, *Democratic Ideals and Reality*, 265–78. New York: Norton, 1962.

———. "The Round World and the Winning of the Peace." *Foreign Affairs* 21, no. 4 (1943): 595–605.

MacLachlan, Ian, and Adrian Guillermo Aguilar. "Maquiladora Myths: Locational and Structural Change in Mexico's Export Manufacturing Industry." *Professional Geographer* 50, no. 3 (1998): 315–31.

Mahan, Alfred T. *The Influence of Sea Power on History: 1660–1783*. Boston: Little, Brown, 1890.

———. *The Problem of Asia and Its Effect upon International Policy*. Boston: Little, Brown, 1900.

Malin, James. "Space and History, Part 2." *Agricultural History* 18 (July 1944): 65–126.

March, Andrew L. *The Idea of China*. New York: Praeger, 1974.

Martin, Lisa L. "Self-Binding." *Harvard Magazine* (Sept.–Oct. 2004): 33–36.

McCants, William, ed. *The Military Ideology Atlas: Research Compendium*. West Point, NY: Combating Terrorism Center, 2006.

Merk, Frederick. *The Monroe Doctrine and American Expansionism, 1843–1849*. New York: Knopf, 1966.

Meyer, Karl E., and Shareen Blair Brysac. *Tournament of Shadows: The Great Game and Race for Empire in Central Asia*. Washington, DC: Cornelia and Michael Bessie/Counterpoint, 1999.

Modelski, George. *Long Cycles of World Politics*. Seattle: University of Washington Press, 1987.

———. "The Study of Long Cycles." In *Exploring Long Cycles*, edited by George Modelski, 1–15. Boulder, CO: Lynne Rienner, 1987.

Montesquieu, Charles-Louis de. *The Spirit of Laws*. Book XIV. Translated by Thomas Nugent. 1906. Reprint, Library of the Classics, New York: Hafner, 1949.

Murphy, Alexander B. "International Law and the Sovereign State System." In *Reordering the World*, edited by George J. Demko and William B. Wood. Boulder, CO: Westview, 1999.

"Myanmar's Where the Indian and Chinese Navies Meet." *Stratfor Commentary*, January 27, 2000.

Mydans, Seth. "East Timor's Dream of Oil." *New York Times*, October 20, 2000, A13.

———. "Religiosity, Not Radicalism, Is New Wave in Indonesia." *New York Times*, July 2, 2007, A7.

National Interest. "The End of History?" *National Interest* 16 (Summer 1989): 3–18.

Newbigin, Marion. *The Mediterranean Lands*. New York: Knopf, 1924.

News Central Asia. "Tehran Summit Unites Caspian States on Major Issues." *News Central Asia*, October 17, 2007. http://www.newscentralasia.net/Regional-News/179.html.

New York Times. "St. Kitts Ponders Request for Bombing Range." March 22, 2001, 5.

Nijman, Jan. *The Geopolitics of Power and Conflict: Superpowers in the International System, 1945–1992*. London: Belhaven, 1993.

Nitze, Paul H., Leonard Sullivan Jr., and the Atlantic Council Working Group on Securing the Seas. *Securing the Seas*. Boulder, CO: Westview, 1979.

Nordhaus, William D. *The Climate Casino: Risk, Uncertainty and Economics for a Warming World*. New Haven, CT: Yale University Press, 2013.

O'Brien, R. *Global Financial Integration: The End of Geography*. New York: Council on Foreign Relations Press, 1992.

Olopade, Dayo. *The Bright Continent: Breaking Rules and Making Change in Modern Africa*. New York: Houghton Mifflin Harcourt, 2014, 272.

O'Loughlin, John, and Paul F. Talbot. "Where in the World Is Russia? Geopolitical Perceptions and Preferences of Ordinary Russians." *Eurasian Geography and Economics* 46, no. 1 (2005): 23–50.

O'Loughlin, John, and Herman Van der Wusten. *The New Political Geography of Eastern Europe*. New York: Belhaven, 1993.

———. "Political Geography of Panregions." *Geographical Review* 80 (1990): 1–20.

O'Neill, Robert. "Australia and the Indian Ocean." In *The Southern Ocean and the Security of the Free World*, edited by Patrick Wall, 177–89. London: Stacey International, 1977.

Onishi, Norimitsu. "African Bloc Hoping to Do Better as the 'African Union.'" *New York Times*, July 12, 2001, A3.

O'Sullivan, Patrick. "Antidomino." *Political Geography Quarterly* 1 (1982): 57–64.

Ó Tuathail, Gearóid. *Critical Geopolitics: The Politics of Writing Global Space*. Minneapolis: University of Minnesota Press, 1996.

———. "Introduction." In *The Geopolitics Reader*, edited by Gearóid Ó Tuathail, Simon Dalby, and Paul Routledge, 19–24. London: Routledge, 1998.

———. "Thinking Critically about Geopolitics." In *The Geopolitics Reader*, edited by Gearóid Ó Tuathail, Simon Dalby, and Paul Routledge, 1–11. London: Routledge, 1998.

Ó Tuathail, Gearóid, Simon Dalby, and Paul Routledge, eds. *The Geopolitics Reader*. London: Routledge, 1998.

Painter, Joe. *Politics, Geography and "Political Geography."* London: Arnold, 1995.

Paret, Peter, ed. *Makers of Modern Strategy*. Princeton, NJ: Princeton University Press, 1986.

Parker, Geoffrey. *Geopolitics: Past, Present and Future*. London: Pinter, 1998.

———. *The Geopolitics of Domination*. London: Routledge, 1988.

———. *A Political Geography of Community Europe*. London: Butterworth, 1983.

Perle, Richard, and David Frum. *An End to Evil*. New York: Random House, 2004.

Perlez, Jane. "Blunt Reason for Enlarging NATO: Curbs on Germany." *New York Times*, December 7, 1997, A17.

Pierre, Andrew J. *The Global Politics of Arms Sales*. Princeton, NJ: Princeton University Press, 1982.

Population Reference Bureau. *2007 Population Data Sheet*. Washington, DC: Population Reference Bureau, 2007.

Prescott, J. V. R. "Africa's Boundary Problems." *Optima* 28 (1980): 3–21.

Rand McNally. *World Facts and Maps*. 2000 ed. Skokie, IL: Rand McNally, 2000.

Ratzel, Friedrich. *Politische Geographie*. 3rd ed. Munich: Oldenbourg, 1923.

———. *Politische Geographie der Vereinigtnen Staaten*. Leipzig: Oldenbourg, 1897.

———. "Die Gesetze des Raumlichen Wachstums der Staaten." *Petermanns Mitteilungen* 42 (1896): 97–107. Reprinted as "The Laws of the Spatial Growth of States." Translated by Ronald Bolin. In *The Structure of Political Geography*, edited by Roger Kasperson and Julian Minghi, 17–28. Chicago: Aldine, 1969.

Reid, T. R. *The United States of Europe—The New Superpower and the End of American Supremacy*. London: Penguin, 2004.

Renner, George T. *Human Geography in the Air Age*. New York: Macmillan, 1942.

"Restriction in EU Immigration Policies against the New EU Member States (NMS)," http://www.Europeananalysis.org.uk, 2007.

Revkin, Andrew C. "Lake's Rapid Retreat Heightens Troubles in North Africa." *New York Times*, May 27, 2001, F4.

Rifkin, Jeremy. *The European Dream*. London: Penguin, 2004.

Rosecrance, Richard. *The Rise of the Trading State*. New York: Basic, 1986.

Rupp, George. *Globalization Challenged*. New York: Columbia University Press, 2006.

Ryan, Bruce. "Australia's Place in the World." In *The Australian Experience*, edited by R. L. Heathcote, 305–17. Melbourne: Longman, 1988.

Said, Edward. *Culture and Imperialism*. New York: Vintage, 1994.

Salvo, Joseph J., and Arun Peter Lobo. *The Newest New Yorkers*. 5th ed. New York: New York City Planning Department, 2013.

Schwarts, Mattathias. "A Mission Gone Wrong." *New Yorker*, January 6, 2014, 44–55.

Schwartz, Benjamin I. "The Maoist Image of World Order." In *Image and Reality in World Politics*, edited by John C. Farrell and Asa P. Smith, 92–102. New York: Columbia University Press, 1968.

Sciolino, Elaine. "It's a Sea! It's a Lake! No. It's a Pool of Oil." *New York Times*, June 21, 1998, 16.

Segal, Gerald. "Does China Matter?" *Foreign Affairs* 78, no. 5 (June 1999): 24–36.

Semple, Ellen Churchill. *American History and Its Geographic Conditions*. Boston: Houghton Mifflin, 1903.

———. *The Geography of the Mediterranean World*. 1915. Reprint, New York: Henry Holt, 1931.

Shelley, Fred., J. Clark Archer, Fiona M. Davidson, and Stanley D. Brunn. *Political Geography of the United States*. New York: Guilford, 1996.

Siegfried, André. *The Mediterranean*. Translated by H. H. Hemming and Doris Hemming. London: Jonathan Cape, 1948.

Singh, Govand. *A Political Geography of India*. Allahabad, India: Central Book Deposit, 1969.

Slessor, John. *The Great Deterrent*. New York: Praeger, 1957.

Smith, Dan. *The State of War and Peace Atlas*. London: Penguin, 1997.

Smith, Laurence C. *The New North: The World in 2050*. London: Profile, 2011.

Smith, Neil, and Jan Nijman. "Alfred Thayer Mahan." In *Dictionary of Geopolitics*, edited by John O'Loughlin, 156–58. Westport, CT: Greenwood, 1994.

Smith, Rupert. *The Utility of Force: The Art of War in the Modern World*. New York: Knopf, 2006.

Solana Madariaga, Javier. "Growing the Alliance." *Economist*, March 13, 1999, 23–28.

Spear, Percival. *Modern India*. Ann Arbor: University of Michigan Press, 1961.

Spencer, Herbert. "The Social Organism." Reprinted in *The Man versus the State*, edited by Donald Macrae, 195–233. Baltimore: Penguin, 1969.

Spykman, Nicholas. *America's Strategy in World Politics: The United States and the Balance of Power*. New York: Harcourt, Brace, 1942.

———. *The Geography of Peace*. New York: Harcourt, Brace, 1944.

State of the World 2007—Our Unborn Future. Washington, DC: Worldwatch Institute, 2007; New York: Norton, 2007.

Sulzberger, C. L. *The Coldest War*. New York: Harcourt Brace Jovanovich, 1974.

Tambs, Lewis. "Geopolitical Factors in Latin America." In *Latin America: Politics, Economic and Hemispheric Security*, edited by Norman Bailey, 36, 42–43. New York: Praeger, 1965.

Taylor, Peter J. *Political Geography*. 2nd ed. Harlow, England: Longman Scientific and Technical; New York: Wiley, 1989.

———, ed. *World Government*. New York: Oxford University Press, 1990.

Trubowitz, Peter. *Defining the National Interest*. Chicago: University of Chicago Press, 1998.

Tung, William L. *China and the Foreign Powers*. Dobbs Ferry, NY: Oceana, 1970.

Turner, Frederick Jackson. "The Significance of the Frontier in American History." Paper presented at the American Historical Association Meeting, Chicago, 1893. Reprinted in Turner, *The Frontier in American History*. New York: Henry Holt, 1920.

Tyler, Patrick E. "The China Threat, Some Experts Insist, Is Overrated." *International Herald Tribune*, February 16, 1999, 2.

US Department of Energy, Energy Information Administration. "Annual Energy Review." In *World Almanac and Book of Facts 2000*. Mahwah, NJ: Primedia Reference, 1999.

———. "Annual Energy Review." In *World Almanac and Book of Facts 2007*, 113. New York: World Almanac Education Group, 2007.

US Department of State. *Patterns of Global Terrorism—2000*. Washington, DC: Office of the Coordinator for Counterterrorism, 2001.

Wallerstein, Immanuel. *The Capitalist World-Economy*. Cambridge: Cambridge University Press, 1979.

———. "European Unity and Its Implications for the Interstate System." In *Europe: Dimensions of Peace*, edited by B. Hettne, 27–38. London: Zed, 1988.

———. *Geopolitics and Geoculture: Essays on the Changing World-System*. Cambridge: Cambridge University Press, 1991.

———. *Historical Capitalism*. London: Verso, 1983.

———. "The World-System after the Cold War." *Journal of Peace Research* 30, no. 1 (1993): 1–6.

Walsh, Brian. "Who Won and Lost at Bali." *Time*, Dec. 16, 2007.

Walsh, Edmund. "Geopolitics and International Morals." In *Compass of the World*, edited by H. W. Weigert and V. Stefansson. New York: Macmillan, 1944.

Weigert, Hans. *Generals and Geographers*. New York: Oxford University Press, 1942.

Werner, Heinz. *Comparative Psychology of Mental Development*. Rev. ed. New York: International University Press, 1948.

Werner, Heinz, and Bernard Kaplan. "The Developmental Approach to Cognition." *American Anthropologist* (1956): 866–80.

White, George W. *Nationalism and Territory*. Lanham, MD: Rowman & Littlefield, 2000.

Whittlesey, Derwent. *The Earth and the State*. New York: Henry Holt, 1939.

———. "The Horizon of Geography." *Annals of the Association of American Geographers* 35, no. 1 (March 1945): 1–36.

———. "The Impress of Effective Central Authority on the Landscape." *Annals of the Association of American Geographers* 25, no. 2 (June 1935): 85–98.

———. "The Regional Concept and the Regional Method." In *American Geography: Inventory & Prospect*, edited by Preston E. James and Clarence F. Jones. Syracuse: Association of American Geographers and Syracuse University Press, 1954.

———. "Sequent Occupance." *Annals of the Association of American Geographers* 19, no. 3 (September 1929): 162–65.

Wook-ik Yu. "Seoul: The City of Vitality." *IGU Bulletin* 50, no. 1 (2000): 5–19.

World Almanac and Book of Facts 2000. "Nations of the World." Mahwah, NJ: Primedia Reference, 1999.

World Bank. *Global Development Finance*. Washington, DC: World Bank Publicaitons, 2006.

———. *World Bank Atlas: 1999*. Washington, DC: World Bank Publications, 1999.

———. *World Bank Report Africa Development Indicators (ADI)*. Washington, DC: World Bank Publications, 2007.

Worldwatch Institute. *Vital Signs 2006–2007*. Washington, DC: Worldwatch Institute, 2007; New York: Norton, 2006.

Index

Note: Maps and tables are designated by page numbers in italics.

Abbas, Mahmoud, 399, 401
Abe, Shinzō, 280, 343
Abkhazia, *57,* 192, 232, 249, 257–58, 452
ABM. *See* antiballistic missiles
Abuja, Nigeria, 428, 439
Abu Sayyaf, 325
accommodation, 30–33, 55, 84, 104, 134, 204, 213, 346–47, 455
Aceh, 56–*57,* 90, 328–32
Acheson, Dean, 29
Adalet ve Kalkınma Partisi (Justice and Development Party), 407
Addis Ababa, Ethiopia, 422, 428, 431–32, 442
Aden, Gulf of. *See* Gulf of Aden
Aden, Yemen, 68, 74, 76–77, 85, 92, 231, 376–77, 380–81, 420, 442
Adjara, 232, 258
Afghanistan, 30, 55, 62, 358, 368, 383, 405–6, 447–50, 453; boundaries, 363, 395; Cold War and, 86–87; Pakistan and, 58, 62, 354, 370, *397,* 405–6, 415–16, 449–50; political instability of, 370; political organization of, 383–84; Soviet invasion/war, 83, 86–87, 354; US and, 5, 29, 147; US war in, 11, 39, 44, 91, 247, 310, 354–55, 375, 385, 449
Africa. *See* African Horn; Central Africa; Maghreb; Sub-Saharan Africa
African Horn, 49, 74–77, 90, *92,* 441–43
African Union (AU), 389, 419, 422, 426, 428, 431, 441
AFRICOM, 417
Agnew, John, 16, 32
Agricultural Act of 2014, 114–15
agriculture, 3, 12–13
air power, 19, 28, 53, 66, 83, 89, 113, 316–18, 373
AKP (Adalet ve Kalkınma Partisi), 407
Al-Aqsa Intifada, 398
Alaska, 100–101, 103–4, 108, 122, 125–26, 131, 225, 265, 294
Alaska Highway (Alcan), 103, 134
al-Assad, Bashar, 409, 448
al-Assad, Hafez, 75, 409
Albania, 7, 29, 70, 73, *92,* 201, 254–56, 278
Algeria, *53, 57,* 66, *92,* 182, 188–89, 201, 209–14, *396,* 434, 448
Algerian War of Independence, 201
Allende, Salvador, 82, 163
Allied leaders, 6
al-Nimeiry, Mohammed, 381
al-Qaeda, 1–2, 4–5, 93, 157, 375, 383–84, 402, 405, 442, 444, 447, 449, 454
al-Shabab, 6, 449
Amaru, Túpac, 176
Amazon basin, 162–63, 172, 454
American Mediterranean, 148, 152
American Samoa, 105, 110
Amin, Ash, 32
Amin, Idi, 434
Anatolia, 378, 382, 384, 386, 412
Anatolian Railway, 17, 377
Anbar, 403
Andean Group, 170–71, 177
Andes mountains, 163
Andorra, 197
Anglo-America, 23, 26–27, 66, 163
Angola, 279, 292, 311, 419–20, 422–25, *430,* 436–37, 441, 443–44, 448; Cold War and, 73, 78–79, 90, *92*
Antarctica, 167–68
antiballistic missiles (ABM), 43, 103, 123, 136, 267
Antiballistic Missile Treaty, 250, 267
Antigua and Barbuda, 154
anti-immigrant bias, 202–3, 345
Antioquia, 152

ANZUS, 320, 342
apartheid, 435
APEC, 300, 335, 342–43
Arab-American Oil Company (ARAMCO), 378
Arab Cooperation Council, 392
Arab Gulf. *See* Persian/Arab Gulf
Arabian Peninsula, 76–77, 382, 388, 407, 412, 453
Arab-Israeli conflict, 29, 49, 91, 214, 379, 388, 398–401, 453
Arab League, 392, 400
Arab Spring, 1–2, 49, 213, 375, 389, 393, 409
Arafat, Yasser, 398–99
Aral Sea, 220, 243, 262, 264
ARAMCO, 378
Archangel (Arkhangelsk), Russia, 221–22, 228, 243, 247
Arctic, 13, 27, 72, 122, 126, 130–31, 224–25, 229, 234, 238, 240, 242–44, 250, 294; global warming and, 62, 244, 268, 386, 455
Arctic Ocean, 103–4, 122, 183
Argentina, 53, 66, 82, *92,* 161, 163–65, 167–74, 176–78, 423, 454
Aristide, Jean-Bertrand, 150
Aristotle, 15–16
Armenia, 40, 89, 192, 227, 230–32, 248–49, 257, 259–60, 383, 407, 409, 452
arms and weapons, 74, 82–84, 147; antiballistic missiles (ABM), 43, 103, 123, 136, 250, 267; chemical weapons, 44, 91, 123, 410. *See also* nuclear weapons
arms race, 82–83
Aruba, 155
Arusha Declaration (1967), 426
ASEAN, 47, 80, 292, 300, 306, 320, *322,* 335, 341–43, 455
Asia: continental, 10, 312. *See also* Asia-Pacific Rim; East Asian realm; offshore Asia; South Asia; Southeast Asia
Asia, Central. *See* Central Asia
Asia, East. *See* East Asia
Asia, South. *See* South Asia
Asia, Southeast. *See* Southeast Asia
"Asian century," 282
Asia-Pacific Economic Cooperation Forum (APEC), 300, 335, 342–43
Asia-Pacific Rim, 84, *92,* 282, 315–47; Australia in, 282, 315–16, 319–20; boundaries, 339–41; ecumene, 335–37; effective national territory (ENT), 337–38; empty area, 338–39; evolution of region, 317–18; geopolitical features, 333–41; historic core, 333; and immigration, 337; Japan as core of, 282, 317, 345, 347; political capitals, 335; political stability and instability, 323–33; population in, 321; trade and, 320–23; US and, 316, 343
Assam, 81, 353, 357, 362, 367, 371
Association of Southeast Asian Nations. *See* ASEAN
ASSR (Autonomous Soviet Socialist Republic), *227,* 230, 233
Asunción, Treaty of, 170
Aswan Dam, 75, 380
Atatürk, Mustafa Kemal, 378, 384
Atlantic Alliance. *See* NATO
Atlantic Fleet, US, 157
AU. *See* African Union
Aung San Suu Kyi, 358
Australia, 12, 27, 46, 57, 282, 315–24, 342–43, 357, 455; China and, 47, 342; East Timor and, 5, 329–30; economy of, *322–23,* 345; effective national territory (ENT), 337–38; empty area, 338–39; the future and, 455; immigration to, 345, 455; Japan and, 318–19, 323, 342; Papua New Guinea and, 331; political stability of, 324; as regional power, 3, *53,* 342, 447; and trade, 47, 306, 318–21, 323; US and, 5–6, 46, 319–20, 329–30, 339, 342
Australia, New Zealand, United States (ANZUS), 320, 342
Australia Act (1986), 319
Austria, 17, *57,* 73, *92,* 194, 198, 201–4, 208, 210, 238, 452
authoritarianism, 31, 42–43, 174, 177, 217, 265–66, 324, 407, 409, 436, 448, 452, 454
Autonomous Soviet Socialist Republic (ASSR), *227,* 230, 233
Azerbaijan, 40, *59,* 70, 89, *92,* 192, 220, 227, 230, 232–33, 245, 247–49, 257–61, 263, 377–78, 394, *396–97,* 413
Azeris, 259, 375, 383, *397*
Azores, *57,* 75, 183, *205,* 208

Baath Party, 75, 380, 448
Baghdad, 403
Baghdad Pact (1955), 68, 70–71, 379–80
Bahamas, 152–55
Bahrain, 1, 33, 54, *57, 92,* 123, 376–77, 385, 389, 392–93, *396,* 404, 412
Bakken Formation, *102*
balance of power, 1, 19, 28–30, 46, 218, 378
Bali, 80, 328, 332–33, 373
Balkans, 254–57
Balkan War (1913), 256
Baltic Pipeline Project, 250
Baltic States, 43, 55, *59,* 90, 192, 201, 218–19, 228, 232, 249–50
Baluchistan, 365
Bangalore, India, 353, 363–64
Bangladesh, 13, 81, *92,* 280, 311, 349–*51,* 354, 358, 363–65, 367–68, 456
Bank of the South, 177
Banse, Ewald, 25–26
Bao Dai, 71
Barak, Ehud, 398
Barbados, 154
Barre, Mohamed Siad, 77, 89

Basque country, 204–6
Batista, Fulgencio, 81, 149, 156
Bay of Iskenderun, 259, 392
Bay of Pigs incident, 73, 81–82, 149
Beijing, China, 276, 287, 290
Belarus, 40, 43–44, 56, *59,* 69, 90, 183, 219, 232, 237–38, 248, 250–51, 262, 300. *See also* Belorussia
Belgian Congo, 418
Belgium, 24, 78, 183, *196*–98, *205,* 207, 394, 418
Belize, 144, 151, 154
Belorussia ("White Russia"), 226–29, 232, 250–51. *See also* Belarus
Ben Ali, Zine El Abidine, 1, 213
benevolent policeman policy, 149–50
Benghazi, Libya, 92
Benin, 78, 438, 440
Berbera, Somalia, 74, 77, 395, 420, 431–32, 442
Berbers, 211
Beria, Lavrentiy, 73
Bering, Vitus Jonassen, 225
Bering Sea, 103, 224, 244, 455
Bering Strait, 122, 294
Berlin blockade, 65
Bermuda, *57*
Bertalanffy, Ludwig von, 30, 60
Bharatiya Janata Party, 353
Bhutan, 68, 70, 297, 349–*51,* 362–65, 367, 371
Bhutto, Benazir, 355, 449
Biafra, 419, 438–39
bin Laden, Osama, 2, 93, 354, 383–84, 405, 449
bipolarity, 7, 9, 30, 40, 66, 312
Bishop, Maurice, 86, 150
Black Sea, 19, 32, 43, 190, 192, 219–24 *passim,* 230–38 *passim,* 247–49, 253–54, 257–61, 268, 379, 411, 450, 452; Cold War and, 69–70, 74–75, 77
Blagoveshchensk, Russia, 241
blitzkrieg, 26, 69
"blue-water" fleets, 279–80, 344, 380
blut und boden (blood and soil), 25
Boko Haram, 39, 438, 449
Bolívar, Simón, 161, 177
Bolivarian revolution, 46, 148, 161, 171, 175, 177, 454
Bolivia, 7, 82, *92,* 141, 147, 149, 162–72 *passim,* 174–76, 178, 454
Bolshevik Revolution, 7, 218, 223, 227
Bolshoi Kamen, Russia, 241
Bombay, India. *See* Mumbai, India
Border Industrialization Act (Mexico, 1965), 142
Borneo, 68, 279, 328–29, 332, 341
Bosnia, 58–*59,* 89–91, 249, 254–55
Boston Massacre, 96
Boston Tea Party, 96
Botswana, *430,* 432–33, 435
boundaries, 40
Bourguiba, Habib, 212
Bowman, Isaiah, 17, 23–24, 249
Boxer uprising (1898–1900), 283
Bracero program, 139
Brandt, Willy, 74
Bratsk, Russia, 240
Brazil, 3, 51, 173, 178, 454; Caribbean and, 158; China and, 170, 172; Cold War and, 66, 82; economy and trade, 162, 167, 170–73, 454; ecumene, 166–67; energy policy in, 170–72; the future and, 11, 53, 158, 454; and major powers, 447, 454–55; and oil/gas production, 172; as regional power, 11, *53,* 177; São Paulo, 162, 165, 167, 170, 173; significance of, 7, 158, 172–73, 454; US and, 161, 170–72. *See also* Mercosur
Brazil, Russia, India, China, South Africa (BRICS), 172
Brezhnev, Leonid, 73–74, 87, 278
Brezhnev Doctrine, 30
BRICS (Brazil, Russia, India, China, South Africa), 172
The Bright Continent (Olopade), 440
Britain, 4–5, 17, 19, 23, 44, 48, 180, 183, 186, 191–202 *passim,* 206, 208, 214–15, 452; Asia-Pacific Rim and, 319–20, 326, 339; Cold War and, 68, 70, 76, 78–79, 81; East Asia and, 274–76, 288, 298; economy and trade, 196–97; Middle East and, 68, 376–81, 393, 397, 404; North/Middle America and, 104, 106–8, 110, 123, 125, 138; population of, 196; as regional power, 53; Russia/Eurasian convergence zone and, 220, 255, 262; South Asia and, 350, 353–54, 356, 359–60, 362, 370, 373; Sub-Saharan Africa and, 418–22, 430
British East India Company, 360
British Empire, 17, 112, 319, 350, 360
British North America Act (Canada, 1867), 128
British Raj, 47, 350, 357, 360
British Togoland, 421
Brittany, *57, 205*–6
"brown-water" fleets, 279
Brunei, 80, 315–16, *321–22,* 332, 340–42
Brussels, Belgium, 10, 183, 185, 195, 207
Brzezinski, Zbigniew, 29–30, 30, 32, 89, 192
Buddhism, 234, 283, 295, 297, 333, 350, 356, 359, 362–63, 367
Buganda, 419
Bulgaria, 29, 43, 70, 90, 182, 192, 202, 204, 220, 238, 254, 256, 407, 452
Bullitt, William C., 28–29
Burkina Faso, 429, 432
Burma. *See* Myanmar
Burundi, 62, 89, *92,* 422, 431–32, 434–35, 441
Bush, George H. W., 31
Bush, George W., 5, 29, 113, 120, 126, 192, 214–15, 250, 267, 316, 399

CAFTA-DR (Dominican Republic-Central America Free Trade Agreement), 150, 158
Cairo, Egypt, 75, 243, 380–82, 390, 392, 394, 408, 453

Calcutta, India. *See* Kolkata, India
California, 8, 98–100, 104–5, 107, 110, 115–17, 119–20, 119–22, 137–39, 144–45, 147–48
Cambodia, 27, 43–44, 68, 80, 84–85, *92,* 271, 289, 298–99, 305–9 *passim,* 315–20 *passim,* 326, 341, 372; UN Transitional Authority in Cambodia (UNTAC), 308, 320
Cameroon, 421, *429–30,* 432, 440, 449
Camp David; Camp David Accords, 75, 382, 398
Canada, 12, 42, *53,* 124–32, 343; ecumenes, 128–29; effective national territory (ENT), 129–30; empty areas, 130–31; geopolitical features, 127–32; historic cores, 127–28; migration, 131–32; oil/gas production and, 101–2, 131, 133–35, 145; political capital, 128; population distribution, 132; and trade, 133; US and, 101–2, 104, 125–27, 131–36. *See also* Quebec
Canada-US Free Trade Agreement (1989), 133
Canadian Shield, 129–30
Canary Islands, 55, *57,* 183, *205,* 208
Canberra, Australia, 5, 185, 319–20, 339, 342
Canton, China. *See* Guangzhou
CAP. *See* Common Agricultural Policy
Cape Verde, 55, *57,* 421
capitalism, 3, 12, 17, 31–33, 41–42, 50, 70, 73, 78, 84, 217, 266, 306, 384, 443; China and, 42, 272, 283–84; Russia and, 217, 219, 266–67
capitals, 39
Cárdenas, Lázaro, 139
Caribbean, 41, 46, 48–49, 51, 55–56, 95, 140, 147–49, 151–58; Cold War and, 66, 74, 81–82; as gateway, 124, 454; South America and, 154, 158, 454; US and, 66, 105–6, 109–11, 124, 138, 147–49, 153, 158. *See also* Middle America
Caribbean Community (CARICOM), 158
CARICOM, 158
Carranza, Venustiano, 139
Carter, James Earl, 382
CASAREM, 260
Caspian Sea, 189, 220, 222–23, 234, 236, 240, 245, 247, 249, 257, 259–63, 311, 377, *396,* 413
Castro, Fidel, 7, 46, 81–82, 149, 156–57, 454
Catalonia, 56–*57,* 204–6
Catherine the Great, Empress of Russia, 223
Catholicism, 207, 376
Caucasus. *See* Trans-Caucasus
Cayman Islands, 55, *57,* 155
Celebes. *See* Sulawesi
CENTO. *See* Central Treaty Organization
Central Africa, 440–41
Central African Republic, 124, 388, 431–32, 448
Central America, 11, 29, 105, 109, 111, 127, 140, 143, 147–48, 164. *See also* Middle America
Central Asia, 6–7, 10, 32, 247, 260–64, 452. *See also* Trans-Caucasus
Central Asia-South Asia Regional Electricity Market (CASAREM), 260
Central Europe, 30, 48, 69–70, 191, 203, 215, 218, 227, 238, 250
Central Intelligence Agency (CIA), 70, 76, 92, 178, *196, 322, 351,* 419
Central Pacific Railroad, 108
Central Powers (WWI), 139
Central Treaty Organization (CENTO), 68, 353
centrifugal forces, 38, 156, 168, 424
centripetal forces, 38, 152–53, 163
Ceylon. *See* Sri Lanka
Chad, 62, 76, *92,* 311, 388, *396,* 422, *429–32,* 434, 438–41
Champlain, Samuel de, 127
Charles XII, King of Sweden, 223
Chávez, Hugo, 4, 7, 46, 148, 153–54, 172, 177, 454
Chechnya, *57,* 219, 233, 258–60, 266, 384, 450
Chelyabinsk, Russia, 237–38
Chiang Kai-shek, 276–77, 287
Chile, 53, 82, *92,* 141, 147, 161–65, 167–68, 172, 176–78, 316, 343. *See also* Andean Group; Mercosur; Southern Cone
China, 3, 42, *92,* 172, 271–98, 343, 449; accommodation with, 30, 84; Afghanistan and, 368; anti-imperialist movement in, 276; Asia-Pacific rim, Chinese populations in, 321; Australia and, 47, 319, 342; Bhutan and, 70; boundaries, 70, 81, 84, 295–98, 309, 341, 349, 352–53, 367, 372; BRICS, 172; and capitalism, 42, 272, 283–84; capitals, 285–87; continentality vs. maritimity in, 273–78; as core of East Asia, 10, 284; Cultural Revolution, 88, 278, 285, 293, 305; dam projects in, 288; economy of, 40, 84–85, 191, 272, 282, 284, 289–92, 299; ecumene, 289–92; effective national territory (ENT), 292–94; empty area, 294–96; environmental issues of, 42, 62, 272, 288, 290, 292, 456; Europe and, 279; as first-order power, 264, 271, 309, 352; geopolitical features, 285–98; global warming and, 214, 456; the "Golden Coast," 6, 12, 42, *57, 59,* 272–73, 290–91, 299, 454; Great Leap Forward, 73, 88, 277, 284; Great Wall of, 273, 287, 293; historic core, 285; income in, 289–90; India and, 70, 81, 295, 297, 310, 349, 352, 365, 367, 373; industry in, 287–92; Japan and, 47, 278, 298, 318, 323, 341–44, 346, 449; languages in, 273–74; locational perspective, 282–85; Maoist era in, 277–78; maritimity, 273–82; Mexico and, 147; as Middle Kingdom, 283; Myanmar and, 70, 280, 357–59, 372; navy of, 279–80; Nepal and, 70; Nixon's opening of, 122; North Korea and, 299–304; and nuclear weapons, 293, 296, 354; and oil/gas production (*see under* oil/gas production); one-child policy, 289; Pakistan and, 296–97, 352–54, 367–68; political capitals, 285–87; population of, 289; railroads in, 277, 283, 293, 295; Russia and, 32, 224, 244, 264, 275, 284, 310, 312; South Asia and, 311, 358; South Korea and, 47, 278; Soviet

Union and, 39, 66, 80, 84, 244, 276, 299; strategic position of, 284, 299; String of Pearls (strategy), 111, 280; Sub-Saharan Africa and, 279, 311, 444; Taiwan and, 5–6, 47, 278, 291, 299–300, 309, 324, 346–47, 449; and trade, 40, 47, 50, 110, 170, 172, 278–80, 282, 284, 298, 311, 323, 346, 372; US and, 5–6, 110, 122, 278, 279, 298, 302–3, 310–11, 321, 449; Vietnam and, 53, 80, 84, 292, 298, 305–7, 340, 449; WWII and, 275–77, 302, 323. *See also* Mao Zedong
Christianity, 120, 207, 234, 236, 256, 283, 331, 376
Chrone, G. R., 31
Chunnel, 196, 198
Churchill, Winston, 29, 215, 276
CIA. *See* Central Intelligence Agency
CIS (Commonwealth of Independent States), 232
Clark Amendment (1928), 111
climate change, 62, 214, 268, 365, 432, 445, 455–56. *See also* global warming
Clinton, Bill, 150, 250, 260, 307, 310, 398
Clive, Robert, 360
closed space theory, 23, 112
Cohen, Saul B., 30, 351
Cold War, 65–93, 162, 443; Afghanistan, war in, 86–87; the arms race, 82–83; containment, ring of, 65–72; counter-encirclement, fear of, 149; and geopolitical restructuring, 65; major powers and, 84–85, 378–82; maritime realm, Communist power and, 72–74, 83; Middle America and, 149; Middle East and, 75–77, 85–86, 378–82; nuclear stalemate and deterrence, 65–72; Phase I: 1945–46, 65–72; Phase II: 1957–79, 72–83; Phase III: 1980–89, 83–87; and post–Cold War, 16, 19, 31–33, 61, 89–90; shatterbelts and other geopolitical regions, 75–82, 443; South America and, 66, 162; South Asia and, 66; Soviet influence, waning, 85–87; Soviet penetration, regions of, 74–75; Soviet superpower, collapse of, 87–88; state-centered geopolitics and, 28–30; twenty-first century, transition into, 88–93. *See also under specific locations,* e.g., Cuba
Colombia, 10, 53, 86, *92,* 111, 141, 146–48, 151, 161–71 *passim,* 174–75, 178, 448, 454; drug trade and, 146–47, 151–53, 155, 168–69, 174–75
Colombo Plan, 68, 369
colonialism, 7–8, 41; end of, 378; in Middle East, 376–78; in Southeast Asia, 325; in Sub-Saharan Africa, 418–19, 432. *See also* imperial hegemony
COMECON, 73, 305
COMESA, 46, 422
"comic opera war," 150
Cominform, 73
Comintern, 70
Common Agricultural Policy (CAP), 188, 199, 422
Common Market for Eastern and Southern Africa (COMESA), 46, 422
Commonwealth of Independent States (CIS), 232
Communism, 28–29, 43, 54, 60, 149, 193, 198, 217–18, 227, 264, 312, 320; anti-Communists, 29, 74, 76, 78, 80; Cold War and, 65–66, 68, 70, 72–73, 87, 217; post-Communist countries/economies, 192, 196, 204. *See also* Cold War
Comoros, 373, 392, *429,* 435, 445
competition, 30–33
Comprehensive Test Ban Treaty (CTBT), 266, 296
compression zones, 9, 37, 40, 43, 49, 58, 89, 389, 421, 433
Concert of Europe, 24
condominium states, 56–*57, 205*–7, 307, 370, 376, 453
confederations, potential, *59*
conflict mediation, 8, 91
Congo, Democratic Republic of. *See* Democratic Republic of the Congo
Congo, Republic of. *See* Republic of the Congo
connections, 16
Constitution Act (Canada, 1867), 128
Constitution Act (Canada, 1982), 125
Constitutional Convention (of the US), 98
containment, ring of. *See* ring of containment
Continental Congress, 96, 98
continentality, 41–43, 108–9, 115, 183, 203, 265, 272–73, 277, 282
continental-maritime East Asia. *See under* East Asian realm: continental-maritime East Asia
continental settings, 38, 122
convergence zones, 37, 40
Copperbelt, 418, 428, 436
cordon sanitaire, 69–70, 249
Correa, Rafael, 175
Corsica, *57, 205*–7, 209–10
Cossacks, 222, 224, 262
Costa Rica, 54, 141, 151, 154, 158
Côte d'Ivoire (Ivory Coast), 54, 439
Council for Mutual Economic Assistance (COMECON), 73, 305
counter-encirclement, 149
Cressey, George, 112–13
Crete, *57, 205,* 207
Crimea, 19, 180, 192, 223, 226, 232–33, 251, 253, 449–50, 452
Crimean War, 224, 247
Croatia, 59, 89–*92,* 194, 200, 254–55
crush zones, 48, 190. *See also* shatterbelts
CTBT (Comprehensive Test Ban Treaty), 266, 296
Cuba, 3, 23, 29, 48, 53–54, 127, 148–58, 174, 177, 304; Cold War and, 51, 73, 77–82 *passim,* 86, 93, 149, 162, 436–37; and the future, 11, 46, 454; US and, 73, 81–82, 110–11, 121, 127, 139, 149–52, 156–57. *See also* Castro, Fidel; Guantánamo Bay
Cuban missile crisis, 73, 139
Cultural Revolution (China), 88, 278, 285, 293, 305
Curzon, George Nathaniel, Lord, 23, 190
Curzon Line, 190, 229

cyberspying, 6
cyberwarfare, 2, 62
Cyprus, 8, 44, *57, 59, 92,* 183, 191, 194, 200, 204–*5,* 207, 376, 378, *396,* 407, 453
czarist Russia. *See under* Russia: czarist
Czech Republic, 43, 187, 191, 201, 203, 214, 219, 250

Dagestan, 233, 259–60, 266
Dalai Lama, 294–95
D'Arcy, William, 377
Darfur, Sudan, 13, 62, 90, 292, 388, *397,* 422, 426, 438, 440, 444
Darién Gap, 151–52
Dayton Agreement, 254–55
de-development, 37, 46, 388, 418
deindustrialization, 95, 113
Delhi, India, 360, 363
Demilitarized Zone (DMZ), 300, 302–4, 336
democracy, 31–32, 41, 49; Angola and, 420; Arab Spring and, 375; Brazil and, 454; Côte d'Ivoire (Ivory Coast) and, 439; EU and, 193; Ghana and, 426; Haiti and, 156; India and, 349, 353–54; Indonesia and, 328, 333; Iraq and, 29, 402, 448–49; Kenya and, 443; Mongolia and, 264; Myanmar and, 310, 358, 372; NATO and, 192; Nepal and, 371; Philippines and, 324; Russia and, 217, 265–67; South Africa and, 90; South America and, 161; Taiwan and, 324; Thailand and, 324; Turkey and, 384; US and, 2, 109, 118, 123–24, 149, 156, 161, 448–49
Democratic Ideals and Realities (Mackinder), 19, 218
Democratic Party, US, 123
Democratic Republic of the Congo (DRC), 39, 419, 424, *429*–31, 437, 440–41, 445
Deng Xiaoping, 42, 84, 278, 284
Denmark, 24, 111, 122, 183, 186, 194, 197–98, 208–9, 223, 244
depression, 7. *See also* Great Depression
De Seversky, Alexander, 27–28, 113
détente, 30, 74–75, 83
developmental stages, 9–11
DEW (Distant Early Warning) defense system, 72, 125, 136
Diaz, Porfirio, 138
dictatorships, 171, 194, 207, 213, 271, 276, 324, 385, 419; Arab Spring and, 49, 375; Washington's support of, 2, 29, 124, 156, 158
Diego Garcia, Island of, 79, 99, 359, 373
differentiation, 60
diplomacy, 13
Distant Early Warning Line. *See* DEW
Djibouti, 4, 54, *57, 92,* 123, 280, 377, 392, 420, *429,* 431–32, 441–42, 444
DMZ. *See* Demilitarized Zone
Doe, Samuel, 438
dollar diplomacy, 162
Dominican Republic, 118, 149, 153–54, 158
Dominican Republic-Central America Free Trade Agreement (CAFTA-DR), 150, 158
domino theory, 28–29
dos Santos, José Eduardo, 419–20
DRC. *See* Congo, Democratic Republic of the
drones. *See* unmanned aerial vehicles
Drucker, Peter, 49
drug trade, 55, 140, 146–47, 151–53, 155, 162, 168–69, 174–75, 357–58; Afghanistan and, 55, 358; Colombia and, 146–47, 151–53, 155, 162, 168–69, 174–75; Mexico and, 146–47; Middle America and, 147, 155; South America and, 147, 169, 174–75; US and, 55, 146–47, 153, 155, 168
Dubai, 50, 54, *57,* 404, 412
Dulles, John Foster, 29, 353
Durand Line, 350, 370, 450
Durban Conference on Climate Warming (2012), 214
Dust Bowl, 110, 122

East African Community (EAC), 421, 426
East Asia Coastal Seas gateway region, 454–55
East Asia geostrategic realm, 40, 43–44, 55, 88, *92,* 271–312; China, 10, 271–98; continental-maritime East Asia, 10, 41, 43; East Asia Rim periphery, 298–309. *See also under* oil/gas production
Eastern Europe, 40, *92,* 249–57, 401, 449
East Timor, 5, 68, 329–30
Exclusive Economic Zone (EEZ), 244, 279–80, 341, 368
e-commerce, 120, 198
Economic Community of Central African States, 422
Economic Community of West African States (ECOWAS), 422, 426, 434, 445
Economic Community of West and Central Africa, 422
economic crisis, 202–3. *See also* recession
economy, global, 11–13, 31, 41, 50, 60, 89, 118, 181–82, 278, 301, 335, 452
ECOWAS. *See* Economic Community of West African States
ECSC (European Coal and Steel Community), 183, 193
Ecuador, 7, 53, *92,* 152, 155–75 *passim,* 178, 279. *See also* Andean Group; Bolivarian revolution; Southern Cone
ecumenes, 39
EEC (European Economic Community), 183, 194
EEZ. *See* Exclusive Economic Zone
effective national territory (ENT), 39–40, 96
effective regional territory (ERT), 39
Egypt, *53,* 394, 395, 408–9, 412, 453; Arab-Israeli conflict and, 398–99; Arab Spring and, 375, 409; Israel and, 75, 380, 390; oil/gas production, 390, 408; Soviet Union and, 75, 380; the Suez Canal and, 408; Syria and, 380; US and, 75, 147. *See also* Middle East
Eisenhower, Dwight, 29, 83, 123

Ejército de Liberación Nacional (People's Liberation Army), 174
ELN (Ejército de Liberación Nacional), 174
El Salvador, *92,* 149, 154–55, 158
el-Sisi, Abdel Fattah, 409
emissions, greenhouse gas, 62, 173, 214, 456
empty areas, 40
Energy Silk Road Strategy Act (1999), 260
enosis, 207
ENT. *See* effective national territory
entrepôt, 360, 432
environmental issues, 50, 95–96, 126, 132. *See also specific topics,* e.g., climate change
Equatorial Guinea, *429,* 440
equilibrium. *See* global equilibrium
Erdoğan, Recep Tayyip, 406–7, 452
Eritrea, 76–77, 86, *92,* 201, 377, 381, 389, *396,* 408, 413, 420–21; in African Horn, 441; boundaries of, *429;* rebellion of, 420, 431, 435, 441; refugees from, 6, 431
ERT. *See* effective regional territory
Estonia, 55, *57, 59,* 191, 201, 203, 219, 223, 227, 229, 245, 248, 250
Estrada, Joseph, 324
ETA (Euskadi Ta Askatasuna), 205
ethanol, 100, 114, 170–73, 454
Ethiopia, 3, 53, 73, 76–77, 79, 86, *92,* 149, 201, 377, 381, 389, 417, 420–22, 428–*29,* 431–32, 435, 441–42
ethnicity, 121
EU. *See* European Union
Eurasian continental realm, 40, 43–44, 66, 84, 87, 272
Eurasian convergence zone, 40, 44, 49, 245–49
Eurasian Customs Union, 40, 249, 261–62
Eurasian Heartland, 19, *22, 57, 59, 92,* 112–13, 218–19, *235,* 244, 265, 273, 309
Euro-African Free Trade Agreement, 424
"Euro-Asia," 265
Euro-Atlantic alliance, 182
Euromediterranea, 401, 448, 452–54
Euro-Mediterranean geopolitical region, 33, 415
euro (monetary currency), 44, 182, 194–96
Europe, 455. *See also* Central Europe; European Union; Maritime Europe
Europe, Eastern. *See* Eastern Europe
European Coal and Steel Community (ECSC), 183, 193
European Common Market, 125
European Community (EC), 185
European Court of Human Rights, 198, 255
European Court of Justice, 185, 198
European Economic Community (EEC, or the Common Market), 183, 194
European Free Trade Association, 185
European Union (EU), 44, 191–95, 198–200, 407 and *passim*; agriculture policy of, 188, 199; Bosnia and, 255; eastward advance of, 204; emergence of, 193; as first-order power, 53; forerunners of, 185; formation of, 179, 193; Frankfurt as financial capital, 186; Germany as leader, 8; history of, 179, 193; membership in, 200; merging of Eastern and Western Europe with, 203–4; Middle East and, 401, 453; military-strategic equation, 191–93; as model, 426; "New Member States" (NMS) or "New Europe," 187–88, 202; "Old Member States" (OMS) or "Old Europe," 187–88, 202; political accommodation within, 204; and regional unity, 179; and trade, 50, 195–*96, 321, 351;* Turkey and, 200, 452; Ukraine and, 199–200; US and, 39, 216, 456
European Union (EU) rapid reaction force, 192, 214–15, 407
Europoort, 179
Euroskepticism, 194, 215
Eurotunnel, 179
eurozone, 8, 44, 46, 179, 186, 194, 196
Euskadi Ta Askatasuna (ETA), 205
extraterritoriality, 283
ExxonMobil, 268
Exxon Valdez (ship), 103

Faeroe Islands, *205,* 207
failed states, 8, 49, 58, 370
Fairgrieve, James, 17, 25, 48, 190
Falkland Islands (Islas Malvinas), 168
Fallujah, 403
FARC (Fuerzas Armadas Revolucionarias de Colombia), 174–75
farm belt, 100, 110, 114–16
FATA (Federally Administered Tribal Areas of Pakistan), 4, 365
Fatah, 399, 401
features. *See* geopolitical features
Federated States of Micronesia. *See* Micronesia, Federated States of
Federation of Arab Republics (1969–70), 75, 392
Federation of Rhodesia and Nyasaland, 421
fifth-order states, 53
Fiji, 62, *322,* 327, 456
Finland, 69, 73, 186–87, 191, 194, 197, 218–19, 221, 223, 227–29, 241, 250; as gateway, 54, *57*
Finnish-Russian War, 69
First Gulf War. *See* Gulf War, First
first-order states. *See* major powers
First World War. *See* World War I
Five Dynasties, 287
Flanders, *205,* 207
Flemish Community (Belgian Flanders), *205*
Flemishland, 57, 207
Ford Motor Company; Fordlândia, 162
Former Soviet Union (FSU), 61, 90, 231–32, 238–39, 242–43, 258, 260, 262, 264, 296
Formosa, 283, 318, 337. *See also* Taiwan
four pillars of power, 2–3
fourth-order states, 3, 53
Fox, Vicente, 144

fracking, 100, 386, 456

France, 4, 7–8, 12, 17, 24–25, 42, 49, 53, *92,* 180, 183, 186–215 *passim,* 318, 449; Algeria and, 211; Asia-Pacific Rim and, 318, 320, 340; autonomy-seeking regions in, 56, 206–7; Cold War and, 68, 71, 78; East Asia and, 299, 305; economy of, 188, 201; geopolitics in, 31; Maghreb and, 7, 66, 182; Middle East and, 376, 377, 379–80, 380, 402, 404, 408; and North/Middle America, 107, 124, 127, 138; Russia/Eurasian convergence zone and, 227, 255; Sahara Deaert and, 188; Sub-Saharan Africa and, 420, 422, 426, *429,* 440, 444; Vietnam and, 305

Franco, Francisco, 205, 406

Frankfurt, Germany, 186, 195

Franklin, Benjamin, 180

free market, 12, 31–32, 133, 158, 176, 217, 219, 241, 307, 437, 440

Free Papua movement, 329, 331

free-trade accords, 131

Free Trade Area of the Americas, 46, 171

free zones, 142

Frelimo (Mozambique Liberation Front), 79, 437

French Guiana, 163, 189

French-Indochina War, 71

French Polynesia, 188

frontiers, 17, 124, 168, 180; US, 107, 122–23, 159n1

FSU. *See* Former Soviet Union

Fuerzas Armadas Revolucionarias de Colombia (Revolutionary Armed Forces of Colombia), 174–75

Fujiang, China, 42, 272, 274, 275, 279, 287, 290–91, 298, 300, 337

Fujimori, Alberto, 176

Fukushima reactor, 345

Fukuyama, Francis, 31

future, mapping, 6–7, 450–56

Gabon, 311, *429,* 440

al-Gaddafi, Muammar, 76, 93, 123, 381

Gadsden Purchase of 1853, 104, 138

Gagauzi ethnic group, 254

Gakwandi, A. S., 419

Galicia, *57, 205–6*

Gambetta, Léon, 210

Gambia, 421, *429,* 438, 440

Gandhi, Indira, 354, 356, 371

Gandhi, Mohandas K., 70

Gandhi, Rajiv, 356

GAP (Guneydogu Anadolu Project), 384, 407

García, Alan, 176

gas production. *See* oil/gas production

gastarbeiters, 201

gateway states and regions, 54–55, *57,* 450

GATT (General Agreement on Tariffs and Trade), 42

Gaza, 8, 33, *92–93,* 375, 380, 385, 387, *396–400,* 408, 413, 449, 453

General Agreement on Tariffs and Trade (GATT), 42

general systems, 30, 59–60

genocide, 25, 89, 179, 190, 407, 426

geographical settings, 38–39

geography: geographical geopolitical theory, 32; geopolitics and geographical change, 7–9; globalization and, 11; impact of, 4–6

geopolitical analysis, 1

geopolitical features, 39–41; boundaries, 40; capitals or political centers, 39; ecumenes, 39; effective national territory (ENT) and effective regional territory (ERT), 39–40; empty areas, 40; historic or nuclear cores, 39; nonconforming sectors, 40

geopolitical map of the future, 6–7

geopolitical regions, 44–47; as dynamic, 346; as meso-order, 9; realms vs., 46

geopolitical structure, 37–55, 41–49; centrifugal vs. centripetal forces in, 38; features, 39–41; gateways, 54–55; geographical settings, 38–39; geopolitical regions, 44–47; geostrategic realms, 41–44; levels of, 41–49; orders of national power, 51–54; shatterbelts, 48–49; states, 49–51; and theory, 60

geopolitics, 15–16; Cold War–state-centered vs. universalistic approaches, 28–31; equilibrium, turbulence, and world order, 60–62; general systems approach to, 30, 59–60; and geographical change, 7–9; geopolitical structure, 37–55; German *geopolitik,* 24–26; modern, stages of, 16–33; national states, proliferation of, 55–59; post–Cold War, 31–33; race for imperial hegemony, 16–24; survey of, 15–33; in the US, 26–28. *See also geopolitik*

geopolitik, 15–16, 23–26, 24–26, 28, 317, 418

géopolitique, 31

Georgia, *59,* 220, 452; capital of, 248; civil war in, 232, 249; ecumene, 248; NATO and, 43, 452; Russia and, 40, 233, 247, 249, 257, 452; Soviet Union and, 227, 230; US and, 220, 258–59, 452

geostrategic realms, 41–44; description of, 41; as macro-order, 9; regions vs., 46

German-Soviet pact (1939), 25

Germany, 17, 30, 42, *92;* boundaries, 189–90; economy of, 192–93; Frankfurt, 186, 195; *gastarbeiters,* 201; German school (of geopolitical thought), 25; as great power, 24, 53–54; historical formation, 189–90; immigration to, 201; Nazi Germany, 7, 25, 69, 218, 228; in nineteenth century, 17; reunification of, 8, 87, 90, 191–92, 194, 215; WWI and, 7, 24–26, 190, 418; WWII and, 190–91, 240, 245, 247, 249. *See also* European Union; *geopolitik*

Ghana, 54, 78, 421, 426, *430,* 440

Gibraltar, *57,* 191, 198, *205–6,* 209

Gibraltar, Strait of, 201

Ginsburg, Norton, 283

glasnost, 87, 219

global equilibrium, 6, 13, 60–62, 88, 216, 312, 448–49; isostasy, 40

globalization, 11–13, 455; theories of, 50
global stability, 46, 61, 90, 447–50, 452
global warming, 4, 13, 62, 103, 122, 130, 173, 242, 244, 359, 386, 444, 455–56; Kyoto Protocol, 214, 342. *See also* climate change
Golan Heights, 75, *396,* 410, 412
Gold Coast, 418, 421
"Golden Coast," China. *See under* China: the "Golden Coast"
Golden Horde, 222
Good Neighbor policy, 111, 139, 149, 162
Goodyear, Charles, 162
Gorbachev, Mikhail, 87, 219, 268
Gore, Al, 120
Great Britain, 68, 107, 183, 196, 274, 419
Great Depression, 41, 110, 125
Greater Antilles, 152
Greater East Asia Co-Prosperity Sphere, 315, 318
Great Game strategy, 220, 261–62
Great Leap Forward (China), 73, 88, 277, 284
great powers. *See* major powers
Great Wall of China. *See under* China: Great Wall of
Great War. *See* World War I
Greece, 8, 29, 44, 69–70, *92,* 179, 183, 200–202, 238, 254, 256–57, 280; as shipping nation, 197, 322; Turkey and, 191, 194, 200, 207, 254, *396,* 407
Greek Orthodox Church, 234, 236
Greenland, *57,* 183, *205,* 208–9, 244, 455
Grenada, 48, 82, 86, 149–50
Group of Seven (G-7), 42
Guam, 23, *57,* 74, 105, 110, 315, 344
GUAM (Georgia, Ukraine, Azerbaijan, Moldova), *59,* 220
Guangdong, China, 42, 272, 274–75, 287–91, 337
Guangzhou, China, 108, 241, 272–74, 287–88
Guantánamo Bay, 66, 74, 81, 105, 110, 149, 152, 157
Guatemala, 82, *92,* 144–45, 149–51, 154–55, 158
Guevara, Che, 82
Guinea, 78, *92,* 421, *429*–30, 439
Guinea, Gulf of, 417, 423, 439
Guinea-Bissau, 421, 434, 440
Gulf Cooperation Council, 392, 404, 412, 449
Gulf of Aden, 4, 74, 77, 86, 231, 377, 381–82, 420, 442–43
Gulf of Guinea, 417, 423, 439
Gulf of Mexico, 81, 95–96, 101, 104, 107, 115, 143, 148, 411
Gulf States, 1, *59,* 68, 76–77, 149, 387, 390, 395, 403–4, 413, 415, 443, 447
Gulf Stream, 180
Gulf Wars, 83, 89, 359, 381; first, 91, 127, 381–83, 385, 387, 393, 397–98, 410
Guneydogu Anadolu Project (GAP), 384, 407
GUUAM (Georgia, Ukraine, Uzbekistan, Azerbaijan, Moldova), 220
Guyana, *57,* 82, 118, 148, 151, 163, 170
Guyot, Arnold Henry, 16
Habibie, B. J., 329, 333
Habyarimana, Juvénal, 432
Haider, Jörg, 202
Haig, Alexander, 29
Hailemariam Desalegn, 442
Haiti, 32, 58, 105, 111, 149–50, 154–56
Hamas Party, 8, 33, 93, 387, 399–401, 449
Han dynasty, 285
Hanseatic League, 54, 181, 189, 226, 234
hard power, 123, 215
Hardt, Michael, 49
Harper, Stephen, 131
Hartshorne, Richard, 15, 48
Hashemite dynasty, 377
Haushofer, Albrecht, 25–26
Haushofer, Karl, 15, 25–26, 317
Hawaii, 23, 108, 110, 122, 344
Hazara people, Hazaras, 383, 405
heartland, 17, 218. *See also* Anglo-America; Eurasian Heartland
Heartlandic Russia. *See* Russia
Hegel, G. F., 16, 25
hegemony, imperial, 16–24
Hejaz, Saudi Arabia, 377, 389
Hennig, Richard, 25–26
Henrikson, Alan, 13
Hepple, Leslie, 29
Hérodite (journal), 31
Hess, Rudolf, 26
Hezbollah, 8, 33, 93, 399, 402–3, 409, 415
hierarchical order of power, 3–4
highways, 8, 27, 103, 111, 197, 293, 393
Himalayan mountains, 70, 295, 297, 349–50, 352, 360, 362–63, 366–67, 371, 382
Hinduism, 69, 274, 333, 350, 353, 356, 359–60, 362, 367, 371, 373, 383
Hindustan Plains, 351, 360, 362–63, 371
historic (nuclear) cores, 39
Hitler, Adolf, 26
HIV/AIDS, 424, 435
Ho Chi Minh, 71, 305
Holocaust, WWII Jewish, 25, 179, 190
Honduras, 55, *57,* 111, 151, 153–55, 157–58
Hong Kong, 42, 84, 119, 243, 272, 274–75, 287–89, 291, 305, 308, 337, 341, 357; China and, 205; as gateway, 54–55, *57;* and trade, *321*
"Hong Kong Plus" model, 299–300, 347, 454
Honshu ecumene, 335
Horn of Africa. *See* African Horn
Houphouët-Boigny, Félix, 439
House of Rothschild, 181
Howard, John, 342
Hukbalahaps, 80
Humala, Ollanta, 176
human rights, 2, 50, 58
Humboldt, Alexander von, 16
Hungary, 74, 84, 191, 201, 203–4, 219, 230, 250
Hun Sen, 80, 308

Huntington, Samuel, 32, 89, 439
Hussein, Saddam, 1, 5, 29, 76, 89, 375, 383, 385, 393, 397–98, 402–3, 405, 454
Hutus. *See* Rwanda
Hyderabad, India, 364, 366
Hydro-Québec (utility), 131

Ibn Ali, Husayn, 377
Ibn Saud, 377
ICBM. *See* intercontinental ballistic missiles
Iceland, 183, 185, 194, 197, 200, 209
ICJ. *See* International Court of Justice
Iles Glorieuses, 373
immigration, 5–7, 38, 337, 345, 455; anti-immigrant bias, 202–3, 345; Asia-Pacific Rim and, 337, 345; Australia, 345, 455; Canada, 131–32; Japan and, 345, 455; Maritime Europe and the Maghreb, 6, 55, 182, 200–203, 455; Mexico and, 6–7, 147; Middle America, 154–55; New Zealand, 319; Russia and, 455; US and, 109, 121, 131, 147, 154–55. *See also* migration
imperial hegemony, 16–24. *See also* colonialism
imperialism, 11, 23, 49, 73, 87, 179, 213, 276–77, 285, 317, 329, 408, 417, 433; WWI and, 41; WWII and, 38
India, 3, 47, 352–55; Bangladesh and, 350, 364, 368; Bhutan and, 70, 362; boundaries, 70, 81, 297, 349, 352, 364, 367–68; BRICS, 172; Britain and, 45, 350, 353, 356, 360, 362, 370, 373, 376–77; China and, 70, 81, 295, 297, 310, 349, 352, 357–59, 365, 367, 373; economy of, 351, 364–65, 372–73; ecumenes, 363–65; effective national territory (ENT), 366; as first-order power, 53; future of, 372–73, 447, 450, 452, 455–56; the geostrategic realm, 41; and global warming, 456; growing strength of, 310; high-tech industry in, 364, 372–73; infrastructure, 372; Kashmir and, 47, 56, 367–70, 373; and major/world powers, 8, 349, 372–73, 447, 450; Muslims in, 353, 360, 369; Myanmar and, 280, 357–59, 372; Nepal and, 70, 362, 368; neutrality of, 70, 353, 370; and nuclear weapons, 366, 369–70; and oil/gas production, 358; Pakistan and, 202, 350, 352–54, 366–70; partition of, 297, 353, 367; population of, 353; as regional power, 10, 349, 370, 373; Russia and, 310, 373; Sikkim and, 297; technology industries in, 364; threats to unity of, 353; and trade, *351,* 365, 372; United Arab Republic and, 365; US and, 11, 353–54, 365. *See also* Hinduism
Indian Ocean geostrategic realm, 373
India-Pakistan War of Partition, 202, 350
Indochina, 304–9
Indonesia, 5, 10–12, 49, 68, 201, 280, 315, 318, 320–*22,* 326–33, 341–42, 353, 448; China and, 298, 342; Cold War and, 71–73, 80, 85; composition and core of, 328; economy and trade, 12, 56, *321–23*; effective national territory (ENT), 338; the future and, 49, 59, 333; Muslims in, 331–32; political instability of, 327–33, 455; as second-order power, *53. See also* Aceh; *specific locations,* e.g., Java
industrial age, 43, 179
industrialization, 19, 38, 41–43, 108, 110, 142, 167, 221, 238–39, 241, 276, 290, 296, 384, 418
industrial revolution, 180
Indus Water Basin Treaty (1960), 368
information technology, 12, 95, 129, 196, 202, 278, 373
in-migration, 131
Interamerican Development Bank, 177
Inter-American Highway, 139, 177
intercontinental ballistic missiles (ICBM), 72, 74, 83, 103
International Court of Justice (ICJ), 126, 168, *430*
International Criminal Court, 215
International Monetary Fund, 177
International Settlement (1863), 274
international trade. *See* trade
Internet, 12, 198, 323
Interservice Intelligence (ISI), 355, 449
Iran, 1, 13, 30, 32–33, 48–50, 53, 403–5; Arab Spring and, 389; Azeris in, 259, 375, 383, *397;* boundaries, 245, 249, 263, 395–98; Cold War and, 230; containing, 404; economy and trade, 50, 384–85; ecumenes, 394; and the future, 59, 401, 415, 447–48, 453; Iraq and, 85, 392, 395–97, 402–3, 405, 412; Kurds in, *397,* 405; Kuwait and, 392, 397–98; Majlis (parliament), 76; in Middle East, 5, 7–8, 402–3; negotiations with, 13, 123, 267, 401, 404; nuclear weapons in, 5, 91, 123, 267, 292, 404, 447; oil/gas production in, 384–85, 413; population of, 394, 405; as regional power, 3, 7–8, 39, *53,* 402–3, 447; revolution (1979) in, 76–77; Russia and, 32, 44; Soviet Union and, 70, 230; US and, 13, 76, 147, 404. *See also* Middle East
Iran, Shah of (Mohammad Reza Pahlavi), 70, 76, 379, 381, 405
Iraq, 3, 5, 90, 402–3, 448–49, 452–54; boundaries, 395–*96;* and democracy, 29, 402, 448–49; Iran and, 85, 392, 395–97, 402–3, 405, 412; Kurds in, 383, *397,* 403, 405, 407, 409, 448, 453; Kuwait and, 392, *396*–98; Soviet Union and, 76; US and, 5, 448–49; US invasion of (2003), 402–3, 444. *See also* Gulf Wars; Middle East
Iraq War, 5, 39, 62, 85, 114, 152, 320, 344, 375, 385, 448–49
Ireland, *57,* 118, 180, 183, 186–87, 194, *196*–97, 202; Northern, 90–91, 191, 204–*5,* 207
Irian Jaya, 56–*57,* 329, 331–32, 338
Iron Curtain, 29
irredentist movements and areas, 29, 58, 395, *397,* 413, 455
ISI (Interservice Intelligence), 355, 449
ISIL (Islamic State in Iraq and the Levant), 448
ISIS (Islamic State in Iraq and Syria), 409, 448–49

Islam, 213, 256, 259, 331, 333, 375, 406, 438; fundamentalism, 54, 91, 189, 212–13, 233, 249, 262–63, 295, 333, 354–56, 370, 449–50; Islamic law, 51, 381, 388, 409, 438. *See also* Muslims; Taliban
Islamabad, Pakistan, 363
Islamic State in Iraq and Syria (ISIS), 409, 448–49
Islamic State in Iraq and the Levant (ISIL), 448
isolationism, 23, 28, 68, 109, 112, 162, 357
isostasy, 40
Israel, 447, 449, 452–53; boundaries, 395–*96;* Cold War and, 381; ecumene, 394; Egypt and, 75, 380, 390; Europe and, 380, 401; Jordan and, 380, 386–88, 394; as regional power, *53,* 447; Syria and, 75, 380, *396;* technology industries in, 394; US and, 68, 77, 380, 401, 413, 453; War of Independence (1948), 379, 400; water scarcity in, 386–88. *See also* Arab-Israeli conflict; Jerusalem; Levant; Middle East
Istabu, 327
Itaipu Dam, 170
Italy, 9, 12, 42, *92,* 125, 182–83, 186–88, 193–213 *passim,* 238, 255, 257, 276, 408, 420; autonomy-seeking regions in, 56; economy, 188; immigration to, 6, 201–3; Libya and, 209, 377; population of, 202
Ivan, Czar of Russia, 222
Ivan IV, Czar of Russia, 222, 226
Ivory Coast, 54, 439

Jackson, Andrew, 107
Jamaica, 55, *57,* 82, 105, 118, 153–56
James Bay hydroelectric development (Quebec), 131, 134
Japan, 42, 71, 343; Asian-Pacific rim, as core of, 282, 317, 321, 342, 345, 347, 455; Australia and, 318–19, 323, 342; boundaries, 309; capital of, 335; China and, 47, 278, 298, 318, 323, 341–44, 346, 449; economy of, 84, *322*–23, 345–46; ecumene, 335–36; effective national territory (ENT), 338; emergence of, 321; as first-order power, 10; the future and, 455; and immigration, 345; maritime realm and, 346; Middle East and, 346; military issues in, 343–44; and nuclear power, 345; and oil/gas production, 241; political stability of, 324; as regional power, 321, 342; Russia and, 225, 241, 244–45, 318, 339–40; Self-Defense Forces (SDF), 344; South Korea and, 316, 323, 335, 345; Soviet Union and, 228, 230, 244; Taiwan and, 337, 340; Thailand and, 318, 325, 337; and trade, 47, 50, 306, 318, 323, 345–46; US and, 32, 39; US personnel stationed in, 68, 74, 123, 343–44; Vietnam and, 84, 306, 318. *See also* World War II
Java, 80, 328–33, 336, 338, 373
Jemaah Islamiya, 333
Jerusalem, 379, 390, *397,* 400, 453
Jewish Pale of Settlement, 190
Jiang Zemin, 278, 310
jihadists, 12, 39, 93, 409, 433
Jiménez, Marcos Pérez, 156
Johnson, Lyndon B., 119
Jones, Stephen, 27–28
Jordan, 68, *92,* 379–80, 385–88, 392, 394–95, 398–99, 408, 410, 412–13, 453; refugees to, 6, 62, 410, 413
Jordan River, 400
Juan de Nova Island, *429*
Juarez, Benito, 138

Kabila, Laurent, 419, 422, 431, 435, 441
Kaczyński, Jarosław, 199
Kaesong Free Trade Industrial Zone (KIZ), 303, 347
Kagame, Paul, 431–33
Kalimantan, 298, 328–29, 332, 338
Kaliningrad, 123, 190, 192, *222,* 229, 245, 250
Kant, Immanuel, 15–16
Kaplan, Robert, 16, 31, 90
Karakoram Highway, 296–97, 354, 367
Karmal, Babrak, 86
Karzai, Hamid, 406
Kasa-Vubu, Joseph, 419
Kashagan oil field, 260–61
Kashmir, *57,* 363, 373, 384; China and, 297, 352–53, 367; India/Pakistan and, 47, 56, 297, 352–54, 367–70, 373
Katanga (Shaba), 78, 418–19, 424, 445
Kazakhstan, 4, 40, *59, 92,* 189, 201, 219, 223, 232, 239–40, 243, 251; boundaries, 244–45, 249, 262–64, 292, 295–96, 396; capital of, 248; ecumene of, 248; as locus of the Soviet/Russian space activity, 243; and oil/gas production, 250, 257, 260–62, 311, 411; population of, 262; as regional power, 262–64; Russia and, 243, 247, 250, 262
Kelly, Philip, 48
Kennan, George, 29
Kennedy, John F., 29, 81
Kennedy, Paul, 50
Kenya, 62, 78, *92,* 373, 411, 413, 421, *430,* 434, 449; capital of, 428; as leading East African nation, 442–43
Kenyatta, Jomo, 443
Kenyatta, Uhuru, 443
Kerry, John, 399
Keystone XL pipeline, 101–*2,* 131, 134–35
Khabarovsk, Russia, 225, 241, 244
Khan, Genghis, 287
Khan, Kublai, 287
Khmer Rouge, 80, 85, 298, 305, 308, 320
Khomeini, Ruhollah, 76, 381, 385
Khrushchev, Nikita, 73, 81, 239, 277–78, 353
Kibaki, Mwai, 442–43
Kiev, Ukraine, 226, 230, 234, 236, 248, 251
Kievan Rus, 225, 232, 234, 236, 251
Kim Dae-jung, 303
Kim Jong-il, 303
Kirchner, Cristina Fernández de, 177

Kirchner, Néstor, 176
Kiribati, 62, 456
Kissinger, Henry, 29–30, 32
KIZ (Kaesong Free Trade Industrial Zone), 303, 347
Kjellén, Rudolf, 15, 17, 24–25
Kolkata, India, 280, 360, 363–64
Korean Peninsula, 43, 61, 71, 268, 271, 298, 304, 310, 312, 342, 346–47. *See also* North Korea; South Korea
Korean War, 66, 301–2, 317, 335, 340
Kosovo, 29, *59,* 89, *92,* 200, 249, 254–56
Krasnovodsk, Russia, 223, 240
Kuomintang (Nationalist Party), 275–76, 299, 302, 324
Kurdistan, *57,* 201, 378, 382, 395, 405, 407, 410, 448–49, 453
Kurds, 375, 382–84, *397,* 403, 405, 407, 409, 412, 448, 453. *See also* PKK
Kuril Islands, 71, 225, *227*–28, 230, 244–45, 339
Kuwait, 89, *92,* 376–77, 385–86, 392, 395–98, 409–10, 413
Kyoto Protocol, 214, 342
Kyrgyzstan, *59, 92,* 249, 260–64, 267–68, 295–96

Lacoste, Yves, 31–32
Ladakh, 81, 297, 367
lage (location), 17
Lake Chad, *429,* 432, 439
land communication, 27, 169, 210, 327
languages, 38, 54, 316; in China, 273–74; in EU, 199, 205; in Indonesia, 328
Laos, 27, 43–44, *92,* 175, 271, 289, 299, 305, 308–9, 315, 318, *322,* 341–42, 357, 372; Cold War and, 68, 80, 85
latifundia, 169
Latin America, 81–82, 86. *See also* South America
Latvia, *59,* 191, 195, 203, 219, 223, 226–29, 245, 248, 250
League of Arab States (the Arab League), 392, 400
League of Nations, 19, 24–25, 109, 125, 420
Lebanon, 8, 33, 49, 59, 85, 90, *92*–93, 182–83, 376–77, 387–88, *396,* 399, 402–3; civil war in, 75; gateway function of, 54, 412; refugees to, 6, 62, 410, 413; Syria and, 402, 409–10; US and, 68, 413. *See also* Levant; Middle East
lebensraum, 25–26
Leopold, King of Belgium, 418
Le Pen, Jean-Marie, 202
Lesotho, *430,* 432–33, 435
Lesser Antilles, 152
Levant, 183, 209, 376, 378–79, 382, 385–86, 407, 415, 448, 453
Liberia, 89, *92,* 417, 422, 430, 438–39
Libya, 13, 75–76, 85, 90, *92*–93, 201, 209, 211, 213–14, 238, 377–79, 381–82, 388, 392, 415, 434; Arab Spring and, 375; Benghazi, 92; boundaries of, 395–*96, 429–30;* Italy and, 209, 377
Liechtenstein, 185, 197, 205
linchpin states, 13, 28, 30, 49, 213, 224, 342
linkage principle, 29–30
Lippmann, Walter, 65
liquid natural gas (LNG), 100, 241, 408
Lithuania, 25, *59,* 190–92, 222, 225–*27,* 229, 234, 245, 250; capital of, 248
Livingstone, David, 418
Livonia, 226
location, 38
Lombard League, 181
Lomé Agreement (1975), 422
Lukacs, John, 89
Lukashenko, Alexander, 251
lumber, 154, 156, 224, 241
Lumumba, Patrice, 78, 419
Lushun (Port Arthur), 224–25, 275–76
Luxembourg, 9, 183, 185, 197–98

MacArthur, Douglas, 302
Macau, 274, 289
Macedonia, 29, 90, *92,* 192, 194, 200, 254, 256
Mackinder, Halford, 17, 19, 23–26, 108, 218, 249
macrolevel, 9, 37
Madagascar, 373, 422–23, *429,* 445
Madeira Islands, *57, 205,* 208
Maduro, Nicolás, 153, 172, 177, 454
Maghreb: France and, 7, 66, 182; migration from, 182; as strategic annex, 209–14. *See also* Maritime Europe and the Maghreb
Magnitogorsk, Russia, 237–39
Mahan, Alfred T., 17, 23, 25–26, 48, 110
Majlis (parliament of Iran), 76
major powers, 3–4, 9–11, 19, 24, 28, 31, 37, 41, 51, 53–55, 60–62, 79, 90, 95–96, 112, 123, 181–82, 189, 216, 271; African Horn and, 441; Asia Pacifica and, 315; Brazil and, 447, 454–55; China as, 264, 271, 352; climate change and, 456; the Cold War and, 84–85; emerging, 84–85, 447; and Eurasian convergence zone, 268; four pillars of major powerdom, 349; India and, 349, 372–73, 447, 450; Middle East and, 375, 448; more open borders and, 88; and Paris Peace Conference of 1919, 276; rivalry of (Cold War period), 378–82; Russia as, 234, 268, 293; shatterbelts and, 48, 71, 443; South Asia and, 349, 369; US as, 10, 28, 31, 95–96, 123, 268, 293, 447, 456; and US-EU partnership, 216, 456; Vietnam War and, 71
Makka (Mecca), 377, 389
Malawi, 421, *430,* 432–33
Malaysia, 11–12, 53, 80, 85, *92,* 143, 221, 280, 298, 315–26 *passim,* 329, 332, 336–42 *passim;* economy and trade, 12, *321–22;* political stability of, 324, 326
Maldives, 280, 349, 351, 359, 373, 445, 456
Mali, 4, 10, 12, 78, 91–*92,* 124, 421–22, 429, 432–34, 448
Malin, James, 112
Malta, *57*

Maximilian, 138
Manchuria, 84, 224–25, 228, 272, 275–77, 287–90, 293, 315, 318, 336; Korea and, 302–4
Manchurian Railroad, 318
Mandarin Chinese, 273–74
Mandela, Nelson, 428, 435–36
"Manifest Destiny," 108–10
Maoism, 86, 174, 176, 277–78, 421
Maoist Revolutionary Armed Forces of Colombia (FARC), 174–75
Maori people, 319
Mao Zedong, 42, 72, 84, 87–88, 272, 283, 293, 305, 353; the Maoist era (1949–76), 277–78
Maputo Development Corridor, 428
maquiladoras system, 121, 140, 142–43, 145
Marañón War (1942), 168
Marcellus Shale, 99–100
Marcos, Ferdinand, 324
Mariam, Mengistu Haile, 77, 86, 431
Maritime Europe and the Maghreb, 11–12, 44, *92,* 179–216; boundaries, 189–91; ecumene, 186–87; effective regional territory (ERT), 187–88; empty areas, 188–89; EU as core of, 44; Euro-Atlantic alliance as core of, 182; European integration, 191–200; the European integration model, 193–95; geopolitical features, 183–91; global economic and political hegemony of, 181; historic core, 183–85; immigration patterns, 182, 200–203; Maghreb as strategic annex, 209–14; merging of Eastern and Western Europe with, 203–4; military, 191–93, 215; oil/gas production and, 196–98, 211, 237; political capitals, 185–86; population of, 187–88, 202, 418; regional geopolitical unity in, 8; state proliferation, 204–9; and trade, 191, 195–97, 210; transportation and telecommunications, 197–98; unification, politics of, 27, 198–200. *See also* European Union
maritime realm, 6, 40–44, 46, 48, 55, 452; the Asia-Pacific Rim, 315, 320–21, 339, 342, 346; Cold War and, 65–66, 68, 84–87, 89; Communist penetration of, 72–75, 218, 381; Communist power retreat from, 83; East Asia geostrategic realm and, 271, 273, 284, 303, 309–10, 312; East Asia rim periphery and, 307; Europe and, 180, 182, 200, 214–15, 452; Japan and, 346; the Middle East and, 378–79; North and Middle America and, 148, 158; Russia and Eurasian convergence zone, 219–20, 245, 254; South America and, 161, 177–78; South Asia and, 359, 373; Sub-Saharan Africa and, 445; US and, 95, 115, 122, 124, 214–15, 452, 455. *See also* Asia-Pacific Rim; Maritime Europe
maritime ring, 115–24
maritime settings, 38
maritimity, 41, 108, 115, 118, 181, 272–73, 277–79, 282, 287, 316
Marshall Islands, 103, 105
Marshall Plan, 8, 66, 147, 193, 384
Martin, Paul Edgar Philippe, 126
Marx, Karl, 49
Marxism, 31, 149–50, 162–63, 174, 231, 283, 354, 380, 419–20, 431, 436, 437, 440, 443; Cold War and, 73, 77–79, 78, 82, 85–87
Mason-Dixon line, 98
Massachusetts, 96, 98, 131
Matamoros, Mexico, 142–43, 147
Maull, Otto, 25–26
Mauritania, 188, 212, 422, 429–*30,* 433
Mauritius, 280, 359, 373, 445
Mayak, Russia, 238
Mayotte, 373, 429, *429*
Mbeki, Thabo, 436
McKinley, William, 23
McMahon Line, 70, 297, 357
Mecca. *See* Makka
Medina, Saudi Arabia, 389
Mediterranean, American, 148, 152
Mediterranean basin, 209, 213
Mediterranean union, 213, 415
megalopolis, 8–9, 98, 119, 141, 336
Mein Kampf (Hitler), 26
Mercado Común del Sur, the Southern Cone Common Market. *See* Mercosur
mercantilism, 41
Mercosur, 46, 125, 168, 170–71, 177, 445, 455
Merkel, Angela, 8, 214
mesolevel, 9, 37
Mesopotamia, 378, 382, 385–86, 394–95
Metaxas, Ioannis, 207
Métis people, 136
Metternich, Klemens von, 203
Mexican Revolution, 138–39
Mexico, 6, *92,* 136–49, 343; boundaries, 143–45; capital and historic core, 140–41; economy and trade, 141, 143–44; ecumene, 141–42; effective national territory, 142–44; empty areas, 144; geopolitical features, 140–45; geopolitical forces of attraction, 145–48; and oil/gas production, 135, 141–42, 145; population of, 144; as second-order power, *53;* US and, 105, 143–44, 147; US-Mexican War, 104, 107, 137; War of Reform (1858–61), 138
Mexico City, Mexico, 137–41, 143–44
microlevel, 9, 37
Micronesia, Federated States of, 103, 105, 122, 315
microshatterbelts, 174, 177
Microsoft, 120
microstates, 197
Middle America, 148–58
Middle East, 44, *92,* 375–416, 453; boundaries in, 395–98; Cold War and, 68, 75–77, 85–86, 90, 378–82; colonialism and, 376–78; conflicts, major, 398–402; countries in, selected, 402–10; ecumenes, 392–95; effective regional/national territory, 395; empty areas, 395; the future and, 54, 182, 390, 399–401, 415, 447–49, 453; geographical setting, 382–90; geopolitical

features, 390–98; Golan Heights, 75, *396,* 410, 412; historic core, 390; Intermediate Zone, 385–88; Iran's power in, 7–8, 402–4; irredentist movements and areas, *397;* Japan and, 346; major conflicts in, 398–402; major powers and, 448; modern colonial penetration, 376–78; Northern Highlands Zone, 382–85; and nuclear weapons, 380, 404; oil/gas production and, 145, 378, 386, 389–90, 392, 408, 410–12, 448; population of, 375; regional political capitals, 390–92; Russia and, 44, 410; as shatterbelt, 44, 375–416; Southern Desert Zone, 388–90; Soviet Union and, 7, 380–81; territorial dispute resolutions, recent, *396;* Turkey and, 410–11; US and, 68, 147, 410; US influence in, declining, 1–2, 124, 375, 401; water-based disputes in, 85, 395–97, 405, 412; water bodies in, 412; water scarcity in, 386–88. *See also* Arab-Israeli conflict; Arab Spring; *specific locations,* e.g., France: Middle East and
Midway, 105
migration: effects of, 6–7; illegal, 62. *See also* immigration
"migro-dollars," 145, 155
MIGs, 303
military-industrial complex, 83, 123
Milošević, Slobodan, 91, 254
Ming dynasty, 287
Miskito Indians, 155
Misseriya tribes, 90
Mobutu Sese Seko, Joseph, 78, 419, 431, 441, 448
Modelski, George, 31, 61
modernization, 11, 32, 122, 187, 221, 227, 280, 287, 290, 301, 337, 351, 380, 404, 453
Moldova, 40, 44, 183, 219–20, 232, 249, 251, 254
Moluccas (Malaku) Islands, *57,* 328–29, 331–32, 338
Monaco, 54, *57,* 197
monarchy, 1, 125, 209, 212, 362, 371, 379–80, 393, 401
Mongolia, 90, 228, 230, 233–34, 244, 247–48, 261, 264–65, 268, 272–73, 276, 285, 287, 292–94, 296, 303
Monroe Doctrine, 111, 138–39, 161–62, 178
Montcalm, Louis, 127
Monterey Shale, 100
Montesquieu, Charles-Louis de, 15–16, 169
Montreal, Canada, 128–30, 132, 135
Morales, Evo, 175
Morocco, 53–54, 66, *92,* 182, 188, 191, 196, 201, 209–12, 214
Moros, 80
Morsi, Mohamed, 51, 123, 409, 453
Mosaddegh, Mohammad, 70, 76, 379
Moscow, 236–37
Movimento Popular de Libertação de Angola (MPLA, People's Movement for the Liberation of Angola), 419–20
Mozambique, 78–79, 86, *92,* 424, 428, 430, 436–37, 448
Mozambique Liberation Front (Frelimo), 79, 437
MPLA (Movimento Popular de Libertação de Angola), 419–20
Mubarak, Hosni, 51, 382, 409
Mughal (Mogul) Empire, 350, 360
Muhammad, 377
mujahideen, 87, 354–55, 383
multilateralism, 84, 88, 93, 127, 341
multinational corporations, 50, 335
multipolarity, 7, 13, 33, 346, 448
Mumbai, India, 353, 360, 363, 366
Musharraf, Pervez, 355, 369
Muslim Brotherhood, 123, 408–9, 453
Muslims. *See* Islam; *specific locations*
mutual economic dependence (MED), 311, 447
mutually assured destruction (MAD), 9
mutual strategic dependence (MSD), 311
Myanmar (Burma), 70, 81, *92,* 276, 294, 318, 341, 350, 356–59, 362; capitals of, 362; China and, 70, 280, 357–59, 372; Cold War and, 68, 70–71; cyclone emergency, 2008, 358; democracy in, 310, 358, 372; economy and trade, *351,* 372; ecumene, 310; government of, 310, 358, 372; India and, 70, 280, 357–59; neutrality of, 71; oil/gas production, 358

NAFTA, 46, 50, 113, 121, 126, 133, 140–43, 146, 193, 195, 455
Nagaland, India, *57,* 357–58, 371
Nagorno-Karabakh, 232, 249, 259–60
Nairobi, Kenya, 92, 428, 443
Namibia, *92,* 420, 422, *430,* 435, 441
Nanjing, China, 275–77, 287
Napoleonic Europe, 183
Napoleonic Wars, 223, 247
Napoleon III, 138
narco-guerrillas, 152
Nasser, Gamal Abdel, 75, 375, 379, 408–9
National Action Party (PAN), 138
nationalism, 17, 49, 51, 65
national missile defense (NMD) program, 267, 307, 339
national power, five orders or levels, 51–54
National Security Agency (NSA), 6, 123
national states. *See* states
National Union for Total Independence of Angola. *See* UNITA
NATO (North Atlantic Treaty Organization/Atlantic Alliance), 1–2, 5, 28–30, 43, 58, 124–25, 200; Cold War and, 66, 70, 77, 84, 88, 90–91; East Asia geostrategic realm and, 311–12; in the future, 43, 449–50, 452; Maritime Europe/the Maghreb and, 179, 182–83, 191–94, 196, 207–8, 213, 215; Midde East and, 379–80, 385, 405–6, 415; Russia/Eurasian convergence zone and, 218–20, 247, 249–51, 253–59, 267
natural gas. *See* oil/gas production
Nauru, 8

naval power: China and, 279–82; Soviet vs. US, 74, 77; US and, 74, 105, 108, 125, 152, 157, 282, 323, 381, 393
Navassa Island, 105
Nazi Germany. *See under* Germany: Nazi Germany
Negri, Antonio, 49
Nehru, Jawaharlal, 68, 349, 352–53, 357
neoconservatism, 5
neocritical geographers, 32
neoliberalism, 32
Nepal, 53, 68, 70, 90, *92,* 349–*51,* 362–65, 367–68, 371
Netanyahu, Benjamin, 399
net-centric warfare, 123
Netherlands, *92,* 173, 180, 183, 186, *196*–99, 201–2, 207, 394, 456
Neutrality Acts, 109
New Delhi, India, 11, 70–71, 80–81, 353–56, 358–60, 362–65, 369, 371, 373
"New Europe," 187–88
New Guinea, 56, 68, 329, 331
"New Member States" (NMS) or "New Europe," 187–88, 202
new world order, 7, 23, 31, 89
New Zealand, 68, 105, 315–16, 319–24, 338–39, 342–43
Ngo Dinh Diem, 71
Ngok Dinka people, 90
Nguyễn Tấn Dũng, 292
Nicaragua, 48, 86, *92,* 111, 141, 148–51, 158, 167–68, 454; Sandinistas, 82, 149–50
Niger, 4, *92,* 311, *396,* 423, 429–*30,* 432, 434, 438–39, 445
Nigeria, 3, 7, 39, *53*–54, *57,* 91–*92,* 280, 419–23, 425, 432–35, 437–39, 443, 445; and the future, 59, 448–49; as West Africa's most powerful country, 428–*29*
Nitze, Paul, 29
Nixon, Richard, 29–30, 42, 74–75, 122
Nkrumah, Kwame, 78, 421, 426
nonconforming sectors, 40
NORAD, 125, 243
Noriega, Manuel, 150, 153, 156
North American Aerospace Defense Command, 126, 243. *See* NORAD
North and Middle America, 95–158
North and Middle American Free Trade Agreement. *See* NAFTA
North Atlantic Alliance, 28
North Atlantic Drift, 180
North Atlantic Treaty Organization. *See* NATO
Northern Ireland, 90–91, 191, 204–*5,* 207
Northern League, 208
Northern Mariana Islands, 105
Northern Sea Route, 4, 224–25, 241, 247, 455
North Korea, 3, 53, 91, 271, 299–304, 312, 347
North Pole, 27, 113, 122, 131, 136, 244
North Sulawesi, 332
Northwest Passage, 130–31, 134, 455
Norway, 122, 180, 182, 185–87, 196–98, 229, 244–45, 455
nuclear cores, 39
Nuclear Non-Proliferation Pact, 296, 339
nuclear waste, 101, 119, 198, 238, 240
nuclear weapons, 5, 9, 28, 51, 91, 126–27, 127, 339, 447; China and, 293, 296, 354; Cold War and, 9, 72, 87, 240, 243, 354; India and, 366, 369–70; Iran and, 5, 91, 123, 267, 292, 404, 447; Israel and, 380, 404; Middle East and, 5, 354, 366, 380, 404; North Korea and, 92, 299–300, 347; Pakistan and, 354–55, 366, 369; Russia and, 54, 192, 219, 234, 238, 243, 250, 266–67; stalemate and deterrence, 65–72; START treaties, 266
Nunavut, 130–31, 136
Nyasaland. *See* Malawi
Nyerere, Julius, 79, 421, 426

Obama, Barack, 6, 29, 101, 121, 123, 267, 404
Obregón, Álvaro, 138
Obst, Erich, 25–26
Odinga, Raila, 442
offshore Asia, 66, 68, 72, 74, 84–85, 132, 274, 284, 309, 315, 318–20; shatterbelts, 80
Ogallala Aquifer, 100, 135
oil/gas production, 410–11, 452; Asia-Pacific Rim and, 332; Canada and, 101–2, 131, 133–35, 145; East Asia/China and, 280, 284, 292, 295–96, 304, 311–12, 358, 452; in the future, 386, 448, 450, 452; gateway regions and, 55; geopolitics of, 260, 410–11; India and, 358; Maritime Europe/the Maghreb and, 196–98, 211, 237; Mexico and, 135, 141–42, 145; Middle East and, 145, 378, 386, 389–90, 392, 408, 410–12, 448; Russia/Eurasian convergence zone and, 43, 55, 198, 220, 225, 233, 236–38, 241–42, 247, 250–51, 258–61, 284, 304, 386, 450, 452; South America and, 170–72, 174–75, 177, 454; South Asia and, 358; Spratly Islands and, 340; Sub-Saharan Africa and, 420, 424, 428, 437, 440, 442; Trans-Caucasus/Central Asia and, 247, 257–61, 311, 452; US and, 99–103, 124, 131, 133–35, 145, 175, 378, 386
oilseed, 114, 176
oil tar sand resources, 131
Okinawa, 74, 123, 298, 344
"Old Member States" (OMS) or "Old Europe," 187–88, 202
Oleg, 234
Olmert, Ehud, 399
Olopade, Dayo, 440
O'Loughlin, John, 251
Olympic Games, 217
Oman, 377, 386, 392, 396
Omsk, Russia, 240, 248
Ontario, Canada, 99, 127–30, 132–33, 135
OPEC, 131, 154, 330, 397, 437
open borders, 88, 90, 124, 347

Open Door policy, 110, 306
Operation Barbarossa, 228
Operation Condor, 82
Opium Wars, 274
Order of the Teutonic Knights, 189
orders of national power, 51–54
organic theories, 17
Organization of African Unity (OAU), 422, 426, 431
Organization of American States (OAS), 151
Organization of Petroleum Exporting Countries . *See* OPEC
Orient Policy, 307, 310
Ortega, Daniel, 111, 150
Oslo I (1993) and Oslo II (1995) agreements, 398
ostpolitik, 74
Ottawa, Canada, 125–30, 132–36, 185
Ottoman Empire, 376–77
Ottomans, 223–24, 230, 251, 256, 376–77, 393, 402
Ó Tuathail, Gearóid, 16, 32
out-migration, 54, 131, 197, 231, 371
outsourcing, 11

Pacific strategy, 271
"Padania," 208
Pago Pago, 105, 110
Pahlavi, Mohammad Reza. *See* Iran, Shah of
Pahlavi dynasty, 378
Painter, Joe, 32
Pakhtunistan, *57*–58, 370, *397,* 405–6, 450
Pakistan, 30, *53,* 352–55; Afghanistan and, 58, 62, 354, 370, *397,* 405–6, 415–16, 449–50; boundaries, 353; capital of, 363; China and, 296–97, 352–54, 367–68; Cold War and, 354; FATA (Federally Administered Tribal Areas of Pakistan), 4, 365; and the future, 59, 415–16, 448–50, 453; India and, 202, 350, 352–54, 354, 366–70; Kashmir and, 47, 56, 367–70; nuclear weapons and, 354, 366; political instability of, 370; and trade, *351;* US and, 147, 353–55, 369
Palau, 105, 315
Palestine, *57, 59,* 75–76, 85, 90, *92,* 182–83, 214, 385, 387–88, 394, *396*–402, 410; Britain and, 377; division of, 379; Europe and, 401; the future and, 54, 390, 399–401, 453; refugees from, 402, 413
Palestine Liberation Organization (PLO), 398
Palestine Mandate, 412
Palestinian Authority, 392, *396, 398*–99, 412. *See also* Levant
PAN (National Action Party), 138
Pan-African Common Market, 422
Pan-Africanism, 78, 426
Panama, 110–11, 149–53, 155–58, 162–63, 171
Panama Canal, 23, 81–82, 95, 110–11, 116, 124, 130, 149, 152–53, 156, 162–63
Panama City, 139
Pan-American Highway system, 151
Pan-Americanism, 11, 161–62
Pan-Arabism, 51, 408
Pan-Asianism, 317–18
Pan-Eur-Africa, 25, 162, 418
panregionalism, 25, 162, 317, 418
Pantanal, 167
Papua New Guinea, 315, *321*–22, 331, 342
Paracel Islands, 296, 298, 311
Paraguay, 46, 82, 165, 167, 170–71, 174, 178, 454
Paris, Treaty of (1920), 245
Paris Peace Conference of 1919, 276
Parker, Geoffrey, 16
Parti Québécois, 136
Partition of Tordesillas, 163
Partiya Jiyana Azad a Kurdistanê (Party for Freedom and Life in Kurdistan). *See* PJAK
Partiya Karkerên Kurdistan (Turkish Workers Party). *See* PKK
Pashtuns, 4, 58, 69, 349, 355, 370, 375, 383, *397,* 405, 450
Pax Americana, 60, 88–89
Peace Treaty of Nystad (1721), 223
Pennsylvania, 98–99, 106, 116–17, 133
People's Liberation Army (ELN), 174
perestroika, 87, 219
Perón, Juan, 163, 176
Peronista, 82, 163, 176
Pershing, John, 139
Persia, 223, 261, 376–78
Persian/Arab Gulf, 77, 123, 127, 261, 376–78, 381–82, 385–86, 389, 392–93, 397, 412–13, 415; Britain and, 68
Peru, 86, 90, *92,* 147, 155, 157, 161–65, 168–71, 174–76, 178, 316, 343
Peter the Great, Czar of Russia, 217, 221–23, 225–27, 236
petrodollars, 50–51
Petróleos Mexicanos (PEMEX), 139, 141–42
petroleum production. *See* oil/gas production
Philadelphia, Pennsylvania, 96, 98, 118
Philippines, 6, 11, 23, 30, 105, 110, 132, 279, 298, 309, 315, 318–25, 340–43, 345, 448–49; Cold War and, 68, 72, 74, 80, 91–*92;* economy and trade, 143, *321*–23; effective national territory (EFT), 338; political stability of, 324–26; US and, 68, 72, 122, 343
pipelines. *See* oil/gas production
piracy, 332, 376
pivot area, 17, 19, 87, 218–19, 227, 265
PJAK, 397, 405
PKK (Turkish Workers Party), 384, *397,* 403, 405, 407, 410
places, defined, 16
Plains of Hindustan. *See* Hindustan Plains
Plan Colombia, 152, 174
Platt Amendment, 110
P5 + 1 nations, 404
Poland, 25, 30, 43, 55, 191–92, 201–4, 214–15, 218–19, 249–50; boundaries, 183, 189–90, 219, 223,

225–30; Cold War and, 65, 69–70, 74, 190–91, 218; economy and trade, 55; ecumene, 187; EU and, 182, 199, 204; NATO and, 191–92, 194, 215, 250–51; partitions of, 226; population of, 202; as regional power, 53; Russia and, 226, 267; Solidarity movement in, 84
political capitals, 39
political centers, 39
pollution, 42, 115–16, 141, 144, 200, 239, 241, 272, 288, 290, 292; major powers and, 62, 456
Pol Pot, 80, 85, 298, 305, 308
population density, 4
Porfirio Diaz, José de la Cruz, 138
Port Arthur (Lushun), 224–25, 275–76
Portugal, 8, 44, 79, 179–80, 183, 187, 194, 202, 208, 274, 419, 436–37; Partition of Tordesillas and, 163. *See also* Azores; Madeira Islands
postindustrial age, 38, 95
power: four pillars of, 2–3; hard and soft, 123, 215; hierarchical order of, 3–4; national, orders of, 51–54
Prague, 186–87, 203
Pretoria, South Africa, 428
Primakov, Yevgeny, 307, 310
Proclamation of 1763, 106
Puerto Rico, 23, 55, *57,* 66, 105, 110, 121, 149, 151–54, 157
Puntland, *47, 429,* 442
Putin, Vladimir, 12, 217, 219, 239, 241, 253, 259, 266–67, 307

Qatar, 50, 53–54, *57,* 123, 377–78, 385–86, 392–93, *396,* 404, 407–9, 412
Qin dynasty, 273, 285
quasi states, 33, 37, 56–59, *205,* 207–9, 211, 233–34, 254, 260, 331, 370, 454–55
Quebec, *57,* 107, 125–31, 133–36

race, 32, 38
railroads, 17, 79, 107–9, 120, 129, 138–39, 181, 197–98, 223, 258, 303–4, 318, 335, 371, 393, 423–24, 424, 432. *See also* Trans-Siberian Railroad
Rajasthan, India, 359–60
Rajputana, 359
Rajput Princely Territories, 359
Rann of Kutch, 366–68
rasse und raum (race and space), 25
Ratzel, Friedrich, 17, 23–25, 108
raum (space), 17
Rawlings, Jerry, 440
Reagan, Ronald; the Reagan administration, 74, 83, 127
realms. *See* geostrategic realms
realpolitik, 2, 15, 29, 123
recession, 8, 12, 44; of 1948, 193; of 2001, 119, 145; of 2007–2009, 2, 12, 99, 113, 123, 145, 179–80, 197, 202
Reclus, Élisée, 31
refugees, 6, 62, 256, 363, 402, 413, 425
regional powers, 3, 7–8, 52–54. *See also* second-order states
regional unity, 46, 179, 182, 197, 199, 204, 213, 333, 369–72, 376, 390, 392
regions. *See* geopolitical regions
Reid, T. R., 215
religions, world, 32. *See also specific religions*
Renner, George, 27
Republican Party, US, 123–24
Republic of Gran Colombia, 161
Republic of Rhodesia, 421
Republic of the Congo-Brazzaville, 78, 124, 437
Réunion, 373
Rhodesia, 79, 418, 421
Riau, Sumatra, 332
rimland, 26–29, 245
ring of containment, 65, 69–72, 75, 218, 284, 381
Ritter, Carl, 16
Riyadh, Saudi Arabia, 389, 392–93
rogue states, 40, 51, 304
Rohingya, 359
Romania, 43, 69–70, 90, 182, 191–92, 201–2, 204, 218, 220, *227*–29, 249, 254, 407
Roosevelt, Franklin D., 111, 139, 162, 276
Roosevelt, Theodore, 23, 111, 139, 162
Roosevelt Corollary, 111
Roosevelt Roads naval station, 157
Ross, Colin, 25–26
Rostow, Walt, 29
Rothschild, House of, 181
RSFSR (Russian Soviet Federal Socialist Republic), *227–29*
rubber, 78, 112, 162, 322, 326, 328, 330, 351, 364, 418, 430
Rudd, Kevin, 342
Rurik, 234
Russia, *92,* 217–45, 265, 343; agriculture in, 239–40, 248, 262; Armenia and, 40, 232, 257, 259–60, 452; Azerbaijan and, 40, 232, 247, 258–60, 377; Baltic States and, 192, 250; boundaries, 244–45, 249, 263, *396;* BRICS, 172; Central Asia and, 6–7, 263; challenges faced by, 40, 267; China and, 32, 224, 244, 264, 275, 284, 310, 312; and conflict mediation, 91; as core of Central Asia, 10; czarist, 41, 43, 69, 190, 222–27, 377; Eastern Europe and, 40, 449; economy of, 239, 265–66; ecumene, 237–39; effective national territory (ENT), 239–42; empty area, 242–43; energy policies of, 449; Eurasian continental realm and, 40, 43–44, 66, 84, 87, 272; Eurasian convergence zone and, 217–68; Eurasian Heartland, 218; Far East of, 241, 247; as first-order power, 54, 234, 268, 293; foreign policy of, 266; future of, 447, 449–50, 452, 454–55; geopolitical features, 234–45; Georgia and, 40, 232, 247, 249, 257, 452; historic core, 232, 234–36, 251; and immigration, 455; India and, 310, 373; infrastructure, 217, 240; internal conflict in,

223; Iran and, 32; Japan and, 225, 241, 244–45, 318, 339–40; Middle East and, 44, 410; military of, 263, 266; modernization of, 221; Moldova and, 40; NATO and, 250; North Korea and, 304, 312; nuclear weapons of, 54, 192, 219, 234, 238, 243, 250, 266–67; and oil/gas production (*see under* oil/gas production); Pacific coast of, 223–24, 304; political capitals, 236–37; population of, 231, 455; problems in, 259; railroads in, 258; Serbia and, 249, 254–55; South Korea and, 304, 312; Soviet State, implosion of, 231–34; strengths of, 266; territory, changing, 220–34, 261, 376–77; trade and, 55; Trans-Caucasus and, 452; Ukraine and, 40, 55, 180, 218, 226, 251–54, 449; US and, 266–67, 410; Vietnam and, 307. *See also* Putin, Vladimir; Soviet Union
Russia, "White." *See* Belorussia
Russian Soviet Federal Socialist Republic (RSFSR), *227*–29
Russo-Georgian war of 2008, 452
Russo-Japanese War (1904–5), 224, 318
Russo-Polish War of 1667, 226
rust belt. *See under* United States: rust belt
Rwanda, 62, 89, *92,* 422, 431–34, 441–42, 444

Saakashvili, Mikheil, 258
SAARC (South Asian Association for Regional Cooperation), 369
SACU (Southern African Customs Union), 435
Sadat, Anwar, 75, 380–82, 409
SADC, 422, 433–37, 441, 445
Sahara Desert, 188, 210
Said, Edward, 50
Saint Lawrence Seaway, 112
Sakhalin, 71, 225, *227*–28, 230, 340
Sakhalin I and II pipelines, 241
SALT I and SALT II, 74, 83
Samoa, 105–6, 110
Sandinistas, 82, 149–50
San Marino, 205
São Paulo, Brazil, 162, 165, 167, 170, 173
São Tomé, 280
Sarkozy, Nicolas, 199, 213
Saudi Arabia, 389, 392–93, 393, 395; Arab-Israeli conflict and, 399; Arab Spring and, 389, 393; Britain and, 377, 389; foreign workers in, 413; the Gulf Cooperation Council, 392; Hejaz, 377, 389; oil/gas production in, 51, 145, 378, 410; as second-order power, 51, *53;* US and, 68, 378, 410, 413. *See also* Middle East
Savimbi, Jonas, 420, 436–37
School of the Americas, 82
Schuman, Robert, 199
Scotland, 4, 56–*57,* 92, 179, 186, 204–*5,* 208
sea, importance of, 41
SEATO, 68, 71, 80, 320, 335, 353, 357
Second Neutrality Act (1936), 109
second-order states, 3, 51, *53*–54, 309, 434
Second World War. *See* World War II
Security Council, UN. *See* United Nations Security Council
Selassie, Haile, 77, 431
self-sufficiency, 23, 38, 54, 60
Semple, Ellen Churchill, 25, 109, 148
Senegal, 421, *429–30,* 440
Senegambia, 421
Seoul, South Korea, 4, 302, 336
separatism, 56–*57*
September 11, 2001, 1, 5, 92–93, 432
Serbia, *59,* 91, 183, 194, 200, 249, 254–57, 284
Serbian Orthodox Church, 256
Seward's folly, 101, 103
Seychelles, 280, 373, 445
Shaba. *See* Katanga
Shah of Iran. *See* Iran, Shah of
Shanghai, China, 28, 243, 272–75, 277–78, 287, 289, 291, 296
Shanghai Cooperation Council, 264, 312
Shanghai Free-Trade Zone, 289
Shariah law, 331, 438
Sharif, Nawaz, 355
Sharon, Ariel, 398–99
Shatt-al-Arab waterway dispute, 85, 395–97, 405, 412
shatterbelts, 9, 48–49; distinguishing feature of, 48, 349; Eurasian convergence zone, 44; and the future, 44, 450; microshatterbelts, 174, 177; Middle East as, 44, 375–416; offshore Asia, 80; South Asia and, 349; Southeast Asia, 80; Sub-Saharan Africa as, 44, 49, 77–79, 417–45
shatter zone. *See* shatterbelts
Shenzhen Special Economic Zone, 289
Shia Islam, 1, 39, 58, 89, 375, 383–84, 389, 393–94, 399, 402–4, 406, 409, 412, 415, 454
Shi Yunsheng, 280
Siberia, 13, 17, 19, 122, 201, 218–44 *passim,* 248, 250, 262, 264–65, 304, 317. *See also* Trans-Siberian Railroad
Sierra Leone, 10, 89–90, *92,* 422, 430, 438–39
Sikhs, 56, 371
Sikkim, 297, 363
Silk Road, 223, 260–61, 354
Sinai War, 75
Singapore, 8, 60, 80, 84–85, 280, 308, 315–20 *passim,* 340–42; economy and trade, 50, 220–21, 306, *321*–24, 326, *351;* ecumene, 336, 338; effective national territory (ENT) of, 338; as gateway, 54, *57;* political stability of, 326; as political capital, 335; population of, 321; significance of, 220–21, 326, 335
Singh, Govind, 367
Sino-Japanese War (1894–95), 318
Sino-Japanese War (1937), 318
Slessor, Sir John, 28
SLORC (State Law and Order Restoration Council), 358
Slovakia, 43, 90, 182, 191, 201

Slovenia, 43, 55, *57,* 90, 192, 201, 203–4, 254
Smith, Adam, 61
Smith, Laurence, 268
Smith, Neil, 32
Smoot-Hawley Tariff bill, 109
SNAP (Supplemental Nutrition Assistance Program), 115
Snowden, Edward, 6
socialism, 11, 25, 30, 46, 48, 148, 158, 163, 212, 272, 282–84, 357–58, 380, 409, 421, 426, 448, 454; Cold War and, 71, 75–76, 79, 82, 84
soft power, 215
Solana Madariaga, Javier, 192
Solomon Islands, 327
Somalia, 3–4, 10, 32, 58, 65, 76–77, *92*–93, 381, 389, 392, 413, 420–22, *429*–30, 432, 441–42, 448–49; refugees from, 6, 62; US and, 89, 442, 444
Somaliland, *57,* 77, 420, *429,* 432, 441–42
Somoza dictatorship, 82
South Africa, 172, 202, 373, 411, 420, 422–25, 434–37, 440; boundaries, *429–30;* capital of, 428; Cold War and, 78–79, 86, 90–*92;* as ecumene, 428; as regional power, 3, 7, *53*–54, 447; and trade, 50
South America, 161–78; boundary and territorial disputes and wars, 167–68; Brazil as powerhouse of, 7, 172–73, 454; Caribbean and, 454; Cold War and, 66; Eastern South America as most important part, 162; economy of, 162; ecumene, 165, 167; effective national territory (ENT), 167; future of, 178, 454; geographical setting of, 162–65, 169; geopolitical features, 165–68; geopolitical forces of separation and attraction, 168–72; independence, prospects for, 172–77; indigenous peoples in, 164, 173, 175, 177; north-south strategic alignment concept, 162; oil/gas production and, 170, 174–75, 454; population of, 164–65; regional economic organizations, 170–72; Southern Cone, 163, 170, 178, 454; US and, 66, 161–63
South American realm, 51
South American Union (UNASUR), 171
South Asia, *92,* 349–74; boundaries, 367–68; Britain and, 350; capitals, 360–63; challenges to unity, 368–72; China and, 311, 358; Cold War and, 66, 80–81, 85; ecumenes, 363–65; effective regional/national territory, 365–66; empty areas, 366–67; Federally Administered Tribal Areas (FATA), 365; geopolitical features, 359–68; historical background, 350–52; historic core, 359–60; independence of, 47, 68; India as core of, 349; political capitals, 360–63; population and trade, *351;* regional geopolitical overview, 352–59
South Asian Association for Regional Cooperation (SAARC), 369
South Asian realm, 51
South Asia Preferential Trade Association, 369
Southeast Asia, 9–11, 26–29, 32–33, 41, 44, 46, 48–49, 61, 218, 274–75, 284, 298, 307, 312–21 *passim,* 333, 337, 342, 345, 351–52, 357, 372, 418; Cold War and, 68, 70–71, 73, 75, 80, 84–85; colonialism and, 325; as shatterbelt, 80. *See also* ASEAN
Southeast Asia Treaty Organization. *See* SEATO
Southern Africa, 434–37
Southern African Customs Union (SACU), 435
Southern African Development Community. *See* SADC
Southern Cone, 163, 170, 178, 454
Southern Cone Common Market, 125
southern continents, 10, 46, 162, 418
Southern Rhodesia (Zimbabwe), 421
South Georgia and South Sandwich Islands, 168
South Korea, 6, 30, 47, 68, 271, 300–304, 322–24, 343, 347; boundaries, 309; China and, 47, 278, 312; economy of, 301, *322,* 335; ecumene, 335–36; Japan and, 316, 323, 335, 345; North Korea and, 300–304; political stability of, 324; as regional power, *53*–54; and trade, 47, 50, *321,* 323; US and, 68, 122, 343. *See also* Korean War
South Moluccas, 328–29, 331–32, 338
South Ossetia, 232, 249, 257–58, 452
South Stream Pipeline, 452
South Sudan. *See under* Sudan: and South Sudan
South Sulawesi, 332
Southwest Africa, 79, 420
South West Africa People's Organization (SWAPO), 79, 420
South Yemen, 75–77, 85, 380, 392
Soviet Union: Afghanistan and, 83, 86–87, 354; boundaries, 84, 190; China and, 39, 66, 80, 84, 244, 276, 299; collapse of, 9–10, 40, 48, 60–61, 87–88, 161, 183, 191, 194, 231–34, 245, 271, 279, 299–301, 312, 354; de-Stalinization in, 73, 277; détente with, 30, 74–75, 83; economic core of, 66; Egypt and, 380; Germany and, 25; influence of, 85–87; Iran and, 70, 230; Iraq and, 76; Japan and, 228, 230, 244; Latin America and, 82; Middle East and, 75, 380–81; Sub-Saharan Africa and, 78, 86; Syria and, 75, 85; territory/territorial expansion of, 74–75, 227–31; Turkey and, 230; Vietnam and, 80. *See also* Cold War; Russia; World War II
Soviet Union, Former. *See* Former Soviet Union
Spain, 8, 12, 44, 55, *92,* 109–10, 138, 140, 161, 177, 179, 182–83, 194, 204–13; autonomy-seeking regions in, 56, 205–8, 255; boundaries, 191, 205–10; economy of, 179–80, 182, 188, 196, 198, 201; immigration to, 55, 201, 213; Partition of Tordesillas, 163; Spanish civil war, 109
spatially structured geopolitical theory, 60
special economic zones, 248, 278, 289, 325
specialization, 60
specialized integration, 60
Spencer, Herbert, 59–60
Spice Islands. *See* Moluccas (Malaku) Islands
Spratly Islands, 341

Sputnik, 72, 243
spying, 6, 123, 339
Spykman, Nicholas, 26–27, 42, 148
Sri Lanka, 44, 47, 68, 90, *92,* 143, 311, 349–*51,* 356, 362, 364–66, 371, 448
St. Petersburg, Russia, 69, 191, 221–22, 227–28, 236–37, 245, 247–48, 250
stability, global. *See* global stability
Stalin, Joseph, 28, 72–73, 276, 302
Stanley, Henry, 418
START treaties, 266
state-centered geopolitics, 28–30
State Law and Order Restoration Council (SLORC), 358
states, 49–51; organic theories of, 17; proliferation of, 55–59; prospective, 56–59; state system, five orders or levels of, 51–54
states, failed. *See* failed states
states, quasi-. *See* quasi states
"states of concern," 304
Strabo, 16
Strait of Gibraltar, 201
Strategic Arms Limitations Talks. *See* SALT I and SALT II
String of Pearls (strategy), 111, 280
Sub-Saharan Africa, *92,* 417–45; African Horn, 49, 75–77, 90, *92,* 441–43; boundaries, 429–32; Central Africa, 440–41; China and, 311, 443–44; Cold War and, 77–79, 86, 417; colonial/imperial background, 418–19, 432; East Africa, 441–43; economy of, 424–26; ecumenes, 428; effective regional territory, 428–29; geographical background, 423–26; geopolitical features, 426–33; historic regional core, 426; infrastructure, 444; landlocked areas in, 432–33; oil/gas production in, 420, 424, 428, 437, 440, 442; political capitals, 428; postcolonial political frameworks, 419–23; regional power center prospects, 434; regional subdivisions, 433–34; as shatterbelt, 44, 49, 77–79, 417–45; Southern Africa, 434–37; Soviet Union and, 78, 86; transportation, 423–24; US and, 311, 444; West Africa, 437–40
Sudan, 53, 68, 230, 279, 304, 373, 375–79, 381–82, 388–89, 392, 395–97, 408, 415, 429, 432–33, 441, 444, 453; and South Sudan, 90, *92,* 388, 395, 411, 413–*14,* 432, 442, 448–49. *See also* Darfur
Suez Canal, 23, 68, 74, 76–77, 127, 181, 231, 376, 379, 381, 390, 394, 443; closure of, 411; Egypt, importance to, 408
Sufism, 371
Suharto, 80, 328–33
suicide bombing, 403
Sukarno, 71, 73, 80, 320, 328–29, 333
Sukarnoputri, Megawati, 333
Sulawesi (the Celebes), 328, 332, 338
Sumatra, 162, 328, 330, 332–33, 338, 373
Sung dynasty, 287
Sunni Islam, 1, 5, 33, 53, 58, 355, 375, 383–85, 389, 393, 402–5, 408–9, 412, 415, 448–49, 453–54
Sunshine Policy, 303–4, 347
Sun Yat-sen, 276, 287
superpowers: Soviet, collapse of, 87–88; US as no longer world's superpower, 447, 449
supertankers, 411
Supplemental Nutrition Assistance Program (SNAP), 115
Suriname, 154, 156, 163, 201
Svalbard Archipelago, 183, 229, 245, 248
SWAPO (South West Africa People's Organization), 79, 420
Swaziland, 428–*29,* 432–33, 435
Sweden, 24, 186–87, 189, 194, *196*–98, 202, 221, 223, 226
Switzerland, 182, 185, 190, 195, 198, 203, 205, 257
Syria, 409–10, 412, 448–49; Arab Spring and, 375, 409; boundaries of, 387, 395–*96;* Egypt and, 380; and the future, 59; Iraq War refugees and, 62; Israel and, 75, 380, *396;* Kurds in, *397,* 409; and Lebanon, 402, 409–10; rebellion in, 90, 402, 449; refugees from, 6, 62, 402, 410, 413; Soviet Union and, 75, 85. *See also* Levant; Middle East

Taft, William H.; the Taft administration, 111
Taiwan, *53*–54, 299–300, 315, 323–24, 346–47; China and, 5–6, 47, 278, 291, 299–300, 309, 324, 449; economy of, *322,* 337; ecumene, 291; as gateway, *57;* Japan and, 337, 340; political stability of, 324; and trade, 47, 50, *321;* US and, 68, 337, 343
Tajikistan, *59, 92,* 233, 249, 260–61, 263–64, 267–68, 295, 297, 368
Talbot, Paul, 251
Taliban, 1–2, 4, 39, 51, 89, 93, 175, 247, 263, 354–55, 368–70, 375, 383–84, 405–6, 444, 447, 449, 454
Tambs, Lewis, 175
Tamils, 350, 356, 364, 366, 371
Tanganyika African National Union (TANU), 421
Tan-Zam Railway, 79, 424
Tanzania, 54, 78–79, *92,* 280, 373, 421, 423–24, 426, *430,* 434, 442, 444–45
Tataria. *See* Tatarstan
Tatarstan, 219, 223
Taylor, Charles, 430, 438
Taylor, Maxwell, 29
Taylor, Peter, 31–32, 50
Tazara (Tan-Zam) Railway, 79, 424
Tea Party, Boston, 96
Tea Party Republicans, US, 123–24
territoriality, 38, 51
terrorism, 8, 91–93, 403, 443, 449; antiterrorism, 220, 385, 417; war on, 5, 93, 267, 359, 368, 399, 442. *See also* September 11, 2001
Texas, 100, 107, 109, 112, 115–17, 119–21, 137–39, 145, 147–48, 157
Texas Revolution (1835), 137

Thailand, 323–26, 337; boundaries, 326, 341; economy of, 12, 143, *322,* 326, 337; Japan and, 318, 325, 337; political stability of, 324–26; as regional power, *53*–54; and trade, *321, 351,* 372; US and, 325, 343
Thani, Tamim bin Hamad Al, 407–8
Thar Desert, 354, 366
Third Neutrality Act (1937), 109
third-order states, 53–54
Third World, 29, 53, 71, 73, 188, 283–84, 321, 329, 354, 357, 425–26
Three Gorges dams and reservoir system, 288
Thrift, Nigel, 32
Tibetan Buddhism, 234
Tibet (Xizang), 43, *57,* 70–71, 81, 261, 272, 274, 276, 294–97, 312, 352–53, 357, 362, 367, 372, 454
Timofeyev, Yermak, 222
Timor Gap, 330
Timor-Leste, *92,* 315, *322,* 327, 330, 342. *See also* East Timor
Togo, 422, 426, *430*
Tok Do islets (Liancourt Rocks), 341
Tokyo, Japan, 335
Tomsk, Russia, 240
Tordesillas, Partition of, 163
Torrijos, Omar, 153, 156
totalitarianism, 23
Touré, Ahmed Sékou, 78
trade, 5, 40–43; Asia-Pacific rim and, *321;* cores of, 50; European system of, 195–*96;* US and, 121–24
trade-dependent maritime realm, 41, 66, 181
TransCanada pipeline, 133–34
Transcarpathia, 227, 230
Trans-Caspian Railroad, 223
Trans-Caucasus, 32–33, 44, 49, 60, 123, 192, 218–19, 239, 257–65, 406, 450. *See also under* oil/gas production
Trans-Dniester Republic (Transnistria), 232, 254
Trans-Jordan, 377, 379
transnational megalopolis, 9
Trans-Siberian Railroad, 17, 218, 223–25, 230, 238, 240–41, 265, 304
Treaty of Asunción, 170
Treaty of Paris (1920), 245
Treaty of Utrecht, 191
Treaty of Verdun (843), 189
Treaty of Versailles (1919), 24–25, 190
treaty ports, 274–76
Trentino-Alto Adige, *57, 205,* 208
Trinidad, 54, *57,* 152, 154
tropical regions, 164, 388, 418
Truman, Harry S., 29
Truman Doctrine, 29, 66
Tsin dynasty, 287
Tunisia, 1, 53–54, 66, 76, *92,* 182, 201, 209–14, 382, 388, *396,* 434
Tupamaros urban guerrilla movement, 82
turbulence, 60–62
Turkestan, 17, *59,* 223, 244, 285, 295
Turkey, *92,* 378, 406–7, 447–48, 452–53; boundaries, 395; economy of, 384; EU and, 200, 452; Gagauzi ethnic group, 254; Greece and, 191, 194, 200, 207, 254, *396,* 407; Kurds in, 383–84, *397,* 409; Middle East and, 395, 410–11; as NATO cornerstone, 200; refugees to, 6, 62, 410, 413; as regional power, 3, *53,* 447; Russia and, 232; Soviet Union and, 230; and trade, 50; US and, 384; the West and, 76, 378; WWII and, 384
Turkish Workers Party. *See* PKK
Turkmenistan, 55, *57, 59,* 245, 249, 257, 260–61, 263–64, 279, 311, 383, *396*
Turk-Sib railroad, 223
Turner, Frederick Jackson, 108, 112
Tusk, Donald, 199, 204
Tutsis. *See* Rwanda
Tutu, Bishop Desmond, 436
Tuvalu, 456
twenty-first century, transition into, 88–93

UAVs. *See* unmanned aerial vehicles
Uganda, 78–79, *92,* 419, 421–22, 431–32, 434, 442
UGVs (unmanned ground vehicle), 2
Uighurs, 292, 295, 312
Ukraine, 3, 53, *57, 59,* 220, 250–54, *252;* boundaries, 245; capital of, 248; EU and, 199–200; the future and, 55, 450, 452; "Land of the Little Russians," 226, 251; NATO and, 43, 452; partition of (Russo-Polish War of 1667), 226; Romania and, 249; Russia and, 40, 55, 180, 218, 226, 251–54, 449, 452; trade and, 55
UN. *See* United Nations
UNASUR, 171
undifferentiated stage, 60
União Nacional para a Independência Total de Angola (National Union for Total Independence of Angola). *See* UNITA
unilateralism, 5
Unión de Naciones Suramericanas (Union of South American Nations), 171
Union of Soviet Socialist Republics (USSR), 7. *See also* Cold War; Russia; Soviet Union
Union Pacific Railroad, 17, 108
UNITA (União Nacional para a Independência Total de Angola), 79, 86, 420, 430, 436
United Arab Emirates (UAE), 50, 385–86, 392, 404–5, 412
United Arab Republic, 365, 380
United Arab States, 380
United Empire Loyalists, 128
United Kingdom, 26, 28, 42, 56, *92,* 125, 168, 194, *196,* 198, 207, 227, 319, 369
United Nations Emergency Force, 127
United Nations Security Council, 61, 93, 230, 300, 320, 329, 343, 447, 455
United Nations Transitional Authority in Cambodia (UNTAC), 308, 320

United Nations (UN), 60–61; and Asia-Pacific Rim, 320, 324, 329–30, 340; Cold War and, 70–71, 89–91; and East Asia geostrategic realm, 300, 302, 308; future of, 441, 453–56; irredentism and, 58; and Maritime Europe/the Maghreb, 202, 212; membership of, 55–56; and Middle East, 379–80, 389, 397–400, 402–3, 407, 410, 415; and North/Middle America, 125, 127, 136, 150–51; and Russia/Eurasian convergence zone, 230, 244, 254–55; and South America, 191; and South Asia, 357, 362; and Sub-Saharan Africa, 419–21, 426, 431, 436, 438–39

United States, 2–3, 13, 42, 95–124, 343; agriculture in, 12, 100, 114–16, 188; American exceptionalism, 2, 216; Asia-Pacific Rim and, 316; boundaries, 71, 104–6, 143–44; Canada and, 101–2, 104, 125–27, 131–36; Central Asia and, 32, 260, 262, 264; centrality of, 95; China and, 5–6, 110, 122, 278, 298, 302–3, 310–11, 321, 449; and conflict mediation, 91; continental-maritime stage, 108–12; continental stage, *106*–8; as core of North/Middle American geopolitical region, 95; economy of, 5, 95–96, 126, 132; ecumenes, 98–100, 118; effective national territory (ENT), 100–101, 118; empty areas, 101, 103; Europe and, 215; farm belt, 100, 114–16; as first-order power, 10, 28, 31, 53, 95–96, 123, 268, 293, 447, 456; and foreign economic aid, 147; and foreign policy, 5, 32, 58, 121–24; frontiers, 107, 122–23, 159n1; geopolitical development stages, 106–15; geopolitical features, 96–106; geopolitics in, 26–28; and global warming, 62, 214, 456; and hard power, 123, 215; historic core, 96, 98; and immigration, 109, 121, 131–32, 147, 154–55; Israel and, 68, 77, 380, 401, 413, 453; Japan and, 32, 39, 68, 74, 123, 343–44, 344; Latin America and, 82; and "Manifest Destiny," 108–10; maritime-continental stage, *106,* 112–15; maritime ring, 115–24; maritime stage, *106*–7; Mexico and, 105, 143–44, 147; Middle America and, 148–51, 154–55; Middle East, declining influence in, 1–2, 124, 375, 401; Middle East and, 68, 147, 378, 410, 413; military, 32, 46, 68, 72, 74, 83, 103, 111, 123, 152, 156, 324–25, 342–44, 403, 447 (*see also* naval power; *specific events and locations*); and oil/gas production, 99–103, 124, 131, 133–35, 145, 175, 386; Pacific coast of, 101, 103, 107, 110, 115, 122, 134, 294; Pacific strategy of, 271; political capital, 98; political power, national, 120–21; population of, 118–19, 121; presidency of, 111–12, 120–21; railroads, 107–9, 120, 138; role of, 13, 149–50; Russia and, 266–67, 410; rust belt, 99, 113, 187, 239, 290; and soft power, 215; South America and, 66, 82, 161–63, 174–75; Sub-Saharan Africa and, 442; the Sunbelt, 117; as (no longer) superpower of world, 447, 449; territories, 104–6; terrorism and, 1, 5, 92–93, 267, 359, 368, 432, 442; and trade, 50, 121–24, 170–72, 306, 323; Trust Territories, 105; US-European Union partnership, 216; West Coast of, 116, 119, 242; WWI and, 41, 109–10. *See also* Cold War; World War II; *specific locations,* e.g., Caribbean: US and; *specific topics and events,* e.g., Keystone XL pipeline; Gulf Wars

United States Africa Command (AFRICOM), 417

unity, regional. *See* regional unity

universalistic geopolitics, 30–31

unmanned aerial vehicles (UAVs), 2, 4, 123, 447

unmanned ground vehicle (UGVs), 2

UNTAC. *See* United Nations Transitional Authority in Cambodia

U Nu, 357–58

urbanization, 38, 43, 110, 115, 142, 164, 220, 239, 241, 266, 337, 366

Uruguay, 82, *92,* 141, 149, 161–62, 165, 167–71, 174, 176–78, 454–55

US-Canada Auto Pact (1965), 113, 133

US-Canada Free Trade Agreement (1987), 126

US-Japan Security Treaty (1951), 71

US-Mexican War (1846–48), 107, 137, 139

USS *Manhattan,* 130

USSR. *See* Union of Soviet Socialist Republics

US Trust Territories, 105

Utrecht, Treaty of, 191

Uzbekistan, 55, *57, 59, 92,* 220, 243, 249, 260, 262–64, 267–68, 311, 383–84

Uzbeks, 58, 375, 383, 405–6, 450

Vancouver-Victoria, Canada, 129

Vanuatu, 315

Varangian dynasty, 234

Venezuela, 3–4, 7, 46, 48, 51, 141, 148–58 *passim,* 161–67 *passim,* 170–77 *passim,* 279; as bridge country, 148, 158, 454; Cold War and, 82, 135; the future and, 11, 454; oil/gas production and, 135, 145, 154, 177, 386; as second-order power, 51, *53;* US and, 82, 177. *See also* Andean Group; Bolivarian revolution; Chávez, Hugo; Mercosur

Verdun, Treaty of (843), 189

Versailles, Treaty of (1919), 24–25, 190

viceroyalties, 140, 163–64

Vieques, 105, 157

Vietnam, 54, 84, *92,* 304–8, 341; China and, 53, 80, 84, 292, 298, 305–7, 340, 449; Cold War and, 80, 84; division of, 305; as dominant state in Indochina, 308–9; France and, 305; Japan and, 84, 306, 318; 1954 partition of, 80; as regional power, *53,* 447; reunification of, 84, 307; Russia and, 307; Soviet Union and, 80; and trade, 306; US and, 306

Vietnam War, 71, 73, 80, 114, 122, 126, 271–72, 277, 279, 304–5, 307, 317–18, 320, 325–26, 359

Villa, Francisco "Pancho," 138–39

Virgin Islands, 105, 111, 155

Virgin Lands program, 239–40, 248, 262

Vladimir, 234

Vladivostok, Russia, 72, 218, 223–25, 228, 230, 241–42, 244, 247, 296, 304, 336
Vostochny, Russia, 241

Wahid, Abdurrahman, 333
Wake Island, 110
Wales, *57, 205,* 208, 339
Wallerstein, Immanuel, 31, 61
Wallonia (French-speaking Belgium), *57, 205,* 207
Walsh, Edmund, 15
war crimes, 91, 426
War of 1812, 107
War of Independence (Israel), 379, 400
War of Partition (1947–48), 202, 350
War of Reform (Mexico), 138
Warsaw Conference on Climate Warming, 214
Warsaw Pact (1955), 9, 66, 70, 73–74, 88, 181, 191, 194, 245
Washington, DC, 98
weapons. *See* arms and weapons; nuclear weapons
Wellington, Duke of, 107
Werner, Heinz, 30, 60
West Africa, 55, 78, 86, 202, 418, 422, 428, 433–34, 437–40, 448
West Bank, *92,* 385–86, 394–401, 412–13, 453
Western (Dutch) New Guinea, 56, 329, 331
Western Hemisphere, 27, 81, 111, 149, 162, 163
Westernization, 217, 378
Western Sahara, 188, 212
White Russia. *See* Belorussia
Whittlesey, Derwent, 15, 127–28
Wilson, Woodrow, 24–25, 109, 111, 139
Wolfe, James, 127
World Bank, 177, 262, 309
World Citadel, 112–13
World-Island (Mackinder's terminology), 19, 25–26, 218
world order, 60–62
world-systems theory, 31
World Trade Organization (WTO), 42, 49, 122, 291, 405
World War I, 125, 222, 225–27, 249, 256, 264, 275, 376–78, 397, 420; Germany after, 7, 24–26, 190, 418; Mexico after, 139; US after, 41, 109–10
World War II, 7, 10–11, 38, 125, 139, 190, 207, 218, 276, 319; China and, 275–77, 302; geopolitical restructuring after, 7–8, 10, 19, 23, 38, 40, 48, 65–67, 410; Japan and, 47, 71, 225, 228, 276, 316–18, 323, 325, 337, 339–40, 345, 356; Soviet Union and, 65–71, 190, 218, 222, 225, 227–31, 238, 247, 302; US and, 41, 46, 65–68, 71, 98, 103, 106, 109, 111–12, 119, 124–25, 139, 152, 208, 215, 302

Xinjiang, 43, *57,* 84, 244, 263, 272, 276, 285, 292–97, 312, 352–54, 367–68, 384, 454
Xizang. *See* Tibet

Yacyretá Dam, 170
Yakutia, 224, 233–34, 266
Yalta agreement, 69, 71, 244, 276
Yanukovych, Viktor, 251, 253
Yaounde Convention, 422
Yekaterinburg, Russia, 237–38
Yeltsin, Boris, 217, 219, 239, 241, 250, 267, 310
Yemen, 4, 75–77, 85, *92–93,* 230, 377–78, 380, 389, 392, 395–*96,* 408, 412. *See also* Aden
Yin dynasty, 273
Yudhoyono, Susilo Bambang, 333
Yugoslavia, 7, 29–30, 54, 65, 70, 88–90, 191, 201, 254–57
Yushchenko, Viktor, 251

zaibatsu, 318
Zambia, 53, 79, 418, 421, 424, 428, 430, 432–33, 436, 441
Zanzibar, 54, *57,* 78, 373, 421–22, 445
Zapatistas, 144–45
Zedillo, Ernesto, 144
Zeitschrift für Geopolitik, 25
Zenawi, Meles, 431, 442
Zhou dynasty, 285
Zhou Enlai, 278
Zimbabwe, 54, 58, 79, 86, *92,* 421–22, 424, 428–36 *passim,* 441, 448
Zimmerman, Arthur, 139
zones of marginality, 161, 443

About the Author

Saul Bernard Cohen is a teacher, author, and lecturer in the field of political geography. Among the leaders in the revival of political geography as a discipline following World War II, he has consulted to US and foreign government agencies. His first volume, *Geography and Politics in a World Divided* (1963, revised 1973), and other works and numerous articles have focused on geopolitical theory and issues inherent in world order. He has also written extensively on the Arab-Israeli conflict and Middle East geopolitics.

Professor Cohen's works in geography and educational policy include thirteen volumes and over one hundred articles focusing on such additional themes as environment, resource networks, and location analysis. He is editor-in-chief of the *Columbia Gazetteer of the World* and the *Oxford World Atlas*.

In his university career he has been professor of geography at Boston University, visiting professor at the US Naval War College, professor and director of Clark University's School of Geography, and president of Queens College, CUNY, and is university professor emeritus at Hunter College, CUNY.

A Boston native and World War II veteran, he received his AM, MA, and PhD degrees from Harvard College and Harvard University. A lifelong commitment to education improvement has led to service on numerous national governmental research and policy committees. Elected to the New York State Board of Regents in 1993, he has chaired the Regents Committee on Higher Education and currently chairs the Regents Committee on Revising New York State's School Learning Standards. He lives in New Rochelle, New York, with his wife, Miriam. They have two daughters and seven grandchildren.